P9-AOG-172

The Federal
Judicial System
Readings in Process and Behavior

The Federal Judicial System
Readings in Process and Behavior

Sheldon Goldman
University of Massachusetts

Thomas P. Jahnige
Smith College

Holt, Rinehart and Winston, Inc.
New York Chicago San Francisco Atlanta Dallas Montreal Toronto London

Copyright © 1968 by Holt, Rinehart and Winston, Inc.

All rights reserved

Library of Congress Catalog Card Number: 68-19663

2696557

Printed in the United States of America

1 2 3 4 5 6 7 8 9

Preface

A collection of readings can usually be justified by citing the great convenience to students, teachers, and college librarians of gathering materials from a wide variety of sources and making them easily accessible in one book. Indeed, this *is* one justification for the present collection. The field of public law within the Political Science discipline has been undergoing fundamental changes in the last decade. Empirical-behavioral research has expanded the field in both theory and methodology, and extensive research is now being conducted on topics previously neglected or unconsidered by political scientists. All this has produced a growing amount of judicial process and judicial behavior studies, much of it concerning the federal judiciary and federal courts, the results of which are scattered in many journals and books. One purpose of this book, then, is to provide a handy compilation of important and largely recent research findings and analyses concerning the federal judicial process and federal judicial behavior. But a justification of this collection of readings does not end with mere considerations of convenience.

The major purpose of this book is to provide the student with a logical framework for meaningfully relating diverse materials concerning the federal judicial process and federal judicial behavior. The framework which, in our judgment, accomplishes this task of integrating the process and behavior approaches is systems theory as developed by David Easton. The main categories of systems theory—input, conversion, output, and feedback—therefore provide the principal organizing concepts for presenting these materials. The system with which we are concerned is, of course, the federal judicial system.

Although systems theory is broadly used to organize the readings, it should be emphasized at the outset that the materials themselves exhibit a wide variety of approaches. Indeed, this collection demonstrates that valuable insights can be derived from a methodological and theoretical pluralism. The utilization of a broad systems framework in no way limits the selections for those who reject systems theory. However, the outlines of a systems framework are there for those who may agree with the editors that it is a useful heuristic and integrating device.

The Federal Judicial System is divided into six parts and each part subdivided into sections. Each part and section contains introductory comments written by the editors. These serve to bridge gaps, suggest to the student points of special concern to be found in the readings, and generally relate the selections to the broad version of systems theory we have employed.

We wish to acknowledge the supportive behavior of our colleagues at Smith College and the University of Massachusetts. We are grateful to Professor Joel B. Grossman of the University of Wisconsin for his comments on the material written for this book. We are also indebted, of course, to the authors and publishers who have permitted us to reprint their original works. Finally, a very special acknowl-edgment is due our families to whom this collection is affectionately dedicated.

Amherst, Massachusetts   S.G.
Northampton, Massachusetts   T.P.J.
April 1968

Contents

The Federal
Judicial System
Readings in Process and Behavior

Introduction

The following readings on the federal judiciary are organized according to certain concepts of systems theory. This introduction contains a brief outline of the theory and concepts utilized. We use systems theory as an analytical framework because we believe it to be beneficial for understanding the federal judiciary as a policy-making institution. First, as a form of general theory, systems theory brings order and coherence to the increasingly vast range of materials and studies on the federal courts, many of which use different and seemingly contradictory approaches and methodological techniques. Second, we are convinced of its explanatory potential. Systems theory illuminates interrelationships and processes otherwise unexplained. Third, although this seems its least merit thus far, systems theory has predictive value. Last, and perhaps most important, is the heuristic quality of this approach. It suggests new lines of research and new questions to be asked about the judiciary for us to understand more fully its role and function in American society.

Basic to systems theory is the notion of a *system*. The solar system is an example of a system. Like all systems, it consists of elements. The sun, comets, planets, moons, asteroids, and meteors are some of these elements. The behavior of each element is related to and in some way affected by the behavior of every other element. The earth's motion, for example, is dramatically affected by the sun, the moon's motion by the earth. Each, in turn, affects the motion of its larger companion. Certain relationships among the elements imply others. The gravitational attraction of the planets to each other and the sun, for example, implies that they follow certain paths at specific speeds in the past, present, and future. These relationships are so well known that even amateur astronomers can predict with a high degree of accuracy the relative positions of the planets a year, a hundred years, or even a thousand years from now. The analysis of the solar system *qua* system is highly developed both mathematically and theoretically.

When we turn to social and political systems we find less mathematical precision and theoretical sophistication. We also cease to deal with only non-living, material elements. Social systems also have material, living elements—human beings—as well as non-material, non-living elements—ideas and institutions. Yet the notion of a system as a set of elements which interact (or are interrelated) in a more or less orderly fashion is still highly useful.

Can we conceptualize the federal judiciary and its courts as comprising a system? Utilizing the broad definition of a system just given it should be clear that we can. Federal judges, lawyers who practice before the federal courts, federal juries, interest groups that support and sponsor litigation, and the litigants themselves are some of the material, living elements of the federal judicial system. Many of the interactions between them are obvious to even the most casual observer. Litigants hire lawyers to represent them; lawyers argue cases before federal judges, and so forth. Traditional judicial institutions such as *stare decisis* and judicial restraint; legal rules of procedure, evidence, and statutory construction; accepted codes of ethics; and political and economic ideas and theories are among the non-material, non-living elements of this system. These too can be observed to be interrelated with one another and with the material living elements of the system. Not only are the material and non-material elements interrelated with one another, but these interrelations have some degree of order to them. Regular procedures and patterns of behavior, for example, are involved in appealing a case from a federal district court to a United States court of appeals or from a court of appeals to the United States Supreme Court. Of even greater import and interest are the somewhat ordered relationships among individual judges and the other elements of the system in rendering judicial decisions. For example, relationships of leadership and group reference occur that are far from patternless or random. The conceptualization of a federal judicial system in the technical sense of *system* should be even more apparent after reading this book.[1]

The identification of a system does not end with specification of the elements and observing how they interrelate in a more or less orderly fashion. All systems, except perhaps the universe, have boundaries. Outside these boundaries is the system's environment. In the environment of our solar system, for example, are other stars, galaxies, stellar dust, and other solar systems. Surrounding a political system are physical, biological, social, economic, and cultural environments. Each of these, it should be noted, can itself be conceptualized as a system. Meaningful definition of a political system, then, requires specifying its limits or boundaries. We can do this by defining "politics" as the authoritative allocation of values for a society.[2] Politics, in other words, concerns those decisions ultimately backed by state-enforced sanctions as to who gets what, when, where, and how.[3] A political system, therefore, consists of those elements and the interactions among them that are concerned with the authoritative allocation of values for a society.

The boundaries of a political system are not impermeable. Every political system is open to influences from its environment and is thus considered an "open" system. With an open system, the environment is the source of stresses and disturbances. These enter the system and must be processed or in some manner dealt with. Otherwise, the system may not survive. Because political systems are open systems, politics and political life are intimately influenced by and, in turn, influence their physical, biological, social, economic, and cultural environments. This makes the study of political systems at once extraordinarily complex and of the utmost relevance for every aspect of human existence.

Let us now look at the federal judicial system as a political system. (Technically, of course, it may also be viewed as a subsystem of the larger American political system.) It might be asked, at this point, why we do not consider the state judicial processes along with the federal judiciary as one judicial system. It is true, after all, that federal courts considering diversity cases interpret state law and that certain cases may be appealed from the highest state courts to the United States Supreme

---

[1]Systems theory has been previously used to study the judiciary but in a form somewhat different from that employed here. See, Glendon Schubert, *Judicial Policy-Making* (Chicago: Scott, Foresman and Co., 1965), especially chapter 5, and Walter F. Murphy, *Elements of Judicial Strategy* (Chicago: The University of Chicago Press, 1964), pp. 31–36.

[2]This is David Easton's definition contained in his *The Political System* (New York: Alfred A. Knopf, 1953).

[3]This is a paraphrase of Harold Lasswell's famous definition.

Court. However, we believe that state judicial processes are sufficiently distinct from the federal judicial system to warrant separate systems analysis. For example, different states recruit judges by different methods. One state judiciary has no direct relationships with any other state judiciary. The relations of the state judiciaries to the federal judiciary occur infrequently and only with the Supreme Court. Moreover, vast areas of state law, both substantive and procedural, lie outside the reach of the federal courts. The federal courts, on the other hand, constitute integrated sets of relationships. It therefore seems appropriate to examine the federal courts as one system and consider the state judiciaries individually as separate systems.

The boundaries of the federal judicial system can be defined as the authoritative allocation of values presented in the form of litigation which the larger political system allows by its rules of jurisdiction and which the courts further define by their notions of justiciability and standing. The federal judicial system is not only bounded by nonpolitical environments but also by its various political environments. The political environments can be thought of as containing all other political systems within the larger American political system. Included among these, for example, are the judicial systems of the fifty states, the fifty state plus federal legislative systems, the fifty-one bureaucratic systems, the institutionalized Presidency, and so forth. Because the federal judicial system is an open system, it is subject to influences, stresses, and disturbances from these political as well as the nonpolitical environments.

The way in which a political system reacts to and copes with the influences, stresses, and disturbances emanating from the environment shapes the nature of that system. Systems theory uses four theoretical constructs to explain how this occurs. The first is *input*. A system has two types of input: (1) the *demands*, which are the stresses and disturbances emanating from the environment to which the system must respond if it is to survive; and (2) *supports*, which determine whether the system will be sustained as an institution for making political decisions. Supports can either be positive or negative; that is, they may either strengthen or weaken the system as a forum for political decision-making. The supports imply that only a certain range of alternatives can be legitimately used to process demands. The second concept is *conversion*. This refers to the stage when the system's political decision-makers in their institutional roles confront, reshape, and evaluate the inputs in making decisions. The third construct is *output*. The outputs of a political system are the resulting decisions and policies that are made. These are the end products of the conversion process. Output may have far-reaching effects or *impact* on the broader society of which a political system is a part. This brings us to the fourth construct—*feedback*. Feedback is the label given to new demands, generated by the system's output and impact, which become part of the new input into the system.

The federal judicial system can be treated analytically by these four interrelated constructs. The input to the federal judicial system consists both of demands in the form of litigation and supports in the form of lay and professional attitudes about the way the courts fulfill their role. To maintain positive support, the courts must behave according to the role expectations of these publics. This includes, among other things, a conformance to formal legal rules and the norms and mores of the legal and judicial professions. Following these role expectations determines to a large degree what demands can be processed and in a broader sense represent the limits of authority within which the federal judiciary will receive positive support from the larger political system. The conversion or judicial decision-making stage occurs as the inputs are processed, reshaped, and evaluated by federal judges. The

output consists of actual decisions or outcomes of particular cases as well as specified or implied policies concerning how similar cases are to be processed in the future. Judicial output has an impact on the larger political system and its component
subsystems. It also has an impact on other parts of the environment such as the
social and economic systems. The reactions from these systems are fed back into the
federal judicial system as feedback. Feedback influences the nature of the new demands and supports at successive input stages. Figure 1 illustrates the major elements and concepts used in our analysis of the federal judicial system.[4]

FIGURE 1   The Federal Judicial System

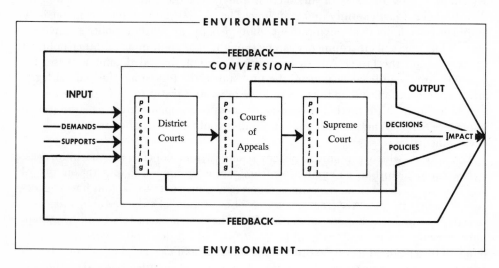

This, then, is a brief outline of the major systems concepts which we have used to
organize the readings in this book. They will be further explained and clarified in
the following parts and sections. The immediately following part considers the
principal elements of the federal judicial system. Subsequent parts consider the input stage, the conversion process, output and feedback. The concluding part is concerned with the relationship of the federal judicial system to the larger American
political system.

[4]The diagram, of necessity, is a simplification of reality. The diagram is applicable to cases which
begin in the district courts and are appealed to the appeals courts and then to the Supreme Court.
But certain demands in the form of litigation take other routes not illustrated by the diagram, and the
student should be aware of them. For example, some cases of special constitutional significance or types
of cases specified by Congress (such as appeals from the Interstate Commerce Commission) are heard
by three judge district courts and then are appealed to the Supreme Court, bypassing the appeals
courts. Most federal agency appeals bypass the district courts and go directly to the appeals courts.
Appeals from the highest state courts are demands made exclusively on the Supreme Court.

Part 1
Elements
of the Federal
Judicial System

The readings in this part are devoted to a consideration of the elements of the federal judicial system. These are the actual participants as well as the ideas and institutions associated with the legal setting in which the federal judicial system functions. The first eight readings concern the participants in the system. Greatest attention is given to the judges. There are also readings about the role of interest groups and lawyers in the judicial system. This, of course, does not exhaust the list of participants. Federal juries,[1] law clerks and ancillary administrative personnel as well as the litigants are also elements of the system. It should also be noted that governments at all levels, interest groups, and private persons, as litigants, are the major source of demands for the federal judicial system.

The last three readings in this part concern the legal setting. This term subsumes a constellation of elements, both ideas and institutions, which are vitally important for understanding the federal judicial system. This is so because the key positions in the system—judges, attorneys, and prosecutors—are all occupied by members of the bar. The legal setting thus affects a judge's or lawyer's motivations, his norms, the way he conceptualizes and performs his role, and his notions of what is legitimately open to judicial determination. In the section concerning the legal profession, we shall briefly consider elements of professionalism. Then we shall consider other elements (*stare decisis* and judicial self-restraint) which comprise the legal setting of the system.

A. Judges: Judicial Selection

Federal judges are the principal elements of the federal judicial system. To become a judge one must first be nominated by the President and then appointed by him after the United States Senate gives its advice and consent. Who are the people

[1] The most thorough recent treatment of jury behavior is that of Harry Kalven, Jr., and Hans Zeisel, *The American Jury* (Boston: Little, Brown & Company, 1966). Their sample includes both state and federal juries.

who become judges and what is the process by which they receive their appointments are questions of the utmost importance. As Jack Peltason has noted, "[t]he decision as to *who* will make the decisions affects *what* decisions will be made."[2] The following three readings present an overview of the selection of federal judges for the two principal lower federal courts—the district courts and the courts of appeals.

The reading by Joel Grossman contains a persuasive argument for viewing the judicial selection process as in itself an important variable in the socialization of would-be judges. Study of the selection process not only informs us about the kinds of judges chosen, but also the norms of selection which provide cues to would-be judges as to the type of training, preparation, and activity appropriate for seeking appointment to the federal bench. Appointments to the district courts are the subject of the article by Harold Chase. Appeals court appointments are discussed by Sheldon Goldman. Both articles trace the variables of the appointment process and suggest the political interactions which characterize judicial selection.

Appointments to the United States Supreme Court are of a somewhat different order in that the White House and not the Justice Department is usually the focal point of activity. Furthermore, Supreme Court appointments are at the center of public attention and thus involve many groups and individuals in behind-the-scenes activity. It is clear from both the Chase and Goldman articles that a great deal of subsurface activity also occurs with lower court appointments. But since Supreme Court appointments have been so few in number, it is more difficult to generalize about the appointment process *qua* process. What can be said, however, is that appointments to the Supreme Court as well as to the lower federal courts are the result of an appointment *transaction*. David Danelski has developed transaction theory to explain judicial appointments[3] and has observed:

In transactional explanations, events are understood within the situation in which they arise, and are explained in terms of postulated relationships among activities. The phenomena of man perceiving, describing, and otherwise acting in process with his environment are observed in fields of connected activity called *transactions*. The prefix *trans* means that the fields of activity are seen in overview just as they appear in time and space. They are not broken up into their so-called component parts, such as perceiver and thing perceived . . . . In other words, perception can be understood only within the situation—that is, the transaction—in which it arises.[4]

It is prudent to remember that while we may generalize about district and appeals court appointments, each appointment represents a unique transaction.

[2]Jack W. Peltason, *Federal Courts in the Political Process* (New York: Random House, 1955), p. 29.
[3]David J. Danelski, *A Supreme Court Justice Is Appointed* (New York: Random House, 1964).
[4]*Ibid.*, pp. 146–147.

1 JUDICIAL SELECTION AND THE SOCIALIZATION OF JUDGES

Joel B. Grossman

"All members of societies go through common socialization experiences."[1] But these experiences do not prepare them for the specialized roles that every society must have, including the roles of political leadership. It is the recruitment function to draw members of a society out of particular subcultures and "induct them into the specialized roles of the political system, train them in the appropriate skills, provide them with political cognitive maps, values, expectations, and affects."[2] Recruitment thus consists of special role socializations built on the foundation of general socialization.

As used here, recruitment is a generalized description of a variety of activities designed to produce judges with certain types of training, certain sets of values, and certain sets of expectations. The socialization of judges necessarily involves a variety of factors. After the obvious ones such as adequate legal training and experience, basic honesty, and judicial temperament, we can identify such basic role-expectation alternatives as devotion to procedure versus concern for substantive issues, judicial self-restraint versus judicial activism, concern for "the law" as an abstract doctrine versus concern for arriving at "just" settlements of individual cases, and a view of the courts as instruments for social change versus a view of the courts as conservators of the status quo. Judicial selection, considered as one part of the overall recruitment process, is not the only means by which judges are socialized. Thus . . . the American Bar Association does not limit itself to seeking influence

via the selection of judges. Through its canons of legal and judicial ethics, and through its influence and control over legal training and bar membership, it seeks to set some of the norms of the institutionalized judicial role and seeks to orient lawyers toward these norms. In its meetings and journals it provides forums for evaluation of judicial actions; and through these same media it tries to educate judges as well as lawyers and the lay public as to proper handling of great constitutional questions or proper responses to judicial actions.

In one sense judicial selection comes "near the end" of the judicial-recruitment process. It acts to reinforce the socialization process by choosing those lawyers who have conformed to the established norms and who therefore give promise of fulfilling the judicial role in an expected manner. But though the act of selection may contribute little to the socialization of the new judge, it demonstrates visibly and effectively the types of behavior to which prospective judges ought to conform. If a particular selection system appeared to favor a high degree of prior political involvement rather than intensive legal experience as a necessary prerequisite, the types of preparatory activities in which prospective judges would engage would vary accordingly. At first, these changed patterns might be latent rather than manifest. But they would be very real indeed! Thus, in another sense, the act of selection could be considered the "initial" act in the process of socializing would-be judges. The norms of selection give the initial cues as to the type of training and preparation which might lead to the federal bench.

The ways in which prospective judges are socialized depend partially on the nature of the selection process. And that process is not susceptible to simple categorization or description. Rather it consists of a variety of forces whose interaction produces a phenomenon called the "selection process." But what are these forces? And which among them is responsible for particular aspects of the process? Which, if any, dominate the process, or make most of the important decisions?

The process of political socialization is necessarily a dynamic one. As the values or

Reprinted by permission of publisher from Joel B. Grossman, *Lawyers and Judges: The ABA and the Politics of Judicial Selection* (New York: John Wiley & Sons, Inc., 1965), pp. 19–20. Footnotes renumbered.

[1]Gabriel Almond, "A Functional Approach to Comparative Politics," in Almond and James Coleman (eds.), *The Politics of the Developing Areas* (Princeton, N.J.: Princeton University Press, 1960), p. 31.

[2]*Ibid.*

conditions of a society change, the training of its future leaders must change accordingly. Thus, any attempt to describe the process by which federal judges are socialized through recruitment is at once limited by the dynamics of the situation. Any description of it must recognize that change itself is a constant factor.

2 APPOINTMENTS TO THE FEDERAL DISTRICT COURTS

Harold W. Chase

Baseball games are played under a well-defined set of rules and customs by players manning prescribed positions, yet it is probable that no two games have been identical. These generalizations about the national pastime provide a good analogy for the process of appointing federal judges. These appointments are made pursuant to law and custom largely by a line-up of individuals occupying prescribed positions. While there are established patterns, the participants interact differently in each appointment within the framework of law and custom.

In one respect, the analogy breaks down. A baseball team fields nine men and has a roster of eligible players limited by statutory baseball law. In the appointing process, there are certain players who must participate in the game: the President; United States Senators; the Department of Justice; the candidates for the judgeship; the Standing Committee on Federal Judiciary of the American Bar Association; and political party leaders. But there is no statutory prescription limiting the game to only these participants. Frequently, others may voluntarily or involuntarily be drawn into the process.

A. LAW AND CUSTOM
. . .

1. Senatorial Courtesy. . . . Senators, whether chosen by state legislatures or by the

Reprinted by permission of author and publisher from Harold W. Chase, "Federal Judges: The Appointing Process," *Minnesota Law Review*, 51 (1966), pp. 185, 188–200, 203–204, 210–218. Footnotes omitted.

voters of the state, must continuously nurture their political support back home if they desire re-election. Senators, since the first Congress, have recognized that Senators from the state where the appointment is to be made have a much greater stake in a particular appointment than the other Senators. It is, of course, exceedingly useful to a Senator to be able to reward supporters with good posts in the federal government. Conversely, it is enormously damaging to a Senator's prestige if a President of the same party ignores him when making an appointment involving the Senator's home state. It is even more damaging to a Senator's prestige and political power for the President to appoint to high federal office someone who is known as a political opponent of the Senator. Senators soon realized that if they united to protect their individual interests in appointments, they could assure that the President could make only such appointments as would be palatable to them as individuals. Out of such considerations grew the custom of senatorial courtesy.

. . .

Senatorial courtesy has come to mean that Senators will give serious consideration and be favorably disposed to support an individual Senator of the President's party who opposes a nominee to an office in his state. But, as the Chief Clerk of the Senate Judiciary Committee put it, "he just can't incant a few magic words like 'personally obnoxious' and get away with it. He must be prepared to fight, giving his reasons for opposing the nominee." If his reasons are not persuasive or if he is not a respected member of the Senate, he may lose.

. . .

As a result of senatorial courtesy, there developed a corollary custom by which Senators of the President's party suggested candidates to the President for federal offices in their home states. If these candidates passed the President's muster, he appointed them. The basis for this custom was laid in Washington's administration. One of his nominees to a federal post in Georgia was rejected by the

Senate in courtesy to the Georgia Senators. Washington yielded with a mild protest and appointed the nominee of the Georgia Senators. Had Washington, with his tremendous prestige, held his ground, he might well have established a precedent which would have stunted the growth of senatorial courtesy. When later Presidents sought to reassert for the presidency the leading role in making appointments to federal offices within specific state boundaries, they met with only limited success.

Although some Presidents, and indeed, some Senators, have tried to verbally punch the Senate into giving up the custom of senatorial courtesy, the custom, albeit in modified form, retains vitality. Senate devotion to the custom can readily be understood in terms of self-interest. . . .

It has become common to overexaggerate the role and power of individual Senators in the matter of district court appointments. When a President chooses to inject himself into the appointment of district judges, he can do so effectively, as Presidents T. Roosevelt, Wilson and Hoover did. Even granting that senators of the party in power once may have owned district judgeships, they have not under the last four Presidents. Appointments are not made by Senators alone; other parties are deeply involved. And, just as the legal power to confirm with its corollary custom of courtesy provides a Senator with formidable practical power to employ toward securing a particular nomination, other parties in interest have special powers which can be used as counters. It does not follow that because individual Senators may be in a position to veto the appointment of judges that they must do the appointing. In fact, close examination of the appointment process suggests otherwise.

2. The President: Expectations and Powers. Curiously, while knowledgeable people have considered it a fact that Senators appointed district court judges, other knowledgeable people have been quick to hold the President responsible for the quality and character of judicial appointments. . . . Consequently, Presidents generally have been very concerned that the quality of appointments made during their incumbency be high. This has been especially true of the last three administrations. And, where a President wants to insure a high level of appointments, he has legal powers which afford him considerable coin with which to bargain with the Senators individually and collectively. First, the President must submit the nomination for formal consideration of the Senate. He is under no legal compulsion to make nominations within a prescribed time limit. He can, therefore, stall or refuse to fill a vacancy. In fact, doing so may be very effective in forcing some concessions from a Senator. Refusal to nominate can be particularly effective when coupled with a suggestion leaked to the press that a distinguished lawyer or state judge is the President's choice. The Senator is then in the position of publicly opposing the President's distinguished candidate, which may have a much different impact in legal circles and on public opinion than in a situation in which the only apparent candidate is the Senator's. The pressure on a Senator may even be greater if both his and the President's candidates are known and if there is feeling among bar and press that the President's candidate is superior.

A second important presidential power is his constitutional mandate "to fill up all Vacancies, that may happen during the Recess of the Senate, by granting Commissions which shall expire at the End of their next Session." There has been stout argument throughout our history as to what the word "happen" means in this context. Some have argued that the President could fill any vacancy which happened to exist during the recess; others have urged that he could only fill those which happened to occur during the recess. In practice, Presidents tend to take the broader view of their powers and fill both kinds of vacancies. Recently, this practice received judicial sanction from the United States Court of Appeals for the Second Circuit.

. . .

Because of the prestige of his office and his access to the mass media, the President can exert a powerful influence upon public expectations as to judicial appointments which may, in turn, affect the play leading to appointment. If the public can be conditioned to expect high level appointments, it may become poor politics for a Senator or state party leader to seek to place men on the bench who do not measure up to the expectation. In such a case, a President may be hoisted with his own petard, for he, too, may find it poor politics to make a particular appointment if that appointment does not measure up to the level of expectation he has helped to create. For example, when it was rumored that "President Kennedy wants to name Boston Municipal Judge Francis X. Morrissey, his former secretary and a life long friend of the Kennedy family, to the single new federal judgeship now available in Massachusetts," members of the Boston and Massachusetts bar associations and the press were outraged because Morrissey seemed poorly qualified for the post. Influential elements of the press were quick to point out the irony of a President considering the nomination of a man who did not meet the standards for the office that the President himself had set.

3. The Deputy Attorney General. . . . If a President takes seriously his legal responsibility for nominating and appointing federal judges, the search for and screening of candidates requires more time than he can personally give to it. But, even if he eschews a major responsibility and is willing to have Senators name appointees, he will at least want to be sure that appointments will not reflect adversely upon him. To obtain such assurance requires a more intensive investigation than the President has time to make. Consequently, it has become customary for the President to assign his Attorney General the responsibility for advising him as to judicial appointments. In turn, it has become customary, at least in the last three administrations, for the Attorney General to make it a primary responsibility of the Deputy Attorney General to make recommendations for such appointments. In the last two administrations, where there were an unusually large number of judicial appointments to be made,

the day-to-day leg work of acquiring data on prospective nominees and negotiating with Senators was assigned by the Deputy to an assistant. . . .

Because the relationship between the Attorney General and the Deputy must be close in an organizational and personal sense, the Attorney General is kept apprised of important developments as the Deputy seeks to fashion a recommendation. At any time, the Attorney General may indicate that he would like the Deputy to proceed in a specific way. The Attorney General may even make the initial suggestion as to a possible nominee, asking the Deputy to check him out. Whatever communication the Attorney General receives from Senators and others will be passed on to the Deputy with or without comment.

To a lesser extent, the Attorney General will keep the President informed. If it appears that a particular recommendation may cause difficulty with a Senator or party leaders, there may be some discussion. Conversely, if the President has had communications from a Senator or party leaders, he will relay the information to the Attorney General with his comments. The President can, of course, at any time specify whom he wants nominated and that settles the matter. But, Presidents rarely do so; rather, Presidents generally are willing to have the Attorney General make the recommendation. In the end, the President will take one good, hard look at the recommended nomination. At that point, the President may seek assurance from the Attorney General that the nomination will stand up when it goes to the Senate or that he has been informed of any anticipated difficulties and the reasons for making the nomination in spite of them.

Although the President or the Attorney General may at any time direct the Deputy Attorney General to follow a prescribed course of action or refuse to accept his recommendations, the Deputy in practice plays the leading role in exercising the President's power. In the last three presidencies, the office of Deputy Attorney General has attracted men of extraordinary ability. . . . Such men have not been content to sit back and screen recommendations offered by Senators. Whenever possible, they took the initiative in seeking out and proposing candidates. As an assistant to one of these Deputies put it: "we take all the ground the Senators let us take." But there have been some very interesting differences in degree of zeal with which Deputies have sought to take ground, largely traceable to their respective President's general attitude toward the Senate. The Eisenhower team was much more aggressive in urging their own nominees on Senators than the present team. Evidently President Johnson, as a consequence of long years in the Senate, believes in senatorial prerogative and is deferential where he can be. President Eisenhower, on the other hand, was not so impressed with senatorial claims to appointments and backed his team strongly in their efforts to take ground against Senators.

Thus, while the Deputy has no legal power in his own right to make nominations, to the extent that he can influence the Attorney General and the President, he can invoke the President's power. This is known and understood by other principals in the appointment process and it facilitates direct negotiations between them and the Deputy.

4. The White House Staff. During the Kennedy administration, the contact between the Attorney General and the President was very close and direct. No member of the White House staff participated actively in the process of judicial selection. Of course, members of the staff who dealt with Senators liked to be informed of the progress of nominations. Shortly after Robert Kennedy's resignation, however, President Johnson asked John Macy, the President's Special Assistant on personnel matters and Chairman of the Civil Service Commission, to review nominations suggested by the Department of Justice. As Macy sees it, his function is to maintain a kind of quality control. To this end, he endeavors to have his office make an independent investigation and evaluation of each suggested nominee.

One could speculate that the President's original purpose in imposing a White House screening was merely to protect his own political interests at a time when he could not be sure about the political loyalties of the team at the Department of Justice. But Macy feels that his search for men and women to fill important vacancies in Government must include judgeships, since a person might well be considered a good prospect for both a seat on the bench and a high administrative post at the same time. Whatever the reasons, Macy and his small staff now take a hard independent look at recommendations of the Department.

5. The American Bar Association. In 1945 the American Bar Association established the Special Committee on Federal Judiciary, later to become the Standing Committee on Federal Judiciary which passes on the qualifications of nominees to the federal bench. It has become customary for the Senate Judiciary Committee to consider these reports from the ABA Committee. Further, the ABA Committee customarily submits an informal report to the Department of Justice on any person the Department is seriously considering for appointment. The Committee will indicate whether a particular person is "Exceptionally Well Qualified," "Well Qualified," "Qualified," or "Not Qualified" for a judicial post. Needless to say, the Committee has a profound impact on the selection process. As experience attests, a rating of "Not Qualified" will not necessarily mean that a particular man will be withdrawn from consideration, but no administration is eager to have very many of its appointments so classified. For this reason, the ABA Committee is significantly involved in the selection process.

6. The Senate Judiciary Committee. Senate rules require that the Judiciary Committee pass on all nominations to the federal bench and make recommendations to the Senate. Customarily, a subcommittee holds hearings on all such nominations, but in most cases the hearing is perfunctory. The Committee members do not regard it as their function to actively help select judges. Rather, they regard themselves as watchdogs, safeguarding the interests of the public and the Senators, individually and collectively.

To safeguard the interests of individual Senators, the Committee checks with the Senators of the state where the nominee will hold his post, in the case of a district judge, or the Senators of the state where the nominee is from, if he is to serve on a circuit, special, or District of Columbia court. With rare exception, the Committee tends to support an individual Senator who objects to a nominee. The Committee reviews the report from the ABA Committee on Federal Judiciary. In addition, the chairman is apprised of the information developed by the FBI investigation of the nominee on behalf of the Department of Justice. . . .

The Committee can affect the selection process markedly in three ways. First, it can delay Senate action on confirmation in the hope of embarrassing the President or testing his determination to make a particular appointment. Delay may be used to afford the Committee or individual members the opportunity to seek Senate support in opposing the nomination. Although effective at times, delay is not effective against a determined President who can expect support from a majority of the Senators. If the Judiciary Committee as a whole refuses to act, a majority of the Senate can take the matter out of the Committee's hands via a discharge petition.

A second way in which the Committee can affect the selection process is through Committee hearings. These hearings afford the Senators—individually and collectively—their best means for influencing judicial selection by attuning the Senate as a whole, the press, and the public to the objections against a nominee. Committee members can dispel or enhance this informational process significantly by their arrangement and questioning of witnesses. In the sense that the Senate Judiciary Committee's hearings provide an opportunity to expose real or alleged weaknesses of nominees, they can exert a powerful influence on the conduct of parties to the nomination process.

In the same fashion, Senate debate over confirmation affords still a third opportunity for Senators to seek to embarrass the administration by questioning the wisdom of a particular appointment. Here, individual members of the Senate Judiciary Committee who have dissented from the majority's recommendation can be expected to play a leading role, for they will have a familiarity with the nominee's record. A Senator who is unable or unwilling to invoke senatorial courtesy can still throw some telling punches. Such action will rarely defeat a nomination, but the prospect of denunciation on the Senate floor may weigh heavily in the deliberations of appointing principals.

B. PRESSURES AT WORK

. . . It is axiomatic that one path to appointive office is to ingratiate oneself with those who hold the appointing power. Baldly stated, the axiom has disturbing overtones. One implication is that appointments are obtained as a quid pro quo for service rendered without regard for qualifications. Looking at it from another perspective, a person working in a campaign has a unique opportunity to demonstrate his ability to a candidate. If the candidate wins and then has the opportunity to appoint or help appoint to high office, he has a coterie who have demonstrated that they are like-minded as to political philosophy and are capable. What is more natural in such a situation than to seek to place such people in high governmental posts? To the degree that an appointment is made on qualifications and ability, it is inaccurate to describe it as a purely political appointment. But political considerations lay enormous pressures on the appointment makers.

. . . Rewarding the faithful has become so much a part and parcel of our system that it would be fair to say that it has the significance and meaning of custom; appointment makers are expected to follow custom and are under pressure to do so. However much an appointment maker might want to make his selection on merit alone, he cannot ignore custom without risk of sparking great discontent among the professionals in his party. . . . [But] no one is promised a judgeship for services rendered nor will anyone be appointed to a judgeship if he does not have the qualifications for the post. But there is a frank recognition that it is incumbent upon the appointment makers to take care of those who contributed heavily to the efforts of the past campaign and that somewhere in the vast spectrum of posts available they can find a spot becoming to the talents of those who have a substantial claim to consideration.

. . .

C. THE INTERPLAY OF FORCES IN THE APPOINTMENT [OF DISTRICT JUDGES]

The appointment process cannot be described adequately as a series of formal and automatic steps. An appointment grows out of the interaction of a number of people with varying and, to some extent, countervailing powers attempting to influence each other within a framework imposed on them by law, custom, and tradition.

Once it is known that there is or will be a vacancy on the federal bench, the jockeying for position begins in earnest. Some groundwork undoubtedly will have been laid far in advance. Some provident aspirants may have established themselves by their political activity in anticipation of the day when the opportunity would surely arise. The President, at the beginning of his administration, will have indicated implicitly or explicitly what he wishes done with respect to appointments. His men in the Department of Justice will have been actively or passively collecting names and information about good prospects. The appropriate Senators will have been importuned from time to time with suggestions for future judicial appointments. If there has been a recent appointment to a post in a particular state, all parties to the nomination process have in mind the also-rans, some of whom must be contenders for the next vacancy. A large percentage of nominees have been considered one or more times before actually being designated.

While the aspirants have others generate support for their candidacy, the President's men in the Justice Department canvass people whom they know, in and outside of the Department, as to qualified candidates. Strategic in this situation are members in the Depart-

ment who have or are thought to have special knowledge about lawyers in their native states. They may recite the virtues of particular individuals from memory or they may contact people back home and relay the information so garnered. Others who have worked in the political hustings with the crucial Department officials will also be queried. Or as is frequently the case, they will not wait to be queried but will offer gratuitous advice.

At the same time, the Senators of the President's party will be actively or passively collecting information on candidates. . . .

. . . [Many] Senators will submit a list of candidates and suggest to the Department that any one of those named on the list will be acceptable to them, inviting the Department to make the selection. The reason for such an approach can be readily understood. As the old saying goes, "In making an appointment, you make fifty enemies and one ingrate." By drawing up a list and placing the onus for decision on the Department, a Senator can satisfy more and disappoint fewer candidates. As indicated earlier, the team at the Department of Justice is happy to move into the breach and make the selections. But Senators who submit lists do not always do so for the purpose of letting the President's men pick and choose; some use the list as camouflage. For, while they send a letter with the list to the Department with copies for all interested parties, they call upon or phone officials to indicate who their real choice is.

Most Senators feel that if they are of the President's party, they should designate the nominee subject to the approval of the Department of Justice. . . .

When a Senator feels strongly about what he considers to be his prerogative, the President's men may have considerable difficulty thwarting his attempt to impose on them an unfavorable nominee. Thus, it is understandable why there is a ready disposition in the Department to accept a good suggestion for nominee from the Senator without much question. If there are two Senators of the President's party from a particular state, Department arithmetic has it that the effect of two Senators wanting a particular man for a district judgeship in their state is more than one plus one. The sum is more like infinity, for it would only be with great trepidation that the President's men would attempt to counter the will of both Senators.

Interestingly enough, the fact that two Senators are involved may give the President's men a wedge for taking more ground in the appointment process. If the Senators are not agreed on a candidate, as is frequently the case, the President's men can jockey suggestions to them trying to find a nominee who is their choice primarily but acceptable to both Senators. In such situations, it is important for the President's men not to convey the impression to either Senator that they have favored the candidate of the other. But Senators are not unaware of the effectiveness of these divide and conquer tactics and many of them will seek to work out an arrangement with the other Senator from their state so that they will always appear to make common cause on appointments. The easiest device for doing so is to split up appointments, including nonjudicial appointments.

Despite the efficacy of presenting a united front, some Senators are so estranged politically from the other Senator of the state that they just cannot work out a satisfactory arrangement. . . .

As indicated previously, when a Senator or two Senators of the state has or have settled on a candidate, the President's agents are predisposed to accept him, unless they feel he does not meet their standard for character and competence. But this does not mean that they have played a passive role. Operating on the basis that "you can't beat someone with no one," the President's men frequently take initiative in proposing candidates to the Senator. It may turn out that all interested parties have had the same person in mind all along. But such initiative on the part of Department officers may put the Senator in the dual position of presenting his own candidate while actively opposing the man suggested by the Department. This can become embarrassing for the Senator if word is leaked to the press as to whom the Department is considering and the state press finds the Department's

choice worth lauding. The Senator is then placed on the defensive locally. His position may be untenable if the Department has fixed on a prestigious lawyer or state judge who has considerable support in his own right among party and bar leaders in the state.

The Senators, however, have a counter strategy. If a Senator beats the Department and issues a press release stating that a particular person will be the next federal district judge, he has placed his own prestige on the line. For the presidential assistants to contest the Senator's choice at this point involves the politically important issue of face-saving. It is, however, a daring maneuver, for should the Department oppose his choice and it turns out that they have good grounds for doing so, the Senator will have difficulty saving face. On the other hand, the President's men may prefer to swallow hard and take the Senator's man without contest, in preference to embarrassing him. This is particularly true if the Senator is regarded as powerful.

When several appointments are to be made to the bench in a particular state, the Department and the Senators may be able to compromise. For example, in the Kennedy Administration, it was easier to get Senators to accept a Republican appointment for one of several vacant positions than it would have been where only one vacancy was to be filled.

Basically, the presidential assistants and the Senators, when they are of the same party, want to avoid open conflict. Both sides appreciate that each has the ability to inflict heavy damage on the other. The President's men view with heavy heart a knock-down-drag-out fight in Judiciary Committee hearings, just as Senators dread having it bruited about in the press back home that their candidate does not meet Presidential standards. Negotiations, therefore, begin in a spirit of accommodation. The principals want to avoid a fight, but most of them are prepared to take all the ground they can.

Depending upon personality, the principals may be frank and direct in their approach or they may play it close to the vest, trying to gauge the true feelings of the others without giving up the same information on themselves.

Frequently, pointed banter in face-to-face situations is a useful device for drawing out information. How does the Senator react when the Deputy Attorney General or his assistant says to him, with a smile: "Oh you can't be serious about putting Joe Smith on the bench?" Conversely, the Senator may watch closely for a reaction when he tells the Attorney General in what appears to be a joking manner: "If Jack Jones doesn't get that judgeship, I'm going to be MIGHTY unhappy."

If it turns out that the Senator has a man that pleases the Executive branch, the negotiations are swiftly closed, provided the reports of the FBI and the ABA Committee on the Judiciary are in the candidate's favor. If the Senator's candidate does not please Department officials, or the President's advisors are pressing a candidacy which is not to the Senator's liking, or both are happening at the same time, the jockeying for position becomes a serious business. The best strategy for the President's agents at this point is to sit tight and not move forward in the formal process of appointment. This will cause immediate concern for the Senator. If the Senator had not been very strong on his proffered candidate, he may quickly back down and seek agreement on another choice. On the other hand, the Senator may try to force the issue by dragging his feet in some endeavor which means a great deal to the President.

Despite frequent allegations to the contrary, appointment makers do not like to be put in a position in which votes in the Senate on the President's program depend upon a particular judicial appointment. Few Senators want to bargain away their independence to vote as they see fit on major issues. It is often more important to them politically to vote against the President on a particular issue than to have a specific individual named judge. The President's assistants may at times feel that going along with a Senator on a judgeship in return for a key vote would be in the public interest. Yet, there is good reason for avoiding such trading. . . . Undoubtedly, there have been occasions when there has been an unspoken quid pro quo, Presidential acquies-

cence to a Senator's wishes with respect to a judicial appointment in return for a vote, but it has been rarer than is generally believed. And it must be remembered that when a President does attempt to bargain with judgeships he is limited in what he can do. For reasons already explored, the President cannot just go ahead and name someone whom the Senator from the state and of his party will oppose, and expect to have him confirmed. Thus, his best currency for purchasing compliance is delay and favoring one Senator in the state over another.

. . .

When the President's assistants employ Fabian tactics and the Senator chooses not to succumb, a ready and available strategy is to try and out wait them. They normally like to fill the vacancies quickly in order that the work of the judiciary keep somewhat apace with the demands on it. This gives the Senator an opportunity to test the resolve of the Executive branch. However, the Senator is at a disadvantage at this point, for the political pressure to fill the vacancy comes from within the state and means more to the Senator than to national officers. Also, the President might make a recess appointment and this might make the situation more difficult for the Senator. When things reach such an impasse, there will generally be more effort to seek accommodation rather than resort to open warfare. For the President's aides are not eager to go the route of the recess appointment which will not avoid, but merely forestall, an open fight with the Senate which they stand a good chance of losing. However, the President's assistants may, in their efforts to dissuade a Senator from backing a particular candidate, receive a big assist from an adverse report from the FBI or the ABA Committee. Not many Senators will want to bear such a cross, particularly if the grounds for the unfavorable reports are the kind which will engender public opprobrium if aired.

When accommodation cannot be reached, one of three possible results occur: The President's men make no effort to fill the vacancy; the President formally designates a nominee unacceptable to the Senator and invariably loses the contest for confirmation, if the Senator fights to the bitter end; or, the President makes a recess appointment and loses the contest for confirmation at the next session of Congress. As suggested earlier, when a President employs either of the last two courses of action, the pressure may be too great for the Senator to persist in opposition. But the outcomes indicated are based on the assumption that the Senator will go the full route in opposition. It is important to stress that ultimately the Senator is not in a position to initiate the action which constitutes a throwing down of the gauntlet when the impasse has been reached. In a very real sense, the President's constitutional power to make the formal nomination provides him with the advantage that is inherent in taking offensive action, whereas the Senator in the moment of truth has only defensive weapons.

3 JUDICIAL APPOINTMENTS TO THE UNITED STATES COURTS OF APPEALS

Sheldon Goldman

This article seeks to explore the complex judicial selection process for appointments to the United States Courts of Appeals. The data utilized have been largely gathered from a systematic study of certain Justice Department files for each of the eighty-four judges in active service on the appeals courts during part or all of the period between 1961 and 1964. The object of this paper is to analyze the various components of the selection process and, in particular, to examine the role of politics and ideology in the process and thus the kind of people appointed. Our attention is focused on the Eisenhower and Kennedy Administrations. . . .

Reprinted by permission of author and publisher from Sheldon Goldman, "Judicial Appointments to the United States Courts of Appeals," *Wisconsin Law Review*, Winter, 1967, pp. 186–214. Footnotes omitted.

I

The judges on the United States Courts of Appeals were nominated for their positions by the President and were appointed by him after the United States Senate had given its advice and consent. Behind this simple statement lies a complex reality of customs, pressures, expectations, and constraints that operate on the participants in the appointment process. The first reality—and an obvious one to casual observers of the process—is that the President's men in the Justice Department, *i.e.* the Attorney General and especially the Deputy Attorney General and his assistants, are primarily responsible for judicial selection. Thus, our attention must focus on the Justice Department rather than the White House.

The appointment process "begins" (at least analytically) by the President's men considering various lawyers or judges for a particular vacancy. The sources of names of prospective candidates for appeals court judgeships are varied. The President occasionally will have his personal choice whom the Justice Department will then promote. But, in more cases, the Deputy, or, indeed, the Attorney General, will take the initiative and activate candidacies of those thought to be well suited for the particular vacancy. . . .

Justice officials use their vast network of friends, acquaintances, and friends of friends as a source for possible appointees. This is not done out of personal favoritism but out of a desire to insure the selection of highly competent people who will reflect credit on the administration. Illustrative of the personal involvement of a high Justice official is a letter to the Attorney General from a candidate who was later appointed to the bench. The candidate had been extremely active in the preceding presidential campaign and had made the acquaintance of the Attorney General, who had also been active in the campaign. The letter began with a first name salutation and continued:

Further in connection with our conversation of last week regarding the vacancy on the United States Court of Appeals for the — Circuit, this is to advise that both Senators — and — will support me. You will be receiving letters from them within a few days, and I told them, as you suggested, to send copies to [the deputy].

Enjoyed visiting with you and hope to see you again before too long.

It is hard to determine the number of appeals court judges who were initially selected and promoted by the Justice Department officials on their own or at the instigation of the President. The difficulty is that for political reasons the department prefers its suggestions to become the recommendations of the senators of the President's party from the appointee's state. However, it is probably no exaggeration to suggest that close to one out of five Eisenhower or Kennedy appeals court appointees had his nomination initiated by the Justice Department.

The next obvious source of names of potential judicial candidates is the senator or senators from the President's party representing the state for which the appointment is slated. . . .

Another source of suggestions for candidates is the political leaders in the President's party, such as veteran congressmen, state party chairmen, governors, national committeemen, and mayors of large cities. Prospective candidates are also often suggested by high-level administration men, by law school deans responding to queries from Justice officials or writing on their own initiative, by friends of Justice officials, and by friends of friends. Indeed, those desiring their own appointment have been known to directly inform the Justice Department of their availability. Still another source of suggestions is the judiciary; about forty percent of the Justice Department files of the Eisenhower and Kennedy appointees contained letters of recommendation from state or federal judges.

When a vacancy occurs on an appeals court due to death or retirement, the sources mentioned will readily suggest candidates to fill the vacancy. The Justice Department maintains files on some of the likely candidates. Usually the Department will consider those candidates proposed by the senators and the party organization before promoting their

own candidate. Often it turns out that the varied sources will independently recommend the same individual for a particular vacancy. This is ordinarily taken as evidence of a strong candidacy.

The problem for the President's men is to investigate informally and evaluate the proposed candidates in the light of certain expectations and constraints. . . .

When the senator(s) and party leaders from the state scheduled to receive the appointment agree on one candidate who subsequently appears qualified by the Justice Department's standards, that candidate's nomination is virtually certain, and confirmation by the Senate is only a matter of time. However, when Justice officials select a man from many submitted names, or have their own candidate to promote and are willing to challenge the senator(s) and state party's nominee, extensive negotiations have to be undertaken with these political leaders. Once the Justice officials have secured the necessary political clearance for the selected candidate, the FBI is instructed to investigate the candidate. When the FBI report is in and nothing adverse has unexpectedly been uncovered, the Attorney General makes his recommendation to the President. Shortly thereafter, the nomination is announced from the White House and sent to the Senate.

The Senate Judiciary Committee is usually briefed on impending nominations, and committee members, particularly the chairman, may indicate what trouble, if any, there will be in having the committee render its approval. The committee meets in closed sessions to discuss the nominations and to decide when to hold hearings. The committee chairman, presently Senator Eastland, has been known deliberately to delay confirmation proceedings for numerous reasons, such as the nomination of a Negro.

In all, it is not unusual for the time span between the opening of a vacancy and the administration of the judicial oath to the appointee to be approximately one year or longer. The average time it took to appoint the eighty-four appeals judges actively serving during part or all of the 1961–1964 period was seven months. The process is long and involved, yet, for appointments to the appeals courts, the Justice Department ordinarily has much leeway in determining who will finally be appointed. Therefore, it is useful to focus our attention on the expectations and constraints, some of which have been mentioned in passing, within which the President's men in the Justice Department operate.

II

A. Qualified Appointees. The President's men in the Justice Department strive to appoint competent people to appeals court posts. They strive because they wish to do a "good" job, *i.e.* to support these important courts, and, in general, avoid the damaging image of "playing politics" with the judiciary. The criteria for being "qualified" or "well qualified" are ambiguous and difficult to define but include being a "respected" lawyer or judge and having the professional competence and judicial temperament thought to befit an appointee to the appeals courts. Trial court experience is usually a plus mark in the evaluation of candidates. Public legal experience seems to be prominent in the backgrounds of the appointees.

There are also external pressures to appoint unquestionably qualified people to appeals court posts. Newspaper editorial writers are fond of delivering sermons on the necessity of "high quality" judicial appointments. By lauding good appointments, newspapers help cultivate an image that most administrations presumably seek.

While Justice officials would like to appoint the "magnas" and "summas" of the legal-judicial profession, they often find that only "cums" have survived the hurdles of the appointment process. The American Bar Association, through its Standing Committee on Federal Judiciary, believes it can discern the "magnas" and "summas" of the profession and has taken upon itself the task of promoting such candidates for federal court appointments. The committee has played an active role in the appointment process since the Eisenhower Administration. Lawyers and judges from the states of the leading contenders (whose names are supplied by Justice officials) are canvassed, and the candidates are given ratings. A recent sample survey of lawyers indicated that only 7.7 percent of the sample had actually been contacted by the ABA committee, and, of these, 70 percent held national, state, or local bar association positions. From 1957 through 1960 Judge Walsh was Deputy Attorney General and was on exceptionally cordial terms with committee chairman Bernard Segal. The committee and the Kennedy Administration were also on friendly terms, but members of the Justice Department, in several instances, would find that only the "Wall Street type" lawyers in the large cities were being initially contacted by the committee. "Wall Street types" are presumably different in attitudes or values from labor union or individually practicing lawyers.

The problem, ultimately, is the large degree of subjectivity involved in separating the "cums" from the "summas." At times the ABA committee itself has had difficulty reaching a consensus for a rating. On those occasions when both the committee and the President's men agree that among the contenders there are many "cums" but only one "summa," other constraints on Justice officials might encourage them to bypass the "summa" and support a "cum." In such cases, the committee can help Justice officials withstand the political pressures to bypass the "summa" by exerting and rallying outside pressure in favor of the "summa." The committee, it would then seem, could define its role as that of providing countervailing power to the political pressures inherent in the appointment process that might be impelling the Justice Department towards the nomination of a "cum" instead of an acknowledged "summa."

In practice, the ABA committee works with Justice officials and often strengthens the hand of the Department in dealings with senators and other political actors. . . .

In sum, there is often great difficulty in defining not only who is qualified, but who is *best* qualified for a particular post. In the final analysis, the ABA committee provides the major external pressure on the Justice Department to appoint obviously qualified people to the federal courts. The expectations of the committee, as spokesman for the legal fraternity, as well as the desire of the President's men in the Justice Department to make "good" appointments, provide a major constraint underlying the appointment process: only those with solid professional credentials can be appointed to the United States Courts of Appeals.

B. Political Considerations: Party as a Factor. Of the 84 judges in active service during part or all of the 1961–1964 period, 79 (ninety-four percent) were affiliated with the same political party as the President who appointed them. Furthermore, about 4 out of 5 appointees, during some portion of their pre-judicial careers, were political activists. It is evident that party organizations expect that qualified lawyers or judges with some record of partisan activism and party affiliation be given preferential consideration for appointment. The Justice Department files, in fact, contain letters from party officials exhorting Justice officials to remember their partisans. . . .

On occasion, the President's supporters in the state from which the appointee is to be chosen will remind Justice officials of the stakes involved in ignoring their wishes. The following excerpt is from a letter written by a state leader to the Attorney General:

If [X] is not named this would damage seriously the Kennedy forces in [the state]. [X] was openly for Kennedy before L.A. and stood strong and voted there. He is known as one of my closest friends. He is an excellent lawyer—and on the merits alone, better qualified than Judge [Y].

The Senators will give you no trouble, but we have put this on the line in public and if [X] is not appointed it will be a mortal blow.

X was appointed. . . .

While there has not been an administration in our history whose judicial appointments were equally divided between both political parties, there is still the tradition that a few appointments to the federal courts are made to persons affiliated with the opposition party.

Both the Eisenhower and Kennedy administrations attempted to make such "nonpartisan" appointments to both the federal district courts and the appeals courts. The "nonpartisan" appointments occurred when there were multiple vacancies, almost all of which involved the elevation of a district judge to an appeals court vacancy. In many cases the Justice Department had to negotiate "package" arrangements with the political actors in the process so that "nonpartisan" appointments could be made.

C. Political Considerations: Political Clearance. . . . The formal procedures for judicial appointments imply a negotiations process involving senators and the administration. In practice, senators have a veto power in the appointment process so that judicial appointments, at the very least, must be "cleared" with the senator(s) of the President's party from whose state the appointee will be picked. In addition the state party organization and party leaders will, in some situations, also "clear" the prospective nominee. . . .

In some cases, shortly after a vacancy occurs, the congressional delegation and the state's political leaders will meet for the purpose of choosing one candidate to support. Such a united front is usually very persuasive when the backed candidate is clearly qualified. In such situations, of course, "clearance" is but an euphemism for a more powerful role played in the selection process. But, typically, the state's political leaders and congressional delegation cannot agree on one candidate to support. . . .

Political clearance is not necessarily synonymous with active support of particular candidacies. Rather, political clearance is considered an exercise of patronage and it is important for the prestige and power of the senator and other party leaders of the President's party to be able to "clear" all appointments made to individuals from their state. That senators, and in many cases, state party leaders of the President's party expect to be able to "clear" —and conversely veto—prospective appointees, provides a major constraint upon the President's men at Justice.

D. State Representation. Party leaders expect that their state will be represented on their federal court of appeals by a citizen of their state. . . .

Justice officials readily acknowledged in interviews that state claims for "representation" are usually accepted. However, there are several situations when the state of the retired or deceased judge may not receive the subsequent appointment. One such situation occurs when the retired or deceased judge was not the only representative of his state on the court. If another state in the circuit does not have a representative on the court and at least one of the senators is of the President's party, that state will receive the appointment. . . .

When the senators are not of the President's party, their state's claim can be ignored by the Justice Department. However, this can bring unforeseen and unwanted consequences, as was demonstrated by the Eisenhower Administration's appointment of Simon Sobeloff of Maryland to the Fourth Circuit Court of Appeals. South Carolina had been in line for that appointment. The Democratic controlled Senate Judiciary Committee obliged the Democratic senators from South Carolina by delaying confirmation proceedings for close to one year. The nomination was finally forced out of committee and onto the floor, where it was approved, although not without a bitter fight. Apparently the Eisenhower Administration got the point, for the next vacancy on the Fourth Circuit was filled by a South Carolinian.

The custom of state representation on the appeals courts, then, places a constraint upon the President's men in their efforts to find a suitable candidate for nomination. The efficacy of this custom is underscored by the fact that close to seventy percent of the judges in active service during 1961–1964 (filling other than newly created seats) came from the same states as the judges they replaced.

E. Pressures from Contenders. The prospective nominees themselves are a source of pressure on Justice officials. Most typically they urge their senators, their friends, and their friends' friends to write letters of recommendation to the Justice Department. Fre-

quently, when urged by the candidates, local bar associations will issue endorsements or circulate petitions supporting candidates for judicial office. The candidates expect that such activity will encourage the Justice Department to consider them seriously.

. . .

In general, when judicial candidates themselves initiate their candidacies by encouraging a barrage of recommendations from lawyers, political activists, and judges to the Justice Department, the resulting pressures provide another constraint on the Justice officials. This constraint may result in prolonging the appointment process. An avalanche of recommendations for one serious contender cannot be tactfully answered by the immediate appointment of another serious contender. The Justice Department officials may feel it important for each serious contender to make his move and articulate his backing so that they can then better grasp the politics involved as well as assess the qualifications of the candidates.

F. Quasi-Ideology and Policy Orientation. In general, Justice officials from both administrations stood ready to reject "extremists," but "extremism" was somewhat differently defined by the two administrations. The Kennedy Administration, a Justice official revealed, would not consider a Democrat who was a "Goldwater Conservative" type. Although candidates during the Kennedy Administration, according to one official, were not given "a saliva test for their liberalism," judicial philosophy was an important consideration in the evaluation of candidates, especially for candidates on the "leading" circuits. A close observer of the Kennedy Administration noted that the President's men wanted to appoint Democrats with the "liberal" point of view of the administration but in many cases were not able to do so—or else made some bad guesses.

The Justice Department files yield some evidence that quasi-ideology was an articulated consideration for a few appointments made by the Kennedy Administration. For example, the following was written to Attorney General Robert Kennedy by a federal district judge concerning a particular candidate (subsequently appointed): "He is our kind of Democrat. . . . I am well acquainted with his views for we have had many occasions upon which to exchange them."

The quasi-ideological assessment of candidates is, of course, a tricky business, and such assessments are usually made under the general standard of "our kind" of Democrat (or Republican). There was one appointment made by the Kennedy Administration for which quasi-ideology was the decisive consideration. The Democratic senators and the Justice officials had narrowed the list of candidates to two, and the senators (friends of both candidates) decided to leave the final selection to the President's men. A Washington, D.C., attorney, himself once a member of the Justice Department, wrote a letter to the Attorney General that undoubtedly crystallized the alternatives faced by the President's men. The letter began by noting that the choice of candidates involved two: "X" and "Y".

Both of these men would make competent judges and are quite superior to the present composition of the — Circuit bench, which is not saying much. . . .

Assuming that I exaggerate and that these men are actually comparable in competence and judicial temperament, there are I think the intangibles which weigh more heavily in favor of [X] than [Y]. I must tread softly here for, by definition, intangibles are hard to weigh. Nonetheless, I submit the trend as toward [X] and against [Y]:

First, not only is the — Circuit a weak bench, it is a conservative bench quite out of step with the premises of the New Frontier as almost all of us understand those premises. In the great run of cases it does not matter whether a judge is liberal or conservative if he is a good judge. There are a handful of cases, however,—and, Heaven knows, they always seem to be the important ones!—where the judicial mind can go either way, with probity, with honor, self-discipline and even with precedent. This is where the "liberal" cast of mind (we all know it, few of us can define it) can move this nation forward, just as the conservative mind can and does hold it back. This is intangible truth, but every lawyer knows it as reality! [X] would go forward, [Y] would hold back.

Second, the political point of view of a candidate deserves weight when other things are equal, or almost equal. . . . I know of [X's] devotion to the Democratic Party. . . . I personally know that over the years he has contributed vast amounts of time and money to good Democrats. On this point, both of his Senators will strongly attest. . . .

[Y] is entitled, as aren't we all, to his convictions and if his convictions in the 1950's happened to be Eisenhower that was not only his privilege, it was his duty. But I also think privilege and duty carry with them the consequences of their acts. I do not think it is unduly partisan of me if I feel a good man cannot and should not live in both worlds.

The President's men chose "X."

In general, however, the Kennedy Administration probably did not use a "liberalism" checklist as part of the selection process. Indeed, the President's men would probably have scorned any suggestion that only the most ideological "liberal" should be chosen. However, there is an indication that the President's men were alert to the candidacies of those harboring a "conservative" orientation. In practice, those appointed by the Kennedy Administration were likely to be categorized as "liberal" in newspaper articles, while the Eisenhower appointees were more likely to be labeled "conservative."

It seems evident from an inspection of the files of the Eisenhower appointees that President Eisenhower's men in the Justice Department proceeded cautiously when considering candidates with a "liberal" orientation, although again it should be emphasized that the Justice officials were not interested in using a candidate's "conservatism" as a criterion. However, just as with the Kennedy Administration, friends of the administration would write letters recommending certain candidates and espouse quasi-ideological reasons for so doing. For example, one letter on behalf of a candidate contained the following: "His [the candidate's] great belief in the democratic form of Government and its protection through the courts is something that is greatly needed in our judicial system today after twenty years of neglect." Or note the following from a former senator:

[X] is conservative in politics and one who would not have radical social theories that would influence his interpretations of the Constitution. . . . I sincerely believe that the administration wants to appoint to all of our courts young men of good quality who will hold the fort against New Dealism as it develops in the future.

In a few cases, apparently, the President's men made special efforts to discover the orientation of particular candidates. In one case, for example, this was done by an appeals judge who, at the request of the Attorney General, made some discreet inquiries and reported that the candidate's views "are not those of [Y, a quasi-ideological liberal] and are quite different."

Quasi-ideological considerations are difficult to discern, but the preceding data suggest that consciously or inarticulately they played some role, perhaps a very limited one, in the appointment process of the last two administrations. Table 1 presents in tabular form the number of files of appeals judges on the bench between 1961 and 1964 that contained references to quasi-ideology or specific policies. To be sure, a large part of the appointment process is conducted over the phone or in person and undoubtedly much does not find its way into the files. Nonetheless, such references, whether by Justice people, by those close to the administration, or in newspaper clippings inserted in the files, are suggestive.

Table 1 indicates that the Roosevelt group had the largest and the Truman appointees the smallest percentage of judges whose files contained general references to quasi-ideology. About the same percentages of Eisenhower and Kennedy appointees' files included quasi-ideological references. However, more Kennedy than Eisenhower appointees' files indicated a concern with specific policy areas.

The candidates' views on specific policies are likely to be ascertained by the Department's informal investigation or, if the candidate is a federal district judge or state judge, by at least a perusal of his decisions. . . . . . . [T]here is some indication that in the Eisenhower Administration, as well as the Kennedy Administration, one specific policy area, that of criminal law, was of concern because of the Justice Department's own organizational maintenance and enhancement needs. . . .

The specific policy area that occupied most, if not all, of the attention of the Kennedy people in the Justice Department was that of segregation. The Kennedy Administration appointed six men to appeals courts who were citizens of southern states. In every case, the administration sought to discover the candidate's views on racial segregation. A Justice official emphasized that it was determined policy of the Department not to appoint a racist to the Fourth or Fifth Circuits. Concern with the candidates' views on this policy area was in evidence in the southern candi-

TABLE 1 Number of Justice Department Files of Appeals Judges Serving Between 1961 and 1964 Containing References to Quasi-Ideology and Specific Policy Outlook

	Number of Files Containing References							
Administration	Quasi-Ideology		Policies		Both Ideology and Policies		Total References	
	No.	%	No.	%	No.	%	No.	%
Kennedy	4	19.0	4	19.0	1	4.7	9	42.7[a]
Eisenhower	7	18.4	1	2.6	2	5.2	10	26.2[b]
Truman	2	14.3	—	—	—	—	2	14.3[c]
Roosevelt	4	40.0	—	—	3	30.0	7	70.0[d]

[a]Out of 21 Kennedy appointees in active service during part or all of 1961–1964
[b]Out of 38 Eisenhower appointees in active service during part or all of 1961–1964
[c]Out of 14 Truman appointees in active service during part or all of 1961–1964
[d]Out of 10 Roosevelt appointees in active service during part or all of 1961–1964

dates' files. Consider, for example, this memo to the Attorney General in reference to a candidate: "The contact says that he has no doubt whatever that [X] will be all right on civil rights questions." The Justice official noted in his memo that he had met with the candidate who "volunteered that he has no feelings of racial bias or prejudice whatever, and that if appointed he would apply the law in the civil rights field as laid down by the Supreme Court without any hesitation, and would feel quite comfortable about it."

The files of the Eisenhower southern appointees do not yield any evidence that the candidates' views of segregation were investigated, but probably such views were known. Several of the appointees had close ties with the administration (for example, Judges Sobeloff, Tuttle, and Wisdom), and their federal supremacy and anti-racist attitudes were undoubtedly important for their appointments to the Fourth and Fifth Circuits. . . .

On balance, it seems that the candidate's quasi-ideological viewpoint or his position on specific policy areas occasionally plays a decisive role in the appointment process. To some extent it is probably an inarticulate force operating to favor "our kind," other things being nearly equal. However, because quasi-ideology and specific policy areas usually do not explicitly concern the political actors involved in the process (with Negro civil rights as a possible exception), quasi-ideology and specific policy views are not a pronounced feature of the selection process.

III

Any assessment of the relative importance of the components of the appointment process —particularly the six expectations and constraints discussed in this article—must be tentative and imprecise. An analysis of unsuccessful candidates for appeals posts would contribute to a more precise knowledge of the process, but even if such an analysis were made (assuming access to these files) the findings would still be incomplete. The appointment process is highly complex, with each appointment involving a different combination of participants, circumstances, and considerations. In addition, those responsible for the crucial decisions in the process (notably the Attorney General, the Deputy Attorney General, and his assistants) base their decisions upon their perceptions and weightings of the qualifications of the candidates, the political situation involved, the extent to which the candidates are "our kind" of Democrat or Republican, and the needs of the various circuits (as they see them). Different Justice officials perceive and weigh the factors involved somewhat differently. Thus, while it is possible to isolate what appear to be the most important aspects of the process, it is extremely difficult to assess the relative importance of these aspects. Nonetheless, a few tentative generalizations will be attempted.

The custom of state representation is an important custom. When a vacancy occurs on an appeals court, the state of the judge responsible for the vacancy or an unrepresented state on the circuit is generally the one from which the appointee will be chosen. The choice of candidates is thus narrowed.

A fundamental prerequisite for appeals court appointments seems to be that Justice officials must be convinced of the candidate's professional competence. The standards of the Justice Department, as we have seen, compare favorably with the ABA committee's standards. However, while the ABA officials strive to promote the candidacies of those that they believe are the "magnas" and "summas" of the legal profession, Justice officials tend to be satisfied with the "cums" if the other components of the process favor them.

Two types of appointment situations seem to be typical: (1) where one or both senators of the state from which the appointee will be selected belong to the President's party; and (2) where both senators belong to the opposition party. In the first situation, senatorial clearance is of overriding importance, and senators generally narrow the range of candidates to be considered. In the second situation, clearance with important congressmen, or party leaders is considered "good politics," but unless there is a united front of the state party leaders and congressmen, Justice officials can select their own candidate and can ordinarily secure "clearance" for that candidate.

In both types of appointment situations (and especially the second type) the Justice officials can choose among several qualified candidates. Other considerations then come into play: Is the candidate "our kind" as evidenced by past partisan activism or quasi-ideological outlook? Who (party organizations, politicians, bar groups, newspapers) will be happy or unhappy with a particular appointment? If the elevation of a district judge is involved, is the elevation part of a "package" that must be worked out with local party leaders or senators? Could a particular circuit bench be strengthened by a certain kind of appointment (such as a legal scholar or a lawyer with extensive trial experience)? Which of these considerations will carry more weight than the others depends entirely upon specific circumstances. In general, though (and with some exceptions), political considerations have taken precedence over quasi-ideological considerations, and "our kind" considerations have been more important than the appointment of brilliant

legal scholars or ABA designated "summas." No doubt Justice officials are delighted to appoint brilliant or "summa" type lawyers or judges who have strong political backing and are "our kind." But the process tends to produce the appointment of qualified people who best satisfy the particular political requirements of the specific situation.

Generally, then, the judges on the appeals courts were appointed largely due to fortuitous circumstances; they were in the right place at the right time. Many had the right contacts, or friends with contacts, who could influence Justice officials to consider seriously their candidacies. Some received their appointments through a process of elimination. In general, the appointment process can be characterized as a highly complex negotiations process consisting of several components. Those selected for appointment have tended to be political activists reflecting (to some extent) the values and outlook of the appointing administration. This undoubtedly has far-reaching consequences for judicial decisional behavior and for the development of law in the United States.

B. Judges: Judicial Backgrounds

Closely associated with the selection process of federal judges is the question of who (in terms of backgrounds and attributes) those chosen few are. The following two readings are concerned with this. The selection by Sheldon Goldman contains an examination of some background and attribute data of the Eisenhower and Kennedy appointees to the two principal lower federal courts. John Schmidhauser in the second selection presents a collective portrait of all Supreme Court judges appointed through 1959. The focal point of both readings is social class analysis and the determination of the segments of American society from which our judges are or have been drawn.

4 CHARACTERISTICS OF EISENHOWER AND KENNEDY APPOINTEES TO THE LOWER FEDERAL COURTS

Sheldon Goldman

The study of socioeconomic, political, and other characteristics of American political decision-makers has been of continuing interest to political scientists and political sociologists. The questions often raised reveal a concern with the extent of social mobility during given historical and contemporary periods. The spectre of a socioeconomic "power elite" has emerged from some of this research. Political scientists have also expressed interest in the extent that background characteristics reflect the social composition and political commitments of the two major political parties. Attempts have been made to measure the relationships between specified characteristics and the decisional behavior of the political actors under study. These lines of inquiry have recently been systematically applied to the judiciary. The burden of this paper is to present some background and political characteristics of the Eisenhower and Kennedy appointees to the two principal lower federal courts (the United States district courts and courts of appeals) and to discuss briefly the import of the findings on the questions of: (1) social mobility; (2) the possible existence of a class-based "power elite"; and (3) the social composition and political commitments of the major political parties.

President Eisenhower made 125 appointments to the district courts and 45 to the courts of appeals. President Kennedy made 103 district court and 21 appeals court appointments. Data on these appointees were primarily collected from published sources including *Who's Who in America, Martindale-*

Reprinted from Sheldon Goldman, "Characteristics of Eisenhower and Kennedy Appointees to the Lower Federal Courts," *Western Political Quarterly*, 18 (1965), pp. 755–762. Most footnotes omitted, others renumbered. Reprinted by permission of the University of Utah, copyright owners.

Hubbell's Law Directory, Congressional Quarterly, The New York Times, and other newspapers.

THE BACKGROUNDS OF EISENHOWER AND KENNEDY JUDICIAL APPOINTEES

It is difficult to assess the class origins of the appointees. Although the most reliable indicator of this variable probably is the father's occupation, this information tended not to be available in the published sources consulted. Geographically, the judges were drawn from all parts of the country and almost all were residents of the judicial district or circuit to which they were appointed. The majority of the appointees, however, were born in urban or metropolitan areas and at the time of their appointments all were working in urban areas. This suggests the possibility that the judges tended to come from middle-class backgrounds. This is reinforced by Table 1 which presents data on the undergraduate and law school education of the Eisenhower and Kennedy judges that show that the majority of appointees attended private or Ivy League schools.

Almost all of the Kennedy and Eisenhower appointees graduated from law school. In this sense, the judges are an educated elite. However, an examination of the schools they attended failed to reveal a predominance of the "exclusive" schools which Mills suggested are the training grounds of the "power elite." There was a fairly large diversity of colleges and law schools represented although 27 per cent of all the appointees attended Ivy League schools.

More Kennedy-appointed district court judges than Eisenhower appointees received their undergraduate training at public institutions, and more Eisenhower appointees attended Ivy League schools. If one considers attendance at a public institution evidence that the appointee's roots were lower socioeconomically than those who had attended private and especially the "exclusive" schools, one might conclude that the Kennedy appointees tended to come from a relatively lower socioeconomic class background than

TABLE 1   Undergraduate and Law School Education of Eisenhower and Kennedy Appointees to the Federal District and Appeals Courts *(in percentages)*

Education	Eisenhower Appointees		Kennedy Appointees	
	District	Appeals	District	Appeals
Undergraduate				
Public-Supported	24.0	26.7	44.6	14.3
Private (not Ivy)	34.4	17.8	35.9	57.1
Ivy League	16.0	24.4	7.8	14.3
None Indicated	25.6	31.1	11.7	14.3
Total	100.0	100.0	100.0	100.0
Law School				
Public-Supported	37.6	31.1	36.9	33.3
Private (not Ivy)	38.4	37.9	41.8	47.6
Ivy League	21.5	28.8	18.4	19.1
Other or Unknown	2.5	2.2	2.9	—
Total	100.0	100.0	100.0	100.0
Total N	125	45	103	21

did the Eisenhower appointees. When we control for region, we find that approximately 43 per cent of the Eisenhower appointees from the eastern states attended Ivy League institutions as opposed to about 26 per cent of the Kennedy eastern appointees. More Eisenhower appellate judges than Kennedy judges had an Ivy League undergraduate education.

More Eisenhower than Kennedy district court appointees graduated from Ivy League law schools. An examination of the regional subgroups suggests that the aggregate data obscure relevant regional differences. In the East, about 41 per cent of the Kennedy appointees attended Ivy League law schools while 59 per cent of the Eisenhower appointees attended such schools. This possibly indicates a relative tendency for the Eisenhower people to have come from higher socioeconomic backgrounds than the Kennedy appointees. Outside the East, very few appointees attended Ivy League law schools. The southern and midwestern Eisenhower and Kennedy appointees tended to be evenly divided between state and private law schools. The Eisenhower and Kennedy western subgroups had close to 60 per cent of their members attending state schools with the remainder attending private schools. On balance, the figures for the eastern subgroup seem to

indicate that the Republican appointees tended to come from a higher socioeconomic class than the Democratic appointees. This is probably somewhat akin to the social composition of the two parties in the eastern states.

It is difficult to obtain complete data on the first self-supporting jobs of the appointees so that this indicator of social mobility is unavailable. Table 2, however, does tell us the major occupations of the appointees at the time of appointment. This gives us some hint as to the social status of the appointees.

The data indicate that Kennedy appointed more people who occupied elective office or who were in some form of government administration than did Eisenhower, who in turn appointed more men than Kennedy who were associated with relatively large law firms or who were government lawyers.[1] The data for the district judges suggest that Kennedy had more of a tendency than Eisenhower to appoint lawyers engaged in individual or small

[1] The information presented in *Martindale-Hubbell's Law Directory* concerning the number of partners and associates in the law firm and the nature of the practice provided the criteria for the categories of "large law firm" and "individual or small law firm." Generally, a law firm consisting of two lawyers was placed in the "small law firm" category. There are, of course, limitations to this method.

TABLE 2 Major Occupation at Time of Appointment of Eisenhower and Kennedy Appointees to the Federal District and Appeals Courts *(in percentages)*

Major Occupation	Eisenhower Appointees		Kennedy Appointees	
	District	Appeals	District	Appeals
Politics-Government.	7.2	2.2	10.7	9.5
Government Lawyer.	14.4	13.3	5.8	4.8
Judiciary.	18.4	55.6	29.1	47.6
Large Law Firm	42.4	22.2	32.0	19.0
Individual or Small Law Firm.	12.8	4.4	21.4	4.8
Other	4.8	2.2	1.0	14.3
Total	100.0	99.9	100.0	100.0
Total N	125	45	103	21

(and presumably "modest") law firm practice. Again, our data suggest the possibility that the Eisenhower appointees tended to come from a higher socioeconomic class than the Kennedy appointees.

The breakdown, by region, for the district court appointees reveals that in the East, of the Kennedy appointees, about 30 per cent were serving on courts, 26 per cent were in relatively large law firms and 26 per cent were in individual or small law firm practice at time of appointment. Of the Eisenhower eastern appointees, 9 per cent were serving on courts, 45.5 per cent were members of relatively large law firms, and 15.9 per cent were in individual or small firm practice. The data for the southern appointees indicate that no Eisenhower appointee but about 21 per cent of the southerners Kennedy appointed were judges at the time of appointment to the federal district bench. This indicates that south-

ern Democrats have had much greater access to state and local judicial posts than southern Republicans. In the Midwest, approximately 45 per cent of the Eisenhower appointees were practicing law in relatively large law firms and about 3 per cent were in individual or small firm practice at time of appointment. This contrasted with 25 per cent of the Kennedy midwestern appointees practicing in large law firms and about 19 per cent in individual or small law firm practice. In the West, Eisenhower appointed more men who were state or local judges, more men from large law firms, and fewer from presumably "modest" practices.

In general, among non-southern appointees, Eisenhower appointed more men from relatively large law firms and fewer men from individual or small law firm practices than Kennedy. This seems to suggest that appointees of the Democratic Kennedy Admin-

TABLE 3 Religion of Eisenhower and Kennedy District and Appeals Courts Appointees *(in percentages)*

Religion*	Eisenhower Appointees		Kennedy Appointees	
	District	Appeals	District	Appeals
Protestant	77.6	80.0	60.2	66.6
Catholic	16.8	13.3	28.1	28.6
Jewish	5.6	6.7	11.7	4.8
Total	100.0	100.0	100.0	100.0
Total N	125	45	103	21

*Note that some estimates of religion based on family name and other background information were made.

TABLE 4   Political Affiliation of Eisenhower and Kennedy District and Appeals Courts Appointees (in percentages)

	Eisenhower Appointees		Kennedy Appointees	
Party	District	Appeals	District	Appeals
Democratic	7.2	6.7	90.3	95.2
Republican	92.8	93.3	9.7	—
Liberal	—	—	—	4.8
Total	100.0	100.0	100.0	100.0
Total N	125	45	103	21

istration had more of a tendency to come from a lower socioeconomic background than the Republican Eisenhower Administration appointees. This, perhaps, is a reflection of the social composition of the two parties.

The data on religious origin or preference, especially for the district court appointees, as shown in Table 3, confirm what one might expect given the facts that "Catholics have had a long history of association with the Democratic Party," and that the "Jewish minority comprises one of the most Democratic groups to be found in the electorate."[2] The Kennedy Administration appointed more Catholics and Jews to district court posts than did the Eisenhower Administration revealing, if anything, the political commitment of a Democratic Administration to its loyal supporters.[3] About 26 per cent of the eastern Kennedy appointees to the district courts were Jewish as opposed to about 7 per cent of the Eisenhower subgroup. Approximately 37 per cent of Kennedy's eastern appointments were Catholic while about 25 per cent of the eastern district judges appointed by Eisenhower were of Catholic origin. In the other regions, Kennedy appointed more Cath-

olics and Jews than Eisenhower. Kennedy also appointed about twice the percentage of Catholics to the courts of appeals than did Eisenhower. It should be noted, however, that a majority of *all* district and circuit posts went to Protestants, reflecting the facts that the dominant religious faith within the United States is Protestant and that its members are prominent within both major political parties.

President Kennedy named four Negroes to district court posts and one to an appeals court. President Eisenhower did not appoint any Negroes to these posts. This again suggests that the judicial appointees of Democratic and Republican administrations will have a tendency to reflect the differing social composition and hence political commitments of the two parties. But the greatest and most obvious difference between the Eisenhower and Kennedy judicial appointees is that of political party affiliation. This is demonstrated in Table 4.

That Republican administrations largely appoint Republicans, and Democratic administrations primarily appoint Democrats is well known. Each administration tends to look for technically well-qualified men who are also partisans for judicial appointments. The latter criterion for selection results from pressures and expectations of party organizations and elected officials (particularly congressmen), as well as a desire to reward the party faithful and appoint "our kind" of Democrat or Republican. The prior political activity of Republican and Democratic appointees is, then, of great interest. Data on the types of partisan activism the appointees

[2]Angus Campbell *et al., The American Voter* (New York: Wiley, 1960), p. 159.

[3]Samuel Lubell, *The Future of American Politics* (Garden City: Doubleday, 1956), pp. 83–84, presented data from which the following percentages were calculated: Of Harding, Coolidge, and Hoover's combined appointments to the lower federal courts, 82.1 per cent were Protestant, 3.9 were Catholic, and 3.9 were Jewish. Of Roosevelt's appointments, 67.0 per cent were Protestant, 26.4 were Catholic but only 3.6 were Jewish. Of Truman's appointments, 59.0 per cent were Protestant, 29.9 were Catholic, and 9.5 were Jewish.

TABLE 5   Types of Partisan Activism at Any Time Prior to Judicial Appointment of Eisenhower and Kennedy Appointees to the Courts of Appeals

Partisan Activity	Eisenhower Appointees		Kennedy Appointees	
	Number	Per Cent	Number	Per Cent
Party or Party Campaign Office*.	11	24.4	12	57.1
Candidate for or Elected to Political Office . . .	9	20.0	1	4.8
Closely Associated with Political Figure	5	11.1	3	14.3
Active Party Worker.	5	11.1	1	4.8
Total Activists	30	66.7	17	81.0
Non-Activists	13	28.9	4	19.0
Activist in Opposite Party.	2	4.4	—	—
Total	45	100.0	21	100.0

*Includes delegate to National Convention.
Note that each appointee was categorized by what seemed to be the most important political activity in which he engaged.

to the appeals courts engaged in during some part of their non-judicial careers are presented in Table 5.

It seems clear, from Table 5, that some form of conspicuous partisan activism has been prominent in the backgrounds of the Eisenhower and Kennedy appointees. Although we do not have data on campaign contributions or minor party work, undoubtedly almost all of the appointees had contributed time and/or money to their party. Congressmen as well as other party leaders are willing to promote party supporters. The administration, the data also hint, might look favorably upon a well-qualified lawyer who supported the President before "Chicago" or "West Virginia" or during the campaigns.

The data, although involving only a small number of appointees, tend to indicate that the Kennedy Administration appointees may have been more "political" in their backgrounds than the Eisenhower appointees. However, it should be noted that according to the Standing Committee on Judiciary of the American Bar Association, the large majority of *both* administrations' judicial appointments were among "the best qualified" judges and lawyers available. Table 6 shows that judicial experience was probably one consideration for appointment. Over one-half of both administrations' appointees to the courts of appeals had judicial experience while slightly more than a quarter of the district court appointees had judicial experience.

TABLE 6   Percentage of Eisenhower and Kennedy Appointees to the District and Appeals Courts with Judicial Experience

Court	Eisenhower Appointees		Kennedy Appointees	
	District	Appeals	District	Appeals
Federal*.	—	40.0	—	38.1
Non-Federal	26.4	22.2	33.0	14.3
Total	26.4	62.2	33.0	52.4
Total N	33	28	34	11

*Appeals courts judges with both prior federal and state court experience were counted once under the federal category.

SUMMARY AND CONCLUSIONS

Some background and political characteristics of the Eisenhower and Kennedy appointees to the federal district and appeals courts were studied for the purpose of determining similarities and differences between the two sets of appointees. The results were examined for their relevance to three research problems, those of (1) social mobility; (2) the existence or non-existence of a socioeconomic "power elite"; and (3) the social composition and political commitments of the major political parties. Implicitly raised in this paper were questions pertaining to judicial recruitment and selection.

The slim data presented were only able very generally to suggest that both the Eisenhower and Kennedy appointees tended to come from "middle-class" backgrounds, and that whatever mobility did occur was probably predominantly within that class. The route to judicial appointment by mid-twentieth-century America most certainly included a law school education and this rather than social origins was all-important for providing opportunities for occupational as well as social mobility. There was little to support any claim of a class "power elite" either by the schools attended or the occupations of the judges at the time of appointment. What was suggested by the data, however, was that the Eisenhower Administration appointees tended to be of a higher socioeconomic status (determined by education and major occupation at time of appointment) than the Kennedy appointees. While the differences between the two groups were relatively small, the observed differences were thought to reflect the differing social composition and political commitments of the two parties. This was reinforced by the data on the religion of the appointees. However, it is well to keep in mind that the differences were those of degree, and the results, on the whole, underscore the absence on the American scene of a party system built on pronounced class and ethnic cleavages. . . .

5   THE SOCIAL AND POLITICAL BACKGROUNDS OF THE JUSTICES OF THE SUPREME COURT: 1789–1959

John R. Schmidhauser

From what levels of American society have the ninety-two individuals who served on the Supreme Court been chosen? . . . Among the diverse criteria available for the establishment of social status, paternal occupations, patterns of occupational heredity, individual career patterns, ethnic origin, religion, and education have been considered most useful by social scientists. Of these, paternal occupation has been accepted as the most trustworthy clue to the determination of social origin. The great amount of work in judicial biography completed in the last three decades has resulted in the accumulation in readily available form of much of the material necessary for such a synthesis.

PATERNAL OCCUPATIONS

Throughout the entire history of the Supreme Court, only a handful of its members were of essentially humble origin. Nine persons selected in widely scattered historical periods comprise the total. The remaining 83 (91 per cent) not only were from families in comfortable economic circumstances but were chosen overwhelmingly from the socially prestigeful and politically influential gentry class in the late eighteenth and early nineteenth century or the professionalized upper-middle class thereafter. A large number of justices (55, comprising 60 per cent of the total) came from politically active families. The politically

Reprinted from *The Supreme Court:Its Politics, Personalities and Procedures* by John R. Schmidhauser, pp. 31–39, 43–49, 52, 55–59, footnotes omitted. Copyright © 1960 by John R. Schmidhauser. Reprinted by permission of Holt, Rinehart and Winston, Inc.

active families were essentially those enjoying high social status (99 per cent of the political activity was concentrated in families of high social status).

. . .

After 1862, a definite shift in the occupational emphasis of high social status families took place. The trend began in the Jacksonian period, but before the 1860's the preponderance of high social status families had been engaged in nonprofessional occupations such as farming or manufacturing. A rather high percentage of the heads of these families had pursued active and successful political careers. After 1862, the majority of fathers of justices selected from high social status backgrounds were engaged in professional activities, largely in the fields of law, medicine, and religion, and occasionally in higher education. In social composition, the over-all tendency was a gradual transition from selection largely from the families of the aristocratic landholding and mercantile class of the late eighteenth and early nineteenth century to choice from among members of the professionalized upper-middle class. Lest this transition from selection from the old gentry class to predominant influence by the upper-middle class be interpreted as a liberalizing trend, it might be noted that the appointees from professionalized upper-middle class families were firmly in the ascendancy from 1889 through 1937, a period in which the Court virtually surpassed John Marshall's Court in its decisions in support of economic conservatism.

OCCUPATIONAL "HEREDITY"

The social transmission of attitudes, beliefs, values, and aspirations has as its most effective vehicle the family. Since political participation of a very advanced kind appears as a crucial ingredient in the life careers of all but one of the members of the Supreme Court, the nature and extent of family conditioning for such participation deserves special attention.

The United States has never produced an aristocracy comparable to Namier's "inevitable Parliament men," but it has developed, especially in local and state politics, families with consistent and frequently successful records of political involvement. America's "political families" have been able to transmit intangible, yet real advantages to their children. These advantages have included not only the prestige of possession of a "political" name and family connections in a local, state, or even national political organization, but also a true political education which is derived from the practice and familiarity with political activity, the encouragement of political ambitions, expectations, and perhaps a veritable sense of destiny respecting high political achievement.

Nearly two thirds of the members of the Supreme Court were raised in this far from commonplace type of American family. . . .

. . . To an even greater extent than the function of over-all political participation, that of judicial service is exceedingly rare in America. Yet twelve justices were the sons of prominent judges (usually of the highest court of a state). Six (including one of the above) married the daughters of judges. An additional fifteen were related to prominent jurists. Excluding duplication, thirty-two members of the Supreme Court (over one third) were related to jurists and intimately connected with families possessing a tradition of judicial service.

Several of these families have had members or close relations on the Supreme Court for periods extending over a half century. For example, Sarah Williamson of Georgia was the grandmother of Justice John Archibald Campbell (who served on the Court from 1853–1861) and the great-grandmother of Justice Lucius Q. C. Lamar (1888–1893). Later Joseph Ruckner Lamar, a cousin of Lucius, also served on the Court from 1910–1916. The Livingston family of New York and New Jersey has also had an intimate relation to Supreme Court service through many generations. John Jay, the first Chief Justice (1789–1795), was married to a Livingston whose father was a prominent colonial judge. Jay's wife's brother, Brockholst Livingston, served on the Court from 1806 to 1823. And

Brockholst was succeeded on the Supreme Court by Smith Thompson, who had married into the Livingston family. Thompson served on the highest court from 1823 to 1843.

. . .

. . . This . . . does not imply that a deliberate effort has been made by successive Presidents to choose Supreme Court justices from such families; rather, that it frequently was very advantageous for a successful lawyer and a member of the President's political party to be a member of a family with a political background, and especially with a strong tradition of judicial service. This situation was as true in 1955 for John Marshall Harlan, the namesake and grandson of the famed dissenter in *Plessy* v. *Ferguson,* as it was in 1799 for Alfred Moore, the son of a well-known colonial judge of North Carolina, or in 1874 for Morrison R. Waite, the son of a former Chief Justice of the Supreme Court of Connecticut.

WHERE WERE THE JUSTICES BORN?

Closely related to the question of the determination of social origins and the nature of the relation of family background to social outlook is the additional environmental factor of place of birth and the setting for the formative years of the justices. Even in the earliest period, a greater number of the justices (75 per cent) were born (and usually reared) in cities or towns. Because most of the families of the justices possessed unusual social and economic advantages, the justices who were born in an urban environment were not subject to the tensions and crowded conditions of the tenement areas and slums. For many, the fact that they lived in a city brought all the urban cultural advantages but maintained the serenity and security also enjoyed by the justices living on plantations and town or country estates.

In a few instances, place of birth also had a special relation to United States citizenship. An overwhelming number (94.6 per cent) of the justices were, of course, born in the United States of parents who were citizens of the United States. Six justices were born abroad, Justice David Brewer in Turkey of

American missionaries. Three of the foreign-born justices were chosen for the Supreme Court by President Washington: James Iredell (England), James Wilson (Scotland), and William Paterson (Ireland). The remaining two, George Sutherland (England) and Felix Frankfurter (Austria), were chosen in modern times. Leaving aside Washington's appointees, both Sutherland and Frankfurter came to America at an early age. Their childhood experiences were similar to those of first-generation Americans rather than aliens. Although nativists raised objections to Frankfurter's appointment, other factors were present to assure presidential nomination and to assure senatorial confirmation.

. . .

ETHNIC ORIGINS OF THE JUSTICES

The ethnic origins of members of the Supreme Court represent another important source of data available for the determination of their social background. Throughout the entire history of the Supreme Court, judicial recruitment has granted a virtual monopoly to natives or the descendants of natives of northwestern Europe. And among those selected, individuals of English, Welsh, Scotch, or Irish ethnic origin have predominated, comprising 88 per cent of the appointees. . . .

. . .

The patterns of ethnic representation are additional evidences of the virtual monopolization of Supreme Court appointments by the socially privileged segment of the population dubbed the "old Americans."

RELIGIOUS AFFILIATION OF THE JUSTICES

Religious diversity in America has at its root a social basis as well as a doctrinal rationale. To some denominations are attached factors of prestige and social status, while others are viewed socially as "churches of the disinherited," of unpopular immigrant groups, or of ethnic groups which, because of color, have not been fully accepted. In keeping with the fact that most of the justices were selected from among socially advantaged families was the heavy incidence of affiliation with high social status religious groups by the justices. An overwhelming majority were Protestant. A substantial majority of the justices were affiliated with the Episcopalian, Presbyterian (or French Calvinist), Congregational, and Unitarian churches. Slightly over 10 per cent were affiliated with Protestant religious groups which historically were considered of lower social status. In a special category were the slightly less than 10 per cent of the justices who were either Roman Catholic, Jewish, or Quaker. Only one Quaker, Noah Swayne, has been appointed to the Supreme Court. Since the Roman Catholic and Jewish groups in America have frequently been subjected to nativist and religious criticism and attack, members of these groups have, historically, been at a considerable disadvantage in the competition for Supreme Court appointments.

In recent years there has been considerable discussion of the existence of a custom of maintaining on the Supreme Court a member of the Roman Catholic and Jewish religious faiths. . . . The very controversy over the existence of the "custom" has political significance, and it may be assumed that . . . religious representation, whether accepted or not, must play a part in subsequent presidential considerations of judicial selections.

EDUCATIONAL BACKGROUND OF THE JUSTICES

Of all the advantages which were incidental to birth into the early gentry class or the professionalized upper-middle class, that of the opportunity to acquire a good education was perhaps of greatest importance to the later formative period in the career patterns of a majority of the justices. A college education has, until comparatively recent times, been a prize available only to a small minority of American adults. An advanced education in a college or university of high standing has been even more rare. And finally, such an education coupled with professional training in law has been exceedingly difficult to attain. A rather large number of justices have been able to acquire such education, usually in the

better colleges and universities. Over a third did their college work in the Ivy League schools, while nearly a third did their law studies in them. Aside from the manifest professional advantages which might be derived from such educational opportunities, the personal associations which were established and the notions of social responsibility and civic leadership inculcated at these educational institutions must all be taken into account as aids in the individual career patterns of the justices and as factors conditioning their attitudes toward the challenges and responsibilities of judicial decision making in later maturity.

The justices who studied under private tutors and who served law apprenticeships were not recipients of inferior types of education. In fact, these justices were often afforded several unique advantages from this educational opportunity, for in most instances the tutors or law teachers not only were unusually talented but were leading practitioners of law in the community or state, and were among the top political leaders in the contemporary scene. One may conclude that in the period before the full development of law schools, members of the Supreme Court who were taught law by outstanding legal and political leaders gained incalculable educational and political advantages in the process. Throughout the history of the Supreme Court, the recruitment process has generally rewarded those whose educational backgrounds, both legal and nonlegal, have comprised the rare combination of intellectual, social, and political opportunities which have generally been available only to the economically comfortable and socially prominent segment of the American population.

THE NONPOLITICAL OCCUPATIONS OF THE COURT MEMBERS

. . . All of the ninety-two justices of the Supreme Court had legal training of some kind. All practiced law at some stage in their careers. For eighty-eight of the total (97 per cent), law was a major nonpolitical occupation. The justices who had not practiced law as a major nonpolitical occupation (Stone,

Frankfurter, Douglas, and Rutledge) were all law school professors or deans. With the exception of Stone, all were chosen by President Franklin Roosevelt and were, in essence, instruments of constitutional protest against the highly restrictive attitude of earlier appointees. . . .

. . .

. . . [A]n overwhelming number of Supreme Court appointees selected in the first two historical periods (1789–1828 and 1828–1861) pursued primarily political careers. . . . After 1862 a substantial, but not large, number of corporation lawyers were appointed to the Supreme Court, constituting 19 per cent in 1862–1888, 22 per cent in 1889–1919, 29 per cent in 1920–1932, and then declining to 14 per cent in 1933–1959. Although all except the last of these periods corresponded with historical eras in which corporate influence was, with brief contrary interludes, ascendant in the national government, it would appear at first glance that the process of appointing members of the Supreme Court had remained relatively immune from such influence. This was not true, however, because ideological soundness, from the corporate point of view, actually found its most reliable advocates among the appointees with extensive judicial careers.

The number of appointees who had pursued primarily political careers took a sharp decline after 1862, dropping from 63 per cent in the Jacksonian era to 32 per cent in 1862–1888, 33 per cent in 1889–1919, and 29 per cent in 1920–1932. In the final period, 1933–1959, political careerists on the Court rose to 62 per cent. None of these periods rivaled the original one, 1789–1828, in which 85 per cent of the Court appointees were lawyers who had pursued primarily political careers. It should be noted, however, that with only one exception, George Shiras, every member of the Supreme Court had actively participated in politics before his appointment to the nation's highest tribunal.

In actuality, the most important change in the pattern of judicial selection which occurred after 1862 was the great increase in the percentage of men chosen who had pri-

marily judicial careers. For two periods, judges from state courts or inferior federal courts constituted the largest single group of appointees, totaling 45 per cent in 1862–1888 and 1889–1919, declining to 29 per cent in 1920–1932 and then dropping sharply to a mere 6 per cent in the final period, 1933–1959. Not all the members of the Supreme Court who had prior judicial experience were included in this group. It was felt to be more realistic to include only those whose prior judicial experience represented a major portion of their adult careers. For example, from among the Eisenhower appointees only William Brennan pursued primarily a judicial career. Harlan, Whittaker, and Stewart had short federal judicial tenures before appointment to the Supreme Court, but through most of their adult careers they were corporation lawyers.

The very fact that all the members of the Supreme Court were members of the legal profession in itself merits consideration as a conditioner of social, economic, and political attitudes. Whether one accepts the belief of Alexis de Tocqueville that "the seat of the American aristocracy is with the judges on the bench and the lawyers at the bar" or the contradictory view of a contemporary critic that "the members of the legal profession . . . are not the aristocracy but the agents of the aristocracy . . . [which] is constituted by the owners of accumulated wealth," there has been rather general agreement that the influence of the bar in America has been essentially conservative. This does not imply that every lawyer appointed to the Supreme Court has succumbed to this conservative influence, but it is clear that all are exposed to it. There is considerable evidence to indicate that many lawyers on the high bench willingly espoused the sort of legal conservatism exemplified in the leadership and ideology of the American Bar Association. Furthermore, a number of the members of the Court, such as William Howard Taft and George Sutherland, were among the leaders of the bar, both before and after their appointments to the Supreme Court, who developed and cherished its conservative traditions and attitudes.

POLITICAL PARTY
AND IDEOLOGICAL CONSTANCY

The mere recitation of the changing patterns of legal careers represented on the Supreme Court lacks meaningfulness except as a descriptive contribution. When considered in connection with the most important of the customary "rules" of the judicial selection process, however, these patterns assume greater significance. The choice of men ideologically committed or thought to be committed to the values of the President making the selection has been the policy most rigidly adhered to throughout American history.

One clue to the explanation for the pre-Civil War tendency toward choice of lawyers who pursued primarily political careers lay in the fact that during much of this period party affiliation generally included acceptance of certain clearly defined social, economic, and constitutional attitudes. One need consider only the following statement of Thomas Jefferson to recognize the clarity with which early party leaders identified party loyalty and "right thinking" on philosophical, social, and economic ideas. Jefferson, writing to President Madison's Postmaster, Gideon Granger, suggested that the old Federalist justice William Cushing be replaced with "a firm unequivocal republican, whose principles are born with him, and not an occasion ingraftment, as necessary to complete the great reformation in our government to which the nation gave its fiat ten years ago." Even in the pre-Civil War era, this identity of party and values was not always present, as the appointment of Joseph Story so amply demonstrated, but after 1862, the relation between party affiliation and ideological commitment became, if anything, increasingly less clear.

The judicial selection process reveals rather convincingly that the selection of individuals of the President's political affiliation served not only as a method of rewarding political supporters but also as one of several means of identification of a judicial candidate's ideology, although there has usually been strong pressure for both party and ideological consistency. To be sure, presidents have occasionally paid off political debts (as may have been true in the appointment of Justice Catron), or perhaps have "kicked upstairs" bothersome cabinet officers (as has been alleged in the selection of Justice McLean), but the so-called crasser political motives have not generally been determinative in the appointment of members of the Supreme Court. During historical periods when party attachment actually meant commitment to certain recognizable social, economic, or philosophical values, the choice of justices rather consistently followed party lines. When the identity of party label and ideology was uncertain, presidents usually exercised greater care in their assessment of ideological consistency.

Among the biographical materials on presidents, the frank correspondence between Theodore Roosevelt and Senator Henry Cabot Lodge . . . concerning Horace Lurton, a Democrat, and a federal judge, is . . . precise with reference to the ideological prerequisites of his appointees. Wrote Roosevelt,

Nothing has been so strongly born in on me concerning lawyers on the bench as that the nominal politics of the man has nothing to do with his actions on the bench. His *real* politics are all-important. In Lurton's case, Taft and Day, his two former associates, are very desirous of having him on. He is right on the Negro question; he is right on the power of the federal government; he is right on the Insular business; he is right about corporations, he is right about labor. On every question that would come before the bench, he has so far shown himself to be in much closer touch with the policies in which you and I believe than even White because he has been right about corporations where White has been wrong.

It is rather important to note that Democrat Horace Lurton, despite his ideological soundness, *did not* get this appointment. (Lurton was, however, later chosen for the Supreme Court by Theodore Roosevelt's successor, William Howard Taft.) Instead, Roosevelt appointed his Republican Attorney General, William Henry Moody. In all probability, Senator Lodge's reply to the letter quoted above contains both the explanation for Roosevelt's failure to appoint Lurton and further insight regarding the traditional balancing of factors in the judicial selection process. Lodge wrote,

> I am glad that Lurton holds all the opinions that you say he does and that you are so familiar with his views. I need hardly say that those are the very questions on which I am just as anxious as you that judges should hold what we consider sound opinions, *but I do not see why Republicans cannot be found who hold those opinions as well as Democrats.* . . .
>
> Of course you know my high opinion of Moody. . . . Nothing would give me greater pleasure than to see him on the bench.

. . .

It is interesting to note that presidents and their Senates have always had nominees whose political *bona fides* were matters of wide knowledge. Every member of the Supreme Court except George Shiras held a political post of some kind prior to his appointment to the high bench. Several of the justices had also been unsuccessful candidates for political offices which were of greater importance than those which they actually attained prior to their appointment to the Supreme Court.

Since state or federal judicial service is included among the political posts categorized, special consideration should be given to the factor of prior judicial experience.

THE PRIOR JUDICIAL EXPERIENCE OF MEMBERS OF THE SUPREME COURT

. . . Well over 50 per cent of the justices had served in a judicial capacity at some time before appointment to the Supreme Court, but only slightly more than 25 per cent had had really extensive judicial careers. It is upon this latter group of justices whose life careers prior to appointment to the Supreme Court had been primarily judicial that attention will be centered.

The considerations which governed the choice of these judicially trained men varied according to changing circumstances. During the period of Jeffersonian and Jacksonian dominance of the national administration, Supreme Court appointments were often viewed with an eye to the local responsibilities

of the justices while on circuit duty. Thus, acquaintance with the peculiarities of the land laws of the states within a circuit was occasionally considered a prerequisite, as, for example, in the choices of Thomas Todd and Robert Trimble. Particularly before 1891, experience in the "federal specialities," such as admiralty law, was also of importance. However, it is not at all clear that experience on an inferior federal court or a state court is necessary to or intimately related to the sort of service performed on the nation's highest court. . . .

. . .

There is little in the history of the Supreme Court to suggest that justices with prior judicial experience were more objective or better qualified than those who lacked such experience. As a matter of fact, despite the examples of Holmes and Cardozo, some of the Supreme Court's most distinguished members, notably Marshall, Taney, Curtis, Campbell, Miller, Bradley, Hughes, Brandeis, and Stone, were totally lacking in this experience before their appointments to the Supreme Court.

THE SIGNIFICANCE OF SOCIAL AND POLITICAL BACKGROUND FACTORS

. . .

Throughout American history there has been an overwhelming tendency for presidents to choose nominees for the Supreme Court from among the socially advantaged families. The typical Supreme Court justice has invariably been white, generally Protestant with a penchant for a high social status denomination, usually of ethnic stock originating in the British Isles, and born in comfortable circumstances in an urban or small town environment. In the earlier history of the Court, he very likely was born in the aristocratic gentry class, although later he tended to come from the professionalized upper-middle class. Whereas nearly two thirds of his fellows were selected from politically active families, a third of his fellows were chosen from families having a tradition of judicial service. In college and legal education, the average justice was afforded opportunities for training and associations which were most advantageous. It seems reasonable to assume that very few sons of families outside the upper, or upper-middle, social and economic classes have been able to acquire the particular type of education and the subsequent professional, and especially political, associations which appear to be unwritten prerequisites for appointment to the nation's highest tribunal.

Educational opportunity emerges as a crucial ingredient in judicial recruitment. Every member of the Supreme Court was the recipient of law training and a great number were afforded college or university educations prior to their law training. Law training not only fulfilled an unwritten educational requirement for judicial appointment but frequently represented an important stage in the development of individual political careers. Especially during the periods before the widespread acceptance of law schools as the primary centers for legal education, the internship of subsequent members of the Supreme Court in the law offices of prominent practitioners afforded the student not only a unique educational opportunity and valuable professional associations, but frequently the political sponsorship of men who held high office or were influential in the councils of their political organizations.

The influence of family background, while less tangible in certain respects, may be considered of great importance. In an economic sense, birth in a family in comfortable circumstances was generally a precondition for the advanced educational opportunities afforded most Supreme Court members. However, it is important to note that the families of the justices generally were not of the type one identifies with the modern middle class, a type which has become increasingly apolitical, interested more in comfort and economic security than in the assumption of social responsibility. On the contrary, a high percentage of the families of the justices demonstrated a very deep sense of social responsibility and political involvement. It would be a gross oversimplification to assume a direct transferal of the particular political attach-

ments of these families to their sons. Yet the biographical data on the justices evidences a considerable conditioning of broad attitudes toward social and political participation.

. . . Just as training in law has been a necessary educational step in the achievement of a Supreme Court appointment, so has political activism been a virtual precondition for such an appointment. The degree of political involvement of aspirants to the Supreme Court has, of course, varied considerably. In a large number of instances the justices, prior to their appointments, not only held high political office but were deeply involved in party and campaign management and had close political associations and personal ties with the men who later nominated and appointed them. Thus, political activism of a rather intense kind emerges as a necessary stage in career ascent to the Supreme Court.

. . .

The appointment of men with prior judicial experience, especially those with extensive careers in the inferior federal courts or the state courts, was of great importance in particular historical periods. These appointments frequently served the practical function of identifying ideological partisans, as did selection from the ranks of the openly avowed political activists.

The picture that emerges in the pattern of recruitment of Supreme Court justices is one which emphasizes the intimacy of judicial and political affairs. Since the most important function of the Supreme Court is the settlement of fundamentally political issues through the medium of judicial review, the political background of the justices undoubtedly represents a very necessary and valuable source of experience and training.

It is not at all clear that the social and political background factors in themselves may serve as reliable indicators of precise patterns of judicial behavior. Explanations based entirely upon the causal influence of such factors as family, economic and social status, ethnic background, or religious affiliation could scarcely take into account such important considerations as the impact upon individual justices of the traditions of the

Supreme Court itself or of the interaction of intelligent and frequently forceful personalities which has been an integral part of the internal procedure of the Court. Complete dependence upon background factors would also ignore the complexity and subtlety of intellect and motivation which is part of the collective picture of the ninety-two individuals who have sat on the high bench.

The difficulty is illustrated by looking at the over-all judicial reputations of the nine justices of humble origin. It might be argued, for example, that the choice of men of humble origin for the Supreme Court could scarcely be considered dangerous to the rights of private property because the group included James Wilson, John McLean, John Catron, Pierce Butler, and James Byrnes. Perhaps one would be tempted to accept the acid comment, made by a contemporary concerning Catron's personal characteristics, as a sociological explanation of the decision-making predilections of these justices. Catron was described as "profoundly aristocratic in all his habits and bearing *as all men raised to wealth and station by concurrence of accidents.*" Yet as appealing as such a pat explanation seems, there are certain difficulties inherent in the unqualified use of such biographical data. For one thing, the over-all judicial reputations of the other four justices of humble origin— Henry Baldwin, Samuel F. Miller, Sherman Minton, and Earl Warren—can hardly be accounted for by this explanation. Furthermore,

a variety of other explanations involving such things as political associations, educational conditioning, or ideological commitments to nationalism or states' rights might appear just as plausible as the emphasis upon family background.

It would be a serious mistake, however, to conclude that the background factors have had no influence upon judicial behavior whatsoever. The social attitudes of families in the gentry class or professionalized upper-middle class, and particularly the traditions of the families with judicial associations, may be accounted subtle factors influencing the tone and temper of judicial decision making. While such influence cannot ordinarily be traced in cause-and-effect formulas in specific decisions, it frequently emerges in the careers of individual justices as setting implicit limits on the scope of theoretical decision-making possibilities. Justice Frankfurter once wrote that "by the very nature of the functions of the Supreme Court, each member of it is subject only to his own sense of trusteeship of what are perhaps the most revered traditions in our national system." If it is in this sense that the Supreme Court is the keeper of the American conscience, it is essentially the conscience of the American upper-middle class sharpened by the imperative of individual social responsibility and political activism, and conditioned by the conservative impact of legal training and professional legal attitudes and associations.

C. Interest Groups

Organized interest groups have long been considered important participants in the federal judicial process. Interest groups, especially the American Bar Association (as noted in the Chase and Goldman readings), seek to influence the judicial appointment process. But of even greater import, interest groups have been thought to be responsible for most of the demands made on the federal judicial system. By financing and guiding litigation through the federal courts and by submitting *amicus curiae*[1] briefs, interest groups have been thought to account for much of the in-

---

[1] An *amicus curiae* (friend of the court) brief is one submitted by a party not directly involved in the litigation. In theory, the brief is supposed to provide the judges with additional information and analyses which can help them resolve the legal questions. In practice, it has been used by interested groups to plead their cause. In recent years, the Supreme Court has restricted its use.

put to the system. The activities of organized labor and the National Association for the Advancement of Colored People in the federal courts have frequently been cited as examples of extensive interest group participation. But little systematic study of interest group participation has been undertaken. One exception to this is a study by Nathan Hakman from which the following reading is drawn. Hakman examines in detail the extent of interest group activity before the Supreme Court from 1958 through 1964. In so doing, he also presents data about other litigants, both governmental and private. Hakman's conclusion that organized group activity is, in actuality, relatively minor and has been exaggerated by previous political science analyses should not be taken to mean that we can ignore interest groups in the analysis of the federal judicial system. However, his article does provide a better perspective with which to evaluate interest groups as well as other litigants as elements of the federal judicial system.

6   LOBBYING THE SUPREME COURT

Nathan Hakman

I.   INTRODUCTION

Lobbying in judicial affairs refers to the organization and management of influence by persons and groups who are not necessarily the principals in a litigation. These parties differ from the ordinary litigant in terms of their interest in developing long range policy rather than merely winning a given case.

While lobbying or pressure in the judicial process is believed to be widespread, writers are usually careful to note important differences in the ways lobbyists behave in the judicial and legislative arenas. Judges are ordinarily not contacted directly, correspondence is definitely discouraged, and picketing, demonstrations, and even milder forms of outside pressure seldom accompany pending cases. All forms of persuasion are pursued with a maximum regard for judicial dignity and protocol.

The tactics of judicial lobbying are assumed to be of a different order, and they are frequently listed as follows: (1) the "class action" replacing individual litigants; (2) the

test case; (3) *amicus curiae* participation; (4) the granting by an outsider (usually an organization) of advice, information, and service; (5) the providing of expert testimony and research assistance by a non-principal; (6) the granting of financial assistance by a non-principal; (7) the outsider assuming control of a litigation.

Besides describing these techniques, commentators on Supreme Court litigation also describe the use of other strategies and tactics. These include: (1) bringing alternative litigations in different judicial forums; (2) "broadening the issues" through research and publication; (3) engaging in other kinds of litigation planning.

In the published literature, the bringing of alternative litigations is reported to be used to achieve the following objectives: (1) achieving the most favorable forum; (2) emphasizing issues differently in different courts; (3) taking advantage of the differences in procedure and rulings in state and federal courts; (4) dropping or compromising cases with unfavorable records; (5) stalling some cases, and pushing others to ensure that the "good ones" reach the Supreme Court first; (6) creating conflicts among courts in order to encourage assumption of jurisdiction by the Supreme Court.

According to this kind of political folklore the judicial lobbyist reinforces conventional legal argument by broadening the issues through a "Brandeis" or "sociological" brief, or includes policy arguments in his briefs or

Reprinted by permission of copyright holder from Nathan Hakman, "Lobbying the Supreme Court—An Appraisal of 'Political Science Folklore'," *Fordham Law Review*, 35 (1966), pp. 15–50. Business office: Fordham Law Review, Lincoln Square, New York, N. Y. 10023. © 1966 by Fordham University Press.

oral presentations. Participants in Supreme Court cases are expected to secure the help of research organizations and similar groups in presenting new social theories before the highest court. Since courts do not decide cases in a vacuum, a large dose of planned publicity is sometimes deemed desirable. This publicity is occasionally secured by "flooding" law reviews with articles presenting an interest group's general point of view. In consequence of this and other complex litigation tasks, it is also assumed that the planning of Supreme Court litigation is too great a task for the "small" or moderate-sized law firm. Success in the Supreme Court, it is argued, "is no longer the result of a fortuitous series of accidents." Instead "groups plan their forays into litigation just as meticulously as they do in other political areas."

. . .

II. SOURCES AND METHODS OF INVESTIGATION

A great deal of information about parties, attorneys, *amici curiae,* and arguments, are matters of public record. Until now, these records have not been used to study these data and to challenge important assumptions about Supreme Court litigation. One must go beyond the records, however, to get information about litigation finance, sponsorship, cooperation, research, coordination, planned publicity, and other litigation strategies. . . .

To "test" the propositions . . . information was gathered in 837 cases in which the Supreme Court rendered signed or *per curiam* opinions. The cases, covering seven Supreme Court terms from 1958 to 1964, were classified both in terms of their basic subject matter and the clientele interests involved. Commercial litigations included antitrust, public utilities, transportation, public lands, tax, labor relations, government law suits (private property transactions), private litigations, and private personal injury cases. Non-commercial cases included criminal cases (involving serious anti-social crimes), civil liberties cases (governmental or government supported infringements of individual liberties), cases involving political offenders (communist and

internal security cases) and cases involving race relations. The survey provided data about the types of formal parties, the *amici curiae* involved [see Table 1] and in many instances the reasons given for participating as *amici curiae.*

For more detailed information about litigation support and strategies in Supreme Court cases questionnaires were sent to more than 500 attorneys who participated in 127 opinion cases during the 1960–1961 Supreme Court Term.[1] Many of the attorneys contributed very little to the survey because their participation was confined to giving general advice or merely commenting on the legal briefs. However, a definitive reply was received from attorneys in 78 cases. The comments that follow are essentially the author's own interpretations derived from responses to questionnaires, unstructured interviews, and exact tabulations.

III. THE FINDINGS

A. Formal Parties: The Role of Governments in Supreme Court Litigation. Before commenting on activity in support of litiga-

---

[1] Information about litigation management, however, is not confined to the sample of cases surveyed. It is frequently difficult to tell which attorneys control a given case. Names of attorneys or law firms making little or no contribution sometimes appear in the appellate briefs. Attorneys who argue cases before the Supreme Court occasionally assume control after other attorneys have borne most of the preparation burdens. This is especially true in a situation when there is a voluminous transcript and record. The attorney of record, more frequently than not, accompanies the attorney at the time of Supreme Court oral arguments, and participates significantly in the preparation of the briefs.

Appellate attorneys interviewed were frequently proud of their ability to "give the record a broader perspective," but this claim was often disputed by the trial attorneys interviewed.

In this study, "control" of a case, insofar as strategy and tactics were concerned, was assumed to be in the hands of the law firm or attorney who answered the letter of inquiry. Information about litigation strategy was gathered by letters as well as from interviews. Occasionally, an attorney referred the request to another attorney "who did most of the work," but in most cases, especially commercial cases, the responding attorney or interviewer answered as spokesman for the law firm. While demonstrable proof is difficult the investigator did not feel that lack of candor or evasion affected the validity of the responses.

TABLE 1   Participation as Principals and *Amici Curiae* in Supreme Court Litigations (1958–1964)

Type of Litigant	Commercial Cases (499 cases)		Non-Commercial Cases (349 cases)	
	Principal	Amicus	Principal	Amicus
United States Government & Administrative Agencies	273	38	137	23
States, Agencies, and Their Political Subdivisions	82	26	203	18
Private Companies and Corporations	375	30	13	1
Trade and Business Associations	20	69	—	—
Professions	—	17	—	28
Labor Unions	81	32	1	2
Social Defense Organizations	—	—	13	65
Individuals	117	22	310	5
TOTAL	948	234	677	142

tion, a few remarks about the role of governments and government attorneys seem appropriate. Although the fact is seldom stressed in the political science literature, the United States Department of Justice and attorneys from other federal agencies, primarily the ICC, NLRB, FPC, and FTC, participate in well over half the cases on the Supreme Court's opinion docket. In their prescribed supervisory roles in the Federal legal system, the Supreme Court and administrative agencies are preoccupied with settling technical questions in administrative law. Occasionally substantive policy issues emerge. . . .

In administrative law cases, especially those involving the regulatory processes, state and local governments often appear among the formal legal adversaries. Intergovernmental conflict is also involved in constitutional cases where issues surrounding the limits of state taxation, state regulation of labor, problems of intergovernmental tax immunity, and national-state confrontations concerning private property transactions (e.g., bankruptcy proceedings in which questions of national supremacy or priority arise) are involved. Information about Court-state and other federal relationships growing out of litigations remains largely unexplored by political scientists.

In its *amicus curiae* activity, the federal government behaves very much like a private litigant. Most of its participation in commercial cases is designed to promote narrow proprietary or operational interests that would otherwise be pursued in government litigations. For example, the Antitrust Division of the Department of Justice may instruct the Court on how a statute or patent should be construed because of the way it affects the Department's patent enforcement program. Other regulatory agencies use the device to maximize their administrative efficiency. State Department views are interposed in state and private litigation to avoid embarrassing the Federal government. Sometimes the government participates as *amicus curiae* to pursue even narrower proprietary interests. In personal injury cases, for example, the government's role as land owner, shipper, or banker comes in conflict with other private claims.

The participation of state and local governments in Supreme Court cases differs from that of the federal government in the role of both principal and amicus. When its activity is viewed in relation to other states, each state can be observed pursuing independent interests though degrees of cooperation among them are sometimes achieved in spe-

TABLE 2 Participation as Principals in Supreme Court Litigation (1958–1964)

Type of Litigation	No. of Cases	Social Defense Organizations	United States Government	Trade Associations	Professional Organizations (including Bar Associations)	State and Local Governments	Labor Unions	Private Companies and Corporations	Individual and Ad Hoc Groups
Commercial									
Labor Relations	100	—	54	—	—	7	72	77	8
Trade & Business Regulation	38	—	35	3	—	11	—	39	4
Taxation	93	—	68	1	—	28	1	62	21
Torts, Public Contracts & Other Civil Actions Involving Governments	33	—	24	1	—	9	—	8	15
Power-Utility Regulations	22	—	21	—	—	9	1	20	—
Transportation	36	—	31	6	—	4	3	32	—
Anti-Trust	43	—	26	2	—	—	4	38	—
Public Lands	21	—	14	—	—	14	—	8	9
Private Law Suits	48	—	—	—	—	—	—	39	14
Personal Injury	55	—	—	—	—	—	—	52	46
Total Commercial	499	—	273	13	—	82	81	375	117
Non-Commercial									
Civil Liberties	98	—	24	2	—	76	—	9	84
Political Offender Cases	57	5	34	—	—	15	1	—	46
Race Relations	60	8	10	—	—	47	—	4	46
Criminal	134	—	69	—	—	65	—	—	134
Total Non-Commercial	349	13	137	2	—	203	1	13	310
TOTAL	848	13	410	15	—	285	82	388	427

cific cases. In commercial cases, for example, states having "right to work" laws have occasionally cooperated in joining or supporting another state's amicus brief. Similar cooperation was achieved in "off-shore oil cases," cases involving agricultural regulation, and in public utility cases. This cooperation is, on very rare occasions, facilitated through the National Association of Attorneys General, but more frequently through informal exchanges of briefs and correspondence.

The Supreme Court litigation activities of political subdivisions within states approach in complexity those of corporations and other private business groups. Though state Attorneys General function as the equivalent of "house counsel," they do not always coordinate the litigation work of the state administrative agencies, and they have little or no control of commercial litigation activity of the political subdivisions.

B. Other Formal Parties in Commercial Cases. Court records reveal little or nothing about litigation costs in commercial cases, but a study of the formal parties involved casts doubt on widely held views about the "representational character" of Supreme Court cases. This doubt is further strengthened by questionnaires and interview responses indicating that the costs in almost every commercial case were "borne exclusively by the clients."

Self-financing is to be expected among the types of corporations or public utilities that get involved in business regulation cases—e.g., antitrust, public utility, securities and exchange cases, etc. However, in cases involving taxation, government law suits, private law suits, and personal injury cases the client is more likely to be an individual with limited financial resources. The breakdown of principals classified as "individuals" in Table 2 shows that they appear as parties most frequently in commercial cases involving taxation, government law suits, private law suits, and personal injury cases. Though the results and implications of these cases are watched by claimants' attorneys, and attorneys from insurance companies, banks, and specialized bar associations, none of the participating

attorneys reported any direct financial help from any of these sources. In most of the commercial cases in which individuals, or small business interests, participated, the stakes were sufficiently inviting to justify clients "going all the way." Some of the attorneys noted the availability of "contingent fee" arrangements and economies which aided them in getting their cases to the Supreme Court as cheaply as possible.[2] Trial records in most Supreme Court cases are short with the legal or constitutional issues clearly defined. By keeping records short, or by having the government assume the printing costs, the expense of appellate litigation can be made economically feasible to a broader spectrum of social and economic interests.

The so-called big commercial cases usually involved, as party principals, a plethora of governments, utilities, corporations, and private companies. The complexity of the formal party interests is usually too great to be unravelled meaningfully. Yet a casual glance at transcripts and records shows that interests are combined and consolidated through various formal and informal procedures. Few of the attorneys listed in the records participate significantly at the trial, administrative, or appellate levels though usually all the principals involved in a litigation are at one stage or another represented by counsel. As a matter of common practice locally retained attorneys begin the work, and they are subsequent-

---

[2]The questions pertaining to financial sponsorship and support included in the questionnaires and interviews were as follows:

"Was the litigation in this case financed by your client exclusively, or was additional financial support secured from other interested parties?"

"If the litigation was financially supported by other persons or organizations, do such persons or organizations maintain a legal fund to defray legal expenses in test cases in which they take an interest?"

"If the litigation was financially supported by others, apart from your client, at what stages of the proceeding was the support given?"

Among sixty commercial litigations investigated, information was secured in only forty cases. Attorneys in only two cases reported that they had solicited financial aid from a national trade association. In another case an attorney reported receiving financial aid from "another party who was a competitor and a direct beneficiary of the law suit." Those who reported such aid gave the desire to "broaden the issues" as their reason.

ly joined by corporation "house counsel," and finally by "outside counsel" brought in from the major law firms. The lawyers in the sample reported that the preparation of briefs and other legal materials is carried on by correspondence, conferences, and consultations. These kinds of arrangements, it was noted, are familiar procedure in all kinds of litigation.[3]

1. *Private Companies and Corporations.* The largest group of principals participating in commercial cases are private companies and corporations. Even though information about the size and wealth of these parties has not been gathered, the prominence of many of the companies involved, and the amounts of money in controversy, should convince anyone that cost is not a controlling factor in the planning of most Supreme Court cases.

Attorneys in only two cases indicated that they had solicited trade associations for financial support in behalf of their clients, and there were only four occasions reported in which the United States Solicitor General was asked to participate in behalf of a litigating party. Those who requested such aid gave as their reasons a desire to "broaden the issues," "make a show of strength," or "educate the court on related aspects of public policy." Several attorneys mentioned "the preferred status that government attorneys deservedly enjoy" with the Supreme Court.

[3]The questions pertaining to participation by "extra" attorneys were as follows:

"Were you or your law firm the original attorney of record?"

"If not, how and when did your law firm begin to participate in the case?"

"Did you consult with other attorneys or other interests who were not parties or participants in the litigation?"

"If so, what contribution did these persons or attorneys make toward the preparation of the case? At what stages of the proceedings did they make their contributions?"

"Who played the most important part in pressing the litigation forward?"

Attorneys participating in 37 commercial cases responded "meaningfully" to these questions. Attorneys and law firms in 13 cases reported cooperation with other attorneys consisting of conferences, exchanges of briefs, consultations, or having other attorneys read the briefs. Some of these attorneys noted that this was common practice even though it did not occur in the particular case about which they were reporting.

2. *Trade and Business Associations.* In political life, trade associations can be expected to represent their members in a variety of ways. Some are in a position to control the standards and practices of an industry or trade. Truckers, railroads, banks, and others have associations which behave in this way. Others like insurance underwriters, stock exchanges, industrial information bureaus and similar agencies specialize in providing advice, information and service to their members and other interested parties. Finally, there is a type of association that gives the business or industrial viewpoint on a variety of broader business issues. The Chamber of Commerce and the National Association of Manufacturers seem to fit this pattern. While these organizations on rare occasions participate as principals it is the amicus role of these groups that is of greater concern to the political observer.

If trade associations behaved politically one would expect more *amicus curiae* activity than the public records indicate. (See Table 3 *infra*). The low rate of participation is probably explained by the fact that it is difficult to achieve consensus within an important range of an association's clientele. A broad consensus is occasionally achieved in labor relations "right to work" cases and other issues where an association can unite broad segments within an industrial community. The absence of trade association participation in most commercial cases suggests, however, that the issues are too specialized for such groups to participate in a politically meaningful way. When an association is formed along narrow and specialized lines, participation is more likely, but the number of times this happens is relatively rare.

3. *The Professions.* If the litigation practices of trade associations do not comport with a political view of litigation, professional groups, as indicated by their formal or *amicus* activity, are even less political. These groups in fact are barely visible. In the seven years of litigation studied they did not appear as formal parties and they appeared as *amicus curiae* in only seventeen commerical cases. Most of the appearances were occasioned by professional bar groups or by individual law-

yers seeking technical clarification of laws governing taxes, government contracts, or specific business regulations. To this observer it is somewhat remarkable that so few professional groups play any role in Supreme Court cases. Accountants, engineers, teachers, bankers, economists, and others may individually appear as expert witnesses but rarely provide policy appraisal to guide the Supreme Court. Apparently the issues in most commercial cases are considered too narrow or private to encourage even that kind of participation.

4. *Labor Unions.* . . . [A]n examination of the unions' formal and *amici* appearances shows that their participation is confined almost exclusively to representing the union as an organizational entity. An individual worker having a grievance against the union or a "non-contractual" grievance against a company will usually have to go elsewhere for legal assistance. The cases involving unions concerning "unfair labor practices" under the Labor Management Relations Act included activities such as strikes, lockouts, illegal picketing, use of hiring halls, and suits against unions and companies in their representational or institutional capacities. In cases where individuals pressed grievances, personal injury cases, or other problems, the individuals had to get their legal support from other sources.

While international unions sometimes assume the litigation burdens of their local affiliates, the unions as a whole generally stick to their own knitting and rarely intervene in the litigation of others. Unions participated as amici in only 32 cases, but half of this participation was by the house counsel of the AFL-CIO Federation. Within the labor law, and in other business fields, there is specialization in the way amicus curiae activity is conducted. A so-called narrow labor relations issue, such as the specific use of a hiring hall, may bring another union into the case because the second union has a similar litigation pending. The arguing of broader policy issues, however, is generally left to the counsel of the federation.

This survey of the formal side of commercial litigation suggests a portrait of litigation

activity that is quite different than the one presented in political science literature. It suggests that Supreme Court cases are not representational but narrowly focused private controversies. Companies, individuals, unions, and others pursue narrow interests confined to the immediate litigation. Although more than forty percent of the cases have *amici curiae* of some kind, much of this activity is conducted in pursuit of narrow private interests. If broader types of organized interests do participate in judicial processes they are more likely to be found "behind the scenes" supporting the formal party litigants.

C. Other Supporting Activity in Commercial Cases. To secure information about other kinds of lobbying that may be present, attorneys were asked "whether all significant social or economic interests" were adequately represented in the trial of their cases, and if not, "what significant social or economic interests were not represented?"[4] Questions were also asked about sponsorship and finance as well as other tactics described earlier. While the purport of some of these questions may not have been fully understood by all the attorneys, the responses provided no support to a theory of judicial lobbying. Instead the response verified a not unexpected ethnocentricity or "egotism" within most of the Supreme Court's practicing bar. Attorneys participating in commercial cases frequently volunteered the comment that their litigation was a "straight out economic battle between the parties" or that the "important" or "garden variety" cases involved "solely legal or financial issues." In several instances the attorneys noted that their cases were "not a landmark in any social or economic sense" even though the case was "of great interest to lawyers." Many attorneys stressed the fact that the cases concerned only the parties and

---

[4]In interviews, the following additional questions were occasionally asked:

"Do you consider your client representative of a class of people similarly situated?"

"Was any effort made to get additional representation for the people represented by your client?"

Among those responding, only seven attorneys or law firms felt that "other interests" were not adequately represented.

were conducted without any "behind the scenes" groups or interests.

In a number of cases attorneys representing commercial litigants were antagonistic or even hostile to *amicus curiae* participation arguing that opposing interests such as state governments, labor unions, or other opponents had adequate opportunities to participate at earlier stages of the proceeding. They indicated that they were opposed to persons or groups who stand aside at the trial or administrative stages only to appear with new arguments at the appellate level. Even where attorneys perceived an important social impact to their cases, they noted that the character of the parties and the amounts of money in controversy made the litigation stand on its own bottom. In these cases, it was argued, other interests were "too remote" from the specific issues involved.

Even in cases where smaller financial stakes were involved, the attorneys almost always regarded their cases as private fights. A few of them lamented the fact that policy issues were not developed at the trial or pleading stage, and occasionally an attorney criticized lawyer colleagues for "narrow legalistic viewpoints." Nevertheless, most responses cited technical legal requirements, the attitudes of judges, and of opposing counsel as justifications for strictly legalistic approaches to litigation. A few attorneys warned that policy considerations interposed at trial or pleading stages of litigation would make litigations unduly expensive, introduce irrelevancies, and obscure the resolution of specific issues. From a lawyer's point of view, litigation is a very private form of conflict, and from all indications they expect to keep it that way.

. . .

Further support for a private or legalistic view of litigation is also suggested by the observations of some attorneys that those affected by their litigations were too poorly organized and too isolated to be helpful. In one case an attorney, engaged in self-criticism, noted his own egotism and his failure to solicit such help from trade and business associations. "It might have helped," he said, "but I just didn't think of it." Thus, in tax cases, private litigations, personal injury cases, and other

instances where concerted action may have been helpful, the attorneys gave no hint that they availed themselves of the assistance of "behind the scenes" interests.

Though evidence of lobbying in the judicial process can be found in appearances and briefs contributed by *amici curiae*, such participations seem rare and, more often than not, the amicus has a specific and separate pecuniary interest in the litigation itself. In some of these cases, the *amici* are themselves parties to pending litigations. Attorneys representing trade associations, labor unions and individual taxpayers were among the most frequent amici but in this capacity they were pursuing specific institutional or individual interests and not really supporting the litigations of others[5] (see Table 3). While occasionally a policy-minded bystander would participate in a commercial case, such participation was criticized or even ridiculed as introducing irrelevant and confusing considerations.

If commercial litigants behaved politically,

[5]The questions pertaining to *amici curiae* activity were as follows:

"Did you or your client attempt to secure amicus curiae participation? Were you successful? If so, how and why was this participation secured?"

"Did any other parties, other than the parties you sought, participate as amicus curiae? Did you approve or disapprove of such participation? Why?"
The following questions were asked of *amicus curiae* participants:

"Why did your client find it necessary to participate as an amicus to the proceeding?"

"What specific contributions did your brief make to the facts and issues before the court?"

"Was any offer made to participate at earlier stages of the court proceeding? If so, what contributions did you make?"

"Was any effort made to coordinate your participation with that of any other persons or organizations interested in the proceedings? If so, how was this coordination achieved?"

"Did your amicus participation emphasize legal or extra-legal considerations? If extra-legal, what was the nature of these considerations?"
In 1960 *amici curiae* appeared in 15 of the 60 case situations investigated. In five other cases efforts were made to solicit *amicus* participation of trade associations, and in two other cases the solicitation of the Solicitor General was reported. Attorneys in six cases expressed opposition specifically or in principle to the kind of *amicus* activity involved. These numbers are too small to support firm conclusions, but there is little evidence suggesting that amicus curiae plays a strategic role in commercial cases.

TABLE 3   Distribution of Amicus Curiae Interest Activity in Supreme Court Litigations (1958–1965)

Types of Litigation	No. of Cases	Social Defense Organizations	United States Government	Trade Associations	Professional Organizations (including Bar Associations)	State and Local Governments	Labor Unions	Private Companies and Corporations	Individuals and Ad Hoc Groups
Commercial									
Labor Relations	100	—	7	20	4	3	28	5	1
Trade & Business Regulation	38	—	3	15	3	6	—	10	1
Taxation	93	1	4	6	3	5	—	5	13
Torts, Public Contracts & Other Civil Actions	10	—	—	—	—	—	—	—	—
Involving Governments	33	—	10	2	1	2	—	2	1
Power-Utility Regulations	22	1	2	2	1	6	4	—	1
Transportation	36	—	1	3	2	1	—	2	—
Anti-Trust	43	—	8	—	—	—	—	1	2
Public Lands	21	2	3	4	2	3	—	3	1
Private Law Suits	48	—	—	5	1	—	—	—	—
Personal Injury	55	—	—	7	—	—	—	2	1
Total Commercial	499	4	38	64	17	26	32	30	22
Non-Commercial									
Civil Liberties	98	26	8	5	12	8	—	—	1
Political Offender Cases	57	13	—	—	9	1	2	—	3
Race Relations	60	5	15	—	1	5	—	1	—
Criminal	134	14	—	—	6	4	—	—	1
Total Non-Commercial	349	58	23	5	28	18	2	1	5
TOTAL	848	62	61	69	45	44	34	31	27

their attorneys, together with others representing similarly situated clients, would coordinate their activities to establish more effective litigation strategy. Multiple litigations involving similar issues were found to occur most frequently in the taxation and labor relations fields, and attorneys in these litigations sometimes reported that they managed more than one case at a time. However, even if the circumstances and mutuality of interests made coordination feasible, the situations never permitted litigants to "pick their own cases for Supreme Court review." "Even where cases are managed," said an experienced union attorney, "an unmanaged case gets there first."

Most attorneys reported that the case "most ripe for review" or "most advanced in the legal mill" was the one that the Supreme Court reviewed first. During the interviews, lawyers occasionally complained that "the case selected turns out, from our point of view, to be the wrong one." Counsel from international labor unions, or house counsel of large corporations, may carefully pick their own cases—they may even anticipate the probability of Supreme Court review—but it seems unlikely that any attorney can ensure that a particular case will get there.[6]

Among the cases studied none were found in which attorneys and others planned substantial public relations campaigns in connection with a pending litigation. The usual news handouts and house organ publicity accompanied some cases, and contact with other interested parties followed the conventional pathways of correspondence and informal exchange of ideas.

In summary, attorneys representing commercial litigants seem unable or unwilling to become political actors in the judicial process. In a few instances *amici curiae,* expert witnesses, or conventional legal argument may broaden the issues involved, but most Supreme Court commercial litigation is conducted in a purely private manner, and public consequences apparently flow from "a series of fortuitous circumstances."

D. Non-Commercial Cases: Formal Parties and Amici. Though the distinction is not stressed in political science literature, it may be that the "theory of the judicial lobby" is intended to apply exclusively to non-commercial cases. In these cases, individuals representing political, cultural, religious, and social minorities are more likely to need the financial and legal backing of others. While considerations of this kind are sometimes pertinent, few of the cases clearly present this situation. Business interests are often commingled with civil liberties issues and the cases are processed in a manner sim-

---

[6]The questions pertaining to multiple litigation were as follows:

"Was your case one of several similar cases brought simultaneously in different judicial forums?"

"If so, was coordinative effort made in carrying on the litigations?"

"If there was coordinative effort, why was this particular case selected for appeal?"

In a few cases where coordination was reported, questions like the following were asked in interviews and questionnaire follow-ups:

"What was the nature of the coordination?"

"Did you agree to stress different issues in different cases?"

"Did you succeed in getting any litigants to drop their cases?"

"Even though your client was a defendant in a criminal case, was there an effort to present a 'united front' or coordinate the manner in which the defenses were presented?"

Multiple litigation was reported in 14 of the 60 commercial cases studied. In none of the cases did an attorney report a successful coordinative effort to pick the right case. In many of these cases there were exchanges of briefs and other forms of cooperation.

Both government and private attorneys in commercial cases denied any experience in managing litigations so as to set up the right case, although several attorneys believed that this kind of strategy was occasionally attempted. At least a dozen attorneys representing private clients intimated that the government attorneys managed cases, and a few felt that labor unions and trade associations were able to stage test cases "in circumstances of their choosing." In the tax field an attorney described the situation as follows:

"In my principal field—taxation—a majority of the cases that reach the Supreme Court, particularly on an appeal initiated by the Government, can be classified as 'managed litigation.' A look at the percentage of opinions for certiorari granted tend to bear this out. Frequently years will be permitted to pass, even in the face of repeated adverse decisions by the Court of Appeals, before a case is selected to present to the Supreme Court. . . . Many cases which should perhaps be taken up by the taxpayer do not involve enough money to the litigant to warrant the expense. Few businessmen today can afford to fight on 'principle.' Litigation costs are too expensive. Also the Internal Revenue Service is notorious for stretching a Supreme Court announced principle to the utmost."

ilar to other private commercial litigations. In some of these cases civil liberties organizations participate, but when they do so their activity is usually confined to *amicus curiae* activity at the appellate level. Also, a large number of Supreme Court cases classified as "noncommercial" do not involve issues that stimulate the activity of organized civil libertarians. Thus, immigration cases, military cases, criminal cases, and others are frequently decided on technical procedural grounds without arousing the interest of others. Unless the litigant is affiliated with, or has some special connection with an organization, he or she is unlikely to get this type of assistance. The litigant is thus forced to finance the case himself, or enlist the aid of friends and relatives. Finally, there are some litigants who do not get financial or other legal support simply because they do not ask for it.

1. *Civil Liberties Cases.* In a number of cases, individuals, business, and organizations of various kinds invoke constitutional and legal principles against the actions of public officials. Though the American Civil Liberties Union is known for its work in this area, its spokesmen maintain that the group is not a legal aid society, or a general social defense organization, but an organization solely devoted to constitutional principles. As such, it sponsors only a few cases in which constitutional issues are clearly presented.

This organization, like other social defense groups, operates with a small legal staff and a large network of "cooperating" and consulting attorneys. Local affiliates of the organization decide if and when to intervene in a case, and also decide the character and the amount of legal aid to be rendered. In the case of weaker affiliates the litigation program, if any, is augmented by assistance from the national organization. In its circulating memoranda and official statements emphasis is placed upon the organization's policy of referring prospective litigants to "cooperating attorneys" who control the cases under organization sponsorship. Even if the organization chooses not to sponsor a given case, an attorney recommended by the ACLU may decide to press the litigation forward unilaterally.

Though cooperating attorneys participate in an increasing number of cases, there are many more cases involving civil liberties issues in which the organizations do not participate. Even including those in which they participate as *amici*, the activity of organizations is visible in only one-third of the civil liberties cases.

2. *Political Offender Cases.* Another somewhat different pattern of activity is found in cases involving political offenders. In these cases—especially those involving Communists or "fellow travelers"—litigations are handled by a small and decreasing number of attorneys associated with or cooperating with *ad hoc* defense committees, or small radical defense organizations. Those cases are occasionally supported by civil liberties foundations,[7] and the lawyers retained are frequently associated with the National Lawyers Guild.

. . .

The most common political offender cases involve naturalization and deportation proceedings, non-Communist affidavit cases, employment security (loyalty), passports and travel, registration or membership in the Communist Party or front organizations, contempt charges in congressional investigations, and civil disabilities imposed on Communists and other political dissenters. The ACLU sometimes sponsors cases of this kind but only if the constitutional issue is the dominant issue in the litigation.

3. *Race Relations Cases.* After more than a

[7]According to Ann Fagin Ginger, editor of *Civil Liberties Docket,* "Of the 270,000 attorneys in the United States today [Martindale-Hubbell as of 1964 estimates the total as close to 300,000] fewer than 1,000 represented either a plaintiff or defendant in constitutional litigations. Also, less than half that number instituted even one action for a plaintiff seeking vindication of 'constitutional' rights. In fact, fifty law firms handled the bulk of the 2,600 cases. These fifty firms included those specializing in constitutional litigation and general staff counsel for the NAACP Legal Defense and Educational Fund, Inc., the NAACP, the American Civil Liberties Union, the Emergency Civil Liberties Committee, the Committee to Assist Southern Lawyers of the National Lawyers Guild, and the Commission on Law and Social Action of American Jewish Congress." Ginger, "Litigation as a Form of Political Action," *Wayne Law Review,* 9 (1963), at 464.

If the list were confined to those who handle the trial of political offenders it would undoubtedly be considerably smaller.

decade and a half of harassment in the southern states, the NAACP and its Legal Defense and Education Fund legal staff have established constitutional legitimacy for the main lines of its "representational" litigation activity. In a line of cases culminating in *NAACP* v. *Button*, the Supreme Court majority's dicta have sanctioned at least some forms of litigation sponsorship and management. . . .

At the present time the NAACP staffs and their "cooperating" attorneys control most of the race relations cases that reach the Supreme Court. Questions surrounding legal tactics may, however, become moot due to the surge of litigation connected with more recent race relations activity. Picketing, demonstrations, sit-ins, and other forms of protest have substantially changed the litigation picture. The NAACP lawyers are no longer alone in defense of the movement for racial reform. Their tactical approaches once characterized as "radical" by some or "slow" by others now compete with those being developed by attorneys representing the National Lawyers Guild, the American Bar Association, and the American Civil Liberties Union. It is not yet possible to evaluate the behavior of each of these groups of lawyers, but preliminary indications are that each set of attorneys operates more or less at arms length from the other. The ABA-sponsored attorneys operate in the tradition of legal aid societies and "of counsel" to overtaxed trial attorneys in race cases. While occasionally cooperating with the Committee to Aid Southern Lawyers of the National Lawyers Guild, it is almost certain that this kind of volunteer did not enlist to "defend the movement" or to "avoid tactics of individualized defense and litigation which will wind up in the Supreme Court three years from now." Lawyer spokesmen from the National Lawyers Guild speak the language of collective militancy though their actual legal practices may reflect more attention to conventional lawyer-client procedures. Finally, if past behavior is precedent, lawyers representing the American Civil Liberties Union and affiliated groups will avoid direct identification with the Negro protest by supporting and seeking out selected constitutional cases for ultimate Supreme Court test.

4. *Criminal Cases.* A separate pattern of lawyer activity involving an essentially separate set of attorneys is observable in the case histories of criminal litigations which reach the Supreme Court. The largest number of cases result from prisoner applications and cases brought forward by public defenders or court appointed attorneys. Most of the attorneys in these criminal cases had no connection with the American Civil Liberties Union or similar groups, and according to their responses, they did not request aid from that organization or any similar group. Other criminal lawyers were financed exclusively by their clients and litigated their cases in the manner that private law practice would dictate. The patterns of activities described provide some degree of regularity in the Supreme Court Bar's non-commercial cases. . . .

Any taxonomy of litigation routes to the Supreme Court cannot, of course, overlook the conventional and sometimes idiosyncratic paths that some cases take. As already noted, cases classified as "non-commercial," particularly those involving civil liberties, turn out in some cases to be pocketbook actions with constitutional by-products. In other instances determined individuals press their own principles against organizational advice and at high cost to themselves. Finally, lawyers take cases for sport, and the prestige of arguing before the highest tribunal. Attorneys in all kinds of cases often state that their case was their fight in which they alone had to carry the major burden.

E. Supporting Activity in Non-Commercial Cases. One would expect that a different breed of attorney inhabits the world of non-commercial Supreme Court litigations. This belief is only partially justified because most of the non-commercial litigations involve private complaints about the use of public authority. Most of the cases that reach the Supreme Court involve the troubles of public servants, lawyers, home owners, soldiers, union officials, civilians in military posts, and a variety of other persons complaining about official actions. Though the cases are considered "important" enough for Supreme Court review, they ordinarily do not qualify for support by organized civil libertarians. In any event, the parties in civil liberties cases usually secure their own attorneys without soliciting or receiving help from any outside source. Only a few lawyers handling civil liberties cases see their cases as representing the interests of large classes of citizens.

In civil liberties cases involving movie censorship and church-state relationships, the litigation was primarily commercial with constitutional overtones. Though many cases were brought "simultaneously," local censorship statutes differed in detail and any important degree of coordination was not feasible. Also, litigation enthusiasm varied with different commercial litigants who brought cases of this kind.[8]

Even where mutuality of interests over-

comes specific circumstances, attorneys differ in the way social defense litigation should be conducted. In 1961, a prominent attorney in the American Civil Liberties Union proposed that the organization's "cooperating" attorneys coordinate all contempt of Congress litigations in which a First Amendment defense was raised. The proposal was rejected because of the organization's continuing policy of confining intervention to those cases "where the issues are exclusively and predominately those of civil liberties." Participation in all similar cases, it was argued, would drain the organization's resources by getting it involved in cases clouded by evidentiary considerations. Since ACLU attorneys consider the organization a constitutional rather than a general defense organization, defendants with weak constitutional cases would have to get help elsewhere or fight their own legal battles. Attorneys in particular civil liberties cases cited examples where attorneys agreed to focus particular issues in certain ways, but even in these cases, the facts and circumstances of the individuals concerned were controlling considerations.

In race relations and political offender cases the opportunities for control are at least more favorable. As already noted, political offenders always have had few available attorneys to appeal these types of cases. In the last seven Supreme Court terms the NAACP Legal Defense and Education Fund, Inc., controlled about two-thirds of the race relations cases, and three law firms managed more than 40 percent of the political offender cases that reached the Supreme Court. This legal monopoly, at least in principle, gives these attorneys a strategic role in channeling cases upward.

Lawyers in non-commercial cases also disagree on the use of publicity in pending cases. Some attorneys argue that the Supreme Court does not decide cases on strictly legal grounds, and publicity, when discreetly used, serves as an educational vehicle. Others point out that publicity is essential to counteract unfavorable public opinion, stimulated by government, in cases involving politically or even socially unpopular defendants. The lead-

[8]In The Sunday Closing Cases, *Braunfeld* v. *Brown*, 366 U.S. 599 (1961); *Gallagher* v. *Crown Kosher Super Mkt., Inc.*, 366 U.S. 617 (1961); *Two Guys from Harrison-Allentown* v. *McGinley*, 366 U.S. 582 (1961); *McGowan* v. *Maryland*, 366 U.S. 420 (1961), business firms or businessmen were the "formal parties in interest" though religious interests were deeply involved and appeared at the trial stage of litigation. Attorneys representing some of the respondents in these cases indicated that they consulted with attorneys of the American Jewish Congress, but noted that the litigations were brought separately and involved no comprehensive coordination even on the part of the religious interests involved. The American Jewish Congress Committee and the American Jewish Congress appeared as *amicus curiae* at the Supreme Court level. An attorney in one of these organizations reported that he first learned of the case in U.S. Law Week, and decided that it was the kind of case in which his group was interested. He tried to enlist many other Protestant church and lay organizations to "go along with his brief." Reasons given by these other organizational spokesmen for refusing to cooperate reflect the difficulties in securing cooperation even in the signing of a brief. For example, leaders indicated that they would have to "consult their organizations," or "take a vote." Others reported that there was not enough time to achieve consensus within the organization. For another report of The Sunday Closing Cases, see Lund, "The Sunday Closing Cases," in Pritchett & Westin, *The Third Branch of Government—8 Cases in Constitutional Politics* 275 (1963). Though movie censorship cases in 1961 were brought "simultaneously" in different judicial forums, there was no reported evidence of any conscious coordination. Attorneys indicated that the interests involved were too unique to invite such coordination.

ing organizations do not use this tactic in order to get financial support as money is available in their general funds. They confine their publicity in pending cases to house organs and standard news handouts. General publicity in pending cases is carefully avoided.[9]

Though opinions differ on other techniques, there is widespread agreement among non-commercial lawyers on the value of amicus curiae briefs. In non-commercial cases other social defense organizations are occasionally represented, but the ACLU is far and away the most active organization. From 1958 to 1964 it participated in 20 civil liberties cases, 12 criminal cases, 11 political offender cases and 3 cases involving race relations. The distribution of *amici* activity is shown in Table 3.

As one would expect, the forces at work in criminal cases are markedly different than those involved in civil liberties, political offender and race relations cases. Criminal cases are almost never regarded as "representative" proceedings in any sense. The ACLU over the past seven years has participated in only a dozen criminal cases which resulted in Supreme Court opinions. Attorneys handling criminal cases often regard themselves as "lone wolves" and "independent operators" who feel they are "perfectly

capable" of handling their own cases. Some of the attorneys indicated that they were opposed to seeking or getting outside help, and in two interviews the attorneys complained that the "ACLU was trying to take my case away." While some criminal cases involved notorious clients and presumably large fees, a much larger number of cases involved attorneys who had "assumed a lonely burden of fighting a cause without pay and without help from any source."

IV. CONCLUSION

. . . [This] picture of Supreme Court litigation is at odds with that usually presented in political science literature. The actual judicial process appears to be a close approximation of the traditional *legal* model in which judicial policy-making emerges through *ad hoc* private controversies. The parties, attorneys, and issues in Supreme Court cases, more often than not, remain narrowly private so as to prevent irrelevancies and outside pressure.

. . .

If "lobbying" of litigation were to become widespread as "a form of political or pressure group activity," a fundamental change in thinking about judicial process would be necessary. Businessmen, companies, unions and corporations would have to abandon traditional attorney-client relationships and interpose trade associations and labor federations between themselves and their attorneys. In social and political litigations, "social defense" or defense by civil liberties organizations would have to supersede the limited functions performed by legal aid and public defender groups, and members of the organized bar would have to abandon traditional notions about the "independence of the bar" and "attorney-client relationships and privileges" in order to recognize their collective group responsibility for the making of public policy. The individual who seeks to vindicate his private rights in the Supreme Court would have to recognize that the judicial process is no place for idiosyncratic notions of public policy.

The evidence suggests, however, that neither the legalistic world of individual attorney-

[9]The questions asked pertaining to the use of publicity in litigation were as follows:

"Did you or your client do anything to publicize the issues involved in this case? If so, was publicity conducted while the case was pending? If not, when?"

In subsequent interviews, the following question was included:

"How do you feel about publicity in pending Supreme Court litigation?"

Only seven commercial cases had elements of publicity connected therewith, but the publicity was passive and apparently not a part of litigation strategy. In one instance where the issue in litigation involved public relations, the public relations firm reported that the matter was taken out of its hands and "placed exclusively in the hands of attorneys." A midwestern attorney in another case involving bankruptcy "suspected that the government chooses midwestern cases because midwestern lawyers do not generally solicit publicity." Some attorneys in important public utility cases voiced the opinion that most Supreme Court cases bring with them "a retinue of lawyers, experts, and a public relations counsel and even the nudging of senators and representatives." In most of the interviews conducted, this view was not volunteered—even though several attorneys granted its plausibility.

client relationships nor a world of organized or "managed" litigations reflects the actualities of Supreme Court litigation processes.

Almost all lower court litigations raise important issues of law and policy but few attract the participation of outside groups because the principles involved are too closely intermingled with the private interests of the litigants. As we move from the lower to the higher courts, we find that most of the judicial work has a narrower scope and that it is carried forward, beyond the trial stage, only insofar as the litigant is able to pay for it. Most of the issues that receive judicial attention in appellate court opinions are those involving technical legal matters. These issues are often interlocutory in nature, and are usually confined to the clarification of legal tasks.

The private parties involved in Supreme Court cases usually represent individual, commercial, proprietary or pecuniary interests. The "real party in interest" in these cases is the same as the formal party, and there are usually no "behind the scenes" groups intervening between the attorney and his business client. Sponsorship of such litigation by persons other than the formal parties is rare, but it occurs most frequently in cases involving political offenders or racial discrimination.

The lawyer's role in influencing governmental policymaking is even more apparent in the judicial sphere than in connection with lobbying in the legislative and administrative processes. Large bureaucratically sophisticated commercial law firms are particularly sensitive to the possibilities of raising new issues, whether for offensive or defensive purposes, and they have the ability to bring to bear resources such as money, files, organization, and expertise in order to respond quickly and sensitively before significant judicial decisions are made.

Criminal defense attorneys prefer to work alone and to insulate the case within the narrow confines of their client's private interests. Social defense organizations, on the other hand, participate in support of litigants whose cases provide "public relations" or "educational value." In cases involving the politically unpopular, these attributes provide the basis for the raising of funds for legal expenses and attorney's fees. Civil liberties organizations, and most private organizations supporting civil liberties causes, do not usually intervene at the trial level unless the issues are clearly focused and disentangled from other legal and evidentiary considerations.

Though coordination or management of multiple litigations is theoretically possible, there are too many intervening variables to prevent its success. Litigation management involves problems of timing, the choice of a litigant, selection of judicial forum, the strategic choice of pleadings, and the cooperation of the attorneys. Despite these obstacles, coordination is sometimes attempted. Lawyers exchange briefs and extend courtesies, but unless there is a common client, there is likely to be very little planning or coordination even among litigants who are similarly situated.

Participation in the role of *amicus curiae* is generally aimed at furthering independent pecuniary or proprietary interests, but, in commercial cases, there is evidence that the participation of the United States government is sought to strengthen the legal position of the formal party. In social and political litigations, the ACLU plays an *amicus* role similar to, but less effective than, the role assumed by the United States government in commercial cases. Other *amici* in social and political litigations participate primarily as advocates on behalf of the general position advanced by the party litigant. Some coordination of *amicus curiae* activity among private groups is achieved through clearance procedures which include conferences and exchanges of information and briefs. In social and political cases a great deal of effort is expended in enlisting endorsements to "strengthen" a litigant's position and in avoiding duplicative and unnecessary "me too" briefs. In the last analysis, however, *amicus curiae* briefs reflect the independent work products of individual attorneys or law firms.

On the basis of this study, organized interest groups would appear to play a relatively minor role in Supreme Court decision-making. . . .

D. Lawyers

Lawyers, "the professional judicial persuaders,"[1] are, of course, major participants in any judicial system. The following two selections, both by Herbert Jacob, describe the activities of two types of lawyers—government lawyers and non-government lawyers. Lawyers employed by the federal government almost exclusively participate in the federal judicial system. They are also an identifiable group about whom generalities may be attempted. Non-governmental lawyers can run the gamut from solo practitioner to chief counsel for General Motors. Relatively few non-governmental lawyers practice exclusively before the federal courts. Some never handle federal cases. It is much more difficult to generalize about these lawyers. However, a few broad comments about what lawyers do are presented in the second selection by Jacob.

[1]Jack W. Peltason, *Federal Courts in the Political Process* (New York: Random House, 1955), p. 43.

7 LAWYERS FOR THE FEDERAL GOVERNMENT

Herbert Jacob

As the scope of federal activity has grown in the twentieth century, the range of litigation involving it has also increased. Now more than thirteen thousand lawyers work for the federal government.[1] Some of them serve particular agencies, such as the regulatory commissions, the Department of Agriculture, and Department of Defense. The largest single civilian group works in the government's principal legal office, the Department of Justice.[2]

The Justice Department was not organized until 1870, although its head, the Attorney General, was one of the original cabinet officials authorized by Congress in 1789. Until after the Civil War, litigation involving the

From *Justice in America: Courts, Lawyers, and the Judicial Process* by Herbert Jacob, pp. 67–73. Copyright © 1965 by Little, Brown and Company (Inc.). Reprinted by permission of the publisher.

[1]U.S. Bureau of the Census, *Statistical Abstract of the United States, 1963* (Washington, D.C.: Government Printing Office, 1963), p. 158.
[2]Commission on Organization of the Executive Branch of the Government, *Legal Services and Procedure* (Washington, D.C.: Government Printing Office, 1955), p. 1.

federal government did not justify a separate department; the Attorney General could operate in a small office. Today, however, he supervises ninety-one United States Attorneys attached to each district court, an equal number of United States Marshals, the F.B.I., and more than seventeen hundred[3] attorneys in Washington.

The Justice Department's impact on the judiciary is manifold. The Attorney General is a key participant in the selection of federal judges. He supervises the prosecution of all violations of federal criminal law and the initiation of major civil litigation to carry out the President's antitrust and civil rights policies. Another official of the department, the Solicitor General, supervises the appeal of government cases to the courts of appeals and to the Supreme Court.

Since the Civil War the scope of criminal statutes passed by Congress has increased greatly. They prohibit: interference with federal elections, transporting stolen cars over state lines, white slavery, bank robbery, mail fraud, kidnapping, tax fraud, and similar offenses. Whenever anyone is charged with a federal crime, he is arraigned before a commissioner of a federal district court and his case is turned over to the United States At-

[3]*Ibid.*

torney for that court. The U.S. Attorney functions much like a district attorney. He prepares the prosecution case, he negotiates with the defendant, he conducts the trial.

U.S. Attorneys also handle a large number of civil cases for the federal government. The government initiates numerous suits over its contracts for materials and services, tax matters, and its regulatory programs. Private individuals also sue the government over such matters. Of the 61,836 civil cases begun in federal district courts in 1962, 33 percent involved the federal government as either plaintiff or defendant.[4]

Many of the civil cases are handled by government attorneys employed by operating agencies rather than by the Justice Department.[5] Some of their legal staffs are quite sizable and process thousands of claims. The legal staff of the Treasury Department, for instance, must litigate all challenges to its rulings before the tax court. It also must assist the Justice Department in preparing civil and criminal cases involving tax evasion. Such attorneys also handle many matters that never reach trial. They represent the government in bankruptcy proceedings in order to press the government's tax claims; they file claims before probate courts to pay for federal inheritance taxes. Similar services—though on a much smaller scale—are performed by the legal staff of other departments. Attorneys working for regulatory commissions play a key role in carrying out their programs. They investigate violations of the regulatory statutes; they conduct hearings before the commissions; and they prepare to defend the commissions' decisions when appeals are brought to the courts.

Most of the attorneys working for the government are civil servants. Many make government work their career. They enter by winning a position through competitive examinations. Like most other federal civil servants, they may not participate in overt political activity. In the Justice Department, however, many of the attorneys are political appointees. This is true not only of the key policy-making officials in the department but also of the principal trial lawyers, the U.S. Attorneys.

The U.S. Attorneys are political appointees of the President. Each serves for a term of four years, although he may be asked to resign earlier. The term of office coincides with the President's term, so that each new President may appoint his own U.S. Attorneys. The post is one of the few patronage positions still available to the President for rewarding his political supporters. Consequently, those appointed are often lawyers who have been active in their party's political affairs. The office allows its incumbent to become prominent on the local political scene; it is sometimes used as a stepping-stone to a congressional seat, a judgeship, or a high state office. Few of the attorneys serve more than two terms before returning to private practice or proceeding to a higher public office.[6]

Although U.S. Attorneys resemble prosecuting attorneys, they usually enjoy much less independence.[7] The local prosecutor is usually an elected official operating under no one else's direct supervision. On the other hand, the U.S. Attorney is part of the Justice Department's bureaucracy. Consequently, he has to carry out the orders he receives from Washington. In most instances, Washington gives him considerable latitude in dealing with the ordinary cases that constitute most of his business. He apparently has as much latitude in dealing with a bank robber as the local prosecutor would have if the man had robbed a supermarket. However, those cases to which Washington attaches a special importance are prosecuted according to instructions. When a prominent union leader like James Hoffa is on trial or when a major industrial firm is accused of violating the anti-

[4]*Statistical Abstract, 1963,* p. 159.
[5]Even though somewhat dated, the best discussion of government lawyers is still in Esther L. Brown, *Lawyers, Law Schools and the Public Service* (New York:Russell Sage Foundation, 1948), pp. 43–90.

[6]Based on comparison of names listed in U.S. Civil Service Commission, *Official Register of the United States* (Washington, D.C.: Government Printing Office, 1944–1959).
[7]*United States Department of Justice, A Brief Account of Its Organization and Activities* (Washington, D.C., 1954; mimeographed), p. 4.

trust statutes, the U.S. Attorney operates under the close supervision of the Justice Department. In Washington the Justice Department maintains specialists to assist U.S. Attorneys with their difficult cases. When a particularly important case arises, the department often sends a specialist to the trial court to help prosecute the case. Supervision of such cases allows the Attorney General to use his field staff of U.S. Attorneys to promote particular policies through litigation. This is particularly important to the Attorney General, since some administration policies can only be promoted through litigation. The federal government, for instance, has had no other means of assisting Negroes in their attempts to register to vote in the South. Litigation is also the principal means of enforcing antitrust policies.

Moreover, control over the prosecution of a case is important in order to lay the proper groundwork for an appeal. Controversial policy issues are rarely settled at a trial; they are usually appealed to a Court of Appeals and to the Supreme Court. To win a favorable ruling, the government must be careful to raise the right questions during the trial so that an appellate court can later rule on them. It must avoid mistakes that would raise irrelevant questions on appeal.

The Justice Department exerts a much tighter control over appeals than over original prosecutions. Most appeals must be approved by the proper division of the Justice Department.[8] Appeals are argued by one of the Justice Department's lawyers from Washington rather than by the U.S. Attorney who originated the case. Still more centralized control is imposed on appeals to the Supreme Court. The Solicitor General passes on all such appeals. Although he is also a presidential appointee, he traditionally has remained somewhat independent of the Attorney General. He clears cases for appeal to the Supreme Court on the basis of his estimate of whether the government can win its case, the probable damage that would result if the government lost, the work load of the court, and the policy significance of a particular case.

Appeals to the Supreme Court and to Courts of Appeals are handled by the specialized staff of the Justice Department in Washington. The Antitrust Division supervises litigation on restraint-of-competition cases; the Civil Rights Division handles cases involving civil rights; ordinary civil actions are usually prepared by members of the Civil Division. The other sections of the department (Criminal Division, Internal Security Division, Lands Division, and Tax Division) operate similarly.[9]

One important consequence of these activities by the Department of Justice is that it operates with a higher level of expertise than most private litigants. Many of the Justice Department's Washington lawyers are career officials. They specialize in a narrow range of conflicts and gain enormous experience with the appellate courts before which they appear. The Solicitor General's office is not staffed quite so heavily by career employees. It recruits top-ranking graduates from the leading law schools, who serve for a few years before moving to other positions in government or private practice. Although its lawyers are young, they argue more cases before the Supreme Court than anyone else. They learn through experience the personal proclivities of the Justices and are better prepared for unexpected questions that the Justices may pose during an oral argument.[10]

Because the volume of government litiga-

[8]For the role of the Justice Department on appeals see Leon I. Salomon, "The Government's Law Business: The Solicitor General and His Clients" (paper prepared for delivery at the 1962 Annual Meeting of the American Political Science Association, Washington, D.C., September, 1962). See also the memoirs of former Solicitor General and Attorney General Francis Biddle, *In Brief Authority* (Garden City: Doubleday, 1962), pp. 97–151; Robert L. Stern, "The Solicitor General and Administrative Agency Litigation," *American Bar Association Journal*, XLVI (1960), pp. 154–58, 217–18.

[9]Detailed descriptions of the various divisions' work can be found in *Annual Report of the Attorney General of the U.S.*, issued for the fiscal year.

[10]Salomon, *op. cit.*, pp. 2–5.

tion is large, the Solicitor General can often choose to delay the appeal of an issue to the Supreme Court until the right case or the right moment comes. Most private litigants cannot do this, for they do not control a large enough volume of cases so that at any moment one can be chosen to submit a question to the Supreme Court.

The Justice Department's control over appellate cases has been used to advantage. It has gained the gratitude of the Supreme Court by helping the court restrict its work load. While private requests for Supreme Court rulings (in the form of requests for a writ of certiorari) doubled between 1930 and 1960, the government's requests declined.[11] However, many more government than private applications were accepted by the court.[12]

The Solicitor General's control over government suits that are appealed to the Supreme Court gives the Justice Department considerable influence over the kind of cases that the Supreme Court decides. If the time does not appear propitious, the Solicitor General may decide to accept a lower court defeat that affects cases in only one circuit rather than to risk an unfavorable Supreme Court ruling that would affect the entire country. Not all cases, of course, are subject to review by the Solicitor General; private individuals may appeal their cases to the Supreme Court if they have lost in the lower courts regardless of the Justice Department's desires. However, the Supreme Court accepts a much smaller proportion of such private appeals. In addition, most policy issues involve the government and allow the Justice Department either to block review or to oppose Supreme Court action on a private application for review. By restricting the flow of cases to the Court, the Justice Department influences the scope of judicial policy-making.

Moreover, the Justice Department can prevent judicial review of certain government actions by advising another agency to evade litigation. The Post Office Department, for instance, sometimes stops the delivery of mail that it considers pornographic; when it does so, it acts as a censor. Its legal right to censor reading material is questionable under the First Amendment. Rather than risk judicial review of its policies, the department has often resumed the delivery of particular items as soon as it was sued in court. Such action moots the case and halts court action. Postal policy is not affected: the next shipment of pornographic literature may again be impounded.

In the same way that the Justice Department can block action by the courts, it can also promote judicial activity by initiating suits that will induce judicial declarations of policy. It may take the lead in forcing a judicial test of the constitutionality of a statute. It may support private test cases through the submission of *amicus curiae* briefs.

Although litigation is a risky venture, the Justice Department's operations make it a more manageable tool of policy. Sometimes a President uses the department to enforce a particular policy—such as the civil rights policy. On other occasions an ambitious Attorney General may use the department to further his own political career by engaging in spectacular litigation. A. Mitchell Palmer sought to win the Democratic presidential nomination in 1920 by capitalizing on the Red Scare: the Department hunted for "subversive Bolsheviks" and staged a few spectacular prosecutions.[13]

In summary, the federal government uses its lawyers for quite diverse purposes. It employs them to prosecute violations of federal laws and to defend the government in legal actions. The Justice Department also uses its staff to influence judicial policy-making by promoting the appeal of some cases while blocking the appeal of others. Such a use of government attorneys helps to make the federal court system a weapon in the political arsenal of a President.

---

[11]*Ibid.*, p. 13, note 23.
[12]*Ibid.*, p. 1; Stern, *op. cit.*, p. 156.

[13]Stanley Coben, *A. Mitchell Palmer: Politician* (New York: Columbia University Press, 1963), pp. 196–267.

8   WHAT LAWYERS DO

Herbert Jacob

. . . Although the popular image of the lawyer is that of an attorney fighting a case before judge and jury, many lawyers rarely see a courtroom. Most of their work takes place inside their office. Attorneys write contracts for their clients so that, if trouble arises, the contracts will be enforceable in a court. They arrange the sale of a client's property or, inversely, the purchase of some property for a client. They write wills and arrange trusts. They advise on tax problems. Lawyers handle matters before governmental agencies, such as arranging to rezone a small tract of land or helping to float a multimillion-dollar stock issue. When a client comes to a lawyer, the first action the attorney takes is to see whether the matter can be settled without litigation. The attorney may file a suit to indicate how seriously his client regards the matter, but most such suits are settled long before they reach the courtroom. While a lawyer must be prepared to act like a gladiator, most of the time he assumes the role of advisor and negotiator.

The growing complexity of American law and the need for highly specialized legal services have led to profound changes in the conditions under which legal services are offered. Before World War I the typical lawyer ran his own office. He probably had a clerk or two and perhaps even a young associate. The law office was principally a one-man operation. The typical lawyer took a great variety of cases, and every case received his personal attention.

By 1961 less than half the country's lawyers practiced on their own.[1] Even in the smallest cities (those with a population under 50,000)

only 51.9 percent of the lawyers were solo practitioners. Across the country one quarter of the lawyers were partners in a firm, 6 percent were associates (employees) of a firm, 8.9 percent worked for private industry as house counsel, and about 10 percent worked for governmental agencies. Not only are more lawyers now working in firms, but the firms are also getting larger. The largest on Wall Street have over a hundred partners and associates.

The practice of law in a firm is quite different than on one's own.[2] Law firms do complicated work for wealthy clients, many of whom retain the firm on a continuing basis. Law firms operate in the legal field as clinics do in medicine: they allow lawyers to specialize and to economize on the overhead expenses (office, library, clerical help) of legal practice. Each partner in a firm is likely to be a specialist in a particular aspect of the law. When a technical problem arises, it is sent to the appropriate specialist in the firm, although contact with the client is likely to remain with the partner who initiated the case. New lawyers for the firms are recruited from the leading law schools of the country. Young lawyers are hired as associates. Only one of six or seven new men eventually becomes a partner. The remainder leave for another firm, begin their own practice, or more frequently go to positions with large business firms as a house counsel or an executive.

The position of house counsel is a relatively new one. Lawyers in such positions are employees; they handle only the work of their corporate employer. Some of the larger corporations possess legal departments that vie in size and excellence with those of the largest law firms. The difference is that house counsels serve only one master, their corporate employer, and must serve him regardless of their

From *Justice in America: Courts, Lawyers, and the Judicial Process* by Herbert Jacob, pp. 59–64, footnotes renumbered. Copyright © 1965, by Little, Brown and Company (Inc.). Reprinted by permission of the publisher.

[1]The following statistics are from the *1961 Lawyer Statistical Report*, pp. 62–63.

[2]The work of large firms is described by Spencer Klaw, "The Wall Street Lawyers," *Fortune*, LVII (1958), pp. 140–144; Martin Mayer, "The Wall Street Lawyers," *Harper's Magazine*, CCXII (1956), pp. 31–37, 50–56; Emily P. Dodge, "Evolution of a City Law Office," *Wisconsin Law Review* (1955), pp. 180–207, and (1956), pp. 35–56; Erwin O. Smigel, *The Wall Street Lawyer* (New York: Free Press of Glencoe, 1964), pp. 141–310.

personal estimate of the matter. In some cases such counsels enable the corporation to do without outside legal work; the company can obtain whatever legal services it needs without divulging its secrets to outsiders.

Still another novel service that lawyers perform is that of becoming advisers to businessmen on other than strictly legal problems. Although a business may at first engage a lawyer's service to solve legal difficulties, it often finds that as the result of his legal work the attorney has gained a good deal of insight into the company's operations and its position vis-à-vis competitors. Thus, the lawyer may become a business counselor, advising clients on economic matters, the introduction of new products, and marketing strategies.

One consequence of the specialization of legal work and the shift of most lawyers from individual practice to large partnerships is that relatively few lawyers are prepared to practice before the courts. This is most strikingly true in criminal law. As in other fields, criminal law has become a specialty of its own; but, whereas becoming a tax specialist in a large firm gives a lawyer prestige, becoming a criminal lawyer is likely to cost the attorney whatever prestige he has acquired.[3] A criminal law practice requires close contact with the seamy side of life. In many cases the work does not pay very well, for the clients are not wealthy. If the lawyer defends a notorious criminal, the community may misunderstand and associate the lawyer with his client. For all of these reasons, relatively few lawyers desire criminal cases, and when at all possible, they avoid taking them.

Litigation in civil cases has also become less frequent except for lawyers who specialize in personal injury suits. Lawyers from large firms that specialize in business cases rarely find themselves before a judge. In one midwestern firm that catered to business clients, litigation declined from the relatively low point of 19.3 percent of its affairs in 1908 to 11.1 percent in 1950. By contrast, 27.7 percent of the firm's business involved counseling in 1908, and such activities increased to 47.1 percent in 1950.

The withdrawal of many prominent lawyers from the courtrooms of the nation is felt in appellate tribunals as well. Appellate judges increasingly complain about the quality of oral arguments.[4] Appellate courts depend less and less on oral arguments because, in part, they find that many attorneys who bring appellate cases are ill-prepared to engage in a give-and-take colloquy. Thus, one consequence of the specialization of the bar and its withdrawal to the office is that the character of the judicial process is slowly being changed.

Perhaps the most striking difference today between "firm" lawyers and "solo" lawyers lies in the background of the attorneys and the kind of cases they deal with. Firm lawyers come from the best law schools and handle the affairs of wealthy clients. Solo practitioners—at least in metropolitan areas—are lawyers who have graduated from substandard law schools, that is, either proprietary or night law schools.[5] Moreover, while the firm lawyers are likely to have come from upper middle class families who were relatively well-to-do themselves, solo practitioners usually come from immigrant ethnic groups and working-class or small-merchant families. Typically the firm lawyer makes a much higher income than the solo practitioner.

The solo practitioner is also concerned with quite different legal business from the firm lawyer. The individual practitioner's clients are likely to be small businesses or private

---

[3]A. L. Wood, "Informal Relations in the Practice of Criminal Law," *American Journal of Sociology*, LXII (1956), pp. 48–55.

[4]"The Second Circuit: Federal Judicial Administration in Microcosm," *Columbia Law Review*, LXIII (1963), p. 890.

[5]This and the other differences mentioned below are discussed at length by Jerome E. Carlin, *Lawyers on Their Own* (New Brunswick, N.J.: Rutgers University Press, 1962) pp. 41–122; Jack Ladinsky, "Careers of Lawyers, Law Practice, and Legal Institutions," *American Sociological Review*, XXVIII (1963), pp. 47–54; Jack Ladinsky, *Career Development among Lawyers: A Study of Social Factors in the Allocation of Professional Labor* (unpubl. Ph.D. dissertation, University of Michigan, 1963); Dan C. Lortie, *The Striving Young Lawyer: A Study of Early Career Differentiation in the Chicago Bar* (unpubl. Ph.D. dissertation, University of Chicago, 1958).

individuals with legal problems. Many of his clients come to him by chance; he locates himself on a busy street and depends on "walk-up" clients. In large metropolitan areas solo practitioners are forced by their limited opportunities to specialize in petty matters, which sometimes require unethical practices. They handle doubtful automobile accident claims. They rely on ambulance chasers (euphemistically called investigators), for that is the only way in which they can procure cases. They split fees with other lawyers because they feel that they must pay to get further referrals. They distribute bonuses at Christmas to court clerks and other administrative officials because they know that, unless they do so, their cases will be held back and their clients will leave them, dissatisfied.[6] All of these activities are condemned by the organized bar as unethical. Yet it appears that in some metropolitan areas (and perhaps all of them) prominent members of the bar who work in large firms promote these activities by sending cases that require fixes to solo practitioners, apparently sensing or knowing how the solo lawyer will handle the case. Upper-status lawyers themselves undermine what they consider to be the essential ethics of the legal profession by referring questionable cases to other lawyers. A small-firm lawyer explained his experience as follows: "It's a case of *noblesse oblige*—I remember being asked by a big firm to fix up a phony divorce. I refused; they didn't want to soil their hands."[7] Whereas large-firm lawyers find it disadvantageous to violate legal ethics, some small-firm lawyers and solo practitioners cannot afford to abide by the canons.

The rather sharp distinctions between firm and solo practitioners are reflected in the limited number of lawyers who become active in politics.[8] Large-firm lawyers—the cream of the bar—rarely run for public office. Law firms do not find political activity a wise investment of time for associates or partners.

Lawyers in a firm have relatively little need to go into politics: their clients are obtained through social and business connections, not through politics. When firm lawyers become politically active, it is usually to seek or be appointed to high national office. Many Wall Street firm lawyers have received cabinet or subcabinet positions in Washington. It is rare, however, to find a firm lawyer in local or state politics.[9]

The lawyers engaged in local politics are for the most part solo practitioners and criminal lawyers.[10] Both find that political activity produces useful contacts which help to build up an individual practice. The criminal lawyer must get to know the police well as a matter of professional concern, since he must deal with them every day. He must negotiate constantly with the prosecutor. If the criminal lawyer is a political ally of the district attorney, he will at least receive more courteous treatment than if he were politically inactive. Other solo practitioners find politics a useful way to supplement their incomes. Many receive appointments to sinecure positions, which supplement their meager law income. Others get cases from governmental agencies or from judges whom they have met through their political activity. A solo practitioner has most to gain from running for public office. He may seek the district attorney's post because it allows him to publicize himself without facing disciplinary action by the bar association. If he wins, the office will bring him enough private business so that he can eventually retire from it. Likewise, legislative positions enable a young attorney to publicize his name, become known to business concerns that lobby in the state capital, and supplement his income until his legal practice can stand on its own or until he gets defeated.

---

[9]It is significant that while political activity occupies a prominent role in Carlin's description of solo lawyers, Smigel scarcely mentions it.

[10]Carlin, *Lawyers on Their Own*, pp. 135-35; Wood, *op. cit.*, pp. 48-55. For a more critical view of the role of the lawyer in politics see Joseph A. Schlesinger, "Lawyers and American Politics: A Clarified View," *Midwest Journal of Political Science*, I (1957), pp. 26-39; Heinz Eulau and John D. Sprague, *Lawyers in Politics* (Indianapolis: Bobbs-Merrill, 1964), pp. 11-86.

[6]Carlin, *Lawyers on Their Own*, pp. 155-67.
[7]Smigel, *op. cit.*, pp. 270-71.
[8]Walter J. Wardwall and Arthur J. Wood, "The Extra-Professional Role of the Lawyer," *American Journal of Sociology*, LXI (1956), pp. 340-47.

Some of these lawyer-politicians are lured into politics as a career; most, however, retire from active politics as soon as it becomes financially possible.

Accordingly, the best trained minds of the legal profession and the highest-status members of the bar do not ordinarily seek public office or engage in political activity. Lawyers engaged in public service are more likely to represent the lower echelons. Often they render distinguished service. Rarely, however, do they live up to the expectation that they are experts in the law and therefore especially qualified to serve in the legislature or other public office. As a whole, they render no better and no worse service than other occupational groups.

E. The Legal Setting: Professionalism

Lawyers are not only members of a functional group, such as ditch diggers or insurance agents, they are also members of a very old and well-established profession. Members of the bar are expected to act with a regard to the traditions and norms of their profession. Entrance is granted only to those with professional training and after passing rigorous examinations. Once admitted, a lawyer's further movement up the legal hierarchy and the respect which he is accorded depends to some degree upon how well his actions meet with the expectations of his professional peers. To a large degree, recognition within the profession depends upon the lawyer's skill in playing the legal game according to the rules. The same is true for judges.

The pressures of legal professionalism, as they apply to judges, give judicial decision-making a character different from other forms of decision-making. Roscoe Pound, a famous legal scholar, noted this phenomenon:

There are checks upon the judge which do not obtain or are ineffective as to legislative and executive officers. Three such checks are of especial importance: (1) The judge, from his very training, is impelled to conform his actions to certain, known standards. Professional habit leads him in every case to seek such standards before acting and to refer his action thereto. (2) Every decision is subject to criticism by a learned profession, to whose opinion the judge, as a member of the profession, is keenly sensitive. (3) Every decision and the case on which it was based appear in full in public records. Moreover, in the case of appellate courts, all important decisions and the grounds thereof and reasons therefor are published in the law reports, so that materials for accurate judgment upon judicial decisions are always available and readily accessible.[1]

The pressures from such elements of professionalism are undoubtedly subtle. But there are also unsubtle aspects to them. To maintain his position as a member of the bar or bench, a lawyer or judge must conduct himself according to professionally maintained normative standards. These standards are stated in the American Bar Association's Canons of Professional and Judicial Ethics. For a lawyer, gross failure to live up to these standards may mean censure, disbarment, fine, or even imprisonment. For a judge, it may result in removal or impeachment.[2] But professional or judicial enforcement is relatively rare. The selection drawn from a survey of the New York City Bar by Jerome Carlin discusses what actions the bar and courts have taken with lawyers who have violated the profession's norms.

[1] Roscoe Pound, "Justice According to Law, III," *Columbia Law Review*, XIV (1914), p. 108.
[2] See Joseph Borkin, *The Corrupt Judge* (New York: Potter, 1962).

9 LAWYERS' ETHICS: FORMAL CONTROLS*

Jerome E. Carlin

In New York City, as in most other jurisdictions in the United States, the organized bar relies primarily upon formal disciplinary measures to maintain and enforce standards of professional conduct. . . .

The Appellate Division of the Supreme Court in New York State has the principal responsibility for disciplining lawyers. Preliminary investigation into professional misconduct is carried out by the bar associations. Complaints against lawyers in New York City are almost all (98 per cent) referred initially to the Grievance Committee of the Association of the Bar of the City of New York. After an initial inquiry, unsettled cases with sufficient merit and evidence are heard before a panel of the committee, which may drop the charges, admonish the lawyer, or recommend prosecution. The final decision on recommendations to prosecute rests with the Executive Committee of the Association.

Prosecuted cases are heard in the Appellate Division of the Supreme Court of New York. A court-appointed referee hears the evidence presented by the Association prosecutor and by the respondent, and recommends acquittal, censure, suspension, or disbarment. The court then makes its decision and enters an appropriate order.

Reprinted from *Lawyers' Ethics: A Survey of the New York City Bar,* pp. 150–162, by Jerome E. Carlin by permission of the Russell Sage Foundation. Copyright © 1966 by the Russell Sage Foundation. Most tables and footnotes omitted.

*This analysis is based mainly on data from the following sources: an analysis of the approximately 1,000 disciplinary cases handled by the Appellate Division, First Department, of the Supreme Court of New York State from 1929 to 1962; statistics on the number, type, and disposition of complaints filed against lawyers with the Grievance Committee of the Association of the Bar of the City of New York from 1951 to 1962; and various other published materials (such as statutes, rules of court, the constitutions and by-laws of the bar associations, bar association reports, and articles) pertaining to the disciplinary procedures of the New York City Bar.

The record of the proceeding does not become public until final action is taken by the court. In cases of consent disbarment, however, which account for one quarter of the disciplinary matters processed through the court, the record is never made public. In these noncontested cases, the charges against the attorney are sealed and placed on file at the Appellate Division.

FLOW AND DISPOSITION OF COMPLAINTS

Between 1951 and 1962 an average of 1,450 complaints a year were filed against lawyers with the Grievance Committee. Over 65 per cent involved charges of client neglect or disputes over fees. Virtually all these complaints were disposed of informally by the staff of the Committee by a telephone call to, or brief meeting with, the complaining client or the lawyer in question. Apparently one of the Committee's more important functions is to smooth over the hurt feelings of clients and to clear up misunderstandings between lawyers and clients.

Each year from 1951 to 1962, on the average, 60 cases (4 per cent of the complaints) were brought to a formal hearing before a panel of the Grievance Committee. Of these, a little over 20 per cent were dismissed, 37 per cent ended with an admonition, and 40 per cent, or an average of 19 cases per year, brought a recommendation for court prosecution. Thus, of the approximately 1,450 complaints filed each year, only about 19 were adjudicated by the Appellate Division.

Of the total number of cases handled by the Appellate Division from 1951 to 1962, 9 per cent were dismissed, 12 per cent brought censure, 23 per cent led to suspension, and 56 per cent, or an average of 10 cases per year, resulted in disbarment.

THE OFFENSES AND THE OFFENDERS

The limited data available show that lawyers who have been disciplined by the court (disbarred, suspended, or censured) tend to be newer to the practice of law and more

TABLE 1 Distribution of All Disciplinary Cases Adjudicated by the Appellate Division, 1929–1962, by First Charge

First Charge[a]	Per Cent of Cases (in which Charges Are Known)	Number of Cases[b]	
Client: financial	32		207
Conversion		178	
Overcharging, commingling		29	
Client: other	12		77
Neglect		61	
Misinforming		11	
Other		5	
Justice: payoff (bribery, fixing—mainly of court officials)	1		8
Justice: fraud			
Court (misrepresentation, concealing evidence, actions in bad faith, submission of false testimony)	9		54
Government agencies (mainly submission of false or misleading evidence)	5		29
Colleague: direct (breaking agreements, deceiving another attorney)	3		21
Colleague: solicitation	9		53
Other professional misconduct (not arising out of regular practice of law, abuses in connection with admission to the bar or disciplinary proceedings)	4		25
Nonprofessional misconduct (offenses not related to the lawyer role, such as passing bad checks, failing to pay debts, filing fraudulent income tax return)	5		31
Felonies (lawyer has pleaded guilty to or been convicted of a felony or misdemeanor involving moral turpitude)	20		130
Larceny		43	
Conspiracy		14	
Forgery		13	
Other		60	
Charges not known	—		364
Total	100 (635)		999

[a]The first charge is the offense given the greatest attention and weight in the opinion of the court.

[b]Excludes cases resulting in acquittal.

frequently graduates of lower-quality law schools than other lawyers. . . .

The offenses for which lawyers have been formally processed are shown in Table 1 by type of first charge. The most frequent charges against lawyers involve wrongdoing against clients, usually misappropriation of clients' funds. Much less frequent are accusations of offenses against the administration of justice, mainly the submission of false or misleading testimony in a court or administrative agency. Also infrequent are offenses against colleagues, usually some form of client solicitation. Twenty per cent of the lawyers dealt with by the court have pleaded guilty to, or have been convicted of, a felony or a misdemeanor involving moral turpitude; they are automatically disbarred.

Aggrieved clients are more likely to institute and pursue complaints against lawyers than are colleagues or courts and agencies. Lawyers are notoriously unwilling to lodge complaints against colleagues. This reluctance may result from a fear of retaliation, as suggested by the following comment:

You don't like to get involved. . . . It's a long road, and not a pleasant road. . . . Naturally you make a bitter enemy of the other lawyer and his friends. There's no question about that.

It may also be the case that economic sanctions, such as cutting off referrals, are felt to be more effective. Finally, the unwillingness to file complaints against colleagues may simply reflect a lack of concern:

I don't feel that my job is to be a cop.
I would never call the cops. Why should you? You aren't a policeman.
The unethical guys can't hurt you if you take care not to put yourself into their hands. Guys who are cutting up their own clients don't really concern you. It's the fellow who knows his business that you want to be careful of.

Court and agency officials rarely report offenses either because they have become inured to them or because of their own involvement.

A comparison of the distribution of offenses in disciplinary cases to the misconduct reported by lawyers in our sample discloses that the most frequent type of violation (client solicitation) is least likely to constitute the main charge in the adjudicated cases. The least frequent type of violation (misappropriating funds from or otherwise taking advantage of clients), on the other hand, constitutes the largest proportion of main charges in the adjudicated cases.

Since client solicitation is only rarely condemned by rank and file members of the bar, and taking advantage of clients most widely condemned, it would appear that official enforcement simply reflects the ethical priorities set by the majority of lawyers in practice. In other words, lawyers are more likely to be charged with violations of ordinary standards of morality (the bar norms) than with violations of less widely accepted, but more distinctively professional, norms.

SEVERITY OF THE SANCTION

Neither number of years in practice nor quality of law school attended is related to the severity of the sanction. Older lawyers are as likely to be disbarred as newer lawyers, and graduates of Ivy League law schools as likely to be disbarred as graduates of lower-quality schools.

Important in determining the severity of the sanction is the kind of charge brought. Violations of bar norms are most likely to result in disbarment. Of lawyers charged with client-related financial offenses or bribing public officials, 54 per cent were disbarred compared to 37 per cent of lawyers charged with client solicitation. . . . Thus, lawyers who offend ordinary standards of morality are more likely both to be caught and severely sanctioned than those charged with violations of more uniquely professional norms.

Three other factors are positively correlated with the severity of the sanction: the amount of money, if any, involved in the alleged offense . . .; the number of acts of misconduct . . .; and the extent of publicity or notoriety connected with the violation. Notoriety was presumed present when there was some indication in the record of a public inquiry, involvement of a large number of individuals or a prominent lawyer in the commission of the offense, or coverage by the mass media. . . .

The amount of money and the number of acts of misconduct are related: the more money involved in the case, the greater the number of charges and counts against the lawyer. . . . Where a large amount of money figures in the offense, the result is very likely to be disbarment regardless of the number of acts of misconduct. In all other cases, however, both amount of money and number of acts affect likelihood of disbarment. . . .

Combining amount of money involved in the case and the number of acts of misconduct into a measure of seriousness, we find that the seriousness of the offense and the ethical salience of the charge have an additive effect on disbarment. Amount of money and number of acts may also be considered as indicators of the visibility of the offense. Thus, as the amount of money and number of acts increase, so does the likelihood of some notoriety or publicity in the case. . . .

We have combined these three factors—amount of money, number of acts of misconduct, and notoriety—into a Visibility Index. Considering the joint effect of the visibility of the offense and the ethical salience of the charge, it appears that, although both increase the likelihood of disbarment, visibility has a somewhat greater impact. . . . A lawyer charged with soliciting whose offense is highly visible is more likely to be disbarred than a lawyer who is alleged to have misappropriated his client's funds yet whose act received little or no attention. The importance of visibility is further demonstrated by the fact that even when we control for amount of money, number of acts, and ethical salience of the norm violated, notoriety still increases the likelihood of disbarment. . . .

POSSIBLE FUNCTIONS OF FORMAL CONTROLS

Two of the ostensible functions of official enforcement of ethical norms are to police the bar and to deter potential violators. We turn now to an examination of the extent to which these aims are realized.

Policing the Bar. On the average, 85 lawyers a year are either brought before a panel of the Grievance Committee of the Association of the Bar of the City of New York for a formal hearing or are investigated by the Coordinating Committee on Discipline of the Association of the Bar of the City of New York and the New York County Lawyers' Association. Let us assume that the number of lawyers in private practice in New York City who commit serious violations of professional standards may be estimated on the basis of the proportion of lawyers classified "low" on the Index of Ethical Be-

havior. [Editor's Note: Carlin conducted extensive interviews with a large sample of New York City lawyers in private practice. The responses to the questions relating to ethical behavior were classified on an Index of Ethical Behavior.] The estimated number of serious violators would then be about 4,500 (22 per cent of the 20,500 active practitioners of law in Manhattan and the Bronx). If this estimate is reasonable (it is more likely to be an underestimation of violations, since it is based on lawyers' self-reporting of unethical activities), in any given year fewer than 2 per cent of lawyers who violate the generally accepted norms of the bar are formally handled by the official disciplinary machinery; only about 0.02 per cent are publicly sanctioned by being disbarred, suspended, or censured.

It appears that the formal machinery of the bar does not, and probably could not, do an effective job of policing the profession. Too few violators are formally charged and punished to suggest that this activity by itself does much to weed out or discipline unethical lawyers.

Deterring Violators. While very few violators are caught and punished, it might be argued that the penalties are so severe, and the damage to reputation so serious, that the mere possibility of detection deters lawyers from engaging in unethical activities. Two factors probably limit this deterrent effect. First, the most widespread violations (fraud and solicitation of clients) generally receive the mildest sanctions and are least likely to be formally adjudicated.

A second fact difficult to reconcile with the deterrent function is that over half the disbarments (excluding automatic disbarments for felony) are by consent, in which case the record of the proceedings and the charges are not made public. Thus, the deterrent effect, which depends in part on publicity, is minimal.

CONCLUSION

The organized bar through the operation of its formal disciplinary measures seems to be less concerned with scrutinizing the moral integrity of the profession than with forestalling public criticism and control. We have seen that although violations of ordinary, community-wide standards are far less frequent than violations of standards peculiar to the profession, they are far more likely to receive the attention of official enforcement agencies, and to result in disbarment. The official agencies, therefore, to the extent that they enforce any norms, not only reflect the ethical priorities set by the rank and file of the bar, but do little more than discipline those regarded in the wider community as committing essentially criminal offenses. Standards that are distinctive to, and that arise from, the special requirements of the legal profession are only weakly enforced.

Further evidence that the organized bar is responding primarily to a concern for preserving its public image is the considerable importance of the visibility of the offense to the general community in the handling of disciplinary cases. Although visibility in general tends to force the hand of enforcement officials, it seems here to be the overriding consideration, having an even greater effect on the severity of the official sanction than the nature of the offense itself. It is consistent, however, with a desire to avoid lay interference and control that the most widely publicized violations should be the most severely and publicly sanctioned. Failure to punish visible violations might result in public criticism of the bar, and the visibility itself offers the profession an opportunity to demonstrate to the public that it can discipline its own members. Without publicity, the decision-maker has more leeway. He can offer to preserve the secrecy of the charge in return for a confession of guilt, or if there has been no confession, he is free to impose a relatively mild sanction. Furthermore, if little attention is focused on the violation, little if any official effort need be made to apprehend, let alone punish, the violator.

Finally, in assessing the significance of formal controls for the integrity of the bar, it should not be forgotten that the few lawyers who are officially disciplined are, for the most part, precisely those whose low status renders them least capable of conforming to the ethical standards of the bar.

F. The Legal Setting: Conceptual Elements

The legal setting contains numerous conceptual elements which undoubtedly influence the manner in which judges perform their role and process and decide cases. Included among these are *stare decisis*, due process, the distinction between questions of law and fact, judicial restraint, standing to sue, and the case or controversy doctrine. Judges uniquely use such elements in reaching, explaining, and rationalizing decisions. Each element can be seen as a practical admonition indicating either the boundaries of the judicial function or the limits of judicial discretion. These elements, in other words, indicate the variables associated with the judicial role. It is with this latter viewpoint in mind that we shall look at two of these elements—*stare decisis* and judicial restraint.

Stare decisis is the rule that states that courts should follow precedent in reaching decisions. All who are legally trained profess their allegiance to the broad outlines of this rule, although there are differences as to how closely it should be followed, particularly in Supreme Court decision-making. The first selection, by Theodore Becker, presents a behavioral experiment testing the extent to which an orientation towards precedent is internalized by legal training.

While *stare decisis* deals with the question of how much weight should be given to previous cases in deciding the law of a case, the concept of judicial restraint deals with the question of how broadly a new rule of law should be stated (or even if it should be stated at all) if the court finds no precedents or decides that those that exist should be bypassed. The second selection, from Justice Brandeis' concurrence in *Ashwander* v. *T.V.A.*, deals with this element. It is suggested to the reader that instead of viewing this selection as a description of how courts actually operate, he treat it as Brandeis' conception of how courts should operate. In urging judicial restraint, Brandeis was forwarding his conception of the judicial role. It should be emphasized that there is less agreement about the general efficacy of this institution than there is about *stare decisis*. Even Brandeis' opinion, it should be noted, was a concurrence to which less than a majority of the members participating in the case agreed.

10 LEGAL TRAINING AND *STARE DECISIS*

Theodore L. Becker

GENERAL HYPOTHESIS

Once a legal precedent reaches a point of being clearly controlling in a dispute presented in an appellate litigational context, it will inhibit a substantive value preference of the decision-maker who assumes the judicial role, thus resulting in an objective decision. . . .

DEFINITIONS

Appellate judge: the decision-maker in the appellate litigational context.

Appellate litigational context: a decision-making situation where each of two parties presents a dispute on appeal to a decision-maker for decision in his favor, making reference to the existence of legal precedent as containing principles which would constrain the judge to decide in his favor.

Clear legal precedent: legal precedent which has reached a point where it furnishes explicit guidelines as to which party in a dispute presented in the appellate litigational context ought to prevail.

Judicial role: the expected behavior of the judge characterized as being precedent-oriented, i.e., in an objective decision by referring to established legal precedent as the grounds for such a decision.

Reprinted by permission of author from Theodore L. Becker, *Political Behavioralism and Modern Jurisprudence* (Chicago: Rand McNally, 1961), pp. 99–104, 106–112, 114–116, 127–131, 150–151, and 153.

Legal precedent: a constitution, statute (legislation), or case law of the Supreme Court of the United States or the highest court of the jurisdiction in which the court is sitting.

Objectivity and objective decision: when a decision is actually based upon general principles, or when a decision differs, or the degree to which a decision differs, from that decision or those decisions which would have been reached by the decision-maker had he rationally decided in accordance with his own personal substantive value preferences.

Precedent orientation: the belief of an appellate judge that his decision in an appellate litigational context should directly relate to, be constrained by and be justified by, or be derivable from the established relevant, clear legal precedent.

Substantive value preference: that personal value or attitude or those values or attitudes of the appellate judge which are related to the particular social, economic, or political relationships which are the subject of the litigation and which result in a personal tendency to decide for one of the parties presenting his case for decision in the litigational context.

OPERATIONS FOR THE KEY CONCEPTS

Appellate Litigational Context. . . . [I]n order to study the possible objectivity of the appellate decision, it is essential to present to all of our respondents (subjects) a case on appeal which must be decided by them. All of the respondents must be afforded equal opportunity to assume the position of appellate judge. Whether or not anyone will assume the judicial role as an incumbent of that position remains to be seen.

[Because i]t would be highly unfeasible and expensive to set up a mock courtroom situation and argue a full case, . . . I have settled on the device of presenting hypothetical cases (facts, plus the extant relevant precedent) to all of the people involved in our quasi-experiment, using a questionnaire-type form. By explaining, on this questionnaire and through oral reinforcement of the written instructions, that they (the respondents) are to decide the case as a good judge should and give reasons for such a decision, the general outline of the appellate litigational context in which any appellate judge decides will have been created: He is a judge; there is a case on appeal which confronts him for decision; he is informed as to what the relevant legal precedent is; he is to present, in writing, for scrutiny, the reasoning upon which he bases his decision.

Obviously, this is not exactly the same situation or context in which the judge decides. However, its failures as such are in some ways *less* conducive to bringing about objectivity than they are biased in favor of it. After all, the judge's decision is made in the collegiate and somber atmosphere of the institutional trappings and tradition of the real appellate situation. Thus, if a finding of significant objectivity should be obtained (the null hypothesis not confirmed) in our study, it would seem to augur well for finding a similar result in the real world.

. . .

Law Training Factor. Judges before they become judges are invariably lawyers. And lawyers before they are lawyers must go through the rigors of legal training in a law school. Law school, to describe it for those who have not had that experience, is a dreadfully difficult and tedious process (particularly in the first year). It is in this environment of extremely great tension and pressure that the legal mind is forged. Theoretically, fresh and keen minds are molded from the nonlegal thinker into the legal thinker through the law school process. The legal thinker (theoretically) is he who is a dispassionate seeker into

the law, determined to find out whether any law is controlling in the litigation in which he is involved, and, if such law is found, to abide by it. Non-lawyers could never understand this process; this nagging belief that the law may well furnish the answer or very compelling guidelines which will dispose of the case correctly and justly. This is a main part of what was termed precedent orientation, and it composes what is believed to be the essence of what is usually considered to be the heart of the judicial decision-making role as opposed to any other decision-making role as it becomes manifest in the judicial decision. For purposes of the present exploratory and working theory, it is considered to be the pivotal factor.

As noted above, the treatment which induces this role posture does not have to be created and applied. Rather, in classic quasi-experimental style, one need only to go into the real world and find those who have received the experimental treatment and those who have not. The former will be the experimental group, the latter will comprise the control group. . . . Those who have been through at least one and preferably two or more years of law school will be considered to have become sufficiently inducted into the process of legal thinking.

Substantive Value Preference (SVP). In order to determine whether or not acceptance of law-school-wrought precedent-orientation by one assuming the judicial role does in fact significantly neutralize his own personal predisposition for decision based upon his own attitudes and values, one must also obtain accurate knowledge about the individual substantive value systems involved in any cases to be decided. We need to learn what they are and how intensely they are held by all of the respondents in both experimental and control groups.

The first step towards isolating this variable is the development of a device by which the direction of the predisposition in the relevant areas of the hypothetical litigation can be discovered. In other words, one must be able to discern with great precision *how the respondent would want to see each specific case decided if he had the power to make the law*. In the abstract, it seems that either open-ended (unrestricted) questions or structured (closed) questions are both capable of eliciting this data. Generally speaking, each type of question offers distinct advantages and disadvantages. The major difficulty in the open-ended question involves coding problems which lead to substantial unreliability of results. Two general difficulties in the structured or closed-ended question are the problems of phrasing the questions clearly and the distinct possibility that the experimenter may be putting words in the respondent's mouth.

. . . The solution was to start off with the open-ended query, then to employ several much more specific questions, and finally to end with a direct question or questions closely related in detail to the factual situation of the hypothetical case. . . .

In order to make certain that the rating of predisposition was accurate and objective in relationship to the specific factual situations of our hypothetical cases, a questionnaire consisting of two main parts was developed. There was (1) the attitude questionnaire discussed above (The substantive value questionnaire on the . . . hospital case [is] attached as Appendix B-1. . . .), and (2) a presentation of only the factual segment of our hypothetical cases (that part of the hospital case which was considered to be the factual segment is indicated in Appendix A-1 and A-2 by brackets). The respondents were asked to express their opinions in the first part and then were asked to play the role of *legislator* in the second part by checking an appropriate box as to *how they would want the law to be* in each particular factual situation. They were to indicate how the law should *favor* one party or another.

In order to maximize objectivity in coding the direction of the individual respondent's predispositions, a panel of experts was set up. This panel consisted of four men holding Ph.D. degrees (two political scientists, one economist, and one psychologist . . .). Each panelist read the substantive value preference statements of the respondents and, keeping in mind the nature of the facts which would subsequently be presented to the respondent via the questionnaire, rated the predisposition

of each respondent to favor one party or the other for each case. . . . [W]e decided to use only those respondents upon whom the panel unanimously agreed as to their predisposition. . . .

Although it would probably be possible to develop an intersubjective rating scheme in order to measure the intensity with which each of the values is held by each respondent, this seemed unnecessary. A simple, objective, and probably more accurate calibration device commonly used is one which asks the respondents themselves to rate their own intensity of feeling. This was easily accomplished by placing the following type of question at the bottom of each substantive value preference question page and requesting the respondents to check the appropriate response.

How strongly do you feel about this?

1. Extremely strongly _____
2. Very strongly   _____
3. Strongly   _____
4. Not strongly at all _____

. . .

Clarity of Legal Precedent. . . . The problem of how to go about developing hypothetical cases in which the precedent is very clear and cases in which the precedent is very cloudy seems open to various solutions. Once again the panel of experts was used. . . .

Through personal contacts, several law professors who reputedly had an interest in the social science approach to various problems of the judicial process were approached and persuaded to join the panel. The four who comprised the final panel did not need much persuading, however. . . .

Each professor was given a rating sheet which instructed him to circle a number from 0 to 3 next to a letter which represented each hypothetical case he was to read. Zero stood for "highly ambiguous," which was defined as "precedent is no guide to deciding for either party," while the 3 (the other extreme) stood for "perfectly clear." This was defined as "the precedent leaves no doubt as for whom the court must decide."

Only one of the four experts on the final panel made the 3 and 0 choices throughout the original four sets of hypothetical cases.

The others, through their rating sheet circles, personal statements, and conversation indicated that they felt a bit too constrained by the word "perfectly." However, as they now stand, the four experts are unanimous in their opinion that there is at least a two-point difference between the cases rated as clear and as ambiguous. That is the ambiguous cases were approximately between the 0 and the 1, while the clear ones were between the 2 and the 3. This is so in the hospital cases which are used for analysis. . . . Their conceptualization preference is as "clear" and "not clear" rather than "perfectly clear" and "perfectly ambiguous." Again, for the immediate purposes of testing the hypotheses this would seem to be sufficient.

Objectivity of Decision. The conceptual definition of an objective decision includes decisions which are in accord with the decision-maker's substantive value preferences *if* that decision has been derived from a general principle. However, it is clear that it would be impossible to identify such decisions within the confines of the experimental situation. In other words, this would necessitate being able to discern the difference between a reasoning process and a rationalization process in the questionnaire answer. This is quite a risky business. One can only be certain that a decision is objective when it is in opposition to the coded substantive value preference of the respondent decision-maker. Thus, objective decisions are those decisions which are opposed to the rated substantive value preference.

Administrative Details. The questionnaires which supplied the data which are the subject of the subsequent analyses were administered from June through September, 1963. The control group (nonlaw students) consisted of undergraduate students in political science courses at Wayne State University. Approximately one hundred students participated. A like number of students were drawn primarily from Wayne State University Law School's senior class. The remainder were students from the law schools at The University of Michigan, Northwestern University, and Washington University of St. Louis. . . .

All in all, the questionnaires took about 35 minutes to complete. The front page briefly introduced the respondent to the project. Then came the substantive value preferences questionnaire. Following that, the respondent came to what might be termed the appellate judge position page. The statement therein which reads that the respondent should decide the subsequent cases (there were four) "as you believe a good judge should decide it," was meant to be as ambiguous as it is. It was believed that differing role orientations would lead to differing perceptions of the word "good." The final stage was that of the hypothetical cases which the judges were to decide. . . .

Choice of Cases and Techniques. The cases selected for analysis are the two hospital cases (Appendices A-1 and A-2) *Charney v. St. Mary's Mercy Hospital* and *Arthur v. St. Mary's Mercy Hospital.* The Charney case was one which was rated as "clear" by the experts, and the Arthur case was deemed "ambiguous" by them. . . .

The rating procedure on the questionnaire indicating predisposition-towards-charitable-institutions . . . , given to approximately 100 undergraduate and 100 law students, yielded 77 of the former and 87 of the latter which all four raters agreed as to direction of decisional predisposition. Thus, the total N of this analysis is 164.

[Professor Becker then subjected his data to two different statistical tests—chi-square analyses (two-, three-, and four-dimensional) and analysis of variance. These analyses are not presented here. They may be found on pages 117–127 of Professor Becker's book. His conclusions were as follows.]*

Upon analysis by [these] two reliable statistical techniques, the data gathered from the 164 students involved in our testing indicates that the hypothes[i]s [given above] . . . [has] not been disconfirmed. This, then, is encouraging. It would not be unduly rash to place some confidence in the model as a guide to further research. . . .

Content Analysis: Detecting Judicial Role. Although the findings indicate the exis-

*Editors.

tence of objectivity in the decision-making process, they still cannot be taken to indicate the existence of the judicial role or of precedent orientation. Although the objective decision and the judicial decision are quite similar, they need not be precisely the same. The judicial decision, or that decision which results from the operation of the judicial role, presupposes a certain sophistication with respect to both the guidance and *justification* of the decision by prevailing, pertinent, clear case and statutory law. In a sense it manifests an *explicit deference* of man to law, of whim to continuity.

There would be no way at all to tell from the frequency data used to determine the existence (and the conditions of the existence) of objective decision-making, whether or not an objective decision resulted from a playing of the judicial role by a decision-maker or from the operation of other factors. For instance, given the particular facts and his reaction to them, despite his more abstractly conceived values to the contrary, the decision-maker might simply *reason* his way to a decision opposed to those values. However, reasoning, though part of the appellate process and of judicial role, is not the warp and woof of it. In the judicial process, *the reasoning process must be directly and expressly related to precedent.* And, when the precedent is clear, then the amount of reasoning involved is minimized, and in fact may well be anywhere from negligible to naught.

In developing the decision-making appellate litigation context flavor in this study, care was taken to include a space for the judge to present the reasons for his decision. This was done to serve the purpose in testing that some believe it to serve in the real appellate process, i.e., as an additional relevant institutional constraint upon the judge's free expression of personal values through judicial decision. Moreover, it was included to serve for various types of content analyses. In this study content analysis can assist in discovering whether or not judicial role-playing was responsible for the objective decision-making . . . , and whether or not there is any difference between the objective decision-making of the law students and that of the nonlaw

students. . . .

[T]here were only 22 law students and ten nonlaw students who (we have reason to believe) decided against their values in the Charney case. . . . In looking at the reasons offered by these judges for their decision, there is a noticeable difference. The law students, as one could expect, are virtually unanimous in their dependence upon and reference to precedent as the foundation for their decision. Some even expressed their rue at having to do so, i.e., go against their own preference for decision because of the law: "It's against my own personal beliefs to do so, but precedent would probably have to be followed here." Only one law student neglected to justify his decision by the existence of the precedent afforded; but even he relied on some law. That is, he utilized some other law that he already knew: "As agent of the hospital, we could probably hold the hospital responsible."

Only half of the nonlaw students, however, even alluded to precedent as the basis of their decision against their own values. They were far more prone to go looking for other reasons —which is a bit strange since they were probably being influenced by the precedent to which they were exposed. One explanation for this might be that the clear precedent actually changed the values of the nonlaw student (i.e., the law was internalized by the layman as his own value), and forced him to seek a rationale to justify this new position. But this is surely not what precedent orientation means. Thus, this is a fine illustration of an apparently objective decision being unrelated to the assumption of the judicial role.

Interestingly enough, no two reasoning processes of the nonlaw students who did not assume the judicial role were alike. One of these respondents found in his reading of the case that the hospital was not "directly" responsible and therefore only the nurse ought to be sued. Another, though deciding *mostly* on precedent, also felt that a decision against the hospital was a trifle unfair. That is, there is no reward if the hospital "saves the man's life" but a penalty is levied if they fail. This comes from a respondent, it must be noted, who felt strongly and explicitly in the SVP

TABLE 1   Judicial Role-Playing of Law Students and Nonlaw Students

	Nonlaw	*Law*
Expressly use precedent to justify objective decision	5	19
Use reasons other than precedent to justify objective decision	4	1

$$N = 29 \ (p < .04)^a$$

*a*The N is 29 instead of 32 since I could not decipher the handwriting of three of the respondents well enough to include them.

questionnaire that a hospital was "at fault for hiring the employee" and should be suable. A third reasoned that such decisions against hospitals would create a great burden on them in their hiring practices. A fourth argued that the patient assumed the risk; while a fifth reasoned that the glare of adverse publicity was too great a price to pay.

Table 1 demonstrates the frequencies involved in the interaction between the law training factor and the reliance upon legal precedent as a justification for decision. In using Latscha's extension of Finney's Table in testing for significance, we find a significance of difference well beyond the 4 per cent level.[1]

The research technique and this data seem to yield further evidence to support the long-standing theoretical notions of classic American jurisprudential thinking on this subject. However, I want to clarify what the results of this brief content analysis seem to reveal. It could be said that this data demonstrates that the law-trained person assumes the judicial role to a significantly greater degree than he who has not been legally trained. From the chi-square analysis and the analysis of variance, we know that the law students tended to decide more objectively than nonlaw students under the circumstances of the model. This fact, in addition to the fact that almost all of the legally trained students explicitly relied on precedent when they were being objective, while only one-half of the nonlegally trained did so, justifies the statement that judicial

role does seem to exist and that it is substantially a function of law-school training. As we have seen, judicial role is manifest as an objective decision justified by precedent, made in an appellate litigation context, in interaction between precedent orientation and the existence of relevant (to the litigation), clear precedent [see Figure 10-1 on page 73].

Now, it would be brash to say that this demonstration of the existence of that which we have termed judicial role proves that this is something which operates at all times and under all circumstances in the way which the present study has shown. I simply want to note that this work is indicative that something may well exist which should be recognized by the political scientist in his study of politics as the decision-making process which authoritatively allocates values for the society.

APPENDIX A-1

Charney v. *St. Mary's Mercy Hospital.* [Mr. Charney was seriously injured in an automobile accident. He was rushed to the St. Mary's Mercy Hospital where an emergency blood transfusion was found to be necessary. In the handling of the blood, one of the nurses of the hospital made an error and supplied the doctor with the wrong type of blood. It was proved at the trial that this error was directly responsible for the death of Mr. Charney. Charney's widow sued the hospital for negligence for $100,000. Negligence was clearly established by the evidence, and] the jury returned a verdict for the plaintiff, Mrs. Charney. The hospital appeals.

The law of the jurisdiction is based on several cases. *Karrin* v. *Curtis* (1940) held, in reversing a jury verdict for the plantiff, that a charitable organization is not responsible for damages occasioned by the negligence of its

[1]R. Latscha, "Tests of Significance in a 2 × 2 Contingency Table: Extension of Finney's Table," *Biometrika,* 40 (June, 1953). This table is ordinarily used when the marginals are less than 20. A 2 × 2 chi-square analysis yielded a score of 3.50 which was almost significant at the .05 level. I did not want to use the chi-square, however, since two of the four expected frequencies were less than 5.

FIGURE 10–1

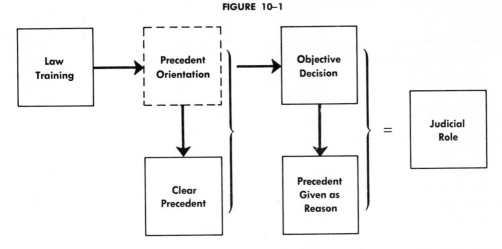

employees, if the negligent act is done while the employee was pursuing the course of employment. The case of *Rick* v. *Castberg* (1958) held that an overdose of barbiturates given to the plantiff-patient by an intern in a hospital did not constitute a breach of warranty in a sale and, therefore, the private hospital employing the intern was not liable for damages to the plaintiff.

Decide this case as a good judge of the State Supreme Court should:

Reverse the lower court decision
                (for the hospital) _____

Affirm the lower court decision
                (for Charney in
                the full amount
                that the jury
                agreed upon) _____

Reasons:

APPENDIX A-2

Arthur* v. *St. Mary's Mercy Hospital. [Mr. Arthur was seriously injured in an automobile accident. He was rushed to the St. Mary's Mercy Hospital where an emergency blood transfusion was found to be necessary. In the handling of the blood, one of the nurses of the hospital made an error and supplied the doctor with the wrong type of blood. It was proved at the trial that this error was directly responsible for the death of Mr. Arthur. Arthur's widow sued the hospital for $100,000. The jury returned a verdict for the plaintiff,

Mrs. Arthur, in the full amount sought. The hospital appeals.]

There is a state statute which reads as follows:

No charitable institution shall be held liable for damages in a suit at law brought about by the negligence of its employees, whether such negligent act was done during the course of the employment or not.

However, the case of *Williams* v. *Fleming Hospital* (1956) held that a hospital was liable for breach of warranty where a person suffered severe food poisoning in the hospital cafeteria. The law of the state is that goods sold carry an automatic warranty that the seller must compensate financially for damages caused by the fact that such goods were not fit for the purposes for which they were sold. The case of *City of Richards* v. *Dawson* (1961) held that the sale of blood (all blood used in this hospital must be paid for) could not be considered to be a "sale" within the meaning of the City Sales Tax.

Decide this case as a good judge of the State Supreme Court should:

Reverse the lower court decision
                (for the hospital) _____

Affirm the lower court decision
                (for Arthur in
                the full amount
                that the jury
                agreed upon) _____

Reasons:

APPENDIX B-1

Responsibilities of Charities.

1. What are your *personal* views as to whether charities ought to have certain privileges, under the law, that other corporations do not have?
2. Do you think that charities, unlike most other organizations, ought to be tax exempt?
3. It is the law that corporations are liable in money damages to a person injured through a negligent act of an employee of the corporation when that act was done while the employee was carrying out the work of the corporation. Do you think that this law ought to be applicable to charitable corporations (charities)?
4. Do you consider:

   the Salvation Army to be a charity?
   hospitals?
   (a) municipal hospitals?
   (b) religious hospitals?
   (c) private hospitals?
   (d) federal hospitals?
   the Red Cross?
5. What if someone was seriously injured or killed by the negligent act of an employee of a hospital but that this occurred while the injured or killed person was receiving the benefits of the hospital—should the hospital or just the employee be liable for money damages, or neither?
6. If the negligent employee was an intern or a hospital nurse, should the hospital be suable in court for money damages or just the nurse or the intern?

   Would your answer hold true for each type of hospital listed in Question 4?

11 *ASHWANDER* v. *T.V.A.*

Louis D. Brandeis

The Court developed, for its own governance in the cases confessedly within its jurisdiction,

Reprinted from **Mr. Justice Brandeis' concurring opinion to** *Ashwander* v. *T.V.A.*, 297 U.S. 288 (1936), 346 ff.

a series of rules under which it has avoided passing upon a large part of all the constitutional questions pressed upon it for decision. They are:

1. The Court will not pass upon the constitutionality of legislation in a friendly, non-adversary, proceeding, declining because to decide such questions is legitimate only in the last resort, and as a necessity in the determination of real, earnest and vital controversy between individuals. It never was the thought that, by means of a friendly suit, a party beaten in the legislature could transfer to the courts an inquiry as to the constitutionality of the legislative act. . . .

2. The Court will not anticipate a question of constitutional law in advance of the necessity of deciding it. . . . It is not the habit of the Court to decide questions of a constitutional nature unless absolutely necessary to a decision of the case. . . .

3. The Court will not formulate a rule of constitutional law broader than is required by the precise facts to which it is to be applied. . . .

4. The Court will not pass upon a constitutional question although properly presented by the record, if there is also present some other ground upon which the case may be disposed of. This rule has found most varied application. Thus, if a case can be decided on either of two grounds, one involving a constitutional question, the other a question of statutory construction or general law, the Court will decide only the latter. . . . Appeals from the highest court of a state challenging its decision of a question under the Federal Constitution are frequently dismissed because the judgment can be sustained on an independent state ground. . . .

5. The Court will not pass upon the validity of a statute upon complaint of one who fails to show that he is injured by its operation. . . . Among the many applications of this rule, none is more striking than the denial of the right of challenge to one who lacks a personal or property right. Thus, the challenge by a public official interested only in the performance of his official duty will not be entertained. . . . The Court affirmed the

dismissal of a suit brought by a citizen who sought to have the Nineteenth Amendment declared unconstitutional. In *Massachusetts v. Mellon* . . . the challenge of the federal Maternity Act was not entertained although made by the Commonwealth on behalf of all its citizens.

6. The Court will not pass upon the constitutionality of a statute at the instance of one who has availed himself of its benefits. . . .

7. When the validity of an act of the Congress is drawn in question, and even if a serious doubt of constitutionality is raised, it is a cardinal principle that this Court will first ascertain whether a construction of the statute is fairly possible by which the question may be avoided. . . .

Part 2
Input

The inputs to the federal judicial system are of two basic types—demands and supports. The demands fed into the federal judicial system are many and diverse. They stem from expectations and desires, fact situations and social theories, ideologies and ideals. They are generated by the needs and interests of the various individuals, groups, classes and organizations of our economically complex, socially pluralistic society. Some of the demands fed into the federal judicial system are not greatly different from those fed into the other institutions of the American political system such as Congress or the bureaucracy. Others, such as occur in "routine" civil and criminal cases, are unique to the judiciary. In either case, judicial processing of demands is substantially different from bureaucratic and especially legislative processing. This difference is maintained by the supports fed into the judicial system. In this part we shall first look at these supports and their implications before turning to a consideration of the demands.

A. Supports

Maintenance of the federal judicial system as an institution for political decision-making depends upon its receiving an influx of positive support both from the political community at large and from those more intimately and professionally involved in the system's operation and output. If these positive supports are lacking, the federal courts may be removed from their role in political policy-making. This, in fact, occurred in part, at least as far as the Supreme Court was concerned, during the Civil War and its aftermath.

One of the criteria that must be met in order to receive a positive flow of supports is that the courts must operate in a "judicial" manner. This has important implications both for the range and type of demands processed.

The first reading in this section is by John Kessel. He presents the results of a public opinion poll made in the Seattle area testing popular attitudes toward the Supreme Court. Kessel, therefore, empirically measures the dimensions of popular support for the Supreme Court in at least one part of the country.

The second and third readings discuss the legal rules and procedures that must be followed if demands are to be processed in a "judicial" manner. These readings stress how these rules and procedures limit demands and structure the way they are processed. The second reading is from a book by Carl Auerbach, Lloyd Garrison, Willard Hurst, and Samuel Mermin. It gives a brief overview of the steps involved in preparing and processing a lawsuit. The third reading, by Thomas Jahnige, deals with some of the implications that these rules and procedures have for the non-professional participants in a lawsuit.

12 THE SUPREME COURT AND THE AMERICAN PEOPLE

John H. Kessel

This [is] . . . an exploratory study of [public] attitudes about the United States Supreme Court. Our data were gathered in

sample in important respects. The Seattle sample contains more political independents, more persons with college education, more members of the middle class, and more Caucasians. Hence this paper should be regarded simply as an analysis of the attitudes of persons we happened to interview. This analysis does contain a number of interesting sugges-

TABLE 1   The Seattle Sample and a National Sample: A Comparison of Selected Statistics

	Seattle Sample	National Sample
Party Identification		
Strong Democrat	16.9%	27.3%
Weak Democrat	12.4	25.0
Independent Democrat	17.2	9.4
Independent	11.3	7.9
Independent Republican	14.9	5.7
Weak Republican	11.5	13.6
Strong Republican	12.7	11.1
Education		
Grade School or Less	6.2	24.4
Some High School	9.9	20.0
High School Graduate	30.4	31.5
Some College	24.2	12.9
College Graduate	28.2	11.1
Subjective Class Identification		
Middle Class	65.1	41.3
Working Class	34.9	58.7
Sex		
Male	50.1	44.6
Female	49.9	55.4
Race		
White	96.6	88.4
Negro	2.0	10.3
Other	1.4	1.3

Seattle, Washington, in February, 1965. . . . [As can be seen in Table 1, i]t is clear that our Seattle sample varies from the national

Reprinted from "Public Perceptions of the Supreme Court," *Midwest Journal of Political Science*, X, no. 2, 1966, by John H. Kessel by permission of the Wayne State University Press. Some footnotes omitted, others renumbered.

tions about what the attitudes of a national population might be. . . .

I

Just what are the public attitudes about the Court? These attitudes were measured in two ways. The first was an open-ended question (Speaking generally, how would you describe

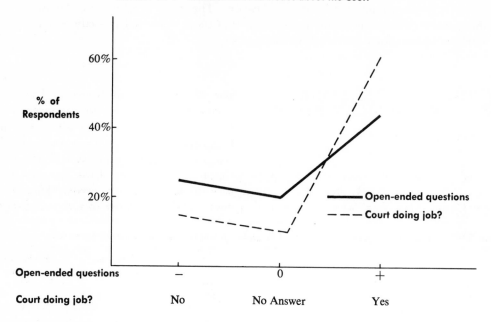

FIGURE 12–1 Distribution of Attitudes about the Court

your own feelings about the Supreme Court?) and two associated probes. (Is there anything [else] you particularly like about the Supreme Court? Is there anything [else] you particularly dislike about the Supreme Court?) The answers to these questions were scaled by assigning a + 1 to each positive comment and a − 1 to each negative comment, and then calculating a sum for each respondent.

The second means of ascertaining opinions about the Supreme Court was a series of questions about the preferred role of the Court. (What do you think the job of the Supreme Court should be? Do you think the Supreme Court is doing this job now?) This sequence of questions was concluded with a standard query about intensity. (How strongly do you hold these views? Very strongly? Fairly strongly? Or doesn't this make too much difference to you?) The intensity items were combined with the responses about whether the respondent thought the Court was doing its job to form a Likert scale.

Figure 12-1 shows the overall results. However measured, the attitudes were supportive of the Court. The question on whether the Court was doing its job produced more positive answers than the scaling of the open-ended responses, but the basic pattern was the same. The pattern resembled a J-curve. By far the largest proportion of respondents had positive attitudes toward the Court, and there were almost as many neutral attitudes as negative attitudes. Comparison of the open-ended responses with the Likert scale,

TABLE 2   Distribution of Attitudes about the Court

	−3* or Lower	−2	−1	0	+1	+2	+3* or Higher	Non-Scale	N
Open-End Questions	8.5%	7.0%	8.5%	22.5%	22.0%	14.4%	11.0%	6.2%	356
Likert Scale	11.3%	2.8%	2.0%	14.1%	13.5%	31.0%	21.7%	3.7%	356

*There were some scores higher than +3 and lower than −3 on the scale formed by the open-ended questions, but these were the maximum and minimum scores possible with the Likert scale.

as in Table 2, reveals the effect of the addition of the intensity component. The positive attitudes about whether the Court is doing its job tends to be fairly strongly held while a large majority of the negative attitudes are very strongly held. The open-ended responses are more evenly distributed. Finally, a direct comparison of the open-ended responses with the Likert scale shows that the answers to both sets of questions tend to be correlated. The only striking departure is to be found in the cases in the upper right-hand cells of Table 3. There are a number of respondents whose feelings about the Supreme Court were negative, but who nonetheless thought that the Court was doing its job.

The comments themselves reveal a fairly low level of informational support for these attitudes. The largest category of feelings about the Court can best be described as generalized approval. The 36.9% of the respondents in this category were not specific in their discussions, but clearly approved of the Court. A retired secretary answered:

It's an institution—a government institution—worked out by the finest minds in the United States with the purpose of giving fairness to people on

Well, gosh, they probably know what they're doing.

The second largest category of supportive responses (9.9% of the respondents) stressed the need for a Supreme Court. Though unable to say why, these people felt that we had to have one. A machinist put it this way:

I'd say it has been with us . . . (pause) . . . since government started. It's a useful and necessary part of the government. That's what I'd say offhand.

A smaller group of respondents (4.8% of the total) made the point that the Court was doing its best with a difficult job. When a middle-aged plastering contractor was asked to describe his feelings about the Supreme Court, he replied:

That's kind of hard to describe. They know more legal things than I would. I wouldn't want their position. You can't satisfy everybody. The hardest thing to do is to satisfy everybody. They really have to have a head on their shoulders.

Two per cent of the sample said in one way or another that they regarded the Supreme Court as the court of final appeal or as the

TABLE 3 Comparison of Open-Ended Responses with Likert Scale Open-Ended Responses

Likert Scale	Strong Supporter (+2 or Higher)	Supporter (+1)	Neutral (0)	Critic (−1 or Lower)	N
+3	36	23	6	12	77
+2 or +1	47	42	36	26	151
0	0	8	31	6	45
−1, −2 or −3	5	2	7	40	54
N	88	75	80	84	327

(Kendall's) Tau-b = .41

trial. People on the Court are well trained and well informed, and they have years of experience. Though they may be small in number, their opinion does need to have consideration. They make their decisions on fairness of law. Someone has to make the decisions, and with the experience they have they give opinions from a humanitarian standpoint.

A riveter used fewer words to say essentially the same thing:

ultimate arbiter of our governmental system. A young secretary said simply:

It's very necessary to our way of life because it is the court of last resort and final judgment.

The largest number of critical answers were coded under the miscellaneous heading of "other critical comments." This category included 10.4% of the total. On examination, it appeared that many of these answers came from persons who disapproved of Supreme Court holdings. Although they were as well informed as most of the other people we interviewed, many of the persons in this category seemed disturbed about legal complexities they could not understand. An insurance adjuster described his feelings as:

Generally unfavorable. The outcome as to what is constitutional or unconstitutional depends too much on one individual. The Court recently has been relying too much on technicalities to let the guilty off. One little error and they let a guy go free. In the area of criminal law, they seemed to be concerned with "Did Oswald get a fair trial?"! Well, they had enough on him to kill him anyway—so why worry about detail?

An English-born candy store manager complained:

I just don't understand them. How can they come to these conclusions? Something must be wrong with the rest of the courts. There are too many contradictions.

Nine per cent of the respondents said that they felt the Supreme Court was acquiring too much power or that it was going beyond its proper role. A truck driver replied in this vein when asked to describe his feelings:

Very unfavorable. I feel it is going far beyond its legal authority in most cases—finding too many loopholes. This isn't right and we should say so.

A special assistant for the telephone company put it this way:

Well, I believe in checks and balances and our system of safeguards. The Supreme Court has usurped power and bypassed the Constitution. I have been interested in this for many years. My father was in politics. . . .

Another group of critics, three per cent of the sample, felt that the Court was too favorable to some particular class. Sometimes this favored category of litigants was thought to be wealthy, sometimes not. A home builder told us:

I would say (my feelings were) very unfavorable. . . . They are getting too technical . . . just too technical. . . . It's getting where the more money you have the better deal you can get. . . . Sort of buy justice, you know. . . .

A seamstress who had immigrated from Finland was worried about what her co-workers had told her concerning the Court's handling of Communist cases:

I am disgusted with the way they are soft on Communism. They turn so many decisions around and let Communists off. I . . . uh . . . suppose the Chief Justice is the major cause. That's all I really feel about them.

Finally, a little more than a fifth of our sample (21.4%) was unable to articulate any opinion about the Supreme Court. Nearly two-thirds of these individuals stated frankly that they didn't feel they knew enough to have an opinion. A small businessman who had just bought a new sound truck company admitted:

I've never given it much thought.

And a retired longshoreman told the interviewer:

I haven't studied it. Read about it a little. Just taxes and atomic war bother us. We leave things like the Court to you young people who will do most of the future worrying.

Similar characteristics were to be found in the responses to the queries about the preferred role of the Supreme Court. A typical answer to the question, "What do you think the job of the Supreme Court should be?" was that of an elderly man:

To study the law, I guess, and help decide what it should be for everyone.

Most of the answers to this question likewise revealed considerable attitudinal support for the Court resting upon a modest understanding of what the Court actually was about.

The distribution of the answers about the preferred role of the Supreme Court is given in Table 4. It is perhaps significant that taken together they add up to a composite portrait of the tasks which presently concern the Supreme Court. The Court is our tribunal of ultimate appeal. It does interpret the Constitution and the laws according to specified and impartial procedure. And so on. Since the Court is now doing what most of our respondents want it to do, it should follow that most of them will support it. This would suggest that how the Court reaches its decisions may be quite as important in maintaining public support as what it decides.

This is not to say that the content of the Supreme Court decisions is unimportant in shaping the public perception of that institution. While it is true that only a few cases are sufficiently dramatic to rise above the public's threshold of attention, these decisions do stimulate some public discussion. When our respondents were asked what they had read or heard about the Supreme Court during the last year, three-quarters of them referred to Court activity or decisions in four areas: civil rights, prayers in schools, redistricting, and Communists. Civil rights was mentioned by twice as many people as school prayers, school prayers by twice as many people as redistricting, and redistricting by twice as many people as referred to Communists. The exact percentages were civil rights, 42.0%; school prayers, 19.6%; redistricting, 8.0%; and Communism, 4.5%.

This was a bit of luck because the four areas most discussed happened to be the four preme Court. The rank-order correlations (Kendall's Tau-b) between these hypothetical decisions and attitudes toward the Court were Heart of Atlanta Motel, .25, Schempp, .14, *Wesberry* v. *Sanders*, .12, and Scales, .18.

When the findings about the frequency of discussion of controversial topics are juxtaposed with the tendency to decide hypothetical cases in particular ways, it is possible to conclude something about how each of these decisions contributed to public attitudes about the Court. Civil rights activities are being widely discussed and the activities of the Court are well thought of in this area. The school prayer case and redistricting are being discussed by smaller groups of people and are having less effect on general attitudes about the Court. And while the Court's handling of Communists is being discussed by fewer people than any of the other three subjects, a person who mentions this topic is rather more likely to be critical of the Court.

II

Why do people hold these attitudes about the Supreme Court? What disposes some to have a favorable view of it while others have

TABLE 4   The Preferred Role of the Court

Description of Supreme Court's Proper Job	% of Respondents
Interpret the Law or the Constitution	30.7%
Be Ultimate Arbiter, Court of Final Appeal	18.0
Continue Exercising Present Responsibilities	9.0
Protect Our Freedoms, the Individual, or the Little Man	5.4
Settle Cases Impartially, without Bias	5.4
Settle Basic Questions, Questions Affecting Entire Country	4.2
Maintain Balance of Power, Check Other Branches	3.9
Assume More Restricted Role	3.9
No Answer	19.5

subjects about which the respondents had been asked to decide "hypothetical" cases. The responses to these queries were related to attitude about the Court. A decision in favor of the public accommodations section, against a required school prayer, for "one man, one vote," and against sending a person to jail simply because he was a Communist was associated with a favorable view of the Su-

an unfavorable image? The answer to this simple question is rather complicated. In order to thread our way through the jumble of evidence, we shall confine our attention to a single dependent variable, the respondent's opinion of the Court as measured by the number of positive and negative comments about it, and use a single measure of association, Kendall's Tau-b.

If pure measures of attitudes could be devised, it might be possible to explain attitudes toward the Court on the basis of three independent variables: some measure of liberalism-conservatism, agreement with what the Court has done, and the favorability of communications received about the Court. Or, if one could tap basic attitudes about the cases before the Supreme Court, one might be able to construct an explanation using just these attitudes and what the respondent has read or heard about the Court's activities. This study, however, was not designed in any experimental utopia. We shall have to do the

TABLE 5 Opinions of Supreme Court in Terms of Selected Variables

Independent Variable Party Identification	Attitude about the Supreme Court			
	Strong Supporter (+2 or Higher)	Supporter (+1)	Neutral (0)	Critic (−1 or Lower)
Strong Dem.	28.4%	22.7%	10.5%	7.1%
Weak Dem.	12.5	14.7	18.4	7.1
Independent Dem.	20.5	14.7	18.4	13.1
Independent	11.4	13.3	10.5	10.7
Independent Rep.	12.5	13.3	14.5	20.2
Weak Rep.	10.2	12.0	13.2	15.5
Strong Rep.	4.5	9.3	14.5	26.2
	100.0	100.0	100.0	100.0
N	88	75	76	84
Tau-b = .244				
Support for Specific Procedural Rights (McClosky Items)				
Support 7–9 Rights	56.2%	25.6%	26.2%	24.7%
Support 5 or 6 Rights	22.5	37.2	34.2	42.4
Support 0–4 Rights	21.3	37.2	39.5	32.9
	100.0	100.0	100.0	100.0
N	89	78	76	85
Tau-b = .163				
Agreement with Court Decisions				
Agree 3 or 4 Cases	46.0%	30.8%	26.9%	29.6%
Agree with 2 Cases	34.9	39.7	30.8	35.7
Agree 0 or 1 Case	19.5	29.5	42.3	35.7
	100.0	100.0	100.0	100.0
N	87	78	78	84
Tau-b = .144				
Prior Information				
Quite Favorable	35.1%	35.6%	20.0%	7.1%
Favorable	33.3	28.9	24.0	25.7
Mixed	15.8	24.4	20.0	30.0
Unfavorable	12.3	4.4	28.0	20.0
Quite Unfavorable	3.5	6.7	8.0	17.1
	100.0	100.0	100.0	100.0
N	57	45	25	70
Tau-b = .287				

best we can with four independent variables: subjective party identification, support for specific free speech and procedural rights, agreement with four controversial decisions made by the Court, and the favorability of information received about the Court.

Party identification was measured by the familiar Survey Research Center queries: "Generally speaking, do you usually think of yourself as a Republican, a Democrat, an Independent, or what?" and "Would you call yourself a strong (Republican, Democrat) or a not very strong (Republican, Democrat)?" or "Do you think of yourself as closer to the Republican or Democratic party?"

Support for specific applications of procedural rights was measured by nine items developed for this purpose by Herbert McClosky.[1] Although the answers given by our respondents did not fall into the neat scale obtained by McClosky, it was possible to divide our sample into thirds on the basis of the number of items on which each respondent took a pro-libertarian stand. As Table 5 indicates, the extent of agreement with these procedural rights is positively related to opinion about the Supreme Court. The Prothro-Grigg queries about the general principles of democracy, majority rule, and minority rights,[2] also made it possible to divide the sample so the pro-democratic respondents were more likely to have pro-Court attitudes. The association was weaker than that obtained with the McClosky items, probably because the McClosky questions about procedural and free speech rights asked about specific applications in areas in which the Supreme Court has been active.

The extent of agreement with Supreme Court activity in some controversial areas was investigated by responses to "hypothetical" cases. We could not assume that the

interviewees would know what the Supreme Court had done. Therefore the respondents were asked to listen to some "arguments similar to those heard by the Supreme Court," and give their opinion as to how the Court should have decided the case. For *Wesberry* v. *Sanders*, for example, the argument was:

Attorney White argues that the boundaries of congressional districts must be drawn so that as nearly as practicable one man's vote in an election is worth as much as another's. Attorney Black argues that the Constitution states that as long as Congress does not object, the states may draw the boundaries in any way they see fit. Do you feel this case should be decided in favor of Attorney White or Attorney Black?

And *Heart of Atlanta Motel, Inc.* v. *U. S.* suggested this question:

Attorney Smith argues that Congress has no right to pass legislation telling the owner of a private business that he must serve Negroes or any other particular class of customers if he does not choose to do so. Attorney Jones argues that Congress may pass legislation regulating any economic activity at any time that it decides that a barrier to interstate commerce exists which should be removed. Do you feel that this case should be decided in favor of Attorney Smith or Attorney Jones?

Similar queries asked the respondents how they would have decided the Scales and Schempp cases.

The answers to these items were doubtless responsive to the information contained in the questions themselves, even though 61% of our respondents indicated some prior awareness of such cases. But these queries did tap opinions on four controversial areas: redistricting, civil rights, internal security, and school prayers. And so far as possible, the information contained in these items represented the question presented to the Court for decision. Hence such queries may be an effective way of investigating attitudes when the respondents do not have adequate prior information. Whether or no, these questions were effective for our purposes. They generated responses which could be combined into

---

[1]Herbert McClosky, "Consensus and Ideology in American Politics," *American Political Science Review*, 58 (June 1964), p. 367.

[2]James W. Prothro and Charles M. Grigg, "Fundamental Principles of Democracy: Basis of Agreement & Disagreement," *Journal of Politics*, 22 (1960), p. 282. Note that we used only the questions about the general principles. We did not use the Prothro-Grigg items about the specific applications of these democratic principles.

a scale measuring the extent of agreement with the Court.

Data on the favorability of prior information were derived from questions asking about communications the respondent had received concerning the Court. The first of these queries was:

There has been some public discussion about the United States Supreme Court lately, so I'd like to begin with a few questions about it. Do you recall reading, or hearing, or talking with anyone about the Supreme Court during the past year?

A couple of questions later, the interviewee was asked:

Would you say that this (person, article, program) was favorable or unfavorable to the Supreme Court?

Up to three information sources were coded as predominantly favorable, mixed, or predominantly unfavorable. These, in turn, were sorted into a scale with five magnitudes: quite favorable (2 or 3 favorable contacts), favorable (1 favorable or a mixture with a favorable balance), mixed (mixed contacts of an equal balance between favorable and unfavorable), unfavorable (1 unfavorable or a mixture with an unfavorable balance), and quite unfavorable (2 or 3 unfavorable contacts). Table 5 shows that favorability of prior information—as party identification, support for specific procedural rights, and agreement with Court decisions—did have an effect on attitudes about the Supreme Court.

In order to pursue the analysis, each of the four independent variables was used as a test factor and the relationships between attitudes about the Court and the other three independent variables were stratified in terms of the test factor. When party identification was used as a test factor, for example, the relationships between attitudes about the Court and support of specific procedural rights, agreement with Court decisions, and favorability of prior information were investigated for Democrats alone, Independents alone, and Republicans alone. Three demographic variables which had shown some association with attitudes about the Court, age, sex, and education, were also used as test factors. None

of the original relationships was eliminated with one level of stratification, although most of the effect of support for specific procedural rights was eliminated in certain of the subsamples produced. It is easier to comprehend the effects of each of the independent variables if we look at what happened when it was used as a test factor, so the data shall be presented in that way.[3]

It is apparent from Table 6 that the three independent variables have quite different effects on the three partisan groupings. In each case, the relationship is stronger for the Independents alone than it is for the total sample. It would appear that the directly relevant attitudes and information play a larger role in the formation of the Independents' attitudes because the effects of these attitudes are not dampened by other partisan considerations. In the case of the Republicans, their support for procedural rights and their agreement with the Court's decisions can be explained by the fact that they are Republicans. On the other hand, one can explain much of what the Democrats hear on the basis that they are Democrats. In other words, members of the minority party are

[3]For those who are unacquainted with multivariate analysis, a few words of explanation might be in order. The purposes of this procedure are to guard against the danger of spurious correlation and to evaluate the relative importance of several variables. If the association between two variables can be reduced or eliminated when the relationship is stratified according to a test factor, the original association is regarded as spurious and the interpretation concentrates on the relationship between the test factor and the original dependent variable. If the original association is unchanged on stratification, the relationship is not spurious. If the original association is increased on stratification, it is an indication that the relationship between the original independent and dependent variables is particularly strong. To interpret these tables, therefore, one should compare the association (actually Kendall's measure of rank-order correlation) for each subsample to that for the total sample. In the top line of Table 6, for example, the Tau-b for the original association between support for procedural rights and an attitude toward the Court is .16. The Tau-b for Republicans is −.03, for Democrats .15, and for Independents .24. Hence one concludes that for Republicans the important relationship is between party identification and an attitude toward the Court; for Democrats, party identification does not affect the relationship between procedural rights and attitude toward the Court, and for Independents, support for procedural rights is particularly important in explaining attitude toward the Court.

TABLE 6   Effect of Party Identification as a Test Factor

(All data are Kendall's Tau-b for the relationship between the independent variable and attitudes toward the Court in the sample or subsample noted.)

Independent Variable	Total Sample	Democrats	Independents	Republicans
Support Procedural Rights	.16	.15	.24	−.03
Agree with Court Decisions	.14	.08	.19	.03
Overall Prior Information	.28	.15	.32	.25

more likely to be motivated by strongly held attitudes while members of a majority party maintain their attitudes because they receive continual social reinforcement for them.

Agreement with the McClosky test items on specific procedural and free speech rights seems to be the least basic of the four independent variables we are working with. Of the four, it was the only one which was eliminated in certain subsamples by demographic controls. As shown in Table 7, specific rights as a test factor does not affect the relationship between party identification and opinion about the Court. The reader will recall from Table 6 that the converse is not true. Party identification as a test factor does affect the relationship between specific rights and opinion about the Court. Hence party identification must be regarded as the more important consideration. The relationship between agreement with Court decisions and attitudes toward the Court is unaffected by a pro-libertarian attitude, but is depressed by less libertarian attitudes, perhaps because these attitudes and doubt about the wisdom of the Court's decisions are both related to some more basic attitude. It would seem that favorable communications about the Court are received by those who support 7 to 9 pro-

cedural rights in part because of their pro-libertarian attitude, while relatively rare unfavorable news supports and strengthens the effect of an anti-libertarian attitude.

Table 8 illustrates the effects of the extent of agreement with the more discussed decisions of the Court. This barely affects the relationship between party identification and attitudes about the Court. It does, however, change the influence of attitudes about the procedure and prior information. The pronounced effect of agreement with Court decisions on support for procedural rights (a stronger effect than when the latter was the control) hints again that both of these attitudes are related to some basic attitude, and suggests that agreement with what the Court has done is more important. The influence of prior communication is reduced if one agrees with what the Court has done, but is much more important if one is in disagreement.

The effects of prior communication are quite clear. In the case of each attitudinal variable, the presence of prior information strengthens the relationship while the absence of prior information depresses it. Some kind of communication is absolutely necessary for the attitude about procedural rights to affect attitude toward the Court, although the

TABLE 7   Effect of Support for Procedural Rights as a Test Factor

(All data are Kendall's Tau-b for the relationship between the independent variable and attitudes toward the Court in the sample or subsample noted.)

| Independent Variable | Total Sample | Number of Specific Rights Supported | | |
		7–9	5–6	0–4
Party Identification	.24	.25	.28	.24
Agree with Court Decisions	.14	.16	.05	.08
Overall Prior Information	.28	.15	.29	.38

TABLE 8   Effect of Agreement with Court Decisions as a Test Factor

(All data are Kendall's Tau-b for the relationship between the independent variable and attitudes toward the Court for the sample or subsample noted.)

Independent Variable	Total Sample	Number of Decisions Agreed With		
		3 or 4	2	0 or 1
Party Identification	.24	.25	.28	.24
Support Procedural Rights	.16	.22	.15	−.002
Over-all Prior Information	.28	.02	.36	.45

TABLE 9   Effect of Over-all Prior Information as a Test Factor

(All data are Kendall's Tau-b for the relationship between the independent variable and attitudes toward the court in the subsample noted. The measures for quality of information should be compared with the subsample which had heard about the Court.)

Independent Variable	Heard about Court?		Quality of Prior Information		
	Yes	No	Favorable	Mixed	Unfavorable
Party Identification	.26	.17	.18	.16	.38
Support Procedural Rights	.28	−.09	.23	.29	.30
Agree with Court Decisions	.18	.12	.05	.16	.39

favorability or unfavorability of the communication does not affect the relationship very much. The effect of quality of information on party identification and agreement with the Court's activities is sharp and uniform. Favorable prior communication depresses the relationship suggesting, especially in the case of agreement with the Court's holdings, that favorable prior information can produce a pro-Court attitude directly. Conversely, unfavorable prior information markedly strengthens the relationship, suggesting the adverse information reinforces attitudes which lead one to a critical position.

In sum, having pro-Court attitudes (being a Democrat, supporting 7 to 9 procedural rights, agreeing with 3 or 4 decisions) seems to explain much of what one hears and reads about the Court. At the same time, favorable information makes it less necessary to have such an attitude in order to take a pro-Court position. This implies a circular relationship in which the attitudes of the majority and the communications heard most frequently feed upon and support one another. The minority attitudes (being a Republican, agreeing with 2 or fewer Court decisions) are strong enough to survive in a hostile informa-

tional environment, but when persons holding these attitudes do encounter relatively rare anti-Court information, their attitudes are sharply reinforced.

There are several means of noting the joint influence of the four variables. One is to combine classes so that one group has several pro-Court influences. For example, one can create one group made up of Democrats who support 7 to 9 specific procedural rights and who agree with 3 or 4 Court decisions; a second made up of Independents who support 5 or 6 specific procedural rights and who agree with 2 Court decisions; and a third made up of Republicans who support no more than 4 specific procedural rights and who did not agree with more than 1 decision made by the Court. Such a classification of persons who should be pro-Court, neutral, and anti-Court, respectively, produces a Tau-b of .36 when checked against attitudes about the Court. This is a higher degree of association than any one of the attitudinal variables produced by themselves.

The difficulty with this approach is that these four variables are somewhat independent of each other. If all Democrats agreed with the decisions of the Court, or if all

Republicans were opposed to procedural and free speech rights, it would be easy to divide the world of Court perceptions into liberal and conservative and be done with it. But this is *not* the case. For example, there was only one respondent who was at the midpoint of all four scales. So one comes to a dead end when he follows this path of statistical analysis.

Fortunately, there are other variables available which reflect the effects of those we have been discussing thus far. Perhaps the most dramatic example of this is provided by the respondents' votes in 1964. There should have been some relation between votes and attitudes about the Court because of party identification alone (Tau-b = .24). This association is increased when one adds the effect of the candidates. Here there was a marked contrast on the Republican side. Presidential candidate Barry Goldwater, a conservative, made opposition to Supreme Court decisions one of his important campaign themes. Gubernatorial candidate Dan Evans, on the other hand, was a moderate who campaigned successfully on the basis of a "Blueprint for Progress." He did not concern himself with the Supreme Court, but was known to be favorable to civil rights. Consequently, one finds that the association between presidential vote and attitude toward the Court has climbed to .34, while the association between the gubernatorial vote and attitude toward the Court has dropped to .18. Finally, we can add the effect of information about the Court

to the constellation of attitudes brought together by the campaign. In the case of those who heard unfavorable information about the Court, there was an even stronger relationship between presidential vote and attitude toward the Court. Having heard favorable information about the Court, however, almost completely eliminated the remaining association between gubernatorial vote and attitude toward the Court. Table 10 shows this contrast.

III

Who are the supporters of the Court? Who are its critics? Which persons are neutral in their opinions of the Court? The most direct answer is that every type of person is to be found in each category. These attitudes were analyzed in terms of a series of demographic variables: age, sex, education, religion, occupation, union membership, social class, income and ancestry. No significant relationships were found. As a general explanation for the existence of these attitudes, a demographic approach is not very powerful.

If, however, we are careful to keep in mind that we are working with weak statistical tendencies rather than with any cause-and-effect relationships, there are some things which can be noted. The most important findings are presented in Table 11. The effect of age is noticeable in that those under 30 are most inclined to be strong supporters of the Court, while those over 50 are likely to be critical. Men are more likely to be found among the strong supporters or critics of the

TABLE 10 Some 1964 Votes and Attitudes about the Court

Vote	Strong Supporter	Attitude about the Court Supporter	Neutral	Critic
	(Respondents receiving over-all unfavorable information)			
Johnson (D)	87.5%	66.7%	62.5%	11.5%
Goldwater (R)	12.5	33.3	37.5	88.5
N	8	3	8	26
Tau-b = .613				
	(Respondents receiving over-all favorable information)			
Rosellini (D)	31.4%	37.5%	33.3%	23.8%
Evans (R)	68.6	62.5	66.7	76.2
N	35	24	9	21
Tau-b = .043				

TABLE 11 Opinions of Supreme Court in Terms of Selected Demographic Variables

Demographic Variable	Opinion of Supreme Court			
	Strong Supporter	Supporter	Neutral	Critic
Age*				
Under 30	33.3%	26.9%	29.1%	17.6%
30–49	36.6	34.6	30.3	37.6
Over 50	30.1	38.5	40.6	44.8
N	90	78	79	85
C = .25, X^2 = 21.806, .20 > p > .10				
Sex				
Male	55.6%	50.0%	37.5%	55.3%
Female	44.4	50.0	62.5	44.7
N	90	78	80	85
C = .14, X^2 = 7.061, .10 > p > .05				
Education				
Not H. S. Graduate	12.8%	19.4%	14.9%	16.0%
H. S. Graduate	26.7	30.6	31.1	18.5
Some College	24.4	27.8	28.4	24.7
College Graduate	36.0	22.2	25.7	40.7
N	86	72	74	81
C = .17, X^2 = 10.006, .40 > p > .30				

*These data are presented in condensed form in the interests of clarity. The statistics for the data, however, were calculated on the basis of 6 age categories.

Court, while women are much more likely to be neutral. Education appears to have a similar, if weaker, effect. Those with college degrees are found disproportionately among those who are strong supporters or critics while those who did not go beyond high school tend to be among those who are neutral or weak supporters.[4]

More isolated linkages could be seen here and there among other variables tested. Jews and Italian-Americans were among the strong supporters of the Court. (Neither of these

[4]Age, sex, and education also had effects on agreement with specific rights and party identification when they were used as test factors in the manner discussed in Section II. The effect of the McClosky items was sharply increased for those who had been to college, and was completely eliminated for the age group between 30 and 50. Party identification was a little more relevant for women, and those who had been to college. Party identification was less important in explaining opinions about the Court for those under 30, but much more important for those over 50. (Aside from the normal strengthening of partisanship with age, this may reflect memories of the Court fight of the 1930's.) These demographic controls did not have any influence on the effect of agreement with Court decisions or prior information about the Court.

categories included very many cases.) Those whose ancestors had come from Great Britain, Germany or Austria were likely to be supporters or critics of the Court while those with an Eastern European or Scandinavian heritage were more likely to be neutral. There was some tendency for those with upper white collar occupations (an accountant, for example, rather than a file clerk) and those with moderately high incomes ($6,000 to $10,000) to be found among the supporters or critics of the Court. Neither union membership nor social class had any bearing whatsoever on attitude toward the Court.

To the extent that any generalizations can be drawn from these rather weak relationships, there is one theme which runs through the data. This is that the supporters and critics of the Court have more in common with each other than either grouping does with those who take a neutral posture. This holds up when one looks at intensity of opinion. Strong supporters have the same demographic characteristics as strong opponents. Mild supporters resemble mild critics. And so on.

There are exceptions to this. It would be a fairly good bet that a young Jew or a young Italian-American would take a pro-Court position. But a middle-aged man with a college education whose ancestors came from England who had a white collar job and a moderately high income would be likely to have a strong attitude in one direction *or* the other. On the other hand, an older woman with little formal education whose ancestors came from Poland and whose late husband had been a laborer would be likely to lack any firm attitude or, at most, to take a neutral posture. As we read back over these characteristics, the meaning of the differences becomes more obvious. The socioeconomic groups who take neutral stances are those

who are more isolated from our political culture. Hence, *having an attitude depends on being involved in the political culture while the direction of the attitude depends on the nature of the political environment to which one is exposed.*

If questions can be raised about the weak demographic relationships in Table 11, they can be answered with additional data which support the same conclusions. In Table 12, attitudes about the Court are compared with some measures of involvement in the political culture. We first note that those who have talked about or read about the Supreme Court during the past year are more likely to be found among the supporters or critics of the Court than among those who are neutral. We also see that critics are more likely to

TABLE 12 Opinions of Supreme Court in Terms of Political Involvement

Measure of Involvement Read or Heard about Court in Last Year?	Opinion of Supreme Court			
	Strong Supporter	Supporter	Neutral	Critic
Yes	73.3%	68.5%	45.2%	89.2%
No	26.7	31.5	54.8	10.8
N	86	76	73	83
$C = .32$, $X^2 = 36.275$, $p < .001$				
Heard about Cases Before?				
Yes	70.1%	57.9%	48.7%	78.6%
No	29.9	42.1	51.3	21.4
N	87	76	76	84
$C = .23$, $X^2 = 18.187$, $p < .001$				
Intensity of Attitude about Court				
Very Strong	40.9%	34.2%	17.5%	51.8%
Fairly Strong	48.9	39.7	39.7	32.5
Doesn't Care	10.2	26.0	42.9	15.7
N	88	73	63	83
$C = .31$, $X^2 = 36.543$, $p < .001$				
Number of Political Activities				
5–6	10.1%	12.8%	3.9%	8.8%
1–4	73.0	61.6	68.8	71.8
0	16.9	25.6	27.3	14.1
N	89	78	77	85
$C = .19$, $X^2 = 12.58$, $p = .05$				

have paid some attention to the Court than its supporters. The same thing is true regarding persons who gave some indication in the course of the interview that they were aware of at least one of the four controversial areas in which the Court had been active. A third measure of involvement, intensity of feeling about the Supreme Court, is related to the respondents' comments in a way we have come to expect. Supporters of the Court tend to hold their opinions fairly strongly; more opponents of the Court hold their opinions very strongly; and those who are neutral are also likely not to care too much one way or another. And as a measure of general political involvement, the Survey Research Center list of campaign-related activities (talking about candidates, giving money, going to meetings, etc.) was included. The association between campaign participation and attitude about the Court is weaker than that obtained with forms of political involvement which directly concern the Court, but it is included here because it supports the general point that those who take stands are more likely to be the politically involved.

IV

Now let us recapitulate our major points. Important differences were found between those who had attitudes about the Supreme Court and those who did not. Essentially the differences between those who had attitudes and those who did not were the differences between the politically involved and the politically isolated. Among those possessing attitudes, the direction of the attitude concerning the Court was jointly determined by a cluster of related political attitudes and by communications concerning the Court. The attitudes related to a critical view of the Court were well enough organized to survive in a hostile informational environment, but could be sharply reinforced if a respondent encountered relatively rare supporting information. A circular relationship was found between attitudes related to a favorable view of the Court and information which supported a pro-Court attitude. The cluster of attitudes heightened a respondent's sensitivity to pro-Court communications, and these relatively frequently encountered communications reinforced the already existing attitudes. Finally, the over-all distribution of attitudes was favorable to the Supreme Court.

There are important implications in these findings relating to the probability of changes in these attitudes. We have three types of respondents, each of which has rather different characteristics. Let us ask what would happen to each in the event that pro-Court or anti-Court propaganda were directed at them. Supporters of the Court are already receiving a sufficient number of pro-Court communications to maintain their attitudes. Additional pro-Court messages might result in a modest strengthening of their attitudes, but this is about all. Anti-Court communications, on the other hand, are unlikely to come to their attention at all because their attitudes produce such a high threshold of awareness. Identical threshold mechanisms make it unlikely that those who are now neutral in their stance would be aware of either pro-Court or anti-Court propaganda. In addition, their isolation from our political culture makes it improbable that they would have much contact with political communications to begin with. The critic of the Court is not likely to assimilate pro-Court propaganda, but an increase in the frequency with which he encounters anti-Court communications can perceptibly increase the intensity of his conviction. In sum, the minority may become more highly motivated but is unlikely to become a majority.

There is one interview which typifies the problems of anti-Court propagandists:

What did you hear about the Supreme Court?
Warren is a Communist.
Where did you hear this?
I read it. Something by a right wing individual.
Speaking generally, how would you describe your own feelings about the Supreme Court?
I think the setup is working out all right.
Is there anything you particularly like about the Supreme Court?
I like the decisions of the last fifteen to twenty years.
Is there anything you particularly dislike about the Supreme Court?
No.

So there it is. The decisions of the Supreme Court have had more effect on the reputation of the Court than the activities of its antagonists. The attitudes of the majority are favorable to the Court. In this informational environment, such decisions as the Court has been making (or at least the majority of those few decisions which rise to the public's threshold of awareness) are likely to be favorably communicated. To the extent that we can generalize from this study, we can expect a continuing consensus which is supportive of the Court.

13 A DISPUTE BECOMES A LAWSUIT

Carl A. Auerbach,
Lloyd K. Garrison,
Willard Hurst,
and Samuel Mermin

A. THE PARTIES TO A LAWSUIT

The party who starts the lawsuit is known as the plaintiff, the person who complains; the party against whom the action is brought is known as the defendant. The party appealing is known as the appellant; the other party as the respondent or appellee (in some cases, "petitioner" and "respondent," respectively). Generally, in the published report of a case decided by an appellate court, the name of the plaintiff appears first and the name of the defendant next, regardless of which party becomes the appellant and which the respondent. Thus "*Smith* v. *Brown,* 60 Mo. 126" means that in volume 60 of the Reports of the Missouri Supreme Court, at page 126, appears the report of a case decided by that court on appeal, which was started in the trial court by one Smith as plaintiff against one Brown as defendant. But whether it was

From *The Legal Process: An Introduction to Decision-Making by Judicial, Legislative, Executive, and Administrative Agencies* by Carl A. Auerbach, Lloyd K. Garrison, Willard Hurst, and Samuel Mermin. Published by Chandler Publishing Company, San Francisco. Copyright © 1961 by Carl A. Auerbach, Lloyd K. Garrison, Willard Hurst, and Samuel Mermin. Reprinted by permission.

Smith who appealed, or Brown, you couldn't tell from the title; you would have to get out the volume and look at the case.

B. THE COMMENCEMENT OF AN ACTION

The job of courts is to settle the controversies which persons bring to them. Courts do not start lawsuits. They have no investigating staff and do not conduct investigations. They do not arrest criminals or prosecute them. Their sole job is to decide the cases that are brought before them. To get the proceedings going, the plaintiff will have to do three things: he will have to pick the proper court, he will have to see that the defendant or his property is brought before it, and he will have to state his complaint and what he wants the court to do about it.

Picking the Court. This is a technical matter. The point is . . . that there are various courts with different powers and it is essential to get started in the one whose jurisdiction fits the case.

Catching the Defendant. Courts do not hear lawsuits for the fun of it. It must be clear before they start that if they finally do render a decision it can be enforced. And since the power of every court has territorial limits prescribed by the constitution or the legislature (such as the boundaries of a municipality, a county, a state, or a federal district), it is necessary to demonstrate at the outset that either the defendant or the property involved can be found within those limits, so that the judgment (that is, the court's ultimate decision) can be carried out. In criminal cases, if the defendant is an individual, he is caught quite literally, by being arrested within the territorial jurisdiction of the court, or by being extradited from some other territory. In civil cases the catching is normally symbolic. A "summons" is served on the defendant within the jurisdiction. This demonstrates that he could be arrested if necessary, and also gives him notice that a lawsuit has been started against him, and in what court and by whom. The summons does not, however, compel him to attend court. If it were a subpoena, he would have to obey it or be arrested. But the only result of disregarding a summons is that judgment is likely to be entered against him by default. If the summons cannot be served personally, because the defendant is not there, it may commonly be served by leaving it at his house, if he has one, in the jurisdiction. If he is a non-resident, and does not come into the state, the suit may be started if some property of the defendant can be found and seized, by a proceeding usually called attachment. If none of these things can be done, there may be statutes allowing the lawsuit to be begun in certain situations in which it seems reasonable to do so—e.g., if a non-resident is "doing business" in the state or is a motorist who became involved in an accident in the state. Fixing the precise limitations of the legal doctrines involved in the latter types of cases is beyond our present purposes.

Stating the Claim. The plaintiff must also tell the court and the defendant what it is that he complains of and what he wants the court to do about it. Conceivably this could be done by having the judge orally question the plaintiff in the presence of the defendant. But we have deemed it more expeditious to have the parties, in advance of the trial, attempt to narrow down the issues of fact and law on which they differ by exchanging written statements of their respective claims. This conforms, as we shall see, with our notions of the adversary nature of our litigation. The written statements that are exchanged by the parties are called pleadings. Thus the plaintiff is the first to state his claim and request for relief, in a written document now commonly called the complaint (formerly sometimes called declaration, bill, or petition).

C. PLEADINGS AND OTHER PROCEDURES PRIOR TO TRIAL

Once the plaintiff has picked his court, caught the defendant or his property, and filed his complaint, the lawsuit is on its way and the next move is up to the defendant. The defendant will no doubt see his lawyer, who will find out from him what the row is all about. The claim may be admitted and paid up, or compromised. If so, the suit will be

dismissed by the lawyers, and the court will hear no more about it. Or the claim may be allowed to go by default, in which case, after a certain time lapse, the court will enter judgment for the plaintiff. But if the claim is really in dispute, and is not compromised, the defendant's lawyer will have to file an "Answer."

The answer, too, is a formal document. It states the defendant's position in the controversy, and its first job is to state his position on the things which the plaintiff says in his complaint. If, for example, the complaint states that the defendant owes the plaintiff $1000 for money lent by plaintiff to defendant and not repaid by the defendant on the due date, the answer may deny that the defendant ever borrowed any money of the plaintiff, or it may say the loan is paid, or that it has been discharged by a proceeding in bankruptcy (under the Federal Bankruptcy Act, which permits insolvent debtors, upon surrendering their non-exempt property, to be freed or discharged from their debts by order of a U.S. district court). Whatever the answer says about the plaintiff's claim, it may assert some counterclaim which the defendant has against the plaintiff. Formerly, such additional pleadings could be filed by plaintiff and defendant as were necessary to raise at least one disputed issue of fact or law determinative of the result in the case. But in most states today the pleadings terminate with the answer or with the plaintiff's reply to the defendant's answer.

If the defendant thinks that the complaint fails to state a claim for relief, even though all the statements therein may be true, he may file *a motion to dismiss* the complaint. In many states today, the same objective is achieved by filing a *demurrer*. The demurrer or motion to dismiss may, if appropriate, be used by a plaintiff to attack the answer. This procedural device challenges the *legal* sufficiency of a pleading (i.e., on the temporary assumption that the *facts* alleged in the pleading are true) and the issues it raises will be decided by the judge, not the jury. The defendant need not necessarily choose between the two kinds of responses we have mentioned; he may combine them in one pleading, making his claims in the alternative. He could say: such and such facts alleged in the complaint are not true, but even if they are, the plaintiff's claim for relief is not legally valid.

In addition to the pleadings, other proceedings prior to trial are worth noting. To shorten the trial and reduce the element of surprise, various "discovery" devices are available, including the taking of "depositions" from expected opposing witnesses and asking the court to order production of certain documents by the opposing party. "Pretrial conferences" of the judge with the opposing attorneys often narrow the issues of fact and law in real dispute, or lead to settlement of the case without trial.

D. THE TRIAL

If the only issue on which the parties are in dispute is one of law, the dispute is submitted to the court by the process known as argument. The lawyers appear before the judge, argue the disputed point or points, and perhaps also submit written arguments called briefs. Witnesses and jury are not necessary because there are no disputed facts to pass on. The judge decides the matter himself, on the basis of the arguments and of his own knowledge and study. In most lawsuits, the main dispute disclosed by the proceedings before trial is on the facts. To resolve such a dispute there has to be a trial. This is the familiar courtroom process and consists chiefly of the presentation by the two competing sides of their views of the facts, through documents, physical exhibits, and the oral testimony of witnesses. The decision is based on what is thus offered. Neither the judge nor the jury is supposed to make any independent investigations.

The issues of fact are tried either before the judge alone, or before the judge and a jury, depending on the kind of case. The distinction, for the most part historical, is between cases "at common law" (in which event juries were generally used) or "in equity" (in which event juries were not used). For the present it is enough to say that, in general, in criminal cases, except very minor ones, there will always be a jury (unless, as often

happens, the defendant expressly chooses to forego, or in legal language "waives," a jury); and in civil cases there will be a jury if all the plaintiff wants is money damages (and if he asks for a jury, or the defendant does). But if the plaintiff seeks a remedy which, historically, only a court of equity could grant (e.g., a divorce, or the foreclosure of a mortgage, or an injunction to prevent some threatened wrong) the case is normally tried without a jury. Because of this peculiar and still surviving distinction between cases "at common law" and "in equity," it happens that many very important business cases are regularly tried and decided by a judge alone.

E. THE JUDGMENT

If the case is tried by a jury, the issues of fact are settled, within limits determined by the judge, by the jury's *verdict*. If it is tried without a jury, they are settled by the judge's findings. The verdict or findings will be followed by a judgment or order of the court. If the defendant has won, the judgment will read substantially as follows: "Adjudged: that the plaintiff recover nothing by this action." If the plaintiff has won, let us say, a judgment for money, it might read: "Adjudged: that the plaintiff recover from the defendant one thousand dollars ($1000.00) with interest thereon at 6% per annum from this date until paid."

F. APPELLATE REVIEW

The judgment or order of the court is subject to appeal, or to be set aside or corrected by the court that entered it. The time within which either of these steps may be taken is strictly limited. When that time has passed and neither of these steps has been taken or the appellate court of last resort has upheld the judgment or order, it becomes final. The court will generally not hear applications to correct it. Even if the court became convinced, as a result of subsequent disclosures, that the case was wrongly decided, either in fact or law, while that might affect later similar cases between other people, it would not affect the judgment or order previously entered. For that controversy has been settled.

"Nothing is settled until it is settled right," is not a maxim of judicial conduct, and for obvious, practical reasons.

When appeal is taken from the judgment or order of the trial court, the appellate court is given a condensed record of the proceedings in the trial court. It will usually contain the pleadings, verdict and judgment and so much of the proceedings at the trial as the attorneys for the parties regard as important. No testimony is heard by the appellate court; just argument by the lawyers as to the pros and cons of what the trial court decided. In addition, the lawyers are permitted to file *briefs* for the parties—printed documents containing legal arguments in much more detailed form than can be presented orally.

G. ENFORCEMENT OF THE JUDGMENT OR ORDER . . .

The simplest judgment to enforce is one for the defendant. No private or public person need do anything to enforce it, unless the plaintiff continues to assert the same claim or brings another lawsuit on it. If he does that, the defendant will simply plead the prior judgment in defense, and if it is really the same claim and between the same parties he will automatically prevail again. A judgment for the plaintiff for money is more difficult to enforce. You should notice that the court's judgment that the plaintiff recover money is not an order or command by the court to the defendant to pay the money; it is simply a declaration by the court that the law applicable to the facts obligates the defendant to pay the plaintiff a certain sum. The judge does not concern himself personally with seeing to it that the defendant satisfies his legal obligation to the plaintiff; he merely states what the obligation is.

How, then, does the plaintiff collect from the defendant if the defendant refuses to honor the judgment by paying up? He will get from the clerk of the court a writ (order) of "execution," which is a document directing the sheriff to satisfy the judgment out of the defendant's property. (*Note:* The *sheriff* is a county official, generally elected; he is an officer of the court; that is to say, he is subject to judicial supervision in the performance of his duties, which also include various police functions.) When the sheriff (or the United States Marshal in the federal system) receives the "execution" from the plaintiff he will proceed to take into his custody the property of the defendant which has not been exempted by statute from execution; to sell it at public auction; to pay the plaintiff's judgment out of the proceeds; and to remit the balance, if any, to the defendant. All the details of this process are regulated by statute. Judgments for the possession of specific property are enforced in much the same way. The sheriff takes away from the defendant the cow or the car which the defendant has improperly appropriated, and turns it over to the plaintiff. If the defendant has no property out of which the judgment can be satisfied, the plaintiff can do nothing unless and until the defendant acquires property; imprisonment for debt, which used to exist in England and to some extent in this country, has long since been abolished.

14 A NOTE ON THE IMPLICATIONS OF LEGAL RULES AND PROCEDURES*

Thomas P. Jahnige

Traditionally, judicial decision-making has been lauded as being endowed with an objectivity and fairness not found within other political decision-making forums. Every citizen is entitled to his "day in court." There, the merits of his case are considered without bias or favoritism no matter how despicable his character or lowly his status. The rules of judicial procedure, the right to counsel, the adversary presentation of questions of law and fact, and the use of the jury stand as the guarantors of this promise. Or so we are told. It is not my purpose to deny the relevance of these time-honored promises as the normative standard at which the courts should aim;

*This reading was especially prepared for this volume.

rather, I would like to point out how the very rules and procedures which are supposed to promote "equal justice for all" may in fact undercut the achievement of this goal in many serious ways. I shall do this by focusing on some of the burdens legal rules and procedures inflict upon the non-professional participants in litigation—i.e., the parties themselves, witnesses, jurors, and others in society having a stake in a case.

The origin of most litigation lies within disputes between individuals lacking legal training. Yet, once an action is begun, the litigants themselves play only a very minor role. Except in the most insignificant courts of the land, being a litigant implies having a lawyer. Hiring a lawyer, especially a good lawyer, costs money. Even though in criminal cases and certain types of civil suits, in some jurisdictions, free counsel is available to the poor, such legal representation is rarely as good as that which can be hired. The middle-class litigant is probably most heavily burdened by the costs of going to court. He, no doubt, must pay out of his own pocket for counsel and court costs. The time he spends with his lawyer and in court may decrease his wages or other income. Individuals and institutions with wealth, on the other hand, are in a vastly different position. They can not only afford more easily to go to court with good counsel, they can also afford the legal advice necessary to keep them out of court. These greater resources available for carrying on litigation may grant more than just a relative advantage to those with wealth. If this wealth is combined with a litigious nature, the threat of going to court can be used as a club for obtaining ends which are either legally questionable or even unwarranted.

The "right to counsel"—even when this right assures an equality of expertise—is not the right to a professionally trained advocate who will promote his client's cause to the bitter end. In representing his client, the lawyer actually plays two different roles. On the one hand, he is a professional advocate hired to represent his client in an adversary proceeding which is typified by formal motions and countermotions prior to the trial, argu-

ment in court, a judgment, and, in a very small number of cases, an appeal. On the other hand, the lawyer plays the role of bargainer in which he, the opposing counsel, and often the judge act as intermediaries in achieving a consensual accommodation between the litigants. In terms of volume of cases, the second role is by far the most important. Only about 10 percent of the civil and criminal cases filed in the federal courts actually go to trial.[1] As this figure suggests, a major function of judges and lawyers is to prevent trials from occurring by achieving accommodations.[2]

Accommodation is without a doubt a worthy goal. It relieves the perpetually overloaded courts from some of their work load. It saves litigants from many of the burdens and frustrations of trial. It may even, in fact, achieve the most equitable solution possible. Yet, in seeking accommodation, the lawyer may sacrifice the legitimate interests of his client. Let us look at the reasons why this may be so.

Although a lawyer's formal position in a lawsuit is that of representative for his client, informally he may be more properly seen as a member of a courthouse bureaucracy. This is especially true for a lawyer who specializes in pleading particular types of cases before a specific court. With such a lawyer, his relationship to his client is probably temporary and casual. His relationship to the judges of the court, its administrative personnel, and the other private and government lawyers operating in the same area is much deeper and more permanent. To maintain his position in such a bureaucratic system, promote its smooth operation, and enjoy the psychic and financial benefits thus produced, may lead a lawyer to seek accommodations which are against the interests of his client. Abra-

[1]Glendon Schubert, *Judicial Policy Making* (Glenview, Ill.: Scott, Foresman and Co., 1965), p. 79.
[2]In the federal courts this function is formalized through procedures for "discovery" (the presentation prior to trial by opposing counsel of the evidence available to them) and the pretrial conference (a set of meetings between the judge and opposing counsel formally for discussing the case but often resulting in accommodation).

ham Blumberg, in a study of criminal lawyers operating in a metropolitan court has found,[3] for example, that these considerations cause lawyers in such a court often to persuade their clients to plead guilty as a mode of accommodation even though the clients themselves may feel the plea is incorrect. He further has found that these lawyers, with the tacit knowledge of the judges, often use formal motions to delay trial as a method of forcing full payment of fees from their clients before the trial. This latter situation is obviously unethical and has been the subject of professional criticism and reprimand. It is indicative, however, of the more subtle conflicts arising from the dual position of the lawyer as both representative of his client and courthouse bureaucrat and his dual role of both advocate and accommodator.

When and if a case does come up for trial, the overt behavior of the lawyer emphasizes his role as an advocate operating within an adversary framework. This role requires presenting his client's case in the strongest light possible. This entails presenting both legal rules and precedents and evidence which support his client's claim. It means producing witnesses whose versions of what happened are favorable. In handling such witnesses only those questions which encourage favorable testimony are asked. Questions which might elicit harmful or confusing answers are suppressed. It is even common for counsel to coach his client and witnesses on how to conduct themselves in court in order to make a good impression on the jury.

The role of advocate also entails destroying his opponent's case. Primarily this is done during cross-examination. As Jerome Frank notes,[4] standard courtroom practice requires using cross-examination for bringing into question the character and veracity of an opponent's client and witnesses. This can be done by eliciting testimony from them which

seems to contradict that given earlier and then not providing a chance for explaining these contradictions. It also entails making the witness under cross-examination display any unpleasant personal traits he may have. The courtroom situation aids the lawyer in this task. Its unfamiliar rules and contentious atmosphere make the witness under cross-examination confused and suspicious.

This mode of proceeding does, of course, have its functional aspects. Traditionally these have been the ones most emphasized. Pitting trained adversary against trained adversary, it is argued, promotes full consideration of all relevant questions of fact and law. At least formally, neither litigant is denied the *chance* for having his side presented in the most favorable light. At the same time, judge and jury are removed from the sometimes bias-inducing tasks of legal research, fact-finding, and interrogation. Both can maintain their neutrality until the very end of the trial. Only then, when the whole record is complete, need they decide what is the law and what happened. According to traditional legal theory, the prize of a favorable judgment goes to the party whose counsel has persuaded the jury into accepting his version of the law and the jury into accepting his version of the facts.

In practice, of course, both judge and jury may have formed earlier impressions which color their decisions. "Law" and "fact" may be difficult to separate, and both judge and jury may privately respond to both. Furthermore, the value and attitudinal proclivities of judge and jury may make the task of one or the other lawyers far more difficult or easy than might otherwise be expected. When certain values—such as racial integration or rights of criminal defendants—are involved, judge and jury may use their positions to promote their values against the formal requirements of the law. This, however, occurs *sub rosa*. On the surface, there is a radical separation between advocacy and decision-making which gives judicial decisions an aura of objectivity lacking in other political decision-making contexts.

The *sub rosa* behavior referred to above is

[3]Abraham S. Blumberg, "The Practice of Law as a Confidence Game: Organizational Cooptation of a Profession," *Law and Society Review*, I, no. 2 (1967), pp. 15–39.

[4]Jerome Frank, *Courts on Trial* (New York: Atheneum, 1949), pp. 81–85.

considered a perversion not a product of the adversary method. The most devoted proponents of adversary proceedings would criticize such behavior even though they may find it understandable given that judges and jurors are human. There are, however, other aspects of the adversary method which only the most "radical" jurists have criticized.[5] These aspects are integral elements and products of the way the process operates. Criticism of them is, at heart, criticism of the adversary method itself as a way of processing disputes. Foremost among these are the psychological costs occasioned by courtroom proceedings.[6] To the court professional the "rough and tumble" manner of proceeding may seem obvious. In fact, under the rules by which the game is played, no other approach is possible. To litigants and witnesses, however, this may be an extremely disturbing experience. The litigant, especially the litigant never before involved in a lawsuit, may go to court because he feels he has been dealt with unfairly. His dispute may seem to him quite clear. But once in court, he is fortunate if he can recognize it. Facts which seemed so clear become obscured in the hands of his opponent's lawyer. Rules of evidence and procedure block what is to him the clear presentation of the issues. The case itself may be decided on a legal technicality or ruling which to the layman may, at best, seem arbitrary, at worst, stupid. The extremely partisan nature of the proceedings may encourage dishonesty on the part of the parties, their lawyers, and the witnesses for both sides. This may produce feelings of guilt, especially on the part of the non-professional participants in the case. For the most part they have not been immunized by repeated courtroom appearances to accept such behavior as normal. Moreover, they are probably already made sensitive to this problem by their treatment under cross-examination.

The members of the jury face similar, if more subtle, problems. Out of the barrage of conflicting evidence and argument they are called upon to decide for one side or the other. Yet, the various rules governing the admissibility of evidence may block many facts which to them seem crucial. This is especially true for those accustomed to making decisions within other contexts. The businessman, for example, is accustomed to investigating a man's financial position and community background before making a decision to hire or extend credit. In the context of the courtroom, such "vital" pieces of information cannot be presented. In a criminal case, even the fact that a defendant has a criminal record may be ruled inadmissible. The juror also may be troubled by guilt feelings if he decides or is talked into deciding against a litigant not on the basis of the evidence but because of negative feelings he or his fellow jurors have toward the litigant's personality or status. Potentially, then, the litigants, witnesses, and jurors may leave the courtroom psychologically dissatisfied and with their respect for the courts greatly lowered.

To the non-participating but interested member of society, the results of litigation may also have their disappointments. Litigation often forces or encourages the courts to reach decisions with important policy implications. For this reason groups often use litigation as a way of achieving policy decisions blocked by the system's other policy-making institutions. At other times, laws or schemes of regulation cannot be enforced on a society-wide basis until they have been legitimized by the courts. To the student of constitutional law, this is patently obvious. Yet, the fact that the courts render policy decisions as a byproduct in the resolution of concrete disputes between unique individuals has important implications of timing, scope, and clarity. In a constitutional challenge to a law or regulation, for example, interested members of the political community would probably most like a decision which is rapidly given, which is comprehensive in scope, and which clearly covers all points in contention. The nature of judicial decision-making often prevents these *desiderata* from being obtained.

[5]Perhaps the leading spokesman was Judge Frank. See *ibid*.
[6]See Robert S. Redmount, "Psychological Discontinuities in the Litigation Process," *Duke Law Journal*, 1959, pp. 571–587.

In fact, that element of the legal setting called judicial restraint is concerned with techniques designed to relieve the courts from meeting them. Even when these techniques are not consciously used, many procedural aspects of the judicial process thwart those who would use the courts for getting decisions of grand policy.

Litigation, especially if it must pass through several levels of the judiciary, can be ponderously slow. The National Industrial Recovery Act, for example, was not declared fully unconstitutional in the Schechter case[7] until a few weeks before the statute was to expire. This case illuminates another problem facing those who would use the courts for achieving decisions on grand policy. This is the unpredictability of the process in determining which case the courts will respond to in making policy pronouncements. As a test case for the government, Schechter was notoriously badly framed. The NIRA was designed to bring order to an economy characterized by vast industries with continent-wide operations. The business involved in the case, however, was a poultry wholesaler in Brooklyn.

On the other hand, constitutional law is replete with cases carefully and expensively nurtured through the courts, which are denied definitive resolution either because they fail to win review by the Supreme Court or because they are decided on grounds other than constitutional. The history of the litigation leading to the final striking down of Connecticut's anti-birth control law provides us a classic example. It took over twenty years and three cases before the constitutional issues were finally decided by the Supreme Court. In the first case, *Tileston* v. *Ullman,*[8] the plaintiff was found to lack standing by the Supreme Court. In the second case, *Poe* v. *Ullman,*[9] the case was found to lack the essentials of a true "case or controversy," even though under Connecticut rules it was found to be justiciable. Thus a third case, *Griswold* v. *Connecticut.*[10] had to be launched, appealed up the hierarchy of the Connecticut courts, and then appealed to the United States Supreme Court before a definitive resolution occurred in a finding that the Connecticut statute was unconstitutional.

Typically, adjudication as a means of deciding questions of policy has an *ad hoc* quality to it. One case may only indicate the state of the law for one set of facts. To find it for another set a new case is required. Thus courts, unlike legislatures or administrative agencies, rarely give forth their schemes for social ordering fully developed and articulated.

It should be obvious that this is not a balanced treatment of the implications of legal rules and procedures. By focusing on the negative implications, I have underplayed their positive aspects. I have done so because most of the literature, particularly that written by lawyers, has so emphasized these positive aspects.

It should also be obvious that some of the faults mentioned are conceptually, if not empirically, peripheral. These are the ethically questionable aspects of behavior which can be controlled. Other, perhaps more common deviations from the behavior normatively demanded, reflect the fact that judges, jurors, lawyers, litigants, and witnesses are all human. As such, they are subject to their emotions and biases. It is not surprising to see these at play within the courtroom. In fact, it might be argued that any mode of processing disputes less rigid than that used by the judiciary would give even greater weight to these subjective factors.

Other "faults" which have been noted may not even be "faults." The fact that a businessman-juror finds "vital" pieces of information blocked by rules of admissibility may merely mean that courts and businesses in order to fulfill their societal roles must use different decision-making criteria. Perhaps in this same category is the charge that court-fashioned policies lack the comprehensiveness and sharp articulation of legislatively or bureaucratically made policies. Lastly, it might be noted that certain faults mentioned—for example, the greater litigious resources of the wealthy and the power this grants—reflect deeply rooted

[7]295 U.S. 495 (1935).
[8]318 U.S. 44 (1943).
[9]367 U.S. 497 (1961).
[10]381 U.S. 479 (1965).

elements within the cultural environment. These cannot be eliminated without changing the cultural environment.

But once these warnings and reservations have been made, it must be emphasized that certain of the negative aspects cited do represent true dysfunctionings of the way cases are processed. Among these are: (1) the role and institutional conflicts which may cause the lawyer to sacrifice his client's interests to promote the needs of the system, (2) the psychological costs inflicted by the partisan nature of the adversary process, and (3) the uncer-

tainties and unproductive expenditure of resources created by the fact that courts exist both for resolving disputes and for making policies, it being impossible to tell, prior to judgment, which role the courts will emphasize in any particular case with policy implications. These negative aspects are the price we must pay for maintaining the present structure and procedures of the judicial process. Even though upon reflection we may decide that this is not a bad bargain, we should realize that these limitations to judicial justice exist.

B. Demands

The rules of the federal judicial system require that demands come in the form of cases. It is these case-demands which we shall consider in this section. The vast majority of cases adjudicated in the United States are processed by the state judicial systems and are never treated by the federal courts. Statutory and constitutional requirements of jurisdiction allow only a limited range of cases to be processed by the federal judicial system.

For a case to be initiated before the federal district courts it must be either a civil suit between citizens of different states ("diversity" cases) in which at least $10,000 is involved, or a question involving federal law or the U. S. Constitution ("federal question" cases). The jurisdiction of the U. S. courts of appeals includes appeals from the federal district courts and from rulings of various federal administrative agencies. In its appellate role, the U. S. Supreme Court has jurisdiction over cases coming from the lower federal courts as well as cases involving a federal question decided within the various state judicial systems. The original jurisdiction of the Supreme Court, which relates to cases where states or foreign diplomats are parties, is only rarely used.

Many of the diverse fact and legal situations which make up the case-demands processed by the federal judicial system are found in the typical legal casebook. It is assumed that the reader has used such a book (most probably one on constitutional law) or is otherwise familiar with the type of materials in it. Although this knowledge is useful, perhaps even essential, for understanding how the federal courts function and their role in the American political system, it has certain limitations. Foremost among these is that it leaves the student without any quantitative sense of what kind of cases the federal courts process and at which level in the system cases of various classes are disposed. Thus, for example, although the typical student of constitutional law may know that the federal courts have played an important role in promoting civil liberties in the last decade, he probably has little knowledge about how many federal cases touch on these issues and the extent to which they are treated by the district courts, the courts of appeals, or the Supreme Court. These are important questions. The impact of the federal judicial system on the larger American political system is as much a function of how often it makes policy decisions of various types as what these decisions are. Furthermore, there may be differences in policy and/or impact resulting from whether a case is finally disposed of by a district court, a court of appeals, or the Supreme Court. The following selections discuss these questions.

The first selection, by Glendon Schubert, gives a quantitative overview of the types of cases processed by the United States district courts and the courts of appeals in 1962. Following this is a table from the *Harvard Law Review* presenting analogous data for the Supreme Court's 1961 term. In the third selection, Richard Richardson and Kenneth N. Vines compare the issues of cases as argued in district courts with the issues as they emerge on appeal in the courts of appeals. The last selection, by Joseph Tanenhaus, Marvin Schick, Matthew Muraskin, and Daniel Rosen, concerns how the Supreme Court in its appellate role decides which cases to consider fully on their merits and which to deny review.

15   THE FLOW OF CASES

Glendon Schubert

Both district courts and courts of appeals decide civil and criminal cases, and this constitutes, in one sense, their most important function. In addition, the courts of appeals have a specialized function of administrative supervision. The district courts have a different function of administrative supervision, as well as many primarily administrative tasks.

the approval of passport applications, which constitute the largest number of items for the district courts, are direct administrative functions that require only a small amount of judicial time for their accomplishment. Bankruptcy and parole are next most numerous, and together they constitute about half as many cases (approximately 175,000) as are in the direct administrative category. Bankruptcy and parole cases require administrative supervision by the district courts and consume, relatively, considerably more judicial time. The judges must appoint referees to

TABLE 1   Major Components of Decision-Making of Lower National Courts (1962)

Type of Case	District Courts	Courts of Appeals
United States Civil	19,793	936
Private Civil	38,203	1,508
Total Civil	57,996	2,444
Criminal	34,392	622
Total, Civil and Criminal	92,388	3,066
Administrative Appeals	—	1,024
Bankruptcy	137,709	128
Parole	36,663	—
Aliens Naturalization	98,573	—
Passport Application	249,655	—

Table 1 shows the number of cases in each of these categories that were docketed in a recent year. The naturalization of aliens and

Reprinted from *Judicial Policy-Making* by Glendon Schubert. Copyright © 1965 by Scott, Foresman and Company.

supervise the management of estates in bankruptcy, and approve their decisions. Parole supervision is closely related to the sentencing of convicted criminals, either under the more traditional system in which the judge determines sentences or under the newer "flexible" procedures of indeterminate sentencing through which the judge delegates much of his discretion to the parole (administrative) officials. Very few of either these direct or these supervisory administrative functions of the district courts are reviewed by the courts of appeals. Even in the bankruptcy cases, which are among the exclusive functions of the national court system, less than a tenth of 1 per cent are appealed beyond the district court level.

The district courts docket almost thirty times as many civil and criminal cases as do the courts of appeals, but only about 11 per cent in each category go to trial; the remainder are resolved by negotiation and agreement between the parties. There were 6260 civil trials in 1962, about half of which were tried with a jury. Almost three fourths of the 3788 criminal cases that went to trial, however, involved the participation of petit juries. . . . The average allocation of the time of the district courts is about 3 to 1 in favor of the civil cases. Moreover, the courts of appeals review proportionately almost two and a half times more civil cases tried by the district courts: about 40 per cent of the civil cases (2444 out of about 6200) but only about 16 per cent (622 out of about 3800) of the criminal cases. Therefore, the ratio of civil to criminal cases docketed by the courts of appeals is about 4 to 1 (2444 to 622), but criminal appeals constitute less than a sixth of the total caseload of the courts of appeals, and their disposition requires an even smaller proportion of the time of these appellate courts. The point is that both the district courts and the courts of appeals give most of their time and attention to civil cases—i.e., to what are predominantly questions of property rights rather than personal rights.

About three fourths of the cases reviewed by the courts of appeals come from the district courts, but the remaining quarter constitute many of the most complicated and important policy questions. The latter come under the rubric of what lawyers call "administrative law," and they are appealed directly from the so-called regulatory commissions, from one of the specialized national courts, or from the executive departments. For example,

almost 10 per cent of all the cases docketed with the courts of appeals come from the National Labor Relations Board, either as Board petitions to have a court order the enforcement of the Board's decision or as petitions from private litigants who seek to have a court declare invalid an order or proposed action of the Board. Only about 5 per cent of these N.L.R.B. cases come before the Court of Appeals of the District of Columbia; the remainder are divided among the courts of appeals for the ten numbered circuits. About 5 per cent of the cases docketed with the courts of appeals consist of attempts, either by the Tax Division of the Department of Justice or by counsel for taxpayers, to overturn decisions of the Tax Court of the United States. Practically none of these cases come before the District of Columbia Court of Appeals. This court does, however, somewhat specialize in the supervision of administrative decision-making, in addition to its special function in relation to the municipal courts of the District of Columbia and its general function in relation to the usual jurisdiction of United States district courts. About 7 to 8 per cent of the cases docketed with the courts of appeals consist of appeals from a large variety of regulatory commissions and administrative agencies, including the Civil Aeronautics Board, the Federal Communications Commission, the Federal Power Commission, the Federal Trade Commission, the Secretary of Agriculture, the Securities and Exchange Commission, the Immigration and Naturalization Service of the Department of Justice, and the Court of Tax Appeals of the District of Columbia. Of these, about a third go to the Court of Appeals of the District of Columbia, while another third go to the Court of Appeals for the Ninth (Far West) and the Fifth (Deep South) Circuits. Most appeals from the Interstate Commerce Commission (it will be recalled) do not come to the courts of appeals at all but go instead to special three-judge district courts, which has the nominal effect of "expediting" the disposition of such cases and the practical effect of maximizing the probability that the Supreme Court will review the trial courts' decisions in such cases. Since the Supreme Court, at the present time, has a more liberal orientation than the great majority of the panels of the courts of appeals, the effect of bypassing the courts of appeals in most I.C.C. (and other three-judge district court) cases is to provide a more liberal base for policy-making in appellate review than obtains generally for cases that must be filtered through the courts of appeals.

The "United States" (viz., the five divisions of the courts subsystem of the Department of Justice) was the plaintiff in about two-thirds and the defendant in the remaining cases classified as "United States civil" in Table 1. Of the "private civil" cases in that table, almost half are diversity-of-citizenship cases, over a third raise "federal questions," and the remaining sixth are "local" cases. We have already explained what lawyers mean by "diversity" and "federal question" jurisdiction; for present purposes, we shall simply summarize by stating that "diversity" cases—the most numerous subcategory of the "private civil" cases—require that the national courts apply what they understand to be public policy of the various states in regard to questions that are conceptualized, for substantive purpose, as being matters of "state law"; while, quite to the contrary, in "federal question" cases the national courts are asked to interpret the Constitution, statutes, administrative orders and regulations, and the judicial decisions that embody the policies of the national political system. In deciding diversity cases, the United States district courts are supposed to follow the policy guidance of the state courts, while in deciding federal question cases, the district courts are supposed to follow the policy guidance of the Supreme Court and of the courts of appeals for their own circuit. The third subcategory of "local" cases we have not previously discussed. These "local" cases arise exclusively in the national territories, and they consist (like the diversity cases) of policy questions that are decided, in the states, by state courts. They differ from the diversity cases in two respects: (1) they include many types of questions that rarely can involve diversity of citizenship among the parties; and (2) in terms of policy guid-

ance for United States district courts, they are like federal question rather than diversity cases, since there is no relevant "state law" and the national political system, in combination with the local political system in each territory, makes the policy norms that are supposed to guide the territorial district courts.

The largest subcategory of the diversity category consists of tort cases, and the most frequent type of tort, about 7000 in 1962, was "motor vehicle, personal injury" claims. The major subcategories of the federal question cases were "marine, tort, personal injury," about 3700; "marine, contract," about 2200; antitrust, electrical equipment industry," about 1700; and Federal Employers' Liability Act, about 1100.

There were over 7000 local cases in 1962, of which over 50 per cent arose in the District of Columbia. The largest subcategory of local cases—2750—consisted of insanity commitments; 96 per cent of these were in the District of Columbia. Second were about 1200 "motor vehicle, personal injury" claims, and third were some 466 domestic relations cases. These three together comprised over 60 per cent of all local cases in the national courts.

Approximately 35,000 criminal cases were docketed by the district courts in 1962, and a majority of these were sufficiently serious to have been based upon indictment by a grand jury. About four-fifths of the total were classified among the following eight categories: embezzlement and fraud; liquor and internal revenue; forgery and counterfeiting; auto theft; larceny; immigration; narcotics; and juvenile delinquency.

Of the approximately 35,000 criminal defendants in 1962, some 86 per cent were convicted either of the offenses with which they were charged or of lesser offenses. The highest rates of conviction were for violations of the immigration laws (96 per cent of 2349) and for forgery (94 per cent of 2887); the lowest rates were for the defendants in antitrust prosecutions (61 per cent of 114) and for defendants charged with perjury (50 per cent of 32). Of the 28,511 persons who were sentenced, half received jail terms that averaged two and two-thirds years, and 40 per cent were placed on probation; the remaining 9 per cent received fines only. Analyses of trial time indicate that antitrust and robbery cases require, on the average, about the same amount of time in court. But analyses of the types of sentence, in relation to the types of crime, suggest a consistent relationship between judicial leniency and the social status of the defendants: businessmen convicted of violations of economic regulatory legislation simply do not go to jail. None of the sixty-nine businessmen sentenced for violation of the antitrust laws were imprisoned or even put on probation, sixty-six were fined, and three received "other" punishment. Similarly, none of the businessman defendants convicted of violations of the Motor Carrier Act went to jail, although 86 per cent were fined, 11 per cent were put on probation, and 3 per cent received "other" punishment. Of the 283 bank robbers, however, 83 per cent were sentenced to five or more years in jail, and, similarly, 82 per cent of the 875 violators of the narcotics acts (other than the Marijuana Tax Act and the border registration legislation) were sent to jail for five or more years.

16   THE BUSINESS OF THE SUPREME COURT

Harvard Law Review

TABLE 1   Cases Disposed of with Full Opinion, 1961 Term[a]

	Principal Issue		Decision[b]		
	Constitutional	Other	For Gov't	Against Gov't	TOTAL
CIVIL ACTIONS FROM INFERIOR FEDERAL COURTS	6	47	21	10	53
Federal Government Litigation	0	26	20	6	26
Taxation	*0*	*5*	*4*	*1*	*5*
Review of Administration Action	*0*	*12*	*8*	*4*	*12*
Direct Enforcement of Federal Statutes	*0*	*2*	*2*	*0*	*2*
Other Actions by or against the United States or Its Officers	*0*	*7*	*6*	*1*	*7*
State Government Litigation	3	2	1	4	5
Private Litigation	3	19	—	—	22
Federal Question Jurisdiction	*0*	*18*	*—*	*—*	*18*
Diversity Jurisdiction	*3*	*1*	*—*	*—*	*4*
FEDERAL CRIMINAL CASES	2	9	4	7	11
FEDERAL *HABEAS CORPUS*	0	1	0	1	1
CIVIL ACTIONS FROM STATE COURTS	8	9	6	6	17
Federal Government Litigation	0	2	2	0	2
State or Local Government Litigation	8	2	4	6	10
Private Litigation	0	5	—	—	5
STATE CRIMINAL CASES	13	1	4	10	14
TOTAL	29	67	35	34	96

[a]This table deals with only those full opinions of the Court which dispose of cases on the merits. . . . .
[b]"Government" refers to federal, state, or local government or agency, or individual participating in the suit in an official capacity. A case is counted "for" the government if as a party it prevails in part on the principal issue. When the federal government opposes a state or local government, a decision is counted "for government" if the federal government prevails.

Reprinted by permission of the publisher from "The Supreme Court, 1961 Term," *Harvard Law Review,* LXXVI (1962), table iii. Copyright 1962 by The Harvard Law Review Association. A further breakdown of the cases into subcategories in the original table has been omitted.

17 THE APPELLATE PROCESS: A POLITICAL INTERPRETATION

Richard J. Richardson
and Kenneth N. Vines

. . .

From a political point of view, the formal norms which govern intercourt relationships are important, for they set the context in which the federal courts operate. Moreover, they set limits to the activities of the courts and prescribe important movements in the judicial process. The difficulty lies not in the use of formal terms or even in the conceptions of the formal model, but in the fact that theories implied by the use of the terms have not been explained by functional, behavioral, or even political description.

Among these formal conceptions of the process, often utilized when describing judicial politics, are such ideas as: (1) the judicial hierarchy with its assumptions concerning power and responsibility among the courts, (2) the appellate process with attendant notions concerning the flow of cases through appellate filters, and (3) appellate review with its implications of institutional authority. Since these and other elements of the judicial process are seldom pictured in interactional terms, they tell us little about power relationships within and between the courts. In turn they suggest the need for a model with a greater capability for political analysis and description.

. . .

It is our purpose to undertake an exploration of judicial activity in a systematic context, that is, through a study of some of the distinctive interactions within the system with respect to processes of review, the flow of judicial business, and the process of appeal. The pivotal point of the study is the United States Courts of Appeals, but interrelationships are extended beyond this level to the entire judicial system. We assume that the study of judicial activities properly involves several varieties of interaction. We suggest, first of all, that litigants and parties to the case interact differently among themselves and with the courts in different levels in the federal system, for example, before the courts of appeals and the district courts. Another level of interaction involves the courts as institutions and their relationships among different courts on the same level and with courts on different levels. Examples are the manner in which courts of appeals behave toward district courts and the Supreme Court, in turn, acts towards the lower courts . . . . These interactions by no means exhaust the content of the judicial system but they do represent crucial elements in its operation.

Our method involves an examination of cases decided in the United States Courts of Appeals for which we have coded both decision-making and process data. To make up our sample we have collected all civil liberties cases from the Third, Fifth, and Eighth Circuit Courts of Appeals with district court antecedents for the years 1956–61, a total of 649 cases.[1] We have chosen civil liberties cases because of their great policy interest and unusual salience in the judiciary as well as in the country at large during the '50's. Our choice of circuits was designed to include courts located in contrasting political and socioeconomic regions.[2] Finally, we determined upon cases decided in the courts of appeals as a base of analysis because of the intermediate position of the Circuit Courts, their direct relationships with both the district courts and the Supreme Court as well as their central position in the process of appeal.

[1] A "civil liberties case" is defined as one in which a claim is made under the Bill of Rights, Thirteenth, Fourteenth, and Fifteenth Amendments, or Article I, Section 9 of the Constitution (*Habeas Corpus, Ex Post Facto*, Bills of Attainder). For a modified use of this standard, see S. Sidney Ulmer, "Supreme Court Behavior and Civil Rights," *Western Political Quarterly*, XII (1960), p. 288.
[2] The Third Circuit is composed of New Jersey, Pennsylvania, Delaware and the Virgin Islands; the Fifth of Georgia, Alabama, Mississippi, Louisiana, Texas, and the Canal Zone; the Eighth of Minnesota, Iowa, Missouri, Arkansas, Nebraska, North Dakota, and South Dakota.

Reprinted with permission of authors and publisher from "Review, Dissent, and the Appellate Process: A Political Interpretation," *Journal of Politics*, XXIX (August, 1967). Some footnotes omitted and others renumbered.

I. THE APPELLATE PROCESS

Figure 1 describes the flow of cases in the federal system, using the sample of cases identified as civil liberties in the courts of appeals as the base of investigation. Other methods could be used for describing the flow of cases that emanate from the districts and tracing their course in the judicial process. Our purpose is to describe both the antecedents and the subsequent progress of civil liberties cases that were identified in the courts of appeal. Moreover, the intent is to describe the development of judicial policies rather than merely to reconstruct the history of litigation.

FIGURE 17–1   The Flow of Civil Liberties Cases in the Judicial System*

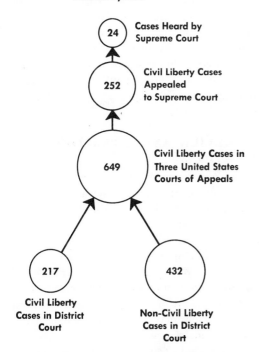

*Owing to the fact that trial cases in the district courts were often decided without written opinions, it was necessary in some instances to decide upon the civil liberties nature of the district case on the basis of case reporting in the appellate decision.

The most striking feature of our diagram is the enlargement of the civil liberties policy function at the appellate level, the emergence of a substantial civil liberties policy docket from cases whose origins were largely non-civil liberties cases in the district courts.[3] These data indicate that one of the important political functions of the appellate process in the federal courts is the metamorphosis of cases, the transformation of cases that were routine trial types in the district into cases with greater political significance as civil liberties issues. Obviously the circuit courts do not actively seek such transformations for they may hear only those cases appealed to them, in the form and with the issues that are raised by the litigants. However, the courts of appeals do provide the environment, the institutional tendencies that support such efforts, and also the structure which makes the metamorphosis possible.

The development of district trial cases into civil liberties cases in the courts of appeals may be illustrated by the following two examples. In *Reyes* v. *United States* the defendant was convicted of a narcotics violation in the district court and the judge sentenced him to less than the minimum term provided under the law. Upon learning of his error, the district judge, three days later, had the defendant brought into the court where he increased the sentence. The defendant then appealed to the court of appeals on the grounds that his constitutional rights had been violated. In a second case, *Proffer* v. *United States*, defendant was convicted in the district court of mail fraud and false and fraudulent misrepresentation in selling stocks. The defendant, who was a lawyer, had waived right to counsel. But upon conviction, he appealed to the circuit court claiming that his constitutional right to counsel during trial had been violated.

As it happened, neither of the appeals to the courts of appeals was successful. However, both cases do exemplify the process by which trials in the district courts, often involving no formal written opinion, may upon the ini-

[3]Technically, legal issues raised in a higher level of court must have been raised consistently in all prior actions or else, not raised, they are deemed waived in the case. In practice, however, there are many exceptions to this rule, especially in the area of civil liberties on such subjects as due process of law, and there seem to be few legal difficulties to obstruct the process of transforming what was a trial case at the district level, into a civil liberties case at the appellate level.

tiative of litigants become civil liberties cases in the appellate courts. Here they are heard by a collegial court, bring forth a formally written opinion, and sometimes evoke important policy decisions with significant impact.

Like the two cases described above, the district court antecedents of our sample of circuit civil liberties cases frequently had no civil liberties character in the district courts. In their district court form they evidenced little policy salience but functioned as routinized federal trials of little individual political impact. Because of their lack of policy salience and interest, such cases often do not evoke opinions from the judges.

To assume, therefore, that the appellate process is largely a "filtering" operation and to base political analysis upon this assumption is inadequate. The fact that fewer cases are heard at each higher level of the judiciary indicates that in terms of numbers alone, filtering does take place. But what escapes the formal notion of the appellate process is the fact that the cases which are appealed are often radically different in their second hearing than in their first. Often the substance of the case shifts on appeal, and while the litigants remain the same, the judicial system permits a case to undergo significant transformation as it moves within the appellate process.

At their foundation in the Judiciary Act of 1891, the intermediate appellate courts were hardly intended to perform the functions our data reveal. Created originally to shoulder the appellate burden for the Supreme Court and make it possible for that court to deal more selectively and more deliberately with appellate work, the circuit courts have also provided the seedbed where numerous important policy cases are begun and often finally decided. The circuit courts, far from simply refining and echoing the work of the district courts, have, in effect, developed into courts of first instance for large numbers of civil liberties cases. Though placed in an intermediate position in the appellate process, they both initiate and conclude many policy questions in federal litigation. Their in-between location in the judicial system belies their actual functions. . . .

Indeed, the whole array of concepts by which many civil liberties are claimed in federal appellate courts is of recent development and, at the time of the circuit courts' creation, limited possibilities existed for civil liberties litigation.[4] But certain features of the circuit courts make such development not implausible. District courts with their atmosphere of the trial courts and their roots in the parochial character of district organization and judicial recruitment, hardly provide an environment for the consideration of important constitutional issues that may grow out of litigation. Courts of appeals, on the other hand, present a collegial atmosphere that is at once less parochial in all respects than the district courts and promise more for policy modification. Finally, the norms and perceptions that grow out of civil liberties concepts present a distinctive and cogent evaluation of the way in which verdicts may be reached and the grounds upon which decisions may be based, and these decision-making norms are best appreciated at the appellate level.

II. REVIEW AND INTERCOURT RELATIONS

The nature of the appellate process, the linking of courts in any hierarchical structure, necessarily involves the act of review by a higher court of a lower court's decision. Indeed the work of the court of appeals is entirely that of inspection of other court or administrative agency decisions and that of the Supreme Court almost entirely a review function. As we have pointed out *supra,* appellate review may involve the creation and development of new policy issues in the circuit courts and the same is true in the Supreme Court; yet, it is true that a major part of the appellate work in the federal judicial process involves review of cases already decided on grounds and in forms set in a lower trial court in the districts.

Clearly, the process of review is an important potential source of conflict in the

[4]Whether the appeals courts performed similar functions in the classic judicial disputes of the 1890's and 1920's or whether this function is peculiar to civil liberties litigation of the present has not been established.

judicial system, perhaps the most important area of institutional conflict. In reviewing the cases from the lower courts the appellate judges pass on cases already decided by a judge and adjudicated often with the cachet of his written opinion, personifying his handling of the case and his judgment upon it. If an opinion is lacking from the lower court, what is at stake is the manner in which the judge conducted or allowed the case to be tried in his court. Moreover, despite some professional ties of bar and bench, district, appellate, and Supreme Court judges are recruited from different constituencies and from different political structures; their allegiances are very often to quite different support groups. Differences among the courts are also emphasized by the different ways in which business is conducted among the courts and sharpened by different institutional perspectives.

Indeed, among the many opportunities available in the judicial system for the potential eruption of conflict, that of reversing a decision by one judge over another is especially dramatic. It calls for a much more deliberate act on the part of the individual judge than would be the case when simply affirming system. It is generally, although not always, a more passive act and one which connotes less policy initiative.

In large part the sources of disagreement in the process of review are institutionalized by the manner in which statutes and judicial codes organize and outline their functions and specify the manner in which their members are recruited. What these formal arrangements do not tell us, however, is either the frequency of concurrence among the court levels as measured by the affirmation-reversal dimension or the functions that patterns of reversal or affirmation perform in the judicial process. A careful examination of review interaction among the courts is required to suggest such answers.

The significantly higher proportion of appeals courts cases reversed by the Supreme Court compared to the circuit courts' reversals of district decisions suggests that reversal is utilized in a different manner by the Supreme Court than by the lower appellate bench. Not only is it more frequently used, but the right to limit its docket by the denial of *certiorari*, suggests that those cases heard in the Supreme Court are highly susceptible to reversal. The lower appellate courts, un-

TABLE 1   Rates of Reversal—Civil Liberties Cases 1956–1961

Circuit	Percentage District Cases Reversed by Circuits (N = 177)	Percentage Appeals Courts Cases Reversed by Supreme Court (N = 16)
Third	27.5	66.7
Fifth	29.4	77.8
Eighth	21.0	00.0

the action of a colleague. It necessitates rationalizing of conflict in proper terms, discounting the arguments honored in the lower court and posing alternative values. Reversal is also an exceptional act, in that the norms of the judiciary place great value on the action of the trial judge, aware and involved as he was in the actual courtroom case. Reversal is therefore not just a disagreement; it is an exceptional assertive, expression of lack of confidence in the lower court judge. Affirmation, on the other hand, expresses support, builds consensus, and expresses the common interest of the courts in maintaining a stable legal able to control their review functions, reverse in a smaller percentage of cases simply because many cases are automatically appealed which have low potentiality for reversal, but must be heard. The relative reversal rates between Supreme-Appeals Court and appellate-district also indicate that the constituency relationships between circuit and district involve more common ground for consensus than those between Supreme Court and circuit. The remnants of parochialism which are maintained in the judicial system by the circuit courts—the fact that judges are appointed from the circuit, often with district

TABLE 2   Relation of Circuit and District Courts in Civil Liberties Cases, When Supreme Court Reversed

	Supreme Court Reversed (Number)	Percentage
When District-Circuit Agreed	13	81.3
When District-Circuit Disagreed	3	18.7

TABLE 3   Libertarian and Non-Libertarian Decisions Appealed* and Reversal Rates by Circuits

Circuit	Libertarian Decisions from Districts Appealed	Reversed	Percentage
Third	9	4	44.4
Fifth	36	11	30.6
Eighth	6	1	16.7
Circuit	Non-Libertarian Decisions Appealed	Reversed	Percentage
Third	111	29	26.1
Fifth	355	104	29.3
Eighth	132	28	21.2

*As used here a libertarian decision is one made for the civil liberty claimed; a non-libertarian decision is made against the civil liberty claimed.

court experience and values, and adjudicating in circuit boundaries drawn along state lines —make the circuit courts responsive to the district courts. However, the insulation of the Supreme Court from parochial concerns and the demands made upon it by a national constituency permit a more frequent expression of conflict with the lower courts than is found among the lower courts themselves.

Analysis of the cases reversed by the Supreme Court on appeal from the circuits also shows that the higher court is, in a greater percentage of cases, inclined to both hear and reverse those cases in which the appeals courts have affirmed the districts, rather than in those cases reversed by the appeals courts. The deliberate act of reversal by a circuit court closes the appellate process in a significant percentage of cases. The conflict expressed by a Supreme Court reversal is therefore most often directed toward lower court consensus, rather than lower court conflict, when this conflict is in the relationship between appeals court and district. The legal notion that a primary function of the Supreme Court is to arbitrate lower court conflict is not applicable to district appeals courts rela-

tions. Here, the Supreme Court intervenes more often in consensus rather than conflict situations.

The conflict which reversals reflect is more often a part of the judicial relationship in some circuits than in others. In the fifth circuit, for example, the high percentage of civil liberties cases reversed reflects the tensions existing between appellate and original courts in this sensitive area of litigation. In the Eighth Circuit, on the other hand, the civil liberties cases caused less lower court conflict than was average for the circuit's entire docket during the same time sample. Further analysis of reversal in the appellate courts confirms that a court of appeals will, when it reverses, usually reverse toward a pro-libertarian position.[5] Table 3 distributes the cases of the districts into libertarian and non-libertarian cases under review and the number of each reversed by the appellate courts.

The reversal process in the appellate courts

[5]The terms "libertarian" and "non-libertarian" are used in the study to distinguish judges and courts who hold for and against the civil liberty being claimed by the defendant.

is primarily concerned with granting liberties denied in the district courts. Constitutional, statutory, and informal provisions which limit the appealing of cases once a liberty has been granted, make the circuit courts' reversal role mainly that of liberalizing decisions handed down in the initial court.

. . .

An analysis of conflict and consensus in the judicial process, its direction and frequency, reveals important information about the role of the courts in the political system; it helps explain the political results that emanate from the judiciary and informs concerning the form and frequency with which they occur. Especially does a behavioral analysis of the judicial process yield insight into the manner in which the courts are interrelated. More than the national legislature and the administration, the members of the courts system are linked into a highly interdependent system. . . .

We find that while legal notions assume a filtering function in the appellate process, in actuality, the appellate process sometimes transforms and increases certain political issues in federal court litigation; whereas the legal notion provides substantial opportunity for appealing cases and equal opportunity for reversing them; in political reality, among the civil liberties cases primarily non-libertarian decisions are appealed and non-libertarian reversed. . . .

18 THE SUPREME COURT'S *CERTIORARI* JURISDICTION: CUE THEORY

Joseph Tanenhaus,
Marvin Schick,
Matthew Muraskin,
and Daniel Rosen

1. INTRODUCTION

. . .

Ever since the effects of the Judiciary Act [of 1925] came to be fully felt, *certiorari* has

Reprinted with permission of The Macmillan Company from *Judicial Decision-Making* by G. Schubert (ed.) Copyright © The Free Press of Glencoe, division of The Macmillan Company, 1963.

provided the bulk of the cases that go to oral argument each term [before the Supreme Court.] According to data reported by Schubert, for example, 465 cases were decided after oral argument during the 1953–1956 terms. Of these cases 76.6 per cent reached the Court via the *certiorari* route.

Certiorari petitions are of two types: those submitted *in forma pauperis*, which, since 1947, have been placed on the Miscellaneous Docket, and other (not *in forma pauperis*) petitions, which go on the Appellate Docket. Applications of both kinds are very numerous. During the 1950–1959 terms, 695 appellate docket and 571 *in forma pauperis* petitions were disposed of, on the average, per term.

Appellate docket petitions for the writ are fairly standardized in format. They are printed documents, usually 10 to 30 pages in length, that must set forth the basis for the Court's jurisdiction, frame the questions presented for review, state the facts material to a consideration of those questions, and, in the words of the late Chief Justice Vinson, "explain why it is vital that the question involved be decided finally by the Supreme Court." The opinions and judgments of the tribunals below, and any administrative agencies involved, are appended to the petitions, as well as at least one copy of the record. Respondents may counter with briefs in opposition seeking to show why *certiorari* should be denied, and petitioners may file supplementary briefs in reply. Individual copies of all these documents, with the frequent exception of copies of the record, go to each member of the Court. Most justices ask their clerks to prepare a memorandum on each application before attacking the documents themselves.

Applications *in forma pauperis* are very different in nature. Usually the petitioner submits but a single copy of a typewritten document prepared without legal assistance and without access to the complete record of his case. As a result the petitions follow no particular form, tend to contain much that is irrelevant, and omit materials essential for a thorough understanding of the facts and issues involved. When only a single copy of an application is filed, it goes to the Office of the Chief Justice. Its processing there seems to be as follows. The Chief's clerks prepare memoranda analyzing each application and send copies to every Justice. The petitions themselves tend to be circulated only if a prisoner's life is at stake or if some matter of particular interest and importance seems to be involved.

Both appellate docket and *in forma pauperis* petitions are handled in much the same way in conference. Every petition is placed on the agenda of at least one conference and will be discussed if even a single justice so desires. What makes the system manageable at all is that normally half of the appellate docket certioraris and an overwhelming majority of the *in forma pauperis* petitions receive little or no conference discussion. In fact, Chief Justice Hughes, in an effort to expedite the processing of *certiorari* applications, initiated a practice which has apparently been carried on by Chief Justices ever since. He prepared and circulated to the members of the Court before each conference a special list of petitions that in his judgment did not merit conference discussion. Only rarely did a justice exercise his right to have a petition removed from these "blacklists" and discussed.

It has long been the practice of the Court to grant *certiorari* if as many as four justices so desire. If *certiorari* is granted, the Court may either decide the case on its merits on the basis of the documents in hand, or earmark it for argument in open court.

Although applications for *certiorari* provide a large share of the cases that go to oral argument, these successful applications make up only a small proportion of the total applications for discretionary review. The Administrative Office of the United States Courts reports that 6946 appellate docket applications for *certiorari* were disposed of during the 1950–1959 terms. Of these, 15.5 per cent were granted, ranging from a low of 13.0 per cent for 1953 to a high of 16.9 per cent for 1954. Petitions *in forma pauperis* for the 10-term period were almost as numerous: 5708. Only 4.1 per cent of these petitions were granted, however, ranging from a low of

1.9 per cent for 1953 to a high of 6.9 per cent for 1959. It must be noted, moreover, that the percentages of applications granted include a goodly number that were decided without going to oral argument.

Both the importance of *certiorari* as an avenue of access to the Court and the rather small proportion of *certiorari* applications granted have been widely known for many years. It is small wonder, then, that there has been a substantial interest in the standards the Court uses in evaluating applications for the writ.

2. RULE 19*

The most important official statement of the standards used by the Court in granting or denying *certiorari* is Rule 19. This Rule has remained largely unchanged for more than three decades. Its opening sentences state:

A review on writ of certiorari is not a matter of right, but of sound judicial discretion, and will be granted only where there are special and important reasons therefor. The following, while neither controlling nor fully measuring the court's discretion, indicate the character of reasons which will be considered.

The reasons mentioned may be summarized as follows:

1. A Court of Appeals decides a point of local law in conflict with local decisions.

2. A Court of Appeals departs from or sanctions departure from the usual course of judicial proceedings.

3. A lower court ruling conflicts with a ruling of the Supreme Court.

4. A conflict in circuits exists.

5. An important question has been decided on which the Supreme Court has not yet ruled.

Other than Rule 19 there is only the group of rules on technical requirements such as format, the number of copies of documents to be submitted, and filing dates.

Analyses of the utilization of Rule 19 reveal

---

*Prior to the 1954 revision of the Court's Rules, the contents of Rule 19 were contained in Section 5 of Rule 38. For reasons of style both the old 38(5) and the new 19 will be referred to as Rule 19.

that it does not constitute a very adequate explanation of the standards the Court uses in evaluating applications for *certiorari*. The first analyses were undertaken by Frankfurter and his associates for the 1934–1936 terms.[1] Apparently these early studies had been prompted by Chief Justice Hughes' 1934 address to the American Law Institute in which he suggested that the Court would not be so deluged with frivolous petitions for the writ if lawyers paid more careful attention to the contents of the Rule. Harper made an analysis roughly similar to Frankfurter's for the 1952 Term, and we have followed suit for the 1956–1958 terms. Our data appear in Table 1. While these analyses are not comparable in all respects, because of somewhat differing methods of data collection, they do warrant a number of conclusions about the Court's employment of the Rule.

For one thing, only rarely does the Court give any reason for refusing to grant the writ. In fact, our data for these reasons for denying *certiorari* span the 1947–1958 terms. On less than 40 occasions in a systematic sample of more than 3000 unsuccessful applications for the writ during those 12 terms did the Court explain why it had denied *certiorari*. And then the most commonly offered explanation was that a petition had been dismissed on the motion of one or both parties. Another reason sometimes offered was that the application was not filed in time. It should be noted, what is more, that these are not Rule 19 explanations.

Explanatory comments in cases decided with opinion are more frequent. They appeared in about one case in three for the 1934–1936 terms and in more than 66.8 per cent of the opinions of the Court during the 1956–1958 terms. It might seem at first glance, then, that the widespread criticism

of the Court for its failure to explain why *certiorari* was granted has been extraordinarily effective. More careful analysis substantially discounts any such conclusion. For as Table 1 shows, the reason offered in 20.1 per cent of the Court's opinions for the 1956–1958 terms was simply "to decide the issue presented"—and this in reality is no different from offering no reason at all. Realistically, then, the Court gave reasons of the type mentioned in Rule 19 in only 46.7 per cent of its opinions during the 1956–1958 terms. This is, to be sure, something of an increase over the 32.4 per cent for the 1934–1936 terms. But the increase, while statistically significant at the 0.01 level of confidence ($X^2 = 11.65$), is not very impressive when one bears in mind the repeated scholarly pressures on the Court to disclose more fully its reasons for granting review.

The several analyses of the utilization of Rule 19 further disclose that the first three items on the list of five reasons summarized above are rarely cited. Only a conflict in circuits, the importance of the issue, or a combination of the two are referred to very often. Importance is cited somewhat more frequently than conflict in circuits. If one considers only cases in which Rule 19 reasons were actually given, importance alone was cited 48.5 per cent of the time during the 1935–1936 terms, 55.1 per cent during the 1952 Term, and 56.9 per cent during the 1956–1958 terms. Using this same group of cases as a universe, conflict in circuits (whether alone or in combination with other reasons) was mentioned 40.6 per cent of the time during the 1935–1936 terms, 40.0 per cent during the 1952 Term, and 40.0 per cent during the 1956–1958 terms. The increase in the frequency of Rule 19 reasons cited in more recent terms, it thus appears, is almost entirely attributable to Reason 3, "the importance of the issue."

Although importance was officially cited more frequently than any other reason, it is not of much assistance in enabling students of the Court to understand the basis of its exercise of its *certiorari* jurisdiction. This is so because the Court has sedulously avoided providing any metric for determining what is

[1] Felix Frankfurter and Henry M. Hart, Jr., "The Business of the United States Supreme Court at October Term, 1933," *Harvard Law Review*, 48 (1934), p. 262 ff. [these data are not refined enough to be of much value]; Frankfurter and Hart, "The Business of the United States Supreme Court at October Term, 1934," *Harvard Law Review*, 49 (1935), p. 83; Frankfurter and Adrian S. Fisher, "The Business of the Supreme Court at the October Terms, 1935 and 1936," *Harvard Law Review*, 51 (1938), p. 595.

TABLE 1   Reasons Offered by the Supreme Court for Granting Review in *Certiorari* Cases Decided after Oral Argument: 1956–1958 Terms*

Reason	1956 Term		1957 Term		1958 Term		Three-Term Total	
	N	Per Cent	N	Per Cent	N	Per Cent	N	Per Cent
1. None	28	31.4	43	43.9	21	23.1	92	33.1
2. To Decide Issue Presented	12	13.5	12	12.2	32	35.2	56	20.1
3. Importance of Issue	26	29.2	28	28.6	20	22.0	74	26.6
4. Importance and Circuit Conflict	13	14.6	4	4.1	5	5.5	22	7.9
5. Circuit Conflict: Actual	9	10.1	11	11.2	7	7.7	27	9.7
6. Circuit Conflict: Alleged	1	1.1	0	—	2	2.2	3	1.1
7. Conflict with Supreme Court	0	—	0	—	4	4.4	4	1.4
TOTAL	89	99.9	98	100.0	91	100.1	278	99.9

*Opinions deciding more than one case have been counted only once.

or is not important—other than that which at least four justices wish makes it so.

Conflict in circuits is another matter. There has been, it is true enough, some controversy as to whether the Court has granted *certiorari* in every case of direct conflict without exception. But there is no question but that a clear conflict in circuits usually leads to a grant of the writ. In fact universal recognition of the importance of this ground for access to the Court is reflected in the heroic efforts of skilled lawyers to work in some sort of conflict angle, however tenuous. A few terms back the Court seemed to be encouraging this practice by stretching the concept of conflict in circuits to cover sweeping ground. "Alleged conflict," "apparent conflict," and "seeming conflict" began to be cited as reasons for granting *certiorari*. But during the 1956–1958 terms such reasons were mentioned on only three occasions.

However, the most serious limitation of conflict in circuits as a satisfactory explanation for the way the Court exercises its *certiorari* jurisdiction is neither that sometimes square conflicts do not result in *certiorari*, nor that the Court sometimes stretches the concept to cover cases where the existence of direct conflict is most doubtful. Rather the most serious limitation of conflict of circuits as a key to the Court's *certiorari* behavior is that conflict is cited as a reason for granting *certiorari* in less than 20 per cent of the *certiorari* cases decided with full opinion: 14.3 per cent during the 1935–1936 terms, and 18.7 per cent during the 1956–1958 terms.

· · ·

3.   THE CUE THEORY

The theory that underlies our study . . . [w]e call . . . "the cue theory of *certiorari*." In constructing it we have proceeded from three assumptions, each of which is grounded in established knowledge. The first assumption, that Rule 19 does not provide a very satisfactory explanation for the Court's exercise of its *certiorari* jurisdiction, has already been discussed at length. . . .

Our second assumption is . . . that *certiorari* petitions are so sizable and so numerous that justices saddled with many other heavy obligations (e.g., hearing argument, attending lengthy conferences, doing necessary research, and drafting and redrafting opinions) can give no more than cursory attention to a large share of the applications for *certiorari*. . . .

Our third assumption is that a substantial

share of appellate docket petitions for *certiorari* are so frivolous as to merit no serious attention at all. Chief Justice Hughes estimated that 60 per cent of the petitions for *certiorari* were of this character. The usefulness of the earlier-mentioned "blacklists" is additional evidence of the total lack of merit in many petitions, as are statements by other members of the Court.

These three assumptions have led us to hypothesize that some method exists for separating the *certiorari* petitions requiring serious attention from those that are so frivolous as to be unworthy of careful study. We further hypothesized that a group of readily identifiable cues exists to serve this purpose. The presence of any one of these cues would warn a justice that a petition deserved scrutiny. If no cue were present, on the other hand, a justice could safely discard a petition without further expenditure of time and energy. Careful study by a justice of the petitions containing cues could then be made to determine which should be denied because of jurisdictional defects, inadequacies in the records, lack of ripeness, tactical inadvisability, etc., and which should be allotted some of the limited time available for oral argument, research, and the preparation of full opinions. Those remaining could then be disposed of by denying *certiorari* or by granting it and summarily affirming or reversing the court below.

A number of possible cues have occurred to us. These concern the parties seeking review, the reputations of the attorneys of record, the reputations of the judges who wrote the opinions below, several types of dissension (conflict in circuits, conflict in a given case within a court below, and conflict in a given case between the courts and agencies below), and subject matter. Our limited resources permitted us to assemble the data necessary for testing only some of these.

Our justification for selecting the cues we did use for testing, and the methods employed both in collecting the requisite data and in testing hypotheses about the cues, will be discussed in detail in Sections 4 and 5. . . . But in general terms our approach has been to examine lower court reports for the presence of selected cues and then determine whether the incidence of writs granted was in fact greater (to a statistically significant degree) when cues were present than when they were not.

. . .

4.   TECHNICAL PROBLEMS AND PROCEDURES

. . .

The data used in this study were drawn from the published records of the United States Supreme Court and the lower courts and administrative agencies in which the cases were litigated. No use was made of the *certiorari* documents themselves. A codebook was used in assembling the data for a systematic sample of applications for review for the 1947–1958 terms. Since both the codebook and sample were prepared for several purposes in addition to this study, something needs to be said in detail about each.

The sample was drawn as follows: Every fifth petition was coded for the ten terms 1947–1951, 1953–1955, and 1957–1958, and every petition for the two terms 1952 and 1956, with the exception of:

1. Original docket entries
2. Petitions for change of counsel, permission to submit *amicus* briefs or additional briefs and statements, postponement of consideration, etc.
3. Applications for rehearing
4. Entries on the Miscellaneous Docket other than petitions for *certiorari* carrying lower court citations

When two or more applications for review arose from a single lower court decision, each was counted separately. We should also point out that initial disposal only was coded; amended decisions and rulings were ignored.

The sampling design was established for purposes largely unrelated to this study, but the size of the sample was not. A sample as large as this one (more than 3500 cases) was deemed necessary because we were committed in this study to test with nominal data several independent variables, not all of which can be dichotomized. This meant, of course, a heavy reliance on cross-tabulation—a technique notorious for its appetite in consuming cases. In fact, the original design called for coding the 1948 Term in the same manner as the 1952 and 1956 terms, and for larger samples than one case in five from several of the other terms. However, those persistent inhibitors of overly ambitious research projects, time and money, forced us to modify our initial sampling plans.

An indication of the extent to which the sample mirrors the universe can be gained from Table 2. The differences between the sample and universe are slight and fall well within the usual limits of sampling error.

. . .

Data coded included case name and citation, docket and docket number, court immediately below and citation to it, agreement

data had been punched into IBM cards and verified, they were machine-processed for internal consistency, and the errors thereby uncovered were corrected. As a result of these measures we believe that all systematic errors that might have affected this analysis were removed. Whatever errors remain are, we think, random and do not exceed 1 per cent for any one of the variables to be used.

5. HYPOTHESES AND DATA

The cue theory of *certiorari* maintains that the justices of the Supreme Court employ cues as a means of separating those petitions worthy of scrutiny from those that may be

TABLE 2   Appellate Docket *Certiorari* Cases Disposed of during 1947–1958 Terms: Comparison of Study Sample and Actual Universe

	Granted		Denied		Total	
	N	Percentage	N	Percentage	N	Percentage
Universe	1279	15.7	6860	84.3	8139	100.0
Sample	445	16.9	2186	83.1	2631	100.0

within the court immediately below, agreement among the courts and agencies below, parties involved, mode of application for review, disposition by the Supreme Court, exceptions taken by individual justices to the Supreme Court's handling of the case, and subject matter. Several of these classifications required more than 50 mutually exclusive categories.

No difficulties were experienced in using some classifications, such as the citations, courts below, and agreement within and among lower courts. Certain others proved more troublesome. We found it necessary to expand and refine some subject matter and party categories even after hundreds of cases had been coded.

Emending the categories after coding had begun increased the danger of unreliability even though we undertook all the coding ourselves. To compensate for this danger, most of the first 1500 cases coded were subsequently checked by a second coder. In addition, all problem cases in the entire sample— about one in six—were coded at least twice, and many were coded three times. After the

discarded without further study. If the theory is valid, it should follow that:

Proposition I: Petitions that contain no cues will be denied.
Proposition II: Petitions that contain one or more cues will be studied carefully, and 25 to 43 per cent of them granted.

We estimate the percentage of petitions which contain cues and which are granted in the following manner. Previously cited statements by the members of the Court lead us to believe that 40 to 60 per cent of the appellate docket petitions have some merit, and therefore receive more or less careful attention. Since, furthermore, the Court grants the writ in 15 to 17 per cent of all appellate docket petitions, those granted should constitute from 25 per cent to 43 per cent of all meritorious *certioraris*.[2]

[2]The lower range was set by assuming that (1) only petitions containing some merit have any chance of success, (2) 15 per cent of all petitions were granted, and (3) 60 per cent of all petitions contained some merit. If x equals the percentage of cases with merit granted, and N equals the total number of petitions filed, then $15N = (0.6N)(x)$, and $x = 25.0$. The upper range was set

It hardly needs to be said that we cannot expect to find the requirements of the cue theory completely fulfilled, if only because not all the hypothesized cues have been included in our analysis. But if we have accounted for most of the major cues, these requirements should be fairly well satisfied. At the very least, we should find a sizable and statistically significant correlation between the presence of one or more cues and the granting of *certiorari*. Before this relationship can be measured, however, it is necessary to determine whether each of the several possible cues about which we have collected data can properly be regarded as a cue. One method of doing this is to take cases involving none of the hypothesized cues and compare them in turn with those cases containing a given cue but no other. If a given cue is present, the likelihood of *certiorari* should be greater (to a statistically significant degree) than when none of the cues is involved. Whenever this turns out in fact to be the case, we shall accept it as satisfactory evidence that the hypothesized cue does exist. Because the large number of petitions involved causes rather small differences to produce large *Chi* squares, we have set the confidence level necessary to accept an hypothesis at 0.001.

The hypotheses concerning the several cues we wish to test may be stated as follows:

A. *Party as a Cue.* When the federal government seeks review, but no other cue is involved, the likelihood of *certiorari* is greater (to a statistically significant degree) than when other parties seek review and no other cue is involved.

B. *Dissension as a Cue.* When dissension has been indicated among the judges of the court immediately below, or between two or more courts and agencies in a given case, but no other cue is involved, the likelihood of *certiorari* is greater (to a statistically significant degree) than when no such dissension is present and no other cue is involved.

C. *Civil Liberties Issues as Cues.* When a civil liber-

ties issue is present, but no other cue is involved, the likelihood of *certiorari* is greater (to a statistically significant degree) than when no civil liberties issue is present and no other cue is involved.

D. *Economic Issues as Cues.* When an economic issue is present, but no other cue is involved, the likelihood of review is greater (to a statistically significant degree) than when no economic issue is present and no other cue is involved.

We turn now to our reasons for selecting each of these hypotheses for testing, the procedures used in classifying the petitions, and the data we have developed.

Hypothesis A: Party as a Cue. This hypothesis finds some support in the literature. Frankfurter and Landis, in two of their early articles, observed that the Solicitor General speaks with special authority. They pointed out that during the 1929 and 1930 terms the federal government was extremely successful in having *certiorari* granted when it was appellant and denied when it was respondent. More recently Justice Harlan and the authors of a law review note made similar observations.

There are several reasons why the position of the federal government may be regarded as an important cue. For one thing, many of the persons who prepare petitions for *certiorari* are sorely lacking in the required expertise. This is decidedly not the case with the Solicitor General's staff and the other government attorneys who practice before the Court. They have the talent, the resources, and the experience fully to exploit the strong aspects of their own cases, and in reply briefs to expose the most glaring weaknesses of their opponents. We do not mean to imply that government attorneys are grossly unfair in seeking or opposing writs of *certiorari*. In fact, we place credence in the widely circulated gossip that when a clerk or justice wants to get to the nub of a complex case in a hurry he turns to the government's brief. Still, it is surely not invidious to suggest that government attorneys generally turn their assets to the government's advantage.

Another consequence of the government lawyers' expertise is its tendency to prevent them from deluging the Court with applica-

---

by assuming that (1) only petitions containing some merit have any chance of success, (2) 17 per cent of all petitions were granted, and (3) 40 per cent of all petitions contained some merit. If x equals the percentage of cases with some merit granted, and N equals the total number of petitions filed, then $17N = (0.4N) (x)$, and $x = 42.5$.

tions that they know the Court has no interest in reviewing.

Still another reason why the petitions for review submitted by the lawyers for the government tend to be meritorious is that only rarely are they under pressure to carry cases to the Court solely to satisfy a client who insists upon leaving no stone unturned in his search for vindication. Nor is the government lawyer tempted to pursue a case regardless of merit in the hope that he may gain the prestige of having argued once before the highest court in the land.

Finally, we suspect that the Court's deference for the opinions of the executive branch tends to make it especially solicitous of the government's judgment that particular cases do or do not warrant review.

The data used to test Hypothesis *A* appear in Table 3. We have included in the group of cases "federal government favors review" not only those in which the United States and its agencies and officials were petitioners, but

have been excluded from the analysis altogether.

The data reveal that when the federal government favored review and no other cue was involved the writ was issued 47.1 per cent of the time. On the other hand, when all other parties sought review, and no other cue was involved, only 5.8 per cent of the petitions were granted. Since these differences are statistically significant at the .001 level of confidence, Hypothesis *A* is confirmed. We accept these data as satisfactory evidence that party is a cue.

Hypothesis B: Dissension as a Cue. Hypothesis *B* was formulated to determine whether dissension may be regarded as a cue. By dissension we mean disagreement among the judges in the court immediately below (one or more concurring opinions, dissenting votes, or dissenting opinions) or disagreement between two or more courts and agencies in a given case. We have employed the term dissension rather than conflict to avoid any

TABLE 3   Party as a Cue

	Certiorari Granted		Certiorari Denied		Total	
	N	Percentage	N	Percentage	N	Percentage
Federal Government Favored *Certiorari*, Cue Involved	8	47.1	9	52.9	17	100.0
No Cues Involved	39	5.8	637	94.2	676	100.0
TOTAL:	47	6.8	646	93.2	693	100.0
	$\phi = +0.25$		$\chi^2 = 44.72$		$P < 0.001$	

also others if they clearly indicated that review should be granted—e.g., official declarations that review would not be opposed, and cases in which the federal government intervened on the side of the appellant. Cases involving the District of Columbia and the territories were not included unless a federal judge was a party. Cases dismissed for technical reasons, such as the petitioner withdrawing the case or mootness, and cases for which data on the parties were inadequate

possible confusion between the concept we are testing and conflict in circuits. We have not sought to test conflict in circuits, not because we do not regard it as an important cue, but because there was no systematic way to assemble the necessary data without going to the *certiorari* papers themselves. And this we were not in a position to do.

The justification for deciding to test dissension as a cue was suggested by Chief Justice Vinson when he said: "Our discretionary jurisdiction encompasses, for the most part, only the borderline cases—those in which there is a conflict among the lower courts or widespread uncertainty regarding problems of national importance." When lower court judges and quasi-judicial administrators disagree strongly enough officially to reveal their differences, petitions for *certiorari* concerned with these disagreements are, we think, bound to be studied closely by the members of the highest appellate tribunal in the land. This feeling was buttressed by an examination of the *certiorari* cases decided with full opinion during the 1947–1958 terms. At least 52 majority opinions during that period contained specific references to dissension within the court immediately below.

Table 4 contains the data used to test Hy-

er certain types of subject matter can be regarded as cues. They will be considered together.

The supposition that subject matter is a major ingredient of what the Court refers to as "important" has been made so frequently that hypothesizing it as a cue needs no special justification. In fact, much data about subject matter appear in the literature. Petitions for *certiorari* granted and denied have been classified by subject matter by Frankfurter and his associates for the 1929–1938 terms, by Harper for the 1952 Term, and by the editors of the *Harvard Law Review* for all terms since 1955.

We settled upon two subject matter groups (with four subcategories each) as the most likely to attract the interest of the justices

TABLE 4   Dissension as a Cue

	Certiorari Granted		Certiorari Denied		Total	
	N	Percentage	N	Percentage	N	Percentage
Dissension Only Cue Present	37	12.8	253	87.2	290	100.0
No Cues Involved	39	5.8	637	94.2	676	100.0
Total:	76	7.9	890	92.1	966	100.0
		$\phi = +0.12$	$\chi^2 = 13.69$	$P < 0.001$		

pothesis *B*. All appellate docket applications for *certiorari* were included, except the handful decided on the technical grounds referred to just above.

The data disclose that 12.8 per cent of the petitions in which dissension, but no other cue, was present were granted. As earlier noted, *certiorari* was granted in only 5.8 per cent of the petitions without any cue at all. While the phi coefficient shows that the correlation between the presence of dissension and the grant of *certiorari* is rather weak, these differences are significant at the .001 level of confidence, and Hypothesis *B* is confirmed. We accept these data as satisfactory evidence that dissension is a cue.

Hypotheses C and D: Civil Liberties and Economic Issues as Cues. Hypotheses *C* and *D* were formulated to determine wheth-

when scanning the mountainous piles of *certiorari* papers. In the civil liberties group we included petitions pertaining to (1) alien deportation, (2) racial discrimination, (3) military justice, and (4) miscellaneous civil liberties.[3] Our second group, economic issues, contain (5) labor, (6) regulation of economic life, (7) financial interest of the federal government, and (8) benefit and welfare legislation. Some of these categories are self-explanatory; others require a comment.

Miscellaneous civil liberties includes church-state relations, permits and licenses

[3]We decided at the outset not to include applications for review by criminal defendants in the civil liberties category even though the allegation of a deprivation of constitutional rights is usually involved. Our reason for the decision was our belief that such petitions tend to be so completely frivolous that the justices will ignore them unless some other cue is present.

for the use of the streets and parks, postal and movie censorship, state and local censorship of reading matter, loyalty oaths, problems arising from the investigations of legislative committees, disbarment proceedings, regulation of occupations and professions, picketing —free speech, and right to work litigation. The financial interest of the federal government includes excise, gift, income, and excess profit tax cases, and government contract disputes in time of peace and war. The benefit and welfare category refers to litigation concerned with civil service rights, wage statutes, the Federal Employers Liability Act, seamen and longshoremen welfare legislation, servicemen's benefits, workmen's compensation, social security legislation, tort claims, agricultural benefit regulations, and unemployment insurance. About 1 per cent of the applications for *certiorari* could not be classified with satisfactory precision because insufficient data were available. These cases have been omitted from the analysis.

Table 5 contains the data used to test the civil liberties issue hypothesis (Hypothesis *C*).

These data show that about one petition in every three containing a civil liberties cue, but no other, was granted. The differences between the treatment of the petitions with civil liberties cues and petitions without any cues are significant at the 0.001 level of confidence. Hypothesis *C* is therefore confirmed, and we accept these data as satisfactory evidence that the presence of a civil liberties issue constitutes a cue.

The data used to test Hypothesis *D* (economic issue as a cue) appear in Table 6. As the contents of this table make clear, the likelihood of review when only an economic issue is present is not much greater than when no cue at all is involved. The *Phi* coefficient shows the correlation between the presence of an economic issue and the grant of *certiorari* is only slightly positive. Nor can a *Chi* square of the magnitude attained be regarded as impressive for an N of nearly 1400 cases. Hypothesis *D* is not confirmed, and we cannot regard the presence of an economic issue as a cue.

Now that we have determined that party,

TABLE 5   Civil Liberties Issue as a Cue

	Certiorari Granted		Certiorari Denied		Total	
	N	Percentage	N	Percentage	N	Percentage
Civil Liberties Issue Only Cue Present	57	32.9	116	67.1	173	100.0
No Cues Involved	39	5.8	637	94.2	676	100.0
Total:	96	11.3	753	88.7	849	100.0
		$\phi = +0.35$	$\chi^2 = 101.46$	$P < 0.001$		

TABLE 6   Economic Issue as a Cue

	Certiorari Granted		Certiorari Denied		Total	
	N	Percentage	N	Percentage	N	Percentage
Economic Issue Only Cue Present	59	8.5	637	91.5	696	100.0
No Cues Involved	39	5.8	637	94.2	676	100.0
Total:	98	7.1	1274	92.9	1372	100.0
		$\phi = +0.05$	$\chi^2 = 4.11$	$0.05 < P < 0.01$		

dissension, and civil liberties issues are cues, we can return to the two propositions set forth. . . . We then pointed out that if the cue theory were valid, it should follow that: *(Proposition I)* petitions which contain no cue will be denied, and *(Proposition II)* petitions which contain one or more cues will be studied carefully and 25 to 43 per cent of them granted. Data giving some indication of the extent to which these propositions are satisfied by the data in our sample appear in Table 7.

further reduce the number of deviant cases not readily accounted for by the cue theory.

We feel justified in concluding, therefore, that the cue theory of *certiorari* is valid.

6. [PREDICTIONS]

. . . [W]e had no theoretical or empirical bases for hypothesizing in advance of data processing about the interrelationships among the several cues and their usefulness as predictors of what the Court will do with

TABLE 7   Petitions Containing One or More Cues and Petitions Containing No Cue Compared

	Certiorari Granted		Certiorari Denied		Total	
	N	Percentage	N	Percentage	N̄	Percentage
One or More Cues	337	27.5	889	72.5	1226	100.0
No Cues	98	7.1	1274	92.9	1372	100.0
Total:	435	16.7	2163	83.3	2598	100.0
	$\phi = +0.27$		$\chi^2 = 192.20$	$P < 0.001$		

Table 7 makes it quite evident that the requirements of *Proposition II* are satisfied. Of the petitions containing at least one cue, 27.5 per cent were granted. In addition, the petitions containing cues constituted 47.2 per cent of all appellate docket petitions. This falls within the estimate that 40 to 60 per cent of all appellate docket petitions contain some merit.

Proposition I is not fully supported, since 98 petitions containing no cues (7.1 per cent) were granted. But these 98 deviant cases do not in our judgment invalidate the cue theory, since all hypothesized cues have not been tested. Our judgment is reinforced by reading the opinions of the Court in those deviant cases decided with full opinion. In 19 instances the Court specifically pointed to a conflict in circuits, a cue we were unable to test. In one case, the Court pointed to dissents by intermediate appellate judges, and in another to the fact that the federal government did not oppose review. Still another case had civil liberties overtones which had been missed when the case was coded. More painstaking analysis would, we are convinced, still

sets of *certiorari* petitions containing given characteristics.

Insofar as the cue theory itself is concerned, the relative magnitude of the correlations between established cues and the grant or denial of *certiorari* (outcome) is of no particular consequence. All the cue theory requires is that the presence of a cue is enough to insure that a petition for *certiorari* will be studied with care. Hence, the presence of more than one cue, or for that matter the fact that one established cue may be more or less strongly correlated with outcome than another, will not alter the likelihood that a petition will be scrutinized. However, these relationships do have enough intrinsic interest to warrant analysis.

In testing Hypotheses *A*, *B*, and *C*, ϕ coefficients were computed and included in the appropriate tables. The correlation between outcome and party was $+0.25$, outcome and dissension $+0.12$, and outcome and civil liberties $+0.35$. But these correlations are not very adequate measures of the relationship between the individual cues and the outcome because cases containing more than one cue were not taken into account. A more satisfactory method for determining the magnitude of the association between outcome and any given cue, when all other cues are held constant, is to compute the portion of the variance explained by each. The portion of the variance accounted for by a given cue is obtained by multiplying the coefficient of correlation between outcome and the cue by its standard partial regression (β) coefficient.

The β's were obtained by Doolittle's method and appear, together with the data necessary for their computation, in Table 8. Since

sension and civil liberties combined, and all three cues taken together account for nearly twice as much of the variance (13.7 per cent) as party taken alone.

However, these data on the percentage of the variance explained by the three cues, independently and in combination, do not in themselves enable us to predict the likelihood of *certiorari* grants in sets of cases containing various assumed proportions of cues. Such predictions are made possible by solving the regression equation $x_1 = B_2x_2 + B_3x_3 + B_4x_4 + A$, where outcome is the dependent variable

TABLE 8   Multiple Correlation and Regression Data

		x_1	x_2	x_3	x_4
	x_1	—	0.28	0.17	0.19
	x_2	0.28	—	0.16	−0.03
Intercorrelations	x_3	0.17	0.16	—	−0.06
	x_4	0.19	−0.03	−0.06	—
		x_1	x_2	x_3	x_4
$\overline{M}$		0.176	0.076	0.401	0.116
σ		0.379	0.266	0.490	0.319

$\beta_2 = 0.264$ $B_2 = 0.375$ $A = 0.076$
$\beta_3 = 0.140$ $B_3 = 0.108$
$\beta_4 = 0.206$ $B_4 = 0.245$
$r^2 1.234 = 0.138$
$(\beta_2)(\phi12) = 0.074$
$(\beta_3)(\phi13) = 0.024$ $r 1.234 = 0.37$
$(\beta_4)(\phi14) = 0.039$

$$x_1 = 0.375x_2 + 0.108x_3 + 0.245x_4 + 0.076$$

LEGEND FOR VARIABLES

x_1 = Outcome (*certiorari* granted vs. *certiorari* denied) x_3 = Dissension
x_2 = Party (federal government favored *certiorari* vs. other cases) x_4 = Civil liberties issue

only cases for which adequate information about all three cues were available could be utilized, the number of cases used in this analysis was 2293.

As the data in Table 8 show, 7.4 per cent of the variance is explained by the party cue, 3.9 per cent by the civil liberties cue, and 2.4 per cent by the dissension cue. In our sample, therefore, party was relatively three times as important as dissension and almost twice as important as civil liberties in explaining outcome. Since the several contributions to the variance are additive, one may quickly determine the relative importance of the several cues in combination. For example, party alone was slightly more important than dis-

(x_1) and the independent variables are party (x_2), dissension (x_3) and civil liberties issues (x_4). The equation and the data used in computing it appear in Table 8.

One can now substitute any set of means desired for the independent variables in the regression equation and solve for outcome. To illustrate, if in a given set of *certiorari* petitions the federal government sought review in 75 per cent, dissension was present in 50 per cent, and civil liberties issues were involved in 40 per cent, the following substitutions would be made:

$$x_1 = 0.375 (0.75) + (0.108) (0.50) + (0.245) (0.40) + 0.076.$$

TABLE 9 Predicted Percentages of *Certiorari* Petitions That Will Be Granted When All Cases in a Set
Contain Indicated Cues

| | CUES | | Predicted Percentage of |
Party	Civil Liberties	Dissension	Certioraris to Be Granted
+	+	+	80
+	+	0	70
+	0	+	56
+	0	0	45
0	+	+	43
0	+	0	32
0	0	+	18
0	0	0	7

LEGEND

0 = Absence of a cue in all cases in set   + = Presence of a cue in all cases in set

Solving for outcome, $x_1 = 0.434$. Therefore, 43 per cent of the set of petitions will be granted.

Since our particular interest is to determine the predictive powers of the cues if every case in a set contains them in a given combination, we need to substitute 1.00 if we wish to include a cue and 0.00 if we wish to exclude it. For example, for a set in which every case contains all three cues, the following substitutions are made:

$$x_1 = (0.375)(1.00) + (0.108)(1.00)$$
$$+ (0.245)(1.00) + 0.076$$

Therefore, $x_1 = 0.804$, and 80 per cent of the petitions in the set will be granted. Similar substitutions provided the other results reported in Table 9.

We consider it important to reemphasize that the relationships discussed in Section 6, unlike those in Sections 3–5, were not hypothesized in advance of processing. As a result, we do not regard them as established, but only as useful bases for formulating hypotheses that need to be tested with fresh data. . . .

Part 3
Conversion

Once demands (input) are injected into the federal judicial system in the form of litigation and channeled to the appropriate court, the burden is on the judges to convert input to output. Conversion, to use more familiar terminology, is the decision-making stage in the processing of a case. How judges decide cases has been a topic of continuing interest for students of law. Because decision-making is also a primary concern of political science, extensive consideration of the conversion stage of the federal judicial system is given in this part.

The conversion process (or judicial decision-making) has been approached in several ways. At one time legal scholars piously repeated (and both lawyers and laymen apparently believed) that judges in an exact, completely logical, and detached manner merely *found* or *discovered* "the law." Judges, according to this theory, exercised no discretion whatsoever. They merely searched through the statutes, precedents, books by legal authorities, or documents to uncover the law. Then, by standard tools of logic and legal reasoning, they mechanically applied their findings to the case under consideration. In the twentieth century this mechanical explanation of the conversion process has been discredited. The initial attack on the mechanistic view was made by Oliver Wendell Holmes. He set the tone for the eventual development of what came to be generally known as "legal realism." In 1881 he opened his treatise on *The Common Law* with the following words which became justly famous: "The life of the law has not been logic: it has been experience. The felt necessities of the time, the prevalent moral and political theories, intuitions of public policy, even the prejudices which judges share with their fellow men, have a good deal more to do than the syllogism in determining the rules by which men should be governed."[1]

In the first decades of the twentieth century many distinguished legal scholars and judges became identified with this "realistic" approach to the judging process. Among them were Louis Brandeis, Benjamin Cardozo, Roscoe Pound, and Thomas Reed Powell. The realistic approach to judicial decision-making was given greater impetus in the 1930s by the more impassioned and radical writings of such lawyers and legal philosophers as Jerome Frank, Karl Llewellyn, and Morris and Felix Cohen.

In 1935 Felix Cohen sounded the call for "increased use of statistical methods in the scientific description and prediction of judicial behavior . . . to map the hidden springs of judicial decision and to weigh the social forces which are represented on the bench."[2] Cohen's call, for the most part, went unanswered until

---

[1]Boston: Little, Brown and Company, 1881.
[2]"Transcendental Nonsense and the Functional Approach," *Columbia Law Review*, 35 (1935), p. 833.

the late 1940s. Since then political scientists have devoted considerable attention to the conversion process. The readings in this part are devoted to various social science approaches to the central question of why judges decide cases the way they do. Using more technical systems terminology, the question becomes: How can we explain the conversion process by which inputs are converted to outputs? Most of the readings are drawn from frankly exploratory studies. Most concern the Supreme Court. This is a reflection of the fact that relatively little research attention has been given to the lower federal courts. There is also large emphasis on methodology. Some of the approaches may superficially appear inconsistent with one another. But they all attempt to delineate empirically the multifaceted nature of the conversion process within the federal judicial system. The different approaches provide one with a broad perspective of judicial decision-making as well as some inkling of the complexity and subtlety of the variables involved in the process.

A. The Social Science Approach

All the readings in Part 3 are examples of social science approaches. In the following selection, Joseph Tanenhaus presents an overview of social science techniques and how they were used before 1961 (when the article was published) to study various aspects of the judicial process as well as judicial behavior. Tanenhaus ends by briefly considering the validity of quantitative analysis of judicial decision-making.

19 SOCIAL SCIENCE METHODS IN THE STUDY OF THE JUDICIAL PROCESS

Joseph Tanenhaus

. . .

I. SOCIAL SCIENCE AND THE COURTS

"Social science methods" is a portmanteau-like term which contains whatever one chooses to stuff into it. For present purposes I take it to include a variety of devices currently in vogue among psychologists, sociologists, and political scientists—*e.g.*, mail questionnaires, systematic observation and interviewing, opinion and attitude surveys, psychological testing, and statistical, scale, game, factor, and content analyses.[1] Students of the judicial process are fairly familiar with at least some of these methods, for they have been used in one or both of the following ways: (1) to assist or influence the courts in reaching decisions, and (2) to analyze aspects of the judicial process. . . .

. . . Attention is now directed to the numerous studies in which social science techniques have been used to analyze aspects of the judicial process. The bulk of the literature may be said to fall into six categories: (1) descriptive-empirical studies; (2) studies in judicial administration; (3) sentencing behavior studies; (4) psychological studies; (5) experimental studies; and (6) studies of the voting behavior of appellate judges. These categories are admittedly somewhat arbitrary

Reprinted by permission of author and publisher from Joseph Tanenhaus, "Supreme Court Attitudes Toward Federal Administrative Agencies 1947–1956—An Application of Social Science Methods to the Study of the Judicial Process," *Vanderbilt Law Review* 14 (1961), pp. 473, 475–482. Footnotes renumbered.

[1]Convenient introductions to these techniques include: Sellitz, Jahoda, Deutsch, & Cook, *Research Methods in Social Relations* (rev. ed. 1959); Duverger, *Méthods de la Science Politique* (1959); Festinger & Katz, *Research Methods in the Behavioral Sciences* (1953); Goode & Hatt, *Methods in Social Research* (1952).

and certainly are not mutually exclusive. They have been adopted only because they give some indication of the scope and character of a literature so substantial that space precludes a comprehensive survey.

1. Descriptive-Empirical Studies. As is well known, sociological or functional jurisprudence established a firm foothold in some American law schools during the first decades of the present century. The interest of the functionalists in a more realistic appraisal of the law in action led them to undertake empirical investigations of legal institutions, personnel, and doctrine. Important early studies examined the administration of criminal justice in Cleveland[2] and in Illinois,[3] and the business of the United States Supreme Court.[4] Others, conducted under the aegis of either the Yale Law School or the ill-starred Johns Hopkins Institute of Law, attacked such diverse phenomena as divorce,[5] debtor,[6] and mayors'[7] courts, the waiver of jury trial,[8] business failures,[9] wage assignments,[10] stop payment orders on bank checks,[11] and over-all law administration in Connecticut.[12] Similar work has been carried on in more recent years. Among the later studies are Warren's volume on the traffic courts,[13] analyses by

Harper[14] of the summary actions of the United States Supreme Court and by Ewing[15] and Schmidhauser[16] of the background and training of its members, the massive survey of the legal profession undertaken for the American Bar Association,[17] the American Civil Liberties Union's probing into illegal detention practices by Chicago police,[18] and the groundbreaking effort by Cohen, Robson, and Bates[19] to determine whether certain legal doctrines square with the moral sense of Nebraskans. Materials for the descriptive-empirical category of studies were obtained by questionnaires, interviews, and the systematic culling of court records.[20] Occasionally sampling techniques and punched card equipment were employed in collecting and processing data, but only the most elementary kinds of descriptive statistics were utilized in their analysis.

2. Studies in Judicial Administration. The techniques used in studies of judicial administration are so very similar to those employed in descriptive-empirical investigations that both could be properly placed in one category. However, the volume and special character of the administrative studies entitles them to separate consideration. The primary purpose of most of these studies is to assemble the data requisite for organizing and managing judicial establishments more efficiently. Reliable information on the

---

[2]*Criminal Justice in Cleveland* (Pound and Frankfurter, eds. 1922).

[3]*The Illinois Crime Survey* (Wigmore, ed. 1929).

[4]Frankfurter & Landis, *The Business of the United States Supreme Court* (1928). See also the annual articles by Frankfurter and associates which began appearing in 38 *Harvard Law Review* (1925).

[5]Marshall & May, *The Divorce Court* (1932).

[6]Nehemkis, "The Boston Poor Debtor Court—A Study in Collection Procedure," 42 *Yale Law Journal* 561 (1933).

[7]Douglass, *The Mayors' Courts of Hamilton County, Ohio* (1933).

[8]Martin, *The Waiver of Jury Trial in Criminal Cases in Ohio* (1933).

[9]Clark, Douglas & Thomas, "The Business Failures Project—A Problem in Methodology," 39 *Yale L. J.* 1013 (1930); Douglas & Thomas, "The Business Failures Project—An Analysis of Methods of Investigation," 40 *Yale L. J.* 1034 (1931); Douglas, "Some Functional Aspects of Bankruptcy," 41 *Yale L. J.* 329 (1932).

[10]Fortas, "Wage Assignments in Chicago," 42 *Yale L. J.* 526 (1933).

[11]Moore, Sussman & Brand, "Legal and Institutional Methods Applied to Stop Payment of Checks," 42 *Yale L. J.* (pts. 1, 2) 817, 1198 (1933).

[12]Clark & Shulman, *A Study of Law Administration in Connecticut* (1937).

[13]Warren, *Traffic Courts* (1942).

[14]Harper & Leibowitz, "What the Supreme Court Did Not Do During the 1952 Term," 102 *U. Pa. L. Rev.* 427 (1954); Harper & Pratt, "What the Supreme Court Did Not Do During the 1951 Term," 101 *U. Pa. L. Rev.* 439 (1953); Harper & Etherington, "What the Supreme Court Did Not Do during the 1950 Term," 100 *U. Pa. L. Rev.* 354 (1951); Harper & Rosenthal, "What the Supreme Court Did Not Do in the 1949 Term—An Appraisal of Certiorari," 99 *U. Pa. L. Rev.* 293 (1950).

[15]Ewing, *The Judges of the Supreme Court, 1789–1937* (1938).

[16]Schmidhauser, "The Justices of the Supreme Court: A Collective Portrait," 3 *Midwest J. of Political Science* 1 (1959).

[17]Summarized, with full citations to the literature, in Blaustein & Porter, *The American Lawyer* (1954).

[18]American Civil Liberties Union (Illinois Division), *Secret Detention by the Chicago Police* (1959).

[19]Cohen, Robson, & Bates, *Parental Authority. The Community and the Law* (1958).

[20]A valuable manual for the use of trial court records was published by the Johns Hopkins Institute of Law, Marshall, *Unlocking the Treasures of the Trial Courts* (1933).

amount and kinds of litigation coming before the courts and the time needed to process it facilitate the determination of personnel requirements, equalization of work loads, revision of rules and procedures, and the utilization of available personnel in such a manner that the business of courts can be disposed more expeditiously and at reduced expense to both litigants and taxpayers. Detailed data for the federal court system have been regularly collected by the Administrative Office of the United States Courts since 1939, with a growing number of states following suit. In addition, a foundation-supported private organization, the Institute of Judicial Administration, has completed more than eighty studies, many of them quantitative, since its creation in 1952.

3. Sentencing Behavior Studies. Modern criminology has successfully contended that one of the most traditional elements of justice, equality, should be severely modified in favor of the doctrine that punishment be tailored to fit the individual rather than the crime. A variety of aids, such as past criminal histories and reports by social and psychiatric workers, is available for assisting judges in applying modern theory to concrete cases. But the feeling has been widespread that these aids have been a slighter influence than judicial idiosyncracies, that equality has been abandoned for capriciousness rather than for a more refined type of justice. As a result many studies have sought to measure disparities in sentencing behavior, to determine their causes, and to evaluate the wisdom of the sentences imposed. In some ways one of the earliest studies is still the most remarkable. For the years 1914–1930 (1917 alone excepted) data was published disclosing the number of times each New York City magistrate imposed various types of penalties for each of several kinds of offenses. These reports,[21] which cover more than two million cases, reveal both substantial disparities among the magistrates in handling identical offenses, and also striking inconsistencies in

the conduct of some magistrates. Methodologically, some sentencing behavior investigations have been more sophisticated than almost any of the studies mentioned in categories one and two. For example, the psychologist Frederick Gaudet and his associates,[22] in a study of six New Jersey Court of Common Pleas judges over a nine-year period, attempted to control statistically such variables as type of crime, length of time on the bench, imminence of reappointment, and the use of juries. Gaudet also used inferential statistics to determine the likelihood that observed differences in behavior could be accounted for by random error.

4. Psychological Studies. Expert testimony by psychologists and psychiatrists has been widely utilized in litigation, but psychological analysis of aspects of the judicial process has been far more discussed than exploited. Understandably, enough judges, unlike undergraduates, job applicants, and draftees into the armed forces, cannot be, and ought not to be, expected to submit to a battery of aptitude, achievement, and other personality tests. . . .

5. Experimental Studies. Some students of jurisprudence tend to speak of any rigorous application of social science methods as "experimental." The term is used here in a more restricted way, *i.e.*, investigations in which a deliberate effort is made to manipulate one or more independent variables. Only a few legal studies can be classified as experimental in this sense. Best known is the series of experiments undertaken in connection with the University of Chicago Jury Project.[23] Underhill Moore's parking violation experiments are

---

[21]City Magistrates' Court of New York Ann. Rep. (1915–1931).

[22]Gaudet, *Individual Differences in the Sentencing Tendencies of Judges* (1938); Gaudet, "Differences Between Judges in the Granting of Sentences of Probation," 19 *Temp. L. Q.* 471 (1946); Gaudet, Harris, & St. John, "Individual Differences in Penitentiary Sentences Given by Different Judges," 18 *J. Applied Psychology* 675 (1934); Gaudet, Harris, & St. John, "Individual Differences in the Sentencing Tendencies of Judges," 23 *J. Crim. L., C. & P. S.* 811 (1933).

[23]Broeder, "The University of Chicago Jury Project," 38 *Neb. L. Rev.* 744 (1959); Kalven, "Jury, the Law, and the Personal Injury Damage Award," 7 *U. Chi. L. S. Record* 6 (1958).

also familiar to many lawyers.[24] In addition, two other studies may be mentioned. In one,[25] recently reported, a team of several psychologists and a lawyer sought to determine the impact of the personalities of the foremen of juries on the decisions reached by their other members. The second study[26] took place more than 40 years ago. Statistics on the sentencing behavior of every New York City magistrate were published on the assumption that making these data public would pressure those magistrates whose behavior deviated most markedly from group norms into acting more in concert with their colleagues. Methodologically, it hardly needs to be pointed out, such experimental studies as those referred to are apt to be quite sophisticated, both in design and in the techniques used to analyze the data.

6. Studies of the Voting Behavior of Appellate Judges. Some studies of appellate courts have already been mentioned. The present category includes only research in which particular use was made of judicial voting records. Work of this kind began about twenty years ago when C. Herman Pritchett[27] first undertook to analyze the extent of agreement among pairs of Supreme Court justices in nonunanimous cases, the existence and functioning of blocs within the Court, and the voting patterns of the justices with respect to particular values, issues, and groups. Pritchett's methods were used with but slight modification by John P. Frank,[28] and have more recently been considerably refined by Glendon A. Schubert.[29] More intricate tech-

niques, factor,[30] game,[31] and especially scalogram analysis,[32] have also been employed for broadly similar purposes. Almost all work thus far has been confined to the Supreme Court of the United States, although there now seems to be a glimmer of interest in other appellate courts.[33]

II. THE VALIDITY OF QUANTITATIVE ANALYSIS

Unlike other studies employing social science methods to analyze aspects of the judicial process, those making use of the voting records of appellate judges have, on the whole, been harshly received. All too often the objections have not been directed at their technical soundness or the substantiality of their findings—both thoroughly appropriate grounds for criticism. Rather, disapproval has tended to take the form of broadside attacks on quantitative inquiry: "thinkers don't count, and counters don't think;" or "it is naïve or inappropriate to deal with judges as if they were bookmakers or baseball players." . . .

In the current controversy over the suitability of quantitative methods for the study of appellate court behavior, there is a tendency to overlook a rather important similarity among the majority of contenders on both sides. Most contemporary analysts of appellate court decisions, be they lower court judges, practicing lawyers, journalists, professors of law, or political scientists, tend to comb discrete decisions in a search for uniformities and inconsistencies. However much motives may vary, analysts of both schools strive to rise above the particular, to generalize about phenomena, all of which are

[24]Moore's discussion of these experiments in *My Philosophy of Law* (1941) is conveniently reprinted in Cowan, *The American Jurisprudence Reader* 189 (1956).

[25]Bevan, Albert, Loiseaux, Mayfield, & Wright, "Jury Behavior as a Function of the Prestige of the Foreman and the Nature of His Leadership," 7 *J. Pub. L.* 419 (1958).

[26]See Everson, "The Human Element in Justice," 10 *J. Crim. L., C. & P. S.* 90 (1919).

[27]Pritchett, *The Roosevelt Court: A Study in Judicial Politics and Values* (1948); *Civil Liberties and the Vinson Court* (1954).

[28]See his series of perceptive articles which appeared in Volumes 15–20 of the *University of Chicago Law Review* (1947–52).

[29]Schubert, *Quantitative Analysis of Judicial Behavior* 77–172 (1960).

[30]Thurstone & Degan, "A Factorial Study of the Supreme Court," 37 *National Academy of Science Proceedings* 628 (1951).

[31]Schubert, *op. cit. supra* note 29, at 173–267.

[32]Schubert, *op. cit. supra* note 29, at 269–376; Snyder, "The Supreme Court as a Small Group," 36 *Social Forces* 232 (1958); Bernard, "Dimensions and Axes of Supreme Court Decisions: A Study in the Sociology of Conflict," 34 *Social Forces* 19 (1955).

[33]Schubert, *op. cit. supra* note 29, at 129–142; Downing, *The U.S. Courts of Appeals and Employer Unfair Labor Practice Cases, 1936–1958* (mimeo. 1959).

in some ways unique. Utilizing the techniques it considers most apposite, each group collects and classifies data which it hopes to cast into formularies characterizing the behavior of a court and its individual members.

Fundamental though their common objectives may be, the differences between the generalizers who quantify (the quantifiers) and those who do not (the qualifiers) can hardly be put aside. Two seem presently relevant. In the first place, the quantifier tends to place greater emphasis on systematic and objective classification. He seeks to devise procedures which will permit trained analysts to come up with highly comparable results. On the other hand, the qualifier tends to feel that such striving for reliability sacrifices too much that is vital. In his view the richest ore is mined by those who devote their energies to nuances too elusive for systematic objectivity.

In the second place, the quantifier is more disposed than the qualifier to study the voting behavior of judges as distinguished from the opinions they father. To the qualifier, a judge's vote grossly oversimplifies the hard choice he is frequently obliged to make among competing principles, values, and interests. And what is more, votes are counted equally, although some decisions are obviously more important than others. How, the qualifier tends to ask, can one equate *Korematsu* v. *United States*[34] (sustaining the wartime Japanese evacuation) and *Martin* v. *City of Struthers*[35] (invalidating a city ordinance against doorbell ringing by peddlers of literature)? Though each case may have involved a fundamental freedom, *Korematsu* dealt with the physical internment of many thousands of persons, while the *Struthers* case involved only a minor inconvenience to a small group of proselytizers. A vote against the government in the evacuation case was of such vastly greater moment than a vote against the city in the doorbell case that they cannot seriously be treated as equal.

Despite these troublesome objections, the quantifier persists in his use of voting data—in part because of the relative ease in recording them in a systematic and ostensibly value-free way. But only in part. Other reasons are, I think, more important.

For one thing, since an appellate judge normally votes far more frequently than he writes opinions, his voting behavior may often be the only data available. For another thing, what a judge says in one case is not always an accurate guide to what he will do in others. Appellate courts are collegial bodies. Though they employ a division of labor in writing opinions, a majority statement is always in a sense a group product. It reflects the style and sentiments of its author, but only as tempered by necessary deference to the wishes of other members of the majority. Moreover, and this applies to concurring and dissenting opinions as well as to majority opinions, a judge may be unwilling or unable to articulate the premises on which his decision is based. Opinions, in fine, like voting records, have their limitations as data.

B. Backgrounds and Decision-Making

One approach to explaining the conversion process has focused on examining the relationship of judicial background and attribute variables to judges' decisions. The first selection by Kenneth Vines is drawn from his study of southern federal district court judges and their handling of race relations cases. The second selection by Joel Grossman contains an overview and assessment of some other research done in this area. Although Grossman's overview discusses studies of both federal and state judges, it is relevant for our purposes because the broad outlines of the conversion process are somewhat similar for both federal and higher state judges.

[34]323 U.S. 214 (1944).
[35]319 U.S. 141 (1943).

One further point should be stated. Social, emotional, intellectual, and political backgrounds are generally acknowledged to be related to the conversion process in a subtle fashion. They are the building blocks or the foundation of the judicial personality which emerges after being tempered by professional training and experience, by appreciation of political reality, and by the socialization process which occurs first as a lawyer and then as a judge. Nevertheless, background studies thus far have attempted to test directly the relationship of judicial voting to background characteristics. Although the types of cases selected for study are presumed to be able to indicate any direct effects of backgrounds on decisions, the studies thus far have not been conclusive. This is perhaps due to the fact that the effects of backgrounds are far too complex and subtle to show up in aggregate voting studies. The tracing of backgrounds may well have to proceed on an individual basis with the cumulative results providing the basis for a theory of backgrounds and the conversion process.[1]

[1]Joel Grossman has discussed in some detail an alternative research strategy for the analysis of backgrounds and conversion. See his "Social Backgrounds and Judicial Decisions: Notes for a Theory," *Journal of Politics*, **29** (1967), pp. 334–351.

20 FEDERAL DISTRICT JUDGES AND RACE RELATIONS CASES IN THE SOUTH

Kenneth N. Vines

The purpose of this paper is to explore the political activities of officials operating within a judicial environment, in a sensitive, crucial area of Southern politics. This will be done by an examination of race relations cases in Southern federal district courts.[1] The disposition of cases will be described and the distribution of decisions related to judicial districts and to deciding judges. Finally, an attempt will be made to explain the similarities and differences in the decisions. The cases exa-

Reprinted by permission of author and publisher from Kenneth N. Vines, "Federal District Judges and Race Relations Cases in the South," *Journal of Politics*, 26 (1964), pp. 338–340, 343–344, 348–357. Footnotes and tables renumbered.

[1]I am greatly indebted to the *Race Relations Law Reporter* published by the Law School at Vanderbilt University whose collection and publication of race relations cases made this study feasible. In deciding what is a "race relations" case, I have accepted the *Reporter's* definitions. I wish to acknowledge the help of the staff of the *Race Relations Law Reporter* whose generous advice and aid helped at important points in the tabulation and analysis of material.

mined will include all race relations cases decided in the federal district courts of the eleven states of the traditional South from May 1954 to October 1962. Data concerning the disposition of these cases will be used in conjunction with information on the backgrounds and experiences of Southern district judges and with certain information on the judicial districts in which the cases were decided.

Political scientists have shown that a variety of political institutions are molded by their economic and social environment and that political behavior is related to the social backgrounds and political experiences of the participants.[2] Legal theory supposes, however, that courts and judges, because of the myth of legal objectivity and the quasi-insulated position of the courts from the remainder of the political system, are not similarly influenced, except perhaps by their legal environment. Judicial analysts have frequently shown that judges do vary in their behavior but have not

[2]On the judiciary see: Herbert Jacob, "The Courts as Political Agencies," *Tulane Studies in Political Science*, Vol. 8, pp. 9–50; Stuart Nagel, "Political Party Affiliation and Judges' Decisions" *American Political Science Review*, Vol. 55 (1961), pp. 843–850, and "Ethnic Affiliations and Judicial Propensities, *Journal of Politics*, Vol. 24 (1962), pp. 92–111; John Schmidhauser, "The Justices of the Supreme Court: A Collective Portrait" *Midwest Journal of Political Science*, Vol. 3 (1959), pp. 1–57.

often attempted to explain the variations in judicial behavior. Through investigation of a homogeneous group of cases decided by judges in the context of a region with both social similarities and social differences, we have an opportunity to examine the behavior of judges against their social and political environment. Then we may see whether judges and courts are also molded by their social and political environment or whether legal theory correctly describes judicial behavior.

The analysis of cases in this paper is based upon quantitative treatment of cases rather than the more usual qualitative treatments to be found in constitutional law.[3] In constitutional law each case is treated more or less as a distinct phenomenon, related to other cases by precedent, by treatment of similar subject matters, or by legal concepts. Cases on similar subject matters often involve quite different legal formulations of the issues. Thus cases on the desegregation of the schools may involve not just the issue of whether the school should be desegregated, but whether pupil placement plans should be used, how pupil placement plans should be used, and whether states may legislate methods of avoiding school desegregation such as closing the public schools.

The quantitative treatment of cases, which considers cases as part of groups even though they may involve quite different legal statements of the issue, can be justified in political analysis. Let us consider education cases in the federal courts as an example. Even though the cases may be stated legally in quite different ways, as above, the cases are all part of a common political issue conflict. This policy conflict centers on the efforts of Negro interests in the South to secure desegregation of public schools and the attempts of white groups, private and governmental, to thwart these efforts or limit their effectiveness. Liti-

gation of the issue in terms of the conception of pupil placement does not change the basic policy conflict, since white communities have tried to use the technique of pupil placement to curtail desegregation of schools and Negro interests have objected to its use on the grounds that it slows down the process of desegregation. Hence, though legally variable, education and other race relations cases are basically similar politically.

. . .

THE DISTRICTS

An important characteristic of the federal district courts is their dispersion in different states and in different sections of the same state. Twenty-eight of the more than one hundred districts in the nation are located in the eleven states of the traditional South; each of these states is then divided into two, three, or four districts. The boundaries of federal court districts are hardly systematic, following from time to time the needs of different district case loads and the political exigencies of acts of Congress. However, sectional interests are often fortuitously embodied in some districts. For example, Tennessee is divided into an Eastern, a Middle, and a Western judicial district, corresponding roughly to important sectional differences found within that state; the division of Georgia and Alabama into Northern, Middle, and Southern districts encompasses some of the distinctive social and political characteristics of those states.

Federal district judges commonly come from the district which they serve. Not only do federal judges live in the district but in 51.3 per cent of all cases they were born in that same district. Often (in 56.1 per cent of the cases) they have attended law school in the state in which the district is located, and (in 89 per cent of the cases) they have held government positions in the state.[4] Their ties

[3]See Glendon Schubert, *Quantitative Analysis of Judicial Behavior* (New York: The Free Press, 1960). Jack W. Peltason has pioneered in calling attention to the work of the federal district courts in his books *Federal Courts in the Political Process* (1955) and *Fifty-Eight Lonely Men* (1961). The latter work should be consulted for further description of the materials covered in this paper.

[4]Biographical data on federal district judges were gathered from the files of the United States Senate Committee on the Judiciary. When not available (on occasion when the judge was appointed before 1947, the date systematic collection was begun) data were taken from *Who's Who in America*. Mr. Kenneth Casanova assisted in the collection and tabulation of the above data.

TABLE 1 Disposition of Cases by Judicial Districts

Percentage Favoring Negroes	Number of Districts
90–100	3
80–89	2
70–79	1
60–69	5
50–59	5
40–49	2
30–39	3
20–29	2
10–19	0
Below 10	5
	28

with the judicial district in which they serve are consequently deep and of long standing. Moreover, while in office, judges are required by statute to continue living in the district of appointment.[5]

. . .

It is fair to point out that certain characteristics of the district judiciary may also reduce the influence of local political values. While predominantly local influences prepare and bring the judges into office, local influences are not necessary to keep him there. Appointed for life during good behavior, the Southern district judge does not depend for tenure in office upon his success in winning office; the district judge does not have to win the Democratic primary with all the campaigning, contacts with local politicians, and interaction with Southern public opinion that are implied in competition in party primaries. Neither does the federal judge depend in the performance of his duties upon cooperation and good working relationships with local politicians and groups. The operating independence of the federal judiciary can largely insulate the judge from the effects of local and regional political values and practices if he desires it.

. . .

There is considerable variation in the way different judicial districts disposed of race relation cases, as described by Table 1. In dealing with similar political problems often stated in similar legal ways, Southern district

[5]*United States Code,* 28:134, 1958.

courts evidenced quite wide differences in their decisions. Given the differences among the districts in Negro-white population balance, we can find whether or not the two variables are related. A measure of relationship would provide one test of the proposition that courts are influenced by their social environment.

The coefficient of correlation between the two factors is $R = -.48$. That is, the proportion of Negroes in the population of Southern judicial districts is negatively related to the percentage of cases decided in favor of Negroes in the district. The higher the proportion of Negroes in a district, the less apt, at least to the extent of $R = -.48$, is the court to decide the cases in favor of Negroes.

A comparison of the degree of influence exercised by Negro-white population balance in another political situation is instructive. Matthews and Prothro have shown that in Southern counties the proportion of Negroes in the population correlates negatively, $R = -.46$, with the level of Negro registration in the county. The similarity of the correlations in the two situations indicates that a large Negro population has about the same impact on Southern federal judges in district courts as it does upon county officials in the South who register Negroes. In both instances the relationship, though of some significance, explains about twenty-two per cent of the total amount of variance. However, we may infer from the data that localism is of some influence in the district courts since Negro-white population balances affect decision-making in the district courts of the South.

THE DISTRICT JUDGES— INFLUENTIAL FACTORS

Among the 60 judges who sat in the Southern district courts on race relations cases from 1954–1962 there were 23 who participated in fewer than 3 decisions. These included judges who died or resigned during the period, those newly appointed, and some who sat in districts such as the West Texas district that simply had few race relations cases.[6] There were 37 judges who sat on 3 or more cases and among them these judges decided 267 cases. These judges are ranked in Table 2 according to disposition of cases.

cent, while seven judges who decided 60 cases attained a percentage rank of more than 80 per cent in deciding cases favorably towards Negroes.

The extreme differences among the judges in the disposition of race relations cases can be indicated by the fact that there were seven judges who handled 43 cases and who decided no cases in favor of Negroes; but there were four who handled 35 cases and who decided more than 90 per cent of the time for the Negro litigants. We may conclude from this description that the average performance is made up, in part, of extreme pro-Negro decision records in combination with extreme anti-Negro decision records.

Ranked according to the disposition of cases

TABLE 2   Disposition of Cases by Active District Judges

Per Cent of Cases Favorable for Negroes	Number of Judges	Number of Cases Decided by Judges in Each Category
90–100	4	35
80–89	3	25
70–79	0	0
60–69	12	85
50–59	1	4
40–49	2	12
30–39	3	25
20–29	3	19
10–19	2	19
0–9	7	43
	37	267

The 37 judges who were active in the decision of race relations cases reacted to them with varying degrees of favor toward the Negroes involved, as Table 2 shows. There is no outstanding mode which locates a large proportion of judges. Only 18 judges, or about half of them, decided cases in the large middle range of 30 to 79 per cent. Moreover, significant groups may be found at both extreme ends of the distribution. Nine judges who decided 62 cases ranked less than 20 per

[6]One judge, Ronald N. Davies, was sitting temporarily in Little Rock from his regular district in South Dakota. This is the only instance of the participation of a non-Southern judge.

for and against Negroes, the judges fall into three groups: the first group we may call the "Segregationists," and they decided in favor of Negroes in less than one-third of the cases; the second group who decided in favor of Negroes in 34–67 per cent of all cases handled, we call the "Moderates"; the third group whose record in favor of Negro claimants was better than 67 per cent of all cases, we call the "Integrationists." These terms are doubtless not an accurate description of the judicial philosophies of the respective groups, but they can serve as identifications for the three groups and as rough indicators of their roles in Southern politics.

TABLE 3 Relationship of Percent of Cases Decided in Favor of Negroes to the Percentage of Negroes in District of Judge

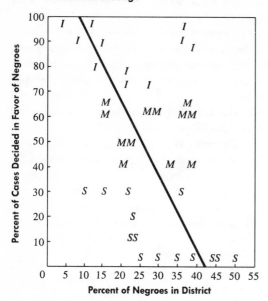

I = Integrationists, M = Moderates, and S = Segregationists

One possibility of the difference among the three groups is that the different policy positions can be explained by reference to the kinds of districts they serve. Thus, those judges from the deep South where Negro populations are proportionately large might be expected to regard Negro interests less favorably than those judges in the hills and mountains outside the black belt areas where there are comparatively few Negroes. Table 3 indicates the differences among the three groups; the Integrationists hear cases in districts which have somewhat fewer Negroes than the two others while Segregationist judges have more Negroes in their districts. Although there is some relationship as indicated by the estimated line of regression, there are some clearly exogenous cases.

The factor of Negro-white population balance, we have seen, has limited explanatory power in accounting for the differences in the disposition of cases within the various districts. For further information on the factors associated with the differential judicial behavior, we may turn to the judges themselves, their backgrounds and experiences. Some studies of judicial behavior in various courts have indicated that judicial behavior is related to the social backgrounds and political experiences of the judges. The general thesis in all these studies is that social and political factors are related to judicial behavior in much the same fashion that social and political characteristics are related to the political behavior of voters and nonjudicial policymakers.

One way in which the personnel of Southern federal courts differ from other Southern politicians is in the larger number of Republicans on the district courts. Of the 37 judges in the three groups, 15 or 40.1 per cent are Republicans. Officeholders who must seek office through popular elections can rarely be identified as Republicans in the South and still win election. For appointments to the Southern judiciary, however, Republican presidents generally seek out Southern Republicans. Because of the appointments of both Republican and Democratic presidents the Southern district judiciary contains judges of both Republican and Democratic affiliation. Historically, the Democratic party in the South has been identified with the maintenance of segregation and white supremacy, while the Southern Republican party has a tradition of a more permissive attitude in race relations. Consequently, we might wonder whether judicial behavior in the South is related to partisan affiliation.

The figures in Table 4 indicate that the

TABLE 4 Party Affiliations of Three Groups of Southern Judges*

Affiliation	Segregationists	Moderates	Integrationists
Democratic	78.6%	50.0%	45.4%
Republican	21.4	50.0	54.6
	100.0 (*N*=14)	100.0 (*N*=12)	100.0 (*N*=11)

* X^2 indicates marginal significance at .08 level.

Republican judges are located disproportionately among the Moderates and Integrationists, half of whose members are Republicans. Only 3 out of 14, or 21.4 per cent of the Segregationist judges, are Republicans. Republican candidates in the South today are often as enthusiastically in favor of segregation and as racially demagogic as their Democratic opponents. Yet, there is some evidence here that the traditions of the Southern Republican party still have some impact upon political behavior. The relative isolation of Southern Republicans may also contribute to their more permissive attitude toward Negroes in race relations cases. Even if active and politically involved, Southern Republicans are apt to have fewer occasions to seek state political office, to attend regional political meetings, and publicly to defend Southern political

values. The political roles which result in white supremacy among the Democratic office seekers and party workers are often lacking in the more restricted political lives of Southern Republicans. A further possible explanation may be found in the character of the Republican judges appointed by Eisenhower. Not restricted by senatorial courtesy, the President was able to appoint with relative freedom and his appointments include the "new" Republicans with urban backgrounds.

The Judges' relationships to their districts, states, and the Southern region is investigated in Tables 5, 6, and 7.

Southern judges like other federal judges, we see in Table 5, tend to be born in the district they serve. A similar number of Integrationists and Segregationists hold court in the same district in which they were born. Few

TABLE 5   Place of Birth of Southern Judges*

Place of Birth	Segregationists	Moderates	Integrationists
In His District	64.3%	50.0%	63.6%
In His State but Not District	7.1	8.3	9.1
Other Southern State	0.0	8.3	9.1
Outside South	14.3	25.0	9.1
Don't Know	14.3	8.4	9.1
	100.0% ($N=14$)	100.0% ($N=12$)	100.0% ($N=11$)

* X^2 indicates relationship not significant.

TABLE 6   Location of Law School of Southern Judges*

Location of Law School	Segregationists	Moderates	Integrationists
South	71.4%	50.0%	63.6%
Border State	28.6	16.7	0.0
Outside South	0.0	8.3	18.2
Don't Know	0.0	25.0	18.2
	100.0% ($N=14$)	100.0% ($N=12$)	100.0% ($N=11$)

* X^2 indicates relationship not significant.

TABLE 7   Location of Law Practice of Southern Judges*

Location of Law Practice	Segregationists	Moderates	Integrationists
In State of District	85.8%	58.3%	81.8%
In Other State	7.1	25.0	9.1
No Practice Listed	7.1	16.7	9.1
	100.0% ($N=14$)	100.0% ($N=12$)	100.0% ($N=11$)

* X^2 indicates relationship not significant.

of any group were born outside the Southern region although a slightly greater number of Moderates had non-Southern birth places.

The local attachments of Southern judges are strengthened in their training and practice of the law. While there is a common core of values and practices in legal training wherever it is taught in the United States, state and regional law schools and particularly state universities have strong ties with the state political system. Lawyers who practice in one state meet only the political values of that state, contact only local politicians, and gain practice only in the political process of that state. On the other hand, lawyers who have gone to law school outside the state or region of their association, receive training in other political symbols and meet a different set of political values. Lawyers who practice in more than one state have an opportunity for contact with several state political structures; they meet different kinds of litigants and may gain a more cosmopolitan perception of law and political life.

Southern judges have had, as a group, few opportunities for such cosmopolitan development in their legal training and practice, as shown in Tables 6 and 7. The legal development of Southern judges has taken place within the framework of the Southern political system and very largely within the state containing the district of their appointment. Moreover, there are few significant differences

have practiced outside the state of their court district more often (25.0 per cent compared to 7.1 per cent and 9.1 per cent). The Integrationists have attended non-Southern law schools slightly more often (18.2 per cent compared to 0.0 per cent and 8.3 per cent). But these differences are not remarkable and the fact remains that Southern judges have received their professional training and experiences very largely within the locality of the court over which they preside.

Religious affiliation, while it cannot be considered of great significance in itself, may provide a clue to the relationship of the judge to the Southern social structure. Very largely (except in quite restricted areas such as Southern Louisiana), Southern society is Protestant and orthodox. The Protestant church, far from providing an exception to the structure of a segregated society, remains an almost totally segregated institution and must be regarded as one of the important institutional supports of traditional Southern values.

The data in Table 8 indicate that there are significant differences among the groups of judges on the matter of religious affiliation. Only about one-third of the Integrationists list orthodox Protestant religions (36.4 per cent) while two-thirds or more of the Moderates (66.7 per cent) and the Segregationists (71.4 per cent) list such religion. The few Catholic judges are found among the Integrationists and almost half of the Integration-

TABLE 8   Religious Affiliation of Groups of Southern Judges*

Religious Affiliation	Segregationists	Moderates	Integrationists
Orthodox Protestant	71.4%	66.7%	36.4%
Catholic	0.0	0.0	18.2
None Listed	21.4	25.0	45.4
Don't Know	7.2	8.3	0.0
	100.0% $(N=14)$	100.0% $(N=12)$	100.0% $(N=11)$

* X^2 indicates significance at .05 level.

among the group of judges. The Moderates have undergone slightly more broadening experiences than the two other groups. The Moderates have attended law schools in the South less frequently (50.0 per cent compared to 71.4 per cent and 63.6 per cent) and

ists (45.4 per cent) list no religion. We may speculate that the non-affiliation of the Integrationists with orthodox Protestant religions provides suggestive evidence that these judges are not closely related to the conventional social structure; this may be one of the sources of their unorthodox conduct of race relations cases.

The path to the district judiciary in the South, as Table 9 shows, has often involved holding public office. Experience in public office has been important in the careers of judges in all three groups, but there are some important differences in the types of experiences. No office, federal or state, judicial or non-judicial, has dominated the political experiences of all three groups with uniform frequency. While close to one-half of the Segregationists (57.1 per cent) and the Moderates (41.7 per cent) have held state office, only 9.1 per cent of the Integrationists have. Federal offices have been occupied by nearly half the Segregationists (42.9 per cent) and the Integrationists (45.5 per cent) but by only 8.4 per cent of the Moderates.

Looking at the variation in the types of offices[7] held by the three groups, we may

attorney or assistant district attorney, the judicial candidate prosecutes cases involving various national political values, meets numerous kinds of litigants and serves in many political situations. Such experiences might be expected to broaden the outlook of prospective judges inducing respect for national values when these conflict with regional ones. However, federal political experience is apparently not enough, by itself, to accomplish this.

Tenure in a state political position, on the other hand, could strengthen the identification of the judge with Southern norms. As a legislator, state administrator, or state judge, he is often called upon to enact or enforce policies which implement the Southern point of view and sometimes to defend these values against what is called federal encroachment. Moreover, in seeking office, regional symbols may be invoked, or at least, paid lip service.

TABLE 9*   **Previous Public Offices Held by Southern Judges****

Public Office	Segregationists (N=14)	Moderates (N=12)	Integrationists (N=11)
State Political Office	57.1%	41.7%	9.1%
Federal Political Office	42.9	8.4	45.5
State Judicial Office	50.0	33.3	9.1
Federal Judicial Office	28.6	8.4	45.5
State and Local Judgeship	35.7	33.3	0.0

*Columns do not add up to 100.0 per cent because some judges held more than one office.

** X^2 indicates significance at .01 level.

advance some suggestions concerning the relationship between political experience on the way to the bench and judicial behavior. Since about half of both the Segregationists and the Integrationists held federal office before coming to the court, we may conclude that political experiences gained in the services of the federal government do not function as an educational experience for the judge steeped in the values of Southern society. As a district

[7]State judicial offices include all state and local judgeships and state and local court officers such as sheriffs, and state district attorneys. Federal judicial offices include all federal law enforcement officials. State political offices include state and local legislative posts and executive and administrative positions, while federal political positions include federal legislative and administrative posts of a non-judicial character.

The difference between Segregationist and Integrationist judges here is striking. Well over half the Segregationists (57.1 per cent) have held state political office while only 9.1 per cent of the Integrationists or less than one-tenth have held state office.

The Segregationist group is clearly distinguished from the Integrationist group by prejudicial experiences in state government. Both in policy making and campaigning the Southern state officeholder can rarely remain indifferent to the issues involving the political and social position of the Negro. The frequency with which Segregationist judges have held state office suggests that state political experience corroborates Southern values. Integrationists, on the other hand, have seldom held state political positions. When they have held public office, it has been a federal one and in all cases also a federal judicial office. Here the service of judicial candidates as federal attorneys, when not combined with office-holding in the state political structure, seems to have marked out many members of the Integrationist group for deviation from traditional Southern values. It is important that the future judge has not undergone commitment to the state political system. Not identified with the state political system the judge may be more sympathetic toward national values and less sympathetic toward Southern state efforts to resist federal policies.

When the district judge has been a state judge before his ascent, his objectivity does not seem to be strengthened. About one-third of both the Segregationists (35.7 per cent) and the Moderates (33.3 per cent) have been judges but none of the Integrationists. We tend to associate dispassionate behavior with judges because of the security and insulation of their position in the political structure. However, the judges of most Southern states are elected. They must seek reelection, they must undergo campaigns and secure nominations from political parties, and they must maintain good relationships with the rest of the state political structure. State judges, far from an insulated isolation from state politics, must master the technique and the symbols of the state political system to obtain and to retain office. As a state judge, the future district judge may be called upon to handle cases involving race relations. In his behavior the judge must be constantly wary, like all elected Southern officials, of the effects of his actions upon his chances for reelection. Usually the safe course of behavior for the elected Southern official is adherence to the traditional Southern norms in political situations involving race relations. Considering these aspects of the role of state judges, we could hardly expect experience gained on the state bench to train Southern officials toward greater objectivity in race relations cases.

CONCLUSIONS

The judicial behavior of district judges was . . . examined in the context of the judges' social and political backgrounds. Few differences were found in the location of births, legal training, or law practices of different judges. All were about equally tied to the region by their pre-judicial experiences. In connection with the social and political structures, however, significant differences were discovered among judges, grouped by their disposition of cases. Segregationist judges were more closely linked to the Southern social system, as measured by religious affiliations, and to the political structures by their more frequent experiences in state government. Integrationist judges had few experiences in government, and what experiences they had were in federal officeholding.

Construed broadly, linkages with the local social and political system can be considered a variety of localism. From this viewpoint we can say that Southern district courts are influenced by local factors: pro-Negro decisions in the courts are negatively correlated to the proportion of Negroes in the districts' population, and district judges are more apt to hold against Negro litigants if these judges have experiences in their backgrounds tying them to the social and political structure of Southern states.

The evidence points to the conclusion that Southern federal judges in district courts are influenced by their social and political environment. In this they join other Southern politicians, state legislators, Congressmen, and state executives, who also respond to local factors. To this extent, we can say that judges, though ostensibly "different," react to environmental factors like other policy makers. We do not exclude the possibility of the influence of the legal environment upon the behavior of judges, but suggest that if legalistic influences are operative, they must be considered along with social and political factors.

21 SOCIAL BACKGROUNDS AND JUDICIAL DECISION-MAKING

Joel B. Grossman

Legal scholars and social scientists, having long since disabused themselves of the aesthetically pleasing but inaccurate view of the appellate judge's task as primarily mechanical and syllogistic,[1] are still seeking answers to the elusive question: to what extent is a judge a creature or a captive of personal values and attitudes developed during his pre-judicial experiences? If it can be assumed that the task of judging—particularly on the Supreme Court of the United States—involves some very practical choices between policy alternatives, and if it can be further assumed that no judge derives all his premises from the courtroom, the sources of these "other" premises and the manner in which they affect the mix of personal and institutional factors which constitute the judicial function must yet be ascertained.

Assessing the role of personal values and experiences in judicial decisions is particularly difficult because of norms which prevent judges from openly casting their decisions in such terms.[2] Yet the inescapable conclusion that judicial decisions—and particularly constitutional law decisions—are at least partially attributable to the personal values and experiences of the judges impels a search beyond mere surface observations.[3]

Efforts to understand and explain judicial behavior in the light of the social backgrounds and experiences of the judges have been a staple of traditional descriptive and biographical studies, but it is only in the past decade that more systematic and theoretically oriented explorations have taken place. While sharing with traditional studies the judicial realists' assumptions about the dynamics of the judicial function, these explorations differ substantially in other respects. They are more concerned with general behavior patterns than with discrete actions or events and therefore tend to focus on properties of behavior which are amenable to generalization —for example, on judges' votes rather than on their opinions. They rely on methods of inquiry which assume that a useful way to examine judicial behavior is to consider the judge not as sui generis, but rather as a variety of *homo politicus*. Such a perspective is not to be confused with the exaggerated notion that judges are *no* different from other political actors.[4] It has the advantage, however, of permitting observations about judicial behavior to be integrated into broader-based studies of human behavior and legal-political institutions.

All research must be understood and interpreted in the light of the organizing principles to which it subscribes. The ultimate goals of social science involve the construction of sophisticated theories of human behavior, in which judicial processes occupy a small but important part. Such theories emphasize systematic formulations of empirical data and place a high premium on generalization and prediction. It may be, as Schubert suggests, that "the power of any science lies in its capacity to make successful predictions."[5] But successful prediction alone is not what distinguishes scientific endeavor. Scholars and ordinary people are constantly making

Reprinted by permission of publisher from Joel B. Grossman, "Social Backgrounds and Judicial Decision-Making," *Harvard Law Review*, 79 (1966), pp. 1551–1564. Copyright © 1966 by the Harvard Law Review Association.

[1]See, *e.g.*, Cardozo, *The Nature of the Judicial Process* (1921); Frank, *Law and the Modern Mind* (1930); Holmes, "The Path of the Law," 10 *Harvard Law Review* 457 (1897).

[2]One famous exception is Justice Frankfurter's denial that his Jewish immigrant background should result in a contrary vote. *West Virginia State Bd. of Educ.* v. *Barnette*, 319 U.S. 624, 646–647 (1943) (dissenting opinion).

[3]*Cf.* Haines, "General Observations on the Effects of Personal, Political, and Economic Influences in the Decisions of Judges," 17 *Ill. L. Rev.* 96 (1922).

[4]*Cf.* Frank, *Courts on Trial* 254 (1949); Frankfurter, "The Judicial Process and the Supreme Court," 98 *Proceedings of the American Philosophical Society* 233 (1954).

[5]Schubert, "Judicial Attitudes and Voting Behavior: The 1961 Term of the United States Supreme Court," 28 *Law & Contemp. Prob.* 100, 102 (1963). The goal of predictability for "reckoning" is also discussed in Llewellyn, *The Common Law Tradition—Deciding Appeals* 11–18 (1960).

predictions—some with greater success than others.[6] The scientist seeks prediction based objectively on the measurement of relationships of observed data; to most people, and often to scientists as well, prediction is intuitive and based on less than complete data. It is this goal of more objectivity and increased reliability of prediction and inference which supplies the major motivation for much of the work described below.

II

Both historically and analytically, attempts to relate social backgrounds to judicial decisions have fallen into three distinct categories. The first, primarily descriptive, involves the systematic collection and organization of a variety of background data. Practically speaking, this means gathering such information about each judge in the sample as age, ethnic and religious affiliations, parental occupations, career patterns, prior judicial office, party affiliation, education, and so forth—the number of factors being limited only by the availability of data or the imagination of the researcher.

Studies of this kind date back to the 1930's, but the most recent and influential has been John Schmidhauser's "Collective Portrait" of the Justices of the Supreme Court.[7] Published in 1959, this study provided the most detailed analysis of the backgrounds of the Justices ever assembled, served to demonstrate clearly the upper middle class bias of judicial recruitment patterns, and stimulated a host of similar inquiries. In addition to identifying patterns of selections shedding considerable light on the judicial selection process, such implications also provide the basis for plausible, though unsystematic, inferences about the sorts of values likely to

dominate a court in a particular period.[8] Furthermore, such efforts illuminate one way in which power and status are distributed among various groups and interests in society—what Krislov has called the "representational question."[9]

The second category involves attempts to relate these background characteristics to actual decision patterns, measuring the degree to which a particular characteristic is regularly associated with a particular type of decision. Of the many studies in this category, those by Nagel,[10] Schmidhauser,[11] Goldman,[12] Sprague,[13] and Danelski[14] have been chosen for specific attention. Though these studies differ somewhat in research design and results, all share certain basic theoretical assumptions. First, they all accept the "dynamic" view of the judicial function outlined in the first section. Second, they all accept the utility—for research purposes—of abstracting a single item, or variable, from a complex process and treating it in isolation. This leads to what may seem to be a contrary and overly simplistic view of the sources and motivations of judicial behavior—almost akin to mechanical jurisprudence. But all these scholars recognize—to differing degrees and in differing weights—the importance of institutional factors in accounting for particular decisions or groups of decisions. None suggests, except in the abstract, that any particular back-

---

[6]Legal scholars frequently attempt to predict judicial actions. Fred Rodell correctly forecast the results and the votes of seven of eight justices participating in *Baker v. Carr.* Rodell, "For Every Justice, Judicial Deference Is a Sometime Thing," 50 *Geo. L. J.* 700 (1962).

[7]Schmidhauser, "The Justices of the Supreme Court: A Collective Portrait," 3 *Midwest J. of Political Science* 1 (1959). For examples of earlier studies see Ewing, *The Judges of the Supreme Court, 1789–1937: A Study of Their Qualifications* (1938); Mott, Albright, & Semmerling, "Judicial Personnel," 167 *Annals of the American Academy of Political and Social Science* 143 (1933).

[8]*Cf.* Grossman, *Lawyers and Judges—The ABA and the Politics of Judicial Selection* 196–207 (1965).

[9]Krislov, *The Supreme Court in the Political Process* 30 (1965).

[10]Nagel, "Political Party Affiliation and Judges' Decisions," 55 *Am. Pol. Sci. Rev.* 843 (1961); "Testing Relations between Judicial Characteristics and Judicial Decision-Making," 15 *Western Pol. Q.* 425 (1962); "Ethnic Affiliations and Judicial Propensities," 24 *J. of Politics* 92 (1962); "Judicial Backgrounds and Criminal Cases," 53 *J. Crim. L., C. & P.S.* 333 (1962).

[11]Schmidhauser, "Judicial Behavior and the Sectional Crisis of 1837–1860," 23 *J. of Politics* 615 (1961); "Stare Decisis, Dissent, and the Background of the Justices of the Supreme Court of the United States," 14 *U. of Toronto L. J.* 194 (1962).

[12]Goldman, *Politics, Judges, and the Administration of Justice,* unpublished Ph.D. dissertation, Harvard University, 1965.

[13]Sprague, *Voting Patterns on the United States Supreme Court: Cases in Federalism, 1889–1959,* unpublished Ph.D. dissertation, Stanford University, 1964.

[14]Danelski, *A Supreme Court Justice Is Appointed* (1964).

ground variable "accounts" for certain types of decisions. All reject theories of causality which seem to establish a direct dependent relationship between a background variable and a line of cases. Rather, they argue that evidence of a highly significant statistical relationship[15] between a background variable and a decisional pattern is both relative and associational. For example, though all but Danelski treat political party affiliation as a major independent variable, none suggests that for a judge to have been a Republican or a Democrat automatically results in certain types of decisions. They do suggest that, when placed on a continuum, Democratic judges are more likely to vote in certain ways than Republican judges in certain types of cases. Finally, with the single exception of Danelski, all operate solely with aggregates of judges and cases; they are interested in generalized patterns of association, rather than in discrete individual actions.

These studies also share some methodological techniques. Regardless of the type or level of court being studied, unanimous decisions are eliminated from all samples. While this emphasis on intracourt division certainly introduces an element of bias, particularly since the majority of all cases are decided unanimously,[16] there is no way of including unanimous cases when *comparing* judges. The mere fact that most judges on most courts tend to agree most of the time tells us something about the common process of condition-

ing and socialization that they undergo and further serves to caution us against placing undue emphasis on the differences among them. But whatever correctives are needed can properly be postponed until we have adequately understood the reasons for patterns of division. In addition, all these authors assume, for purposes of analysis, a simplistic stimulus-response model of judicial behavior: the case is pictured as presenting a clear and uniform stimulus to all judges on a particular court, the judges' votes constitute the primary response, and the background characteristic being tested is the major intervening variable. In fact, of course, all of the judges hearing a particular case may perceive it differently, and their responses may be distillations of complex factors. But techniques of analysis are still too crude to permit the more refined models which would properly account for this complexity.

Nagel's study involved an analysis of the decisional propensities of a sample of the Justices of the United States Supreme Court and state courts of last resort—the sample consisting of the 298 judges listed in the 1955 *Directory of American Judges* who were still serving at the close of 1955.[17] Limiting himself to those courts on which there was at least one member of each party, Nagel analyzed all the 1955 cases for each court in fifteen areas of law, determining decisional propensities for each court and decisional scores for each judge. Hypothetically, if the Ames Supreme Court decided 10 of 21 criminal cases for the defendant, and Judge A, a Republican, voted 3 times for the defendant, he would have a decisional score of 3/21 or .14, considerably below the court's mean defendant-support score of .48. If the decisional scores of Republicans on that court were generally in the .14–.40 range, while the scores of Democrats were in the .50–.80 range, Nagel would conclude that there was a strong and possibly significant relationship between party affiliation and propensity to decide for the defendant in criminal cases.[18]

---

[15]"Statistical significance" is a technical term, not to be confused with "importance" or "validity." To say that a finding is statistically significant at the ".05" level means that the finding would not have occurred by chance more than five times in a hundred. As a matter of convention, a finding which has a random probability of less than .05 is described as "statistically significant."

[16]Goldman found that the rate of division on the courts of appeals varied by circuit, from 2.8% to 15.5% over a three-year period. See Goldman, *supra* note 12, at 191. Unanimous decisions of the United States Supreme Court constitute a much smaller proportion of that Court's decisions. In all cases involving federalism questions from 1910 to 1959, the percentages of divided cases, by decades, were 15, 21, 26, 53, and 56. See Sprague, *supra* note 13, at 78. In the cases decided in its 1964 term, the Supreme Court divided in 61.4% of its full opinion cases and 29.3% of its memorandum orders. See "The Supreme Court, 1964 Term," 79 *Harv. L. Rev.* 103, 109 (1965).

[17]Nagel, "Political Party Affiliation and Judges' Decisions," 55 *Am. Pol. Sci. Rev.* 843 (1961).

[18]*Id.* at 845.

Nagel's findings showed that "in all 15 types of cases the Democratic judges were above the average decision scores of their respective courts (in what might be considered a liberal direction) to a greater extent than the Republican judges."[19] Nagel found that Democratic judges were more prone to favor (1) the defense in criminal cases, (2) administrative agencies in business regulation cases, (3) the private party in cases involving regulation of nonbusiness entities, (4) the claimant in unemployment compensation cases, (5) the libertarian position in free speech cases, (6) the finding of a constitutional violation in criminal cases, (7) the government in tax cases, (8) the divorce seeker in divorce cases, (9) the wife in divorce settlement cases, (10) the tenant in landlord-tenant disputes, (11) the labor union in union-management cases, (12) the debtor in debt collection cases, (13) the consumer in sales of goods cases, (14) the injured party in motor vehicle accident cases, and (15) the employee in employee injury cases. Nine of these findings (1, 2, 4, 6, 7, 10, 13, 14, and 15) proved to be statistically significant relationships.

Nagel concluded that, in these areas of decision, Democratic judges were *more likely than* Republican judges to support the designated liberal position, a result consistent with the findings of Schubert,[20] Ulmer,[21] and Vines,[22] and, in part, with the findings of Goldman and Bowen reported below. Similar policy differences between Democrats and Republicans have been found to exist among Congressmen and the electorate.[23] Nagel did not suggest a "party-line" theory of judicial decision-making but rather that the same factors which resulted in party identification also resulted in more or less liberal decisions, with party affiliation operating as a "feedback reinforcement."[24] In parallel studies, Nagel found that judges who had been public prosecutors, members of the American Bar Association, or Protestants took the "Republican" position more often and were less likely to support the defendant in criminal cases than their brethren, findings which are clearly consistent with existing data on the backgrounds of identifiers with each party.[25]

Schmidhauser's studies focus exclusively on United States Supreme Court Justices. In one study, he examined the relationships of regional backgrounds to the decision in 52 major cases involving "sectional rivalry" between 1837 and 1860. Did the Justices "consistently split on regional lines despite other possibly compelling factors such as attitudes toward national supremacy, the integrity of the judicial institution, or the position of their political parties?"[26] Relying primarily on the technique of scalogram analysis, Schmidhauser was able to isolate regional divisions in the voting patterns and hypothesize that (1) among Justices who took extreme positions, party and sectional background both seemed to strengthen underlying attitudes toward regionally divisive issues, and (2) among moderate and neutral judges, party frequently proved stronger than regional background.

In a second study, Schmidhauser sought to test the *a priori* assertion that prior judicial experience was positively related to judicial restraint, particularly to a strong adherence to *stare decisis*. Focusing on the 81 decisions

---

[19] *Ibid.*

[20] Schubert found Democratic judges on the Michigan Supreme Court more favorably inclined towards workmen's compensation claims. Schubert, *Quantitative Analysis of Judicial Behavior* 129–42 (1959).

[21] Ulmer extended Schubert's analysis and concluded that "Democratic justice is more sensitive to the claims of the unemployed and the injured than Republican justice." Ulmer, "The Political Party Variable in the Michigan Supreme Court," 11 *J. Pub. L.* 352, 362 (1962).

[22] Vines' study of the voting patterns of federal district judges in the South found consistently more Republicans among the "moderate" and "integrationist" blocs than among those judges most disposed to favor segregationist claims. Vines, "Federal District Judges and Race Relations Cases in the South," 26 *J. of Politics* 337, 350–51 (1964).

[23] See, *e.g.*, Campbell, Converse, Miller, & Stokes, *The American Voter* 39–115 (1960); Truman, *The Congressional Party* (1959); McCloskey, Hoffman, & O'Hara, "Issue Conflict and Consensus among Party Leaders and Followers," 54 *Am. Pol. Sci. Rev.* 406 (1960).

[24] Nagel, *supra* note 17, at 847.

[25] Nagel, "Judicial Backgrounds and Criminal Cases," 53 *J. Crim. L., C. & P. S.* 333, 335 (1962).

[26] Schmidhauser, "Judicial Behavior and the Sectional Crisis of 1837–1860," 23 *J. of Politics* 615, 621, 627 (1961).

of the Supreme Court in which a valid precedent had been expressly overruled,[27] he established a "propensity to overrule" score for each Justice participating in one or more of these decisions and then compared these scores with the amount of prior experience each Justice had. The finding was that Justices with experience on lower courts had a greater propensity to abandon *stare decisis* than did Justices without such experience. While the data did not justify a conclusion of such an inverse relationship, it seemed at least to rebut opposite *a priori* assertions.[28] Schmidhauser also found that Justices who most frequently dissented were those with the lowest propensities to overrule, and he concluded from this and other data that contrary to a common impression, the typical dissenter was not a fire-breathing doctrinal innovator, but rather a "tenacious advocate of traditional doctrines which were being abandoned."[29]

Goldman's method was similar to that of Nagel and Schmidhauser, but his results can best be described as ambiguous. Goldman's sample included all nonunanimous cases decided by the United States courts of appeals from 1961 to 1964, a total of 2,510 cases and 2,776 issues.[30] After establishing liberal and conservative divisions within each court (panel), Goldman attempted to correlate the judges' scores with four sets of background variables—political, socioeconomic, professional, and miscellaneous—such as age or ABA rating.[31] He found, like Nagel, that the

Democratic judges had significantly higher liberalism scores in economic cases; but he found no differences between Democrats and Republicans in criminal cases or general civil liberties categories.[32] And he found that the marked differences Nagel noted between Catholic and Protestant judges—the former being more liberal—disappeared when party affiliation was controlled.[33] Part of the difference may have resulted from a different sample, since many of the judges Nagel studied were elected in partisan contests and were presumably more attuned to existing party ideologies.[34] Going beyond the party variable, Goldman's findings led him to conclude that "the background variables . . . tested . . . are not directly associated with uniform tendencies in judicial behavior."[35] Goldman does not discount background characteristics entirely as a generator and predictor of judicial behavior; but he is clearly skeptical of attributing any major significance to them.

Sprague's study of Supreme Court voting blocs in cases involving questions of federalism seems to reinforce Goldman's skepticism. Unlike the aforementioned projects, Sprague's does not focus on individual judicial voting. His unit of analysis is the bloc, or group of Justices who tend to unite consistently in voting. Having established the existence of these blocs, Sprague sought to determine whether personal background characteristics "unambiguously discriminated" between the members of one bloc and those of other blocs. He found that the best discriminator was prior judicial experience, though none of the background variables was very adequate. In contrast to Nagel, he found that political party did not effectively discriminate between blocs except in the very limited area of property disputes.[36]

Danelski's study of Pierce Butler differs

---

[27]Schmidhauser recognizes the vulnerability of this index as a true measure of "propensity to overrule," since it neglects the perhaps more revealing solo dissenting opinions in favor of abandoning precedent. Schmidhauser, "Stare Decisis, Dissent, and the Background of the Justices of the Supreme Court of the United States, 14 *U. of Toronto L.J.* 194, 199 (1962).

[28]*Id.* at 202. Ulmer's finding of a positive relationship between experienced judges and court stability is in point here. Ulmer, "Homeostasis in the Supreme Court," in *Judicial Behavior* 170 (Schubert ed. 1964).

[29]Schmidhauser, *supra* note 27, at 209.

[30]The courts of appeals present a special problem because most cases are decided by rotating panels of three judges. Goldman's technique is specifically attuned to this problem. Goldman, *supra* note 12, at 46.

[31]The "ABA rating" mentioned is the preappointment evaluation of the judge by the Standing Committee on Federal Judiciary of the American Bar Association. See Grossman, *op. cit., supra* note 8.

[32]Goldman, *supra* note 12, at 219.

[33]*Id.* at 237–41. Nagel's findings on religious affiliations were reported in "Ethnic Affiliations and Judicial Propensities," 24 *J. of Politics* 92 (1962).

[34]Nagel did, however, break down his sample into judges who were chosen in partisan or nonpartisan elections, finding no significant difference in the "party effect." Nagel, *supra* note 17, at 848.

[35]Goldman, *supra* note 12, at 254.

from the works already discussed in several ways. He deals only with a single Justice. And most important for analytical purposes, he has introduced an intermediate variable between the judge's background characteristics and his later behavior as a judge. From a total picture of Butler's early life and professional career, Danelski derives several key *values* which are then treated as independent variables. Butler is characterized as a "moralist, patriot, laissez-faire champion. . . . His was a world of . . . black or white, a world in which principle could never be sacrificed to expediency. He had a system of values for which he was willing to fight."[37]

Relating these values to Butler's work on the Supreme Court, Danelski finds significant areas of agreement or correlation, with the exception that Butler proved much more sensitive to procedural due process claims—in fact he was the "Court's champion of those claims from 1923 to 1939"—than his prior speeches and activities would have indicated. Danelski had "predicted," on the basis of a content analysis of Butler's speeches, that freedom, patriotism, and laissez-faire were his dominant substantive values, and adherence to *stare decisis* his dominant procedural value. All predictions in economic cases proved correct, while individual freedom, which probably accounted for Butler's record in due process cases, bowed to patriotism in free speech and internal security cases.[38]

The picture which Danelski draws is that of a strong-willed judge who found support and encouragement for his personal values in the institutional life of the Court. But the question implicit in such a finding concerns the circumstances and conditions in which personal values derived from pre-judicial experiences are most likely to account for judicial decisions. None of the studies described so far has—or could have—gone further than to

speculate about answers to such a question.

It is in attempting an answer to a related question that the third category of analysis becomes crucial. Assuming that statistically significant relationships between certain background characteristics and judicial behavior have been discovered, to what extent can these findings be said to account for the variance in judicial vote patterns? Quantitatively, inquiry can be made through the use of partial correlation coefficients and multiple regression analysis. Bowen's study of state and appellate judges is the only application so far of these techniques, and his findings are both encouraging and disturbing.[39] After replicating most of Nagel's and Schmidhauser's "associational" results,[40] Bowen found that none of the variables most significantly "associated" with judicial decisions explained more than a fraction of the total variance among judges. No single variable accounted for more than 16 per cent of the variance in any particular area, and most were in the 1 to 8 per cent range. With one exception, the combined explanatory power of the six variables tested never exceeded 30 per cent.[41] Even allowing for errors in sampling and measurment, Bowen's findings cast clear doubt on the explanatory power of background variables taken by themselves.[42] Mere tests of association are inadequate, though useful, and more powerful measures indicate the presence of other "intervening variables" between the case and the ultimate decision.

---

[36]Sprague, *supra* note 13, at 144. The only attempt to test the impact of party affiliation at the trial court level has produced similarly negative results. Dolbeare, *Trial Courts in the Political System: Policy Impact and Functions in an Urban Setting* 177–83, 222–29, unpublished ms., University of Wisconsin, 1966.

[37]Danelski, *op. cit., supra* note 14, at 19.

[38]*Id.* at 180–99.

[39]Bowen, *The Explanation of Judicial Voting Behavior from Sociological Characteristics of Judges*, unpublished Ph.D. dissertation, Yale University, 1965. The partial correlation coefficient is a measure of the amount of total variance explained by one independent variable when all other variables are controlled. Multiple regression analysis measures the amount of variance explained by all the independent variables together.

[40]On the basis of tests of association comparable to those used by Nagel, Bowen found party affiliation and age to be the most consistent independent variables. *Id.* at 187–89.

[41]*Id.* at 201.

[42]There is some problem with Bowen's data which detracts from his findings. His inclusion of unanimous cases may operate to depress the "amount of variance" explained. However, even if the amount of variance were doubled, it would seem that his essential pessimism is warranted.

Bowen's study serves to emphasize Schmidhauser's warning:[43]

It is not at all clear that the social and political background factors in themselves may serve as reliable indicators of precise patterns of judicial behavior. Explanations based entirely upon the causal influence of such factors . . . could scarcely take into account . . . the impact upon individual justices of the traditions of the Supreme Court itself or of the interaction of intelligent and frequently forceful personalities . . . . Complete dependence upon background factors would also ignore the complexity and subtlety of intellect and motivation . . . .

But his findings do not justify any inference that background variables are irrelevant. Rather, his results emphasize the importance of describing and analyzing the other intervening variables which interact with personal values, and of finding a way to integrate these variables in a theory which emphasizes their effect on judicial decisions.

III

Those who attempt to explain judicial behavior in terms of the backgrounds of the judges share with historians the problem of never knowing precisely how the past has influenced the present. But even allowing for these failings, background studies have made a contribution by systematically exploring an important dimension of judicial behavior. That early and crude efforts have not yet led to a perfect understanding of such behavior is surely not the measure of these efforts. Such a measure should weigh their contributions against present and potential results to be derived from other methods. A brief catalog of general contributions would include the identification of key background variables and some attempt at explaining their relationship to decisional patterns, the facility for handling quantities of data which extend the basis—in breadth and reliability—of inferences about

the judicial process, and the ability to test conclusions and observations of traditional observers. Schmidhauser, for example, was able to demonstrate the shallowness of Rodell's claim that virtually all of Chief Justice Taney's decisions could be "traced, directly or indirectly, to his big-plantation birth and background."[44] On the other hand, Danelski was able to demonstrate the substantial validity of contemporary observers' predictions that Butler's experience as a railroad lawyer would be clearly reflected in his Supreme Court votes on rate and valuation cases.[45] Danelski did not make the unwarranted generalization that all judges who had been railroad lawyers would have acted the same way as Butler; as Paul Freund has emphasized, the lawyer is not always father to the judge.[46] But an examination of all judges with "railroad" backgrounds might support such a generalization. Inferences and generalizations about the judicial process are all too often made on the basis of a very limited sample— the "great" cases or the work of the "great" judges—which ignore the run-of-the-mill business which constitutes the essence of the judicial process. No theory with any claim to significant explanatory power could afford to rely on such incomplete knowledge.

There is no doubt that preliminary attempts to isolate particular background variables have initially and necessarily overlooked the essentially cumulative and often random nature of human experience, as well as slighting the impact of institutional influences on the judicial mind.[47] That judges are (or were) Republicans or Catholics or corporate lawyers or law professors may tell everything about some judges. More likely, it will tell only part of the story. Furthermore, not all judges can be easily classified as "liberal" or "conservative." Some categorization is inherent in all scholarship, but the demands of quantita-

[43]Schmidhauser, *The Supreme Court: Its Politics, Personalities and Procedures* 57–58 (1960). For another view of these studies see Becker, *Political Behavioralism and Modern Jurisprudence* 31–36 (1964).

[44]Rodell, *Nine Men* 120 (1955).
[45]Danelski, *op. cit., supra* note 14, at 184–88.
[46]Freund, *The Supreme Court of the United States: Its Business, Purposes and Performance* 116 (1961).
[47]See, *e.g.*, Llewellyn's famous "Fourteen Points." Llewellyn, *op. cit., supra* note 5, at 19–61.

tive analysis in this regard may sometimes seem to be fulfilled at too great a cost.[48]

Finally, methods must be developed which measure judges' intensity of preference and which take into account the vast majority of decisions which are decided unanimously. The latter point is particularly crucial at this stage of research development, since it raises

in peculiarly dramatic fashion the question of the actual impact of social backgrounds on judicial behavior. The hypothesis has been that backgrounds are a major cause of division or variance among the judges; but the contrary assumption, that background experiences contribute to consensus and unanimity, has never been carefully examined. In any case, what is required are further efforts in understanding the very subtle ways in which personal values derived from background experiences are articulated in the judicial context.[49]

[48]Nagel's imputation of "liberalism" to supporting the "wife in divorce settlement cases" is an example of the possible arbitrariness in classifying cases, and Schmidhauser's finding on the basis of a single decision that Rufus Peckham had a "propensity to overrule" indicates the difficulty in classifying some behavior. See Schmidhauser, *supra* note 27, at 200.

[49]See Goldman, *supra* note 12, at 20.

C. Small Group Analysis

One facet of the conversion process lies in the interpersonal relationships among the judges of a collegial court. Two of the three principal court structures of the federal judicial system are collegial bodies. The nine-member Supreme Court sits as one court. The eleven courts of appeals hear and decide almost all of their cases by three-judge panels whose membership generally shifts from case to case. Under special circumstances, for example, when constitutional issues are directly raised at the first instance, a three-judge district court (consisting of one appeals judge and two district judges) is convened. (Appeal from such a court is direct to the Supreme Court.) The small group situation may thus generate pressures which have to be taken into account in explaining judicial decision-making by collegial courts. The selections in this section discuss this aspect of the conversion process. In the first selection, Richard Richardson and Kenneth Vines present some aggregate data concerning dissents and bloc voting on three federal appeals courts. From these data certain interpersonal relationships in the small group context of the appeals courts can be inferred. The second selection, by David Danelski, is an analysis of the leadership potential and influence of the Chief Justice in the small-group context of the Supreme Court. This selection underscores the importance of the Chief Justice's conception of his function and how his "role-playing" vitally affects the small-group situation. Walter Murphy, in the third selection, considers the prospects and potential of small-group analysis for the understanding of judicial behavior.

22 INTERPERSONAL RELATIONSHIPS ON THREE UNITED STATES COURTS OF APPEALS

Richard J. Richardson
and Kenneth N. Vines

. . . The relationships within the judicial system are . . . complex, especially when viewed against the background of conflict in the collegial courts. The internal politics of the court tells us not only something about the institutional character of the judicial process but also something of the structure of interpersonal relationships in the judicial system.

Table 1 describes the paucity of dissent [in civil liberties cases] in . . . three appeals courts [the Third, Fifth, and Eighth Federal Courts of Appeals]; only in the Fifth is the rate of dissent of much significance. Even in the Fifth Circuit the 14.1 rate of dissent may be compared to the general average of Supreme Court dissent which is over 50 per cent. Offhand, we would expect civil liberty cases to be a prolific source of dissent, involving as they do many of the most controversial cases of recent political history. In the Fifth and Eighth circuits, the civil liberties litigation was especially active and intense. However, our data corroborate other findings that dissent is simply not a frequent decision-making pattern in the circuit courts.

to inquire into the likelihood of conflict when affirmance or reversal of various kinds of lower court decisions are involved. This, in turn, may reveal something about the political relationships that are involved in the institutional functions of the courts.

Table 1 suggests some important political characteristics in the federal courts, and describes some relationships between internal dissent and institutional review. We learn that dissent on the appeals courts is primarily a function of the reversal of lower court decisions; this is the case on both the Third and Fifth circuits but not on the Eighth where there is simply very little dissent as such. When reversing decisions in the district courts, the Fifth Circuit is three times as likely to be in conflict as when affirming cases; on the Third Circuit, the court is more than six times as likely to be in conflict when reversing the district courts as when affirming their decisions.

Internal conflict in the appellate courts, strong enough to bring forth dissenting opinion, is usually expressed by an appellate judge who is in agreement with a district judge while the majority of the circuit court wants to reverse. Since in all circuits, the reversal of cases by the appeals courts is largely directed toward turning non-libertarian decisions into libertarian ones, we suggest that dissent in the lower appellate courts is usually an expression of non-libertarianism. Table 2 permits an inspection of the libertarian-non-

TABLE 1 Appellate Dissents When Reversing and Affirming Lower Court Decisions

Circuit	Affirmed Per Cent Cases with Dissent	Reversed Per Cent Cases with Dissent
Third	2.3 (2 of 87)	15.2 (5 of 33)
Fifth	8.7 (24 of 276)	27.0 (31 of 115)
Eighth	3.7 (4 of 109)	0.0 (0 of 29)

An important line of inquiry is the relationship of dissent on the circuit courts to their review of lower court decisions; it enables us

Reprinted by permission of authors and publisher from Richard J. Richardson and Kenneth N. Vines, "Review, Dissent and the Appellate Process: A Political Interpretation," *Journal of Politics*, 29 (1967). Most footnotes omitted and renumbered. Tables renumbered.

libertarian nature of dissent.

Analysis of dissents and unanimous votes when reversing libertarian and non-libertarian decisions shows that for the three circuits, dissent, when exercised, was for a non-libertarian position in all cases except one. From a total of 38 dissents, only one was a

TABLE 2 Distribution of Reversed Cases among Libertarian-Non-Libertarian and Unanimous-Non-Unanimous Positions

	Circuit		
Reversed Cases	**Third** (N = 33)	**Fifth** (N = 115)	**Eighth** (N = 29)
Reversing Libertarian Decisions in District Court:	%	%	%
Unanimous	12.1	10.3	3.4
Non-Unanimous	0.0	1.0	0.0
Reversing Non-Libertarian Decisions in District Court:			
Unanimous	72.7	60.9	96.6
Non-Unanimous	15.2	27.8	0.0
	100.0	100.0	100.0

pro-libertarian expression. Within the lower appellate process, therefore, we can conclude that the conflict represented by dissent in the collegial courts is most often found when a lower court is being reversed and that in the reversed cases, dissent in the three sample circuits is an almost exclusive expression of non-libertarianism.

Records of dissent inform us about the nature of conflict in the judicial system. Dissent is also potentially useful for locating voting blocs within the collegial court and relating these blocs to other supporting blocs in the judiciary.[1] However, besides the low rate of dissent, there are other factors that suggest the difficulties involved in sociometric analysis in the circuit courts.

Basic to the difficulty of dissent analysis in the circuit courts is the institutional structure of decision making there. While the Supreme Court sits as a body regularly in all cases and individual absences are idiosyncratic and exceptional to the decision-making process, the circuit courts routinely hear cases in panels of three judges. Moreover, there is no obvious structure or consistency in the make-up of the three judge committees and the

group composition continually shifts and changes. Since there are only three judges to a panel, except in rare instances of *en banc* deliberations, the objective probability of dissent is much less than on a court of nine judges. Futhermore, a judge, when he dissents, always dissents alone. The intrinsic loneliness of dissent on the circuits may well act as a deterrent to a single judge who faces the possibility of lone disagreement with the majority judges in contrast to the Supreme Court judge who more frequently dissents in company with colleagues.

Of special importance in the analysis of conflict is the shifting context of dissent. Usually on the Supreme Court a dissenting judge is reacting to a stable set of associations and the interactions expressed by voting are in the context of the same justices; hence the context of dissent is relatively uniform. In the circuits, on the other hand, since the group context frequently changes, the dissenting judge must continually change the judges that he dissents from. Clearly, a dissent is in part a relational action, given the fact that one dissents from other judges. And when the relationships are unstable, as they are on the circuits, the significance of dissent is more ambiguous and difficult to measure. Our point is not that bloc analysis is impossible but it must be handled with great care.

The insight to be gained of interpersonal relationships in the judicial system by the use of bloc analysis can be tested in this study on

[1] Glendon Schubert, *Quantitative Analysis of Judicial Behavior* (Glencoe: The Free Press, 1959). Studies utilizing bloc analysis on the circuit courts are Louis Strauss Loeb, *Judicial Values in Four Selected United States Courts of Appeals 1957–1960 Terms* (Unpublished Ph.D. dissertation, The American University, 1964); Sheldon Goldman, *Politics, Judges, and the Administration of Justice* (Unpublished Ph.D. dissertation, Harvard University, 1965).

TABLE 3   Voting Blocs in the Fifth Circuit: Percentage "Rates of Agreement" in Non-Unanimous Decisions

	Rives	Wisdom	Brown	Jones	Tuttle	Hutcheson	Cameron
Rives		71.4	81.9	0.0	54.5	0.0	0.0
Wisdom	71.4	—	50.0	x*	x	x	12.5
Brown	81.9	50.0	—	28.6	40.0	50.0	0.0
Jones	0.0	x	28.6	—	40.0	x	40.0
Tuttle	54.5	x	40.0	40.0	—	x	18.1
Hutcheson	0.0	x	50.0	x	x	—	50.0
Cameron	0.0	12.5	0.0	40.0	18.1	50.0	—

*An "x" indicates too few cases to find "Rate of Agreement." Other circuit judges sitting only a part of the time period or on assignment are not included.

only one of the three circuits. Since both the 3rd and 8th courts of appeals had only minimum dissent in the sample cases, the 5th circuit is the example chosen for study of blocs by use of "Interagreement in Split Decisions" methodology.[2]

Table 3 shows a strong voting bloc on the left (libertarian) composed of judges Rives, Wisdom, and Brown. The "Index of Agreement" for this bloc is 68 per cent. No cohesive voting bloc appeared on the right (non-libertarian), although the "Rate of Agreement" for Hutcheson and Cameron was 50 per cent, a low but not insignificant rate. The cohesion of the libertarian position was clearly more regular and consistent than that of the non-libertarian. The bi-polar aspects of blocs in the 5th circuit is revealed by the example of Judge Rives. When Rives sat with either Jones, Hutcheson or Cameron in a split decision, he did not vote with them a single time.[3]

The linkage between the appellate blocs and district judges can only be suggested, since in no instance did the three members of the libertarian bloc and the two members of the non-libertarian group sit in review over a single district judge in a sufficient number of split decisions. However, when the Rives-Wisdom-Brown average approval rate on all cases heard from a district judge is compared to that of Hutcheson and Cameron, noticeable differences of support do occur. Especially was this marked with regard to Judge Ingraham (R-W-B support 58.3 vs. H-C support 87.5), Judge Davidson (R-W-B support 50.0 vs. H-C 70.3). These relationships suggest that the circuit liberal bloc is supporting liberal judges on the district courts while denying succor to such conservative district archetypes as Ingraham and Davidson; the conservative bloc tends to give similar differential support. While space does not permit a more detailed description, these examples suggest a part of the behavioral context of circuit-district court relations.

. . .

23   THE INFLUENCE OF THE CHIEF JUSTICE IN THE DECISIONAL PROCESS OF THE SUPREME COURT

David J. Danelski

In theory, the relationship among the Justices of the Supreme Court of the United States is one of equality, and frequently the

[2]Schubert, *Quantitative Analysis*, 91.

[3]Although our microanalysis reveals little bloc structure in voting on the appellate courts, Sheldon Goldman has pointed out that macroanalysis reveals definite voting structures on the appeals courts. See his "Voting Behavior on the United States Courts of Appeals," *American Political Science Review* LX (1966), pp. 374–83.

Published with the permission of the author. This paper was delivered at the 1960 annual meeting of the American Political Science Association. Except for minor editing (the deletion of a few sentences and paragraphs and some footnotes), the present publication presents the paper as it was delivered in 1960. An abridged version of it was first published in Walter F. Murphy and C. Herman Pritchett (eds.), *Courts, Judges, and Politics* (New York: Random House, 1961), pp. 497–508.

Chief Justice is referred to as first among equals. Rarely, however, is there equality in practice. Some Justices are more able, more persuasive, or more personable than their associates, and, in the calculus of influence which lies behind every decision of the Court, these are the important factors. The Chief Justice, by virtue of his office, has a unique opportunity for leadership. He is the key figure in the Court's *certiorari* practice. He presides in open court and over the secret conferences where he usually presents each case to his associates, giving his opinion first and voting last. He assigns the opinion of the Court in virtually all cases when he votes with the majority, and, as a practical matter, he decides when the opinion will be announced. But the Chief Justiceship does not guarantee leadership. It only offers its incumbent an opportunity to lead. Optimum leadership inheres in the combination of the office and an able, persuasive, personable judge.

The Chief Justiceship has lived and grown in the shadow of judicial secrecy. Data cannot be obtained about it for purposes of analysis by direct observation of the Chief Justice's participation in the decisional process of the Court. Manuscripts, memoirs, interviews, and the Court's official reports are the chief available sources of data. Although one must be wary of coming too close to the present, lest disclosures embarrass Justices still on the bench, a study of the Chief Justiceship, to be worthwhile, must be close enough to the present to yield generalizations useful in understanding the office as it is today. In an effort to avoid both difficulties, the period 1921 to 1946—the era of Chief Justices Taft, Hughes, and Stone—was selected for analysis.

. . .

I. SOME THEORETICAL CONSIDERATIONS

Leadership in the Supreme Court is best understood in terms of influence: CJ influences J to do x to the extent that CJ performs some activity y as a result of which J chooses to do x.[1] Explicit in this definition are the two

concepts, activity and interaction. Activity simply refers to things Court members do, for example, voting and writing opinions. Interaction refers to activity by one member of the Court to which another member responds, for example, conference discussion and opinion assignment. Interaction is indispensable to influence, for if J does not respond to CJ's activity, J cannot choose to do x as the result of y. Influence, however, implies more than surface activity and interaction, for frequently underlying these phenomena are expectations, values, and attitudes of CJ and J.[2]

Expectations are evaluative standards applied to an incumbent of a position, such as the Chief Justice, and a set of those expectations defines his role.[3] The term "expectation" is used in the normative sense (CJ *should* do y) rather than in the predictive sense (CJ *will* do y).[4] Role is an important concept in the analysis of judicial behavior because the expectations the Chief Justice and Justices hold for themselves and each other affect their activity. Conversely, activity affects expectations. The Chief Justice, by his activity, can create new expectations and to some extent thereby redefine his role and even the roles of the Justices. Chief Justice Hughes, for example, did this when he established the "special list" for disposing of unmeritorious *certiorari* cases without conference discussion. Thereafter, the Chief Justice was expected to determine initially which *certioraris* should be considered in conference, and if a Justice wanted a case transferred from the "special list" so that it might be discussed and voted upon, the Chief Justice was expected to do so upon request.

Likeability is an important dimension of influence. Like other men, Court members

[1]See Felix E. Oppenheim, "An Analysis of Political Controls: Actual and Potential," *The Journal of Politics*, Vol. 20 (1958), p. 516.

[2]Cf. George C. Homans, *The Human Group* (New York, 1950), pp. 37–40. For purposes of this study, expectations, values, and attitudes are postulated. The postulation arises out of the observation of activity and is used to observe and analyze other similar activity.

[3]See Neal Gross, Ward S. Mason, and Alexander McEachern, *Explorations in Role Analysis* (New York, 1958).

[4]Cf. Chief Justice Vinson's statement about Charles Evans Hughes: "He was precise and decisive in playing the role he believed the Chief Justice *ought* to play." 338 U.S. xxviii (1950).

tend to like some of their associates more than others, to be indifferent to some, and perhaps even to dislike others. Chief Justice Taft, for example, regarded Justice Van Devanter as "the closest friend [he had] on the Court . . .," and when he was fatally ill in January, 1930, Van Devanter was the only member of the Court who was allowed to see him.[5] Applying sociometry to the personal documents of Justices, the social structure of the Court can be diagrammed, and the various relationships described by Moreno emerge: the "isolated individual" (McReynolds, *ca.* 1921–1926), the "star" or greatly preferred member (Taft, 1921–1930), etc.[6] As this paper will show, the social structure of the Court is significant in decisional process, and likeability is an important variable in influence, for it is related to the degree and kind of interaction between Court members. Thus, the more the Chief Justice is liked, the greater is his influence potential.

Esteem is another important dimension of influence. The member who is regarded as having the best ideas in conference and being best able to handle the tough cases assigned him for opinion is ordinarily highly esteemed by his associates. Of course, there may be differences of opinion as to who is the most able member of the Court, the next most able, etc., but there is no doubt that such ranking occurs.[7] Esteem within the Court may rest on, or be increased by, prestige he carries over from previous high status positions, such as President, presidential candidate, Secretary of State, etc. The position of Chief Justice in itself, however, probably adds only a little to the esteem of its incumbent in the eyes of his associates. In the Court his esteem depends more upon his over-all ability and how well he fulfills his role as Chief Justice.

In terms of influence, then, the ideal Chief Justice is a persuasive, esteemed, able, and well-liked judge who perceives, fulfills, and even expands his role as head of the Court. One might ask: influence for what? The more important objects of influence are the attainment of: (1) a majority vote for the Chief Justice's position, (2) written opinions satisfactory to him, (3) social cohesion in the Court, and (4) unanimous decisions. In the close case, where a Justice is wavering in his vote, influence may be the difference between a decision one way or another. Since the Chief Justice assigns opinions in cases in which he votes with the majority, the content of an opinion is to some degree determined by his selection of the Court's spokesman. Unless there is minimum social cohesion among the Justices, collegial decision-making is virtually impossible. And where there is such cohesion, unanimous decisions tend to be prevalent, for unanimity arises from the give and take of compromise. Thus, the main objects of influence go to the heart of the Court's decisional process.

II. THE DECISION TO MAKE A DECISION

Today, the appellate jurisdiction of the Court is almost entirely discretionary. Therefore, the threshold decision to take or not to take a case for review is crucial; six out of seven cases go no further in the Court's decisional process. Standing at the throat of the Court's discretionary jurisdiction is the Chief Justice. All the Justices examine the petitions for *certiorari* and jurisdictional statements, but the Chief Justice's examination must be particularly careful, for it is his duty to present them in conference. Chief Justice Taft's preparation of *certioraris* was like Holmes's: not done so thoroughly as to decide the cases, but thoroughly enough to decide whether or

[5]Taft to Charles Taft, June 8, 1927; Taft to Horace D. Taft, June 29, 1927; Taft to Van Devanter, Jan. 7, 1930, William Howard Taft Papers, Manuscript Division, Library of Congress.

[6]See J. L. Moreno, *Who Shall Survive?* (New York, 1934); Gordon W. Allport, *The Use of Personal Documents in Psychological Science* (New York, 1942), pp. 46–47, 50, 108–10.

[7]See Henry F. Pringle, *The Life and Times of William Howard Taft* (New York, 1939), II, pp. 968–972; Alpheus Thomas Mason, *Harlan Fiske Stone: Pillar of the Law* (New York, 1936), p. 793; Charles Evans Hughes, Biographical Notes, 1930–1941, p. 12, Hughes Papers, Manuscript Division, Library of Congress; Steven T. Early, Jr., *James Clark McReynolds and the Judicial Process*, Unpublished Ph.D. dissertation, Department of Political Science, University of Virginia, 1954, p. 90; Fred Rodell to Editor, *New York Times Book Review*, July 24, 1960, p. 24.

not they should be brought before the Court.[8] Chief Justice Hughes, however, made very complete and thorough preparation, usually going into the merits of each case and often deciding it "then and there in his own mind."[9] Apparently Chief Justice Stone, who was prone to defer judgment for days and even weeks after cases were argued, usually prepared the *certioraris* and jurisdictional statements only to determine whether the Court should exercise its jurisdiction.[10]

Until the middle 1930's, every petition for *certiorari* was presented in conference by the Chief Justice and voted upon by the Court. At the beginning of a term, some 250 to 300 certioraris would be awaiting disposition. Taft scheduled daily conferences to dispose of them, taking up about 50 to 60 cases a day.[11] At first, Hughes followed Taft's procedure, presenting and disposing of as many as a hundred petitions for *certiorari* in a single afternoon.[12] Then he established a unanimous consent procedure in which the Chief Justice was the key figure. If the Chief Justice decided that a petition for *certiorari* was frivolous or ill-founded and therefore did not merit conference discussion, he placed it on a "special list" which was circulated to the Associates. Upon request, any case on the special list would be transferred to the regular take-up list,[13] but cases remaining on the special list were automatically denied *certiorari* without

discussion. Hughes disposed of about 60 per cent of the petitions for *certiorari* via the special list, and rarely did a Justice challenge his lists. Challenges were also relatively rare during Stone's Chief Justiceship.[14]

The innovation of the special list increased the influence potential of the Chief Justice. Petitions he wants discussed in conference are taken up automatically, but petitions are not so easily transferred from the special to the regular list. The Justice who challenges the special list must be well prepared and willing to disagree openly with the Chief Justice. To the extent, therefore, that a Justice does not prepare thoroughly or is hesitant to disagree with the Chief Justice, because he likes or esteems him or for some other reason, the Chief Justice's influence increases proportionately.[15]

The Chief Justice's second opportunity for influence during this phase of the decisional process arises when he presents the petitions for *certiorari* and jurisdictional statements to the conference, for he gives his views first and usually speaks longer than any of his associates. The influence of the Chief Justice in conference is considered later, but a word as to the time spent on petitions for *certiorari* and jurisdictional statements is in order here. Frequently when Hughes finished his presentation of those cases, his associates had nothing to add,[16] and when there was a discussion, he limited it. In the Hughes Court, the average time devoted to the discussion of a *certiorari* case was 3.6 minutes.[17] During Taft's

---

[8]Holmes to Lewis Einstein, May 19, 1927, Oliver Wendell Holmes, Jr., Papers, Manuscript Division, Library of Congress.

[9]Edwin McElwain, "The Business of the Supreme Court as Conducted by Chief Justice Hughes," *Harvard Law Review*, Vol. 63 (1949), p. 13. McElwain is a former law clerk of Chief Justice Hughes.

[10]See Mason, *op. cit.*, p. 792; William O. Douglas, "Chief Justice Stone," *Columbia Law Review*, Vol. 46 (1946), p. 693; Alfred McCormack, "A Law Clerk's Recollections," *ibid.*, p. 716; Bennett Boskey, "Mr. Chief Justice Stone," *Harvard Law Review*, Vol. 59 (1946), p. 1200.

[11]Taft to Brethren, Sept. 27, 1928; Taft to Horace D. Taft, Sept. 22, 1929, Taft Papers.

[12]Hughes to Stone, Oct. 1, 1931, Harlan F. Stone Papers, Manuscript Division, Library of Congress; Hughes to Brandeis, Oct. 1, 1931, Louis D. Brandeis Papers, University of Louisville Law School; McElwain, *op. cit.*, p. 15.

[13]Hughes to Stone, Sept. 30, 1935, Feb. 25, 1938, Sept. 30, 1940, Stone Papers; Merlo J. Pusey, *Charles Evans Hughes* (New York, 1952), II, 672.

[14]Stone's Papers indicate that his special lists were challenged less than 10 times in five years.

[15]Few of the Justices of the pre-1937 Court under Hughes, said an anonymous writer (probably a former law clerk), "made a careful study of the records or briefs of cited authorities before they went to conference." Quoted by John P. Frank, "Harlan Fiske Stone: An Estimate," *Stanford Law Review*, Vol. 9 (1957), p. 629, n. 31. During Stone's Chief Justiceship, too, Court members were not always fully prepared for the conferences. Frankfurter to Stone, *ca.* Oct. 22, 1942; Rutledge to Stone, Feb. 1, 1946, Stone Papers.

[16]Owen J. Roberts, Address to the Association of the Bar of the City of New York and the New York County Lawyers' Association, December 12, 1948, *Proceedings of the Bar and Officers of the Supreme Court of the United States in Memory of Charles Evans Hughes* (Washington, 1950), pp. 122–123.

[17]McElwain, *op. cit.*, p. 14.

Chief Justiceship, the average *certiorari* case received about 10 minutes, but Taft felt that too much time was devoted to such cases, thus limiting discussion of argued and submitted cases. During Stone's Chief Justiceship, "petitions for *certiorari* and jurisdictional statements," said Justice Douglas, "were never more fully or carefully discussed."[18]

Taft admitted that his conference activity in regard to *certioraris* was not very influential: when the Court votes on *certioraris*, he said, "I'm usually in the minority . . ."[19] Hughes was more influential partly because of his rigorous control of discussion. In the three and one-half minutes allowed each *certiorari* petition, there could be little discussion, for usually it would take that long to present the case and vote. Thus, by virtually monopolizing the time available, he greatly influenced the *certiorari* and probable jurisdiction decisions. Conversely, Stone's influence was probably less than Hughes's because of the expanded discussion of *certioraris* and jurisdictional statements during his Chief Justiceship.

III. ORAL ARGUMENT

When the Court hears oral argument, the Chief Justice is only in a little better position than his associates to influence the decisional process. As presiding officer, he has some discretion in extending counsel's time for argument, but beyond that, his influence depends primarily upon his esteem and interaction.[20] For oral argument is a period of deliberation in which Court members frequently arrive at tentative decisions that usually accord with their final votes.[21]

. . .

IV. IN CONFERENCE

In conference, the Chief Justice is in a favorable position to influence his associates. In order to explain the nature of his influence at this stage of the decisional process a theory of conference leadership is necessary. Relying principally upon the empirical studies of decision-making groups by Bales,[22] Slater,[23] and Berkowitz,[24] the following theory has been constructed: The primary task of the conference is the decision of cases through interaction. In making decisions, some Court members initiate and receive more interaction than others. Usually one member makes more suggestions, gives more opinions, orients the discussion more frequently, and successfully defends his ideas more often than the others. Usually, he is regarded as having the best ideas for the decision of cases and is highly esteemed by his associates. Thus, he emerges as *task leader* of the conference. He is apt to be an intense man, and, in concentrating on the Court's decisions, his response to the emotional needs of his associates is apt to be secondary. The interaction involved in deciding cases tends to cause conflict, tension, and antagonism, which, if allowed to get out of hand, would make the intelligent decision of cases virtually impossible. The negative aspects of interaction are counterbalanced by members of the conference who initiate inter-

[18]Douglas, *op. cit.*, p. 695.
[19]Taft to McKenna, April 20, 1923, Taft Papers.
[20]Chief Justices Taft and Stone were lenient in this regard, but Hughes was not. When the hour ordinarily given counsel for argument was over, Hughes invariably required counsel to stop. See McElwain, *op. cit.*, p. 17.
[21]Charles Evans Hughes, *The Supreme Court of the United States* (New York, 1928), pp. 61–62; Frederick Bernays Wiener, "Oral Advocacy," *Harvard Law Review*, Vol. 62 (1948), p. 58, n. 7; Robert H. Jackson, "Advocacy before the United States Supreme Court," *Cornell Law Review*, Vol. 37 (1951), p. 2.

[22]Robert F. Bales, *Interaction Process Analysis: A Method for the Study of Small Groups* (Cambridge, Mass., 1950); "The Equilibrium Problem in Small Groups," Ch. IV in Talcott Parsons, Robert F. Bales, and Edward A. Shils (eds.), *Working Papers in the Theory of Action* (Glencoe, Ill., 1953); "Task Status and Likeability as a Function of Talking and Listening in Decision-Making Groups," in Leonard D. White (ed.), *The State of the Social Sciences* (Chicago, 1956), pp. 148–161; "Task Roles and Social Roles in Problem-Solving Groups," in Eleanor E. Maccoby, Theodore M. Newcomb, and Eugene L. Harley, *Readings in Social Psychology* (New York, 1958), pp. 437–447.
[23]Philip E. Slater, "Role Differentiation in Small Groups," *American Sociological Review*, Vol. 20 (1955), pp. 300–310.
[24]Leonard Berkowitz, *Some Effects of Leadership Sharing in Small, Decision-Making Conference Groups*, Unpublished Ph.D. dissertation, Department of Psychology, University of Michigan, 1951; "Sharing Leadership in Small, Decision-Making Groups," *Journal of Abnormal and Social Psychology*, Vol. 48 (1953), pp. 231–238.

action relieving tension and showing solidarity and agreement. One member usually performs more such activity than the others. He invites orientation, opinions, and suggestions, and, in general, attends to the emotional needs of his associates by affirming their value as individuals and Court members. Typically, he is the best-liked member of the conference and emerges as its *social leader*. Not only is he well liked; usually he wants to be well liked. He is apt to dislike conflict, and its avoidance may be a felt necessity for him. Thus, it is difficult for him to assume task leadership of the conference.

Yet it is possible for the Chief Justice to be both task and social leader.[25] Although his task leadership is not primarily derived from his office, the fact that he speaks first in conference tends to maintain such leadership if he has an independent claim to it. Also his control of the conference process puts him in a favorable position to exercise social leadership, for he can minimize exchanges which contribute toward negative feelings among Court members and perform other activity which favorably disposes his associates toward him. Assuming he performs both aspects of leadership well and fulfills the important expectations of his role, his influence in conference tends to be high. Other important consequences, stated as hypotheses, are: (1) Conflict in conference tends to be minimal. (2) Court members tend to be socially cohesive. (3) Court members tend to be satisfied with the conference. (4) The conference tends to be productive in terms of the number of decisions made for the time spent. Rarely, however, are both aspects of leadership combined in a single individual. Typically, leadership is shared in conference. If it is positively shared, that is, if a Chief Justice who is social leader forms a coalition with a Justice who is task leader and they work together, a situation prevails which is similar to the one in which both aspects of leadership

are combined in the Chief Justice. Such coalitions ordinarily occur where the personal relations between the Chief Justice and the task leader are fairly close. However, if leadership is negatively shared, that is, if the Chief Justice and the task leader do not work together and even compete against each other, then not only does the Chief Justice's influence in conference tend to decrease, but conflict tends to increase, and cohesion, satisfaction, and production tend to decrease.

There was positive sharing of leadership during Taft's Chief Justiceship: Taft was social leader and his good friend and appointee, Van Devanter, was task leader. Evidence of Van Devanter's esteem and task leadership is abundant.[26] Taft, time and time again, asserted that Van Devanter was the most able Justice on the Court.[27] If the Court were to vote, he said, that would be its judgment, too. The Chief Justice admitted that he did not know how he could get along without Van Devanter in conference, for Van Devanter kept the Court consistent with itself, and "his power of statement and his immense memory make him an antagonist in conference who generally wins against all opposition."[28] The impression Van Devanter's contemporaries had of him was: "Here is a man with great physical vigor, a powerful

[26]Hughes said that Van Devanter's perspicacity and common sense made him a trusted advisor in all sorts of matters. Chief Justice White relied heavily upon him, and before Hughes accepted the Presidential nomination in 1916, Van Devanter was the only member of the Court with whom he discussed the matter. *Biographical Notes*, pp. 220–221, 231. In conference, said Hughes, Van Devanter's "careful and elaborate statements . . . were of the greatest value." *Ibid.*, p. 220. Stone said Van Devanter had "great legal ability" and "an accurate and precise mind," and referred to Van Devanter's service in conferences as "invaluable." Stone to Children, Feb. 13, 1941; Stone to Van Devanter, June 2, 1937, Stone Papers. When Taft wrote to Holmes that "209 was affirmed on Van Devanter's suggestion," it was but an instance of what was typical in the Taft Court. March 12, 1928, Taft Papers. See also Holmes to Laski, May 13, 1919, Mark DeWolfe Howe, *Holmes-Laski Letters* (Cambridge, Mass., 1953), I, 202; Alexander M. Bickel, *The Unpublished Opinions of Mr. Justice Brandeis* (Cambridge, Mass. 1957), p. 248; 316 U.S. xix, xxxii, xlii (1941).

[27]Taft to Helen Taft Manning, June 11, 1923; Taft to Robert A. Taft, May 3, 1925, Jan. 22, 1927; Taft to Charles P. Taft, June 8, 1927, Taft Papers.

[28]Taft to William Lyon Phelps, May 30, 1927, *ibid.*

[25]Though rare, there are such individuals. See Edgar F. Borgatta, Robert F. Bales, and Arthur S. Couch, "Some Findings Relevant to the Great Man Theory of Leadership," *American Sociological Review*, Vol. 19 (1954), pp. 755–759.

intellect and a driving and dominant personality."[29] Though he was absorbed by his work, he had a sense of humor, "not of the frivolous or merry sort," but "always dignified."[30] At times, Van Devanter's ability actually embarrassed Taft, and the Chief Justice wondered if it might not be better to have Van Devanter run the conference himself.[31] "Still," mused the former President, "I must worry along until the end of my ten years, content to aid in the deliberation when there is a difference of opinion."[32] In other words, Taft was content to perform the functions of social leadership. Clearly, he was the best liked member of his Court, and he wanted to be liked.[33] His friendship with Van Devanter was especially close,[34] but he valued the friendship of each Justice with whom he served, even that of McReynolds, whom he characterized as a "grouch."[35] "I am old enough to know," he wrote to one of his sons after an incident with McReynolds, "that the best way to get along with people with whom you have to live always is to restrain your impatience and consider that doubtless you have peculiarities that try other people."[36]

Discussion in the Taft-Van Devanter conference was described in 1928 as being of "the freest character,"[37] and naturally this led to some conflict. But when the Justices disagreed, it was usually, as Brandeis said, "without any ill feeling"; it was "all very friendly."[38] . . . During his Chief Justiceship, the Justices were satisfied with the conferences. "Things go happily in the conference room," Brandeis remarked. "The judges go home less tired emotionally and less weary physically than in White's day."[39] Despite differences of opinion, there was compromise and teamwork among the liberal and conservative Justices alike. And there was production. The Court under Taft, for the first time in more than 50 years, came close to clearing its docket. Taft's influence in conference was probably as great as it could have been, for his coalition with Van Devanter gave him power he would not have had otherwise.

Task and social leadership were combined in Hughes. Overall, he was the most esteemed member of his Court.[40] His prior high positions undoubtedly contributed to his high esteem, but primarily it was due to his performance in conference. His associates could always be sure that he was well prepared. Blessed with a photographic memory, he would summarize comprehensively and accurately the facts of each case. When he was finished, he would look up and say with a smile: "Now I will state where I come out."[41] Then he would outline his views as to how the case should be decided. Sometimes that is all the discussion a case received, and the Justices proceeded to vote for the disposition suggested by the Chief. Where there was a discussion, the Justices gave their views in order of seniority without interruption, stating why they concurred or dissented from the views of the Chief Justice. After the Justices had their say, Hughes would review the dis-

[29]Remarks of former Attorney General William D. Mitchell, 316 U.S. xvii (1941).

[30]*Ibid.*, pp. xvii–xviii.

[31]Taft to Robert A. Taft, Oct. 23, 1927, *ibid.*

[32]Taft to Robert A. Taft, *loc. cit.*

[33]Each summer Taft made it a point to write to his associates friendly letters which were answered in the same spirit. Apparently, he was the only member of his Court who corresponded with all of his associates regularly.

[34]"Van Devanter is really the closest friend I have on the Court, and we ordinarily work together. . . ." Taft to Charles Taft, June 8, 1927; Taft to Horace D. Taft, June 29, 1927. During Taft's last illness, he wrote Van Devanter: "Nobody will be permitted to call me except you and Misch [Taft's secretary] and Nellie [Taft's wife]. . . . Love to Mrs. Van Devanter and yourself. You are a thing of joy forever." Jan. 7, 1930, *ibid.* Cf. Slater, *op. cit.*, pp. 306–307.

[35]Taft to Helen Taft Manning, June 11, 1923, Taft Papers.

[36]Taft to Robert A. Taft, Jan. 10, 1926, *ibid.*

[37]Harlan F. Stone, "Fifty Years' Work of the United States Supreme Court," *American ·Bar Association Journal*, Vol. 14 (1928), p. 436.

[38]Quoted in Bickel, *op. cit.*, p. 203.

[39]Bickel, *loc. cit.*

[40]Frankfurter has said that if Hughes "made others feel his moral superiority, they merely felt a fact. . . . All who served with him recognized the extraordinary qualities possessed by the Chief Justice . . ." *Of Law and Men* (New York, 1956), p. 148. Hughes was the only member of the Court to whom McReynolds would defer. Early, *loc. cit.*, Black said he had "more than impersonal and detached admiration" for Hughes' "extraordinary intellectual gifts." Black to Hughes, June 3, 1941. Hughes Papers.

[41]Roberts, *op. cit.*, p. 123.

cussion, pointing out the agreement and disagreement with the views expressed. Then he usually called for a vote. In terms of inter-action, Hughes was the key figure of the conference. He made more suggestions, gave more opinions, and oriented the conference more than any other member. He not only did most of the talking; his associates' remarks were usually addressed to him, and they discussed the views he initially presented. Clearly, Hughes was conference task leader. His personality was in some respects similar to Van Devanter's. "The Chief Justice was an intense man," said Justice Roberts. "When he had serious business to transact he allowed no consideration to interfere with his operations. He was so engrossed in the vital issue that he had not time for lightness and pleasantry."[42]

Yet Hughes's relationship with his associates was genial and cordial, and he was regarded as being "considerate, sympathetic, and responsive."[43] Never in the eleven years that Roberts sat with Hughes in conference did he see him lose his temper. Never did he hear him pass a personal remark or even raise his voice. Never did he witness him interrupting or engaging in controversy with an associate. Despite his popular stereotype, Hughes had a "keen sense of humor" which aided in keeping differences in conference from becoming discord. On the whole, he was well liked. . . .

Justice Stone's attitude toward Hughes, however, was ambivalent. From the beginning of Hughes's Chief Justiceship, he thought Hughes did not allow adequate time for discussion in conference.[44] Stone was also critical of Hughes' presentation of cases. The Chief Justice, he said, would greatly overelaborate "unimportant details" and then dispose of the vital questions "in a sentence or two."[45] Stone referred to a portion of Hughes's presentation of the AAA case as "painful elabo-

ration."[46] Oddly enough, Hughes was not aware of Stone's attitude, for Stone never openly challenged Hughes' methods, even when he had strong feelings about them. Why did not Stone speak out? If he had pressed his views in conference, Hughes could not have stopped him. It might be suggested that Hughes' esteem among his associates tended to inhibit discussion generally; for, as Frankfurter said, the "moral authority" exerted by the Chief "inhibited irrelevance, repetition, and fruitless discussion."[47] It might have inhibited relevant and fruitful discussion as well. Stone's ambivalence toward Hughes might be also traced to his conception of the Chief Justice's role in conference which he learned during Taft's Chief Justiceship. Since leadership was shared in the Taft Court, the Chief Justice was a more permissive presiding officer, and Stone apparently felt that Hughes should have presided in a similar manner.

Although there was some conflict in the Hughes conference, the Chief Justice used his position as presiding officer to cut off discussion that showed signs of deteriorating into wrangling. Socially, the Hughes Court was fairly cohesive. Justice Roberts said that though the Court was divided on constitutional policy, there was a feeling of "personal cordiality and comradship" among the Justices.[48] . . . Conference production reached the highest point in the Court's history under Hughes and has never been equalled. Unquestionably, Hughes's influence in conference was great.

During Stone's Chief Justiceship, conference leadership was negatively shared. . . . Stone departed from the conference role cut out for him by Hughes. When he presented cases, he lacked the apparent certitude of his predecessor, and, at times, his statement indicated that he was still groping for a solution. In that posture, the case would be passed down to his associates. Justices would speak out of turn, and Stone did little to control their debate. Instead, like his younger asso-

---

[42] *Ibid.*, p. 127, Cf. Frankfurter, *op. cit.*, pp. 147–148.
[43] Roberts, *loc. cit.*
[44] Stone to McReynolds, April 3, 1930, Stone Papers.
[45] Stone Memorandum re *Colgate* v. *Harvey*, Stone Papers, quoted in Mason, *op. cit.*, pp. 401–402.

[46] Stone Memorandum re *U. S.* v. *Butler*, Stone Papers, quoted in Mason, *op. cit.*, pp. 414–416.
[47] *Op. cit.*, pp. 135, 141.
[48] Roberts, *op. cit.*, p. 126.

ciates, he would join in the debate with alacrity, "delighted to take on all comers around the conference table."[49] "Jackson," he would say, "that's damned nonsense." "Douglas, *you* know better than that."[50] In other words, Stone was still acting like an Associate Justice, and in the free and easy interaction of the conference, his presumptive task leadership began to slip from his grasp.

Eventually, Justice Black emerged as leading contender for task leadership of the conference.[51] Although Stone esteemed Black, he distrusted his unorthodox approach, and no coalition occurred as in the Taft Court. Most of the Justices, having served under Hughes, probably expected that Stone should lead in conference much in the same manner as his predecessor. When he did not, a problem arose which is similar to the one studied by Heyns.[52] Heyns's study suggests that when a designated leader of a conference group does not perform the task functions expected of him, the group will tend to accept leadership from one of its other members. But if the designated leader performs his task functions, members who act like leaders will tend to be rejected by the group. Stone's case was ambiguous, for Stone performed some task functions. That may explain why some Justices accepted Black's assertion of task leadership and others did not. Douglas, Murphy, and Rutledge esteemed and liked Black and went along with his leadership which, as senior Associate, he was able to reinforce by usually speaking before them in conference and by assigning opinions when Stone dissented. Roberts, Frankfurter, and Jackson, however, rejected Black's leadership, regarding him as a usurper of functions which were properly

Stone's.[53] Reed, who was inclined toward Black, stood in the middle as did Stone. Since Black asserted task leadership, a word might be said about his personality. His former law clerk, John P. Frank, described him in the following terms: ". . . Black is a very, very tough man. When he is convinced, he is cool hard steel. . . . His temper is usually in close control, but he fights, and his words may occasionally have a terrible edge. He can be a rough man in an argument."[54]

Debates in conference were heated in the Stone Court and a social leader was needed to sooth ruffled tempers, relieve tensions created by interaction, and maintain solidarity. Stone was liked and respected by all of his associates and could have performed this function well, but he did not. He did not use his control over the conference's process, as Hughes did, to cut off debate leading to irreconcilable conflict. He did not remain neutral when controversies arose so that he could be in a position to mediate them. As Professor Mason said, "He was totally unprepared to cope with the petty bickering and personal conflict in which his Court became engulfed."[55] In sum, he did not provide the conference with effective social leadership.

The combination of negative sharing of task leadership and the failure of social leadership increased conflict in conference during Stone's Chief Justiceship. The conflict was not friendly as in Taft's day; rather it was acrimonious, and, at times, descended to the level of personalities. On one occasion, even Stone's integrity was challenged. Cohesion in the Court decreased. Satisfaction with the conference also decreased. Frankfurter warned Stone about the dangers of Justices speaking out of turn after the first conference, and a year later he was appalled at the "easy-going, almost heedless way in which views on Con-

---

[49]Remarks of Justice Reed at unveiling of Chesterfield Memorial Tablet for Stone, Aug. 25, 1948. Quoted in Mason, *op. cit.*, p. 792.

[50]Mason, *op. cit.*, p. 795.

[51]See John P. Frank, *Mr. Justice Black: The Man and His Opinions* (New York, 1949), pp. 134–135, 137; Mason, *op. cit.*, pp. 768, 797; Fred Rodell, "Justice Hugo Black," *The American Mercury*, Vol. 59 (1944), pp. 136–137, 142–143.

[52]R. W. Heyns, *Effects of Variation in Leadership on Participant Behavior in Discussion Groups*, Unpublished Ph.D. dissertation, Department of Psychology, University of Michigan, 1948. Reported in Berkowitz, *loc. cit.*

[53]This is only a partial explanation for Black's rejection by Roberts, Frankfurter, and Jackson. Some further insights into this problem can be obtained by studying the Roberts letter incident, the Jewell Ridge Case controversy, and Jackson's Nuremberg cable. See Mason, *op. cit.*, pp. 641–646, 765–769.

[54]Frank, *Mr. Justice Black, op. cit.*, pp. 134–145.

[55]Mason, *op. cit.*, p. 790.

stitutional issues touching the whole future direction of this country were floated. . . ."[56] Extended discussion meant extended conferences, and frequently they lasted until after six in the evening and sometimes had to be continued on Monday, Tuesday, or even Wednesday of the following week. "On more than one Saturday," Frankfurter noted, "the discussion after four-thirty gave evidence of fatigued minds and occasionally of frayed nerves." He longed for the taut four-hour conference of the Hughes Court and felt that the Justices of the Stone Court were not always well prepared for conference and discussion was not duly focused. Production decreased. The Court under Stone decided as many cases as the Hughes Court did, but the time spent in conference to do this was just about double. It is probably safe to say that Stone's influence in conference was no greater than that of some of his associates.

Hughes was probably the most influential conference leader in modern times because he was able to perform both the task and social functions of leadership. These functions are to some degree incompatible and ordinarily a Chief Justice will be predisposed to perform either the task or social function, but not both. It is possible that Taft's strong dislike of conflict and his desire to be liked would have prevented him from becoming task leader even if he had the ability and esteem of Van Devanter. This, too, may have been the reason for Stone's failure as task leader. For Justice Jackson said, "Stone dreaded conflict"[57] and the description of Black as "a very, very tough man" could not be applied to Stone. Stone, it would seem, was made of the intellectual, but not of the emotional, stuff that task leaders are made of. By comparison, it would seem that these elements were magnificently combined in Hughes. But there was more to Hughes' success as conference leader than that. He had all the advantages of both Taft and Stone and few of their disadvantages. He apparently had more esteem than Taft when he came to the Court as Chief Justice, and on the Court

he had more esteem than either Taft or Stone. Like Stone, he had the advantage of having been a Court member; but he did not have the disadvantage of disassociating himself from his former role of Associate Justice. The principal thing he learned during his service with Chief Justice White was how not to preside in conference. He felt White did not give the leadership he should have in conference and did not control and focus the discussion of the Justices. As Chief Justice, Hughes intended to act otherwise. He had a clear conception of his role in conference and acted accordingly. One might well conclude that Hughes understood the task and social functions of leadership and rationally sought to perform them to maintain his position in conference.

V. ASSIGNMENT OF THE COURT'S OPINION

In all cases in which the Chief Justice votes with the majority, he may write the Court's opinion or assign it to one of his associates who voted with him.[58] The making of assignments is significant in terms of influence because the selection of the Court's spokesman may be instrumental in:

(1) Determining the value of a decision as a precedent, that is, depending upon the writer, an opinion may be placed on one ground rather than another or two grounds instead of one, or deal narrowly or broadly with the issues.

(2) Making a decision as acceptable as possible to the public.

(3) Holding the Chief Justice's majority together in a close case.

(4) Persuading dissenting associates to join in the Court's opinion.

The Chief Justice has an opportunity to exercise such influence in a high percentage of cases. Taft and Hughes assigned more than 95 per cent of the Court's opinions during their Chief Justiceships. Stone's assignment

---

[56]Frankfurter to Stone, Oct. 21, 1942, Stone Papers.
[57]Quoted in Mason, *op. cit.*, p. 769.

[58]One minor exception to this rule is that a newcomer to the Court is entitled to select his first case for opinion. This is a tradition of long standing. Matthews to Waite, Oct. 5, 1881, Morrison R. Waite Papers, Manuscript Division, Library of Congress.

average was slightly better than 85 per cent. Usually assignments by the Chief Justice are accepted without question by the Justices.

The Chief Justice has maximal control over an opinion if he assigns it to himself, and undoubtedly Chief Justices have retained many important cases for that reason. The Chief Justice's retention of "big cases" is generally accepted by the Justices. In fact, the expectation is that he should write in those cases so as to lend the prestige of his office to the Court's pronouncement. In varying degrees, Chief Justices have fulfilled this expectation. Taft wrote opinions in 34 per cent of the "important constitutional cases"[59] decided while he was Chief Justice. Hughes' and Stone's percentages were 28.9 and 17.9, respectively.

When the Chief Justice does not speak for the Court, his influence lies primarily in his assignment of important cases to associates who generally agree with him. From 1925 to 1930, Taft designated his fellow conservatives, Sutherland and Butler, to speak for the Court in 50 per cent of the important constitutional cases assigned to Associate Justices. From 1932 to 1937, Hughes, who agreed more with Roberts, Van Devanter, and Sutherland than the rest of his associates, assigned 44 per cent of the important constitutional cases to Roberts and Sutherland. From 1943 to 1945, Stone assigned 55 per cent of those cases to Douglas and Frankfurter. During that period, only Reed agreed more with Stone than Frankfurter, but Douglas agreed with Stone less than any other Justice except Black. Stone had high regard for Douglas' ability, and this may have been the Chief Justice's overriding consideration in his assignments to Douglas.

[59]The "important constitutional cases" decided by the Court from 1921 to 1946 were determined by examination of four leading works on the Constitution, Paul A. Freund, Arthur E. Sutherland, Mark De Wolfe Howe, and Ernest J. Brown, *Constitutional Law* (Boston, 1954); Alfred H. Kelly and Winfred A. Harbison, *The American Constitution: Its Origins and Development* (New York, 1948); Alpheus T. Mason and William M. Beaney, *American Constitutional Law* (Englewood Cliffs, N. J., 1959); and C. Herman Pritchett, *The American Constitution* (New York, 1959). If a case was discussed in any two of these works, it was considered an "important constitutional case."

It is possible that the Chief Justice might seek to influence dissenting Justices to join in the Court's opinion by adhering to one or both of the following assignment rules:

Rule 1: Assign the case to the Justice whose views are the closest to the dissenters on the ground that his opinion would take a middle approach upon which both majority and minority could agree.

Rule 2: Where there are blocs on the Court and a bloc splits, assign the case to a majority member of the dissenters' bloc on the ground that he would take a middle approach upon which both majority and minority could agree and that the minority Justices would be more likely to agree with him because of general mutuality of agreement.

There is some evidence that early in Taft's Chief Justiceship he followed Rule 1 occasionally and assigned himself cases in an effort to win over dissenters. An analysis of his assignments from 1925 to 1930, however, indicates that he apparently did not adhere to either of the above rules with any consistency. Stone's assignments from 1943 to 1945 show the same thing. In other words, Taft and Stone did not generally use their assignment power to influence their associates to unanimity. However, an analysis of Hughes' assignments from 1932 to 1937 indicates that he probably did. He appears to have followed Rule 1 when either the liberal or conservative blocs dissented intact. When the liberal bloc dissented, Roberts, who was then a center judge, was assigned 46.5 per cent of the opinions. The remaining 53.5 per cent were divided among the conservatives, apparently according to their degree of conservatism: Sutherland, 25 per cent; Butler, 17.8 per cent; McReynolds, 10.7 per cent. When the conservative bloc dissented, Hughes divided 63 per cent of the opinions between himself and Roberts.

Hughes probably also followed Rule 2 to some extent. When the left bloc split, Brandeis was assigned 22 per cent of the cases he could have received, compared with his 10 per cent assignment average for unanimous cases. When the right bloc split, Sutherland was assigned 16 per cent of the decisions he could have received, compared with his 11 per cent average for unanimous cases. He received five of the six cases assigned the conservatives when their bloc was split. One of those cases was *Powell* v. *Alabama* which, it has been said, was assigned Sutherland "probably in the hope that he could bring over Justices Butler and McReynolds while some of the more 'liberal' Justices could not."[60]

If the Chief Justice is to be well liked, he must appear to be generous, considerate, and impartial in assigning cases, particularly the important cases. Taft was considered generous in his assignments, and undoubtedly this contributed to his likeability. Hughes said he tried to assign each Justice the same proportion of important cases and especially took into account the feelings of the senior Justices. Justice Roberts thought Hughes' assignments were generous and considerate, and Justice Frankfurter believed that no Chief Justice equalled Hughes in the "skill, wisdom, and disinterestedness" with which he assigned opinions.[61] Justice Stone, however, thought otherwise. During the early and middle Thirties, he felt that Hughes was not assigning him as many important cases as he should have received. Just as Stone felt slighted by Hughes in the matter of assignments, so did Justices Murphy and Rutledge during Stone's Chief Justiceship. Stone was aware of this, but he did little about it.[62]

How often the Chief Justice uses his assignment power to influence activity of his associates cannot be determined with certainty. Besides influence, there are other reasons underlying opinion assignment such as equality of case distribution, ability, and expertise.[63] Nonetheless, every assignment presents the Chief Justice with an opportunity for influence.

[60]McElwain, *op. cit.*, p. 18.

[61]Frankfurter, *op. cit.*, p. 137.

[62]Mason, *op. cit.*, pp. 602–603, 793.

[63]I have considered the general problem of why Chief Justices make the assignments they do in a previous unpublished paper, "The Assignment of the Court's Opinion by the Chief Justice," presented at the Midwest Conference of Political Scientists, Indiana University, April 28–30, 1960.

VI. THE FINAL PHASE: PERSUASION AND UNANIMITY

In the last stage of the decisional process, opinions are written, circulated, discussed, and approved or disapproved. Final decision near, Court members have their last chance to persuade each other. The results of interaction during this period can be highly significant: opinion modification, increase or decrease in the size of a majority, and even the reversal of a conference decision. Again the Chief Justice is in a favorable position for purposes of influence. Standing at the center of intra-Court communication, he ordinarily knows better than any of his associates the status of each case—who is having trouble writing an opinion, who is overworked, who is wavering in his vote, etc.—and if he is so inclined, he can play an active role in reconciling differences, seeking compromises, and attaining unanimity. Since, as a practical matter, he decides when an opinion will be announced, he can delay the announcement in hope of augmenting the Court's majority. What the Chief Justice actually does greatly depends upon how he views his role in this final phase of the decisional process.

Seldom has a Chief Justice had a more definite conception of his role than Taft. The Chief Justice, he said, is "expected to promote teamwork by the Court so as to give weight and solidarity to its opinions."[64] He believed his predecessor, White, earnestly sought to avoid divisions by skillfully reconciling differences among the Justices, and he intended to do the same. His aim was unanimity, but he was willing to admit that at times dissents were justifiable and perhaps even a duty. Dissent was proper, he thought, in cases where a Court member strongly believed the majority erred in a matter involving important principle or where a dissent might serve some useful purpose, such as convincing Congress to pass certain legislation. But in other cases, a Justice should be a good mem-

[64]Draft of a tribute to Edward Douglas White, *ca.* May 1921, Taft Papers.

ber of the team, silently acquiesce in the views of the majority, and not try to make a record for himself by dissenting.

Taft's conception of the function of the dissent was shared by most of his associates, and when he sought to unite them, his efforts were accepted as proper and consistent with his role as Chief Justice. Justices joining the Taft Court were socialized in the no-dissent-unless-absolutely-necessary tradition, and most of them learned it well. Justice Butler gave it classic expression on the back of one of Stone's slip opinions:

I voted to reverse. While this sustains your conclusion to affirm, I still think reversal would be better. But I shall in silence acquiesce. Dissents seldom aid in the right development or statement of the law. They often do harm. For myself I say: "lead us not into temptation."[65]

Even Stone, who was not so sure about the no-dissent tradition, usually went along with it, acquiescing in the appropriate cases.

Taft enjoyed moderate success in his efforts to attain unanimity. During his first year as Chief Justice, he united the Court in a number of [controversial] cases. . . . Usually he would assign himself such cases and try to write an opinion which would bring in the dissenters. This meant he had to make concessions to Justices like Brandeis, but he was willing to exchange concessions for votes. When there were divisions in cases he assigned to others which could be reconciled, Taft would try to mediate between majority and minority (at times with the help of Van Devanter) in an effort to attain unanimity. If there was a possibility of winning over a dissenter, Taft would frequently let the case go over a few conferences with hope that time would work in his favor.

Hughes easily assumed the role of Court unifier that Taft had cut out for him, for he believed that unanimity should be sought where it could be attained without sacrificing

strongly held convictions. Like Taft, he distinguished two types of cases, those involving matters of important principle and those of lesser importance. The former were dissent-worthy; the latter were not. As to the cases of lesser importance, Hughes felt it was better to have the law settled one way or the other regardless of his own ideas as to the correct disposition of the case; and if the majority voted contrary to his view, he would change his vote. For example, in a case involving statutory construction, Hughes wrote to Stone: "I choke a little at swallowing your analysis; still I do not think it would serve any useful purpose to expose my views."[66]

Like Taft, Hughes mediated differences of opinion between contending factions, and in order to get a unanimous decision, he would try to find common ground upon which all could stand. He was willing to modify his own opinions to hold or increase his majority, and if this meant he had to put in some disconnected thoughts or sentences, in they went. In cases assigned to others, he would suggest the addition or subtraction of a paragraph if by doing so he could save a dissent or concurring opinion. According to Justice Roberts, dissents were thus avoided in some cases in which agreement seemed impossible. But unlike Taft, Hughes apparently seldom held up the delivery of an opinion in an effort to secure another vote or two. He made his attempt to secure unanimity, and if it failed, the case was usually handed down as soon as the opinions were ready.

Hughes' efforts to attain unanimity were fairly successful. During his Chief Justiceship, there was no radical increase in the number of dissents. Even in the cases that invalidated New Deal legislation, the Court was fairly intact. Of the eleven such cases, five were unanimous, and two were decided 8 to 1. The no-dissent-unless-absolutely-necessary tradition continued, and in a host of lesser cases Court members acquiesced in silence. The

[65]Slip opinion, *The Malcom Baxter, Jr.*, 277 U.S. 323 (1928) (9–0), Stone Papers. Butler, apparently thinking this was a good statement or at least one the Chief Justice would like to see, had a copy of it made and sent to Taft. May 19, 1928, Taft Papers.

[66]Nov. 4, 1939, Stone Papers. The case was *Stanford* v. *Comm'r.* 308 U.S. 39 (1939) (8–0). Roberts and McReynolds also acquiesced in silence. The case is cited as illustrative of what was commonplace in the Hughes Court.

Roosevelt appointees, particularly, showed remarkable restraint in the matter of dissents while serving under Hughes. Frankfurter, who had the best record, registered only seven dissents in his three years with Hughes. The New Deal Justices were baptized in the old tradition concerning dissent, but whether they would retain the faith after Hughes left the Court was another matter.

As an Associate Justice, Stone prized the right to dissent and occasionally rankled under the no-dissent-unless-absolutely-necessary tradition of the Taft and Hughes Courts. As Chief Justice, he did not believe it appropriate for him to dissuade Court members, by persuasion or otherwise, from dissenting in individual cases. A Chief Justice, he thought, might admonish his associates generally to exercise restraint in the matter of dissents and seek to find common ground for decision, but beyond that he should not go. Stone usually went no further. His activity or lack of it in this matter gave rise to new expectations on the part of his associates as to their role and the role of the Chief Justice regarding unanimity and dissent. A new tradition of great freedom of individual expression displaced the tradition of the Taft and Hughes Courts. This explains in part the unprecedented number of dissents and separate opinions during Stone's Chief Justiceship.

Chief Justice Stone, nonetheless, exercised some influence in the final phase of the decisional process. In *Edwards* v. *California*,[67] one of the first cases heard by the Court after he became Chief Justice, he persuaded Justice Byrnes to change his conference vote, and the switch resulted in a decision based on the commerce clause rather than on the privileges and immunities clause of the Constitution. He also influenced the content of many opinions, especially those of Justice Murphy, by suggesting additions and deletions. Although Justices who voted against Stone in conference would occasionally go along with his

opinions, he usually made no concerted effort to attain unanimity. He recognized, however, that unanimity in certain cases was desirable, and in a few cases he sought it. . . .

The unprecedented number of dissents and concurrences during Stone's Chief Justiceship can be only partly attributed to the displacing of the old tradition of loyalty to the Court's opinion. A major source of difficulty appears to have been the free and easy expression of views in conference. Whether the Justices were sure of their grounds or not, they spoke up and many times took positions from which they could not easily retreat, and given the heated debate which sometimes occurred in the Stone conference, the commitment was not simply intellectual. What began in conference frequently ended with elaborate justification as concurring or dissenting opinions in the United States Reports. This, together with Stone's passiveness in seeking unanimity, is probably the best explanation for what Professor Pritchett characterized as "the multiplication of division" in the Supreme Court.[68]

VII. CONCLUSION

The task of the political scientist, said John Morley, is not simply to describe governmental institutions, but to penetrate to the secret of their functions. In regard to the Chief Justiceship, that is difficult, for complex relationships among the Chief Justice and Justices are involved. The office provides the Chief Justice with an opportunity for influence, but it does not guarantee it. To exercise influence, he must perform activity that results in his associates choosing to do what he wants them to do; and in this regard, his success depends largely upon his likeability and esteem in the Court and upon how he perceives and fulfills his role.

. . .

[67]314 U.S. 482 (1941) (9–0).

[68]C. Herman Pritchett, *The Roosevelt Court* (New York, 1948), p. 24.

24 COURTS AS SMALL GROUPS

Walter F. Murphy

Collegial courts and juries are small groups in a face-to-face relationship that interact under an obligation to solve a specific problem or set of problems. Reliable theories and perhaps even raw data about human behavior in small groups may thus be relevant to the study of the judicial process. This article will discuss the "state of the art" of small group sociology that may be useful to that study.

The initial problem is to define what is meant by a small group approach.[1] The studies clustered under the "small group" rubric have had many different orientations and objectives and have employed many different assumptions and data, but the focus of most of these investigations has been on collective decision-making.[2] This paper will refer to "a" small group approach rather than "the" approach, meaning research that puts a major emphasis on the processes of face-to-face interaction among members of the same group to produce a decision or a series of decisions.[3]

I

A major stimulus of small group studies of judicial behavior has been the work of C. Herman Pritchett of the University of Chicago. Beginning in the early 1940's, Pritchett published a series of articles and *The*

Reprinted by permission of publisher from Walter F. Murphy, "Courts as Small Groups," *Harvard Law Review*, 79 (1966), pp 1565–1572. Copyright © 1966 by the Harvard Law Review Association.

[1]For discussion of the meaning of "small" and "group" and of related problems of a basic nature, see Golembiewski, *The Small Group*, chs. 2–3 (1962).

[2]For an introduction to the extensive small group literature see Bass, *Leadership, Psychology, and Organizational Behavior* (1960); Hare, Borgatta, & Bales (eds.), *Small Groups* (1955).

[3]The definition thus excludes discussion of such interesting works as Ulmer, "Homeostatic Tendencies in the United States Supreme Court," in *Introductory Readings in Political Behavior* 168 (1961). For a summary of other useful definitions see Verba, *Small Groups and Political Behavior* 11–12 (1961).

Roosevelt Court,[4] demonstrating the existence of cohesive voting blocs on the U.S. Supreme Court during the years 1937–1947. He relied in part on traditional case analysis but also used statistical analysis of the Justices' votes to show consistent tendencies of certain members of the Court to vote together on various classes of issues. The bloc analysis portion of his study depended entirely on the votes of the Justices.

In 1958, Eloise Snyder, a sociologist, published an analysis of the Supreme Court which considered whether the Court over a long-time span (1921–1953) had divided into persistent subgroups, how changes in alignments occurred, and how new Justices found their positions within the larger group.[5] Using as her data the votes of the Justices in all non-unanimous constitutional cases during the thirty-three year period, Snyder found that the Court divided into three subgroups: a liberal group, a conservative group, and a pivotal group that lacked a firm commitment. Snyder reported that these alignments were consistent. While a Justice might switch from a pivotal to a liberal or conservative subgroup or vice-versa, never did a Justice of the liberal subgroup cross over to the conservative bloc, and rarely did a Justice make the conservative-to-liberal transition without a pause in the pivotal group.[6] She noted a general tendency to shift to the right during a Justice's career but attributed this more to the Court's moving to the left so as to make a Justice whose views did not change seem to shift to the right than to any change of views by the individual Justice. Newly appointed Justices tended to join the pivotal subgroup, the group that frequently held the balance of power. After a time on the Court they

[4]Pritchett, *The Roosevelt Court* (1948). This bloc analysis was extended on a more limited set of issues through the end of the Chief Justiceship of Fred Vinson in Pritchett, *Civil Liberties and the Vinson Court* (1954).

[5]Snyder, "The Supreme Court as a Small Group," 36 *Social Forces* 232 (1958).

[6]Snyder was speaking in general terms; she did not mean that "liberals" and "conservatives" never voted together in individual cases. See also Schubert, *Quantitative Analysis of Judicial Behavior* 77–172 (1959); Loeb, "Judicial Blocs and Judicial Values in Civil Liberties Cases," 14 *Am. U. L. Rev.* 146 (1965).

tended to gravitate to the right or left subgroup.

Since Pritchett and Snyder only used voting records, they could discover little more than that Justices could be classified; study of groups also requires consideration of interpersonal interaction and influence. The fact that two or more Justices vote together is rather weak evidence that their votes are the result of interaction; standing alone, voting records tell very little about the force or direction of any interpersonal influence that may exist. Small group analysis requires other kinds of data and a more general understanding of the impact of a group decisional situation on individual behavior.

Especially in the postwar period, social psychologists have produced a mass of literature on group decisional situations.[7] Their research was based on observation of people brought together under laboratory conditions and given a specific problem to solve. The experiments were designed to suggest and to test as rigorously as possible general hypotheses about leadership as a function of group interaction. Professor Robert Bales of Harvard, perhaps the leader in this field, developed a concept of the dual character of leadership: task leadership and social leadership.[8] The former seeks to complete the present task in the most effective and efficient manner; the latter seeks to provide the friendly atmosphere that eases cooperation. Experiments indicated that these two functions often are exercised by different persons within the group.

It is difficult to obtain direct observations of the judicial decision-making process. The private papers of deceased judges, however, constitute a fruitful source of information, and various judges have preserved their working papers—including intracourt memoranda, slip opinions as edited by colleagues, and occasionally notes taken during conference discussions—and arranged for their future use by scholars.

David Danelski, a lawyer and political scientist, was the first to utilize both the theoretical constructs of the small group sociologists and the information in judicial papers to apply a small group approach to a court.[9] Relying on materials found in the unpublished papers of a number of Justices, Danelski applied Bales' concept of dual leadership to the Supreme Court under Chief Justices Taft, Hughes, and Stone. Taft, he concluded, was the social leader of his court and relied on his close friend, Willis Van Devanter, to supply task leadership; Hughes exercised task leadership over his brethren and also offered some social leadership; Stone played neither role and was unable to ally himself with one or more colleagues who could perform these functions.[10]

Danelski concluded that as a result of the comparative ability in social leadership, conflict among the Justices was more muted and cohesion more pronounced on the Taft Court than on the Hughes Court and far more so than on the Stone Court. Danelski ranks the Hughes Court somewhat ahead of that of Taft and well above that of Stone in terms of the effectiveness of task leadership—decisions produced in relation to conference time. Hughes's advantage in playing both roles was offset, Danelski believes, by Taft's greater skill as a social leader.

In a work related to Danelski's, I discussed how a Justice of the Supreme Court could

---

[7]For an account of the historical development of this kind of analysis, see Faris, "Development of the Small-Group Research Movement," in Sherif & Wilson (eds.), *Group Relations at the Crossroads* 155 (1953).

[8]Bales, *Interaction Process Analysis* (1950).

[9]Danelski, "The Influence of the Chief Justice in the Decisional Process," in Murphy & Pritchett (eds.), *Courts, Judges, and Politics* 497 (1961). Other scholars, of course, had used judicial papers, *e.g.*, Mason, *Harlan Fiske Stone* (1956), but they did not use the tools developed by small group sociology. Those who criticize use of this kind of material are answered in Llewellyn, *The Common Law Tradition—Deciding Appeals* 324 n. 308 (1960).

[10]Danelski's conclusion was based primarily on his analysis of the Stone Papers in the Library of Congress and on the divisions within the Stone Court revealed in concurring and dissenting opinions. A later reading and partial analysis of the papers of Mr. Justice Frank Murphy at the University of Michigan indicate that Stone led the conference discussion at least to the extent of getting the other Justices to discuss the issues he thought crucial.

lawfully act to maximize his influence on public policy development through a process of bargaining.[11] My objective was not to demonstrate how the judicial process typically operates but to explain the capability of a single Justice to affect the definition and allocation of values in our society. The Associate Justices of the U.S. Supreme Court are equal in authority, and the Chief Justice has only a small amount of additional authority. It may sometimes happen for a period of time, as with John Marshall, that a judge may by the power of his intellect and the sheer force of his personality lead his colleagues. Certainly one should not underestimate the importance in the judicial process of reasoned argument based on thorough research and grounded in deep learning, nor should one be willing without evidence to deny that even judges may be swayed by a great personality. Yet on many issues a Justice may find himself unable to convince colleagues even after massing all his erudition and dialectical skill, and even after emotional appeals. A Justice may thus find himself either: (a) with the majority on the result but unable to agree with other Justices on the reasoning to support the decision; (b) with the minority on both scores; or (c) with the majority on both points but faced with the publication of an acid dissent. In these situations he can strike out on his own and write his views just as he holds them, or he can negotiate with his colleagues and try to compromise existing differences.

Bickel and Wellington have criticized the Warren Court because some of its opinions appear to be "desperately negotiated documents,"[12] but it would seem that many if not most opinions of the Court on major issues are negotiated documents.[13] I would also hypothesize that this kind of bargaining process occurs on any collegial court that follows similar formal procedures of group decision-making. If this is true, close reading of an opinion should include consideration of the compromises it may contain. What may seem inscrutable wisdom to the traditional case analyst may only be deliberate ambiguity designed to accommodate by its very vagueness conflicting doctrines. One would not expect nine or even five intelligent, individualistic, and strong-willed lawyers to agree readily on controversial and significant issues, much less on the doctrines to be established and reasoning to be used to justify any major ruling. As Justice Frankfurter observed after fourteen years on the bench: "When you have to have at least five people to agree on something, they can't have that comprehensive completeness of candor which is open to a single man, giving his own reasons untrammeled by what anybody else may do or not do if he put that out."[14] The bargaining and resulting compromise may be over trivial matters of literary style or over crucial doctrinal issues. The objects which a Justice has to trade are his vote and his concurrence in an opinion; his sanctions are his right to change his vote and his right to write a separate opinion. Quite clearly, the effectiveness of the first sanction depends largely on the existing division within the Court and of the second on the Justice's literary skill and legal expertise. Bargaining may be the product of open negotiation or it may be accomplished tacitly. Brandeis, Bickel shows, was a master of the latter technique. Often he would circulate a dissent within the Court, then withdraw it when the conservative majority modified the opinion of the Court.[15]

---

[11]Murphy, *Elements of Judicial Strategy*, ch. 3 (1964). My data consisted primarily of material drawn from Columbia University's Oral History Project, the papers of Presidents Coolidge, F. D. Roosevelt, and Truman, of Chief Justices Chase, Taft, Hughes, and Stone, and of Justices Lurton, McReynolds, Sutherland, and Murphy. Much of the analytical framework of this part of my study was built on the work of Danelski, Bales, and other small group sociologists, although I differed with them at several points.

[12]Bickel & Wellington, "Legislative Purpose and the Judicial Process: The Lincoln Mills Case," 71 *Harv. L. Rev.* 1, 3 (1957).

[13]See, *e.g.*, Mr. Justice Frankfurter's discussion of Justice Holmes' compromises in The Pipe Line Cases, 234 U.S. 548 (1914), *Felix Frankfurter Reminisces*, 294–301 (Philips ed. 1960).

[14]*Id.* at 298.

[15]Bickel, *The Unpublished Opinions of Mr. Justice Brandeis* 205–10 (1957).

II

As I indicated in the opening paragraph of this paper, a small group approach offers no magic key to understanding judicial behavior.[16] One has to keep in mind, first, that social scientists have so far only a variety of hypotheses about behavior in small groups, most of which have been tested only in experimental, laboratory situations. Clearly, one must not uncritically apply to the actions of professional judges concepts derived from the behavior of *ad hoc* groups assembled in a laboratory for the purpose of solving only one problem. The findings of small group sociologists should be treated only as working hypotheses until tested outside the laboratory. And of course no social scientist claims that the group environment is the only factor governing behavior. Small group analysis, as Golembiewski points out,[17] merely supplements understanding of individual psychology and of social forces operating in the larger social environment.

More specifically, I have reservations about the orientation of much of the small group literature toward leadership. Stressing leadership as a product of a social situation may leave the impression that because the functions of leadership are needed, they will be performed. But a leadership void may exist and persist, or only be partially filled. Moreover, just as one must be careful not to mistake formal trappings for real leadership, so too one has to be careful not to equate role-playing with effective role-playing. For instance, though Hughes was able to center discussion on the questions he thought important and to conduct that discussion rapidly and efficiently, and though he soothed ruffled feelings and maintained a working level of harmony among the brethren, the vital question remains: having led them to be social and having led them through their tasks, was he able to lead the Justices to vote and to write opinions the way he wanted?[18] The inability of small group theories to pro-

vide answers or even a framework for answers to this question detracts from their usefulness; but it would not appear that the future establishment of such a framework is impossible.

A second set of difficulties with any small group approach involves available data. As already indicated, although voting records are important indicia of group interaction, they are of limited use. Direct observation is probably impossible to obtain. Interviews, however, might be of some help in filling the gaps, if the interviewer makes certain he stays away from issues that are or are likely soon to be *sub judice*.

The private papers of the Justices are extremely valuable here. They often reveal much about the force and direction of interpersonal influence and group interaction, yet they, too, are subject to limitations. Even where a Justice took and kept notes of conference discussion, as Murphy and Burton did, the record is rarely complete and may suffer because of memory lapse and human bias. Further, since no Justice is apt to allow his papers to be used during his own lifetime, there will always be a time lag before they can be utilized.

Even with these difficulties, there are still advantages to a small group approach. Careful attention to assumptions and critical use of unproved hypotheses can avoid most of the theoretical pitfalls. And new research techniques can be invented to reduce problems with data.[19] It might even be worthwhile to try to simulate a court much as the Chicago project has done with juries. The simulation could be made part of an advanced course.[20]

Simulation employing students seems, however, better adapted to teaching participants about the nature of group decision-making

---

[16]For perceptive general critiques of small group analysis, See Golembiewski, *op. cit., supra* note 1, and Verba, *op. cit., supra* note 3.

[17]*Op. cit., supra* note 1, at 17.

[18]*Cf.* note 10 *supra*.

[19]See Ulmer, "Leadership in the Michigan Supreme Court," in Schubert (ed.), *Judicial Decision-Making*, 13 (1963), which applies an imaginative series of methods based on concurrence in opinions.

[20]In a graduate seminar on the judicial process I have required students at one three-hour session to sit as a court, hear oral argument on a hypothetical dispute in constitutional law, and then meet in conference to discuss and decide the case. After the conference the chief justice has assigned the opinion of the court. While allowing dissenting and concurring opinions, I coerced the majority into agreeing on an institutional opinion by giving each the same grade for the court's opinion.

than it is a promising research device. Nevertheless, interaction among the students may suggest some useful ideas that can be tested in other ways. Another kind of panel might be composed of experts, perhaps lawyers with considerable experience in appellate advocacy, law professors, or former judges. This kind of simulation would probably be a more accurate research tool. The NAACP has on occasion utilized a similar procedure to prepare presentations before the Supreme Court.[21]

III

Although it may not be of any immediate use in winning a particular lawsuit, small group analysis has already done much to increase understanding—by social scientists as well as lawyers—of the judicial process; and the various approaches have not yet been nearly fully exploited. There have been few investigations of tribunals other than the U. S. Supreme Court.[22] It would be very useful to

have comparative studies of the influence of the group situation in courts that follow other kinds of formal decisional procedures.[23] What difference does it make, for instance, that in some states the task of writing the opinion of the court is assigned on a strictly rotational basis? Or if, as in England and Canada, there is a tradition of seriatim rather than institutional opinions? Or if, as in civil law countries, there is a rule against separate opinions? Do any of these formal practices affect the exercise of leadership and bargaining among the judges? What kinds of informal rules or customs develop to protect the integrity of the court and maintain harmony between the majority and the minority? Most important, what effect do these formal and informal procedures have on the course of the development of law and public policy?[24]

[21]Vose, *Caucasians Only*, 199–200 (1959).
[22]*But* see Sickels, "The Illusion of Judicial Consensus," 59, *Am. Pol. Sci. Rev.*, 100 (1965); Ulmer, *supra* note 3.

[23]For descriptions of the formal procedures allowed in various American courts see New York University Institute of Judicial Administration, Appellate Courts: International Operating Procedures, Preliminary Report (mimeo., 1957).
[24]For another view of the utility of small group analysis, see Becker, *Political Behavioralism and Modern Jurisprudence* 26–31 (1964).

D. Fact Patterns and Decision-Making

Conventional legal analysis considers the conversion process a relatively straightforward process although one that occasionally allows for judicial creativity to fill in the blank spots of the law. For the most part, it is argued, judges decide specific cases by examining the facts of the case and the law that is supposed to govern that situation. When the law is unclear, judges examine previously decided cases with similar or analogous factual situations and decide in accord with the precedents. If there are conflicting precedents or if no precedent appears applicable, judges are free to distinguish the case before them and decide according to their interpretation of what the law requires. According to this standard interpretation of the conversion process, judges clearly state in their opinions the reasons for their decisions.

The social science approach eschews much (but not all) of this model. Indeed, legal realists of an earlier era would have been quick to point out that in actuality judges have more discretion than the formal model suggests. The very fact that the litigants have gone to trial or sought appellate review is often a good indication that the facts and/or law are unclear. The costs and time involved in going to court screen out most frivolous litigation. At the highest level of the federal judicial system—the Supreme Court—the judges are given wide discretion as to which cases to accept for review and which to reject. This means, particularly at the appellate stage, it is rare that any two cases involve the same questions of fact and law. In addition, there may be so many precedents that judicial discretion can be considerable. Lastly, cases often turn on inarticulated premises rather than the reasons formally stated in opinions. All these considerations make the conventional legal model unsatisfactory as an explanation for the conversion process. This does not mean, however, that the fact situations of certain types of cases are irrelevant.

One line of empirical judicial research relevant for the conversion process seeks to uncover from a statistical analysis of various sets of decisions the fact patterns that are related to the outcomes of such cases. Although superficially this may seem a modern form of the conventional approach, there are several considerations which set this form of analysis apart from the older model. First, in conventional analysis, the assumption is made that courts are consistent in the type of facts they use for the basis of their decisions. No such assumption is made in fact-pattern analysis. Indeed, the existence of consistency in a particular area of adjudication *is* determined *by* fact-pattern analysis. Second, conventional legal analysts are concerned with the relationship of "law" to facts. The fact-pattern approach requires no such focus on legalistic rationalizations of decisions but is only concerned with the facts of particular types of cases. Furthermore, the conventional approach does not enable one to determine what combinations of facts are more important than others for reaching a result for one or the other party involved in the litigation. On the other hand, if the court is consistent, fact-pattern methods can potentially yield precise weightings or combinations of facts that allow one to predict the outcomes of future cases.

The selection in this section is by Fred Kort. He has developed two methodologies for analyzing fact patterns which are associated with the decisions the Supreme Court renders. They are simultaneous equations and Boolean algebra. The student should observe that Kort's approach differs in two ways from the approaches discussed in the two preceding sections. First, the focus is on court decisions rather than on the behavior of individual judges. Secondly, the emphasis is on what Kort refers to as conditional prediction. One can infer from the successful application of this approach in certain legal areas that fact stimuli are relevant components of the conversion process by which judges process inputs and fashion outputs.[1]

---

[1]Cf. Glendon Schubert's comments about this line of research in *Judicial Behavior* (New York: Rand McNally, 1964), pp. 449–455.

25 SIMULTANEOUS EQUATIONS AND BOOLEAN ALGEBRA IN THE ANALYSIS OF JUDICIAL DECISIONS

Fred Kort

INTRODUCTION

In the study of the dependence of judicial decisions on relevant facts, traditional methods of analysis have encountered limitations in

Reprinted with permission from a symposium, *Jurimetrics*, appearing in *Law and Contemporary Problems* (Vol. 28, No. 1, Winter 1963), pp. 143–163, published by the Duke University School of Law, Durham, North Carolina. Copyright 1963, by Duke University.

solving salient problems. In many areas of law, comprehensive sets of facts have been specified by courts as relevant and controlling for reaching decisions, with the understanding that some combinations of these facts would lead to decisions in favor of one party, whereas other combinations would lead to decisions in favor of the opposing party. Beyond the association of *some* combinations of these facts with decisions which already have been reached, it is not apparent, however, what decisions can be expected on the basis of *other* combinations of the specified facts. For example, in reviewing administrative decisions in workmen's compensation cases, appellate courts have indicated that the award or the denial of compensation must be decided on the basis of the particular combination of such facts as the nature of the injury, the conditions under which the accident or the harmful act occurred and became known, the health record of the claimant prior to the injury, and the evidence obtained from expert and lay testimony.

From a series of cases which already have been decided, it can be ascertained to what decisions some combinations of the relevant facts lead. But it cannot be readily inferred what decisions other combinations of these facts would justify. In order to appreciate that this problem is not a unique feature of any particular area of law, it is advisable to consider another example. In the involuntary confession cases arising under the due process clause of the Fourteenth Amendment, the Supreme Court of the United States has clearly stated that each decision depends on the facts pertaining to the pressure applied to the petitioner and to his inability to resist such pressure. Cases which already have been decided indicate what decisions have been reached on the basis of some combinations of such facts. They do not show, however, what decisions would correspond to other combinations of these facts.

The general problem in the analysis of all decisions which depend on various combinations of specified facts is, therefore, the following: to obtain a *precise and exhaustive* distinction between combinations of facts that lead to decisions in favor of one party and combinations of facts that lead to decisions in favor of the opposing party. This distinction can be obtained with the aid of mathematical models. To be sure, it can also be described verbally. But such a description would be extremely complex, and—in any case—it could be formulated only after a mathematical model has been designed.

For the purpose of obtaining the indicated distinction, two alternative models will be introduced in this presentation. One is based on simultaneous equations, and the other utilizes Boolean algebra. The models will be first discussed separately, and then their respective advantages and disadvantages will be compared. In conclusion, attention will be directed to the purposes, the limitations, and the implications of their use in the analysis of judicial decisions.

I. A MODEL BASED ON SIMULTANEOUS EQUATIONS

Before examining situations which actually are encountered in judicial decisions that depend on various combinations of specified facts, it will be helpful to consider a hypothetical example. Assume that in a given area of law facts, f_1, f_2, and f_3 have been accepted by a court as relevant and controlling for the decision of cases. Assume also that these facts have different "weights" in determining the decision, and that these weights are represented by x_1, x_2, and x_3, respectively. Assume, furthermore, that three cases already have been decided. In Case 1, all three facts, *i.e.*, f_1, f_2, and f_3, were present, and the decision was in favor of the party seeking redress. In Case 2, facts f_1 and f_3 were present, and the decision again was in favor of the aggrieved party. But in Case 3, facts f_1 and f_2 were present, and the decision was against the party seeking redress. What decision can be expected on that basis in a case in which facts f_2 and f_3 are present? Neither the stated rule that facts f_1, f_2, and f_3 shall be controlling for the decision, nor any of the decisions which already have been reached, offers an answer to this question. If it can be assumed, however, that the available decisions as well as future decisions form a consistent pattern of judicial action, a set of simultaneous equations can be written, and the solution of these equations provides an answer to this very question.

In the proposed set of simultaneous equations, each case is represented by one equation, and the decision of the case is treated as a function of the combination of controlling facts. Accordingly, the facts of the case are the independent variables in the equation, and the decision is the dependent variable. In this fashion, the cases which already have been decided form the desired set of simultaneous equations, in which the weights of the facts are the unknowns. As these equations are solved, a weight is found for each controlling fact, and—as these weights are substituted in the equation which represents a new case—a numerical value for the particular combination of facts and for the corresponding decision is obtained. Moreover, since the weights of the facts now are known, a numerical value for *any* combination of these facts and for its corresponding decision can be determined.

In order to illustrate this method in its most basic form, the following assumptions are now made with regard to the hypothetical example which has been introduced: (1) The combination of facts is linear, *i.e.*, the relationship among the facts is additive. Further comments about this assumption will be made later. (2) The cases are decided by a court consisting of nine judges, and all judges participate in all decisions. This assumption also will receive further attention later. (3) Each decision is represented by the number of votes of judges favorable to the party seeking redress. The reason for this assumption is that the decisions of multi-judge courts do not necessarily constitute two opposite extremes, but are characterized by various degrees of support (or lack of support) of the aggrieved party by the votes of the judges. (4) Seven judges voted in favor of the party seeking redress in Case 1, five voted in favor of the aggrieved party in Case 2, but only three supported the party seeking redress in Case 3. The three decided cases in the hypothetical example then can be stated in terms of the following simultaneous equations:

$$f_{11}x_1 + f_{12}x_2 + f_{13}x_3 = 7$$
$$f_{21}x_1 + f_{22}x_2 + f_{23}x_3 = 5$$
$$f_{31}x_1 + f_{32}x_2 + f_{33}x_3 = 3.$$

In this set of equations, only the weights of the facts, *i.e.*, x_1, x_2, and x_3, are the unknowns. The coefficients f_{ij} (i = 1, 2, 3; j = 1, 2, 3) are known. They indicate the presence or absence of the respective facts in the cases. More specifically, f_{ij} indicates whether fact j is present or absent in case i. If the fact is present in the case, $f_{ij} = 1$; if it is absent, $f_{ij} = 0$; if the fact has more than one manifestation in the case—for example, more than

one accident occurred in a workmen's compensation case—f_{ij} has a multiple value of 1. Accordingly, in Case 1 of the hypothetical example, f_{11}, f_{12}, and f_{13} each has a value of 1. In Case 2, f_{21} as well as f_{23} has a value of 1. But—since f_2 is absent in Case 2—$f_{22} = 0$, and this means that the second term in the second equation vanishes. In Case 3, f_{31} as well as f_{32} equals 1. However, $f_{33} = 0$ because f_3 is absent in Case 3, and this means that the third term in the third equation also vanishes. The simultaneous equations which represent the decided cases in the hypothetical example can be restated, therefore, in the following form:

$$x_1 + x_2 + x_3 = 7$$
$$x_1 \qquad + x_3 = 5$$
$$x_1 + x_2 \qquad = 3.$$

These equations can be interpreted as follows: In Case 1, the presence and relative importance of facts f_1, f_2, and f_3 persuaded seven judges—*i.e.*, a sufficient majority of the nine-judge court—that a decision in favor of the party seeking redress should be rendered. In Case 2, the presence and relative importance of facts f_1 and f_3 persuaded a smaller, but still sufficient, majority of five judges that a decision in favor of the aggrieved party was in order. But in Case 3, the presence and relative importance of facts f_1 and f_2 gave the party seeking redress the support of only three judges, *i.e.*, a decision in his favor was not reached.

As these equations are solved according to the basic rules of algebra, a weight of $x_1 = 1$ is obtained for fact f_1, a weight of $x_2 = 2$ for fact f_2, and a weight of $x_3 = 4$ for fact f_3. By substituting these weights in the equation which represents the new case in the hypothetical example, a numerical value for the combination of facts f_2 and f_3 and for the corresponding decision—*i.e.*, six votes in favor of the party seeking redress—is obtained. Moreover, a numerical value for any other possible combination of the controlling facts (including any single fact) and for its corresponding decision can now be determined. In this fashion, a precise and exhaustive distinction between combinations of facts which call for a decision in favor of the aggrieved party and combinations of fact which require a decision against the party seeking redress is obtained.

In reality, however, judicial decisions depend on more extensive and more complex combinations of facts than are indicated in the foregoing illustration. For example, in the workmen's compensation cases which have been reviewed by the Connecticut Supreme Court of Errors, 19 relevant and controlling facts appear in the opinions of the court. In the involuntary confession cases decided by the United States Supreme Court, 22 relevant and controlling facts can be identified.[1] It can be readily seen that in these areas of law simultaneous equations for 19 and 22 unknowns, respectively, must be solved in order to obtain the weights of the facts. Moreover, it is apparent from the basic rules of algebra that at least as many equations—*i.e.*, cases which already have been decided—as unknowns must be available for that purpose. With a view to the situations that actually are encountered, the simultaneous equations then would have to be written in the following *general* form:

$$f_{11}x_1 + f_{12}x_2 + \ldots + f_{1j}x_j + \ldots + f_{1n}x_n = D_1$$
$$f_{21}x_1 + f_{22}x_2 + \ldots + f_{2j}x_j + \ldots + f_{2n}x_n = D_2$$
$$\ldots \ldots \ldots \ldots \ldots \ldots$$
$$f_{i1}x_1 + f_{i2}x_2 + \ldots + f_{ij}x_j + \ldots + f_{in}x_n = D_i$$
$$\ldots \ldots \ldots \ldots \ldots \ldots$$
$$f_{N1}x_1 + f_{N2}x_2 + \ldots + f_{Nj}x_j + \ldots + f_{Nn}x_n = D_N.$$

In this form, the simultaneous equations apply to any number of facts and their weights ($j = 1, 2, \ldots, n$) in any number of cases ($i = 1, 2, \ldots, N$). As in the set of equations for the hypothetical example, the only unknowns are the weights of the facts, x_j. Each numerical value of f_{ij} (0, 1, or multiple

values of 1), which indicates the presence or absence of fact j in case i, is known. Likewise, each numerical value of D_i, which indicates the decision in case i in terms of the votes favorable to the party seeking redress, is known. In determining the value of D_i for each case, certain criteria for counting the votes of the judges must be observed. Only the votes of judges who accept the facts as stated in the opinion of the court, and who support the contentions of the party seeking redress on *that* ground, can be included in the numerical value which represents the decision (D_i). If a judge writes a concurring opinion in which he justifies his position in the case only on jurisdictional grounds, his vote cannot be included; for his contribution to the decision is *not a part* of the decision *as a function* of the applicable combination of facts. Furthermore, if a judge supports the aggrieved party in a concurring opinion by accepting *more* facts than are stated in the opinion of the court, his vote also cannot be included; for no indication is given what his position would be on the facts which are accepted in the opinion of the court, *i.e.*, the facts which are controlling for the particular decision. But, if a judge supports the party seeking redress by relying on *fewer* facts than are stated in the opinion of the court, his vote can be included. This is justifiable, because obviously the judge also would support the aggrieved party on the basis of more facts in his favor.[2]

---

[1] For a detailed analysis of the Connecticut workmen's compensation cases, the involuntary confession cases, and the right to counsel cases in terms of the proposed method, see Kort, "Content Analysis of Judicial Opinions and Rules of Law," in Glendon A. Schubert (ed.), *Judicial Decision-Making* 133–197 (1963).

[2] These considerations have an important ramification for the meaning of a majority of votes in terms of this method of analysis. What constitutes a "majority" must be determined in relation to the number of participating judges in the sense in which "participation" just has been defined. In some situations, this may lead to a misclassification of decisions. Assume, for example, that—in a case before a nine-judge court—three judges support the decision in favor of the party seeking redress on the basis of the facts, two judges concur on jurisdictional grounds, and four judges oppose the decision on the merits of the case. In accordance with the criteria which have been advanced, this means that only three out of the seven votes of "participating" judges can be counted in favor of the aggrieved party. In this fashion, a decision against the party seeking redress is indicated, *contrary* to the actual decision. This limitation of the proposed method must be recognized. Empirically it has been found, however, that this limitation does not seriously impair the analysis of judicial decisions in terms of the proposed method. See Kort, *supra* note 1.

A unique and perfect solution of the simultaneous equations can be obtained, provided that the number of cases is equal to the number of facts—i.e., $N = n$, and provided that the equations contain sufficient information. How the equations can be solved if there are more cases than facts—i.e., $N > n$—will be discussed in a moment. But what is of primary concern now is that—in most areas of law in which the decisions depend on the combinations of facts—the available cases do not provide sufficient information, even if their number is equal to or exceeds the number of facts. In other words, the equations which represent the cases do not contain sufficient information for obtaining a unique solution for the unknowns. For the purpose of illustration, assume that Case 2 in the hypothetical example consists of a combination of two manifestations of f_1 and f_2, and that six judges vote in favor of the party seeking redress. With the substitution of the known values of f_{ij}, the equations then would have to be written as follows:

$$x_1 + x_2 + x_3 = 7$$
$$2x_1 + 2x_2 = 6$$
$$x_1 + x_2 = 3.$$

The number of equations equals the number of unknowns, but a unique solution for x_1, x_2, and x_3 cannot be obtained. This is due to the fact that the second and third equations actually state the same relationship between f_1, f_2, and the corresponding decisions. Consequently, the three equations provide information on only *two* relationships in a situation that involves *three* facts. In the more complex combinations of facts that are encountered in actual situations, the lack of sufficient information is, of course, far less obvious than in the given hypothetical example. The problem of insufficient information for a unique solution of the equations can be overcome, however, by restating the original independent variables in the equations—i.e., the relevant and controlling facts in the cases—in terms of a new set of independent variables, which are called *factors*. The method by which the

facts can be reduced to factors is known as *factor analysis.*[3]

For the purpose of illustration, it will be helpful to consider two examples which already have been mentioned, namely, the workmen's compensation cases reviewed by the Connecticut Supreme Court of Errors and the involuntary confession cases decided by the Supreme Court of the United States. Some of the relevant and controlling facts which appear in the workmen's compensation cases can be described as follows: an accident or harmful act occurred in the course of an activity which was permitted by the employer; an accident or harmful act occurred in the course of an activity conducive to efficient work; an accident or harmful act occurred in the course of an activity which was indispensable for the performance of the work; an accident or harmful act occurred on the premises of employment, in an area annexed to the place of employment, or in an area where the work normally is performed; an accident or harmful act occurred during an activity which did not involve unnecessary, self-imposed hazardous conduct, such as taking a "joy ride" on a conveyor belt for unloading coal; the alleged injury became immediately apparent to the employee, as a result of an accident; the accident or the act which caused the alleged injury was observed by other persons; the alleged injury became immediately

---

[3]Various methods of factor analysis have been developed. For the problem under discussion, Hotelling's Iterative Method of Factoring, also known as the Principal Components or the Principal Axes Method, is the most desirable method for locating the factors in terms of which the controlling facts can be restated. See Hotelling, "Analysis of a Complex of Statistical Variables into Principal Components," 29 *J. Educ. Psychology* 417–444; 498–520 (1933); Hotelling, "Simplified Calculation of Principal Components," 1 *Psychometrika* 27 (1936). For a complete exposition of this method, with regard to mathematical proof as well as application, see L. L. Thurstone, *Multiple Factor Analysis*, 480–503 (1947). For restating the combination of circumstances in terms of factors in each case, the Shortened Estimation Method is most suitable. See Lederman, "On a Shortened Method of Estimation of Mental Factors by Regression," 4 *Psychometrika* 109 (1939), and Harman, "On the Rectilinear Prediction of Oblique Factors," 6 *Psychometrika* 29 (1941). For a complete exposition of this method and its relation to the Complete Estimation Method, with regard to mathematical proof as well as application, see Harry H. Harman, *Modern Factor Analysis*, 338–356 (1960).

apparent to other observers, as a result of an accident or harmful act. To a large extent— although not exclusively—these facts can be restated in terms of a factor which can be called "a combination of facts which relate the alleged injury to an accident or observable harmful act."

In the involuntary confession cases, some of the relevant and controlling facts which can be identified are the following: there was a delay in the formal presentation of charges; the defendant was detained incommunicado; the defendant was not advised of the right to remain silent; the defendant was not advised of the right to counsel; the defendant did not have any consultation with counsel prior to the challenged confession. These facts can be restated to a substantial degree in terms of a factor which can be described as "a tactic to keep the defendant in isolation, uninformed of the charges against him, and uninformed of his procedural rights." These examples provide an understanding of the intuitive meaning of restating facts in terms of factors. It should be noted, however, that the applicable factors actually are found by relying *exclusively* on the rigorous mathematical techniques which factor analysis employs. It also should be noted that—in addition to solving the problem of insufficient information in the original set of simultaneous equations— factor analysis fully explores the mutual dependence or independence of the facts.

On the basis of the restatement of the relevant and controlling facts in terms of factors, the decision in each case becomes a function of the combination of factors. Accordingly, the original set of equations can be restated in terms of a new set of equations, in which the factors in each case are the independent variables, and in which the decision is the dependent variable. In general terms, the new set of equations then can be written as follows:

$$\bar{F}_{11}X_1 + \bar{F}_{12}X_2 + \ldots + \bar{F}_{1j}X_j + \ldots$$
$$+ \bar{F}_{1m}X_m = D_1$$
$$\bar{F}_{21}X_1 + \bar{F}_{22}X_2 + \ldots + \bar{F}_{2j}X_j + \ldots$$
$$+ \bar{F}_{2m}X_m = D_2$$

$$\cdots \cdots \cdots \cdots \cdots \cdots \cdots \cdots$$

$$\bar{F}_{i1}X_1 + \bar{F}_{i2}X_2 + \ldots + \bar{F}_{ij}X_j + \ldots$$
$$+ \bar{F}_{im}X_m = D_i$$

$$\cdots \cdots \cdots \cdots \cdots \cdots \cdots \cdots$$

$$\bar{F}_{N1}X_1 + \bar{F}_{N2}X_2 + \ldots + \bar{F}_{Nj}X_j + \ldots$$
$$+ \bar{F}_{Nm}X_m = D_N.$$

These equations apply to any number of factors and their weights ($j = 1, 2, \ldots, m$) in any number of cases ($i = 1, 2, \ldots, N$). Since the object of the factor analysis is to restate the independent variables in the original set of equations in terms of *fewer* independent variables in the new set of equations, it is expected that the number of factors, m, is smaller than the number of facts, n. Each numerical value of $\bar{F}_{ij}$, which is the *factor estimate* of factor j in case i (*i.e.*, the measure of the degree to which factor j appears in case i), is known; it has been obtained as a result of the factor analysis. Likewise, each numerical value of D_i, which indicates the decision in case i in terms of the votes of the judges favorable to the party seeking redress, is known. Consequently, the only unknowns in the new set of equations are the weights of the factors, X_j. Since the facts have been restated in terms of factors, the number of the new equations, N, exceeds the number of unknowns, m. But the equations can be solved by the *method of least squares*, which offers the best possible approximation to a perfect solution.[4]

As new cases arise, the applicable facts can be reduced to the factors which have been identified, and—since the weights of the factors now are known—the decisions can be determined by substituting the weights of the factors in the equations which represent the new cases. It is in this respect that the proposed method for analyzing judicial decisions in the indicated areas of law provides a basis for prediction. Of more fundamental importance, however, is the criterion which this method offers for a *precise and exhaustive* distinction between combinations of facts that call for a decision in favor of the aggrieved

[4]Various references for the method of least squares are available. A convenient source, which contains a concise description and explanation of this method, is Gerhard Tintner, *Mathematics and Statistics for Economists*, 273–286 (1953).

party and combinations of facts that require a decision against the party seeking redress. For each combination of facts can be restated in terms of a combination of factors, and the weights of the factors and the degrees to which the factors represent the facts provide the numerical value for the decision.

As far as the application of the proposed method to the analysis of judicial decisions is concerned, it should be noted that the use of a high speed electronic computer is imperative. The solution of simultaneous equations with 20 or more unknowns, which must be expected in the analysis of decisions in the indicated areas of law, would be prohibitive without the aid of a computer. Moreover, the particular method of factor analysis which is recommended here involves such extensive iterative matrix multiplications that a computer becomes indispensable. It would be proper to say, therefore, that—from the viewpoint of all practical considerations—the proposed method could not be employed without reliance on a computer.[5] It will be seen in a moment that these considerations also are pertinent for the analysis of judicial decisions in terms of Boolean algebra. In this respect, both models provide one of many examples of how research in law and the social sciences has been revolutionized by the invention of the electronic digital computer.

II. A MODEL BASED ON BOOLEAN ALGEBRA

The area of mathematics which is known as *Boolean algebra* was first developed by the British mathematician George Boole during the nineteenth century.[6] It can be employed in the form of compound statements, using symbolic logic, as well as in the context of the theory of sets.[7] In both forms, Boolean algebra has been applied by Reed C. Lawlor

to the analysis of judicial decisions that depend on various combinations of specified facts.[8] It is on the basis of Lawlor's study that the model which uses Boolean algebra for analyzing these decisions now will be examined.

For the purpose of initial explanation, it will be convenient to refer again to the hypothetical example which was introduced earlier. It will be recalled that the cases in this example contain the following combinations facts: f_1, f_2, and f_3 in Case 1; f_1 and f_3 in Case 2; and f_1 and f_2 in Case 3. It also will be recalled that the decisions in Case 1 and Case 2 are in favor of the party seeking redress, but that the decision in Case 3 is against the aggrieved party. It will be desirable now to change Case 1 to a case in which only f_2 and f_3 are present, but in which the decision is the same, and to include in the example another case, in which only fact 3 is present, and in which the decision is against the aggrieved party. An inspection of these four cases shows that the decision is in favor of the party seeking redress, D_{pro}, if and only if f_3 and either f_1 or f_2 are present in the case. Accordingly, the following compound statement, using symbolic logic, can be written:

$$D_{pro} \leftrightarrow f_3 \; \wedge \; (f_1 \vee f_2).$$

The symbols which are used in this statement have the following meanings: "$\leftrightarrow$" represents the "biconditional" relationship ". . . if and only if . . ."; "$\wedge$" denotes logical "conjunction," *i.e.*, "and"; "$\vee$" represents logical "disjunction," *i.e.*, "or," but—more specifically—it means "one or the other *or* both." It can be seen, therefore, that this compound statement indicates that the decision is in favor of the aggrieved party *if and only if* fact 3, *and* either fact 1 *or* fact 2, *or* both fact 1 and fact 2 are present in the case. In this form, the statement provides a precise and exhaustive distinction between *pro* and *con* decisions (*i.e.*, decisions in favor of and against the party seeking redress) in the hy-

---

[5]Although computers can design new methods of analysis, it should be carefully noted that—in this instance—the computer merely executes mathematical and statistical techniques which have been designed by human beings. That the computer performs in this process a task which practically cannot be achieved by human beings just has been seen. . . .

[6]George Boole, *The Laws of Thought* (1854).

[7]See J. G. Kemeny, J. L. Snell, & G. L. Thompson, *Finite Mathematics* 1, 69 (1957).

[8]See Lawlor, "Computer Aids to Legal Decision Making," 63J *Modern Uses of Logic in Law* [M.U.L.L.] (to be published); and Lawlor, "Prediction of Court Decisions," in *Second National Law and Electronics Conference, 1962, Proceedings* (to be published).

pothetical example. It should be noted that, like the method which uses simultaneous equations, the present method treats the decision as a function of controlling facts. Moreover, like the former method, the latter method can accommodate sets of consistent cases in which the number of cases exceeds the number of facts. But, unlike the method which is based on simultaneous equations, this method is concerned only with logical relationships, and does not assign numerical weights or values to combinations of facts and decisions.

The foregoing compound statement also can be written in a different form, using in part the concept of sets and subsets. It can be said that the facts in the hypothetical example form a "set," which can be described by using the following notation: $S = \{f_1, f_2, f_3\}$. This expression indicates that set S contains the elements f_1, f_2, and f_3. Any combination of these elements forms a "subset." Accordingly, $S_s = \{f_1, f_2\}$ would be the subset which contains elements f_1 and f_2. On this basis, the compound statement which provides the distinction between *pro* and *con* decisions in the hypothetical example also can be written as follows:

$$D_{pro} \leftrightarrow f_3 \; \wedge \; L \, (1, S_s).$$

This statement has the following meaning: the decision is in favor of the party seeking redress *if and only if* fact 3 and *at least* (L) one (1) of (,) the elements of subset S_s, consisting of fact 1 and fact 2, are present in the case. In this form, the statement offers the same precise and exhaustive distinction between *pro* and *con* decisions which it provided in its earlier form.

It must be noted again, of course, that in reality judicial decisions depend on more extensive combinations of facts than are suggested by the foregoing illustration. As applied to actual situations, the Boolean equation—*i.e.*, the compound statement which provides the distinction between *pro* and *con* decisions—is therefore more complex. For example, in his study of the right to counsel cases decided by the Supreme Court under

the *Betts* rule,[9] Lawlor has used 39 facts. These facts are relevant and controlling for the decision whether or not a petitioner had been deprived of his right to counsel in a state criminal proceeding, in violation of the due process clause of the Fourteenth Amendment. Lawlor found that the following Boolean equation provided a distinction between the *pro* and *con* cases that had been decided:

$$D_{pro} \leftrightarrow (f_{11} \; \vee \; f_{12}) \; \wedge \; f_{19} \; \wedge \; [L \, (1, S_a) \\ \vee \; L \, (5, S_b)].$$

The terms in this expression represent certain facts and subsets of facts which apply to the right to counsel cases. Facts 11, 12, and 19 can be described, respectively, as follows: f_{11}—the petitioner had no assistance of counsel at the time of arraignment; f_{12}—the petitioner had no assistance of counsel between the time of arraignment and the trial, or between the time of arraignment and the plea of guilty; f_{19}—the petitioner never waived explicitly the right to counsel. Subset S_a contains two facts: (1) the petitioner was convicted of a crime subject to capital punishment; (2) a jurisdictional issue or complicated charges were involved. Subset S_b contains 32 facts, which pertain to the personal handicaps of the petitioner, to circumstances relating to the denial of representation by counsel, and to other procedural irregularities. On this basis, the Boolean equation states the following relationship: The decision in a right to counsel case is in favor of the petitioner *if and only if* fact 11 *or* fact 12 (*or both*), *and* fact 19, *and at least* one element in subset of facts S_a *or at least* five elements in subset of facts S_b (*or both*) are present in the case. Otherwise, the decision is against the petitioner, D_{con}.

The form of the Boolean equation which distinguishes between *pro* and *con* decisions varies considerably in different areas of law. In some instances it might state a relationship exclusively in terms of conjunctions, whereas in other instances it might state a relationship exclusively in terms of disjunctions, or in terms of both conjunctions and disjunctions.

[9]See Lawlor, "Prediction of Court Decisions," in *Second National Law and Electronics Conference, 1962, Proceedings* (to be published).

In some instances it might contain a condition to the effect that all elements of a subset of facts must be present, whereas in other instances it might require the presence of only a given minimal number of elements in a subset. How can it be determined then which Boolean equation applies to a given area of law? Initially, it is not known which combination of facts constitutes a compound statement that distinguishes between *pro* and *con* decisions. If there are 20 relevant and controlling facts, the number of possible combinations of facts is 2^{20}, *i.e.*, approximately one million. If there are 39 relevant and controlling facts—as in Lawlor's study of the right to counsel cases—the number of possible combinations of facts is 2^{39}, *i.e.*, approximately 100,000,000,000. Even though—as will be seen in a moment—not every possible combination of facts has to be explored in order to obtain the applicable Boolean equation, the number of combinations which actually have to be examined still would make human inspection prohibitive. However, the systematic search for the Boolean equation can be performed by an electronic computer, and in this fashion the desired distinction between *pro* and *con* decisions is obtained. Computer programs which are designed to locate the applicable equation for *any area of law* in which the decisions are a function of facts have been developed independently by Lawlor and Kort.

An explanation has to be given now why not every possible combination of facts has to be examined in order to determine the Boolean equation which distinguishes *pro* and *con* decisions. The facts which are relevant and controlling for the decisions in the areas of law under consideration are *monopolar*, or can be restated in monopolar form. In other words, all the facts favor the party seeking redress, or can be restated as facts favorable to the aggrieved party, and thus point in *one* direction. The facts which already have been mentioned as examples in the workmen's compensation cases, in the involuntary confession cases, and in the right to counsel cases are monopolar in this sense. All these facts favor the claimant in a workmen's compensation case in obtaining an award, or favor the

petitioner before the Supreme Court in obtaining a reversal of his conviction. A fact which is disadvantageous to the party seeking redress can be accommodated by including its opposite in all the cases in which it does not appear. For example, "previous experience in court proceedings" is a fact which does not favor the prospects of a petitioner to obtain a reversal of his conviction in a right to counsel case. Instead of identifying this fact in a case to which it applies, the fact "*no* previous experience in court" can be included in the other cases, and the same relative standing of cases then is maintained. In this fashion, all the relevant and controlling facts can be stated in monopolar form.[10]

Since the facts are monopolar in the direction of favoring the party seeking redress, it can be said that a case C_{i+a}, which contains *all* the facts that are present in a case C_i and *other* facts, has a higher rank (Ra) than case C_i. Moreover, it can be said that, if both cases contain the same facts, they have equal rank. On that basis, the following relationship can be stated:

$$[Ra\,(C_i) \leq Ra\,(C_{i+a})]$$
$$\rightarrow (D_{pro,\,i} \rightarrow D_{pro,\,i+a}).$$

In this expression, the symbol "$\leq$" means that the term which follows the symbol is "higher than or equal to" the term which precedes the symbol. The notation "$\rightarrow$" represents the "conditional," and should be read as "if . . . then . . . ." or ". . . implies . . . ." Accordingly, the following meaning can be given to the expression: If case C_{i+a} has a rank *higher than or equal to* the rank of case C_i, then a *pro* decision in case C_i *implies* a *pro* decision also in case C_{i+a}. This relationship assumes that the decisions constitute a consistent pattern of judicial action. In other words, it assumes that the decision in a case is as favorable to the party seeking redress as the decision in another case which is equally

---

[10]With regard to the analysis of judicial decisions in terms of simultaneous equations, it should be noted that the facts are *monopolar*, but that the factors may be *bipolar*, *i.e.*, they may point in two opposite directions. However, the analysis of the decisions in terms of Boolean algebra does not involve a restatement of facts in terms of factors.

or less meritorious. But whether or not the decisions actually form a consistent pattern of judicial action can be initially determined by inspection, and this is a task which also can be assigned to a computer.

For *con* decisions, a similar relationship can be stated:

$$[Ra\,(C_i) \leq Ra\,(C_{i+a})] \rightarrow (D_{con,\,i+a} \rightarrow D_{con,\,i}).$$

This expression means that, *if* case C_{i+a} has a rank *higher than or equal to* case C_i, then a *con* decision in case C_{i+a} implies a *con* decision also in case C_i. Again it is assumed here that the cases constitute a consistent pattern of judicial action, and again it should be noted that the actual existence or nonexistence of such a pattern of consistency can be initially determined. It also should be understood that the subscripts i and $i+a$ do not necessarily indicate the chronological sequence in which the cases are decided.

In order to see how these relationships apply to the location of the Boolean equation which provides the distinction between *pro* and *con* decisions, it is desirable to consider another hypothetical example. Assume that the decisions are a function of four relevant and controlling facts, f_1, f_2, f_3, and f_4. Sixteen different combinations of facts (2^4) and corresponding cases then are possible. Assume, furthermore, that 10 of the cases representing these combinations of facts already have been decided. In the list which follows, it is indicated which cases have been decided—and how they were decided—by using the notation *pro* and *con*. Moreover, set notation is used for representing the cases, in view of the fact that each case can be regarded as a subset of the total set of facts. The cases are *not* listed in the chronological order of the decisions.

$C_1 = \{f_1, f_2, f_3, f_4\}$ *pro*
$C_2 = \{f_1, f_2, f_3\}$
$C_3 = \{f_1, f_2, f_4\}$ *pro*
$C_4 = \{f_1, f_3, f_4\}$
$C_5 = \{f_1, f_2\}$ *pro*
$C_6 = \{f_1, f_3\}$ *pro*
$C_7 = \{f_1, f_4\}$ *pro*

$C_8 = \{f_2, f_3, f_4\}$ *con*
$C_9 = \{f_2, f_3\}$ *con*
$C_{10} = \{f_2, f_4\}$ *con*
$C_{11} = \{f_3, f_4\}$ *con*
$C_{12} = \{f_1\}$ *con*
$C_{13} = \{f_2\}$
$C_{14} = \{f_3\}$
$C_{15} = \{f_4\}$
$C_{16} = \{\}$

In this example, the applicable Boolean equation can be easily found without the use of a computer. Nevertheless, the procedures which apply to the location of the equation in this simple example are the same as the procedures which have to be employed in finding the equation for combinations involving 20 to 40 facts, where the numbers of possible combinations range from one million to 100 billions. For this reason, a detailed examination of this example will be helpful.

It can be seen that case C_7 in the example was decided in favor of the party seeking redress. Furthermore, it can be seen that cases C_3 and C_1, which also were decided in favor of the aggrieved party, have higher ranks than case C_7, inasmuch as they contain *all* the facts that are present in C_7 as well as *other* facts. If the cases form a consistent pattern of judicial action, the combinations of facts in C_3 and C_1 will not have to be considered as possibilities for the applicable Boolean equation, because any equation which designates C_7 as a *pro* decision also designates C_3 and C_1 as *pro* decisions. And—as already has been indicated—whether or not the cases actually form a consistent pattern of judicial action can be initially determined by the computer. If the computer finds in the process of scanning the cases that there is a *con* case which has *all* the facts that are contained in a *pro* case, or *all these* facts and *other* facts, an inconsistency has been established. If such a case is not found, the pattern of decisions can be regarded as consistent. Moreover, if the pattern is consistent, the combination of facts in case C_4 (which has not yet been decided) does not have to be considered, because any Boolean equation which designates C_7 as a *pro* decision also designates C_4 as a *pro* decision. Likewise, the combination of facts in C_2 does not have to be considered, for any equation which designates C_6 as a *pro* decision also designates C_2 as a *pro* decision. This process of eliminating combinations of facts has been called by Lawlor "*pro* truncation." It should be recalled that this process assumes, of course, that the facts are monopolar.

Conversely, it can be shown how the process which Lawlor has characterized as "*con* truncation" applies to the example under consideration. Case C_8 was decided against the party seeking redress. Cases C_9, C_{10}, and C_{11}, which also were decided against the aggrieved party, have lower ranks than case C_8, inasmuch as they do *not* contain *all* the facts that are present in C_8, and do *not* have *any other* facts. If the inspection by the computer shows that the cases form a consistent pattern of judicial action, the combinations of facts in C_9, C_{10}, and C_{11} will not have to be considered as possibilities for the applicable Boolean equation, because any equation which designates C_8 as a *con* decision also designates C_9, C_{10}, and C_{11} as *con* decisions. Moreover, if the pattern is consistent, the combinations of facts in C_{13}, C_{14}, C_{15}, and C_{16} (which have not yet been decided) do not have to be considered, for any equation which designates C_8 as a *con* case also designates C_{13}, C_{14}, C_{15}, and C_{16} as *con* decisions. Again it should be noted that the facts are assumed to be monopolar.

After applying *pro* truncation to the example under discussion, the Boolean equation which distinguishes between *pro* and *con* decisions then can be obtained by taking the "logical sum"[11] of the *pro* cases C_5, C_6, and C_7:

$$D_{pro} \leftrightarrow (f_1 \wedge f_2) \vee (f_1 \wedge f_3) \vee (f_1 \wedge f_4).$$

This expression can be simplified to:

$$D_{pro} \leftrightarrow f_1 \wedge (f_2 \vee f_3 \vee f_4).$$

It states that the decision is in favor of the party seeking redress *if and only if* fact 1 *and*, in addition, either fact 2 *or* fact 3 *or* fact 4 (*or* two *or* all of the latter three facts) are present in the case.

The Boolean equation also can be obtained by taking the logical sum of the *con* cases C_8 and C_{12}:

$$D_{con} \leftrightarrow \sim f_1 \vee (\sim f_2 \wedge \sim f_3 \wedge \sim f_4).$$

The symbol "$\sim$" in this expression is the "negation" of the term which it precedes;

[11]The term "logical sum" becomes fully plausible if it is noted that an alternative notation for disjunction is "+." But, in this sense "+" has the same meaning as "$\vee$," and is not equivalent to "+" in arithmetic.

e.g., $\sim f_1$ means *not* f_1. The statement then means that the decision is against the party seeking redress *if and only if* fact 1 is absent in the case, *or* if none of facts 2, 3, and 4 are present. This statement has the same meaning as the statement in terms of the *pro* decisions.

Aside from providing a precise and exhaustive distinction between the *pro* and *con* decisions in this example, the Boolean equation also makes it possible to predict the decisions which have not yet been reached. Since the equation designates C_2 and C_4 as *pro* decisions, it can be predicted that these cases will be decided in favor of the party seeking redress, provided that future decisions will remain a part of the consistent pattern of judicial action which has been identified. With the same qualification, it can be predicted that cases C_{13}, C_{14}, C_{15}, and C_{16} will be decided against the aggrieved party, inasmuch as the applicable Boolean equation designates C_{13}, C_{14}, C_{15}, and C_{16} as *con* decisions. If—in actual situations—the cases which have been decided do not provide enough information for an *exhaustive* distinction, the best possible approximations must be made.

The location of a satisfactory Boolean equation also involves a task which is more complex than taking the logical sum of the *pro* decisions and the logical sum of the *con* decisions. For it is necessary to determine the subsets of facts and the minimal numbers of their elements which satisfy the equation. In the example under consideration, it is relatively unimportant whether the applicable Boolean equation is stated as:

$$D_{pro} \leftrightarrow f_1 \wedge (f_2 \vee f_3 \vee f_4)$$

or as

$$D_{pro} \leftrightarrow f_1 \wedge L(1, S_s),$$

where

$$S_s = \{f_2, f_3, f_4\}.$$

But where large subsets of facts are involved, the difference between stating the equation in a form which uses subsets and writing the equation in a form which uses exclusively individual facts is crucial. Consider, for example, Lawlor's Boolean equation for the right to counsel cases. Subset S_b in this equation consists of 32 facts. If the last term in this equation would have to be written in a form using only individual facts, it would contain 201,376 disjunctions. It can be seen that such a statement would not be feasible. For practical purposes, it is therefore necessary to instruct the computer to identify the applicable subsets of facts and the minimal number of their elements which satisfy the Boolean equation.

In addition to *pro* and *con* truncation, a reduction in the number of combinations of facts which have to be explored in finding the Boolean equation is achieved by taking into account the cumulative effect of some facts. Consider, for example, the following two facts in the workmen's compensation cases: (1) an accident or harmful act occurred in the course of an activity conducive to efficient work; (2) an accident or harmful act occurred in the course of an activity which was indispensable for the performance of the work. If the first fact is represented by f_j and the second fact by f_{j+1}, it can be said that $f_{j+1} \rightarrow f_j$, although $\sim (f_j \rightarrow f_{j+1})$. In other words, the occurrence of an accident in the course of an activity which is indispensable for the performance of the work *implies* that the accident also occurred in the course of an activity which was conducive to efficient work. On the other hand, the fact that the accident occurred in the course of an activity conducive to efficient work does *not imply* that it occurred in the course of an activity indispensable for the performance of the work, even though— according to the "law of contraposition"— $\sim f_j \rightarrow \sim f_{j+1}$. For this reason, the two facts have to be identified separately. But assume now that the search for the applicable Boolean equation considers the possibility that f_{j+1} and some other facts *must* be present in a case for a *pro* decision. In the process of this search, the combination ". . .$f_j \wedge f_{j+1}$ . . ." does not have to be examined, because in any case in which f_{j+1} is present f_j also is present, and in any case in which f_j is absent f_{j+1} also is absent. In this fashion, a further reduction

of the number of combinations of facts which have to be considered in locating the Boolean equation is obtained.

III. A COMPARISON OF THE TWO MODELS

Each of the models which has been introduced for the analysis of judicial decisions offers some advantages and some disadvantages in comparison with the other model. One significant advantage of the method based on Boolean algebra is that it does not have to make any assumption with regard to the linearity or nonlinearity of the combination of facts. In the method based on simultaneous equations, this is an important consideration. For example, in the workmen's compensation cases the question arises whether a previous illness is a fact which *adds* to the likelihood of an occupational disease as indicated by the other facts, or modifies such likelihood in some other way. If the former is true, the relationship between the fact "previous illness" and the other facts would be *additive*, i.e., the combination would be *linear*. If the latter is true, the relationship between the fact "previous illness" and the other facts would *not* be *additive*, i.e., the combination would be *nonlinear*. Taking the possible combinations of many different facts into account, it is difficult to determine which are linear and which are nonlinear. To be sure, the proposed method of analysis in terms of simultaneous equations actually does not make any assumptions regarding the linearity or nonlinearity of the combinations of facts, inasmuch as the facts are restated in terms of factors. It does assume, however, that the *combinations of factors* in the cases are linear, and this is an assumption which conceivably could be refuted. On the other hand, the method of analysis in terms of Boolean equations makes no assumption in this respect, for it is concerned only with the simultaneous appearance or nonappearance of facts in cases.

Another advantage of the method based on Boolean algebra is that it does not use numerical weights. It is true, of course, that the factor estimates and the weights of the factors in the method based on simultaneous equations are not determined arbitrarily, but are obtained by rigorous mathematical techniques. Moreover, it is plausible to assign numerical values to the decisions in terms of the votes of the participating judges. Nevertheless, the assumption is made that the votes of the judges are the best numerical index for the decisions, and the weights of the factors are obtained from equations in which this index is the dependent variable. On the other hand, the method which employs Boolean algebra does not make such an assumption. And this method does not ignore the degree of support of the aggrieved party by the different judges, inasmuch as it can be applied to the position of each judge. Lawlor has demonstrated this aspect of the analysis in his experimental tests in the right-to-counsel cases.[12]

One of the main advantages of the method using simultaneous equations is that it provides the distinction between *pro* and *con* cases by obtaining a *unique* solution of the equations in which the facts have been restated in terms of factors. To be sure, the fact that a trial-and-error procedure has to be used to locate the applicable equation in the method based on Boolean algebra is not a disadvantage. For it has been shown that this elaborate task can be performed by a computer. But several criteria for the designation of subsets of facts in the Boolean equation that provides the desired distinction are available, and the question then arises on what grounds one criterion should be preferred to another. On the other hand, this problem does not arise in the method using simultaneous equations, for the solution which is obtained is the best possible solution in the *least square* sense.

A further advantage of the method based on simultaneous equations is that it fully explores the mutual dependence or independence of the facts by means of factor analysis. It is quite true that—as has been shown—the dependence of some facts on other facts can be explored in the form of logical implica-

tions. Nevertheless, the latter do not indicate the various degrees of mutual dependence which are obtained through the correlation measures in the factor analysis.

IV. THE PURPOSES, LIMITATIONS, AND IMPLICATIONS OF THE ANALYSIS OF JUDICIAL DECISIONS IN TERMS OF THE PROPOSED MODELS

In spite of the respective advantages and disadvantages of the two methods, identical purposes can be attributed to them. As has already been indicated, their main purpose is to provide a precise and exhaustive distinction between decisions which depend on combinations of facts that have been specified by the courts. It is in this fashion that the proposed methods of analysis offer information about the content and the application of rules of law which the verbal statements of these rules do not provide. For in deciding cases in the indicated areas of law, courts actually employ rules of law which state that the decisions shall be made on the basis of the combinations of facts that appear in the particular cases. The verbal statements of these rules specify which facts shall be regarded as relevant and controlling. But they do not specify which particular combinations of these facts call for a decision in favor of the party seeking redress, and which combinations of facts demand a decision against the aggrieved party. It is the absence of this information which has been criticized,[13] and it is precisely this information which judges and lawyers need for appraising cases in terms of these rules.

To be sure, this information could be provided by a verbal *restatement* of the applicable rule of law. However, such a restatement would be extremely complex and—from a practical point of view—extremely cumbersome. The verbal restatement would have to

[12]Lawlor, "Prediction of Court Decisions," in *Second National Law and Electronics Conference, 1962, Proceedings* (to be published).

[13]For such criticism regarding the right to counsel cases, see Note 33 *Va. L. Rev.* 731 (1947); Comment, 22 *So. Cal. L. Rev.* 259 (1949); Green, "The Bill of Rights, the Fourteenth Amendment, and the Supreme Court," 46 *Mich. L. Rev.* 869, 898 (1948), and the reference to these sources in William M. Beany, *The Right to Counsel in American Courts* 194 (1955).

contain all the possible combinations of the controlling facts and the corresponding decisions, and it already has been seen that in actual situations the number of these combinations would range from one million to several billions. It is hardly conceivable that an intelligent human being could obtain a precise and exhaustive formulation of the applicable rule of law from this number of combinations without reliance on mathematical techniques and without the aid of a computer. It can be seen, therefore, that— even if a verbal restatement of the rule should be preferred—an analysis in terms of the proposed methods would be necessary *before* such a restatement could be formulated.

On the basis of the precise and exhaustive distinction between *pro* and *con* decisions, another main purpose of the proposed methods of analysis becomes apparent, namely, the prediction of new decisions. It has been shown how both methods can serve this purpose. Of course, prediction is possible only if it can be assumed that the consistent pattern of judicial action which has been detected in past cases will continue in the future. This points to an important limitation of the analysis of judicial decisions in terms of the proposed methods—a limitation which will receive further attention in a moment. Moreover, it must be clearly understood that the prediction of new decisions is *conditional* and *not unconditional*. In other words, the decisions are predicted on the assumption that the combinations of controlling facts which will be accepted by the court are known.

To predict which facts actually will be considered by the court in a given case is an entirely different task. If such a predictive device can be found, its combination with the present methods would permit an *unconditional* prediction of decisions. But even conditional prediction offers at least two advantages: (1) It enables an attorney to anticipate rationally—and not merely intuitively—which combinations of controlling facts would lead to a decision in favor of his client and which combinations would be insufficient for such a decision. On that basis, he could appraise more accurately the prospects of his client, and also would be in a better position to know which facts he should emphasize in his presentation to the court. (2) Conditional prediction makes it possible to determine whether or not a new decision represents a continuation of a pattern of judicial action which has been established in previous decisions. For after a new decision, the combination of facts that has been accepted by the court is, of course, known. And, certainly, the initial task of both methods of analysis is to explore whether or not a consistent pattern can be identified.

The proposed methods require not only an explanation of their purposes, but also a clear recognition of their limitations. One limitation just has been discussed, namely, that—at their present stage—the methods in question do not offer unconditional, but only conditional prediction. Another limitation is that the test of consistency and conditional prediction cannot be applied to a case in which a fact *not previously* encountered appears.[14] However, if such a case is included in the analysis, subsequent cases in which this new fact is present can be tested for consistency and can be conditionally predicted. A further important limitation is that the proposed methods are not designed to predict doctrinal changes and the adoption of new rules of law. For example, these methods could not have predicted the overruling of *Betts* v. *Brady*[15]—the case in which the Supreme Court had stated the rule that the decisions of the state right to counsel cases depend on the combinations of certain relevant and controlling facts.

If the utility of the proposed methods is questioned under these circumstances, the

---

[14] A further point in this connection is that some facts might have a special meaning in some jurisdictions. For example, in *Hamilton* v. *Alabama,* 368 U.S. 52, 54 (1961), the Court stated: "Whatever may be the function and importance of arraignment in other jurisdictions, we have said enough to show that in Alabama it is a critical stage in a criminal proceeding. What happens there may affect the whole trial." In order to account for the special meaning which the Supreme Court gave to arraignment in Alabama, Lawlor included in his study of the right to counsel cases, *supra* note 8, the fact that "the case arose in Alabama." . . .

[15] 316 U.S. 455 (1942), overruled in *Gideon* v. *Wainwright,* 372 U.S. 335 (1963).

following considerations should be noted. First of all, the fact that the applicability of the methods to a given area of law is terminated by a doctrinal change does not affect in any way their applicability to other areas of law, where such doctrinal changes have not occurred. For example, the overruling of *Betts* v. *Brady* obviously has no consequences for the analysis of the involuntary confession cases and the workmen's compensation cases in terms of the proposed methods. Secondly, even in the area of the law in which the doctrinal change has occurred, an analysis in terms of these methods will have provided insights which otherwise could not have been obtained. As far as the right to counsel cases are concerned, this means that—even though *Betts* v. *Brady* has been overruled—the analysis has demonstrated that a rule of law which has been condemned as a "nebulous standard," as a complex "*ex post facto* standard," and as an "arbitrary and capricious rule,"[16] actually has been employed with remarkable consistency. In other words, the proposed methods have revealed a pattern of judicial action which traditional methods of interpretation have not been able to detect.

It is the latter consideration which points to important implications of the proposed methods. In examining *past* decisions by means of these methods, *no* assumption is made regarding the existence or nonexistence of a consistent pattern of judicial action. Whether or not consistency does exist in a given area of adjudication is determined by the very use of the methods. And that they can detect the existence or nonexistence of consistency more accurately than traditional methods just has been seen. If a consistent pattern cannot be identified, it must be concluded that judicial action in the given area of law cannot be understood in terms of the dependence of decisions on various combinations of specified facts. A different interpretation of the decisions and an examination of other models for their analysis then would

be appropriate. If, on the other hand, the decisions reveal a consistent pattern, the proposed methods make it possible to determine whether the consistency of judicial action in the given area of law can be explained in terms of *stare decisis*, or must be understood in terms of a pattern of regularity beyond the traditional meaning of this concept.

In an area of law in which a sufficiently large number of decisions have been rendered, the available cases can be chronologically divided into two halves, and an attempt then can be made to predict one-half of the cases from the other half. If the results show that it is possible to predict only the chronologically second half of the cases from the chronologically first half, the conclusion can be reached that *stare decisis*—in the sense of basing later decisions on earlier precedents—has been followed. If, on the other hand, the results indicate that the second half of cases can be predicted from the first half, and the first half can be predicted from the second half,[17] the consistency of judicial action cannot be explained in terms of *stare decisis*. For consistency which can be detected in earlier decisions by prediction from later decisions obviously cannot be attributed to a process of basing earlier decisions on later precedents.

It seems, therefore, that consistency of judicial action—which in many instances would appear to be an application of *stare decisis*—actually would have to be explained in terms of a pattern of regularity which differs from adherence to precedent. Such consistency would have to be understood in terms of an independent—although convergent—recognition and acceptance of similar standards of justice by different judges at different times. It is in this respect that the proposed methods of analysis provide new insights into a principle which has been a pillar of the common law.

[16]See *supra* note 13.

[17]This has been the case, for example, in the analysis of the Connecticut workmen's compensation cases. See Kort, *supra* note 1.

E. Judicial Norms and Judicial Roles

Certain judicial norms, for some judges under certain circumstances, may be crucial for their decision-making. *Stare decisis,* or following precedent, is such a norm. The two readings by Glendon Schubert concern this research area. In the first reading, Schubert's first work on this topic is presented. The second reading is a brief excerpt from Schubert's extensive and masterly work, *The Judicial Mind.* In that work, utilizing complex and sophisticated methods, Schubert uncovered two principal ideological dimensions, (1) liberalism-conservatism and (2) pragmatism-dogmatism. These ideological dimensions account for most of the nonunanimous decisional behavior of Supreme Court judges in the 1946–1963 period. Schubert, in the excerpt presented here, suggests that judges' attitudes toward *stare decisis* are related to the second ideological dimension and range from pragmatic (anti *stare decisis*) to dogmatic (pro *stare decisis*).

The second norm which has been empirically treated is that of judicial restraint. Judges, according to many in the legal profession, should eschew an activist role and embrace judicial restraint—i.e., a deference to the other branches of government. However, it is clear that different judges have different conceptions of the judicial function (or judicial role). To what extent judicial restraint and its converse —judicial activism (or a desire to exercise judicial power)—can be shown to be associated with decisional behavior is the subject of the selection by Harold Spaeth. Guttman scaling is the methodology employed in the Schubert and Spaeth selections and is explained in the readings.

26 CIVILIAN CONTROL AND *STARE DECISIS* IN THE WARREN COURT

Glendon Schubert

. . . [T]he question arises why there has been, during the quarter of a century that has elapsed since 1937, such a dearth of adverse judicial review of federal legislation, assuming the libertarian orientation of the [post-1937 Supreme] Court alleged by [C. Herman] Pritchett and others. Certainly, the lack of such cases does not reflect a commensurate lack of opportunity for the Court. The period of which we speak includes the usual quota of anti-civil liberties legislation that characteristically marks the endeavors of Congress in prosecuting a major war; it

Reprinted with permission of The Macmillan Company from *Judicial Decision-Making* by Glendon Schubert (editor), pp. 56–62, 66–72, 75. © The Free Press of Glencoe, a division of The Macmillan Company, 1963.

also encompasses a postwar period which has been denominated the "Cold War," and was for a time symbolized by the transient but menacing symbol of the late Senator McCarthy, and in which there has been substantial national legislation that has tended to repress civil rights and liberties.

Pritchett's argument is that the Court was able substantially to realize its libertarian goals by relying less upon judicial review and more upon the alternative technique of statutory interpretation. This explanation does, undoubtedly, have some validity. But the fact remains that during a period of almost two decades, thus including both the Roosevelt and Vinson Courts, only three scattered and relatively minor decisions emerged: *Tot* v. *United States*, 319 U.S. 463 (1943); *United States* v. *Lovett*, 328 U.S. 303 (1946); and *United States* v. *Cardiff*, 344 U.S. 174 (1952). Only the second of these decisions attracted much public attention; and none of them is considered to be a landmark case in constitutional law. In all three decisions, however, the Court did uphold claims of constitutional civil rights.

In dramatic contrast, the Warren Court, within a span of half a dozen years beginning in 1955, has in seven cases struck down various sections of the Uniform Code of Military Justice of 1950 and a section of the Nationality Act of 1940, in which the basic question for decision was the extension of military law and trial by courts-martial to include civilian defendants and civilian rights.[1] Although the Chief Justice remarked, in the opinion for a plurality of the Court accompanying the decision upholding the most extreme libertarian claim (and therefore resulting in the closest voting margin of the cases in this set), that "the ordeal of judgment" must be approached "cautiously" when the Court thus exercised the power of judicial review,[2] it is not unreasonable, against the background that has been sketched, to infer that the Warren Court has manifested exceptional zeal in its defense of constitutional claims against military control over civilian rights.

I

Since the inference stated—that the Warren Court has undertaken a zealous defense of civilian rights against Congressional attempts to expand the system of military control—is not the only one that might be drawn from, nor the only interpretation that might be based upon, the data examined thus far, this

inference and other possible alternatives must be deduced from differing theories which purport to explain the Supreme Court's decision-making behavior. The legal scientist, like the political scientist or the psychologist or any other behavioral scientist, therefore has an obligation to articulate precisely the theoretical model of judicial behavior in terms of which he proposes to observe, to measure, to analyze, and to interpret a set of real-life events such as a series of decisions of a court. It will have been more or less obvious—depending upon one's degree of sophistication in sociopsychological theory—. . . that the implicit model for studying such a variable as "judicial hostility towards military control" or "a justice's libertarian attitude toward civil liberty claims" is that of the attitude scale.[3]

Attitudinal scaling of judges constitutes a relatively new development in legal research. Although other techniques of collecting the raw data (such as interview or questionnaire surveys) are commonly employed in the investigation of social attitudes by social psychologists,[4] most of the exploratory studies of recent years have sought to measure judicial attitudes *indirectly* by examining voting data for split decisions of the United States Supreme Court. Such research is premised upon the general stimulus-response model of modern psychometrics and, more specifically, upon the concept of the cumulative scale developed during World War II by Guttman and his associates.[5] The Guttman scale is linear and one-dimensional, and it assumes that an attitude can properly be conceptualized as a continuous variable that ranges over a continuum. Within any segment of the continuum, points lying near one end of the

[1] *Toth* v. *Quarles*, 350 U.S. 11 (1955); *Reid* v. *Covert*, 354 U.S. 1 (1957); *Trop* v. *Dulles*, 356 U.S. 86 (1958); *Kinsella* v. *Singleton*, 361 U.S. 234 (1960); *Grisham* v. *Hagan*, 361 U.S. 278 (1960); *McElroy* v. *Guagliardo*, 361 U.S. 281 (1960); and *Wilson* v. *Bohlender*, 361 U.S. 281 (1960). Cf. *Kinsella* v. *Krueger*, 351 U.S. 470 (1956) and *Reid* v. *Covert*, 351 U.S. 487 (1956). For a typical legalistic analysis of the role of *stare decisis* in these cases, see Robert Girard, "The Constitution and Court-Martial of Civilians Accompanying the Armed Forces—A Preliminary Analysis," *Stanford Law Review*, Vol. 13 (1961), pp. 461–521, esp. pp. 495–499. In the unrelated case of *Bolling* v. *Sharpe*, 347 U.S. 497 (1954), the Warren Court declared unconstitutional several acts of Congress authorizing racial segregation in public schools in the District of Columbia. This also, of course, was a pro-civil liberty decision; but, unlike the courts-martial cases that followed, the nominal scope of the national legislation at issue was local rather than nationwide, or, indeed, international.

[2] *Trop* v. *Dulles*, 356 U.S. 86, 104 (1958).

[3] For a general discussion, see Warren S. Torgerson, *Theory and Methods of Scaling* (New York: Wiley, 1958).

[4] See the special issue edited by Daniel Katz, "Attitude Change," *Public Opinion Quarterly*, Vol. 24, No. 2 (Summer, 1960), and references cited therein. See also Hans J. Eysenck, *The Psychology of Politics* (London: Routledge and Kegan Paul, 1954).

[5] The basic reference is Samuel Stouffer, *et al.*, *Measurement and Prediction*, Vol. 4 of *Studies in Social Psychology in World War II* (Princeton: Princeton University Press, 1950).

segment can be identified as more positive, and points near the other end of the segment as more negative, depending upon how the variable has been defined and how directionality has been attributed to the continuum. It is postulated that as one discerns discrete points moving along the continuum in the direction that has been defined as positive, such points are measures of the increasingly affirmative and intense attitude toward the variable that an individual might possess. Correspondingly, different points might be conceived of as questions of increasing "difficulty" that might stimulate an affirmative response from an individual whose ideal point was located at least as far along the continuum in the stipulated direction as the questions asked. The scale is "cumulative" in the sense that an individual would be assumed to respond affirmatively until the question asked corresponds to a stimulus point that is located beyond (in a more extreme position on the continuum than) his own ideal point; to this and to all questions even more extreme, he would respond negatively. Thus, if an individual respondent's attitude toward a given variable were perfectly consistent, he would respond affirmatively to all questions up to a critical point, and he would respond negatively to all questions that were more extreme than his ideal point. Thus, a group of individuals, responding to a series of questions corresponding to a set of stimulus points on the continuum, might be represented by a set of ideal points on the same continuum. Different individuals in the group might, therefore, respond differently to the various questions (stimuli) and still be perfectly consistent in their respective individual attitudes. To the extent that an individual responds inconsistently to a series of questions that are answered consistently by other members of the same group, one might infer that the inconsistent respondent was committing perceptual errors, or that he had not yet "made up his mind" about the value to which the questions relate.

A Supreme Court Justice is an individual, and a case before the Court for decision can be conceptualized as asking the justice to respond by his vote on the merits, signifying his attitude toward the major value or values at stake in the decision. Certainly, it is not *prima facie* unreasonable to suggest that the seven recent cases dealing with judicial review of courts-martial jurisdiction were testing the individual attitudes of the Justices toward a basic value in our constitutional system: civil supremacy over the military (or, stated reciprocally, civilian freedom from military control). Under such an assumption, the articulation, as judicial opinion behavior, of language which directs attention to other issues than the scale variable, is not necessarily to be construed as evidence that the case is viewed as multivariate by the Justices who associate themselves with such language; the model requires that the analyst examine the consistency of voting behavior, rather than the consistency of opinion behavior (as appears to be so frequently done in traditional legal analysis) as the basis for inferences about the attitudes of the Justices toward the scale variable under investigation.

The number of cases in this particular set is insufficient to permit the construction of a scalogram, even though the sample of seven includes all of the relevant decisions of the Court. (Older cases are not relevant, in terms of the model that we are using, because the personnel of the Warren Court did not participate in the earlier decisions which might, from a legal point of view, be deemed to be relevant as precedents.) A minimum of at least ten decisions in which two or more justices dissented would be required for the construction of a judicial scalogram. It is possible, nevertheless, to arrange the voting data provided by the available cases in the form of a scalogram; however, one would necessarily have considerably less confidence in inferences based upon such a quasi-scale[6] than would be the case if a larger sample of decisions on this subject were presently available for analysis.

[6]A different concept of "quasi-scale" is discussed in Torgerson, *op. cit.*

TABLE 1   Decisions of the Warren Court Declaring Unconstitutional Acts of Congress Extending Court-Martial Jurisdiction over Civil Rights (1955–1957 Terms)

Justice	Toth v. Quarles, 350 U.S. 11 (1955)	Reid v. Covert, 354 U.S. 1 (1957)	Trop v. Dulles, 356 U.S. 86 (1958)
Bl	('+')	('+'	('+'
Do	(+)	(+	(+
Wa	(+)	(+	('+'
Br	*	(+	('+'
Wh	*	NP	(+
Fr	(+)	('+'	'−')
Ha	(+)	('+'	−)
Cl	(+)	'−')	−)
Mi	−)	*	*
Re	'−')	*	*
Bu	−)	−)	−)
Voting Division	6–3	6–2	5–4

LEGEND		Justices	
+ = a vote in favor of holding the statute unconstitutional		Bl	Black
− = a vote against holding the statute unconstitutional		Br	Brennan
		Bu	Burton
' ' = wrote opinion		Cl	Clark
( ) = joined in the opinion of the Court		Do	Douglas
(= concurring opinion		Fr	Frankfurter
) = dissenting opinion		Ha	Harlan
* = not seated at the time of this decision		Mi	Minton
NP = seated but not participating in this decision		Re	Reed
		St	Stewart
		Wa	Warren
		Wh	Whittaker

II

Table 1 is a quasi-scale of the Court's final decisions on the merits in the first three cases in our sample. It should be noted that these decisions, declaring acts of Congress unconstitutional, appeared in successive terms of the Court. (The middle case consisted of two separate cases that were joined for common final disposition in the 1956 Term, although in the previous term each had received what appeared then to be a separate decision on the merits as we shall see in greater detail below; for purposes of the present analysis, the two cases will be considered as one. . . . when reference is made to the later decision of the 1956 Term only.)[7] From the point of

[7]*Reid* v. *Covert,* 354 U. S. 1 (1956 Term); *Kinsella* v. *Krueger,* 351 U.S. 470, and *Reid* v. *Covert,* 351 U. S. 487 (1955 Term).

view of scale theory—although not, we should note, from the point of view of some alternative theories of judicial decision-making—it is only a coincidence that the ordering of the cases corresponds to their chronological ordering. Since the cases and votes are in an ordinal relationship, however, scale theory suggests certain inferences and predictions that we might not otherwise be in a position to see or to make.

As Table 1 indicates, the Justices are, in effect, partitioned among four subsets, corresponding to their ranks or scale scores. Black, Warren, Douglas, Brennan, and Whittaker all would receive the maximal scale score of 3, since each voted affirmatively in the most "difficult" or marginal case, *Trop* v. *Dulles.* But we can also partition further this subset of five justices, according to the degree of confidence that we would place in the scale score assigned to these individuals. Clearly, we should have most confidence in the scoring of Black, Warren, and Douglas, because we have three observations of the voting behavior of each of them, since each participated in the decision of all three cases; and we should put less confidence in Brennan's score, and least in Whittaker's. By the same reasoning, we should have substantial confidence in assigning Frankfurter and Harlan a scale score of 2, Clark a score of 1, and Burton a score of 0; our lesser confidence in the scores of 0 for Reed and Minton is inconsequential, since their retirement from the Court (and replacement by Brennan and Whittaker) subsequent to the decision in *Toth* v. *Quarles* effectively removed them from consideration as relevant factors in the disposition of any other cases in our sample.

Although, as a matter of fact, the Court could not have formed majorities favorable to the claim of civil right in *Toth* and *Covert* without the support of Frankfurter and Harlan, the quasi-scale suggests that if Whittaker had voted in *Covert* and if both Brennan and Whittaker had participated in *Toth* (in lieu of Reed and Minton), minimal favorable majorities would have been formed *irrespective* of Frankfurter's and Harlan's attitudes toward, and votes in, these cases. That is to say, despite our lesser confidence in having correctly identified the underlying attitudes of Brennan and Whittaker toward the basic policy problem of military control over civilians, it seems more probable than not that each would have voted in favor of the claim of civil right had he participated. The votes of Clark and Burton, on the other hand, were not essential, in either fact or theory, to assure a favorable decision in these particular cases; but the fact that Clark did vote favorably to the civil right claim in the "easiest" of these cases, *Toth,* indicates that he was more sympathetic to the principle of civilian control than were Burton, Reed, and Minton. In fact, the quasi-scale, based as it is upon such a small and inadequate sampling of the attitudes of the Justices of the Supreme Court upon this issue, really provides us with more

information about Frankfurter, Harlan, and Clark than about any of the other Justices.

Let us assume an infinite extension of our underlying attitudinal continuum, in both directions. There is some sociological and anthropological evidence that in other societies and cultures, opinions on the subject of military control over civilians, both pro and con, are much more extreme than the range of positions commonly accepted within American society today. Furthermore, the segment of the continuum which includes American lawyers is doubtless a narrower segment than that for American society as a whole; and the Justices' ideal points doubtless lie on a subsegment of the "legal" segment of the continuum. The point is that the range of the continuum within which disagreement among Supreme Court Justices can occur, with consequent split decisions of the Court, is probably a very narrow segment of the total continuum. Although this point may well be "self-evident," it seems desirable to articulate it, in view of the considerable volume of passionate criticism of the Court which either states or assumes that the Court always is in disagreement, and generally by a 5-4 margin. More sophisticated observers are well aware that the Court is unanimous in over 90% of its decisions in each term; they also understand that the Court's division in over half of the decisions that it makes after oral argument and on the merits is a reflection of the value conflicts explicit in the questions (cases) that the Court, by a process of self-selection, undertakes to resolve. Conflict among spokesmen for different values on the Court is as real as it is earnest. However, it is well to remember that this conflict takes place within a milieu whose communication context is such that the value conflict among the Justices is magnified, and the essential homogeneity of values common to the Justices as a group[8] tends to be overlooked.

[8]For some persuasive evidence in support of this proposition, see "Homeostatic Tendencies in the United States Supreme Court," in Ulmer (ed.), *Introductory Readings in Political Behavior* (Chicago: Rand McNally, 1961), pp. 173–178. Ulmer shows that Kendall's W, an index of multiple ordinal concordance, is significantly

Returning to our quasi-scale, we can now say that the stimulus points corresponding to these three cases are bunched more or less closely together, somewhere in the middle of the relatively narrow subsegment (of the extended continuum) which includes the ideal-points of all the Justices who participated in these three decisions. Somewhere not too far to the left of *Toth* is a stimulus point or question which, if it had been asked of the Court, would have evoked favorable responses from Burton, Reed, and Minton as well as from their brethren. Somewhere immediately to the right of *Trop* lies a question which the Court would—given its present composition—answer unfavorably to the claim of civil right; and somewhat further to the right there lie an infinity of questions to all of which the Court would respond, and with increasing vehemence, unanimously in the negative—although most of these latter questions are so extreme that they could never survive jurisdictional screening and so would not appear upon the Supreme Court's dockets for oral argument and decision on the merits of the substantive issues presented.

On the basis of this assumption about the relatively narrow subsegment of the continuum of military control over civilians, within which *Toth, Covert,* and *Trop* are hypothesized as being located, it has been suggested recently that:

It is most reasonable to assume that if another case should come along, asking the Court to support a libertarian claim *more extreme* than that of *Trop,* the liberal bloc might be hard pressed to keep Whittaker in the fold or to attract Stewart, even assuming (as seems warranted) that Stewart's attitudes on this issue are likely to be more liberal than those of the man he replaced, who was the Court's anchor man in defense of the military. In-

deed, the liberal bloc might well have to face up to the defection of Brennan, as in [*Perez* v. *Brownell,* 356 U.S. 44 (1958)]. Even Warren refused to associate himself with the Black-Douglas concurrence in *Trop*; and from all appearances, only those two justices considered the military-control-over-civilian-rights angle to bear a sufficiently important relationship to this case to justify discussion. It seemed most likely, on the basis of the data shown in Table [1], that the Court's trend toward curtailing military control over civil rights had come to an end, and that any case similar to but less deprivational than *Trop* would find the libertarians, as on many other issues of constitutional policy that come before the Supreme Court for decision, exercising the traditional right of dissent.[9]

The above statement, which I wrote for use in an undergraduate text, is not sufficiently precise to be useful for present purposes. Moreover, it is clear that three cases are far too few to justify any statements about a "trend." Nor is it valid to assume that, simply because the chronological sequence in which these three cases arose coincided with their scalar order, such a coincidence could be expected to hold for any future case that might arise. Of course, the assumption explicit in the qualification that the next case to come along should be "similar to but less deprivational than *Trop*" is equivalent, from the point of view of scale theory, to the statement that such a case should raise "a libertarian claim *more extreme* than that of *Trop*."

It is possible to restate the prediction, more precisely, as follows: If the next case (or cases) which the Court accepts for decision raises a question (or questions) for which the corresponding stimulus point lies on the segment of the underlying continuum bounded by *Covert* and *Trop,* the Court's decision will be favorable to the claim of civil right; and if the stimulus point lies in the segment which is bounded determinately by *Trop* and indeterminately by the Court's jurisdictional tolerance to entertain the issue—and the latter point would almost certainly be more

high and positive for the decision-making of the Supreme Court throughout the period from 1888 to 1958; with the single exception of 1941–1945. The exceptional period of discordance is, of course, that of the Stone Court; and the exceptionally high rate of disagreement among the Justices, under Stone's leadership, has been pointed out by many observers, including Stone's biographer: Mason, *The Supreme Court from Taft to Warren* (Baton Rouge: Louisiana State University Press, 1958), pp. 154–155.

[9]Glendon Schubert, *Constitutional Politics: The Political Behavior of Supreme Court Justices and the Constitutional Policies That They Make* (New York: Holt, Rinehart and Winston, Inc., 1960), pp. 204, 206. Emphasis added.

extreme than Brennan's ideal point (since at least four votes are required for a favorable jurisdictional decision)—then the case might be decided either favorably or unfavorably, depending upon the extremity of the libertarian claim. Stated in this form, the prediction is sufficiently precise to be tested empirically by an examination of the decisions of the Court in the next cases to arise in fact, an event which occurred in the 1959 Term. A test of the prediction should prove to be valuable as a means for affording insight into the utility of cumulative-scale theory and analysis as an approach to the understanding, as well as the prediction, of Supreme Court decision-making behavior.

III
. . .

. . . [A]n examination of the facts and opinion data for the *Toth, Covert,* and *Trop* cases corroborates the assignment of positions in the quasi-scale of Table 1 on the basis of cumulative-scale theory and the voting data. *Toth* presents the strongest civil liberty claim, and *Trop* raises the weakest (or most extreme) libertarian claim; and both the opinion and the voting responses of the Justices correspond to the increasing "difficulty" of the questions raised by these cases for decision. We can also summarize, on the basis of the data provided by these three cases, the expected future behavior of the Justices in any related cases that might arise subsequent to *Trop.*

In terms of scale theory, we have no further interest in Minton, Reed, and Burton, since all of them had retired by the opening of the October 1958 Term, and hence a knowledge of their attitudes could be of no help in predicting what the Court would decide in subsequent cases. We are interested in Stewart, but we can say nothing about his attitude toward the scale variable, since he joined the Court too late[10] to participate in any of the three decisions for which we have information. A majority of five Justices (Black, Douglas, Warren, Brennan, and Whittaker)

[10]Mr. Justice Stewart replaced Mr. Justice Burton at the beginning of the 1958 Term.

can be expected—though with varying degrees of confidence—to vote favorably to any libertarian claim less extreme than that of *Trop.* In the case of more extreme claims, we should expect (on the basis of the *opinion* data) Black and Douglas to support more extreme claims than the other three. However, we cannot (on the basis of the *voting* data) differentiate among the ideal points of these five Justices, except in terms of confidence levels and other than to say that all five are located to the right of the *Trop* stimulus point on the continuum, because in terms of our quite limited information, all five Justices must be assigned the same rank or scale score. We should, of course, expect Frankfurter, Harlan, and Clark to vote against any claim more extreme than *Trop's,* and we should expect Frankfurter and Harlan to favor a claim falling between *Toth* and *Covert,* and Clark to reject a claim falling between *Covert* and *Trop.* But we cannot predict Clark's vote in a case lying between *Toth* and *Covert,* nor those of Frankfurter and Harlan in a case lying between *Covert* and *Trop.*

Assuming that all Justices participate in the decision, there are four possibilities:

1. In a case less extreme than *Toth,* eight Justices should vote favorably, but Stewart's vote would be indeterminate.

2. In a case more extreme than *Toth* but less extreme than *Covert,* seven Justices should vote favorably, but Clark's and Stewart's votes would be indeterminate.

3. In a case more extreme than *Covert* but less extreme than *Trop,* five Justices should vote favorably and Clark should dissent, but the votes of Frankfurter, Harlan, and Stewart would be indeterminate.

4. In a case more extreme than *Trop,* three Justices (Frankfurter, Harlan, and Clark) should reject the claim, and six votes (Black, Douglas, Warren, Brennan, Whittaker, and Stewart) would be indeterminate. We could predict that any case less extreme than *Trop* would be decided favorably; but we could not predict the decision in any case more extreme than *Trop.*

Since all three of the cases on the quasi-scale involved trials by courts-martial for capital offenses, but only the first two involved *civilian* defendants—and any claim in behalf of a *civilian* defendant against trial by court-martial might logically be considered to present a stronger civil liberty claim than that of a *military* defendant invoking a civil right—we might expect any case raising a question about the constitutional civil rights of *civilian* defendants to lie to the left of *Trop* on the scale. Moreover, since Frankfurter and Harlan had postulated an explicit distinction between capital and noncapital offenses, we might expect that, *at least for these two Justices,* a case raising a question about court-martial trial of a civilian defendant for a noncapital offense necessarily would fall between *Covert* and *Trop* on the quasi-scale. (Translated into psychological language, we should say that five Justices—Black, Douglas, Warren, Brennan, and Clark—would perceive *no difference* in the locus of the stimulus point of such a case and that of *Covert;* Frankfurter and Harlan would perceive the stimulus point of the new case to be located to the right of the stimulus point of *Covert* on the continuum; but we cannot say whether Whittaker and Stewart would perceive the difference, since neither had as yet revealed his attitude toward this question.) We can, therefore, refine our expectations regarding possibility 3 to this extent: If a case should arise involving the court-martial trial of a civilian defendant for a noncapital offense, the decision should be favorable to the defendant's claim and the voting division of the Court should be 5-4 or 6-3 (in view of the uncertainty about Stewart) with Frankfurter, Harlan, and Clark in dissent; and if another case should arise involving the court-martial trial of a civilian defendant for a capital offense, the decision should be favorable to the defendant's claim and the voting division of the Court should be 7-2 or 8-1, with Clark (and possibly Stewart, too) in dissent. Such a prediction is based, of course, upon the assumption that all of the Justices would perceive to be relevant one major independent variable—*Civilian/Military Control*—and that at least two of the justices also would perceive to be relevant a second independent variable—*Capital/Noncapital Offense.*[11]

IV

It was not long after *Trop* that the Court decided a series of cases in which questions were raised that furnished an appropriate test of our "refined" predictions for both alternative circumstances that might arise under what we have called possibility 3. On January 18, 1960, the Court decided seriatim four cases[12] that centered on the following questions: Can Congress authorize trial by court-martial of the following persons:

1. Civilian *dependents* for *noncapital* offenses?
2. Civilian *employees* for *capital* offenses?
3. Civilian *employees* for *noncapital* offenses?

The first question is consistent with our expectations, and we ought to expect our prediction to hold for the decision of the case, *Kinsella v. Singleton,* 361 U.S. 234, in which this question was raised. But the second and third questions have introduced a new and unanticipated independent variable—*civilian dependent/employee.* In effect, the major independent variable, *civilian/military control,* has now been further subdivided, as follows:

$$\left\{ \begin{array}{l} \text{MILITARY STATUS} \\ \\ \text{CIVILIAN STATUS} \end{array} \right. \left\{ \begin{array}{l} \text{CIVILIAN DEPENDENT} \\ \\ \text{CIVILIAN EMPLOYEE} \end{array} \right.$$

The voting data, of course, provide no information about what effect (if any) might be produced by the recognition, on the part of any or all of the Justices, of this new variable as a relevant consideration. The opinion data indicate that it would be improbable, but possible, for the remaining Justices who participated in *Covert* to attach much weight to this new variable. Certainly we should not expect, if the cases are perceived by the Justices as falling between *Covert* and *Trop* on the continuum, that this new distinction would have sufficient effect to change the

---

[11] A third independent variable, *war/peace,* is referred to in Clark's opinions in the two decisions on the merits in the *Covert-Krueger* cases, but this variable obviously would be of no help in prediction until a case arises under circumstances that at least some of the Justices would consider to be those of a time of war.

[12] *Kinsella v. Singleton,* 361 U.S. 234; *Grisham v. Hagan,* 361 U.S. 278; and *McElroy v. Guagliardo* and *Wilson v. Bohlender,* 361 U.S. 281.

predicted favorable votes of Black, Douglas, Warren, and Brennan, or the predicted unfavorable vote of Clark. Indeed, if the new variable were to be perceived as relevant by any of the Justices, the most likely candidates would be Stewart and Whittaker, who were uncommitted[13] by any previous votes or expression of opinion, and whose attitudes, therefore, could be assumed to be most flexible (i.e., least definitely structured) and most open to advocacy and persuasion on this issue.

If we view the *Covert* case as the most directly relevant precedent for the decisions made in January, 1960, we might array the cases, with the question that each raised, as follows:

(0) *Reid* v. *Covert*, 354 U.S. 1
    Civilian *dependent, capital* offense
(1) *Kinsella* v. *Singleton*, 361 U.S. 234
    Civilian *dependent, noncapital* offense
(2) *Grisham* v. *Hagan*, 361 U.S. 278
    Civilian *employee, capital* offense
(3) *McElroy* v. *Guagliardo*, 361 U.S. 281
    Civilian *employee, noncapital* offense
(3) *Wilson* v. *Bohlender*, 361 U.S. 281
    Civilian *employee, noncapital* offense

The cases and questions might then be considered to fall in a fourfold table (Table 2).

We can now see that the most directly relevant precedent, *Covert* (0), did not provide an unambiguous predictor for any of the four new cases, because of the uncertain effect that might be produced if there were general recognition among the Justices of the presence of a new independent variable (civilian status). As it turned out, however, only the two uncommitted Justices (Stewart and Whittaker) were attracted by the government's suggestion of this new variable, with the result that the stimuli (1-3) evoked the responses from the Justices shown in Table 3.

In other words, Black, Douglas, Warren, Brennan, and Clark voted for the defendants on all three questions (in all four cases); this majority was joined by Whittaker and Stewart, over the dissents of Frankfurter and Harlan, when the defendant was a civilian *dependent* but the offense was *noncapital;* the same majority group of five was joined by Frankfurter and Harlan, over the dissents of Whittaker and Stewart, when the offense was *capital* but the defendant was a civilian *employee;* while Frankfurter, Harlan, Whittaker, and Stewart all dissented against the decision of the majority five, upholding the claims of defendants who were civilian *employees* accused of *noncapital* offenses.

TABLE 2   Stimuli Attributes in the Court-Martial Decisions of the 1959 Term

		Civilian Status:	
		Dependent	**Employee**
Offense:	Capital	0	2
	Noncapital	1	3

TABLE 3   Voting Response in the Court-Martial Decisions of the 1959 Term

		Civilian Status:		
		All	**Dependents Only**	
Offenses:	**All**	Bl, Do, Wa Br, Cl	Wh, St	7
	Capital Only	Fr, Ha		2
		7	2	

---

[13]From a psychological, although not perhaps from a legal point of view.

TABLE 4   A Test of a Scale-Theory Prediction of the Court-Martial Decisions of the 1959 Term

Question	Prediction	Result	Errors
(1) Civilian Dependent, Noncapital Offense			
Outcome:	Pro	Pro	
Division:	6-3 or 5-4	7-2	1 Vote
Dissenters:	Fr, Ha, Cl (St?)	Fr, Ha	Cl
(2) Civilian Employee, Capital Offense			
Outcome:	Pro	Pro	
Division:	7-2 or 8-1	7-2	
Dissenters:	Cl (St?)	Wh, St	Cl, Wh
(3) Civilian Employee, Noncapital Offense			
Outcome:	Pro	Pro	
Division:	5-4 or 6-3	5-4	
Dissenters:	Fr, Ha, Cl (St?)	Fr, Ha, Wh, St	Cl, Wh

V

We can now examine the results of the test of our so-called "refined" prediction; that is, we can compare our prediction, based upon cumulative-scale theory and the data available prior to January, 1960, with the decisions made by the Court at that time. The results are given in Table 4.

The Court's decisions were all favorable to the civil liberty claimants, as expected; and six justices—Black, Douglas, Warren, Brennan, Frankfurter, and Harlan—voted precisely as we had predicted. We were in error about Whittaker's vote in the second and third questions; but Whittaker (and, of course, Stewart also) voted *consistently* in terms of the unpredicted new variable, which also accounts for our failure to predict accurately Whittaker's responses. The really surprising error is our failure to predict Clark's vote in any of the decisions on these three questions; to which should be added the further shock of discovering that Clark wrote the majority opinion for all four cases!

One possible inference might be that Clark, like Harlan in the various decisions in the Covert-Krueger cases, had changed his *attitude* toward the major independent scale variable—military control over civilians. However, this seems unlikely in view of the fact that Clark's votes in these decisions appear as *inconsistencies* in a cumulative scale of all civil liberties cases for the 1959 Term, and

particularly when one takes into consideration that on such a scale Clark ranked at the bottom of the Court in support of civil liberties claims with only one other pro-civil liberty vote, in a split decision, during the entire term. But if Clark did not change his attitude toward the question of military control over civilians, how are we to account for our failure to predict his voting in these cases?

VI

. . . [W]e can turn to the opinion data to complement the insights that we can derive from the voting data. Such a task is considerably facilitated, in this instance, by the circumstance that Clark wrote the opinion of the Court for all four of these cases. An examination of Clark's opinions reveals a perfectly clear and unambiguous reliance upon yet another new independent variable: the time-honored common-law principle of *stare decisis*. Both opinions for the majority in *Covert*, said Clark, agreed that trial by court-martial of *civilian dependents* in *capital* cases, in time of peace, is unconstitutional. (This is Clark's first major premise, which we shall call, for convenience, P-I). Moreover, a clear majority of six Justices (i.e., Black, Douglas, Warren, and Brennan, from the majority; and the two dissenters, Clark and Burton) agreed, said Clark, that the purported distinction between capital and noncapital offenses (urged by Frankfurter and Harlan in concurrence) was spurious and irrelevant. (This is Clark's second major premise, which we shall call P-II.) Therefore, Clark reasoned, P-I + P-II require a favorable response to question (1); that is, *Covert* applies as a precedent to civilian dependents in both capital and noncapital cases, in time of peace. Also, P-I requires a favorable response to question (2); that is, *Covert* applies as a precedent to both civilian *dependents* and *employees,* in capital cases, in time of peace. And of course, the favorable responses to questions (1) and (2) necessarily require, in turn, a favorable response to question (3). That is, *Singleton* and *Grisham—Covert* is not mentioned in Clark's opinion for *Guagliardo* and *Wilson*—apply as precedents to civilian *employees,* in *noncapital* cases, in time of peace. This is the precise logic of Clark's opinions; and this is the precise sequence in which the questions and cases were decided.

The opinion data also confirmed what is implicit in Table 4, namely, that by January, 1960, the Court was *unanimous* on the issue that had created such unusually great dissension and caused difficulty in reaching a final decision that would stick only three and a half years earlier: the unconstitutionality of trial by court-martial of *civilian dependents* in *capital* cases. This *post hoc* unanimity was accompanied, however, by disagreement among the justices on several other related issues, as our analysis of the *civilian status, capital offense,* and now yet a third variable *stare decisis* has demonstrated; so there was no net gain in consensus on the Court.

We are led to conclude that our prediction, based upon scale theory, of the court-martial decisions of the 1959 Term, was very substantially validated by the empirical data. The voting "errors" of Clark and Whittaker can be readily explained by the presence of two additional independent variables that were not present in the *Covert* decision. Of course, one might well have anticipated, from the point of view of Austinian positivism, that *stare decisis* might become an important, or at least a relevant, factor in the decision of a set of cases for which a recent precedent existed. The major error in our prediction must be attributed to our failure to include such a

traditional legal variable as *stare decisis* within the frame of reference deemed relevant.

. . .

. . . [A]ttitudinal analysis of the Justices, . . . on a multivariate basis, . . . suggest[s] the necessity for an even more complex theoretical model of judicial behavior. In measuring judicial attitudes, we must be concerned not only with the externally oriented values which represent the recurrent issues of law and policy raised before the Court for decision; we must also be concerned with the internally oriented values which represent the institutional identifications of the Justices with the Court, its customs and traditions, and their attitudes toward each other as members of the same small decision-making group.

27 *STARE DECISIS* AND THE JUDICIAL MIND

Glendon Schubert

. . . I should like to suggest that further work in the influence of the ideological dimension of pragmatism/dogmatism may shed considerable light upon the importance of what lawyers call *"stare decisis,"* as an attitudinal variable. The extent to which a belief in the obligation of justices to follow precedents, in either the personal or institutional sense, is an important component of the attitudes of judges, is virtually unknown. This is largely because lawyers have attempted to study *stare decisis* by using logical rather than sociopsychological tools of analysis. But the relationships depicted [in Schubert's study] are not inconsistent with the small beginning that has been made, in attempts to study from a behavioral point of view the belief in "following precedent." For example, in my study of the attitudes of the Warren Court toward civilian (versus military) control and *stare decisis,* I arrived at findings that are strictly compatible with the more general structure

Reprinted by permission of the publisher from Glendon Schubert, *The Judicial Mind: The Attitudes and Ideologies of Supreme Court Justices 1946–1963* (Evanston, Ill.: Northwestern University Press, 1965), pp. 267–268. Footnotes omitted.

arrived at in the present study [*The Judicial Mind*], although I did not then appreciate the extent to which the findings of the earlier study—based upon an analysis of only half a dozen decisions dealing with a relatively narrow content area—would have general implications. I think it requires no argument to support the judgment that to believe in the authority of precedent, that rules should be followed until they are formally changed, etc., corresponds with the Dogmatic ideology; while a concern for the present and future consequences of decisions, and a willingness to manipulate precedents to achieve results deemed desirable now, should be associated with the ideology of Pragmatism. So Dogmatism is pro-*stare decisis,* and Pragmatism is anti-*stare decisis.* . . . The conclusion reached by the earlier study was that the basic difference was between liberals and conservatives, but that the conservatives were differentiated by their attitudes toward *stare decisis,* with Clark ranking exceptionally high in his regard for *stare decisis,* and Frankfurter and Harlan ranking exceptionally low. Students of judicial behavior may find it particularly fruitful if they attempt to link their empirical work with the research, in dogmatism and authoritarianism as personality variables, which has been undertaken by such social psychologists as the Berkeley group, Rokeach, and Eysenck. If this is the second most important ideological dimension in Supreme Court decision-making, it probably merits much more careful attention and study than it has received in the past, on the hypothesis that this is a major dimension of judicial behavior generally. It is certainly plausible to assume, for example, that on other courts—or on the Supreme Court at other times—Pragmatism/Dogmatism is a dimension which divides liberal as well as conservative judges. (I would speculate, for example, that Holmes was a pragmatic liberal while his colleague, John H. Clarke, was a dogmatic liberal.)

28 JUDICIAL POWER AS A VARIABLE MOTIVATING SUPREME COURT BEHAVIOR

Harold J. Spaeth

In articulating the bases for decisions, the opinions of the Supreme Court frequently emphasize the propriety (or impropriety) of the Court's attempt to resolve the matter at hand. This concern with the applicability of its powers to specific controversies is not surprising, particularly in view of the substantially complete discretion which the Court has over its workload.[1] However, simply because the Justices who write the Court's opinions articulate their reasoning in terms of their conception of the Court's right to act is no necessary indication that this is the actual basis on which the votes of the Justices turn. It would certainly be presumptuous to maintain that the Court is any less facile in rationalizing its actions than any other group. But be this as it may, recent analyses of Supreme Court decision making have shown that variables of a more value-laden character than the propriety of acting in a given set of circumstances underlie the bulk of the Court's decision making. Thus, in civil liberties cases, the variable dominating behavior has been shown to be the degree of sympathy which the various justices have for the civil liberty

Reprinted from "Judicial Power as a Variable Motivating Supreme Court Behavior," *Midwest Journal of Political Science,* VI (1962), pp. 54–63, 81–82, by Harold J. Spaeth, by permission of the Wayne State University Press. Copyright © 1962 by Wayne State University Press.

[1]See Glendon A. Schubert, *Quantitative Analysis of Judicial Behavior* (Glencoe, Ill.: Free Press, 1959), pp. 26–67.

claim;[2] in workmen's disability actions (Federal Employers Liability and Jones Acts), the dominant variable is support of the claimant;[3] and in cases involving economic regulation of either labor unions or business activities, economic liberalism.[4]

Perhaps the most striking evidence of the generally subordinate character of questions relating to the proper exercise of Supreme Court power is revealed in a study of the universe of business regulation cases.[5] The analysis shows that attitudes of Supreme Court activism/restraint are thoroughly dominated by the variable of economic liberalism —e.g., anti-business, pro-competition, anti-oligopoly sentiments. This is to say that a justice will exercise restraint (or activism) only if it enables him to secure a result compatible with his attitude toward economic liberalism. Aptly illustrating the subordinate character of the Court's right to act is its behavior in agency action items regulatory of business.[6] Analysis shows close correlation between the degree to which a Justice supports economic liberalism and the extent to which he supports agency decision making. For example, the illiberal wing of the Warren Court—Whittaker, Frankfurter, and Harlan —exercises considerably more restraint toward the pro-business Interstate Commerce Commission than toward the other agencies which as a group are strongly anti-business. Furthermore, when members of the pro-business group vote to reverse agency decision making, the effect of their votes is to undo an anti-business agency decision. The behavior of the five most economically liberal members of the Court—Douglas, Black, Warren, Brennan, and Clark—is the direct oppo-

site. Deference is shown to anti-business agency decision making, and, when they vote to reverse an agency decision, it is usually because the agency's decision was pro-business. Alone excepted from the foregoing pattern is Minton and, to a lesser degree, Reed among the members of the Warren Court.

But what of cases that have little or no bearing on value premises? To what extent is the action of the Court in such cases influenced by its conception of the extent of its legal power? This is the question to be taken up in the study that follows.

To put it in a formal context: the purpose of this paper is to ascertain whether or not there exists a dominant variable which motivates the behavior of the justices in what may be termed the "true" judicial power items; namely, those in which the more value-laden variables are either absent or subordinate to considerations of the exercise of power by the Supreme Court. If the existence of a dominant variable can be empirically verified, significant continuity is present in the Court's decision making in the "true" judicial power items. . . .

I

Over the first eight terms of the Warren Court (1953–1960), a total of 52 formally decided cases[7] appear on their face to have been decided on the basis of considerations of Supreme Court power. Three criteria pertaining to the complex of facts, issues, and opinions present in a given case were employed to isolate these cases from the totality of formally decided items.

(1) Where the fact situation, issues requiring resolution, and the points emphasized

---

[2]S. Sidney Ulmer, "Supreme Court Behavior and Civil Rights," *Western Political Quarterly*, 13 (June, 1960), pp. 294–311; "The Analysis of Behavior Patterns on the United States Supreme Court," *Journal of Politics*, 22 (November, 1960), pp. 647–652; "Scaling Judicial Cases: A Methodological Note," *American Behavioral Scientist*, 4 (April, 1961), pp. 31–33.

[3]Schubert, *op. cit.*, pp. 290–297.

[4]Harold J. Spaeth, ["Warren Court Attitudes Toward Business: The 'B' Scale" in *Judicial Decision-Making* (Glendon Schubert, ed.) (The Free Press, 1963), pp. 79–108].

[5]*Ibid.*

[6]*Ibid.*

[7]I define "formally decided" cases as all those appearing in the first part of the *U. S. Reports* (i.e., antecedent to p. 801 or 901 of each volume) which were orally argued. Where a number of cases are gathered together under one opinion of the court, the case is counted as one formally decided item, provided that each participating Justice voted the same way in all of the combined cases. Where one or more Justices distinguished between the cases by concurring in some and dissenting in the remainder, the cases are counted compatibly with the smallest whole number necessary to account for the variant behavior of the Justice or Justices involved.

in the opinions clearly indicate the dominance of considerations of Supreme Court power as the basis for the Court's decisions.

(2) Where a case concerned with issues of Supreme Court power in combination with other issues involving civil liberties, business regulation, labor relations, or disability compensation did not fit compatibly into the relevant substantive universe as revealed by Guttman scale analysis. Under this criterion, only items which contained one or more inconsistent votes when included in the relevant substantive universe are incorporated into the judicial power scale. Five of these items involve regulation of business, one labor relations, and one civil liberties.[8]

(3) Where a case significantly concerned either the matter of comity—the propriety of exercising admittedly existing federal jurisdiction in deference to considerations of federalism—or the Federal Rules of Civil Procedure. Such cases were included in the judicial power universe even though they were of a multi-issue character and fit without inconsistencies into their relevant substantive universe. A goodly number of these items are multi-issue; among the eleven Civil Procedure cases, a total of six are multi-issue, four involving business regulation, two internal revenue.[9] Only three of the eleven comity items, however, are multi-issue. Two of

them involve civil liberties, one, business regulation.[10]

The 52 items comprising the universe admit of division into five component parts: in addition to the comity and Civil Procedure cases, with eleven items each, there are eight diversity of citizenship cases, six involving venue as their primary judicial power issue, and 17 miscellaneous. This breakdown is exhaustive, with one case appearing in both the comity and diversity of citizenship subsets.[11]

The methodology employed to analyze these "true" judicial power items is a modified form of scale analysis. In establishing the existence of the dominant variable, orthodox Guttman scale theory is adhered to as it has been developed and applied to judicial decision-making by Schubert.[12] The modification lies in the extensive use of subscales. . . . [This excerpt does not contain that portion of the Spaeth article which considers subscales.]

Inspection of the 52 "true" judicial power items decided during the first eight terms of the Warren Court reveals that the decision in all but one of them is classifiable in terms of Supreme Court activism/restraint.[13] When the Court decides that it has the power to pass upon the action of other branches of government or—more commonly—to exercise supervisory authority over the decision-making of lower courts, the decision is scored as activist. Where it refuses to do so, the decision is counted as pro-restraint. The resultant array (Figure 1) shows the variable of Supreme Court activism/restraint to produce

---

[8]The business connected items are *Brownell* v. *Singer*, 347 US 403 (1954), *United States* v. *Western Pacific R. Co.*, 352 US 59 (1956), *United States* v. *Chesapeake & Ohio R. Co.*, 352 US 77 (1956), *P.U.C. of California* v. *United States*, 355 US 534 (1958), and *United States* v. *Proctor & Gamble*, 356 US 677 (1958). The labor union item is *Oil Workers* v. *Missouri*, 361 US 363 (1960); the civil liberties case, *Mesarosh* v. *United States*, 352 US 1 (1956). Two business-connected companion cases not containing any inconsistent votes in the business regulation universe are included herein because of their unusually pronounced judicial power character, *Smith* v. *Sperling*, 354 US 91 (1957), and *Swanson* v. *Traer*, 354 US 114 (1957).

[9]Those involving business regulation are *United States* v. *Proctor & Gamble*, 356 US 677 (1958), *Société Internationale* v. *Rogers*, 357 US 197 (1958), *Beacon Theatres* v. *Westover*, 359 US 500 (1959), and *Fox Publishing Co.* v. *United States*, 366 US 683 (1961). The two internal revenue items are *United States* v. *Ohio Power Co.*, 353 US 98 (1957), and *New Hampshire Fire Insurance Co.* v. *Scanlon* 362 US 404 (1960).

[10]The civil liberties connected items are *Harrison* v. *N.A.A.C.P.*, 360 US 167 (1959), and *Wilson* v. *Schnettler*, 365 US 381 (1961). The business item is *P.U.C. of California* v. *United States*, 355 US 534 (1958).

[11]*Clay* v. *Sun Insurance Office*, 363 US 207 (1960).

[12]Schubert, *op. cit.*, chap. 5. For a very brief statement of scale analysis as applied to the Court, see Schubert's "The Study of Judicial Decision-Making as an Aspect of Political Behavior," *American Political Science Review*, 52 (December, 1958), pp. 1014–1017.

[13]The single exception is *Fourco Glass Co.* v. *Transmirra Products Co.*, 353 US 222 (1957), which raised the question of proper venue in a patent infringement proceeding under the Judicial Code of 1948. Harlan alone dissented from the Court's decision.

acceptable coefficients.[14] Hence, this variable is the dominant one in the judicial power scale.

The set of judicial power items produces an R of .934 and an S of .756. Both are comfortably above the minimum requirements for scalability. The cases comprising the scale are far from evenly distributed over the eight terms, as Table 1 shows. Over two-fifths of the 51 items classifiable in terms of the dominant variable were decided during the 1956 and 1959 terms, with only three decided in the 1954 Term and four in 1960. Seven of the 18 extreme marginals (those cases with one or no dissents) were decided in the 1956 Term; a similarly disproportionate share of the inconsistent votes and cases with inconsistencies occurred in the 1959 term—seven of the 19 inconsistencies and seven of the 16 cases with inconsistent votes. There does not appear to be any correlation between the 1959 term inconsistencies and the presence of new personnel on the Court. The composition of the Court during the 1959 Term was the same as it had been at the end of the 1958 Term. The most recent appointee, Stewart, had taken his seat on October 14, 1958, at the

commencement of the 1958 Term. Inspection of the 1959 Term inconsistencies reveals that Brennan cast four of them, Douglas two, and Whittaker one. The inconsistent votes of Douglas and Whittaker occurred in items which appear to be clearly multi-issue. Brennan's inconsistent votes during the 1959 term do not admit of such an explanation, however, with one possible exception. . . .

As for the ranking of the Justices on the activist/restraint continuum of Figure 1, it is no surprise that Douglas and Frankfurter are at polar opposites of activism and restraint, respectively. Although Jackson scored lower than Frankfurter, this is based upon but five participations, Jackson having sat only during the first term of the Warren Court. The broad spread in the Justices' scale scores allows for dividing the members of the Court into two groups, a seven-member activist wing (Douglas, Reed, Minton, Warren, Brennan, Black, and Clark), all of whom have scale score percentages comfortably above 50%, with the remaining six comprising a restraint grouping. The latter is divisible into two groups. Whittaker and Stewart with scale score percentages of 49 and 45, respectively, form the moderate wing of the restraint group, and Burton, Harlan, Frankfurter, and Jackson a strongly restraint-oriented faction. The activists are dominant, as 31 of the 51 items (61%) were decided in an activist fashion. Furthermore, the activists possess an absolute majority of the Court as presently constituted (Douglas, Warren, Brennan, Black, and Clark). Their dominance would have been even more thoroughgoing if Black and Clark had not been considerably more moderate in their activism than the other members of the group. In addition, Clark functions as the Court's equipoise, having voted in dissent only once in the 51 items.[15] Nor would he have been in dissent on this one occasion if either Whittaker or Stewart had voted consistently.

There is considerable disproportion in the distribution of inconsistent votes. Brennan

[14]The R coefficient at the bottom of [the scale] is Guttman's coefficient of reproducibility. An R of .900 or above is evidence of unidimensionality; i.e., that the tested variable dominates behavior in the set of cases. S is Menzel's coefficient of scalability [Herbert Menzel, "A New Coefficient for Scalogram Analysis," *Public Opinion Quarterly,* 17 (Summer, 1953), 268–280]. S provides a more rigid standard than R since it does not capitalize upon the spurious contribution to consistency which arises from the inclusion in the set of extreme marginal distribution of either cases or Justices. An S of .600 or higher is considered evidence of set consistency. In computing S, it is conventional to exclude unanimously decided cases, while R excludes all extreme marginals (i.e., cases with less than two dissenting votes).

It should be noted that in computing S it is virtually certain that the distribution of the Justices is likely to be more extreme than the distribution of the cases. Case division tends to average out about 6–3, i.e., with two majority votes for every dissenting vote. It is most unlikely, however, that the average justice will divide his votes in any scale so evenly. This is evident from the master scale (Figure 1). In counting the ratio of + to − votes for each Justice, we find that only six of the 13 Justices show a ratio of 2:1 or less (Minton, Brennan, Black, Clark, Whittaker, and Stewart). The others are all much more extreme, with Douglas (33:4), Harlan (28:1), and Frankfurter (35:1) most so.

[15]*County of Allegheny* v. *Mashuda Co.,* 360 U.S. 185 (1959).

FIGURE 1 Scale of Universe of Judicial Power Cases

Scale Score	46	40	39	37	37	34	30	25	23	15	11	9	0	Vote
Scale Score Percentage (51 = 100%)	90	78	76	73	73	67	59	49	45	29	22	18	0	
Cases[a] / Justices	DOU	REED	MIN	WAR	BRN	BLK	CLK	WHT	STW	BUR	HAR	FRK	JAC	
Parissi v. Telechron 49/46	+	+	+	+		+	+			+	+	+		9-0
Gibson v. Lockheed 50/356	+	+	+	+		+	+			+	+	'c'		9-0
Petrowski v. Hawkeye Ins 50/495	+	+	+	+		+	+			+	c	'c'		9-0
Sears Roebuck v. Mackey 51/427	+	+	+	+	+	+	+			'+'	c	'c'		9-0
Jaffke v. Dunham 52/280	+	+		+		+	+			+	+	+		9-0
Govt. Employees v. Windsor 53/364	'+'			+	+	*	+	+		+	c			8-0
Swanson v. Traer 54/114	'+'			+	+	+	+	c		c	c	'c'		9-0
Societe Intl. v. Rogers 57/197	+	c		+	+	+	*	+		+	'+'	+		8-0
Nolan v. Transocean 65/293	+		+	+	+	'+'	+	+	+	+	+	+		9-0
Madruga v. Superior Ct 46/556	'+'	c				+	+	'+'		'+'	+	'-'		7-2
Fla. Growers v. Jacobsen 62/73	'(-)'			+	+	+	+	'+'	+	+	+	'-'		7-2
Cold Metal v. United Engr 51/445	+	+	+	+		+	+			'+'	'-'	'-'		7-2
US v. Schaefer Brewng 56/227	+	+		+	+	+	+	'+'		'+'	'-'	'-'		7-2
Bankers Life v. Holland 46/379	c	+	'(-)'			+	'+'	'+'		+	'-'	'-'		6-3
Brownell v. Singer 47/403	'(-)'	+	+	*	+	+	+	+		+	*	'-'		5-3
Dick v. NY Life Ins 59/437	'+'				+	+	+	'(-)'	'c'	'-'	*	'-'	'-'	6-2
Bernhardt v. Polygraphic 50/198	'+'	+		'+'	+	+	+	+		'-'	'-'	'-'		6-3
Mesarosh v. US 52/1	'+'	+		'+'	*	+	+			'-'	'-'	'-'		5-3
PUC of California v. US 55/534	'+'			'(-)'	+	+	+	'+'	'c'	'-'	'-'	'(+)'		6-3
US v. Proctor & Gamble 56/677	'+'			+	+	+	+	'c'	'+'	'-'	'-'	'-'		6-3
Chicago v. AT & SF R Co 57/77									'-'	'-'	'-'	'-'		6-3
Hoffman v. Blaski 63/335	+	+		+	'(-)'	+	'+'	'+'			'-'	'-'		6-3
US v. Am-For SS Co 63/685	+	+		+	'(-)'	+	+	+	'c'		'-'	'-'		6-3
Magenau v. Aetna Freight 60/273									'+'					
US v. Mersky 61/431	+	+		+	'+' 'c'	+	'+'	'+'	'c'	'+'	'-'	'-'		6-3
Byrd v. Blue Ridge Coop 56/525	'+'			+	'+'	+	'+'	'c'	'-'	'(+)'	'-'	'-'		6-3
La Buy v. Howes Leather 52/249	+	+		+	'(-)'	+	'+'	'-'		'-'	'-'	'-'		5-4

Case	51	18	13	49	34	50	48	30	21	30	42	50	5	
US v. Ohio Power Co 53/98	+			+	*	+	+	*						4-3
Smith v. Sperling 54/91	'+'			+	+	+	+				'−'			5-4
Beacon v. Westover 59/500	+			+	+	'+'	+					*		5-3
Allegheny v. Mashuda Co 60/185	+			+	+	(−)	'−'	(+)	'−'					5-4
Oil Workers v. Missouri 61/363	(−)			+	+	'+'			(+)					3-6
Clay v. San Insurance Ofc 63/207	'+'			'−'	(−)	'+'								3-6
Metlakatla v. Egan 63/555	'+'			+	'+'	'+'								3-6
La Power v. Thibodaux 60/25	'+'			+	+				'c'			'−'		3-6
Harrison v. NAACP 60/167	'+'			+	+									3-6
Wilson v. Schnettler 65/381	'+'			+	+							'−'		3-6
Whitehouse v. IC R Co 49/366	'+'	'+'	+	+							'−'			3-5
Olberding v. IC R Co 46/338	(c)	'+'	+	*									—	2-7
PUC v. United Air Lines 46/402	'+'	+	−										—	2-6
Contractors v. Bodinger 48/176	+		−		('+')			c						2-6
Grain Co v. Barge FBL-585 64/19	+													
US v. Western Pacific R Co 52/59	'+'	*				'−'	('+')				c	'c'		2-7
US v. C & O R Co 52/77	'+'	*			*						'−'			1-6
Leiter Minerals v. US 52/220	'+'								'−'			'−'		1-6
Martin v. Creasy 60/219	'+'			c	'c'				'−'					1-8
Brownell v. Chase Bank 52/36	'+'						*				*			1-8
McGann v. US 62/214	'−'													0-7
NH Fire Ins Co v. Scanlon 62/404						'−'	'−'							0-9
Schnell v. Eckrich & Sons 65/260							*							0-9
Fox Publishing Co v. US 66/683												'−'		0-8
Participations	51	18	13	49	34	50	48	30	21	30	42	50	5	= 441
Inconsistencies	4		1	1	5	2		3		1	1	1		= 19

Legend: + activist vote   ' ' wrote opinion   c concurrence
− restraint vote   ( ) inconsistency   * not participating

R = .934
S = .756

[a]Case titles are abbreviated where necessary. The references are to the *U.S. Reports*. The first digit of the volume number is omitted, and numbers following the slash bar are page numbers. For example, *Parissi v. Telechron* is in 349 US 46 (1955).

TABLE 1 Distribution of Judicial Power Items

Term	No. of Items	No. of Extreme Marginal Items	No. of Inconsistent Votes	No. of Items with Inconsistent Votes
1953	5	0	3	3
1954	3	1	1	1
1955	5	3	0	
1956	11	7	1	1
1957	6	1	3	2
1958	7	1	4	2
1959	10	2	7	7
1960	4	3	0	
Totals	51	18	19	16

leads the Court with five, followed by Douglas with four, and Whittaker with three. The twelve inconsistencies cast by these three Justices account for 63% of the 19 total inconsistencies appearing on Figure 1. Among the other Justices, only Black voted inconsistently more than once, with Clark, Harlan, Reed, and Jackson voting with perfect consistency. In relation to total votes, only Brennan and Whittaker have high ratios of inconsistent votes—Brennan 1:7 and Whittaker 1:10. The ratios of Douglas and Minton are 1:13, Stewart 1:21, and Black 1:25. The other members of the Court casting inconsistent votes have ratios of 1:30 or above.

Thirteen of the 19 inconsistent votes were cast by members of the activist group. Of their 13 inconsistencies, 12 were pro-restraint. Consequently, the activists show less consistency in their voting, casting as a group one out of every 20 votes inconsistently. The restraint wing, by comparison, voted inconsistently an average of only once per 30 votes. All but one of the latter's inconsistencies were activist, one of Whittaker's three inconsistencies having been restraint-oriented. In only one item was an inconsistent vote crucial to the outcome of the Court's decision, in County of Allegheny v. Mashuda Co., 360 U.S. 185 (1959), and, interestingly enough, it was inconsistent voting among the restraint group which produced the activist result here.

Only two of the 51 items appearing on the master scale (Figure 1) contain more than a single inconsistency. P.U.C. of California v. United States, 355 U.S. 534 (1958), is clearly multi-issue and contains the sole inconsistent votes cast by Warren and Frankfurter. A statute prohibiting carriers from transporting government property at rates other than those approved by the California Public Utilities Commission was voided by the Court under the supremacy clause. The dissenters, Harlan, Warren, and Burton, held that considerations of comity should have caused the Court to defer judgment until it was known how California intended to apply the statute. Not only does the case involve business regulation, but it is also one of only five non-unanimous cases decided during the 1953–1959 terms in which the business regulation of the state supported business interests. In contrast to the two inconsistencies which the case produced on Figure 1, it appeared with three inconsistencies in the business regulation scale.[16] The other multiple inconsistency item, County of Allegheny v. Mashuda Co., 360 U.S. 185 (1959), although without the egregious multi-issue features of the California case, contains three inconsistent votes, those of Black, Whittaker, and Stewart. The latter's vote is his only inconsistency in the judicial

[16]The vote of Frankfurter and Warren appears inconsistently on both universes. The five non-unanimous items in which the business regulation of the state supported business interests produced a total of ten inconsistent votes on the scale of business regulation cases. Spaeth, loc. cit.

power universe. In *Mashuda*, property owners challenged the validity of a county condemnation proceeding in a federal district court on the ground that their property was being taken for a private purpose. The Court held that the district court's application of comity was improper, the dissenters taking the opposite view.

. . .

In attempting "to map a portion of the hidden springs of judicial decision," this paper has served a three-fold purpose:

(1) Most importantly, significant continuity in the Court's decision making has been established for what has been termed the judicial power universe. A single empirically verifiable dominant variable—Supreme Court activism/restraint—motivates the response of the justices herein. The reader, of course, has noted that the dominant variable is defined in political rather than legal terms.

(2) Considerable data have been provided concerning the specific response of the individual justices to the dominant variable. Much of this is non-relational, not having been presented in a comparative or analogical frame of reference. Given the unplowed character of this area of judicial decision making, emphasis upon collection and simple classification of data is not without warrant.

(3) A measure of comparative data of . . . an . . . interuniverse character has been presented. The interuniverse comparisons are drawn from studies of those areas of the Court's decision making which have in some degree been subject to Guttman scale analysis, most particularly regulation of business.

Finally, a word of caution is in order. What has been said in this paper regarding the behavior of members of the Warren Court in response to the variable of Supreme Court activism/restraint is applicable, so far as is known, only to the universe investigated herein. Although questions of judicial activism/restraint are bound up with virtually all Supreme Court decision-making and are frequently articulated as the ostensible basis of decisions in other areas of litigation, there is no warrant for inferring that the pattern of response manifest in this universe exists elsewhere. Indeed, as mentioned in the introductory portion of this paper, analysis of the business regulation decisions of the first seven terms of the Warren Court shows that the items contained therein which closely involve questions of judicial power were resolved in terms of response to the variable of attitude toward business. As a result, response patterns in the business cases reveal an almost perfect *reversal* of the patterns noted in the judicial power universe. This is to say that such strongly activist Justices as Douglas, Black, Warren, Brennan, and Clark are most deferential and restrained toward agency decision making regulatory of business; while such members of the restraint group as Whittaker, Frankfurter, Harlan, and Burton are thorough-going activists when it comes to these agencies. The reason for this switch is not a result of responses to the variable of activism/restraint, but rather to the Justices' attitudes toward business. And since Whittaker, Frankfurter, and Harlan are the most pro-business-oriented among members of the Warren Court, and since the decisions of these agencies which were reviewed by the Court tended to be predominantly anti-business, this trio voted most often to reverse agency decision-making. For this same reason, our activist group is there transformed into the very model of restraint.

F. Attitudes and Decisions

The largest amount of judicial behavior research has been devoted to the investigation of judicial attitudes and values from an analysis of judicial voting. The findings of the selections presented in this section represent impressive evidence that the attitudes and values of the judge provide a key to understanding the conversion process.

It should be mentioned that most attitudinal studies use non-unanimously decided cases for the raw data. Non-unanimously decided cases are studied because disagreement among judges is considered to ascertain objectively the existence of conflicting paths to the solution of controversies raised in litigation. A study of the voting records of judges in these cases enables one to determine the attitudes and value preferences of each judge. Conflicts in attitudes and values are thus accentuated. Conversely, cases in which no voting disagreement is evident are ignored. But this does not necessarily mean that the attitudes and values of judges have not come into play when cases are unanimously decided. Unanimously decided cases are disregarded because there is no objective way (short of a transcript of judicial conference deliberations) of demonstrating that the "facts" and "law" of such cases allowed the judges sufficient discretion so that the case could be decided either way. Because formal disagreement within and among courts which comprise the federal judicial system is atypical, most attitudinal studies rely on only a fraction of judicial decision-making for their data.

Why are so many cases decided unanimously? As the readings concerning the legal setting emphasized, judges are expected to adhere to the rules of the game and thus live up to professional expectations. The supports of the system are, after all, inputs to the system and as such are relevant variables for the conversion process. The conversion process is thus circumscribed by the nature of *all* the elements and the supports of the system. Thus it is possible that similar attitudes and values of the judges concerning the legal elements and the supports of the system may correctly explain the conversion process for many of the unanimously decided cases.

The selection by Sheldon Goldman concerns voting behavior on the eleven United States Courts of Appeals. Goldman explores the relationship of backgrounds to decisional tendencies as well as the attitudinal voting patterns of appeals judges. The selection by Louis Loeb concerns an analysis of inter-court bloc voting by the United States Court of Appeals for the District of Columbia and the United States Supreme Court. The remaining six selections are exclusively concerned with the Supreme Court. C. Herman Pritchett's article was originally published in 1941 and is the trail-blazing study in the field of judicial behavior. The selection by Sidney Ulmer contains evidence which suggests that attitudes and values and not power considerations underlie bloc voting on the Supreme Court. The study by Joseph Tanenhaus concerns the attitudes of Supreme Court judges toward federal administrative agency cases. David Danelski in his study explores the problem of the identification of values. Danelski also discusses the theoretical implications of his research. Glendon Schubert in the final two selections presents and discusses his psychometric model of Supreme Court voting behavior. Schubert's methods are the most mathematically sophisticated in the field and have enabled him to make predictions which, in the reapportionment area, have been entirely correct (note that Ulmer has some comments about this in the selection of his in part four). The final selection by Schubert is drawn from the conclusion of his study, *The Judicial Mind*. Although Schubert's methodology is further refined in that work, his basic methodology remains the same. Thus his concluding comments have relevance for the preceding selection of his which we have reprinted.

29 VOTING BEHAVIOR ON THE UNITED STATES COURTS OF APPEALS

Sheldon Goldman

Voting behavior of public decision-makers has been of central concern for political scientists. For example, studies of legislatures (notably of Congress) have investigated such research problems as: (1) the extent to which voting on one issue is related to voting on other issues; (2) the potency of party affiliation as an organizer of attitudes and a predictor of voting behavior; and (3) the relationship of demographic characteristics to voting behavior. These and related concerns have more recently occupied the attention of students of the judiciary whose focus has primarily been on the United States Supreme Court.[1]

Reprinted by permission from Sheldon Goldman, "Voting Behavior on the United States Courts of Appeals, 1961–1964," *American Political Science Review,* 60 (1966), pp. 374–383.

[1]C. Herman Pritchett, *The Roosevelt Court: A Study in Judicial Politics and Values, 1937–1947* (New York: Macmillan Co., 1948); Pritchett, *Civil Liberties and the Vinson Court* (Chicago: University of Chicago Press, 1954); S. Sidney Ulmer, "The Analysis of Behavior Patterns in the United States Supreme Court," *Journal of Politics,* 22 (1960), pp. 629–653; Ulmer, "Toward a Theory of Sub-Group Formation in the United States Supreme Court," *Journal of Politics,* 27 (1965), pp. 133–153; Joseph Tanenhaus, "Supreme Court Attitudes toward Federal Administrative Agencies, 1947–1956—An Application of Social Science Methods to the Study of the Judicial Process," *Vanderbilt Law Review,* 14 (1961), pp. 473–502; Glendon Schubert, *Quantitative Analysis of Judicial Behavior* (Glencoe: The Free Press, 1959); Schubert, "The 1960 Term of the Supreme Court: A Psychological Analysis," *A.P.S.R.,* 56 (1962), pp. 90–108; Schubert, *The Judicial Mind: The Attitudes and Ideologies of Supreme Court Justices 1946–1963* (Evanston: Northwestern University Press, 1965); John R. Schmidhauser, "Judicial Behavior and the Sectional Crisis of 1837–1860," *Journal of Politics,* 23 (1961), pp. 615–640; Schmidhauser, "*Stare Decisis,* Dissent, and the Backgrounds of the Justices of the Supreme Court of the United States," *University of Toronto Law Journal,* 14 (1962), pp. 194–212. Glendon Schubert has traced the development of judicial behavior research in two articles: "Behavioral Research in Public Law," *A.P.S.R.,* 57 (1963), pp. 433–445 and "From Public Law to Judicial Behavior," *Judicial Decision-Making;* Schubert (ed.) (New York: The Free Press of Glencoe, 1963), pp. 1–10. The latter work also contains an extensive bibliography of judicial behavior research on pp. 257–265. Also see Martin Shapiro, *Law and Politics in the Supreme Court* (New York: The Free Press of Glencoe, 1964), chap. 1.

State courts of last resort have also provided a testing ground primarily for problems (2) and (3).[2] However, the United States courts of appeals, second only to the Supreme Court in judicial importance, have been largely neglected.[3] This paper considers the above research problems with reference to the voting behavior on all eleven courts of appeals from July 1, 1961 through June 30, 1964.[4]

I. RESEARCH DESIGN

The voting behavior covered by this paper includes non-unanimous decisions and unanimous appeals court reversals of district court

[2]Schubert, *Quantitative Analysis,* pp. 129–142; S. Sidney Ulmer, "The Political Party Variable in the Michigan Supreme Court," *Journal of Public Law,* 11 (1962), pp. 352–362; Stuart S. Nagel, "Judicial Characteristics and Judicial Decision-Making" (unpublished Ph.D. dissertation, Northwestern University, 1961) and the articles derived from that study, especially "Political Party Affiliation and Judges' Decisions," *A.P.S.R.,* 55 (1961), pp. 843–850 and "Ethnic Affiliations and Judicial Propensities," *Journal of Politics,* 24 (1962), pp. 94–110; James F. Herndon, "Relationships between Partisanship and the Decisions of State Supreme Courts" (unpublished Ph.D. dissertation, University of Michigan, 1963).

[3]Only a handful of studies of the courts of appeals have been conducted by political scientists. Among them are: Robert H. Salisbury, *The United States Court of Appeals for the Seventh Circuit, 1940–1950: A Study of Judicial Relationships* (unpublished Ph.D. dissertation, University of Illinois, 1955); Rondal Downing, *The U. S. Courts of Appeals and Employer Unfair Labor Practice Cases, 1936–1958* (mimeo, 1959); Alvin Dozeman, *A Study of Selected Aspects of Behavior of the Judges of the United States Courts of Appeals for the Tenth Circuit* (unpublished Master's thesis, Michigan State University, 1960); Jack W. Peltason, *Fifty-Eight Lonely Men: Southern Federal Judges and School Desegregation* (New York: Harcourt, Brace, and World, 1961); Kenneth N. Vines, "The Role of the Circuit Courts of Appeal in the Federal Judicial Process: A Case Study," *Midwest Journal of Political Science,* 7 (1963), pp. 305–320; Louis S. Loeb, *Judicial Blocs and Judicial Values in Four Selected United States Courts of Appeals, 1957–1960 Terms* (unpublished Ph.D. dissertation, American University, 1964); Loeb, "Judicial Blocs and Judicial Values in Civil Liberties Cases Decided by the Supreme Court and the United States Court of Appeals for the District of Columbia," *American University Law Review,* 14 (1965), 146–177; Marvin Schick, *The United States Court of Appeals for the Second Circuit: A Study of Judicial Behavior* (unpublished Ph.D. dissertation, New York University, 1965).

[4]The time period chosen conforms to the three fiscal years 1962, 1963, and 1964. The Administrative Office of the U.S. Courts bases its statistics on the cases decided or terminated during the fiscal year.

TABLE 1   Voting Positions Assigned High Scores

Issue or Category	Voting Position
Criminal Law	For the claims of criminal defendants or prisoners
Civil Liberties	For malapportionment plaintiffs in reapportionment cases
	For Negro claims in cases involving school desegregation and voting
	For civil libertarian claims of aliens, conscientious objectors, and others
Government Regulation	For the governmental agency in regulation of business cases
Labor Cases	For the labor union and employees in labor-management and NLRB decisions
Private Economic	For the claims of the insured as opposed to the insurance company
	For the claims of the small business or subcontractor when opposed by large business or contractor
	Opposed to alleged antitrust law violators
	For the tenant in landlord-tenant cases
	For the debtor or bankrupt
	For the buyer of goods as opposed to seller
	For the stockholder in stockholder suits
Fiscal Cases	For the government in tax, eminent domain, and other fiscal cases
Combined Injury	For the claims of injured employees
	For the injured or the fatally injured's estate
	For the injured in federal tort cases
Liberalism	All of the above voting positions for only the non-unanimously decided cases
Activism	For federal court jurisdiction
Dissents	Dissenting in non-unanimously decided cases

decisions.[5] Quantification of non-unanimous decisions has been amply justified by students of the judiciary;[6] however, some explanation should be made of the use of district court reversals.[7]

Only those unanimously decided reversals of district court decisions in which the district court judge's interpretation or application of the facts, precedents, principles, or statutes differed from that of an unanimous appellate court were considered. Such cases

indicate that there are alternative paths to decision. The assumptions underlying the study of judicial voting behavior are, of course, that certain types of cases present the judges with reasonable judicial alternatives which can produce contrary results, and that a study of the dispositions of a relatively large number of such cases can reveal certain regularities in judicial voting behavior.[8]

The cases selected for study were assigned to one or more categories depending on the issues involved. Categories with small numbers of cases were either combined with others or discarded. In all, 2,055 cases which yielded 2,260 issues were utilized.[9]

[5]The cases utilized are listed in Appendix A, pp. 274–339, of my "Politics, Judges, and the Administration of Justice: The Backgrounds, Recruitment, and Decisional Tendencies of the Judges on the United States Courts of Appeals, 1961–4" (unpublished Ph.D. dissertation, Harvard University, 1965) microfilm no. 65-9924, University Microfilms, Michigan). A detailed exposition of the methods and statistics used, their justification, and their limitations is presented there.

[6]See, for example, Pritchett, *Roosevelt Court, op. cit.*, p. xii; Pritchett, *Civil Liberties, op. cit.*, pp. 186–192; Schubert, *Quantitative Analysis, op. cit.*, chap. 1.

[7]Note that Vines, *op. cit.*, utilizes district court reversals.

[8]These assumptions are treated as hypotheses and are tested in Goldman, *op. cit.*, pp. 162–163, 175 n. 16, 192–196. The results lend support to the hypotheses.

[9]There were some non-unanimous decisions and unanimous reversals rendered during the time period studied which did not fit the categories and were not used. These cases, for the most part involved patent and trademark issues and various commercial law cases (for example, cases involving disputing insurance companies).

For purposes of uncovering voting tendencies, a scoring system was devised which gave "high" numerical values to designated voting positions on the various issues. The issues and the voting behavior given high scores are presented in Table 1. With the exception of the "dissents" category and possibly "activism," the voting behavior outlined in Table 1 can be considered to be related to a politically "liberal" bent.[10]

Unlike the United States Supreme Court or the highest state appellate courts, all judges on each of the eleven federal courts of appeals do not hear the same cases except on the few occasions when a court will sit *en banc*. Most cases are heard by three-judge panels whose membership usually varies from case to case. The quantification-scoring system thus devised was results-oriented (i.e., oriented toward the disposition of the cases) and did not attempt to discern the intensity of the claims presented in the litigation. By examining the voting behavior of judges on a number of decisions involving choices which present the same general issues, it was thought to be possible to legitimately analyze statistically the judges' scores on the various issues even though the individual scores were based on different cases.[11] Although the different cases present different factual situations, the underlying stimuli of the policy alternatives, in terms of competing interests, are similar. By utilizing relatively large numbers of cases for the scores, the differences in the intensity of the claims should balance out.[12]

The quantification system assigned a high score, the numerical value of 2.0, to the voting positions indicated in Table 1; the value of 1.0 to a vote which in part adhered to those positions; and 0.0 to a vote which was contrary to them. The individual judge's score on each issue or category was determined by averaging the numerical values given to all of his votes for that issue. For example, if a judge voted on ten cases and his vote on seven of these favored the claims of the criminal defendant, while on the remaining three cases he opposed the criminal defendant's claims, the judge's score would be 1.4 on a continuum ranging from 0.0 to 2.0, thus indicating a relative bent towards favoring the claims of criminal defendants.[13]

II. RATES OF DISSENSION AND REVERSALS

The cases utilized for the study were non-unanimous decisions and unanimous district court reversals. Table 2 presents the rates of dissension and unanimous district court reversals on the eleven courts of appeals for the period covered. It is clear, from Table 2, that outright decisional conflict on the appeals courts is the exception not the rule. It is also apparent that the rates of dissension vary considerably by circuit, with the District of Columbia, Second, and Fifth circuits having the largest percentages and numbers of split decisions.

The rate of district court reversals by unanimous appeals courts involving the cases we utilized, also shown in Table 2, gives some indication of intracircuit conflict. The rates of unanimous reversals with the exception of the District of Columbia Circuit (whose rate of dissension is the highest) are larger than

---

[10]See Goldman, *op. cit.*, pp. 36–43 for a discussion of this point.

[11]Note that Vines, *op. cit.*, and in "Federal District Judges and Race Relations Cases in the South," *Journal of Politics*, 26 (1964), pp. 337–357 utilizes the disposition of racial relations cases by various judges on different courts deciding different cases which nevertheless contain the same general issue (i.e., Negro civil liberties).

[12]It might be argued that most or all of the Fifth Circuit cases we examined involving, for example, criminal, civil liberties, or labor issues, are inherently different from such cases raised in the Second or Ninth circuits. While this *may* be true for Negro civil liberties cases, the writer is unaware of any compelling evidence to lead one to suppose that it holds true for the other issues. In any event, the hypothesis that the underlying issues of the various cases subsumed within the categories differ on a geographical basis can only be tested by a content anal-

ysis of the cases themselves. It is relevant to note that students of the Supreme Court apparently reject this hypothesis and do not classify cases by their geographical origins.

[13]Alternatively, simple percentages could have been used. In the example above, the judge would be considered to have favored the claims of criminal defendants in 70% of the selected cases he handled. The method used in this study, however, seemed less cumbersome to work with. In addition, the continuum was considered to be an ordinal scale whereas the percentage implies an interval scale.

TABLE 2   **Rates of Dissension and Unanimous District Court Reversals on the Eleven Courts of Appeals**

Circuit	Number of Split Decisions	Split Decisions as Percent of Total No. of Cases Decided*	Number of Unanimous District Court Reversals	Unanimous Reversals as Percent of Total No. of Cases**
D.C.	168	15.5%	100	13.1%
Second	140	11.5	115	13.4
Fifth	196	11.4	292	23.1
Third	67	9.4	83	17.0
Seventh	63	8.5	88	16.5
Fourth	41	5.9	123	24.8
Ninth	50	4.3	187	22.7
Tenth	23	3.6	70	15.8
Eighth	18	3.3	65	18.1
First	10	3.3	31	16.5
Sixth	20	2.8	105	20.7

*The total numbers of cases are listed in Table B-1 (total cases disposed of after hearing or submission), *Annual Report of the Director of the Administrative Office of the United States Courts* (Washington, D. C.: U. S. Government Printing Office), for fiscal years 1962, 1963, and 1964.

**Ibid., for 1963 and 1964.

the rates of dissension. Differences among the circuits are apparent. The two southern circuits, the Fourth and Fifth, have the highest percentages of unanimous district court reversals. The Ninth and Sixth circuits follow with over 20 per cent of their cases consisting of unanimously decided district court reversals.

When the rates of dissension and unanimous reversals are combined, it is apparent that only a minority of each circuit's total number of cases decided are involved. Judicial consensus is apparently more typical than judicial conflict for the lower federal courts.[14] However, there are differences among the circuits. At one end, with the highest combined rates, are the Fifth, Fourth, Ninth, and District of Columbia circuits. At the other end, with the lowest combined rates, are the First and Tenth circuits. What accounts for these differences cannot be learned from these data. However, it is not unreasonable to assume that judicial strategy, bargaining, persuasion, and the like are at work in the process of fashioning a decision and that these

are relevant variables.[15] Personality characteristics, judges' attitudes, as well as other variables (such as opinion-writing assignments) may be relevant.[16]

The diversity in the rates of dissension and unanimous district court reversals is considered in another context in Table 3, which shows the relative emphasis on the various issues by circuit. Table 3 presents the rank of each appeals court on each issue for the combined number of non-unanimous and unanimous reversals cases. The Fifth Circuit, for example, had the largest total number of cases utilized for our scores, hence its rank for the total number of cases was one. The District of Columbia Circuit had the second largest total number of cases utilized, hence its rank for the total number of cases was two. The differences between the rank for the total number of cases and each of the preceding

[14]Consensus on the United States Supreme Court (in terms of percentage of unanimous decisions) is markedly less. See Table 1 in Schubert, *The Judicial Mind, op. cit.,* p. 45.

[15]See Walter F. Murphy, *Elements of Judicial Strategy* (Chicago: University of Chicago Press, 1964), for examples concerning the United States Supreme Court.

[16]See, for example, Harold D. Lasswell, *Power and Personality* (New York: W. W. Norton & Co., 1948), pp. 61–88; Stuart S. Nagel, "Off-the-Bench Judicial Attitudes," ch. 2 in Schubert (ed.), *Judicial Decision-Making, op. cit.;* Robert J. Sickels, "The Illusion of Judicial Consensus: Zoning Decisions in the Maryland Court of Appeals," *A.P.S.R.,* 59 (1965), pp. 100–104.

TABLE 3   Rank Order of Numbers of Cases Used for Each Appeals Court to Determine Scores for Each Issue

Issue						Rank						
Circuit:	1st	2nd	3rd	4th	5th	6th	7th	8th	9th	10th	D.C.
Criminal Cases	11	3	7	5	2	9	6	10	4	8	1
Civil Liberties	11	3	8	2	1	7	6	10	5	9	4
Government Regulation	9	3	4	7	1	11	5.5	10	8	5.5	2
Labor Cases	11	1	7.5	7.5	3	6	4	9.5	5	9.5	2
Private Economic	11	3	4	10	1	8	6	9	2	5	7
Fiscal Cases	11	5	8	9.5	1	3.5	9.5	6	2	7	3.5
Combined Injury	11	2.5	4	5	1	7	6	8.5	8.5	10	2.5
Activism	11	2	3	4.5	1	8.5	6.5	6.5	4.5	10	8.5
Total Number of Cases	11	3	7	5	1	8	6	10	4	9	2

categories suggest the relative amount of dissent and intracircuit conflict stimulated by that issue on the appeals courts.

Table 3 tells us, for example, that the Fourth Circuit ranks second on civil liberties cases although it ranks fifth on the total number of cases. This would suggest that the Fourth Circuit, whose jurisdiction encompasses three southern and two border states, heard more civil liberties cases (notably, Negro civil rights cases) than any other circuit with the exception of the Fifth (whose jurisdiction covers only southern states). The table also suggests that during the period studied there was disagreement on civil liberties matters between the appeals court for the Fourth Circuit and its district courts as well as disagreement within the appeals court itself.[17] Table 3 further indicates that the Ninth Circuit ranks fourth for the total number of cases utilized yet ranks second on private economic and fiscal cases. The Third Circuit ranks seventh on the total number of cases yet has a rank of four for the government regulation, private economic, and combined injury categories. There are a number of other suggestive findings that need not be spelled out here. What is strongly suggested is that the *sources* of judicial conflict tend to differ among the circuits—perhaps not only a function of the personality-and-attitudes-of-the-judge variables but also of "constituency"

[17]Cf. Vines, "The Role of Circuit Courts of Appeal in the Federal Judicial Process," *op. cit.*

variables manifested by differing numbers of types of cases brought to the various appeals courts.[18]

The differences among the appeals courts in terms of their rates of dissent and intracircuit conflict as well as the sources of conflict presented some difficulties in gathering case data for all the appeals judges. It was not possible to determine scores on all issues for all of the judges.[19] These are obvious difficulties in combining the eleven appeals courts for purposes of analysis. However, these difficulties, indicative of the institutional diversity of the courts, impose limitations but do not preclude analysis. Non-unanimous decisions and unanimous reversals were classified by the issues, and judges were given

[18]It should be stressed that Table 3 is only a very rough approximation (based on the absolute number of cases) of the sources of judicial conflict. A more precise analysis would require the determination, for each issue, by circuit, of the percentage of the total number of cases which comprised non-unanimous and unanimous reversals cases. See Goldman, Table 25, *op. cit.*, p. 170.

[19]A minimum of five cases and typically ten cases were used to determine each judge's score for each category. It is relevant to note that the permanent positions on the appeals courts varies from three on the First Circuit to nine on the Second, Fifth, Ninth, and District of Columbia circuits. These latter circuits also have the most judicial business. The results thus contain some distortion because of the large number of judges from the four largest circuits and the large number of cases which facilitated the collection of case data necessary to determine the scores. The maximum distortion was on the government regulation issue where 25 of the 38 judges with scores were from the four largest circuits.

TABLE 4 Spearman Rank Order Correlations for Issue-Categories

	Criminal	Civil Lib.	Gov't Reg.	Labor	Private Ec.	Fiscal	Injury	Activism	Dissents	Liberalism
Criminal		.61	.38	.44	.34	.16[a]	.38	.60	.06[a]	.54
Civil Lib.			.60	.50	.39	.17[a]	.55	.49	−.37	.72
Gov't Reg.				.40[b]	.12[a]	−.08[a]	.42	.16[a]	−.29[a]	.47
Labor					.49	.12[a]	.47	.39	−.38	.46
Private Economic						.23[a]	.43	.49	−.12[a]	.61
Fiscal Cases							−.02[a]	.26[a]	−.04[a]	.18[a]
Combined Injury								.38	−.02[a]	.59
Activism									−.08[a]	.69
Dissents										−.10[a]

[a]Not statistically significant.

[b]Statistically significant between the .02 and .05 levels.

Note that unless otherwise indicated all the correlation coefficients are positive and are significant at least at the .01 level.

scores based upon their votes on the disposition of the claims of the litigants.

III. INTERRELATIONS OF ISSUES

The first research problem was the extent to which voting on one issue was related to voting on all other issues or categories. The concern was whether, for example, judges who had relatively high scores for civil liberties cases would have relatively high scores on the private economic cases, combined injury, or labor cases. Spearman rank order correlations were calculated and the correlation matrix is presented in Table 4.[20] All the correlations above +.3 or below −.3 were found to be statistically significant at least at the .05 level.

Table 4 suggests that there is a positive relationship among the following seven categories: criminal cases, civil liberties, labor cases, private economic cases, combined injury cases, activism, and "liberalism." The degree of association varies from .720 for the civil liberties and "liberalism" categories to .335 between criminal cases and private economic cases. The judges on the appeals courts, then, show a tendency either to sup-

port or oppose the claims of the following: the criminally prosecuted, the individual presenting a civil liberties claim against the actions of a governmental agency, the labor union or employee in controversies with management, the underdog claim in private economic cases, and the physically injured's claims. The judges who tend to support these claims will also tend to favor the application of federal law and standards as well as federal court jurisdiction when they are challenged. The data also tell us that judges with high scores on the "liberalism" category also tend to have high scores on the above categories. It seems reasonable to infer that the cases subsumed within these categories can be thought of in quasi-ideological politically "liberal" or "conservative" terms. However, three categories (government regulation, fiscal, and "dissents") require special mention because they were not found to be associated with all of the above seven categories.

The government regulation category is positively correlated with the "liberalism" category as well as the criminal cases, civil liberties, labor cases, and the combined injury categories. However, there appear to be no significant correlations with the private economic and activism categories (leaving aside, for the moment, the fiscal cases and "dissents" categories). This suggests that the policy alternatives contained within the government regulation category may be too

[20]The Spearman rank correlation coefficient is described in detail by Sidney Siegel, *Nonparametric Statistics for the Behavioral Sciences* (New York: McGraw-Hill Book Co., 1956), pp. 202–213. The formula used to calculate the coefficients presented in Table 4 was one corrected for ties (found in Siegel, p. 207).

TABLE 5   Party Affiliation and Median Scores by Issue-Category

Issue	Democrats		Republicans		Difference in Medians	Significance Level
	Median	(N)	Median	(N)		
Criminal cases	1.67	(43)	1.71	(37)	0.04	n.s.*
Civil liberties	1.60	(23)	1.50	(24)	0.10	n.s.
Government regulation	1.265	(22)	1.125	(16)	0.14	n.s.
Labor cases	1.50	(29)	0.945	(24)	0.555	.0007
Private economic	1.20	(37)	0.93	(37)	0.27	.0009
Fiscal cases	0.91	(40)	0.80	(35)	0.11	.08
Combined injury	1.155	(34)	1.03	(26)	0.125	.05
Activism	1.33	(33)	1.23	(32)	0.10	.05
Liberalism	1.20	(41)	0.83	(37)	0.37	.003
Dissents	0.68	(41)	0.67	(37)	0.01	n.s.

*Not statistically significant at the .05 level.

complex and thus not amenable to direct quasi-ideological linkage with the other categories.[21]

The fiscal cases category is not associated with any of the other categories. The voting behavior of the judges in cases involving tax and other fiscal matters appears unrelated to the voting positions on any of the categories.[22]

Propensity to dissent was related only to civil liberties and labor cases, for which negative correlations were found. Those who had high scores on civil liberties and labor cases tended to have low scores on the dissents category. Civil libertarians and those sympathetic to employees and labor unions, it would seem, tended to be in the majority when cases were decided non-unanimously.

In brief, while no perfect intercorrelations were uncovered, seven of the categories were shown to be positively related to each other. This provides some evidence of the existence of organized attitudes and the presence of

what can be considered quasi-ideological voting behavior.[23]

IV. PARTY AFFILIATION AND JUDICIAL VOTING

The next research problem concerned the relationship of party affiliation to voting behavior. Examination of the scores of all the Democrats and Republicans on all the circuits yielded several statistically significant differences.[24] Table 5 reports the results and shows that the Democrats, as a group, had higher scores than the Republicans on the labor, private economic, injury, activism, and "liberalism" categories. There is a possibility that the Democrats, as a group, were more

[21]Cf. Harold J. Spaeth, "Warren Court Attitudes Toward Business: The 'B' Scale," in *Judicial Decision-Making, op. cit.*, pp. 79–108; Tanenhaus, "Supreme Court Attitudes Toward Federal Administrative Agencies," *op. cit.*

[22]This finding bears some similarity to Schubert's finding in his article on "The 1960 Term of the Supreme Court," *op. cit.*, pp. 101–102, concerning the F scale (fiscal cases). Schubert noted that "the rankings of the justices on F is different from their rankings on either C [the civil liberties scale] or E [economic liberalism]." Also see Schubert, *The Judicial Mind, op. cit.*, pp. 150–155, and Table 27, p. 173.

[23]Note that another analysis reported in Goldman, *op. cit.*, pp. 179–197, uncovered the existence of voting blocs on all but the First, Sixth, and Eighth circuits. This finding tends to support the interpretation of the rank order correlation analysis in the above text.

[24]The Mann-Whitney U Test was used to determine whether there was a statistically significant difference in medians and distribution of the scores for each of the categories by the Democrats and Republicans. The U test is described in Siegel, *op. cit.*, pp. 116–127. Nonparametric inference statistics were used in this study because the cases utilized are only a sample of the decisions the appeals judges have made in the past and will make in the future. On the appropriateness of inferential statistics see Tanenhaus, "Supreme Court Attitudes toward Federal Administrative Agencies," *op. cit.*, and also Tanenhaus and Albert Somit, *American Political Science: Profile of a Discipline* (New York: Atherton Press, 1964), pp. 144–149.

likely than the Republicans to favor the position of the federal government in fiscal matters (tax and eminent domain)—but this finding did not meet our criterion for statistical significance.

It is interesting to note that, in general, the Democrats appear relatively more "liberal" than Republicans in cases which involve what might be called "economic liberalism."[25] However, Democrats and Republicans appear equally "liberal" on the criminal and civil liberties categories. Perhaps the economic basis of American party politics is most relevant for our understanding of certain kinds of judicial behavior. As there is no strong relationship between civil-libertarian attitudes and party affiliation in the United States,[26] it may be that there are no major differences between Democratic and Republican judges on these matters. However, it must be observed that Democrats had higher scores on the "liberalism" category which included non-unanimously decided criminal and civil liberties cases. This leads us to suspect that on the really "important" cases that force the judges to stand up and be counted, the Democrats may have tended to vote more "liberally" than the Republicans.[27] However, it is also possible to argue that the higher scores of the Democrats on the "liberalism" category were the result of their voting on the other categories. On balance, the findings reported here emphasize that party affiliation as a background variable seems to best "ex-

plain" differences in voting behavior on issues primarily involving economic liberalism.[28]

V. DEMOGRAPHIC CHARACTERISTICS AND JUDICIAL VOTING

The possible nexus of demographic variables to judicial voting behavior was investigated. Religious affiliation was found to be unrelated to the voting behavior of the appeals judges on all but one of the categories.[29] Table 6 presents the results,[30] which suggest that Catholics were more prone than Protestants and perhaps Jews to oppose the position of the government in fiscal cases.[31]

When party affiliation was controlled, the median score of the Catholic judges was still significantly lower than the median score of the Protestant judges. If this relationship is not spurious and can be duplicated for other groups of judges, it will be of interest to discover what, if anything, in Catholic-American culture (or perhaps upper-class Catholic-American culture) may contribute to this behavior. Of course, one could assert that such behavior demonstrates the greater "liberality" of Catholic judges and then argue that the fiscal cases really pit Big Government against the underdog citizen or business. But if Catholic judges are more "liberal" than

[25]See Schubert's definition of "economic liberalism" in "The 1960 Term," *op. cit.*, p. 100, and *The Judicial Mind*, *op. cit.*, pp. 160–170.
[26]See Robert E. Lane, "Political Personality and Electoral Choice," *A.P.S.R.*, 49 (1955), pp. 173–190; Samuel A. Stouffer, *Communism, Conformity, and Civil Liberties* (New York: Doubleday & Co., 1955); Herbert McClosky *et al.*, "Issue Conflict and Consensus among Party Leaders and Followers," *A.P.S.R.*, 54 (1960), pp. 406–427; Thomas A. Flinn and Frederick M. Wirt, "Local Party Leaders: Groups of Like Minded Men," *Midwest Journal of Political Science*, 9 (1965), pp. 77–98. Flinn and Wirt as well as McClosky report that differences between Democratic and Republican party leaders on questions of civil liberties are not as prominent as differences on economic issues.
[27]Had there been more non-unanimously decided cases involving criminal law and civil liberties, we would have been able to test this hypothesis.

[28]See Goldman, *op. cit.*, chap. 7, for the findings concerning additional political variables tested for the study. On the relationship of party affiliation to the judicial behavior on other courts see Schubert, *Quantitative Analysis, op. cit.*, pp. 129–142; Ulmer, "The Political Party Variable in the Michigan Supreme Court," *op. cit.*; Herndon, *op. cit.*; Nagel, "Political Party Affiliation and Judges' Decisions," *op. cit.*; Don R. Bowen, "The Explanation of Judicial Voting Behavior from Sociological Characteristics of Judges" (unpublished Ph.D. dissertation, Yale University, 1965).
[29]These findings contradict those of Stuart Nagel's (for state supreme court justices) reported in "Ethnic Affiliations and Judicial Propensities," *op. cit.* Also see Bowen, *op. cit.*
[30]The test used to determine the statistical significance of the differences among the medians for each category was the Kruskal-Wallis one way analysis of variance by ranks. See Siegel, *op. cit.*, pp. 184–193 for a description of the test.
[31]The number of Jewish judges on the appeals courts is too small for us to draw reliable inferences from the data. The discussion of religious affiliation is therefore confined to a consideration of Catholic and Protestant judges.

TABLE 6 Median Scores by Issue-Category for Appeals Judges by Religious Affiliation

Issue	Catholic		Protestant		Jewish		Signifi-cance Level
	Median	(N)	*Median*	(N)	*Median*	(N)	
Criminal cases	1.655	(16)	1.69	(56)	1.55	(6)	n.s.
Civil liberties	1.60	(9)	1.48	(33)	1.625	(4)	n.s.
Government regulation	1.40	(9)	1.14	(26)	1.33	(3)	n.s.
Labor cases	1.50	(12)	1.115	(36)	1.365	(4)	n.s.
Private economic	1.18	(15)	1.00	(52)	1.10	(6)	n.s.
Fiscal cases	0.585	(16)	0.96	(53)	0.705	(4)	.04
Combined injury	1.30	(13)	1.11	(40)	1.055	(6)	n.s.
Activism	1.33	(15)	1.295	(42)	1.19	(6)	n.s.
Liberalism	1.00	(15)	1.00	(55)	0.86	(6)	n.s.
Dissents	0.61	(15)	0.68	(55)	0.485	(6)	n.s.

Protestant judges, why should their greater liberality be manifest (in our study) only in the fiscal cases?

No differences in voting behavior were found between lower-status Protestants (such as Baptists, Lutherans, and Methodists) and higher-status Protestants (including Congregationalists, Episcopalians, Presbyterians, and Unitarians).[32]

Other demographic variables were tested and did not reveal any relationship to voting behavior either initially or when party was controlled. These background variables included (1) place of birth (no differences in voting behavior among those born in communities with populations under 10,000, over 10,000 but under 50,000, and over 50,000); (2) occupations of the fathers of the judges (no differences in behavior between judges whose fathers had low-status occupations and those whose fathers had high-status occupations); (3) undergraduate and law schools attended (no differences among judges who were educated in Ivy League institutions, other private institutions, or public supported schools); (4) public legal (non-judicial) and/or elective office held any time prior to appointment; (5) federal district court experience; (6) bar association leadership; (7) occupation at time of appointment to the appeals court; (8) judges with more than five years of judicial experience; (9) American Bar Association ratings (judges who received the highest A.B.A. rating, "Exceptionally Well Qualified," did not display different voting behavior from those who received the lowest acceptable "Qualified" rating). Only one category, that of labor cases, was related to the age of the judge. Younger judges (under 60) were found to have had higher scores on the labor category than older judges (over 70) when party was held constant.

It would be easy to dismiss demographic variables other than party affiliation as irrelevant for voting behavior, but this would no doubt be incorrect. Such variables as religious affiliation and socio-economic background are known to be associated in the United States with party identification,[33] and surely judges are not immune to social and economic forces during the development of their political allegiances. Furthermore, the possibility yet remains that demographic factors have played a part in shaping the hierarchy of values, the outlook, and philosophy of individual judges. Our investigation has only suggested that the demographic variables tested are not *directly* associated with judicial voting behavior.

[32]Cf. Nagel, *op. cit., supra*, n. 29.

[33]See Angus Campbell *et al., The American Voter* (New York: John Wiley & Sons, 1960).

VI. SUMMARY AND CONCLUSION

The eleven United States courts of appeals, as we have seen, differ in their rates of dissension and intracircuit conflict as well as the sources of judicial conflict. Presumably personality and "constituency" variables largely account for this. The institutional diversity of the appeals courts thus imposed limitations on data collection and analysis. Nevertheless, the study of judicial voting on the dispositions of selected cases and issues reported here revealed the following principal findings:

1. There appears to be some evidence of organized voting patterns by the judges on the United States courts of appeals. These voting patterns appear, to some extent, to involve "liberal" and "conservative" voting on issues involving political liberalism and economic liberalism.

2. Party affiliation was found to be associated with voting behavior, notably when the issues involved economic liberalism.

3. Other demographic variables such as religion, socio-economic origins, education, and age were found to be almost entirely unrelated directly to voting behavior.

These findings suggest that, for the cases examined, many of the policy choices of judges affiliated with the Democratic party tended to differ from those made by Republican affiliated judges. The data indicate that for some of the types of cases examined, it tends to make a difference (in terms of the disposition of cases) which political party does the appointing to the United States courts of appeals. Furthermore, it seems clear that just as for legislators, party is the principal characteristic associated with voting behavior. However, the correlation matrix presented in Table 4 suggests that more pervasive attitudinal structures may exist. On balance, the findings underscore the absence of a sharp ideological party cleavage in the United States but also give support to the contention that the center of gravity of the Democratic party is more "liberal" than that of the Republican party.

The findings lend support for the continuation of the political selection process involved in appeals court appointments. It can be argued that some degree of policy-making is inherent in the judges' role and that the ideal of party responsibility requires that the large bulk of presidential appointments should be in basic harmony with the values, if not the concrete goals, of the appointing administration. Our findings indicate that although party is the characteristic most strongly associated with voting, this association (when all of the business of the courts is considered) is too limited and imprecise for party affiliation to be consistently identified with specific judicial results by the appeals courts. The differences between Democrats and Republicans are matters of degree—enough to make party affiliation a significant variable, but not enough to create a judicial system so distorted as to resolve dogmatically and predictably even the slightest of legal doubts in favor of any particular class of litigants.

30 JUDICIAL BLOCS ON THE SUPREME COURT AND THE UNITED STATES COURT OF APPEALS FOR THE DISTRICT OF COLUMBIA

Louis S. Loeb

I

Characteristic of recent research in public law and judicial behavior has been the singular interest in the United States Supreme Court. By contrast the eleven United States Courts of Appeals have been almost totally neglected.[1] Perhaps it is because circuit judges

Reprinted by permission of the publisher from Louis S. Loeb, "Judicial Blocs and Judicial Values in Civil Liberties Cases Decided by the Supreme Court and the United States Court of Appeals for the District of Columbia Circuit," *American University Law Review*, 14 (1965), pp. 146–155.

[1]The *Index to Legal Periodicals* is but one indicator of such relative neglect. The triennial issue covering the years 1958–1961 has under the subject entry of "Courts, United States," 179 entries. At least 108 of these have "Supreme Court" or some variant in the title. Only one article was listed dealing with the Courts of Appeals. 12 Index to Legal Periodicals (August 1958—August 1961), pp. 171–73.

are thought of as legal technicians while it has become commonplace to view Supreme Court justices as policy-makers.[2] Court decisions, whether by a court of appeals or the Supreme Court, are expressions of public policy choices. Examining a series of decisions in a particular area made by a court of appeals and the Supreme Court may reveal that the values underlying policy choices are just as explicit at the intermediate level as at the apex of the federal judicial hierarchy. Such an examination may also disclose that there is a degree of similarity in the values articulated at each of these levels of decision, and that opposing blocs of judges exist at each of the levels and are related by their agreement on public policy values. . . .

The importance of the Courts of Appeals in the federal judicial system lies in their function of reducing the appellate burden of the Supreme Court; they serve as a "buffer between the federal District Courts and the Supreme Court."[3] The great majority of litigants who have pursued their cases to a decision in a United States court of appeals have reached their court of last resort.[4]

The Courts of Appeals stand astride two important streams of litigation: appeals from the district courts, except where direct review by the Supreme Court is permitted,[5] and appeals from administrative agency litigation.

[2]"The lack of concern with the work of the other [federal] judges apparently grows out of the assumption that the Supreme Court justices make policy and other federal judges perform the routine task of applying it." Peltason, Federal Courts in the Political Process 13 (1955).
[3]Forrester, Cases and Materials on Federal Jurisdiction 831 (1950).
[4]"In any judicial system where 95% of all litigation is settled finally in one [sic] appellate court and only 5% goes to the Supreme Court, it is, I believe, substantially accurate to say that the appellate courts, the Circuit Courts of Appeals, are the courts of last resort." Evans, address before the Chicago Bar Association, in 3 John Marshall L.Q. 203 (1937).
[5]For provisions permitting direct review see 18 U.S.C. § 3731 (1958) and 28 U.S.C. §§ 1252, 1253, 2281, 2282, 2325 (1958). The existence of direct review leaves a significant gap in the intermediate appellate concept. Cf. Clark, J.: "Direct appeals not only place a great burden on the [Supreme] Court but also deprive us of the valuable assistance of the Courts of Appeals." *United States v. Singer Mfg. Co.*, 374 U.S. 174, 175 (1963).

The eleven United States Courts of Appeals contribute approximately half of all the cases in which requests for review are made to the Supreme Court.[6] Of the more than 2,000 requests for review made each year, the Supreme Court decides considerably less than twenty per cent of its cases on the merits.[7] A test of the degree to which the Courts of Appeals serve as a buffer for the Supreme Court is the extent to which the latter feels plenary consideration of an intermediate appellate decision is necessary. This can be determined by the percentage of the total number of Courts of Appeals' cases (where review by the Supreme Court is sought) decided on the merits. Over the 1954–1961 terms of the Supreme Court, the average was less than fourteen per cent, with a low of barely more than ten per cent being decided on the merits in the 1961 Term.[8] As might be expected, the percentage of petitions for writ of *certiorari* to the Courts of Appeals granted by the Supreme Court is similarly low.[9] These data emphasize the "finality" of decision in about nine out of ten Courts of Appeals' cases where the litigants seek a further review.

When *certiorari* is granted, however, and the intermediate appellate decision is reviewed on the merits, the Supreme Court's decision is an expression of agreement or disagreement with the particular court of appeals. In affirming or reversing the decision below, the Supreme Court is expressing its view on the correctness of the decision of the court of appeals. If decisions of courts are statements of policy, by analyzing those cases in which certiorari is granted some insight may be gained into the policy-making relationships in the federal appellate hierarchy.

II

Although its geographic area is small, the United States Court of Appeals for the Dis-

[6]Based on data derived from the review of the Supreme Court's term published annually in November by the *Harvard Law Review*, "The Supreme Court," [1954–1961] Term[s], 69–76 Harv. L. Rev. (1955–1962), Table II.
[7]Ibid.
[8]Ibid.
[9]Based on data derived from the *Annual Report* published by the Administrative Office of the United States Courts, 1955–1962.

trict of Columbia Circuit is one of the busiest ·in terms of its work load. This court and the courts of the Second, Fifth, and Ninth Circuits handle more than one-half of all the cases decided by the eleven Courts of Appeals.[10] The same four also account for more than one-half of all the petitions for writ of *certiorari* granted by the Supreme Court in Courts of Appeals' cases.[11]

With respect to its internal character as well as the character of its relationship with the Supreme Court, the United States Court of Appeals for the District of Columbia Circuit is markedly different from the three other busiest circuits. During a four-year period, it was reversed by the Supreme Court at a higher rate than the other three; it was a more divided court than the others; and it generated more decisions in which both it and the Supreme Court were divided than did the others.[12]

In this period, the four Courts of Appeals were reversed in just under seventy per cent of the cases reviewed by the Supreme Court.[13] The rate varied from a low of fifty-five per cent for the Second Circuit to a high of almost seventy-eight per cent for the District of Columbia Circuit.

In a normal Court of Appeals' case, the court will consist of a panel of three members; if one of the three dissents from the majority opinion, the result is a divided court. On the Supreme Court, a divided court may occur when from one to four justices dissent,

assuming the normal nine-judge complement. Thus four different possibilities exist when the Supreme Court reverses a Court of Appeals: a unanimous Supreme Court may reverse a unanimous Court of Appeals; a unanimous Supreme Court may reverse a divided Court of Appeals; a divided Supreme Court may reverse a unanimous Court of Appeals; or a divided Supreme Court may reverse a divided Court of Appeals.[14]

Only in the first case can it be said that it is court pitted against court in disagreement. The final alternative, however, presents a situation where groups on both courts are in support of each other; it also would seem to represent cases where there is the most disagreement on both courts as to the public policy choices involved. A Court of Appeals frequently involved in the fourth situation would indicate that such a court is itself greatly divided and precipitates a like division in the Supreme Court.

In the reversal cases during this period, the Court of Appeals for the District of Columbia Circuit was involved in the fourth situation in almost thirty-six per cent of its cases. By contrast, the Second and Fifth circuits were involved in such divided court situations in twenty-one per cent of their reversal cases, while the Ninth Circuit had only nine per cent in this category. When all of the situations in which one or both courts are divided is considered, ninety-two per cent of the District of Columbia Circuit cases fall into these categories. For the Second Circuit, the comparable figure is sixty-two per cent; for the Fifth Circuit, sixty-one per cent; and for the Ninth Circuit, sixty-seven per cent.[15]

Of the total number of cases reviewed by the Supreme Court during the period,[16] about twenty-two per cent involved divided courts at both levels, and nearly one-half of these came from the District of Columbia Circuit. Conversely, of the cases in which both courts

[10]*Ibid.* Each of these courts has nine judges, the only ones of the eleven to have that many.

[11]*Ibid.*

[12]Based on an analysis of cases over a four-year period in which decisions of these four courts of appeals were reviewed by the Supreme Court. The data were obtained by a search of Volumes 355–367 of U.S. Reports covering the 1957–1960 terms of the Supreme Court. The subsequent data in the section involving the four courts of appeals is derived from this analysis. The reasons for the differing character of the United States Court of Appeals for the District of Columbia Circuit are considered outside the scope of this article, but it would seem that its *situs* at the seat of government and the fact that appointees to it need not be residents of the circuit, as is the case with the other courts of appeals, are two predominant factors.

[13]Based on 216 cases, 150 of which were reversed. Over the same period of time, the eleven courts of appeals were reversed at a rate of 70.5%. *Supra* note 6.

[14]Four similar situations are present, of course, when the Supreme Court affirms a lower court's judgment.

[15]If both affirmances and reversals are considered, fairly comparable percentages result.

[16]*Supra* note 13.

were unanimous, only five per cent were cases from that circuit.

This tendency of the Court of Appeals for the District of Columbia Circuit to divide more than the other three is confirmed when only the result at the courts of appeals' level is considered. In this regard the District of Columbia Circuit Court was divided in its decisions sixty per cent of the time. Both the Second and Fifth circuits were divided in about thirty per cent of their decisions, while the Ninth Circuit court divided in only eleven per cent of its decisions. Still further evidence of the divisive nature of the court for the District of Columbia Circuit can be seen in the results of its *en banc* sittings. Normally, a Court of Appeals sits in panels of three judges,[17] but the Judicial Code also provides that "a hearing or rehearing before the court in [sic] banc . . . [may be] ordered by a ma-

unanimous; one of those in the Second Circuit was unanimous. In all of the *en banc* decisions in the District of Columbia Circuit there was a divided court.

The nature of the groups in disagreement on the United States Court of Appeals for the District of Columbia Circuit is revealed when that court is subjected to bloc analysis. By pairing the judges on a collegial court, their rates of agreement with each other can be ascertained. First, the number of times each pair of judges on a court participates with each other in a case in which the court divides is determined. Then, for the same pair of judges, the number of times they voted together is divided by the number of their common participations in cases. The resulting percentage is the rate of agreement between those two judges.[19] Where more than two judges are in agreement with one another

TABLE 1   Agreement in Divided Decisions of the U.S. Court of Appeals for the District of Columbia Circuit (In percentages)

	Edgerton	Bazelon	Fahy	Washington	Danaher	Bastian	Prettyman	Miller	Burger
Edgerton		92	92	60	7	0	0	0	0
Bazelon	92		90	64	0	0	0	0	11
Fahy	92	90		45	8	10	8	7	0
Washington	60	64	45		43	36	31	31	13
Danaher	7	0	8	43		100	100	100	89
Bastian	0	0	10	36	100		92	100	100
Prettyman	0	0	8	31	100	92		100	100
Miller	0	0	7	31	100	100	100		86
Burger	0	11	0	13	89	100	100	86	

Indices of Agreement

Burger — Miller — Prettyman — Bastian — Danaher   97
Edgerton — Bazelon — Fahy   91

jority of the circuit judges of the circuit. . . ."[18] During the period between 1957 and 1960, the District of Columbia Circuit Court sat *en banc* ten times, the Second Circuit Court, five; the Ninth Circuit Court, four; and the Fifth Circuit Court, once. Two of the en banc decisions in the Ninth Circuit were

fairly consistently, a bloc of judges is said to exist.

Table 1 shows quite clearly the existence of strongly cohesive blocs on the United States

[17]28 U.S.C. § 46(b) (1958).
[18]28 U.S.C. § 46(c) (1958).

[19]This type of analysis was first used by Professor C. Herman Pritchett in *The Roosevelt Court* (1948). See also his *Civil Liberties and the Vinson Court* (1954) and Schubert, *Quantitative Analysis of Judicial Behavior* (1959) in which the technique was called "bloc analysis," at 77.

Court of Appeals for the District of Columbia Circuit.[20]

Five judges form a highly cohesive bloc with an index of agreement[21] of ninety-seven; three other judges form an almost equally cohesive bloc with an index of ninety-one. The ninth judge, while agreeing with two of the latter bloc more than fifty per cent of the time, fails to agree with the third judge of this bloc in more than one-half of the cases. Bloc analysis also indicates the polarization of this court. A striking factor is the almost total lack of inter-bloc agreement; the judges in either of the strongly cohesive blocs rarely agree with those of the other bloc. Judge Washington is seemingly able to surmount this sharp division, although he is more closely affiliated with Judges Edgerton, Bazelon and Fahy.

For purposes of identification, the bloc consisting of Judges Edgerton, Bazelon, and Fahy was placed in the left hand corner of Table 1 and is designated as the left-bloc. This was done on the basis of the values supported by these judges in the . . . cases. . . . On the same basis, the block consisting of Judges Danaher, Bastian, Prettyman, Miller and Burger is designated as the right-bloc.[22]

Over the same period of time as the blocs on the Court of Appeals for the District of Columbia Circuit existed, similar left and right blocs existed on the Supreme Court. Table 2 reveals a left bloc composed of Justices Douglas, Black, Warren and Brennan. Justice Burton in one term, and Justice Stewart in three terms, joined Justices Clark, Frankfurter, Harlan and Whittaker to compose the right bloc.[23]

Having determined the existence of blocs on the District of Columbia Court and the Supreme Court it only remains to ascertain whether the left and right blocs on each court are related. That such relationships exist may be demonstrated by constructing a table showing the rates of agreement between pairs consisting of a Court of Appeals judge and a Supreme Court justice. As with tables dealing with but one court, three or more judges on one court who together with three or more judges on the other court have an index of agreement of over fifty per cent constitute an inter-court bloc. The method of counting participations and agreement is the same as when only the judges of one court are involved.

The results are shown in Table 3 and reveal left and right blocs on the United States Court of Appeals for the District of Columbia Circuit and the Supreme Court.[24] The left-bloc judges on the Court of Appeals and the left-bloc Justices on the Supreme Court are related by a rather high index of agreement of ninety-one. This indicates the consistent support given to the decisions of Judges Bazelon, Fahy and Edgerton by the four justices of the Supreme Court left bloc. Justice

[20]Based on 35 cases in which the United States Court of Appeals for the District of Columbia Circuit was divided which were reviewed by the Supreme Court during its 1957–1960 terms. The average number of participations for each pair of judges was ten. The arrangement of the judges is according to the method followed by Schubert, *op. cit. supra,* note 19 at 83–84. The sequence of judges in the vertical and horizontal arrays is determined by adding the top four figures in each vertical column and then dividing the sum by the sum of the four bottom figures in each column. The ratio for each column decreases from left to right. Judges are placed contiguously according to their rate of agreement with one another.

[21]Obtained by averaging the percentages of agreement among the judges in a bloc. Agreement over 50% constitutes a bloc.

[22]The identification is therefore not only a matter of convenience, but also involves a value judgment that the positions taken by these judges in the cases was on the "left" politically. Judges Prettyman (1962), Edgerton (1963), and Miller (1964) have since retired from active service. J. Skelly Wright replaced Prettyman and Carl McGowan replaced Edgerton. On February 27, 1965, President Johnson announced the nomination of Harold Leventhal to succeed Judge Miller and Judge Edward A. Tamm of the United States District Court for the District of Columbia to succeed Judge Bastian who had previously announced his intention to retire. Mr. Leventhal is a Washington attorney and has served as

general counsel to the Democratic National Committee for a number of years. 33 U.S.L. Week 2452 (Mar. 9, 1965).

[23]Based on 133 cases in which the Supreme Court divided. These were cases reviewed by the Court in the four terms, 1957–1960, coming from the District of Columbia, Second, Fifth and Ninth Circuits. The designations of blocs were made on the same basis as those for the District of Columbia Court. Justices Burton, Whittaker and Frankfurter have since retired, the first and last named having subsequently died.

[24]Based on twenty-one cases in which both courts were divided. Justice Burton was not included because his single term during the period did not produce a sufficient number of participants.

TABLE 2   Agreement in Divided Decisions of the Supreme Court in Cases Reviewed from Four Courts of Appeals, 1957–1960 Terms (In percentages)

	Douglas	Black	Warren	Brennan	Stewart	Clark	Burton	Frankfurter	Harlan	Whittaker
Douglas		83	79	68	40	27	31	25	28	29
Black	83		90	72	39	38	36	35	31	33
Warren	79	90		79	48	42	38	39	34	35
Brennan	68	72	79		59	49	49	54	51	45
Stewart	40	39	48	59		65	*	70	75	69
Clark	27	38	42	49	65		77	62	65	64
Burton	31	36	38	49	*	77		61	69	79
Frankfurter	25	35	39	54	70	62	61		83	71
Harlan	28	31	34	51	75	65	69	83		68
Whittaker	29	33	35	45	69	64	79	71	68	

Indices of Agreement

Douglas—Black—Warren—Brennan   79
Clark—Burton—Frankfurter—Harlan—Whittaker   70 (1957 Term only)
Stewart—Clark—Frankfurter—Harlan—Whittaker   69

*No possible agreement.

TABLE 3   Agreement among Judges of the U. S. Court of Appeals for the District of Columbia Circuit and Justices of the Supreme Court in Decisions Where Both Courts Were Divided, 1957–1960 Terms (In percentages)

	Douglas	Black	Warren	Brennan	Frankfurter	Stewart	Harlan	Whittaker	Clark
Bazelon	100	100	82	82	36	17	18	18	0
Fahy	100	92	85	92	31	29	23	8	15
Edgerton	100	92	83	91	36	33	25	17	8
Washington	60	60	60	40	30	50	40	30	40
Burger	11	11	11	11	78	57	67	78	67
Bastian	11	11	11	11	56	67	78	78	89
Miller	0	0	17	17	55	67	75	83	100
Danaher	0	8	8	0	58	67	62	77	100
Prettyman	0	0	0	15	62	60	77	92	100

Indices of Agreement

Douglas—Black—Warren—Brennan—Bazelon—Fahy—Edgerton   91
Douglas—Black—Warren—Bazelon—Fahy—Edgerton—Washington   85
Frankfurter—Stewart—Harlan—Whittaker—Clark—Burger—   74
Bastian—Miller—Danaher—Prettyman

Douglas was the most consistent in this support, agreeing with these three appellate judges in every case in which a pairing was possible.

The relation of the right blocs is not nearly as consistent, the index of agreement being seventy-four. Justice Clark was in complete agreement with three members of the Court of Appeals' right-bloc in every case in which a pairing was possible. As on his own court, Judge Washington maintained ties with both the left and the right blocs on the Supreme Court, but his voting tends to be affiliated with the inter-court left bloc.

While it appears that the majority right bloc on the Court of Appeals is supported by a majority right bloc on the Supreme Court, this is not the case. The minority left bloc on the Court of Appeals attracts support from one or more of the Supreme Court right bloc often enough to have its views sustained more than one-half of the time. Out of the twenty-one cases upon which Table 3 is based, Judges Bazelon, Fahy, and Edgerton participated either singly in a panel decision, or as a group in an en banc decision, sixteen times. In eleven of these decisions (sixty-nine per cent) their position was upheld on review. In fourteen of these sixteen cases, one or more of these judges were in dissent. In ten of these decisions (seventy-one per cent), their judgment was vindicated by a Supreme Court majority. As to the four in which they "lost," the Supreme Court split five-four on three occasions and seven-two once.

These findings indicate the difficulties involved in referring to the rate of reversal by the Supreme Court of a court of appeals' decisions. Only where both courts are unanimous in their decisions is it accurate to characterize this as Supreme Court policy disagreement with the court below. Where both courts are divided, two views of the public policy choices involved are being expressed. In such cases, some of the Justices of the Supreme Court support the views of some of the judges of the court of appeals. In the case of the Court of Appeals for the District of Columbia Circuit, it was most often the situation that a majority of that court was finding itself in disagreement with the Supreme Court. On the other hand, a consistent minority of the appellate court was finding itself in eventual agreement with a majority of the Supreme Court. . . .

31 VOTING BEHAVIOR ON THE UNITED STATES SUPREME COURT

C. Herman Pritchett

"We are under a Constitution," said Charles Evans Hughes when he was governor of New York, "but the Constitution is what the judges say it is. . . ." Several theories of jurisprudence have arisen which attempt to take into account this personal element in the judicial interpretation and making of law. The so-called "realistic" school has argued that law is simply the behavior of the judge, that law is secreted by judges as pearls are secreted by oysters.[1] A less extreme position was taken by the late Justice Holmes, who said: "What I mean by law is nothing more or less than the prediction of what a court will do." While these views go rather far in eliminating any idea of law as a "normative, conceptual system of rules," no one doubts that many judicial determinations are made on some basis other than the application of settled rules to the facts, or that Justices of the United States Supreme Court, in deciding controversial cases involving important issues of public policy, are influenced by biases and philosophies of government, by "inarticulate major premises," which to a large degree predetermine the position they will take on a given question. Private attitudes, in other words, become public law.

Reprinted by permission of author and publisher from C. Herman Pritchett, "Divisions of Opinion Among Justices of the U. S. Supreme Court, 1939–1941," *American Political Science Review*, 35 (1941), pp. 890–898.

[1]This figure and the quotations following are taken from Francis D. Wormuth, "The Dilemma of Jurisprudence," *A.P.S.R.*, 35 (1941), p. 44.

More precisely, it is the private attitudes of the majority of the Court which become public law. As an inexact science, issues at law are settled by counting the noses of jurors and justices. About 150 times every term the judges of the Supreme Court announce to the world in a formal written opinion the result of their balloting on the questions raised by a legal controversy before the Court. Happily, in the great majority of these ballots the decision is unanimous. In such cases, presumably the facts and the law are so clear that no opportunity is allowed for the autobiographies of the justices to lead them to opposing conclusions. It is always possible that the members of the Court may be agreeing for different reasons, but no hint of that fact is given unless concurring opinions are written.

In a substantial number of cases, however, the nine members of the Court are not able to see eye to eye on the issues involved. Working with an identical set of facts, and with roughly comparable training in the law, they come to different conclusions. If our thesis is correct, these divisions of opinion grow out of the conscious or unconscious preferences and prejudices of the Justices, and an examination of these disagreements should afford an interesting approach to the problem of judicial motivation. These cases in which dissent is expressed are particularly deserving of study because they furnish data which are not simply the verbalizations of Justices, to be handled by the typical process of interpretation, analysis, comparison, search for inconsistencies, and general legal exegesis. Instead, they contribute the tangible data of a series of yes and no votes on a variety of issues. Analysis of this voting behavior should be of value in explaining Supreme Court action, in revealing basic relationships among the justices, and, in short, in "predicting" the law.

It may be suggested that the nature of the division of opinion on the Supreme Court at any given time is a matter of common knowledge among those who follow Supreme Court thinking. In the hope, however, that a more precise analysis might have some value, the divisions of opinion in Supreme Court decisions during the past two years (the October terms, 1939 and 1940) have been analyzed. This period was one in which the membership of the Court was fairly stable. The only changes in its composition came when Butler died soon after the beginning of the 1939 Term (without having participated in any cases) and was replaced by Murphy, and when McReynolds resigned during the 1940 Term.

During this two-year period, dissent was registered to more than one-fourth of the decisions rendered by the Court. In the 1939 term, the rate was 30 per cent (42 dissents in a total of 140 decisions), and for the 1940 term it dropped slightly to 28 per cent (47 dissents out of 169 decisions). There were thus 89 decisions during the period in which one or more of the Justices dissented, at least in part, from the conclusion reached by the majority.[2] Table 1 shows the extent of each justice's participation in these dissents. The judge most persistent in disagreement was McReynolds, who took a minority stand in 22 per cent of the decisions in which he participated. Justices Roberts and Hughes were next in order, with records of 18 per cent and 12 per cent respectively. On the other hand, Frankfurter found himself on the losing side in only four of the 309 decisions rendered by the Court, a fact which calls attention to the central position which he appears to occupy on the Court. It should also be noted that he was the only justice whose dissents did not increase in number from 1939 to 1940 (with the exception of McReynolds, who did not serve out the 1940 term). Justices Reed, Murphy, and Stone are also shown by the data to be consistently members of the Court's majority.

Of these 89 dissents, 25 were one-man af-

[2]It should be noted that some 10 or 11 of these dissents were in "companion" cases, i.e., cases involving an issue identical with that decided in a preceding case, and requiring little or no new discussion. For statistical treatment, these cases might have been eliminated, to prevent double weight being given to divisions of opinion in a single situation. However, they have not been excluded, for various reasons, and it is not believed that any distortion has resulted from their inclusion. In two cases (61 S.C. 845, 861), there are dissents by two groups of justices involving separate aspects of the decision; these have been treated as two distinct dissents, and thus there are 91 dissents in the 89 cases.

TABLE 1 Participation of Supreme Court Justices in Dissenting Opinions, 1939 and 1940 Terms

Justice	Number of Dissents			Opinions Participated In	Per Cent Dissents
	1939	1940	Total		
McReynolds*	32	9	41	184	22
Roberts	23	31	54	300	18
Hughes	14	24	38	305	12
Black	4	15	19	306	6
Douglas	4	15	19	303	6
Stone	4	7	11	303	4
Reed	1	8	9	302	3
Murphy**	1	6	7	215	3
Frankfurter	2	2	4	309	1

*Resigned February 1, 1941.
**Began service February 5, 1940.

fairs. McReynolds dissented alone in 13 cases, Roberts in 10, and Reed and Stone once each. In the other 64 dissents, the concurrence of two, three, or four Justices in deviation from the majority view raises interesting problems of judicial interrelationships. Was there a regular pattern of dissent? Did certain Justices tend to agree with each other in expressing dissent? Table 2 attempts to answer such questions by showing the number of times each justice joined each other Justice in a dissenting opinion. A well-defined pattern of relationships was found to exist on the Court, and the names have been arranged in the table so as to bring out this relationship most clearly. Figures on the one-man dissents have been included in parentheses.

The table appears to reveal a marked division of the Justices into two wings or groups. The first is composed of McReynolds, Roberts, Hughes and Stone; the other includes Murphy, Frankfurter, Black, and Douglas. With the exception of two cases, no Justice in one of these groups ever joined in a dissenting opinion with a Justice from the other group. While every one of the eight Justices on occasion dissented in company with other members of his own bloc, in only two out of 89 dissents was there fraternization with the enemy. Both of these exceptional cases saw Roberts crossing the line to vote with Black and Douglas.[3] Justice Reed presents a special

[3]The cases are *Neuberger* v. *Commissioner of Internal Revenue*, 61 S.C. 97 (1940), and *Union Pacific Rr. Co.* v. *U.S.*, 61 S.C. 1064 (1941).

problem, since he was found in company with justices from both groups. His nine dissents included four with judges from each wing, and one lone dissent. He thus appeared to have one foot in each camp.

To the extent that Table 2 appears to show the existence of two self-contained blocs of opinion on the Court, it obviously misrepresents the situation. The pattern of relationships which begins to emerge from the table needs to be made clearer by presenting more complete data which will show all judicial agreements, whether on the majority or minority side. Table 2 reveals that Frankfurter and Hughes were never in dissent together, but it does not tell us how often they agreed with each other when other justices were in dissent. Table 3, consequently, is arranged to show the extent of agreement between each pair of Justices in the 89 controversial cases (or rather, in so many of them as were participated in by that pair). The number of agreements is expressed in percentages of total cases participated in by each pair.

The table reveals some interesting facts. Justices Black and Douglas are shown never to have been on opposite sides of a decision during the entire period. On the other hand, McReynolds disagreed with them in three-fourths of all the decisions in which there was division of opinion. Chief Justice Hughes was closer to Stone than to any other Justice, Stone found himself most often in agreement with Frankfurter, and Frankfurter's views

TABLE 2   Agreements among Supreme Court Justices in Dissenting Opinions, 1939 and 1940 Terms

Justice	McReynolds	Roberts	Hughes	Stone	Reed	Frankfurter	Murphy	Black	Douglas
McReynolds	(13)	26	20	4	2				
Roberts	26	(10)	33	5	3			2	2
Hughes	20	33	—	10	3				
Stone	4	5	10	(1)	1				
Reed	2	3	3	1	(1)			4	4
Frankfurter						—	1	4	4
Murphy						1	—	7	7
Black		2			4	4	7	—	19
Douglas		2			4	4	7	19	—

TABLE 3   Agreements among Supreme Court Justices in Controversial Cases, 1939 and 1940 Terms (In Percentages)

Justice	McReynolds	Roberts	Hughes	Stone	Reed	Frankfurter	Murphy	Black	Douglas
McReynolds	—	64	64	41	35	31	38	24	24
Roberts	64	—	75	51	45	45	39	37	36
Hughes	64	75	—	78	63	64	53	49	49
Stone	41	51	78	—	81	84	75	69	68
Reed	35	45	63	81	—	86	80	79	79
Frankfurter	31	45	64	84	86	—	91	85	84
Murphy	38	39	53	75	80	91	—	89	89
Black	24	37	49	69	79	85	89	—	100
Douglas	24	36	49	68	79	84	89	100	—

coincided most often with those of Murphy. The most important fact about this complex of individual relationships, however, is that it conforms to a basic underlying pattern. Examination of the table shows that the Justices ranked as they are, every member of the Court is placed next to or between the Justice or Justices with whom he is most completely identified in agreement, and farthest away from those with whom he has least in common. The only important exceptions to this rule are found in the McReynolds-Murphy and the Stone-Frankfurter relationships.

or did a number of them involve "purely legal" questions? A proper answer on this point would require the setting up of elaborate criteria for distinguishing between these two kinds of issues, and application of the criteria in a detailed analysis of each case. Such an analysis has been attempted here to only a limited degree, and covering only the dissents of the 1939 term.

A case which requires a decision as to the extent of governmental powers, or presents an issue between the government and an individual, is obviously one in which the

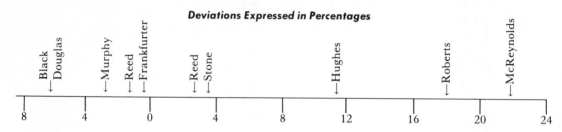

Deviations Expressed in Percentages

The division of opinion thus takes the form of the figure below, which locates the Justices along a continuum from one extreme to the other according to the direction and intensity of their deviation from the normal majority position of the Court, represented by the zero point on the scale. Frankfurter is closest to this point, since he dissented from only one per cent of the Court's decisions. Reed is given a position on both sides of the zero point, since his dissents were divided between the two wings. The scale makes apparent the existence of a fairly cohesive six-judge majority, most of the dissents being entered by the right-wing minority of McReynolds, Roberts, and Hughes.

This use of the term "right-wing" assumes that the division of opinion on the Court results from differences of opinion as to desirable public policy. It assumes that the above scale reflects relative "liberalism" and "conservatism" as those terms are understood by the man in the street. This assumption should be checked by an examination of the issues actually involved in the cases where dissents were filed. Did all of these cases present issues of public policy on which liberals and conservatives might well be expected to differ,

result may be affected by the judges' views on public policy. Our present stereotypes picture the conservative as anti-government (in the sense of opposing new or more effective forms of governmental control over individuals or corporations), and the liberal or New Dealer as pro-government. An examination of the 1939 Term's 42 dissents shows that in at least 36 an issue was presented which required the Justices to vote for or against the government, to uphold or deny a government contention, to approve or disapprove an exercise of governmental authority. The voting record of the Justices in these 36 cases shows that in 27 the dissenters were right-wingers taking an anti-government position; in three more cases, the dissenters were left-wing Justices voting for the government. Thus in 30 of the cases judicial action ran true to form.

Of the six remaining cases in this group, four saw the situation exactly reversed, with the government's support coming from the right wing. The explanation is simple, however. All four were civil liberties cases (involving free speech, the right to picket, and freedom from wire-tapping), and in all four McReynolds was the lone dissenter voting to uphold government restrictions on individuals. His action was in line with the traditional conservative position on the Court. It will be recalled that in 1931 the famous free press case of *Near* v. *Minnesota* brought out a perfect conservative dissenting lineup of Butler, Van Devanter, McReynolds, and Sutherland. By the 1939 Term, only one of this old guard remained to take a stand against civil liberties.

In the remaining two of these 36 dissents, the vote is completely inexplicable in terms of the scale positions of the Justices. One dissent was that of Justice Stone in the well-known flag salute case,[4] in which he alone maintained a strict civil liberties position in the face of the justification for the compulsory salute which the rest of the Court found compelling. The other exception came in a case presenting the thorny question of taxability of trust income, and saw Reed alone voting for the government's contention.[5] Apart from these cases, however, the judicial reaction to a "government" issue was so consistent that it must be considered a definite factor in the Court's divisions of opinion.

Examining the 42 dissents of the 1939 Term from another point of view, we find 18 cases in which the Court was required to make a decision for or against "business." The issue was presented in many forms—the validity of a business tax, an alleged violation of the antitrust laws, the constitutionality of a federal or state regulatory scheme. But wherever the issue was present, the reaction pattern was consistent, support for business coming always from the conservative end of the Court. Specifically, there were 15 dissents by right-wingers taking the side of business, and three by liberals voting against a majority decision favorable to business. Again, in five cases during the 1939 term the Court was dealing with a "labor" issue, and here also the reaction was uniform. There were four conservative dissents to decisions favoring labor, and one dissent by Douglas and Black from a majority decision slightly weakening the effect of a N.L.R.B. order.

The 1939 dissents included seven cases in which state or local action was attacked as violating provisions of the federal Constitution; for example, state and local taxes were resisted as burdening interstate commerce or contrary to due process or infringing a privilege of national citizenship. Here the consistent policy of the Justices at the Black-Douglas end of the Court was to uphold state action, in line with the traditional liberal belief that state legislative powers should be left as unrestricted by federal constitutional limitations as possible. It may also be noted that an issue involving the extent of judicial review was raised in some form in four cases; the left-wing wanted to narrow review, and the right-wing opposed any narrowing. Public operation of a power system was an issue in one case; McReynolds opposed it.[6] The rights of a debtor under the Frazier-Lemke Act were involved in another case; a liberal minority voted in his favor.[7]

One or more of the seven issues just considered was present in every one of the cases where opinion was divided during the 1939 term. In other words, none of these cases appears to present a "purely legal" question, for in each instance the observer can find a facet of the case which might offer an opportunity for the decision to be influenced by judicial views as to desirable public policy. It is not contended, of course, that the decisions were motivated wholly by the personal views of the Justices, but the data clearly indicate that these views had a considerable effect in the process of making up the judicial mind.

It would be interesting to discuss the records of several of the individual Justices in the light of the information which this analysis has supplied. The case of the Court's new Chief Justice is particularly worthy of notice. The participation of Justice Stone in right-wing dissents may seem strange, in view of his reputation as one of the soundest and ablest liberals on the Court. Two explanations suggest themselves. One is that he has deviated slightly to the right in his views with

---

[4]*Minersville School District* v. *Gobitis*, 310 U.S. 586 (1940).
[5]*Helvering* v. *Fuller*, 310 U.S. 69 (1940).

[6]*U.S.* v. *San Francisco*, 310 U.S. 16 (1940).
[7]*Union Joint Stock Land Bank* v. *Byerly*, 310 U.S. 1 (1940).

the passage of time. The other is that he has maintained very nearly his original position, but that the Court has with recent appointments moved so substantially leftward that views which put Stone to the left of the Court ten years ago now occasionally leave him exposed in dissent on the right. Whatever the cause, the process appears to be accelerating, for Stone's dissents with the conservative group numbered three in the 1939 Term and six in the 1940 Term.

The general result of this study has been to emphasize the influence of personal attitudes in the making of judicial decisions and the interpretation of law. To prevent overemphasis on this point, it would be well to recall that even in a Court representing as wide a range of views as has been found during the last two terms, 71 per cent of the cases were decided by unanimous vote. Where there were divisions of opinion, however, they appear to be for the most part explicable in terms of the opinions of the respective judges on public policy. This conclusion hardly comes as a surprise. For few are likely to deny that Justices of the Supreme Court have always, to paraphrase Justice Frankfurter, "read the laws of Congress through the distorting lenses" ground by their own experience. On the other hand, there are many who agree that the Supreme Court's vision is better today than it has been for many years past.

32 SUBGROUP FORMATION IN THE UNITED STATES SUPREME COURT

S. Sidney Ulmer

In recent years those studying the behavior of judges appear to have concentrated on two goals. First, they have attempted to develop methods and techniques for analyzing behavioral data in the judicial area. In addition,

Reprinted by permission of the publisher from S. Sidney Ulmer, "Toward a Theory of Sub-Group Formation in the United States Supreme Court," *Journal of Politics,* 27 (1965), pp. 133–135, 138–139, 140–152 with footnote omissions.

some effort has been made to alert the profession to the advantages of enlarging our span of attention to include "action" as well as "institution." While this research has been suggestive, it is fair to say that little in the way of substantive theory has been produced. In spite of the relatively large amount of resources devoted to the study of judicial voting blocs, for example, attempts to theorize about the dynamics of such groupings have been few indeed. Yet voting blocs in judicial institutions parallel, in many respects, the small groups of the social psychologist. Consequently, the articulation of small group theory with the observed behavior of such blocs might have been anticipated. Schubert, however, reports only one post-Pritchett attempt to do this at the Supreme Court level. That effort does not appear to have been eminently successful.

In this paper, no attempt is made to repair completely the deficiency described. But if we would develop a framework within which sub-group formation in the Court may be better understood, a crude first step must be taken. With that in mind, we shall consider some propositions that may be explanatory for bloc behavior in the Supreme Court. The latter part of the paper will be devoted to evaluating our theoretical expectations using voting data from Supreme Court cases decided in the period 1946–1961.

II

The datum most frequently used by those analyzing judicial behavior is the vote cast by the individual judge in a collegial court. The choice of such data as material for analysis need not be defended merely on the argument of convenience. A theoretical justification is available since decision making in the group is nothing more than the process of forming subgroups which, according to decision-making rules, bind the larger group. Subgroup formation for decision-making purposes can be delineated through the analysis of the votes cast by the members of each group.

The importance of subgroup formation for American politics is, of course, widely recognized. Such formations determine decisional outcomes. And they have pervaded our political life, past and present. This may be seen in the grouping of northern and southern Democratic leaders in support of John F. Kennedy in 1960. It may be seen as well in the cohesion of North Carolina, South Carolina, and Georgia in the Constitutional Convention of 1787. Conceptually speaking, however, it is useful to distinguish these two groupings. The first may be viewed as a coalition, the latter as a clique. A coalition we shall define as an alliance among individuals or groups with diverse long-range goals. As a consequence, coalitions are temporary and means oriented. They not only lack agreement on values, but tacit neutrality on matters beyond the immediate aim is necessary for stability. A clique, on the other hand, can be perceived as a persistently cohering group (or sub-group) organized around and reflecting long-range interests. It follows that a clique is identified by a value-consensus and end-orientation which the coalition lacks.

The United States Supreme Court is a nine-member decision-making group in which outcomes are determined by simple majority vote. The freedom to dissent which prevails in that Court frequently leads to subgroup formation which attracts the attention of social scientists. Contemporary subgroup formation in the Court has been analyzed extensively by Herman Pritchett and Glendon A. Schubert. Both have observed and discussed what they identify as "voting blocs." Other writers have followed their lead. But while gross explanatory hypotheses are sometimes suggested, no attention seems to have been given the conceptual distinction between coalitions and cliques. The primary inquiry has been who votes together rather than why. Yet statements about the characteristics of voting blocs often imply cliques or coalitions and sometimes both. . . .

III

As a small group, the United States Supreme Court seems to meet most of the conditions of a game theoretical situation. It is N-person with N specifed; the alternatives available and the state of information are generally known as are the opportunities for action. Moreover several writers have suggested that subgroup formation in the Supreme Court may be motivated by power considerations. The competition for control of decisional outcome has been viewed as a zero-sum game on the ground that the majority wins all and the dissenters win nothing. The assignment of power (the payoff) within the winning group has been evaluated in accordance with the Shapley-Shubik probability measure. Thus, given a particular voting split in a single case, the exact power gain of each individual may be computed and over many "plays" a mean criterion may be used to evaluate the success or failure of each player. But such measures are, of course, after the fact. If pursuit of power explains subgroup formation, some estimate of the power available in various formations must be made by the players prior to the actual grouping. The focus of the players, then must of necessity be on *expected power*. . . .

Assuming, for the sake of argument, that the power game model is theoretically adequate, i.e., that it tells us how a court would behave if power-oriented, we can draw no conclusions about any "real" court absent empirical evaluation of the model hypotheses. The model itself implies coalition formation, which, in turn, leads to certain empirical expectations. Consider first a nine-member court making a single decision by majority rule. If the measure of probable power is derived by permuting various alignments of judges and computing the probability of each judge occupying the pivotal position, it is assumed that all theoretical possibilities can occur without restriction. Thus, each judge would have .111 of the probable power. For if subgroup formation is coalitional, then any of 362,880 permutations can occur and each group member can be expected to pivot one-ninth of the time.

Such a derivation of power clearly suggests that differences in the values and attitudes of the judges do not restrict subgroup formation. This implies a random distribution of group values across the winning subgroup—an implication entirely consonant with our conceptualization of coalitions. If the subgroups are cliques, however, we cannot expect all the theoretical combinations to occur. For cliques are value based and subgroupings reflecting incompatible values are not expected. We anticipate not a random but a skewed distribution of group values across any set of cliques. In the cases decided by a five-four vote, we do not expect the values of the five to be the same as or similar to the values of the four insofar as the issue at hand is concerned. . . .

A second reason why pursuit of power implies coalition is that power is especially a goal of coalitions. While cliques are held together by common values, coalitions pursue a means by which disparate and even incompatible goals may be accomplished. Power, defined as control of decision, can be that means. At a number of points, the American political system forces coalitions, not cliques. If politics is competition for power, "strange bedfellows" are not unexpected in the coalitions so forced. A president in office, for example, can succor the needs of diverse social, political and economic interests. Awareness of this fact is a watery cement which binds party factions together long enough to accomplish the immediate goal—the election of the candidate.

A Supreme Court decision does not vest the wide powers of a president. A president or a congress, once elected, can act simultaneously on multiple value fronts to satisfy, in varying degrees, incompatible political claims being pressed by competing interests. Though there may be some imbalance in emphasis, a Democratic administration still appoints segregationists to public office and distributes other patronage to southern states while catering to the aspirations of the Negro. One or a series of Supreme Court opinions (at worst or best) cannot match such a performance. The relatively limited number of decisions being made annually by the Court and the restricted access of parties to Court power constitute significant bars to any attempt to play the political role of a president or a congress. Legal traditions, for example, would prevent the court from taking a pro-segregation posture in one case, and an anti-segregation

stand in the next. Precedent and continuity, while often disrupted, still constitute rules for Court behavior. In short, a Court decision is unlike an electoral decision in that it does not vest general authority to make or control subsequent concurrent decisions of an inconsistent nature. Like a streetcar ticket, the power of a coalition in the Court may be good for one case and one case only. This is not the kind of reward which motivates coalition formation, the cost of which, case after case, may be prohibitive. Our reasoning leads us, tentatively, to reject the notion that subgroup formation in the Supreme Court is basically coalitional.

IV

We may now ask whether any hard data support our view that subgroup formation in the Supreme Court is non-coalitional. If Supreme Court subgroups are coalitions primarily seeking to maximize power . . . several expectations seem logical. If coalitions are temporary and means oriented, we may expect coalitional subgroups in the Court to be characterized by a relative lack of membership stability. Likewise, no group should exceed five members, the minimal winning coalition. For proportion of power is greatest in the minimal winning group. Finally, the Court should be composed of two groupings of five and four members respectively, i.e., a minimal winning group and a coalition trying to become a minimal winning group.

On the other hand, stability of memberships in the subgroups are expected for cliques. The number of members in and the composition of each clique may vary when changes in Court composition occur. But otherwise, once aligned, the members of a clique should consistently cohere. As for the number of cliques, there is no theoretical reason to expect any particular number within the limitations imposed by the situation. Thus, if we can think of a single individual as a clique, the number of cliques in the Court may vary from one to nine. . . .

. . . [T]hree propositions [suggested by the work of Eloise Snyder[1]] may be noted.

[1] Eloise Snyder, "The Supreme Court as a Small Group," *Social Forces*, 36 (1958), pp. 232–238.

(1) The first is that members of the Supreme Court tend to form into three cliques. This is implied, of course, by the use of the three categories, A, B, and pivotal. A and B, in effect, are polar cliques separated on a continuum by the pivotal clique. Snyder delineates the three-clique formation in the Court for each of the 16 periods studied in this paper. (2) Her second proposition of interest to us is that changes in clique membership, when they occur, tend to be between pivotal and polar cliques rather than between polar cliques.

While Snyder's first generalization is contrary to our reasoning, her second is entirely compatible. For if cliques are value-based, shifting value alignments should be moderate rather than extreme. This we know from social psychology—judges should be no exception to the accepted generalization in that area. (3) The third proposition asserts that new justices coming to the Court tend to align first with the pivotal grouping before shifting later to a polar group. There seems insufficient reason to expect this in a clique structured Court.

Voting data bearing on our theoretical expectations have been collected for the sixteen terms of the Vinson and Warren courts sitting in the period 1946–1961.[2] We may view these data first in conjunction with our coalitional expectations. But before doing so it is necessary to generate from voting behavior in Supreme Court cases an operational definition of subgroup. The method chosen to accomplish this will, in one sense, be arbitrary. For alternative methods are available. Once chosen, however, the method should be one that will produce the same results when applied to the same data, whoever the practitioner. The writer has suggested elsewhere

that the number of and membership in voting blocs may be determined by factoring a matrix of correlations computed for each pair of justices in the voting group.[3] The arguments for this method are several. First, it is generalizable to other fields in political science (e.g., legislative clique formation) and social science and is a method well known to those in our sister social disciplines with whom improved communication is desirable. Secondly, it is relatively simple and straight forward and can be applied by any political scientist without training in mathematics or statistics. Fifteen minutes of explanation or self-instruction might be necessary for those completely unfamiliar with correlational analysis. Thirdly, the method articulates well with the intuitive analysis pioneered by Pritchett in that those Justices who tend to agree with one another are located in the same cluster bloc. It carries the added advantage of indicating within each bloc the nature of the relationship as between each pair of Justices. Finally, factor loadings extracted from the correlation matrix provide excellent measures of the extent to which each bloc member approximates the group prototype. While other measures of cohesion might be developed to measure "groupness," such measures often require an additional choice of cutting points to determine inclusion and exclusion of members; such choices, unfortunately, may vary with the analyst.

Application of the factor analytic method described, to voting data for each of our sixteen terms produced the sixteen sets of subgroups indicated in Table 1. These structures enable us to make some tentative evaluations.

Mere sight analysis establishes that stability in the membership of the groupings is the rule. Certain liaisons among Justices have been established and have persisted through long periods of time. Most noticeable in that respect is the grouping of Douglas, Black, Warren, and Brennan which has persisted for six years in a row. Douglas and Black have aligned with each other for all

---

[2]The votes were compiled for all participating justices in all split decisions of the court which were accompanied by opinions. Thus, multiple cases were counted once if decided by a single decision. *Per curiams* were included if accompanied by an opinion. The author is particularly indebted to Mr. Gordon Zenk for voting statistics from his own research on the Vinson Court. Alvin Dozeman, Janet Winger, and William Thompson assisted in the collection of voting data for the Warren Court.

[3]S. Sidney Ulmer, "The Analysis of Behavior Patterns in the United States Supreme Court," *Journal of Politics* (1960), pp. 629–653.

sixteen terms. On the other hand, Frankfurter, Harlan, Whittaker, Stewart, and Clark have grouped for four consecutive terms. And Harlan and Frankfurter maintained a close relationship for eight straight terms as did Frankfurter and Jackson. Reed and Burton cohered for nine of ten possible terms. It is to be noted, however, that these groupings have been derived by analyzing dyads or pairs of Justices. By studying all possible pairs, larger groupings can be composed in terms of agreement and disagreement tendencies. Such an approach has characterized the work of Pritchett, Schubert, and others working with judicial blocs. It is clear, however, that the extent to which any identified subgroup votes *en bloc* in deciding cases is another matter. While no one seems to have considered this distinction, it is of obvious importance if control of decisional outcome is postulated as the motivation for sub-group formation in the Court. In order for the cluster blocs to be effective, they must at least vote together.

TABLE 1   Subgroups in the Supreme Court: 1946–1961

		1946 (3)		
BL, MU, DO, RU		RE, BU		FR, JA, VI
		1947 (3)		
BL, MU, DO, RU		RE, BU, VI		FR, JA
		1948 (4)		
BL, DO	MU, RU		RE, BU, VI	FR, JA
		1949 (3)		
BL, DO		RE, BU, VI, CL, MI		FR, JA
		1950 (4)		
BL, DO	FR, JA		BU, MI	RE, VI, CL
		1951 (2)		
BL, DO, FR, JA				RE, BU, VI, CL, MI
		1952 (4)		
BL, DO	FR, JA		RE, BU, MI	VI, CL
		1953 (4)		
BL, DO	FR, JA, MI		WA, CL	RE, BU
		1954 (3)		
BL, DO, WA, CL		FR, HA		RE, BU, MI
		1955 (3)		
BL, DO, WA, CL		RE, BU, MI		FR, HA
		1956 (3)		
BL, DO, WA, BR		RE, CL		FR, HA, BU
		1957 (3)		
BL, DO, WA, BR		BU, CL, WH		FR, HA
		1958 (2)		
BL, DO, WA, BR				FR, HA, WH, ST, CL
		1959 (2)		
BL, DO, WA, BR				FR, HA, WH, ST, CL
		1960 (2)		
BL, DO, WA, BR				FR, HA, WH, ST, CL
		1961 (2)		
BL, DO, WA, BR				FR, HA, WH, ST, CL

Legend:
BL *Black   FR *Frankfurter   HA *Harlan
DO *Douglas   JA *Jackson   BR *Brennan
MU *Murphy   VI *Vinson   WH *Whittaker
RU *Rutledge   CL *Clark   ST *Stewart
RE *Reed   MI *Minton
BU *Burton   WA *Warren

When the subgroups for the 1946–61 terms are compared by the percentage of split decisions in which they voted *en bloc,* sizeable discrepancies are revealed. The data are summarized in table 2. In spite of the disparities, the table clearly establishes that the subgroups identified by tendency of members to agree with one another, actually operated as voting blocs in the period studied. In 16 terms, 47 different blocs were delineated. Of that number, approximately one-third voted *en bloc* in from 70 to 89 per cent of the non-unanimous cases. A total of 34, or 72 per cent of the groupings, cast bloc votes more than half the time. Thus, the groups revealed in the earlier analysis were not only highly stable in respect to tendency to agree within each bloc, but stability was also evident in group voting behavior. This data, therefore, is consonant with a clique conceptualization of Supreme Court subgroups.

The coalitional expectation regarding maximum group size is clearly supported by the data. In 16 terms, no grouping with more than five members appeared. In general, however, the number and size of groups shows considerable variation through the 16 terms. For although the court split (5, 4) in five terms, six terms produced a split of (4, 3, 2); four terms found the Court divided (3, 2, 2, 2); and in one term the Justices were divided into three subgroups of 5, 2, and 2 members, respectively. The proposition suggesting three subgroups, developed from Snyder's work, is, therefore, verified for only seven of the 16 terms examined, a finding entirely compatible with the expectation for cliques.

On balance, conflict between the data and two of the three coalitional expectations lends tentative support to the view that subgroup formation in the Court is essentially non-coalitional. Moreover, subgroup members do not appear to have been primarily motivated by power considerations. For the groupings of two and three justices identified in the decade 1946–1957 did not, once aware of minority status, rush to join a larger grouping. Frankfurter and Jackson constituted a two-member subgroup for five terms; Frankfurter and Harlan for three terms. As a matter of fact, Frankfurter was a member of a two- or three-man grouping for 11 of the 16 terms. The same can be said of Reed for eight of eleven terms. If Frankfurter and Reed were seeking power [i.e., control over decisional outcome] they appear to have been exceedingly ineffective.

It may be noted that beginning in 1953 the Supreme Court has steadily moved to fewer subgroups with larger memberships. In 1953, the split was (3, 2, 2, 2). This became (4, 3, 2) in 1954 remaining so until 1958 at which time a (5, 4) split developed. That split has continued through 1961. This development coincided with the period of Warren's Chief Justiceship and may reflect his influence in leading (and repelling) the members of his Court. It may also reflect the intensified *personal competition* which seems to have increased with Warren's accession to the Court. In short, the possibility remains that power considerations loomed larger after 1953 and began to play a role in 1958 not previously experienced.

Evaluation of the second proposition derived from [Snyder] . . . requires some methodological innovation. That proposition, it will be recalled, asserted that changes in clique membership tended to be between polar and pivotal cliques. It should be noted that, unlike Snyder, the proposition does not assign values, such as conservative or liberal, to the groupings. Meaning can be given the terms "polar" and "pivotal," however, by locating the subgroups in a "psychological space." Thus, we can say that whatever the values or "factors" involved, the two polar groupings are separated from each other in the "factor space" by a greater distance than either is separated from the pivotal grouping. In order to locate groups rather than individuals in a psychological space, we must derive from individual factor loadings an estimate of the group loadings on each of three factors. This is done by using the mean loading of each group on each factor in the city-block metric distance formula. When this is applied to the seven courts with three subgroups each, the polar and pivotal subgroups are identified. The seven Courts which were composed

TABLE 2   Bloc Voting in Non-Unanimous Cases Decided by the United States Supreme Court: 1946–1961

Term Bloc Members	Times Voting En Bloc	As % of Non-U Cases
1946 BL, MU, DO, RU	30	37.
FR, JA, VI	39	48.1
RE, BU	58	71.6
1947 BL, MU, DO, RU	41	53.9
RE, BU, VI	44	57.8
FR, JA	56	73.6
1948 BL, DO	59	71.9
MU, RU	62	75.6
RE, BU, VI	54	65.8
FR, JA	61	74.3
1949 BL, DO	11	19.2
RE, BU, VI, MI, CL	25	43.8
FR, JA	41	71.9
1950 BL, DO	36	59.
RE, VI, CL	35	57.3
BU, MI	43	70.4
FR, JA	37	60.6
1951 BL, DO, FR, JA	8	12.5
RE, BU, VI, MI, CL	21	32.8
1952 BL, DO	47	55.2
RE, BU, MI	57	67.
FR, JA	53	62.3
VI, CL	65	76.4
1953 BL, DO	27	62.8
RE, BU	29	67.4
FR, JA, MI	20	46.5
WA, CL	32	74.4
1954 BL, DO, WA, CL	41	83.6
RE, BU, MI	29	59.1
FR, HA	11	22.4
1955 BL, DO, WA, CL	40	88.8
RE, BU, MI	38	84.4
FR, HA	17	37.7
1956 BL, DO, WA, BR	47	63.5
FR, HA, BU	44	59.4
RE, CL	10	13.5
1957 BL, DO, WA, BR	60	75.
BU, CL, WH	53	66.2
FR, HA	68	85.
1958 BL, DO, WA, BR	49	79.
FR, HA, WH, ST, CL	36	58.
1959 BL, DO, WA, BR	58	77.3
FR, HA, WH, ST, CL	23	30.6
1960 BL, DO, WA, BR	55	67.9
FR, HA, WH, ST, CL	15	18.5
1961 BL, DO, WA, BR	46	58.2
FR, HA, WH, ST, CL	13	16.4

of three subgroups each may be located in Table 1. In each case, the pivotal subgroup is placed immediately under the date with the polar subgroups placed to the right and left of the table.

We are now in a position to determine whether the movement of justices among the subgroups, as we have identified them, was between polar groups or polar and pivotal groups. The changes which occurred are 14 in number and are changes between any pair of the seven years when the Court was composed of polar and pivotal groupings. Of the 14 transfers of a Justice from one bloc to another, every change was between a polar group and the pivotal group. This finding is strong support for Snyder's second proposition and is in the predicted direction in spite of the methodological changes we have introduced. The data here also support the notion of stability in the type of group memberships which characterize each judge. Thus, judges in polar groups tended to remain in polar groups, and those in pivotal groups did likewise. The actual changes from one group to another approximated only 22 per cent of the total possible changes. However, the Justices differed in their tendency toward stability. If we classify those Justices with no change as highly stable, those who shifted less than 50 per cent of the time as moderately stable and those who shifted 50 per cent or more of the

time as unstable, the Justices may be categorized as in Table 3.

The differences in the number of opportunities for change presented each Justice necessitates caution in interpreting this data. But it may be observed that those Justices usually identified as "liberal" seem to have been more stable than those usually classified as "conservative."

Finally, we may evaluate the third proposition derived from Snyder: that new Justices tend to align initially with the pivotal clique. The new Justices absorbed by the Court in the period 1946–1961 were seven in number. Of the seven, the following can be said: Clark and Minton joined the Court in the 1949 Term and aligned immediately with the pivotal clique; Warren came on in 1953, a year when the Court was split four ways. In the 1954 three-way split, Warren is found in a polar clique; Harlan, appointed in 1954, aligned at once with Frankfurter in the pivotal group; but Brennan, who acceded to the Court in 1956, is found in a polar grouping; as for Whittaker, who took his seat in 1957, and Stewart, who joined the Court in 1958, the first went directly into a pivotal clique while the second has yet to sit in a three-bloc Court. Of course, Stewart has not chosen to occupy a pivotal position between the two groups sitting in the Court since 1958. Thus, of seven Justices, four are found initially in the pivotal

TABLE 3   Movement of Supreme Court Justices among Polar and Pivotal Groupings in Seven Selected Terms

Justice	Highly Stable		Moderately Stable		Unstable	
	Chances	Shifts	Chances	Shifts	Chances	Shifts
Black	6	0				
Douglas	6	0				
Rutledge	1	0				
Murphy	1	0				
Jackson	2	0				
Vinson	1	0				
Warren	3	0				
Frankfurter			6	1		
Reed			5	1		
Harlan			3	1		
Minton					2	2
Clark					4	2
Burton					6	4

clique immediately or as soon as such a group came into existence. While this finding is in the direction predicted by Snyder, it is not free of chance influences and no great significance can be attached to it. A possible explanation lies in the extent to which an individual appointee's views are (1) developed and (2) held with conviction. Since individuals differ on these two dimensions, a predictive generalization based on length of tenure in the Court does not seem possible at this time.

V

In conclusion, we have suggested that while the identification and observation of bloc behavior in the United States Supreme Court is important, more attention should now be given to understanding the dynamics of such groupings. Using a conceptual distinction between coalitions and cliques as a point of departure, we have tentatively theorized that subgroup formation in the court is basically clique formation. In so doing, we have rejected power (specially defined) as a primary motivating force for Supreme Court Justices. We have suggested, instead, that pursuit of common value-goals is a more weighty ingredient in subgroup processes. When evaluated in terms of relevant voting data, theoretical expectations flowing from the clique conceptualization were more strongly supported than those derived from a coalition perspective.

33 SUPREME COURT ATTITUDES TOWARD FEDERAL ADMINISTRATIVE AGENCIES

Joseph Tanenhaus

. . . [T]he study here reported makes extensive use of judicial voting records. However, there are three characteristics which differen-

Reprinted by permission of author and publisher from Joseph Tanenhaus, "Supreme Court Attitudes toward Federal Administrative Agencies 1947–1956—An Application of Social Science Methods to the Study of the Judicial Process," *Vanderbilt Law Review*, 14 (1961), pp. 482–502.

tiate it from other voting behavior studies of the United States Supreme Court: (A) the utilization of a conceptual framework; (B) the multiple counting of complex cases; and (C) the use of inferential statistics. Each requires some comment. The first, the conceptual framework, is very much the most important of the three.

A. CONCEPTUAL FRAMEWORK

By conceptual framework I mean a group of related propositions about a phenomenon under investigation. These propositions are, of course, based on available knowledge. A conceptual framework is too diffuse and too lacking in parsimony to be properly termed a theory, but it must nevertheless be comprehensive enough to encompass what seem to be the important facets of the phenomenon in question. The value of any given conceptual framework is determined by the extent to which it (1) takes into account what appear to be critical aspects of available knowledge, and (2) yields testable hypotheses whose confirmation or rejection lead to support for or modification of various aspects of the framework. One hopes, however diffidently, that in this way a satisfactory theory will ultimately evolve. The conceptual framework utilized in this study of the Supreme Court, and certain testable hypotheses drawn from it, immediately follow.

The behavior of the Court at any given time is a product of three factors—the external, the institutional, and the personal. The first factor, the external, refers to the fundamental economic, social, and political forces beyond the control of the Court which limit its freedom of action. These forces make it difficult to believe, for example, that the Court or any of its members could at the present time hold that Old Age and Survivors Insurance is unconstitutional, that executive agreements have no legal standing, that corporations are not persons entitled to due process of law under the Fourteenth Amendment, or that the Congress cannot delegate rule-making authority to administrative officials.

The second factor, the institutional, refers to the formal rules and informal practices which place very real restrictions on the business that comes before the Court and how it is disposed. It is common knowledge that the Court cannot sit in judgment over an incident simply because the Justices read about it in the newspapers. To reach the Court, a dispute must fall somewhere within its jurisdiction and be brought to it in appropriate form and through proper channels. Even if these requirements are satisfied, no matter how anxious a Justice may be to have a petition for review granted by the Court, he cannot have his wish unless at least three of his colleagues concur. Moreover, since the Court handles almost all of its business *en banc,* the number of cases to which it can give serious attention is severely limited. Another restriction on the Court's freedom of action is the slender size of its staff. Limitations of staff not only make it difficult for the Justices to develop data independent of those presented by the parties involved, but even the record may be too voluminous and technical for a justice without access to adequate assistance fully to master.

The third factor, the personal, refers to those differences in personality and values which result in varying patterns of judicial behavior. The first two factors set the broad limits within which the personal is free to operate. There can be no absolute guarantee, of course, that a Justice will not flagrantly disregard external and institutional considerations, but the process by which vacancies are filled makes it fairly certain that persons who are unlikely to act well within the limits set by these two factors will rarely reach the high bench. Since the Court often deals with unsettled questions having substantial policy ramifications, frequent disagreement among the justices is to be expected. Yet the established practice of publicly discussing these divisions in formal opinions makes it all too easy to overstress the importance of dissension within the Court. Crucial though disputed issues may be to the outcome of particular causes, disagreement is generally rather marginal when viewed in terms of the underlying agreement on more fundamental questions— an agreement often explicitly acknowledged by both majority and dissenting Justices in even the most sharply divided cases.

One final limitation on a Justice's freedom to decide as he chooses does not fit squarely into any category, but deserves special attention. The decisions each Justice makes are readily accessible to thousands of lawyers and judges for whom consistency is a cardinal virtue. Since bench and bar constitute the Court's principal public, even the rare Justice who may not share his profession's values is under extraordinary pressure to work out early in his tenure on the Court a point of view to which he can adhere with a minimum of subsequent modification. Barring dramatic changes in the external and institutional factors, fundamental alterations in the pattern each Justice early displays seem rather unlikely. Changes in personnel may, however, be expected to render the position of the Court itself less consistent than that of its individual members.

Only a few additional comments are necessary to relate the conceptual framework just outlined more specifically to federal administrative agency cases for the 1947–1956 terms. First of all, by the opening of the 1947 Term the fundamental questions about the future of the agencies and their work had been resolved for a time at least. The "constitutional revolution of 1937" had been followed in 1942 by President Roosevelt's successful veto of the Walter-Logan bill, and finally, in 1946, by the passage of the Administrative Procedure Act.[1] In giving its sanction to the act, the American Bar Association formally abandoned its long campaign to cripple the administrative process by transferring the settling of all legal controversies to the courts. As Kenneth Culp Davis has put it, "the federal administrative process was secure," and "a period of tranquillity set in."[2] External considerations have made it almost impossible for any justice to question the legitimacy of the administrative process or the type of activity the agencies have been authorized to undertake. Rather, the task of the Court has

[1] 60 Stat. 237 (1946), 5 U.S.C. § 1001–1010 (1958).
[2] Davis, *Administrative Law* 9 (1951).

been confined to acting as overseer and making certain that the agencies conduct themselves in accordance with statutory regulations and with the Constitution.

In the second place, institutional considerations put the Court at something of a disadvantage in dealing with some agencies. Certain agencies have to make large numbers of decisions involving problems of great technical complexity. To cope with this obligation the agencies have developed sizeable and expert staffs. The Justices without access to comparable assistance often find it awkward to sit in serious review over highly technical agency decisions. In addition the agencies have not only long displayed a general disposition to act within the law, but engage outstandingly able lawyers to aid them in determining what the Constitution and laws permit and forbid them to do. Only rarely, as a result, does an agency appear before the Court without a strong argument to support its contentions. There would seem to be relatively few opportunities for the Court to reverse for purely legal reasons (*e.g.*, evidence, procedure, lack of statutory authorization) an agency's action as patently arbitrary and unwarranted. One would then expect the Justices to display strong support for the agencies.

On the other hand, because many agency cases involve questions of policy as well as questions of law, there is room for individual values to manifest themselves: for example, should the Internal Revenue Service or private parties be given the benefit of the doubt in tax cases, the Immigration and Naturalization Service or the alien in deportation proceedings? If a justice is strongly opposed to an agency's position for policy reasons, he can often find some legal ground on which to justify voting against the agency. Questions of policy and value would seem then to be more likely reasons for a justice to disagree with an agency than questions of law.

The foregoing framework of conceptions suggests numerous testable hypotheses about the behavior of the Court and its Justices in federal agency cases during the 1947 to 1956 terms. Among them are the following:

I. Members of the Court agree with one another in federal agency cases to a statistically significant degree.

II. The Court and its individual members favor federal agencies more frequently than they oppose them to a statistically significant degree.

III. A. The voting patterns of the individual justices in federal agency cases display no statistically significant inconsistencies during the ten-year period.

B. The voting behavior of the Court in federal agency cases does display statistically significant inconsistencies during the ten-year period.

IV. If agency is held constant, policy and value preferences of statistical significance are revealed in the voting behavior of the justices: *e.g.*,

A. In cases involving organized labor

B. In cases involving restrictions on competition

C. In cases involving freedom of person

D. In cases involving monetary gain or loss for the government.

V. If agency is held constant, no preferences on legal questions of statistical significance are revealed in the voting behavior of the justices: *e.g.*,

A. In cases involving an agency's statutory authority

B. In cases involving procedures required by statute

C. In cases involving evidentiary questions.

B. MULTIPLE COUNTING OF COMPLEX CASES

The second of the three characteristics which differentiate this study from other voting behavior studies of the United States Supreme Court is the multiple counting of complex cases. How cases were coded, and why these procedures were used, are discussed in the following description of the manner in which the data used in this study were collected and processed.

Several years ago I began a systematic analysis of all United States Supreme Court cases decided with opinion for a ten-year period beginning with the 1947 Term. The purpose of the study was to assemble the information necessary for testing a variety of hypotheses about the behavior of the Court and its several members. Using a pretested code, data pertaining to the parties involved, the issues at stake, the voting behavior of the justices, and a number of other factors were punched into McBee keysort cards. Considerations that seemed important upon reading each case, but which were not provided for in the code, were recorded in writing upon the cards. In preparing the present analysis, cases involving ten federal agencies were drawn from the files and re-analyzed on the basis of an expanded and refined code which sought to offset, wherever possible, the limitations of the earlier one.[3]

The most far-reaching modification on re-analysis was the multiple counting of certain complex cases. Multiple counting was necessitated by a portion of the conceptual framework which had not been adequately developed until after the initial coding was well under way. The system employed for multiple counting, while far from ideal, was the most discriminating that time and resources permitted. Its major elements are these. Cases in which there was dissension *on some but not all* of the issues involved were counted more than once. For example, if all Justices agreed both that an agency had acted within its jurisdiction and that its decision was based on weighty enough evidence, the case was counted only once. But if a Justice dissented on only one point and either agreed with the majority or was noncommital on the second, then the case was counted twice. Multiple counting was, with several exceptions, carried as far as was necessary to enable an unambiguous recording of agreement, disagreement, or noncommitment on the part of every justice with every other justice, with

the Court, and with the agencies. Whenever this could not be accomplished for any justice by double or triple classification, his behavior was treated as indeterminable. As a result, the 197 cases yielded a maximum of 248 issues for decision, although no one actually participated in that many. Throughout the remainder of this paper, N (the number of statistical cases) refers to the issues coded and not to cases in the legal sense.

As coding progressed, occasional reliability checks were made on previously completed cases, but resources did not permit an independent assessment of the reliability of the code. However, data about which I have gnawing doubts have not been utilized in the preparation of this analysis.

Once coded, the data were punched into more than 2200 IBM cards which were verified.

C. USE OF INFERENTIAL STATISTICS

The third distinguishing characteristic of this study of Supreme Court voting behavior is the use made of inferential (or inductive) statistics. Several other legal studies have employed them. . . . But none . . . has dealt with the United States Supreme Court. Social scientists frequently speak of the statistical methods they employ as either descriptive or inferential. By descriptive statistics they mean methods for condensing and summarizing available data (*e.g.,* percentages, ratios, averages, variations of items from averages) as well as methods for ascertaining and describing the association between two or more characteristics of the data (*e.g.,* contingency, correlation, regression, variance, factor analysis). By inferential statistics they mean the methods used when there is need to generalize beyond the data actually in hand. This occurs in either of two situations. In one the data which could be assembled (the universe or whole population) are so numerous that it is feasible only to sample them and from the sample to estimate the characteristics of the universe. In the second situation, one desires to test the validity of certain hypotheses; that is, to determine the likelihood that postulated

[3]Limitations of time and resources restricted the cases used in this analysis to those involving the following agencies: National Labor Relations Board, Federal Trade Commission, Interstate Commerce Commission, Federal Power Commission, Selective Service System, Securities and Exchange Commission, Internal Revenue Service, Immigration and Naturalization Service, Civil Aeronautics Board, and the Federal Communications Commission.

characteristics and relationships could have resulted from random error (or chance). It is the latter situation that occasioned the use of inferential statistics in this study of Supreme Court attitudes toward federal administrative agencies.

In deciding whether to accept or reject a hypothesis, use is made of a non-arbitrary device called a test of significance.[4] An illustration may help to clarify the function of the test for those who may not be thoroughly familiar with it. An assumption (the null hypothesis), which is inconsistent with a research hypothesis, is made about the true character of a whole population—*e.g.*, contrary to Hypothesis II above, the Supreme Court in an infinite number of decisions would oppose federal agencies as frequently as it would support them. Then the actual decisions of the Court are examined to see whether its treatment of federal agencies is consistent with this assumption: the Court opposed the agencies 75 times, and favored them on 168 occasions. If the probability is rather small that such a distribution as did occur in fact would have appeared as a sample drawn at random from the population envisaged in the null hypothesis (in this instance far less than one in one thousand [$P <$ .001] using a two-tailed test),[5] then the null hypothesis is rejected and the research hypothesis accepted. If, on the other hand, the probability is not small (greater than five in 100 [$P >$ .05]), then the null hypothesis is accepted and the research hypothesis rejected.

Now it is extremely important to bear in mind that a test of significance cannot tell us whether a hypothesized relationship is important or trivial, nor can it tell us why a justice acted as he did. All that the test can do, and I do not wish to minimize the value of this service, is to indicate with what probable error we may assume that a postulated relationship exists.

The assumption that a group of Court cases over a given period in time constitutes a random sample drawn from an infinite universe (when in fact the sample includes all the cases that are or can ever be relevant for that period) will no doubt trouble a great many persons. And not without cause. But what makes the assumption desirable in my opinion is the highly unsatisfactory alternative: deciding, for example, whether the hypothesis that the Court is partial to federal agencies is confirmed if agencies were favored 54, or 57, or 60, or 72, or 80 per cent of the time. For, as any baseball fan knows, the stability of a percentage varies directly with the number of cases. The larger the number of cases in a random sample, the less likely its characteristics are to differ from those of the universe; and conversely, the fewer the number of cases in a sample, the more likely are its characteristics to differ from those of the universe. If the Court in the illustration above had made only fifteen decisions instead of 243, roughly 80 per cent would have had to go one way in order to establish significance at the .05 level (using a two-tailed test). Had 25 cases been involved, then 72 per cent; if 100 cases, then 60 per cent; if 200 cases, then 57 per cent; and 500 cases, only 54 per cent. Unless one makes the assumptions necessary to employ inferential statistics, he has no meaningful and non-arbitrary basis for determining whether an observed percentage supports or rejects the hypothesis.

Many statistical techniques are available for testing the significance of a hypothesis. Some of these, the parametric tests, require extensive and strong assumptions about the character of the data and the population from which they were drawn. Other techniques, the non-parametric tests, require fewer and weaker assumptions. All the data in this study are treated as merely nominal, the least elegant of all the levels of measurement.[6] This means that a vote in favor of an agency can be distinguished from a vote against an agency as well as from any other

---

[4]On tests of significance, see Hagood & Price, *Statistics for Sociologists* 313–39 (rev. ed. 1952).

[5]Actually, since direction was predicted, the more powerful one-tailed test would be appropriate. See note 7 *infra*.

[6]On levels of measurement, see Sellitz, Jahoda, Deutsch & Cook, *Research Methods in Social Relations* (rev. ed., 1959), pp. 186–198.

pro-agency vote. But no effort has been made to consider a vote in favor of an agency as any more or less pro-agency than any other pro-agency vote. Because the data are treated as nominal, only the low-powered non-parametric tests appropriate for nominal data are applicable: *e.g.*, the binomial and Chi Square one-sample tests for goodness of fit, the Fisher exact probability and Chi Square two-sample tests for comparing two independent groups, the Chi Square k sample test for comparing more than two independent groups, and the contingency coefficient for measures of correlation.[7] However great the temptation, more powerful statistical operations have been studiously avoided because they require assumptions which, in my opinion, the data do not warrant.

Each of the hypotheses drawn from the conceptual framework is discussed . . . together with the data and the statistical test deemed appropriate for its evaluation. Analysis has not been carried beyond the point where N becomes too small for tests of significance to be meaningful.

ANALYSIS OF THE RESULTS OF THE PRESENT STUDY

Hypothesis I (H_1): *Members of the Court agree with one another in federal agency cases to a statistically significant degree.*—H_1 was tested by assuming that in an infinite number of decisions each justice would disagree with every other justice as frequently as he would agree with him (the null hypothesis [H_0]). Then the actual frequencies of agreement and disagreement were examined to see whether the data are consistent with this assumption. The number of asterisks in the box shared by any pair of justices in Table I indicates the probability that agreement as substantial as that which did occur in fact would have appeared

[7]For an excellent discussion of these and other non-parametric tests, see Siegel, *Non-Parametric Statistics for the Behavioral Sciences* (1956). Siegel defines the power of a test as "the probability of rejecting [the null hypothesis] when it is in fact *false*." (*Id.* at 10). One-tailed tests are more powerful than two-tailed tests, and are generally appropriate when direction has been predicted. For a discussion of when each should be used, see McNemar, *Psychological Statistics* 62–64 (2d ed. 1955).

as a sample drawn at random from the assumed population. Since the direction of deviation from the null hypothesis had been previously indicated, the probabilities were computed by means of a one-tailed Chi Square goodness of fit test. One asterisk indicates a probability of occurrence no greater than five in one hundred, two asterisks a probability no greater than one time in one hundred, and three asterisks a probability no greater than five times in one thousand.

The asterisks alone make clear that in all but a few instances H_0 is rejected in favor of H_1. There is other evidence in favor of H_1 as well. Each of the eight boxes in which there are no asterisks carries a "+" sign above the contingency coefficient denoting that the two justices agreed more often than they disagreed, even though the extent of their agreement was not statistically significant. The binomial expansion applied to these eight cases indicates that positive agreement of this relative frequency is to be expected by chance fewer than five times in one thousand (using a one-tailed test, with $P = Q = \frac{1}{2}$).

Contingency coefficients (C) are given in Table I instead of the "X^2s," because C $\left[\sqrt{\dfrac{X^2}{N+X^2}}\right]$ takes into account the varying number of cases in which each pair of justices took part and thereby enables one roughly to rank the extent to which the justices agreed with one another. The upper limit for the contingency coefficient computed for a 2×2 table (as was here the case) is .707 rather than unity as with Pearson's product-moment correlation. Consequently a C in the upper .60's represents nearly perfect correlation.

An extended discussion of the inferences that may be drawn from the relative size of the eighty-odd C's in Table I would probably be more interesting than germane, since it could do nothing to reinforce or weaken the decision to accept H_1.

Hypothesis II (H_2): *The Court and its individual members favor federal agencies more frequently than they oppose them to a statistically significant degree.*—A decision whether to accept or reject H_2 was reached by the same procedures used in evaluating H_1—a one-tailed Chi Square

TABLE 1   Intercorrelations in Voting Behavior as Measured by the Coefficient of Contingency

	BLACK	DOUGLAS	FRANKFURTER	REED	JACKSON	BURTON	VINSON	RUTLEDGE	MURPHY	CLARK	MINTON	WARREN	HARLAN	BRENNAN
COURT	.43 ***	.28 ***	.51 ***	.57 ***	.47 ***	.57 ***	.63 ***	.52 ***	.57 ***	.68 ***	.66 ***	.66 ***	.51 ***	.68 ***
BLACK		.47 ***	.33 ***	.22 **	.19 **	.24 ***	.26 ***	.67 ***	.64 ***	.33 ***	.31 ***	.55 ***	+ .22	.46 ***
DOUGLAS			+ .07	.27 ***	.19 **	+ .10	+ .13	.59 ***	.59 ***	.23 ***	+ .12	.42 ***	+ .11	.35 **
FRANKFURTER				.35 ***	.55 ***	.48 ***	.31 ***	+ .24	.35 **	.48 ***	.47 ***	.51 ***	.62 ***	.68 ***
REED					.37 ***	.51 ***	.54 ***	.42 ***	.35 **	.53 ***	.56 ***	.48 ***	.33 **	—
JACKSON						.38 ***	.36 ***	+ .16	.28 *	.46 ***	.38 ***	—	—	—
BURTON							.53 ***	.27 *	+ .25	.58 ***	.58 ***	.45 ***	.53 ***	.63 ***
VINSON								.45 ***	.47 ***	.66 ***	.60 ***	—	—	—
RUTLEDGE									.65 ***	—	—	—	—	—
CLARK											.59 ***	.61 ***	.52 ***	.59 ***
MINTON												.51 ***	.45 **	—
WARREN													.37 ***	.62 ***
HARLAN														.60 ***

*P ≤ .05, one-tailed
**P ≤ .01, one-tailed
***P ≤ .005, one-tailed
"+" agreed more than disagreed with P > .05.

TABLE II   Votes Cast For and Against Agencies

	For Agencies (N)	Against Agencies (N)	x^2	P ≤ under H₀: 1-tailed
Court	168	75	35.59	.001
Black	135	95	6.96	.005
Douglas	103	107	.076	*
Frankfurter	129	100	3.67	.05
Reed	143	64	30.15	.001
Jackson	80	59	3.17	.05
Burton	164	74	34.03	.001
Vinson	90	40	19.23	.001
Rutledge	30	11	8.80	.003
Murphy	28	11	7.41	.01
Clark	125	63	20.44	.001
Minton	113	46	28.23	.001
Warren	62	42	3.85	.01
Harlan	33	26	.831	*
Brennan	24	8	8.00	.003

*P > .05.

goodness of fit test. H_0 in this instance assumes that in an infinite number of decisions, federal agencies would be opposed as often as they were favored by the Court and by each of its justices. H_0 is rejected in favor of H_2 if there is little likelihood that the distributions of votes actually cast would appear as samples drawn at random from such a population. As the data in Table II indicate, H_0 is accepted at the .05 level of significance for Justice Douglas and Justice Harlan, H_2 at the .01 level for the Court, and for all the other justices except Frankfurter and Jackson. H_2 is also accepted for them, but with somewhat less assurance that a correct decision has been made.

Hypothesis III-A (H_3A): The voting patterns of the individual justices in federal agency cases display no statistically significant inconsistencies over the ten-year period.—The first step in testing H_3 was to divide the decisions made by each justice into a series of time periods. This was done in such a way as to preclude any manipulation of the data for the purpose of gaining non-random advantages in favor of H_3A. Time periods were set automatically by changes in the Court's personnel:

Time period I (T1)—opening of the 1947 term to the last case in which Justice Rutledge took part;

Time period II (T2)—from the end of T1 until the last case in which Chief Justice Vinson took part;

Time period III (T3)—from the end of T2 until the last case in which Justice Jackson took part;

Time period IV (T4)—from the end of T3 until the last case in which Justice Minton took part;

Time period V (T5)—from the end of T4 until the end of the 1956 term.

H_0 assumes that the differences in the distribution of the votes cast by each justice during his two or more time periods on the Court are so substantial that there is small chance all of these distributions would appear as samples drawn at random from the same population. The probability that the actual distributions would have so appeared was determined for all justices active during three or more time periods by the Chi Square test for k independent samples. When only two time periods were involved, the Chi Square two-sample test with a correction for continuity was used. In both instances, two-tailed tests were deemed appropriate since H_3A would be invalidated by inconsistency in either direction. The voting patterns and test results are presented in Table III. They show that H_0 is rejected in favor of H_3A for every member of the Court except Mr. Justice

TABLE III   Consistencies in Voting Behavior

	T1		T2		T3		T4		T5		X^2	df	P: 2-tailed**
	+ag	−ag	+ag	−ag	+ag	−ag	+ag	−ag	+ag	−ag			
Court	32	10	69	26	16	15	27	16	24	8	7.35	4	*
Black	28	12	59	31	10	19	21	19	17	14	11.56	4	.05
Douglas	23	15	34	38	11	18	19	21	16	15	3.67	4	*
Frankfurter	26	14	44	41	13	18	22	18	24	9	8.25	4	*
Reed	26	11	63	29	20	9	31	12	3	3	1.16	4	*
Jackson	22	14	48	39	9	6	—	—	—	—	.44	2	*
Burton	29	12	58	31	20	11	32	11	25	9	1.89	4	*
Vinson	32	8	58	32	—	—	—	—	—	—	2.40	1	*
Clark	—	—	59	24	17	13	25	17	24	9	3.76	3	*
Minton	—	—	62	25	24	7	27	14	—	—	1.16	2	*
Warren	—	—	—	—	15	15	25	17	22	10	2.60	2	*
Harlan	—	—	—	—	—	—	13	13	20	13	.30	1	*

*$P > .05$.

**Since H_0 was stated positively for the Court and negatively for the justices, P in this table is equal to or less than the probability that the actual voting distributions would have been drawn as random samples from the same population.

Black. In his case H_0 is accepted at the .05 level of significance. Justice Black, then, is the only Justice who did not vote in a fairly consistent fashion in federal agency cases during the 1947–1956 terms.

Hypothesis III-B (H_3B): *The voting behavior of the Court in federal agency cases displays statistically significant inconsistencies during the ten-year period.*—The validity of H_3B was examined in a manner similar to that used for H_3A. But here the conceptual framework led to the expectation that the Court would reveal inconsistencies in its voting behavior. The data and test results, reported in Table III, show that H_3B is untenable and must be rejected. Contrary to expectations, the Court itself acted rather consistently in federal agency cases throughout the years under investigation.

Hypothesis IV-A (H_4A): *If agency is held constant, policy and value preferences of statistical significance are revealed in the voting behavior of the justices—in cases involving organized labor.*—In testing H_4A, all cases in which labor unions were on one *but not both* sides of a dispute were classified into two groups; those in which the agency favored the union and those in which the agency opposed the union. Then the frequency with which each justice supported and opposed the agency in each of the two groups was compiled. H_0 assumes that the actual voting patterns of a justice in each of the two groups (how often a justice supported and opposed the agency when it favored the union, and how often he supported and opposed the agency when it opposed the union) could have been drawn at random from the same population. If the probability that this would occur is small, then H_0 is rejected in favor of H_4A. The Chi Square two-sample test with a correction for continuity was used to determine the probabilities when the data were numerous enough, and the conservative Fisher exact probability test when they were not. In either case, a two-tailed test was considered appropriate because the direction of the anticipated deviations from H_0 cannot be predicted from the conceptual framework. Table IV-A contains the data. These data make it quite clear that H_4A can be accepted only for Justices Black and Douglas, who displayed a marked partiality for labor unions, and for Justice Vinson who revealed hostility toward them. For the remaining justices, H_4A is rejected in favor H_0.

Hypothesis IV-B (H_4B): *If agency is held constant, policy and value preferences of statistical significance are revealed in the voting behavior of the justices—in cases involving restrictions on competition.*—In testing H_4B all cases involving (1) wider access by users to services, and

TABLE IV-A Cases in Which Agency Supported Labor Unions Compared with Cases in Which Agency Opposed Unions

	When Agency for Unions		When Agency against Unions			
	For Agency (N)	Against Agency (N)	For Agency (N)	Against Agency (N)	Direction**	$P \leq under$ H_0: 2-tailed
Court	25	11	11	2	−	*
Black	29	6	5	8	+	.01
Douglas	28	8	2	9	+	.01
Frankfurter	20	15	9	4	−	*
Reed	21	10	4	5	−	*
Jackson	11	10	3	4	−	*
Burton	25	11	11	2	−	*
Vinson	7	10	5	0	−	.01
Clark	18	13	9	2	−	*
Minton	15	9	5	0	−	*
Warren	13	3	5	3	+	*

*$P > .05$.

**"+" indicates that agency was favored in a larger percentage of cases in which unions were supported than cases in which unions were opposed.

"−" indicates that agency was favored in a smaller percentage of cases in which unions were supported than cases in which unions were opposed.

(2) the opportunity to provide them by suppliers, were collected. Then all cases in which the justices disagreed as to whether competition was actually an issue or as to whether an agency's decision furthered or hindered competition were discarded. The competition cases that remained were divided into two groups—one containing cases in which the agencies favored competition and the second cases in which the agencies opposed competition. From this point, analysis proceeded exactly as with H_4A. The data are reported in Table IV-B. From these it follows that H_4B can be accepted only for Black and Douglas. Both favored competition to a degree significant at the .01 level. The voting patterns of the other justices do not reveal statistically significant preferences for furthering or restricting competition.

Hypothesis IV-C (H_4C): *If agency is held constant, policy and value preferences of statistical significance are revealed in the voting behavior of the justices—in cases involving freedom of person.—* With the exception of a criminal proceeding arising out of an Interstate Commerce Commission regulation, the freedom of person cases consist of criminal prosecutions for violations of the draft laws and proceedings against aliens by the Immigration and Naturalization authorities. In each of these cases the agency opposed freedom of person. There were no cases in which the agencies favored freedom. As a result, judicial attitudes toward federal agencies when they opposed freedom cannot be compared with their attitudes toward agencies when they favored freedom. But judicial attitudes in cases where the agencies opposed freedom can be compared with attitudes in cases where freedom was not an issue. This procedure is admittedly less desirable than that used for controlling agency as a factor in testing H_4A and H_4B because a larger number of unknown variables seems to be involved. From this point on, the method used in deciding to accept or reject H_4C is the same as that used for H_4A and H_4B. Table IV-C contains the data which show that H_4C is accepted for Black, Douglas, and Frankfurter at the .01 level of significance. These justices supported the agencies far more strongly when freedom of person was not an issue than when the agencies

TABLE IV-B **Cases in Which Agencies Supported Competition Compared with Cases in Which Agencies Opposed Competition**

	When Agencies for Competition		When Agencies against Competition		Direction**	P ≤ under H₀: 2-tailed
	For Agency (N)	Against Agency (N)	For Agency (N)	Against Agency (N)		
Court	12	5	4	2	+	*
Black	15	1	1	5	+	.01
Douglas	13	2	0	6	+	.01
Frankfurter	6	8	5	1	–	*
Reed	13	3	4	2	+	*
Jackson	5	6	2	2	–	*
Burton	8	9	3	3	–	*
Vinson	9	4	4	0	–	*
Clark	7	4	4	2	–	*
Minton	5	3	5	1	–	*
Warren	3	0	0	2	+	*

*P > .05.

"+" indicates that agencies were supported in a larger percentage of cases in which they favored competition than cases in which they opposed it.

"–" indicates that agencies were supported in a smaller percentage of cases in which they favored competition than cases in which they opposed it.

TABLE IV-C **Cases Involving Freedom of Person Compared with Cases Which Did Not**

	Agency against Freedom of Person		Freedom of Person Not at Issue		Direction**	P ≤ under H₀: 2-tailed
	For Agencies (N)	Against Agencies (N)	For Agencies (N)	Against Agencies (N)		
Court	31	18	137	57	+	*
Black	7	38	128	57	+	.001
Douglas	10	31	93	76	+	.01
Frankfurter	18	29	111	71	+	.01
Reed	31	8	112	56	–	*
Jackson	15	11	65	48	–	*
Burton	36	13	128	61	–	*
Vinson	15	5	75	35	–	*
Clark	27	11	98	52	–	*
Minton	27	5	86	41	–	*
Warren	15	13	47	29	+	*
Harlan	10	6	23	23	–	*

*P > .05.

"+" indicates that agencies were opposed in a larger percentage of cases in which they opposed freedom of person than cases in which freedom of person was not at issue.

"–" indicates that agencies were opposed in a smaller percentage of cases in which they opposed freedom of person than cases in which freedom of person was not at issue.

TABLE IV-D **Cases in Which the Agencies Supported a Financial Interest of the United States Compared with Cases in Which No Financial Interest of the United States at Issue**

	Agencies Favored Financial Interest of U.S.		No Financial Interest of U.S. at Issue			
	For Agencies (N)	Against Agencies (N)	For Agencies (N)	Against Agencies (N)	Direction**	P ≤ under H₀: 2-tailed
Court	41	11	124	61	+	*
Black	44	8	91	82	+	.001
Douglas	25	18	77	85	+	*
Frankfurter	33	17	93	81	+	*
Reed	33	13	108	48	+	*
Jackson	18	13	60	44	+	*
Burton	38	13	123	59	+	*
Vinson	26	6	64	32	+	*
Clark	24	11	99	50	+	*
Minton	22	10	90	34	−	*
Warren	15	5	47	37	+	*

*$P > .05$.

**"+" indicates that agencies were supported in a larger percentage of cases in which a financial interest of the United States was favored than cases in which no such financial interest was at issue.

"−" indicates that agencies were supported in a smaller percentage of cases in which a financial interest of the United States was favored than cases in which no such financial interest was at issue.

opposed it. For the other justices, freedom of person is not shown to be a statistically significant factor in federal agency cases.

Hypothesis IV-D (H_4D): *If agency is held constant, policy and value preferences of statistical significance are revealed in the voting behavior of the justices—in cases involving monetary gain or loss for the government.*—Although there was a sizeable number of decisions in which the United States had a direct financial stake, in only five of these did the agencies oppose the government. It was therefore necessary to proceed as with H_4C. Agency was controlled by comparing the voting patterns of the justices in cases in which the agencies supported a financial interest of the United States with cases in which the United States had no financial interest. Table IV-D contains the data which warrant acceptance of H_4D only for Justice Black. He strongly favored the government when its financial interests were at stake. H_4D must be rejected for all of the other justices.

However, there is some slight evidence that the justices as a group are partial to the gov-

ernment in this type of case. Using the binomial expansion (with $P = Q = \frac{1}{2}$, and a two-tailed test), the distribution of the directional signs is statistically significant at .022.

Hypothesis V-A, V-B, and V-C: If agency is held constant, no statistically significant preferences on legal questions are revealed in the voting behavior of the justices—

(H_5A) *In cases involving the agencies' statutory authority;*

(H_5B) *In cases involving procedures required by statute;*

(H_5C) *In cases involving evidentiary questions.* H_5A, H_5B, and H_5C were all tested in the same manner as H_4C and H_4D. In each of the cases in which one of these legal questions was involved the propriety of an agency's conduct or the soundness of its judgment was, of course, at issue. As a result, the only feasible method of controlling agency as a factor was to compare the behavior of a justice in cases involving one of these legal questions with his behavior in cases which did not. The data are found in Tables V-A, V-B, and V-C.

An examination of these tables leads to

TABLE V-A   Cases Involving Statutory Authority Compared with Cases Which Do Not

	Authority at Issue		Authority Not at Issue			
	For Agency (N)	Anti-Agency (N)	For Agency (N)	Anti-Agency (N)	Direction**	$P \leq$ under H_0: 2-tailed
Court	50	19	116	53	+	*
Black	41	18	94	71	+	*
Douglas	32	24	71	75	+	*
Frankfurter	39	22	89	72	+	*
Reed	44	14	96	49	+	*
Jackson	28	14	52	41	+	*
Burton	42	24	120	47	−	*
Vinson	32	9	58	31	+	*
Rutledge	10	3	20	8	+	*
Murphy	9	3	19	8	+	*
Clark	37	15	87	45	+	*
Minton	41	8	71	38	+	.05
Warren	13	11	49	28	−	*
Harlan	6	9	27	17	−	*

*$P > .05$.

**"+" indicates that agencies were favored in a larger percentage of cases in which authority was an issue than cases in which it was not.

"−" indicates that agencies were favored in a smaller percentage of cases in which authority was an issue than cases in which it was not.

TABLE V-B   Cases Involving Statutory Procedures Compared with Cases Which Do Not

	Procedure at Issue		Procedure Not at Issue			
	For Agency (N)	Against Agency (N)	For Agency (N)	Against Agency (N)	Direction**	$P \leq$ under H_0: 2-tailed
Court	37	18	131	57	−	*
Black	24	24	111	71	−	*
Douglas	20	24	83	83	−	*
Frankfurter	24	24	105	76	−	*
Reed	34	14	109	50	+	*
Jackson	18	14	62	45	−	*
Burton	34	17	130	57	−	*
Vinson	21	11	69	29	−	*
Clark	26	14	99	49	−	*
Minton	26	12	87	34	−	*
Warren	12	8	50	34	+	*

*$P > .05$.

**"+" indicates that agencies were favored in a larger percentage of cases in which procedures were at issue than cases in which they were not.

"−" indicates that agencies were favored in a smaller percentage of cases in which procedures were at issue than cases in which they were not.

TABLE V-C   Cases Involving Evidentiary Questions Compared with Cases Which Do Not

	Evidentiary Questions at Issue		Evidentiary Questions Not at Issue			
	For Agency (N)	Anti- Agency (N)	For Agency (N)	Anti- Agency (N)	Direction**	P ≤ under H₀: 2-tailed
Court	42	8	124	62	+	.05
Black	28	14	105	74	+	*
Douglas	22	14	78	84	+	*
Frankfurter	28	14	99	77	+	*
Reed	37	7	105	51	+	.05
Jackson	23	4	56	50	+	.01
Burton	38	7	124	59	+	.05
Vinson	21	3	69	30	+	*
Clark	30	8	94	48	+	*
Minton	27	5	82	39	+	*
Warren	15	5	47	35	+	*
Harlan	6	4	27	20	+	*

*$P < .05$.

**"+" indicates that agencies were favored in a larger percentage of cases in which evidentiary questions were at issue than cases in which they were not.

"−" indicates that agencies were favored in a smaller percentage of cases in which evidentiary questions were at issue than cases in which they were not.

accepting H_5B for all justices and H_5A for all except Minton. On the other hand, H_5C is rejected for Jackson at the .01 level of significance and for Reed and Burton at the .05 level. All three show particular reluctance to oppose the agencies on evidentiary grounds. Moreover, using the binomial expansion (with $P = Q = \frac{1}{2}$, and a two-tailed test), the distribution of the directional signs is statistically significant at the .01 level. This suggests that when questions of evidence are involved, the justices as a group tend to support the agencies more strongly than they do when such questions are not at issue.

SUMMARY AND CONCLUSIONS

My framework of conceptions about the Court and its personnel was outlined and a series of hypotheses stemming from it formulated. I cannot argue that the hypotheses were logically derived from the conceptual framework because alternative hypotheses, perhaps even some inconsistent with those formulated, could also have been drawn from it. Consequently, acceptance or rejection of

the hypotheses cannot conclusively prove the validity of the framework, but can only add to or detract from the confidence one has in it.

Some of the hypotheses tested were strongly confirmed by the data drawn from Supreme Court cases involving ten federal administrative agencies during the 1947–1956 terms. These were H_1, H_2, H_3A, H_5A, and H_5B. One, H_3B, was not confirmed. The remainder, H_4A, H_4B, H_4C, H_4D, and H_5C turned out acceptable for some justices, but by no means for most.

In retrospect, several comments might be offered about H_3B and the group of less than thoroughly adequate hypotheses. H_3B stated that the voting behavior of the Court in federal agency cases displays statistically significant inconsistencies during the 1947–1956 terms. It grew out of an assumption that changes in personnel would render the behavior of the Court less consistent than that of its individual members. The rejection of H_3B, it now seems to me, raises less serious question about the validity of the conceptual framework than about the cavalier way in which the hypothesis was stated. Changes in personnel may well make the position of the Court less consistent than that of its several members, but there was no particular justification for assuming that the new justices would develop voting patterns in federal agency cases which were dramatically different from those of their predecessors.

H_5C (that no preferences of statistical significance are revealed in the voting behavior of the justices in cases involving evidentiary questions) was confirmed for more justices than not. Yet it does seem that the framework needs refining in such a way as to provide for some differentiation between legal questions of an evidentiary character and those more directly concerned with statutory interpretation.

Finally, the cluster of hypotheses H_4A, H_4B, H_4C, and H_4D reveals more serious inadequacies in the conceptual framework. While differences of voting behavior when questions of policy and value are at issue was an integral part of the framework, it did not provide a satisfactory way of predicting just what the differentiating policies and values would be. Quite obviously the ones tested do not lend impressive support to the assumption that policy and value are in fact important variables for most of the justices in agency cases. On the other hand, policy and value considerations not hypothesized and tested might well turn out to be critical factors in the voting behavior of some members of the Court.

34 VALUES AS VARIABLES IN JUDICIAL DECISION-MAKING

David J. Danelski

I. INTRODUCTION

The scientific study of judicial decision-making began with the pioneer studies of

Reprinted by permission of author and publisher from David J. Danelski, "Values as Variables in Judicial Decision-Making: Notes Toward a Theory," *Vanderbilt Law Review*, 19 (1966), pp. 721–740.

C. Herman Pritchett in the 1940's. For a time his studies stood by themselves; then, in the late 1950's, their methodological thrust was carried forward by a few sociologists and political scientists, principally Glendon Schubert. Schubert's work stimulated a number of studies dealing mostly with methodology and precise description of judicial behavior. The research frontier in this area has now shifted to theoretical considerations—precise definition of concepts, formulation and testing of hypotheses, and development of empirically verifiable theory.

The concept of values is central to the explanation of judicial decision-making. . . . Although students of judicial behavior have used values, or some equivalent concept, in their studies, there has been as yet no thorough, systematic exploration of values with a view toward using it as the central concept in building an empirical theory of judicial decision-making. This paper is a modest step in that direction. It is not, however, a presentation of the empirical theory of values. . . . Rather, it is a presentation of some notes toward such a theory in the hope that they will be useful in the eventual development of a fairly detailed and sound dynamic theory of judicial decision-making.

II. A SCIENTIFIC CONCEPTION OF VALUES

Values are viewed here as constructs anchored in quantifiable human behavior.[1]

This article is a revised version of a paper presented at the 1964 annual meeting of the Midwest Conference of Political Scientists, Madison, Wisconsin. It is a working paper written in connection with a larger study of decision-making in collegial courts that has received financial support from the Walter E. Meyer Foundation and the Social Science Research Council. The writer gratefully acknowledges that support and also the assistance of Carl Hetrick, George Cole, and Thomas Brose in the value-analysis reported in Table 1.

[1]See Bergmann, "Theoretical Psychology," 4 *Annual Rev. of Psychology* 435–58 (1953); MacCorquodale & Meehl, "On a Distinction Between Hypothetical Constructs and Intervening Variables," 55 *Psychological Rev.* 95–107 (1948); Meissner, "Intervening Constructs—Dimensions of a Controversy, 67 *Psychological Rev.* 51–72 (1960). "Few behavioral scientists," wrote Winfred L. Hill, "would regard values (in the empirical, not the transcendental sense) as fundamentally different from such behavioristic constructs as Hull's habit strength or

Such behavior may be either verbal or non-verbal. In ordinary discourse, we move quickly—almost automatically—from the empirical to the abstract in asserting that a man or a judge possesses certain values. This value-labeling process merits close examination so that we might understand more precisely what we mean when we use the term "values." To begin with, value constructs can be anchored only in a certain class of human behavior—behavior that is perceived and labeled as "evaluations" or "value-facts."[2] Evaluations are defined as units of human behavior indicating that an individual regards a thing, condition, property, event, action, or idea as good, useful, or desirable, in itself, or for the achievement of some purpose he is actually pursuing or may eventually pursue. After evaluations are designated, they are labeled in terms of specific value constructs such as freedom, equality, and tradition. Finally, on the basis of certain criteria—such as the number of evaluations in a specific value category or indication of preference for one value over another—an inference is made that the individual whose behavior is under inquiry possesses certain values, some of which are more salient than others. Values and their relative saliency, it is stressed, are always postulated. They are constructs, not empirical entities; their scientific status hinges entirely upon whether they are validly anchored in evaluations and whether the evaluations are validly designated.

For purposes of developing a theory of judicial decision-making, values are viewed as being anchored in individual evaluations. Although we sometimes speak of the values of a group—we say, for example, that freedom is an important value of the Supreme Court—we are actually either making a complex statement about the values of individual Court members, or inferring and postulating

values from group evaluations (court decisions and opinions), which are the end products of a process we are trying to explain. In either case, we are driven back to the evaluations of individuals. This point has important implications not only in terms of theory building, but also in the selection of data for value analysis.

Evaluations always occur within particular situations—"transactions"—which are circumscribed in time and space. Therefore, any inference leading to the postulation of values must be made in the light of the entire transaction in which evaluations occur. Further, the time-space boundaries of transactions limit generalization of the postulated values to future transactions. If, for example, a judge addresses a group in wartime, a number of evaluations indicating patriotism would be expected; and their presence probably would be relevant in analyzing his judicial behavior at that time. But whether patriotism retained the same high place in his value hierarchy after the war is a matter that would bear inquiry. Other situational considerations must also be taken into account in making inferences from evaluations.

III. IDENTIFICATION OF VALUES

The conception of values presented above provides a guide for their identification. Evaluations of individual judges constitute the universe of behavior for observation. Once evaluations are designated, specific values can be inferred and postulated. Personal interviews and written questionnaires are possible research techniques in gathering such value data, as well as content analysis of personal documents, speeches, autobiographies, articles, and books. In this regard, the techniques developed by Ralph K. White ("value-analysis") and Charles E. Osgood ("evaluative assertive analysis") are useful.[3]

Tolman's equivalence beliefs." Meissner, "Learning Theory and the Acquisition of Values," 67 *Psychological Rev.* 318–19 (1960). For a review of the studies concerning values in psychology up to 1955, see Dukes, "Psychological Studies of Values," 52 *Psychological Bull.* 24–50 (1955).

[2]Brecht, *Political Theory* 127 (1959); Dewey, "The Field of Value," in *Value* 64–66 (Lepley ed. 1949).

[3]White, *Value-Analysis* (1953); Osgood, "The Representational Model and Relevant Research Methods," in *Trends in Content Analysis* 23–88 (Pool ed. 1959); Osgood, Saporta & Nunnally, "Evaluative Assertion Analysis," 3 *Litera* 47–102 (1956); White, "Black Boy—A Value Analysis," 32 *J. of Abnormal and Social Psychology* 440–61 (1947). See also Holsti, "Evaluative Assertion Analysis," *Content Analysis* 91–102 (North ed. 1963); Stone, Bales, Namenwirth & Ogilvie, "The General Inquirer," 7 *Behavioral Science* 484–97 (1962).

TABLE 1 Ten Top Values

Brandeis		Butler	
Value	(N = 208) %	Value	(N = 544) %
Individual Freedom	15	Morality	12
Practicality	7	Patriotism	10
Change	7	Tradition	10
Patriotism	7	Individual Freedom	8
Justice	6	Laissez Faire (+)	8
Laissez Faire (−)	5	Religion	5
Social Justice	5	Law	5
Knowledge	5	Safety	4
Unity	4	Justice	4
Equality	3	Order	3

N equals number of evaluation units disclosed by the value-analysis of the speeches mentioned in the text.

For purposes of illustration, White's method of value-analysis will be used to identify the top values of Justices Brandeis and Butler. These Justices have been selected as examples because they were known to have had fairly well-defined, stable value systems.[4] In addition, they were perceived by their colleagues as leading proponents of divergent views on the Supreme Court. The basic hypothesis here is that their disagreement was rooted in a fundamental conflict of values—values to which they had been committed long before they came to the Supreme Court.

The universe selected for value-analysis consisted of two addresses by Louis D. Brandeis given in 1915 and 1916 and two addresses given by Pierce Butler in the same years. The 1915 addresses were on essentially the same subject: Brandeis' address, given on the Fourth of July, was entitled "True Americanism"; Butler's address was entitled "Educating for Citizenship: Duties the Citizen Owes the State."[5] The 1916 addresses were both given to bar associations in the Midwest: Brandeis' address was entitled "The Living Law," and Butler's was entitled "There Is Important Work for Lawyers as Citizens."[6] Brandeis was appointed to the Supreme Court in 1916; Butler was appointed in 1922.

The results of the value-analysis are reported in Table 1. They appear reliable in that they are consistent with independent estimates by contemporaries and scholars. . . .

The value of patriotism in Table 1 merits special comment. In view of the fact that the speeches were given during the World War I period, and that one of them was a Fourth of July speech, patriotism may have been disproportionately emphasized. Therefore, one might suspect that, if a larger universe of evaluations from other time periods were analyzed, the importance of that value would

[4]One of Brandeis' biographers has written: "[Brandeis] . . . knew where he was headed. He did not drift with wind and tide. His actions, his policies, were too sure and definite for sudden impulse or random opportunism." Mason, *Brandeis* 640 (1946). William D. Mitchell, Butler's former law partner, said of him: "He was steadfast, the roots of convictions went deep. They were founded on principles. No one who dealt with him one day was afterwards confounded or nonplussed by any subsequent act or declaration of his on the same subject." *Proceedings of the Bar and Officers of the Supreme Court of the United States in Memory of Pierce Butler* 39 (1940).

[5]Address by Justice Brandeis, Faneuil Hall, Boston, Mass., July 4, 1915, in Brandeis, *Business—A Profession* 364–74 (1925); Address by Justice Butler, Catholic Educ. Ass'n, St. Paul, Minn., 1915, in 12 *Catholic Educ. Ass'n Bull.* 123–32 (1915).

[6]Address by Justice Brandeis, Chicago Bar Ass'n, 1916, in *The Curse of Bigness* 316–26 (Frankel ed. 1934); Address by Justice Butler. Minn. Bar Ass'n, 1916, in *Proceedings, Minn. State Bar Ass'n* 106–19 (1916). A part of Butler's 1916 address appears to have been taken from his 1915 address.

diminish. A cursory check of subsequent public statements by both men indicates that this was the case in regard to Brandeis but not to Butler. Patriotism was a recurrent value in Butler's addresses even after he came to the Supreme Court.

IV. DIMENSIONS OF VALUES

Values are conceptualized as being multidimensional. Although there is no limit to the number of dimensions in which they can be viewed, other than the researcher's verifiable

TABLE 2 Lone Dissents, 1923–1939

Value	Brandeis (*N* = 15) %	Butler (*N* = 10) %
Laissez Faire (+)	0	40
Laissez Faire (−)	40	0

N equals the number of cases in which the named Justice was the lone dissenter.

Table 1 indicates what appears to be a significant conflict between Justices Brandeis and Butler in regard to laissez faire. Proceeding upon the hypothesis that this value conflict was important in Supreme Court decisions while these two Justices were on the bench, an attempt was made to verify the findings by analyzing individual evaluations of each Justice in the judicial process. This was done by examining the lone dissenting votes of Justices Brandeis and Butler during the period they were together on the Court. If the findings in Table 1 regarding their respective valuings of laissez faire are correct, the following could be expected: (1) Brandeis would never dissent in favor of laissez faire (+), (2) Butler would never dissent in favor of laissez faire (−), (3) a substantial number of Brandeis' lone dissents would indicate the value of laissez faire (−), and (4) the precise opposite would be true of Butler. That is what Table 2 shows.[7]

[7]Lone dissenting votes were designated laissez-faire (−) evaluations, and were cast in the following cases: *Donham* v. *West-Nelson Mfg. Co.*, 273 U.S. 657 (1927); *Pub. Util. Comm'n* v. *Attleboro Steam & Elec. Co.*, 273 U.S. 83 (1927); *Murphy* v. *Sardell*, 269 U.S. 530 (1925); *Alpha Portland Cement Co.*, v. *Massachusetts*, 268 U.S. 203 (1925); *Shafer* v. *Farmers Grain Co.*, 268 U.S. 189 (1925); *Ozark Pipe Line Corp.* v. *Monier*, 266 U.S. 555 (1925). Lone dissenting votes, designated laissez-faire (+) evaluations, were cast in the following cases: *United States* v. *American Sheet & Tin Plate Co.*, 301 U.S. 402 (1937); *Burnett* v. *Brooks*, 288 U.S. 378 (1933); *Stephenson* v. *Binford*, 287 U.S. 251 (1932); *Samuels* v. *McCurdy*, 267 U.S. 188 (1925).

insights, only three dimensions—intensity, congruency, and cognitive completeness—are postulated here for purposes of illustration. . . .

The analyses reported in Tables 1 and 2 were based, in large part, upon assumptions about the intensity of Justices Brandeis' and Butler's values. The assumption in the value-analysis was that intensely held values are articulated in speech more frequently than values not intensely held. The assumption in the lone-dissent analysis was that generally a justice does not dissent by himself unless he is expressing some intensely held value.

Although intensity appears to be the most significant value dimension, other dimensions could assume an importance rivaling that of intensity. One such dimension appears to be congruency, which refers to the harmony between a specific value and other values held by a judge. If a specific value is reinforced by a number of other values and is not in conflict with any other value, then it is said to possess high congruency. Butler's value of laissez faire (+), for instance, possessed higher congruency than his value of individual freedom, because in the former there was only reinforcement and no conflict with other top values, whereas in certain cases the latter appears to have been in conflict with the value of patriotism. Those situations involved the freedom of speech or conscience of Communists, members of the Industrial Workers of the World (I.W.W.), and aliens who refused to swear unqualified allegiance to the United States. In every such divided case before the Supreme Court from 1923 to 1939, Butler's vote was inconsistent with his value of individual freedom but consistent with his value of patriotism. This did not mean, however, that he did not highly value freedom; in criminal cases involving issues of due process, no Justice, not even Brandeis, equalled Butler's libertarian record. This is not surprising when one remembers that Butler was the only conservative Justice to dissent in the wiretapping case of *Olmstead* v. *United States*[8] and the only Justice to dissent in the double-jeopardy case of *Palko* v. *Connecticut*.[9]

Laissez faire (−) and laissez faire (+) were highly congruent values for Justices Brandeis and Butler, respectively. As Figure 1 shows, both values were highly reinforced and completely absent of conflict. Hence, viewing laissez faire (−) and laissez faire (+) on two continua, each Justice again is positioned well on the plus side of his continuum.

makes for cognitive completeness of a value frequently occurs in the judicial process itself. Thus, as an increasing number of due process cases are argued before the latter judge and decided by him, his value of due process is apt to become more cognitively' complete. This dimension may provide the basis for explaining why first-term behavior of Supreme Court Justices does not always square with their subsequent judicial behavior.

The cognitive completeness of Justices Brandeis' and Butler's respective values of laissez faire (−) and laissez faire (+) was high. Brandeis had argued the laissez-faire (−) position before the Supreme Court in *Muller* v. *Oregon*[10] in 1908, and Butler argued what amounted to a laissez-faire (+) position in the *Minnesota Rate Cases*[11] before the same tribunal in 1912. Their value positions on laissez faire were so well known before they came to the Supreme Court that their appointments were opposed in part because of them. Moreover, during their tenure on the Court, laissez faire was the dominant issue. From 1923 to 1939, Justices Butler and

FIGURE 1 Illustrations of High Congruency

	Brandeis			*Butler*	
	Change			Tradition	
	↓			↓	
	Laissez Faire (−)			Laissez Faire (+)	
	↗　　↖			↗　　↖	
Equality		Social Justice	Law		Individual Freedom

→ = reinforcement

The dimension of cognitive completeness refers to a judge's readiness to perceive a set of phenomena in terms of a specific value—this readiness being based upon his breadth and depth of experience concerning that value. If, for example, a judge, in his years at the bar, had defended a substantial number of persons accused of crime, his value of due process is apt to be more cognitively complete at the time he ascends the bench than that of a judge who had spent his legal career in corporate practice. The experience that

Brandeis often confronted each other over the conference table in arguments over laissez faire cases. Hence, each of them was well on the plus side of his cognitive-completeness continuum for laissez-faire.

Intensity, congruity, and cognitive completeness are dimensions of "value spaces" corresponding to postulated values. All judges holding a specific value, such as laissez faire (+), have their positions located somewhere in the laissez-faire (+) value space. . . .

[8]277 U.S. 438 (1928).
[9]302 U.S. 319 (1937).

[10]208 U.S. 412 (1908).
[11]230 U.S. 352 (1912).

V. VALUE VERIFICATION
IN THE DECISIONAL PROCESS

The conception of values of individual judges being located in space is similar to Coombs' conception of individuals' ideal points in his theory of data which Schubert has applied in his factor analytic studies of the Supreme Court. According to Coombs, ideal points can be located in single-stimulus data unidimensionally by scalogram analysis and multidimensionally by factor analysis. Situations yielding single-stimulus data are those in which a number of individuals are confronted with the same stimuli eliciting either a positive or negative response. The decision-making process in collegial courts yields this kind of data. Hence, factor analysis and cumulative scaling appear to be useful techniques for verifying the presence of postulated values.

factor analysis and cumulative scaling are useful techniques for value verification, the divided decisions in the 1935 and 1936 terms appear to provide the data for proving it.

Thus the votes of each Justice in the fifty-seven divided cases decided during those two terms were correlated with the votes of every other Justice,[14] and the correlation coefficients obtained were arranged in a nine-by-nine matrix. McQuitty's elementary factor analysis was then used to determine the number of types in the Court and the most representative Justice of each type.[15] This was done because of some comments made by Mr. Chief Justice Charles Evans Hughes in his "Biographical Notes" indicating that he perceived Justices Brandeis and Butler to be the leading proponents of divergent points of view in the Court during that period. It was assumed that these divergent views concerned the value of laissez faire. The first step in the

FIGURE 2   Judicial Types, 1935–1936 Terms

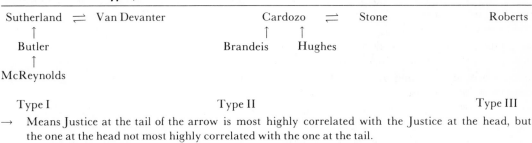

Sutherland $\rightleftharpoons$ Van Devanter	Cardozo $\rightleftharpoons$ Stone	Roberts
↑	↑ ↑	
Butler	Brandeis Hughes	
↑		
McReynolds		
Type I	Type II	Type III

→   Means Justice at the tail of the arrow is most highly correlated with the Justice at the head, but the one at the head not most highly correlated with the one at the tail.

$\rightleftharpoons$ Means reciprocal pairs of Justices most highly correlated with each other.

If the value of laissez faire was ever salient in the Supreme Court, it was during the 1935 and 1936 terms. The proponents of laissez faire had fought a determined rear-guard action during the 1935 Term, chalking up such victories as *Morehead* v. *New York ex rel Tipaldo*,[12] the New York minimum-wage case. Then in the 1936 Term, President Roosevelt announced his "court-packing plan," and the so-called "switch in time" occurred: Justice Roberts defected from the conservative majority in *Morehead* and voted with the liberals to sustain the Washington minimum-wage law in *West Coast Hotel Co.* v. *Parrish.*[13] If

McQuitty analysis revealed the types shown in Figure 2.

The second step of the analysis revealed that Mr. Justice Butler was slightly more representative of Type I than Mr. Justice Sutherland. Mr. Justice Cardozo was clearly

[12]298 U.S. 587 (1936).
[13]300 U.S. 379 (1937).

[14]A case was defined as a perceived decisional unit; that is, if two or more causes were heard together, decided, and reported as a single decision, they were treated as one. In some research situations there are advantages to defining a case as each cause with a separate docket number. This is what Schubert has done.
[15]McQuitty, "Elementary Factor Analysis," 9 *Psychological Reports* 71–84 (1961). For an example of the use of McQuitty's method in an earlier stage of development, see Ulmer, "The Analysis of Behavior Patterns on the United States Supreme Court," 22 *J. of Politics* 629–53 (1960).

TABLE 3 Elementary Factor Loadings, 1935–1936 Terms

Justices	Factors		
	I	II	III
McReynolds	.72	− .78	− .24
Butler	1.00	− .68	− .09
Sutherland	.75	− .56	− .02
Van Devanter	.69	− .46	− .21
Roberts	− .09	− .20	1.00
Hughes	− .28	.42	− .13
Brandeis	− .63	.85	− .06
Stone	− .65	.92	− .22
Cardozo	− .68	1.00	− .20

The numerical figures indicate the correlations of each Justice with the three Justices who are the most representative of their type.

the most representative of Type II. Type III, of course, required no further analysis. Using Justices Butler, Cardozo, and Roberts as reference factors, the factor loadings indicated in Table 3 were obtained. Considering the high correlation of Justice Brandeis with Type II, Chief Justice Hughes' perception of the leading proponents of divergent points of view in the Court was fairly accurate.

If laissez faire was the dominant issue before the Supreme Court during the 1935 and 1936 terms, an examination of Table 3 would lead to an inference that Factors I and II were related to it. In an attempt to verify this, all of the cases in the universe under consideration were examined to determine whether they could be perceived in terms of laissez faire. The operational definition of a laissez-faire case was any case that could have been

perceived as involving governmental activity in economic matters. The definition was broadly applied; tax cases, for example, were viewed as a part of the laissez-faire universe. A vote against government was construed as a laissez-faire (+) response; a vote for government was construed as a laissez-faire (−) response. To minimize bias, all doubtful cases were categorized as laissez-faire cases. They formed the cumulative scale shown in Figure 3, which seems to verify the presence of the values of laissez faire (+) and laissez faire (−).

In a further effort to verify the presence of the laissez-faire values, the entire universe from which the cases in Figure 3 were drawn was factor analyzed by means of the principal-factor method. It was expected that a high loading would be obtained on the first

TABLE 4 Principal-Factor Loadings, 1935–1936 Terms

Justices	Factors					
	I	II	III	I*	II*	III*
McReynolds	.86	.17	.30	.75	.32	.33
Butler	.86	.20	− .12	.48	.52	.07
Sutherland	.78	.29	− .43	.30	.86	− .03
Van Devanter	.73	.47	− .31	.27	.91	.17
Roberts	.003	− .82	− .55	.09	− .09	.98
Hughes	− .45	.36	− .35	− .22	− .09	.06
Brandeis	− .85	.20	− .17	− .88	− .22	− .01
Stone	− .87	.32	− .03	− .88	− .27	.19
Cardozo	− .91	.31	− .09	− .90	− .25	.15

*Kaiser's Varimax Rotation.

FIGURE 3   Laissez Faire Scale, 1935–1936 Terms

Case Vol./Page	Justices										Pro-Con
	McR	Bu	Su	VD	Ro	Hu	Br	St	Ca		
300/297			x								1–8
301/532					x						1–8
301/540					x						1–8
297/288	x										1–8
300/216	x										1–8
301/337	x										1–8
301/402	—	x									1–8
296/268	x	x									2–7
300/308	x	x									2–7
300/577	x	x									2–7
301/619	x	x									2–7
297/88	—	x	x		x						3–6
301/412	x	x	x	*			*				3–4
(12 cases)[a]	x	x	x	x							4–5
(6 cases)[b]	x	x	x	x	x						5–4
301/459	x	x	x	x	—	x					5–4
(10 cases)[c]	x	x	x	x	x	x					6–3
298/393	x	x	x	x	x	x		*			6–2
299/32	x	x	x	x	x	x		*			6–2
299/280	x	x	x	x	x	x		*			6–2
298/441	x	x	x	x	x	x	x				7–2
300/352	x	x	x	x	—	x	—	x	x		7–2
301/655	x	x	x	x	x	x	x	—	—		7–2
Totals	43–5	42–6	38–10	35–12	24–24	16–32	2–46	1–43	1–47	202–225	203–224 427
Scale positions	45	42	37	35½	23	17	3	2	2		
Scale scores	.88	.75	.54	.48	−.04	−.29	−.88	−.92	−.92		

$$R = 1 - \frac{7}{364} = .980 \qquad S = 1 - \frac{11}{75} = .853$$

R = coefficient of reproducibility   S = coefficient of scalability

[a]*4–5 cases:* 296/85, 297/251, 300/324, 300/608, 300/379, 301/1, 301/49, 301/58, 301/103, 301/468, 301/495, 301/548.

[b]*5–4 cases:* 296/39, 296/48, 298/238, 298/513, 298/587, 300/154.

[c]*6–3 cases:* 296/102, 296/299, 296/287, 296/113, 296/404, 297/1, 297/135, 297/266, 298/1, 298/492.

x   = vote against government.

—   = vote for government inconsistent with scale pattern.

blank = vote for government consistent with scale pattern.

*   = nonparticipation.

factor and that each Justice would be correlated with that factor in the same order as on the laissez-faire scale. That factor, of course, would be identified as the laissez-faire value. The results of the factor analysis are indicated in Table 4. Factor I appears to be the expected value of laissez-faire. Varimax rotation provided a solution that is consistent with the initial interpretation.

A comparison of Factor I in Table 3, Factor I in Table 4, and the scale scores in Figure 3 suggests that they are measures of the same thing—namely, laissez faire (+) and laissez faire (−). Those values, it will be recalled, were conceptualized as being located in specific value spaces. The spaces were constructed in terms of the dimensions—intensity, congruency, and cognitive completeness. If these are the most significant dimensions of the laissez-faire values, Factor I in Table 4 could be viewed as a composite of them and positioned in . . . value-space. . . . Butler's position would be in the laissez-faire (+) space .86 from zero on all dimensions. . . . Similarly Brandeis' position would be the laissez-faire (−) space .85 from zero on all dimensions. . . .

VI. TOWARD A THEORY OF JUDICIAL DECISION-MAKING

Implicit in the discussion of values in this paper is a stimulus-response model of judicial decision-making. Responses are decisions of courts defined in terms of judges' behavior at the end of the decisional process. Stimuli are cases before courts for decision, but precisely what constitutes a "case" raises some difficult problems. Values and all the other postulated variables that connect stimuli and responses in some meaningful way are, of course, only theoretical constructs.

In a strict sense, a case before a collegial court is not a stimulus, but rather a set of stimuli—briefs read by judges, arguments of counsel, conference discussions, comments of law clerks, and so forth. These sets of stimuli are not identical for all judges, partly because each judge perceives stimuli uniquely in terms of his own values, experiences, and needs. Lawyers who argue before collegial

courts know this intuitively. Before ascending the bench, Robert H. Jackson, reflecting on his arguments before the Supreme Court, said of Justice Butler:

He was relentless in bringing the lawyer face to face with the issues as he saw them. I think I never knew a man who could more quickly orient a statement of facts with his own philosophy. When the facts were stated, the argument was about over with him—he could relate the case to his conceptions of legal principles without the aid of counsel.[16]

If the sets of stimuli we call cases are considerably different for each judge, it would be fruitless to use techniques such as factor analysis or cumulative scaling in explaining collegial decision-making, for such techniques assume that the sets of stimuli are the same for all the judges. Discussing this problem, Coombs has written: "An anchor point is needed, and the same stimulus being presented to different individuals provides such an anchor. If a stimulus differs in a significant way from one individual to the next, absolutely nothing can be done with just these observations. . . ." Abandoning the hypothesis that individuals differ in their responses "because they perceive the stimuli differently," Coombs concludes, "we concede that each stimulus is more or less the same thing for everyone, not just in its physical dimensions but in whatever its subjective characteristics might be."[17]

In developing a theory of judicial decision-making, the concession to which Coombs refers cannot be made because we have empirical evidence that judges do, upon occasion, perceive the same cases differently. The problem here is how to specify judges' perceptions. A first step in that direction is intensive study of the judges themselves, using data outside of the decisional process. Value analysis is important in this regard. If judges' values are located in value spaces, inferences can be made about how they perceive value phenomena; then there is some basis for

[16]Jackson, *In Memory of Mr. Justice Butler*, 310 U.S. xiv (1939).
[17]Coombs, *A Theory of Data* (1964), at 8.

FIGURE 4   A Decision-Making Model for Collegial Courts

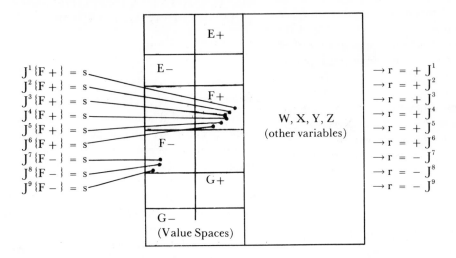

determining whether perceptions overlap. Thus, the exploration of values appears to be a fruitful first step in the development of a theory of judicial decision-making.

In the example discussed in this paper—laissez faire in the 1935 and 1936 terms—it appears that there was sufficient perceptual overlap so that factor analysis and cumulative scaling were useful techniques in verifying the presence of the values under inquiry. It must be stressed, however, that the value and the period were chosen for illustrative purposes because there was considerable independent evidence of perceptual overlap in regard to laissez faire. In the study of other values in other periods, the perceptual problem must be solved if techniques like factor analysis and cumulative scaling are to be used fruitfully.

Although values are important variables in the decision-making process, other variables must be taken into account to explain the process. Anyone who has done extensive research on the manuscripts of Supreme Court Justices is aware of the great amount of evidence in certain historical periods indicating that a Justice's value position on Case A was (−) when in fact his recorded position in the official reports is (+). Obviously his voting behavior was connected with variables other than his values.

A rough outline of a model of judicial decision-making is shown in Figure 4. The sets of stimuli, such as {F+}, are viewed as points located in the same space with values. If a point representing a set of stimuli does not go beyond a judge's value position (that is, it is not more plus than the judge's position if his value is in a plus space), then he acquires a plus value score; otherwise, he acquires a minus value score. Analysis then shifts to the remaining variables in the model.[18] If a judge receives a plus value score and the remaining variables are also plus or zero, then his response—that is, his vote—will be plus.

VII.   CONCLUSION

This paper is a modest step in the direction of developing a fairly detailed, dynamic, empirical theory of judicial decision-making in which the concept of values is central. The identification of values poses no insurmountable problems. Although the data used here to illustrate value identification were public addresses of judges, other and perhaps better sources of value data are readily accessible. In studying the current judiciary, the lone dissenting opinion is an obvious candidate for content analysis. Although White's method of value-analysis was sufficient to identify

---

[18]Among the remaining variables are role, personality, and leadership. . . .

the top values of Justices Brandeis and Butler, other more rigorous techniques, such as Osgood's, may prove more suitable in other research situations.

The multidimensionality of values requires further exploration. The dimensions postulated—intensity, congruency, and cognitive completeness—were considered only for illustrative purposes. They may not be the most important dimensions of value. Nevertheless, if other dimensions are shown to be more important, they can be used to construct value spaces in which values can be located. The problem of measuring the dimensions of values is important, and in light of the advances in psychometric techniques in recent years, it appears to be capable of satisfactory solution.

This paper has demonstrated the utility of factor analysis and cumulative scaling in the study of judicial behavior. In the past these techniques have been used, for the most part, to describe judicial behavior precisely. Here they were used for purposes of verification of hypotheses. They have limitations as research techniques, but only when we have developed an adequate theory of judicial decision-making will we know their precise limits.

The primary purpose in developing a theory of judicial decision-making is not the prediction of judicial decisions before they occur. Rather it is to understand scientifically the complex phenomena we call the judicial process. Some doubt that this is possible, and they may be correct. However, the scientific student of judicial behavior assumes, with Louis L. Thurstone, "that an unlimited number of phenomena can be comprehended in terms of a limited number of concepts or ideal constructs."[19] This paper has explored the utility of one of those constructs.

[19]Thurstone, *Multiple-Factor Analysis* 51 (1947).

35 JUDICIAL ATTITUDES AND VOTING BEHAVIOR

Glendon Schubert

I. LEGAL REALISM: FROM ART TO SCIENCE

Lawyers, political scientists, and other social scientists share an interest in seeking to understand how complex social relationships and patterns of human interaction can be studied so as to increase our stockpile of social knowledge about law and the policy-making processes through which it is formulated. They are not agreed, however, as to how this goal best may be realized.

Recollection of the major emphases of legal realism may be instructive in providing perspective for dispassionate appraisal of contemporary proposals on behalf of a science of judicial behavior. For Holmes, realism was a temper, the mood of pragmatism; while for Llewellyn, realism was only a method, and the "method" was to get at the real facts and issues that underlie legal controversies and the procedures employed to resolve them. For Cardozo, realism meant to understand the values of the judge, since the judge's personality was the only funnel through which policy norms could enter into judicial decisions. Frank, who was more influenced by Freudian psychology, shifted the focus to the sets of unique life experiences of judges which shaped their individual value-patterns; Felix Cohen offered the complementary view that the decisions of individual judges, whatever might be the forces that shaped their individual value-patterns, acquired social significance only when evaluated in the context of complex antecedent and consequent processes involving the interaction of many humans

Reprinted from Glendon Schubert, "Judicial Attitudes and Voting Behavior: The 1961 Term of the United States Supreme Court," *Law and Contemporary Problems*, 28 (1963), pp. 100–142. Reprinted with permission from the symposium *Jurimetrics* appearing in *Law and Contemporary Problems* (Vol. 28, No. 1, Winter 1963) published by the Duke University School of Law, Durham, North Carolina. Copyright © 1963, by Duke University.

besides the judge. There were, of course, other well-known legal realists; but our present sample exemplifies the major emphases which realism brought to the study of American law:

What are the real events that underlie the policy choices urged upon judges?

How does the interaction of other persons limit the range of judicial choice?

What do judges believe, and why?

What are the practical consequences entailed by judicial preference of one policy alternative over another?

One thing that all of these questions have in common is that they direct attention away from the manifest content of judicial opinions, and away from a concern for logical consistency among sets of legal norms. A knowledge of what judges do and say is important, but it is by no means enough; a realistic understanding of judicial decision-making demands that the acts of judges be examined like any other forms of social behavior. The long-standing ties that bind the study of law to the philosophical and historical traditions remain; but they are being augmented by new bridges across interdisciplinary chasms, and more recent links have been forged with sociology, economics, psychology, political science, social psychology, and even with anthropology. Each of these sister disciplines has made some—though differential—progress along the long road that connects art with science. Despite the verbalisms about "legal science," one need only [examine] . . . any of a hundred . . . law journals, in order to perceive the extent to which legal study remains the handmaiden to metaphors that now belong to the ages. Even better, contrast the average legal journal with any of the dozen journals published by the American Psychological Association: it is not the difference in *content;* it is the difference in *ethos* that is significant.

The primary thrust of legal realism was in the direction of reorienting legal study in the spirit of the modern temper, and to redefine its role as that of an applied social science. Just as the profession of medicine had come, earlier in this century, to assume the status of an applied science, dependent upon the theoretical and empirical research done by physicists, chemists, biologists, biochemists, biophysicists, and so on, so has medical science increasingly come to depend also upon the work of social scientists such as psychologists, sociologists, economists, and even political scientists. The legal science of the future doubtless will depend much less than medical science upon basic research in the natural sciences, and much more upon the other social sciences; but its concern increasingly will be not with words in books but rather with the behavior of people. We are all familiar with the harbingers of change; our differences lie in the degree of optimism and pessimism with which we anticipate the impact of the revolution in the behavioral sciences upon the study and practice of law.

II. PREDICTION IN LAW AND JUDICIAL BEHAVIOR

A. Why Is Prediction Important? "The prophecies of what the courts will do in fact and nothing more pretentious," said Holmes, "are what I mean by law." This iconoclasm of three generations ago now has achieved the status of orthodoxy. The model of the laboratory and its associated experimental method has pervaded our cultural understanding; we now are prepared to assume that the power of any science lies in its capacity to make successful predictions concerning the behavior of the particles that constitute its data.

When we focus our attention upon the behavior of judges, the ultimate test of our theory and methods lies in our ability correctly to predict judicial decisions. We should remember, however, that recourse to experimental method in application to other kinds of data almost always results in more unsuccessful than successful predictions, and that this is true in the relatively mature and relatively simple natural sciences; that the development of a systematic, cumulative, communicable store of social knowledge about how and why judges make decisions is strictly a function of the relative quantity and quality of scarce resources that are allocated to its acquisition, and the proportion of such resources allocated to the study of judicial behavior has been and remains very small; and that our present ability to predict the outcomes of other social decision-making processes (*i.e.*, those by legislators, presidents, electorates, business executives, and so on) certainly is no greater than in the case of judges. The relevant questions to ask at this time about the prediction of judicial decisions, therefore, are:

What kind of predictions, about what aspects of decision-making, and within what margins of error, are reasonable to expect of a science which remains in a very primitive stage of development?

To what extent is the non-scientist in a position to make more valid and more reliable predictions than the behavioralist, and to do this with a more parsimonious expenditure of time and other resources?

Obviously, if expectations are unreasonable, behavioralists are foredoomed to fail to satisfy the criteria that are posited for the evaluation of their accomplishments. One seemingly reasonable criterion, which frequently has been suggested in recent years, is whether the judicial behavioralist, with all of his (unnecessarily) complicated (and generally irrelevant) paraphernalia, can do any better than the average, experienced practitioner who is wise in the ways of courts and judges. So stated, the contest is readily recognizable as a recurrent theme in the sociology of knowledge: it is David versus Goliath; the pink-cheeked country lad against the city slicker; it is reason and common sense in opposition to sophism and scholasticism in their contemporary disguise.

B. Professor Rodell versus *Baker* v. *Carr*: *A tour de force majeure?* As a concrete example of prediction by the expert in law who has no need for scientific impedimenta, we might take Fred Rodell's recent and already well-known forecast of the outcome in *Baker* v. *Carr*.[1] Some eleven days before the

event, Professor Rodell correctly predicted that the United States Supreme Court would order the requested redistricting by a vote of five to four. He also stated that the majority would include Justices Black and Douglas, who would adhere to their dissents in *Colegrove* v. *Green*;[2] Chief Justice Warren and Justice Brennan, who would "agree less militantly with Black" and "in that order of enthusiasm"; and Justice Stewart, who would "cast the deciding vote, in the sense that his vote [would] be the least firmly convinced and committed" but "for reasons not basically legal but rather personal and both extra-Court and intra-Court political."[3] Professor Rodell thought that the dissenters would include Justice Frankfurter, who would adhere to his own opinion announcing the judgment of the Court in *Colegrove;* Justice Harlan, who would "join his mentor, Frankfurter, as a matter of course"; and Justices Clark and Whittaker, who would "silently side with Frankfurter." *Colegrove* would be "distinguished or, more probably, overruled"; and the opinion of the Court in *Baker* v. *Carr* would probably be written by Stewart, the most marginal justice in the majority, or possibly by Brennan, the next most marginal justice.

In fact, the decision in *Baker* v. *Carr* was 6–2 rather than 5–4. Mr. Justice Whittaker, who was on the verge of retiring three days later, did not participate; and Mr. Justice Clark concurred in the majority, with an independent expression of his personal view of the case. *Colegrove* was distinguished—indeed, practically embraced—in the opinion that Justice Brennan wrote for the Court; and Justice Stewart's concurrence made it quite clear that he was, indeed, the marginal member of the majority, which also included Black, Douglas, and Warren; and Frankfurter and Harlan wrote reinforcing dissenting opinions. Thus, Professor Rodell was correct in both his general and his specific predictions concerning the case, with the minor exceptions of Clark's vote in support of the majority and of Whittaker's non-participation; and even in this regard, he had ventured the

---

[1] 369 U.S. 186 (1962). Rodell, "For Every Justice, Judicial Deference Is a Sometime Thing," 50 *Geo. L.J.* 700 (1962); the general and specific predictions are stated, *id.* at 707–08.

[2] 328 U.S. 549 (1946).
[3] Rodell, *supra* note 1, at 708.

contingent hedge that he would " not be too astounded to see either Clark or Whittaker join the majority rather than bolster a lost cause," although this too was qualified by the assertion that he would stick to his prediction of a "five-four vote for redistricting." All in all, it seems fair to conclude prima facie that this constitutes an impressive, indeed, a spectacular, example of the skill of the legal expert to anticipate the probable outcome of a specific judicial decision.

One obvious question to ask about Professor Rodell's performance is: how did he manage to do it? In the introductory pages of his article, he informs his readers that it is and has been for many years his assumption that the votes of Supreme Court justices cannot adequately be explained in terms of such theoretical abstractions as judicial beliefs in activism or restraint, or in federalism as a constitutional principle. Much more basic are "a vast complex of personal factors —temperament, background, education, economic status, pre-Court career—of whose influence on his thinking even the most sophisticated of Justices can never be wholly aware." His own approach, therefore, has been to examine "the Justices individually as whole human beings"; and as examples of this approach in action, Professor Rodell next provided brief sketches of Black and Frankfurter, based upon his own subjective evaluation of everything that he then knew about both men. (These sketches make it clear that Rodell empathizes more with Black than with Frankfurter.) In reliance upon undisclosed but presumable similar evaluations of the remaining justices, Rodell then stated his predictions.

Up to this point, there would be little in the *substance* of Rodell's remarks to distinguish him from the judicial behavioralists with whom he appears to find himself in fundamental disagreement. They too have debunked legal principles as factors controlling decisions; it is they, rather than he, who have attempted to undertake systematic investigations of the effect of background characteristics upon decisions. They also affirm the experimental method and the testing of hypotheses by making explicit predictions. The

judicial behavioralists agree that Black is much more liberal than Frankfurter; and some of them (just like Rodell) have suggested that Frankfurter's ostentatious preference for deference is a mask for his own conservative predilections. Indeed, on the basis of my own C (civil liberties) Scale for the 1960 Term of the Court, which also was published in the same month as and prior to the decision in *Baker* v. *Carr, anyone*—not just a legal expert— ought to have been in a position to make precisely the same specific predictions about individual voting as did Professor Rodell— and anyone who had done so would have erred, just as Rodell erred, in regard to Clark. (For reasons that will be explained below, the outcome of *Baker* v. *Carr*—Rodell's general prediction—could not be forecast on the exclusive basis of the C Scale for the 1960 Term.) Therefore, not only would judicial behavioralists agree with the substance of most of Rodell's remarks; they would also have made precisely the same mistake in attempting to predict individual voting in *Baker*.

What, then, is there left to disagree about? Methodology and goals.

C. What Kind of Prediction Is Most Important? Any judicial behavioralist known to me would consider it a waste of professional time to restate the theme of Charles Grove Haines' classic article, which was published in the *Illinois Law Review* over forty years ago.[4] The article is well known, both among law students and undergraduate majors in political science; and no one (including Rodell) has succeeded in restating the general argument, that the personal values of judges are of fundamental importance in their decision-making, in a more articulate or a more thoughtful manner than did Haines. Yet, if one eschews any method more systematic than the necessarily unique, subjective evaluations that are a function of one's total competence, what more is there to be said when one tries to communicate to others the process by which one arrives at his judgments —and makes his predictions? Such a process

---

[4]Haines, "General Observations on the Effects of Personal, Political, and Economic Influences in the Decisions of Judges," 17 *Ill. L. Rev.* 96 (1922).

also is the result of a "vast complex of personal factors—temperament, background, education, economic status, pre-[academic] career—of whose influence on his thinking even the most sophisticated of [Professors] can never be wholly aware."

Rodell concluded his article with the opinion that,

. . . the infinite variety of quirks and causes that may determine human choice on any matter where man is at the mercy of his own mind are fortunately far beyond the predictive capacity of even the most intricately attuned and adjusted calculating machine . . . [and] he who would analyze, predict, or understand the Supreme Court's constitutional decisions will fare considerably better if he concentrates on that same infinite variety of human factors which make precise prediction impossible. . . .

It is not difficult, however, to demonstrate the contrary of this proposition:

(1) Recent research in the social psychology of judicial attitudes indicates that, far from being an infinite set, the number of basic attitudinal dimensions that are relevant to the decision-making of the United States Supreme Court is very small.

(2) Neither calculating machines nor the electronic digital computers (which are, apparently, the intended referent) have any predictive capacity at all; all that computers can do is to perform very simple arithmetic operations. Predictions are made by human beings who design research and write programs which direct computers in their mundane tasks. The fundamental question is this: when the task is to make systematic measurement of the interrelationships among a large number of variables in relation to an extensive set of empirical observations, which instrument is likely to carry out the task with maximal reliability and a minimal number of mistakes? The subconscious mind of some individual scholar? Or the computer?

(3) Neither Rodell nor a computer is capable of concentrating upon an "infinite variety" of factors, human or otherwise.

It is difficult enough to concentrate upon even a relatively small finite number of variables; and one difference between humans and computers is that the former do *not* concentrate upon, for example, *all* of the cells of even a small (say, 10 × 10) matrix, either uniformly, consistently, or simultaneously, while the computer *can* be made to do this. The great virtue, and —from this special point of view—the great weakness of the human mind is that it abstracts from the variable matrix certain relationships for examination; only by thus focusing attention is concentration possible.

(4) For most purposes that I can think of, humans are much to be preferred to computers; but for a few purposes, including some which relate to the processing of data about judicial decision-making, it seems foolish to waste such a scarce human resource as scholarly time and energies by expending them upon tasks that machines can perform better. To argue, therefore, that the legal expert can predict judicial decisions better than a computer is spurious, because such argument distracts attention from the real issue. In any rational allocation of resources, legal experts and computers would be doing different things—for the very good reason, as I have tried to explain, that legal experts are much smarter and, in terms of humanist (though not in terms of economic) criteria, much more valuable than computers.

For Rodell to have predicted correctly many aspects of the decision in the most important case to reach the Supreme Court in almost a decade is of mild interest, from a scientific point of view, but what is the social significance of the event? No doubt, other professors have anticipated the Supreme Court and other courts on previous occasions; and no doubt, successful practicing attorneys develop some skill in making similar predictions, at least in their own cases. What, however, if we were to have assembled a hundred professors of constitutional law, and induced them to make individual predictions about the *Baker* case, utilizing the same method (or, rather, lack thereof) as Rodell: how many would have agreed with him? How many of them would agree now, upon the significance of the decision and its probable effect upon the Court's decision-making in related cases during the current term?

Or, in the alternative, let us suppose that we give our legal expert (I don't care which one) a hundred cases, selected at random from among those set down for oral argument during the term. Although, for technical reasons . . . it would be a difficult experiment to perform empirically, let us assume that the legal expert has access to the records before the Court; and let us also assume that he has been present to hear oral argument for each case in his sample. He makes his prediction for each case immediately after oral argument, both as to outcome and in terms of the more specific details (such as Rodell included in his prediction). What will be his percentage of error?

I think it will be conceded that if perfect prediction were demonstrated to obtain, either in the absolute reliability of the judgments of the one hundred constitutional law professors, or in the absolute validity of the one hundred predictions of our legal expert, we should then have to resort to a theory of chance variation in order to explain the results; we should not expect perfection in either instance, nor should we be likely to encounter it empirically. It seems not unreasonable to make equivalent demands of predictions by judicial behavioralists: that they be correct within some previously stipulated margin of error adequate to assure that the results obtained would be extremely unlikely to have occurred merely as the result of chance variation. But even if the margin of error of the hundred legal experts with the single case, or the single legal expert with the hundred cases, were rather small—say, less than .05—neither performance would have social significance unless the requisite skills could be communicated to other persons. Perhaps they could; but if they could,

we should then still have to talk about the methods of pedagogy which resulted in the inculcation of such a high attainment of professional skill.

For the judicial behavioralist, the question of methodology is not sublimated to the intuitional level; on the contrary, it is a critical consideration in any research design. (This is true, of course, of all scientific research.) Moreover, prediction is not an end in itself; it is, rather, a necessary aspect of the verification of theory; and the goal of scientific inquiry in judicial behavior is theoretical knowledge, not merely the ability to forecast which way some particular case will be decided. Usually, the outcome of any individual case is as irrelevant to the concerns of the investigator as it is to the Court itself. Significance lies not in the individual decision, either of a single justice or of the Court, but rather is found in the uniformities that can be perceived best in the aggregate data for the decisions of several justices in many cases over a substantial period of time.

What *is* important to be able to predict, therefore, is what the Supreme Court (or any other judge or group of judges) is likely to decide in regard to a given issue, or set of issues, through time. The importance of the Supreme Court's policy-making function does not usually flow from the consequences to the immediate parties in a particular case; one evaluates such importance by making (explicitly or implicitly; loosely or precisely) probability statements about the likelihood of other parties inducing equivalent response from the Court if the same issue (or, to speak more exactly, another facet of the same issue) were to be raised again. It is by establishing trends of this sort that the Court makes policy; and these are the uniformities about which judicial behavioralists make predictions, because these are the more meaningful and important kind of predictions to make. The remainder of this paper discusses the attitudinal continuities manifest in both the individual and the group voting behavior of the justices of the Supreme Court during the most recently completed term; that discussion will then provide the basis for the set of predictions about the current (October, 1962) term, with which the paper concludes.

III. A PSYCHOLOGICAL ANALYSIS OF THE 1961 TERM

A. A Psychometric Model of the Supreme Court. Since both a general statement of the theory and a technical description of the method have been published in some detail elsewhere,[5] the present discussion will be limited to a simplified exposition of those aspects of the model that must be understood if the reader is to follow the ensuing analysis of empirical data. Let us assume that each justice entertains relatively well-structured attitudes toward the recurrent major issues of public policy that confront the Court for decision. If it were possible to identify the common issues, and the relevant attitudinal dimensions that are functions of these issues, then it might be possible to speak in some systematic way about the set of attitudinal dimensions that is most important for a particular group of justices—even though there were considerable variation in the direction and intensity of the attitudes of individual justices, as these might be measured on the relevant dimensions. Let us further assume, however far-fetched the notion might seem at first blush, that we can account for most of the important differences among the attitudes of a group of justices by using only three dimensions.

We might then conceive of a syndrome of attitudes for each justice, which we could symbolize and represent graphically as a unique point in the space defined by the three dimensions. Moreover, since the real space that most humans sense and think in terms of is three-dimensional, it will be convenient to employ the attitudinal dimensions

as reference axes for an Euclidean space, and to use sets of Cartesian coordinates to locate in the space the point which represents the unique syndrome of attitudes of each justice. For convenience, we shall refer to such points as judicial "ideal-points," or, more simply, as i-points.

The cases on the Court's dockets might be conceptualized as complex stimuli, which (in effect) ask questions about issues to which the justices are asked to respond. It will be recalled that the number of issues that survive in any case, after appellate review below and the Supreme Court's jurisdictional screening are completed, are few and refined, in sharp contradistinction to the multiplicity of issues that may have been raised during the trial and other earlier stages in the litigation of the case. Characteristically, the effect of what are called "the facts" of the case is to provide direction and intensity in defining the nature of the issue; that is, the issue specifies which attitudinal dimension is relevant, while the facts determine where a particular case is located on the dimension. We already have assumed that the issues raised by cases are the counterparts of the values of the justices, and that judicial attitudes mediate external values (represented by issues in cases) and internal values (which constitute the justices' own beliefs). Therefore, it is not unreasonable to assume that each case can be measured in terms of the same attitudinal dimensions as the justices, and represented by a $[j]$ point in the same three-dimensional space.

If we could locate the i-points for the nine justices, together with the j-points for the one hundred and seventy-five cases decided on the merits in a typical term, in the same joint psychological space, then we should have, at least in principle, a deterministic model for predicting the votes of the justices, and therefore the decisions of the Court. To be more precise, each of our three reference axes would have a defined direction, and therefore the coordinates for *any* point (i or j) in the space would be within the range $+1.00$ to -1.00, in its orthogonal projection on each axis. In order to predict the decision in any case, it would be necessary only to measure the rela-

[5]Schubert, "A Psychometric Model of the Supreme Court," *American Behavioral Scientist*, Nov. 1961, p. 14; Schubert, "Psychometric Research in Judicial Behavior," *62 Modern Uses of Logic in Law [M.U.L.L.]* 9–18 (1962); Schubert, "The 1960 Term of the Supreme Court: A Psychological Analysis," 56 *Am. Pol. Sci. Rev.* 90 (1962); Schubert, "A Solution to the Indeterminate Factorial Resolution of Thurstone and Degan's Study of the Supreme Court," 7 *Behavioral Science* 448 (1962).

tionship between the j-point and the set of i-points. For convenience, let us speak of a *positive* difference between the coordinates, on a given axis, for two points being compared, as a measure of the *dominance* of the point which is more positive, over the lesser point.

We might also assume that in comparing two points, A and B, there might be a negative difference for A on one dimension, and a positive difference on the other two dimensions, so that an excess (of whatever attitudes are being measured) on those dimensions would compensate for a deficiency on the first dimension, and we might then still speak of A as dominating B, in the sense of the over-all balance of their relationships. More generally, any justice would vote to uphold an issue (such as freedom of speech) if, and only if, his sympathy for the issue was equal to or greater than the amount of sympathy required for anyone to agree with the claim raised in a case; or, in terms of our model, he would vote positively if and only if his i-point dominated the j-point.

Obviously, under these assumptions, the decision of the Court in any case would depend upon whether the j-point dominated, or was dominated by, a majority of i-points. In the simplest, one-dimensional case, all ten points would be arrayed along the same continuum; and the justices would be partitioned into two subsets (pro and con the issue) by the locus of the j-point. One subset could, of course, be empty; and unanimous decisions upholding an issue would occur when the j-point is dominated by all i-points, while unanimous decisions in the negative would occur when all i-points are dominated by the j-point. In the three-dimensional case, the justices would be partitioned into two subsets by the plane orthogonal to the vector of the j-point.

Justices who are attitudinally in close agreement with each other ought to be located close to each other in our three-dimensional space; and we should expect such justices to agree in their voting. Justices who hold opposing views on such fundamental issues as civil liberties, or the proper role of government in the economy, ought to be located far apart

in the space, and we should expect them to disagree often in their voting. Cases that raise questions of differing degrees of valuation about the *same* issue would be arrayed as a set of j-points along a single continuum, which we shall hypothesize to be a scale axis which transects the space. Of course, if such a scale axis should coincide with one of the three reference axes, this would be equivalent to saying that such a set of cases raised *only* the single issue represented by the one reference axis, and that these cases were quite independent (in a statistical sense) from the other two reference axes. We should anticipate, however, that most cases decided by the Supreme Court will not be univariate, which is equivalent to saying that most scale axes, representing sets of cases, will not coincide with any of the reference axes.

Moreover, we ought to anticipate that both j-points and i-points will be scattered in non-linear patterns in the space; and when we speak of a scale axis, we refer to a continuum (positioned in the three-dimensional space) which represents the average of the relationships of the relevant j-points *with regard to the particular issue that we define*. Stated otherwise, neither the i-points nor the relevant j-points necessarily *lie upon* a scale axis that represent the issue in which we are interested; but all *project upon* the scale axis, which is the line that is "closest" to all of the j-points in the defined subset.

We can define issues narrowly or broadly, depending upon what seems to be reasonable from an empirical point of view, based upon an examination of the value-content of the cases in any subset that is of interest. Thus, we might be interested in any or all of the following: (1) F.E.L.A. evidentiary cases; (2) all F.E.L.A. cases; (3) F.E.L.A. cases, Jones Act cases, Longshoremen and Harborworkers Act cases, maritime cases raising the question of seaworthiness, and so on; (4) both federal and state cases involving workers' claims for monetary compensation for industrial accidents; (5) any cases involving workers' claims for monetary compensation; (6) any cases involving the rights of workingmen; (7) any cases which raise the fundamental issue of economic liberalism and conservatism. In our model, any of these categories might constitute an issue which we could represent as a scale axis; but the last category clearly is by far the most basic of these seven categories, and we should understand it to include many kinds of public policy issues beyond those involving the rights of labor. If we were to plot a set of seven scale axes, corresponding to these seven categories, we should expect them to be highly intercorrelated with each other, which in geometric terms means that they ought all to traverse the space in the same general direction—indeed, the E scale, representing the seventh category, would define the most general direction, from which the sub-scale axes, representing sub-variables of economic liberalism, could be expected to deviate both from each other and from E.

Methods for locating j-points in the joint decision-making space have not yet been perfected. The relatively simple method which can be used to position i-points, and which we shall describe presently, depends upon the circumstance that there are a relatively large number of cases, and relatively few justices. In the average recent term of the Supreme Court, there have been a hundred split decisions and nine justices. This yields approximately a hundred different observations on the voting of each justice, in relationship to each other justice. If necessary, we could increase the number of observations by extending the time period under analysis. As we shall see, a hundred observations are enough to support stable correlations and analyses thereof; but we are never in a position to observe more than nine votes in a single case. This is too few for statistical manipulation to be meaningful. So voting data can be used to locate the spatial positions of i-points, but not of j-points. It seems most likely that it may be possible to develop methods for analyzing opinion data which will establish the position of a configuration of j-points in a joint space. . . . [S]uch an achievement would be a methodological breakthrough which would facilitate the use of the model for the purpose of predicting decisions

with much greater precision than now is feasible.

In the absence of a methodology for positioning individual cases in the space, we propose to resort to the alternative procedure of positioning *sets of cases*, as scale axes, in the space defined by the analysis of voting data. We shall first explain how we position the i-points. Then we shall explain how, by a quite independent method and set of observations, cumulative scales of judicial voting, on selected major issues, are constructed. We shall then position the cumulative scale axes in the space containing the configuration of i-points, thus (in effect) establishing the approximate location in the space of the cases in the scale sets. We assume that it will not be possible for anyone to fit the scale axes in positions consistent with those of the i-points, except with a specifiably low probability of chance success, *unless* the sets of observations and measurements, represented by cumulative scaling and factor analysis, are indeed equivalent. (They are, of course, theoretically equivalent to each other.) But if they can be demonstrated to be empirically equivalent, with the data for the 1961 Term that we shall examine, we shall then be forced to choose between two hypotheses: either the relationship is due to chance variation, or the votes of Supreme Court justices are determined by their attitudes towards the issues in the cases that they decide.

B. The Data. The sample of decisions to be analyzed consists of all cases in which the Supreme Court divided on the merits during the period of the 1961 Term, which extended from October 2, 1961, through June 25, 1962. Both formal and *per curiam* decisions accordingly are included, but unanimous and jurisdictional decisions were excluded. As Table 1 indicates, almost two-thirds of the Court's formal decisions were reached over the disagreement of one or more justices, while this was true of only one-third of the *per curiam* decisions. In the preceding year, the proportions were approximately three-fourths and one-fourth, respectively. Moreover, it has not been unusual for the justices, in recent years, to disagree in a majority of their decisions

TABLE 1   Summary of Decisions on the Merits, 1961 Term

Decision	Formal	Per curiam	Totals
Split.	63	20	83
Unanimous	39	41	80
Totals	102	61	163

on the merits (combining formal and per curiam), as they did during the 1961 Term; this was also true during twelve of the preceding fifteen terms. The average number of split decisions over the past sixteen terms was ninety-six, and the average number of unanimous decisions on the merits was seventy-nine; in this respect, the 1961 Term provoked somewhat less disagreement among the justices than has been usual.

Each case to which the Court had assigned a unique docket number and for which the Court had made a disposition on the merits, was a unit for voting analysis; and for each case, one set of from six to nine votes was counted. With eighty-three decisions on the merits, there would be potentially a total of 747 votes in the sample for analysis, assuming full participation in each case. In fact, there were a hundred less votes, primarily because of the illnesses which afflicted Justices Whittaker and Frankfurter during the late winter and early spring, resulting, in each instance, in the incapacitation and eventual resignation of the justice. Whittaker's last voting participation was on March 5, 1962, and his resignation became effective on April 1 of that year. Frankfurter's last voting participation was on April 9, but his resignation did not become effective until August 28, 1962. Mr. Justice White, who replaced Whittaker, became a member of the Court on April 16, but he was able to participate, of course, only in cases subsequently argued, or decided summarily. . . .

One of the eighty-three cases could not be used in the analysis, because the Court divided 4–4, without opinion and with Frankfurter not participating, and there was no objective means of identifying the voting positions of the eight participating justices. Justices Douglas and Clark participated in all of the re-maining eighty-two decisions; and Warren, Black, Harlan, Brennan, and Stewart, in all except one each. The remaining three members of the Court during this term voted, however, in less than half of these cases: Frankfurter in thirty-eight, Whittaker in twenty-eight, and White in twelve.

Stated otherwise, Warren and Harlan each filed a jurisdictional dissent in a case which the rest of the Court decided on the merits, and in which at least one other justice dissented on the merits; these two jurisdictional dissents were treated as non-participations. Brennan, Stewart, and Black failed to participate in one case each; Whittaker was absent in five decisions immediately preceding his retirement; Frankfurter missed all forty-five decisions that were announced after he became ill; and White did not participate in thirty-two of the decisions in which the Court divided subsequent to his appointment. To the preceding total of eighty-seven non-participations, we must add the eight votes that could not be specified, in the case in which the Court divided equally, and also the five cases decided by an eight-justice Court, during the interim between Whittaker's resignation and White's appointment. Subtracting these one hundred non-votes from the potential maximum of 747 votes, we are left with 647 votes of ten justices on the merits of the substantive issues in eighty-two cases in which there was dissent; and these 647 votes constitute the universe of raw data which constitutes the basis for our factor analysis and the cumulative scaling.

C. The Factor Analysis. *1. The correlation matrix.* The initial condition precedent to any factor analysis is the construction of a correlation matrix. In the present study, the correlation matrix was based upon a set of fourfold tables which, in turn, were constructed directly from observations of the raw data: the 647 votes on the merits described in the preceding section of this paper. These votes were tabulated in terms of agreement and disagreement with the majority, in the decision of each case, for every pair of justices.

For any such pair, there are five possibilities in each decision: (1) both may agree in the majority; (2) both may agree in dissent; (3) the first member of the pair may vote with the majority, while the second dissents; (4) the second member of the pair may vote with the majority, while the first dissents; or (5) either or both members may fail to participate in the decision, in which event there is no score for the pair for that decision. In the tabulation of votes for the factor analysis, no attention is paid to the substantive variables to which the decisions relate; the sole criterion for the attribution of votes is agreement or disagreement with the majority of justices who controlled the disposition of the case.

It is most convenient to arrange the summary tabulation of agreement-disagreement,

proach was that, by concentrating upon the *agreement* between pairs of justices, the analysts ignored what is at least an equally important aspect of judicial voting behavior, and that is the *ways in which justices disagree*. Table 2, for instance, shows that not only did Douglas and Warren disagree in a dozen of these decisions; they disagreed in a particular way. In all of these instances of disagreement, it was Douglas who dissented while Warren adhered to the majority. This finding certainly suggests that Douglas was more extreme in his dissenting behavior than Warren (or, as we shall observe presently in Table 3, than any other member of the Court except Harlan, during this term). Moreover, the correlation coefficients, which are computed from the fourfold tables, are very sensitive to how votes are partitioned between the two cells of a diagonal, as well as to differences between the diagonals.

In order to measure precisely the relationship among the four cells of a fourfold table, phi correlation coefficients are computed.[6] In the correlation matrix shown in Table 3,

TABLE 2   Fourfold Table of Agreement-Disagreement, Douglas-Warren, 1961 Term

		Warren		Totals
		+	−	
Douglas	+	54	0	54
	−	12	15	27
Totals		66	15	81

for each judicial dyad, in the form of a four-fold table such as Table 2. The table shows that Warren and Douglas dissented together fifteen times; this dis/dis $(-/-)$ cell is the one that contains the kind of information utilized in some earlier studies of "dissenting blocs" of the Court. Similarly, Warren and Douglas agreed in sixty-nine of these eighty-one sets of votes; this is the sum of the major or positive diagonal (*i.e.*, the $+/+$ and the $-/-$ cells), and this is the kind of information that was the basis for the "interagreement" bloc analysis of the earlier studies. . . .

It is apparent from an examination of Table 2 that the weakness of the earlier ap-

[6]The phi coefficient is an approximation of the Pearsonian r correlation coefficient; and it is appropriate to use the phi coefficient when, as is true of these data, the two distributions to be correlated reflect a genuine dichotomy. It certainly seems warranted to consider the voting choice between agreeing with the majority, or dissenting, as a kind of true dichotomy. The phi coefficient is relatively simple to compute: it is the ratio of the difference of the cross-products of the diagonals of a four-fold table, to the square root of the product of the marginals. For the data of Table 2:

$$(1) \quad r_\phi = \frac{(54 \cdot 15) - (12 \cdot 0)}{(66 \cdot 15 \cdot 54 \cdot 27)^{1/2}} = \frac{810 - 0}{(1443420)^{1/2}}$$

$$= +\frac{810}{1201.424} = +.674.$$

Evidently, the sign of the coefficient depends upon which diagonal cross-product is the larger; or, in other words, upon whether or not a pair of justices agree more than they disagree, and *also* whether they agree both in assent

TABLE 3   Fourfold Tables and Phi Correlation Matrix, 1961 Term

	D +	D −	Wa +	Wa −	Bl +	Bl −	Br +	Br −	BW +	BW −	C +	C −	S +	S −	Wh +	Wh −	F +	F −	H +	H −
D			+54	0	46	8	53	0	7	1	31	23	40	14	8	6	9	13	15	.39
			−12	15	12	15	22	6	4	0	27	1	26	1	14	0	16	0	25	2
Wa	.674				+56	10	64	1	9	1	43	23	52	14	13	6	15	13	24	41
					− 2	12	10	5	1	0	14	1	13	1	9	0	10	0	15	0
Bl	.426		.600				+56	1	9	1	36	22	44	13	11	5	13	11	17	40
							−18	5	2	0	21	2	21	2	11	1	12	2	22	1
Br	.389		.471		.343				+10	1	52	23	59	15	17	6	20	13	35	39
									− 1	0	6	0	6	0	5	0	5	0	5	1
BW	−.213		−.100		−.135		−.091				+ 9	2	10	1	—	—	0	0	3	8
											− 0	1	1	0	—	—	0	0	1	0
C	−.407		−.240		−.289		−.178		.522				+45	12	19	6	21	11	33	24
													−21	3	3	0	4	2	7	17
S	−.270		−.137		−.164		−.137		−.091		−.100				+18	4	22	9	34	31
															− 3	2	2	4	5	10
Wh	−.522		−.359		−.276		−.244		.000		−.181		.204				+16	6	16	6
																	− 4	2	2	4
F	−.615		−.431		−.321		−.281		.000		−.008		.291		.055				+21	3
																			− 2	11
H	−.611		−.492		−.596		−.190		−.426		.262		.148		.337		.710			

phi ranges from +.710 (for Harlan and Frankfurter) to −.615 (for Douglas and Frankfurter). Frankfurter, therefore, was the most extreme justice in the range of his agreement and disagreement; and he voted most frequently the same as Harlan, and least often in agreement with Douglas.

Since there were ten justices on the Court during this term, there are fourfold tables and correlation coefficients for each of forty-five dyads.[7] All data were placed on punch cards, and the computation of phi coefficients was programmed for computer analysis. Since both matrices are symmetrical, and in order to conserve space, Table 3 presents the fourfold tables above the major diagonal, and the correlation coefficients below.

Before turning to the results of the factor analysis of the correlation matrix, there are a couple of interesting findings that are apparent from a mere inspection of Table 3. The most obvious is the sharp demarcation of eight of the justices into what appear to be two opposing blocs. Douglas, Black, Warren, and Brennan all correlate positively with each other, and negatively with the six remaining justices. Harlan, Frankfurter, Whittaker, and Stewart all correlate positively with each other, and negatively with the first group. White and Clark are not clearly associated with either bloc, although it should be observed that their relatively high positive correlation with each other hinges upon a

and in dissent, or (in other words) whether their disagreement is divided equally or disproportionately between the cells of the diagonals. The maximum range of the phi coefficient is from +1 to −1; but these limits are rarely attained empirically, since the maximum size of phi is a function of the distribution of the marginals, and can be ±1 only when all four marginal frequencies are equal. See Cureton, "Note on $\frac{\phi}{\phi_{max}}$," 24 *Psychometrika* 89–91 (1959).

[7]When factor analysis is performed by hand use of a calculator instead of utilizing a computer program, it is necessary to arrange the correlation coefficients in the form of a square symmetric matrix, with the major diagonal filled with the estimates of the highest communality for each justice. For the techniques of factor analysis, the interested reader is referred to any of the several standard works on this subject, *e.g.*, Harry H. Harman, *Modern Factor Analysis* (1960); Benjamin Fruchter, *Introduction to Factor Analysis* (1954); Raymond B. Cattell, *Factor Analysis: An Introduction and Manual for the Psychologist and Social Scientist* (1952); Louis L. Thurstone, *Multiple-Factor Analysis* (1947).

single case, *Robinson* v. *California*,[8] in which they dissented together against a pro-civil liberty decision of the six other participating members of the Court.

Obviously, in the light of White's minimal participation during this term, relatively slight confidence should be reposed in the relationships that are denoted for him, either in Table 3 or elsewhere in this article. It should also be noted that White participated in no decisions with either Whittaker, whom he replaced, or Frankfurter, whose illness coincided with White's accession to the Court; in both instances, a zero correlation is reported in Table 3, signifying the absolute statistical independence of White's voting behavior from that of Whittaker or Frankfurter. Clark, however, is positively correlated with Harlan, and his negative correlations with the other three members of the Harlan bloc are generally weaker than his negative correlations with the Douglas bloc. From this we might reasonably infer that Clark was not affiliated with either bloc, but that his disagreement was greater with the Douglas bloc. In view of White's maximal disagreement with Harlan, and his slight negative correlation with Stewart, it seems most likely, on the basis of the slim evidence available, that if he *had* participated in decision with Whittaker and Frankfurter, he would have been negatively correlated with them, too—and this is a proposition that we can re-examine, at a later point in this paper, in the light of evidence bearing upon the psychological distances separating these justices.

The general pattern that emerges from an examination of Table 3, therefore, is that during the first six months of the term, the Court was divided into two opposing blocs of four justices each, with Clark unaffiliated but leaning towards the Harlan bloc. After Whittaker's retirement, the Court was divided into the Douglas bloc of four justices, and the still opposing Harlan bloc, now consisting only of himself and Stewart; and both White and Clark were unaffiliated with either bloc,

although Clark was positively and White was negatively associated with Harlan.

Further evidence of the extent of polarization of the Court is provided by an examination of the dis/dis cells of the fourfold tables in Table 3; for convenience, this information is summarized in Table 4.

It seems obvious that Douglas, Harlan, and the respective justices with whom each tended to associate in these dissents, were in pretty sharp and basic disagreement over something; and unless we are prepared to accept the somewhat implausible notion that they just could not get together over the meaning or application of the principle of stare decisis, then it may not be unreasonable to entertain the hypothesis that these groups may have been in disagreement about the social, economic, and political values that the Court upholds in its decisions.

2. *The factor loadings.* The initial product of a factor analysis is a set of derived correlations or ("loadings," as they customarily are called) which purport to measure the extent to which each element of whatever has been associated in the correlation matrix, is related to the components or dimensions into which the basic correlation matrix has been broken down. In the present study, the elements are the justices, and the factor loadings purport to express the correlation of each justice with the basic underlying dimensions of the phi matrix. Although it is technically possible to extract as many factors as there are elements which are intercorrelated in the phi matrix—ten, in the instant case—only five factors actually were computed, and of these, only three will be used for purposes of testing the principal hypothesis. The reason for limiting the number of factors to three is twofold: (1) the residual matrix, representing the amount of variance unaccounted for by the first three factors, was very small, and less, indeed, than the estimated error variance; and (2) three factors can be given an Euclidean graphical representation which accords with the spatial intuitions of most readers.

The usual procedure in factor analysis is to rotate the orthogonal factor axes, which

[8]370 U.S. 660 (1962).

TABLE 4 Total of Joint Dissents (Selected Justices, by Pairs)

	D	H
Wa, Bl	30	1
C, S, F.	2	38

are the direct product of a complete centroid routine, to oblique positions that are presumed to correspond to some criterion related to empirical reality, and thus to make possible a more meaningful psychological interpretation than would usually be possible if the orthogonal axes were retained.[9] The orthogonal axes have not been rotated in the present study, but for the reason that, contrary to the usual procedure, reliance is not placed upon the association of substantive meaning with the factors. Substantive meaning is associated, instead, with the scale axes which are passed through the space defined by the orthogonal factor axes; and thus the scale axes—which are oblique—perform the same function, for purposes of interpretation, that is usually accomplished by rotation of the orthogonal axes. The orthogonal axes are used, therefore, only as a set of reference axes, which define the three-dimensional space in which the i-points of the justices and the j-points of the cases are located. And the factor loadings, shown in Table 5, function as Cartesian coordinates which locate the i-points of the justices in the factor space.

Factor loadings can vary, in principle, from +1 to −1; in practice, their variance is, of course, bounded by the extremity of the correlation coefficients upon which they are based. It will be observed that, on the average, the highest loadings (both positive and negative) are on the first factor, and that the mean magnitude of the third factor loadings is smallest. This is inherent in the centroid

routine, which assumes that the first factor, to which the largest portion of the variance is attributed, is the most important factor, and so on. The loadings on the first factor range from a high of approximately +.88, for Douglas, to a low of −.67, for Harlan. Obviously, the justices are partitioned on the first factor into the same two blocs that were manifest in the phi matrix; but it is notable that the groupings on the second and third factors are quite different.

Thus, mere inspection of the factor matrix of Table 5 suggests that the multidimensional relationship among the justices is going to be somewhat different, and certainly more complex, than the simple bifurcation of a single dimension which will account for much, but not enough, of the variance in the voting behavior of the justices. For deeper insight than a single dimension—even when it is overwhelmingly the most important dimension—can afford, we must turn to an examination of the richer complexity made possible by work with the three-dimensional factor space.

D. The Cumulative Scales. Cumulative scaling is a research operation that is completely independent from factor analysis. It may be undertaken before, at the same time, or after the factor analysis is completed. In cumulative (or Guttman) scaling, one examines the same universe of raw data that is used for the factor analysis. But instead of tabulating votes by dyads in terms of agreement with the majority, for scaling purposes votes are tabulated by cases, and are classified as being either in support of, or in opposition to, certain defined scale variables. The variables employed in this study were identified on the basis of experimental work in previous terms of the Warren Court. The basic procedures for cumulative scaling have been discussed elsewhere, although the format of Figures 1

[9]Perhaps it should be noted, for the benefit of those readers who are not familiar with the method, that orthogonal axes are statistically independent, while oblique axes are correlated with each other; therefore, the implication of making a factor interpretation based directly upon a system of orthogonal axes is that one is prepared to make the assumption that there is no relationship among the factors, which must be conceived to be independent of each other.

TABLE 5   Factor Loadings for Judicial Ideal Points, 1961 Term

Justices	Factors		
	I*	II	III
D	.883	−.193	−.177
Wa	.769	.074	−.053
Bl	.689	.149	.195
Br	.514	.138	−.136
BW	−.196	−.591	.186
S	−.267	.280	.147
C	−.392	−.514	−.222
Wh	−.430	.268	.487
F	−.627	.370	−.217
H	−.668	.485	−.616

and 2 below differs somewhat from that exemplified in the cited work.[10]

Consistent votes in support of the scale variable are denoted by the symbol x, and inconsistent positive votes by $\underline{x}$. A blank space indicates a consistent negative vote, and the symbol − is used to signify an inconsistent negative vote. An asterisk signifies non-participation, and a slash bar indicates that a justice was not a member of the Court at the time a case was decided. Scale scores are simple functions of scale positions, and a justice's scale position is defined as being fixed by his last consistent positive vote. Where one or more non-participations separate a justice's consistent positive and negative votes, his scale position is assumed to be at the mean of the non-participation or non-participations, since it cannot be determined how he might have voted. A justice's scale score is computed by use of the formula:

$$(2) \qquad s = \frac{2p}{n} - 1$$

where s is his scale score, p his scale position, and n equals the number of cases in the scale. Scale scores, like correlation coefficients and factor loadings, can range in value from +1 to −1, with the significant difference that in practice, scale scores frequently attain these extreme values, reflecting the extremity of attitude of several of the justices in each of the scales shown in Figures 1 and 2.

Two coefficients appear at the bottom of each scale; each of these purports to measure the degree of consistency in the set of votes that is being scaled. R is Guttman's coefficient of reproducibility; .900 or better is conventionally accepted as evidence to support the hypothesis that a single dominant variable has motivated the voting behavior of the justices in the set of cases comprising the sample. S is Menzel's coefficient of scalability;[11] it provides a more rigid standard than does R, because S (unlike R) does not capitalize upon the spurious contribution to consistency that arises from the inclusion in the scale of either cases or justices with extreme marginal distributions. Menzel has suggested that the appropriate level of acceptance for S is "somewhere between .60 and .65"; the scales presented in Figures 1 and 2 are well above the suggested levels of acceptability for both R and S.

1. The C Scale. Figure 1 is a cumulative scale of the thirty-nine civil liberties cases that the Court decided non-unanimously on the merits during the 1961 Term. In content, the C variable is defined broadly to include all cases in which the primary issues involved

[10]Glendon Schubert, *Quantitative Analysis of Judicial Behavior* 270–90 (1959). In Figures 1 and 2 cases are cited to the official *United States Reports*: the digit preceding the slash bar is the third digit of the volume number, and should be understood to be preceded, if 8 or 9, by the digits 36; and if 0, by the digits 37. The number following the slash bar is the page cite; and if more than one case begins on the same page, a docket number follows the page cite, from which it is separated by a colon.

[11]Menzel, "A New Coefficient for Scalogram Analysis," 17 *Pub. Opin. Q.* 268–80 (1953).

FIGURE 1   Judicial Attitudes toward Civil Liberties, 1961 Term

1961 TERM
C Scale
Justices

Cases	Bl	D	Wa	Br	S	BW	Wh	F	H	C	Totals
9/402	x					/	/				1–7
0/530:481	x	x				*	/	*			2–5
0/41	x	x	*				/	*			2–5
9/599	*	x	x			*	/	*			2–4
9/541	x	x	x			*	/	*			3–4
8/139	x	x	x			/					3–6
8/19	x	x	x	x		/					4–5
8/231	x	x	x	x		/					4–5
8/424	x	x	x	x		/					4–5
8/448:56	x	x	x	x		/					4–5
8/448:57	x	x	x	x		/					4–5
0/650	—	x	x	x		*	/	*	x̲		4–3
0/49	x	x	x	x		*	/	*			4–3
0/230	x	x	x	x		*	/	*		x̲	5–2
0/660	x	x	x	x	x		/	*	x̲		6–2
9/367	x	x	x	x	x	/	/				5–3
9/186	x	x	x	x	x	/	*			x̲	6–2
9/429	x	x	x	x	x	x	/	*		x̲	7–1
0/190	x	x	x	x	x	x	/	*		x̲	7–1
9/438	x	x	x	x	x	*	/	*			5–2
9/749:8	x	x	x	x	x	*	/	*			5–2
9/749:9	x	x	x	x	x	*	/	*			5–2
9/749:11	x	x	x	x	x	*	/	*			5–2
9/749:12	x	x	x	x	x	*	/	*			5–2
9/749:28	x	x	x	x	x	*	/	*			5–2
0/288	x	x	x	x	x	*	/	*			5–2
0/375	x	x	x	x	x	*	/	*			5–2
0/717	x	x	x	x	x	*	/	*			5–2
0/724	x	x	x	x	x	*	/	*			5–2
9/661	x	x	x	x	x	x	/	*			6–2
9/662	x	x	x	x	x	x	/	*			6–2
9/749:10	x	x	x	*	x	*	/	*			4–2
8/487	x	x	x	x	x	/	x				6–3
8/439	x	x	x	x	—	/	x	x			6–3
9/705	x	x	x	x	x	*	/	*	x		6–1
0/478	x	x	x	x	x	*	/	*	x		6–1
9/141:64	x	x	x	x	x	/	*	x	x		7–1
9/141:65	x	x	x	x	x	/	*	x	x		7–1
0/421	x	x	x	x	—	*	/	*	x	x	6–1
											187–110
											297
Totals	37–1	38–1	36–2	32–6	23–16	4–2	2–6	3–10	7–32	5–34 187–110	
Scale positions	39	38	36½	33	25	23	17½	6	5	1	
Scale scores	1.00	.95	.87	.69	.28	.18	−.10	−.69	−.74	−.95	

$$R = 1 - \frac{6}{236} = .975 \qquad\qquad S = 1 - \frac{9}{45} = .800$$

a conflict between personal rights and claims to liberty, and governmental authority:

(1) Political equality (*e.g.*, white primary, integration, reapportionment),

(2) Political freedom (*e.g.*, speech, association, press),

(3) Religious freedom (*e.g.*, exercise, separation),

(4) Fair procedure (Fifth, Sixth, and Eighth amendment rights), and

(5) The right to privacy (Fourth amendment, psychological, physiological).

The number of cases included in the scale —almost half of the total—was about the same as in other recent terms; and the ranking of justices on the scale was very similar to the rankings for the 1959 and 1960 Terms, and precisely the same as in 1958; the only differences from the 1960 C Scale, for example, were the reversal of Black and Douglas in 1961, and the tie between Frankfurter and Harlan in 1960. Certainly, these are differences of minimal importance, since the Black-Douglas reversal hangs upon a single vote, and another single vote change would have resulted in a Frankfurter-Harlan tie. However, the extent of non-participation for White, Whittaker, and Frankfurter is so large that, although we are confident that their rank order is correct, much less confidence can be reposed in the precise scale scores denoted for these three justices.

The scale confirms what most scholars certainly believe to be the ideological patterning of the justices on civil liberties issues: Black and Douglas are most extreme in their support, followed by Warren, and then Brennan; Stewart is the marginal justice; and— skipping over the three justices with high non-participation—Harlan and Clark give very slight support to civil liberties claims. Moreover, the differentials are in precise accord with those assumed by Professor Rodell for his prediction of *Baker* v. *Carr,* with the possible exception of Clark's ranking below Frankfurter and Harlan. In this regard, it is notable that three of Clark's four inconsistent votes—those in *Baker* v. *Carr,*[12] *Scholle* v.

Hare,[13] and *W.M.C.A.* v. *Simon*[14]—came in state legislative reapportionment cases. Evidently, on this particular issue, Justice Clark's attitude *was* inconsistent with his more general attitude toward civil liberties questions, or at least, so it seems when all civil liberties issues of the term are squeezed into the less flexible mold of a single dimension. However, reference to Figure 3 and Table 7, *infra,* will show that Clark's votes in these three cases were *not* inconsistent when the civil liberty variable is viewed as an axis in three-dimensional space.

Mr. Justice Stewart was indeed the most critical decision-maker in these civil liberties cases. Because of his central position, and relatively moderate attitude, he was in the majority in thirty-four of these thirty-nine decisions—more than any other justice. A justice in the fifth rank can function literally as the determinative voter, however, only when there is full participation by nine justices, which occurred in only eight of these cases; or else when an even number of justices participate, and in such a way that the justice in the fifth rank might vote to create a tie, thus preventing the formation of a majority which could upset the decision below. In all five of the cases in which his colleagues divided 4-4, Stewart joined with the justices to his right to form majorities against the civil liberties claims; in the 5-3 and 4-2 decisions, he joined the more liberal colleagues to his left rather than to create an even division of the Court.

It is certainly noteworthy that over a wide range of specific issues, Black and Douglas and Warren together cast a total of only four negative votes; while Clark, with the exception of his three votes in the reapportionment cases, discovered only two among the remaining thirty-six civil liberties claims that were sufficiently meritorious for him to uphold. Turning from the extreme voters to the extreme cases, the one which raised the least persuasive civil liberty claim was *Murphy* v. *United States,*[15] a *per curiam* decision which

---

[12]369 U.S. 186 (1962).

[13]369 U.S. 429 (1962).
[14]370 U.S. 190 (1962).
[15]369 U.S. 402 (1962).

confirmed the unanimous ruling, announced two weeks earlier, that pre-indictment motions to suppress evidence on fourth amendment grounds are not appealable. Black wrote no opinion to explain why he alone, among the justices, differentiated between *Murphy*, and the decision in *DiBella* v. *United States*.[16] At the bottom of the scale is *Engel* v. *Vitale*,[17] the New York public school prayer decision announced on the final day of the term; here Stewart *did* articulate his views, which were to the effect that the Court, and not he, was being inconsistent in this decision. Evidently, the inference that one would have to make on the basis of this scale is to the contrary.

2. *The E Scale.* Figure 2 is a cumulative scale of the thirty-four cases dealing with economic policy issues that the Court decided non-unanimously on the merits during the 1961 Term. Economic liberalism (E+) means, in general, to favor the interests of the economically underprivileged, and to oppose affuence and monopoly power. More explicitly, it includes the following major components:

(1) To uphold the fiscal claims of injured workers in Federal Employers' Liability Act cases, in Jones Act and other maritime cases, and in state workmen's compensation diversity-jurisdiction cases; of tort claimants against the government; and of small, inferior claimants against the national government; but to favor the national government over large, corporate claimants (such as banks, railroads, power companies, and gold mining companies) and to uphold the government in eminent domain cases.

(2) To uphold governmental regulation of business "in the public interest."

(3) To uphold unions in labor-management disputes; to favor unions representing workers over unions acting in a management capacity; and to uphold unions rather than individual workers in disputes over dismissals, union security, and hiring halls.

(4) To oppose monopoly; to favor competition in patent infringement or patentability suits; to favor individuals over larger or corporate groups; and to favor small business over larger corporations.

(5) To uphold state taxation on *constitutional* grounds (such as the commerce clause or the due process clause of the fourteenth amendment).

Although research in depth over several recent terms demonstrates that sub-scales of each of these components are very highly intercorrelated, both the highest consistency in judicial voting, and the highest proportion of pro (E+) decisions, occur in the F.E.L.A./Jones Act cases. Indeed, the research done thus far suggests that judicial attitudes toward workmen's compensation, and other fiscal claims of injured workers against employers, are an excellent index to even broader attitudes toward general liberalism, which we might define as a paravariable combining C and E.[18]

The number of cases included in the E Scale—about forty per cent of the total split decisions on the merits for the 1961 Term—is about average for recent terms. The ranking of the justices on this scale was similar to the rankings for the 1960, 1959, and 1958 Terms, although there were three pair reversals in 1961 which differ from the pattern of the previous terms: it is unusual for Warren to precede Black, or for Clark to precede Brennan, or for Frankfurter to precede Harlan on a term E scale. Moreover, the evidence in the scale to support these transpositions, in the present rankings, is so slight, that they would appear to be clearly within the range of error variance for the 1961 Term E Scale. The differential for Warren and Black is a

---

[16]369 U.S. 121 (1962).
[17]370 U.S. 421 (1962).

[18]For an analysis of the interrelationships among scales and scale axes of the first and third of these subvariables, together with the civil liberties and economic liberalism variables, and the liberalism paravariable, during the middle years of the Roosevelt Court, see Schubert, "A Solution to the Indeterminate Factorial Resolution of Thurstone and Degan's Study of the Supreme Court," 7 *Behavioral Science* 454–57 (1962). For other scale analyses, of the second (anti-business) and the third (pro-labor) component subvariables, see Spaeth, "Warren Court Attitudes Toward Business: the 'B' Scale," in Glendon Schubert (Ed.), *Judicial Decision-Making* ch. 4 (1963), and Spaeth, "An Analysis of Judicial Attitudes in the Labor Relations Decisions of the Warren Court," 25 *Journal of Politics* (1963), pp. 290–311.

FIGURE 2 Judicial Attitudes toward Economic Liberalism, 1961 Term

1961 TERM
E Scale
Justices

Cases	D	Wa	Bl	C	Br	BW	S	F	H	Wh	Totals
9/95			<u>x</u>			/					1–8
0/76			<u>x</u>			*		*		/	1–6
0/451			<u>x</u>			*		*		/	1–6
9/60	x					/					1–8
9/134	x					/			*	*	1–6
0/173	x							*		/	1–7
8/403	x	x				/	*				2–6
8/20	x	x	x			/					3–6
9/153	x	x	x			/				*	3–5
0/165	x	x	x					*		/	3–5
0/626	x	x	x			*		*		/	3–4
8/324	x	x	x	x		/					4–5
8/464	x	x	x	x	x	/					5–4
9/463	x	x	x	x	x	*		*		/	5–2
9/482	x	x	x	x	x	*		*		/	5–2
9/527	x	x	x	x	x	*		*		/	5–2
8/81:17	x	x	x	x	x	/				<u>x</u>	6–3
8/81:18	x	x	x	x	x	/				<u>x</u>	6–3
9/355	x	x	x	x	x	/			<u>x</u>	/	6–2
0/114	x	x	x	x	x	x		*		/	6–2
0/195	–	x	x	x	–	x	x	*		/	5–3
8/360	x	x	x	x	x	/	x				6–3
9/404:77	x	x	x	x	x	/	x			/	6–2
9/404:94	x	x	x	x	x	/	x			/	6–2
9/643	–	x	x	x	x	*	x	*		/	5–2
9/698	x	x	x	x	x	*	x	*		/	6–1
0/31	x	x	x	x	x	*	x	*		/	6–1
0/254	x	x	x	x	x	x	x	*		/	7–1
0/460	x	x	x	x	x	x	x	*		/	7–1
8/370:23	x	x	x	x	x	/	x	x			7–2
8/370:24	x	x	x	x	x	/	x	x			7–2
0/607	–	–	x	x	x	*	–	*	x	/	4–3
8/208	x	x	–	x	x	/	–	x	x		6–3
8/35	x	x	x	x	x	/	x	x	x		8–1

											154–119
											273
Totals	28–6	27–7	29–5	23–11	21–13	4–2	12–21	4–14	4–29	2–11 / 154–119	273
Scale positions	31	28	27	23	22	19½	14	7½	3	0	
Scale scores	.82	.65	.59	.35	.29	.15	–.18	–.56	–.82	–1.00	

$$R = 1 - \frac{11}{187} = .941 \qquad\qquad S = 1 - \frac{14}{66} = .788$$

single vote, and an examination of the marginals of Figure 2 shows that Black voted E+ more and E− less frequently than any other member of the Court.

On the other hand, an examination of the case that made the difference, *Blau* v. *Lehman*,[19] shows that Black's vote, upholding stock profiteering through interlocking directorates and trading on insider information, and rejecting the policy position of the Securities and Exchange Commission, was clearly an economically illiberal vote; and in addition, his choice was so consciously made that he wrote the opinion of the Court, having assigned the opinion (as the senior associate justice voting with the majority) to himself, the Chief Justice being in dissent. Such data tend to support the technical requirements of scale construction which account for Black's ranking below Warren this term.

Ranking Clark higher than Brennan also depends upon a single vote, although in this instance, the voting marginals support the order shown in the scale. Once again, moreover, an examination of the relevant case, *Mechling Barge Lines* v. *United States*,[20] indicates that the choices made by the two justices were quite deliberate, and that the discrimination made between them by the E scale for this term is a valid one. Brennan wrote for a majority which upheld an anti-competition decision of a three-judge district court, relating to profits already realized under long-haul/short-haul rate discriminations by a group of railroads, with the support of their acolyte, the Interstate Commerce Commission; Clark wrote the dissenting opinion, in behalf of Douglas and Warren and Black, protesting the Court's unwillingness to facilitate redress of the economic injury suffered by the competing barge lines which were plaintiffs in the case. Since the division was 5-4, Brennan's illiberal vote was decisive, and he made a clear choice to support the more conservative group of four justices on this issue.

The Frankfurter/Harlan reversal stems from two cases that were joined for common disposition, *United States* v. *Drum* and *Regular Common Carrier Conference* v. *Drum*.[21] Frankfurter joined in an opinion of the Court which upheld the extension of governmental regulation over motor carriers; Harlan dissented in behalf of unregulated private enterprise. Notwithstanding Frankfurter's substantial nonparticipation, it should be noted that it is unlikely that full participation would have resulted in any change in his rank position; the same remark applies to Whittaker as well. With White, full participation might have resulted in a higher rank; and with the exception of White, there is a perfect correlation between the proportions of the marginals and the scale ranks of the justices.

Douglas, Black, Warren, and Brennan— the justices who are commonly recognized as the most liberal members of the Court during the past half dozen terms—scale as economic liberals, as well as liberals on the C Scale. Similarly, Whittaker, Frankfurter, and Harlan have negative scale scores, and are among the lowest four ranks, on both scales; while Stewart and White both have moderate scale scores and occupy middle ranks, between the liberal (Douglas) and conservative (Harlan) groups, on both scales.

The only justice whose rank on the two scales shows considerable change is Clark, who is tenth on C but fourth on E, which suggests that Clark is a moderate liberal in his attitude toward issues of economic policy, and a pronounced conservative in regard to civil liberties. This finding is quite consistent with those for other recent terms; in the 1960 Term, for instance, Clark ranked fifth on E and last on C. On the other hand, six of the justices (Douglas-Warren-Brennan-Stewart-Frankfurter-Harlan) maintain precisely the same ordinal relationship, among themselves, on both the C and E scales for the 1961 Term, which suggests that their responses to issues of both civil liberty and economic policy were functions of more generalized liberal and conservative orientations.

[19]368 U.S. 403 (1962).
[20]368 U.S. 324 (1961).

[21]368 U.S. 370 (1962).

The three cases at the top of the E Scale, in which Black alone voted (and in terms of this linear analysis, inconsistently) to uphold the liberal position, raise the question whether these three cases, and the three which follow in which Douglas dissented alone, relate to two different components (or subvariables) of the scale. Examination of these six cases demonstrates, however, that such an assumption is false. In each of the two sets of three cases, there is one case involving the second component (governmental regulation of business), one case involving the third (labor-management relations), and one involving the fifth (the constitutionality of state taxation of interstate commerce). All three Douglas dissents were on grounds which are highly doctrinaire, which supports the attribution to him, by the scale, of the most extremely liberal views of any of the justices on issues of economic policy.

Black's dissents have two obvious common characteristics: in each case, he protested against a decision which had the effect (as he argued) of retreating from previously established liberal salients in what were formerly highly controversial areas of public policy, and each of these issues was one in which Black personally had been intimately involved —either as a Senator or as a Justice—in the struggle for the establishment of a more liberal policy. Thus, in the first case on the scale, Black dissented on behalf of labor's hard-won right to strike.[22] In the second, the invalidation of a regulation (of the Secretary of Agriculture) intended to prevent interstate competition in milk marketing evoked, for Black, the unpleasant recollection of *United States* v. *Butler*,[23] which impelled him to discuss the legislative history of New Deal statutory language that he had helped to create; and in the third, Black dissented on behalf of effective state regulation of the insurance business—but the interpretation of the McCarran-Ferguson Act, which was nomi-

nally at issue, must have been viewed, by Black, in the context of his own role in *United States* v. *South-Eastern Underwriters Ass'n*,[24] which was, in effect, overruled by the McCarran-Ferguson Act.

In short, our interpretation of Black's vote in these cases is psychological rather than legal: the intensity of his earlier personal involvement in these particular issues was so great that he now, years later, committed perceptual "errors" which caused him to evaluate the importance of the contemporary decisions differently than did his colleagues. In more strict psychometric terms, Black's perception of the loci of the j-points of these three cases, in the three-dimensional space of our model, differed from the apparent consensual perception of the other justices. The other justices thought that these cases raised extreme claims, which would locate their j-points near the positive terminus of the E scale axis in Figure 3; but Black perceived these to be moderate claims, represented by j-points located either near the origin or else with negative reference coordinates on the first factorial axis.

3. The Minor Scale Variables. In addition to the two major variables that have been discussed, there are four other variables that have been tentatively identified, on the basis of similar research in other recent terms of the Court. These include F (either the national or state governments versus taxpayers, when the issue is statutory or administrative rather than constitutional); A (judicial activism or restraint in reviewing the decisions of the Congress, the President, and administrative agencies); N (federalism, and conflict between the national and state governments); and J (the supervisory authority of the Supreme Court over the decision-making of lower courts). There were fourteen split decisions on the merits in non-constitutional taxation cases during the 1960 Term, and these formed an acceptable F scale. There were also enough F cases to form scales in the 1959 and 1957 Terms. Working in depth with a sample of cases drawn from several

---

[22]"It took more than 50 years for unions to have written into federal legislation the principle that they have a right to strike." Mr. Justice Black, dissenting in *Teamsters Local* v. *Lucas Flour Co.,* 369 U.S. 95, 109 (1962).

[23]297 U.S. 1 (1935).

[24]322 U.S. 533 (1944).

terms, Spaeth has used cumulative scaling to analyze an attitudinal dimension that seems to be very similar to the variable which we have denominated J.[25] There have been too few cases associated with A, N, or J, for any of these variables to be scaled on the basis of term data, in recent years.

In the 1961 Term, there were three cases on F, three on A, two on N, and none on J; there was one decision that could not be classified in terms of any of these variables; and there was also the one 4-4 decision (the effect of which was E−) for which objective attribution of the votes was not possible. These ten cases, plus the thirty-nine C Scale and the thirty-four E Scale cases, account for the total of eighty-three split decisions, on the merits, for the term; and it is evident that together, the two major liberalism variables account for the variance in the voting behavior of the justices in eighty-eight per cent of these decisions.

E. Scale Axes in the Factor Space. The next step is to position the scale axes, which are considered to be the psychological analogues of the cumulative scales, in the space defined by the factorial reference axes. It will be recalled that the configuration of i-points for the justices is uniquely determined by the set of factor loadings given in Table V. The problem now is to determine whether it is possible to pass a set of axes through the factor space, in such a manner that the rankings of the projections, from the i-points onto the axes, are equivalent, in a statistically acceptable sense, to the rankings of the justices on the scale axes. What is required mathematically, in order to accomplish this, are sets of weights which will determine the position of the axes in the space, and the points on each axis where the projections from the i-points fall. Given such data, it will then be possible to compare the rankings of the justices on the cumulative scales, with the rankings of the projections from their i-points on the counterpart scale axes.

[25]Spaeth, "Judicial Power as a Variable Motivating Supreme Court Behavior," 6 *Midwest J. Pol. Sci.* 54–82 (1962).

It is helpful to prepare a set of two-dimensional plots of the i-points against the reference axes, similar to Figure 3 but without (of course) the scale axes. Initial estimates of weights can be made from an examination of such two-dimensional plots. More precise determination of a set of acceptable weights requires mathematical analysis of the factor matrix of Table 5, and the use of a calculating machine. The distance from the origin of the factor space to the point which is closest to a given i-point, on any scale axis, is computed by use of the formula,

$$(3) \qquad d = \frac{\alpha x + \beta y + \gamma z}{(\alpha^2 + \beta^2 + \gamma^2)^{1/2}}$$

where d is the distance from the origin to the point on the scale axis where it is orthogonal to the projection from the i-point; x, y, and z are coordinates of the factorial reference axes for the i-points; and α, β, and γ are the coefficients which determine the position of the scale axis in the three-dimensional factor space. The same set of coefficients also provides the reference axis coordinates for the positive terminus of the scale axis.

It is not assumed that the positions in which the scale axes have been placed, in Figure 3, constitute a uniquely "best" fit to the configuration of i-points; but it is assumed that the positions defined in Table 6 and shown in Figure 3 are an appropriate and approximately correct solution. One way to conceptualize this question is to think of a cone which intercepts a relatively quite small circular area on the surface of a unit sphere; all axes lying within the cone will array the projections from i-points so as to produce the same set of rankings of the justices as will be produced by any other axis within the cone.

The three plots of Figure 3 may be thought of as three views of a cube. Figure 3a is a top view, Figure 3b is a side view, and Figure 3c is an end view. With relationship to reference axis I*, the C scale axis enters from the lower right octant of the cube, passes through the origin, and emerges at the end through the upper left octant. The E scale axis passes downward and to the right of I*. Reference axis I*, it should be noted, is approximately

FIGURE 35–1   Scale Axes and the Judicial Point Configuration in the Orthogonal Factor Space

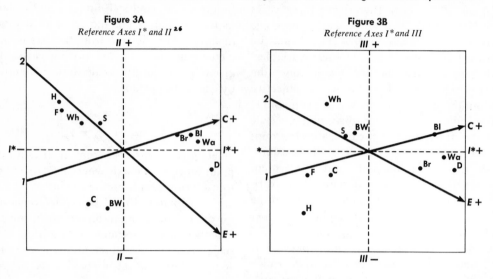

Figure 3A
Reference Axes I* and II [26]

Figure 3B
Reference Axes I* and III

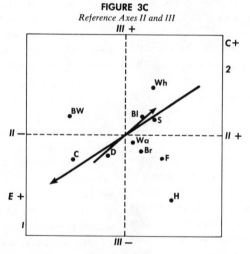

FIGURE 3C
Reference Axes II and III

[26]The direction of orthogonal factor axes extracted by the complete centroid method is arbitrary; the asterisk following the identifying number for the first axis (*i.e.*, 1*) signifies that the polarity of this axis was reversed to facilitate uniformity in inter-term comparisons in the larger study to which this article relates.

TABLE 6   Reference Axis Coordinates, Coefficients, and Cosines for Axes

	C	E
Scale axes	1	2
Coordinates/coefficients:		
I/α	1.00	1.00
II/β	.30	−.80
III/γ	.25	−.50
Cosines		
Figure 3a	$+16\frac{1}{2}°$	− 39°
Figure 3b	+14°	− $26\frac{1}{2}°$
Figure 3c	+40°	−148°

the centroid, or arithmetic mean, of the C and E scale axes. Both the C and E scale axes are positioned almost exactly the same as for the 1960 Term.

The C axis clearly passes closest to Black, who also appears to have the most extreme projection on the positive segment of the axis. (Such a projection would correspond, of course, to Black's position with the highest score on the C cumulative scale.) Douglas, Warren, and Brennan obviously project in that sequence upon the positive segment of the C axis. Stewart clearly will project upon the C axis somewhere near but to the left of the origin, which means that his "loading" on the axis will be low and negative. And the remaining five justices will project upon the negative segment of the C axis.

Douglas, Black, Warren, and Brennan all will project positively upon the E axis, although we cannot be certain, from an examination of Figure 3, whether Black will precede Brennan on the axis, as he does on the cumulative scale. Clark, who ranked fourth on the E cumulative scale, clearly will project to the sixth position on the E axis, behind both Brennan and White; and the remaining justices will project negatively, corresponding to their negative scale scores for this variable.

Figure 3a shows that in terms of the first two factors, which are the most important ones in accounting for the differences among the justices, the latter are grouped into three clusters:

(1) Douglas, Warren, Black, and Brennan, who will project positively upon both C and E;

(2) White and Clark, who will project positively upon E but negatively on C; and

(3) Stewart, Whittaker, Frankfurter, and Harlan, who will project negatively upon both C and E.

F. A Correlational Test of the Theory. The principal hypothesis underlying this study is that differences in the attitudes of the justices towards the basic issues raised by the cases that the Court decides account for the differences in the voting behavior of the justices. In short, Supreme Court justices vote as they do because of their attitudes towards the public policy issues that they decide. We are now in a position to make a statistical test of this hypothesis.

The i-points of the justices are separated in the factor space because of variance in the extent of majority participation of individual justices; but the factor analysis routine knows absolutely nothing about the subject matter of the values to which the decisions relate. The relative degrees of support by the justices for the key substantive issues can be determined by cumulative scaling; but cumulative scaling is a unidimensional measurement device, and each such scale is based upon a different universe of content, and is quite independent *methodologically* (as distinguished from psychologically) from every other scale.

We shall assume, therefore, that if the cumulative scales can be reconstituted as a set of scale axes whose position is consistent with the configuration of i-points in the factor space, then the attitudinal differences of the justices on the cumulative scales must account for the variance in the voting behavior of the justices, which is represented by the spatial separation of their ideal-points in the multidimensional factor space. If the correspon-

TABLE 7   Correlation of Judicial Ranks on Scales and Scale Axes

C				E			
Axis	Ranks		Scale	Axis	Ranks		Scale
.729	1 Bl	1	1.00	.819	1 D	1	.82
.727	2 D	2	.95	.536	2 Wa	2	.65
.725	3 Wa	3	.87	.344	3 Bl	3	.59
.486	4 Br	4	.69	.343	4 Br	5	.29
−.136	5 S	5	.28	.134	5 BW	6	.15
−.212	6 Wh	7	− .10	.095	6 C	4	.35
−.304	7 BW	6	.18	−.411	7 S	7	− .18
−.531	8 F	8	− .69	−.544	8 H	9	− .82
−.560	9 C	10	− .95	−.592	9 F	8	− .56
−.630	10 H	9	− .74	−.646	10 Wh	10	−1.00

Rank correlation coefficient (tau). 911   .867
Significance level, 1-tailed (p) 000015   .000058

dence between the set of cumulative scales and their scale axis analogues can be established in accordance with accepted procedures of statistical proof, then we shall have proved, in a mathematical sense, that the justices of the Supreme Court vary in their voting behavior according to the differences in their attitudes towards the scale variables.

Table 7 presents a comparison of the cumulative scale scores, and the distances along the counterpart scale axes at which the i-points project (as determined by formula 3), together with the corresponding sets of rankings, for all justices on both of the major variables. Although both scale scores and axis loadings range in value, in principle, from +1 to −1, so that some meaning can be attached to direct comparison of pairs of corresponding scores and loadings, it will be recalled that, for mathematical reasons relating to the marginal distributions of the fourfold tables, the intervals on the two types of continua are not genuinely commensurable. Scale scores, indeed, are directly related to the proportion of pro decisions in any set of cases.

This means that the same ranking of justices might reflect a large number of different sets of scale scores; and the variation within such sets is therefore a function not of variation in judicial *attitudes* but rather of the relative extremity of the *stimuli* (cases). Moreover, it has been determined experimentally

that the error variance in the factor analysis routine is usually around ten per cent, while the error variance in the cumulative scales is only slightly less; and there are other sources of error variance implicit in the general method. Therefore, it seems reasonable to employ the nonparametric rank correlation test for the purpose of making the comparison. In spite of the seeming precision of coefficients carried to the third decimal place, it would be fatuous to pretend that the measurement employed in this study can hope to be more than a rough approximation of empirical reality.

As Table 7 indicates, there are two inconsistencies in the two sets of rankings for C, involving Whittaker and White,[27] and Clark and Harlan. However, it will be observed that the probability of such close agreement between the two sets of rankings having occurred by chance is less than one chance in 66,666. Or, in other words, if one were to plot i-points and scale axes on the basis of coordinates drawn from a table of random numbers, and draw a set of numbers in a similar manner for the scale scores, and then compare the two sets of rankings, one would have to expect to repeat these procedures at

---

[27]The rankings of 6 or 7 for Whittaker and White on the C scale and axis demonstrate the extent to which there is homogeneity between the attitudes of White, and the justice whom he replaced, toward civil liberty issues.

least sixty-six thousand times before one could expect to achieve such close agreement between the two sets of rankings more than once on the basis of chance alone.

The correspondence between the two sets of rankings for E also is very close, and again there are two inconsistencies. Frankfurter and Harlan are reversed in order upon the axis; and although, as we already have pointed out, it seems unlikely that Frankfurter's extensive non-participation affected his scale score on E, it is most probable that it did materially affect the location of his i-point, since phi coefficients based upon small cell frequencies (in the fourfold tables) will give more weight to small differences than those based upon more full participation. Therefore, our interpretation of the Frankfurter-Harlan reversal is that it is due to error variance in the configuration of i-points, resulting from Frankfurter's illness during the latter part of the term.

The other inconsistency involves Clark's lower ranking on the axis than on the scale. As we have explained earlier, the E scale's discrimination, in ranking Clark before Brennan, appears to be valid, even though this is the first time that Clark has outranked Brennan on E since they have sat together on the Court—although Clark did rank fourth on E during the 1954 and 1955 Terms, after Warren but before Brennan had joined the Court. We also have pointed out that White's non-participation was so extensive that the E Scale might be in error ranking White below Clark and Brennan. This possible error readily explains the Clark-White reversal in rankings. We are left with Clark-Brennan, and our conclusion is that the i-point configuration is in error with regard to Clark's position in the space. Although Clark has the second highest negative loading on the third factor, it would have to be much more negative than it is, in order for Clark to project consistently upon the E scale axis.

The possibility of chance replication of the pair of rankings observed to obtain for E is so small—about one chance in 20,000—that the most reasonable inference is that these rankings are functions of the same underlying cause: the attitudes of the justices towards the economic policy issues raised for decision in the set of E scale cases. Indeed, the correlation between both sets of rankings is very high, with or without the above explanations, since no reasonable person expects to discover perfect consistency in the exercise of human judgment, even on the part of professional judges.

From a statistical point of view, it should be noted that the probabilities shown in Table 7 relate to the probability of producing, by chance alone, the indicated congruence between any *one* scale and the point configuration. The prospect of chance replication of as good a fit for both scales simultaneously, with the same fixed point configuration, is of course very much more remote; indeed, the joint probability, which is the product of the two discrete probabilities, is a truly astronomical number: $.0^987$, or approximately one chance in a billion. It seems warranted, under these circumstances, to reject the null hypothesis, and to accept instead the hypothesis that the variance in the voting behavior of the justices during the 1961 Term can be adequately accounted for by the differences in their attitudes towards the fundamental issues of civil liberty and economic liberalism.

G. The Psychological Distance Separating the Justices. Now that we have established a basis for confidence in the proposition that the judicial ideal-points in the factor space do indeed function as reasonably adequate symbolizations of the respective attitude syndromes of the individual justices, there remains one final question that we can examine. Discussion about the justices frequently revolves around such questions as which ones tend to share the "same point of view," and which ones are "farthest apart" in their thinking. The factor space provides a convenient vehicle for objective measurement of the psychological distance which separates each justice from each of the others.

Since the measurement of these psychological distances is purely mathematical, we shall carry it out in five-dimensional space, which will afford what may be a slightly more

TABLE 8   Attitudinal Distances among Judicial Ideal Points, 1961 Term

	D	Bl	Wa	Br	S	BW	C	Wh	F	H
D	—	.78	.64	.77	1.29	1.45	1.54	1.55	1.69	1.82
Bl	.78	—	.30	.47	.99	1.19	1.40	1.39	1.42	1.74
Wa	.64	.30	—	.32	1.10	1.22	1.35	1.49	1.48	1.68
Br	.77	.47	.32	—	.91	1.10	1.14	1.26	1.27	1.38
S	1.29	.99	1.10	.91	—	1.00	1.03	.75	.57	1.03
BW	1.45	1.19	1.22	1.10	1.00	—	.51	1.24	1.24	1.58
C	1.54	1.40	1.35	1.14	1.03	.51	—	1.24	1.13	1.24
Wh	1.55	1.39	1.49	1.26	.75	1.24	1.24	—	1.16	1.16
F	1.69	1.42	1.48	1.27	.57	1.24	1.13	1.16	—	.87
H	1.82	1.74	1.68	1.38	1.03	1.58	1.24	1.16	.87	—

accurate basis for measurement than the three-dimensional space depicted in Figure 3, since the fourth and fifth factors will permit us to consider the effect of other dimensions which—assuming that we are not merely interjecting the distortion of error variance—would have to be considered to be a part of the attitude syndrome of each justice. The psychological distance will be measured on the same scale as that employed for the three-dimensional factor space: along orthogonal reference axes, each of which extends from +1 to −1. The standard formula for computing the distance between any two points in orthogonal five-space is:

$$(4) \quad d_{i1-i2} = [(v_1 - v_2)^2 + (w_1 - w_2)^2 + (x_1 - x_2)^2 + (y_1 - y_2)^2 + (z_1 - z_2)^2]^{1/2}$$

where d is the distance, i_1 and i_2 are the ideal-points of a pair of justices, and $v, w, x, y,$ and z are the coordinates (or "loadings") of the justices on factors I–V.

The results of computations based upon the use of this formula are shown in Table 8. Black and Warren are the closest two justices, in terms of their attitudes towards the policy issues that the Court decided in the 1961 Term; they are separated by a distance of only .30 in the five-dimensional factor space, although Brennan, too, is only .32 away from Warren. Black and Brennan, at .47, are the next closest pair, so that the triad of Black-Warren-Brennan constitutes the set of three justices whose attitudes were most similar toward the issues confronting the Court during the 1961 Term. The common misapprehension that Douglas and Black are the two

justices who "are closest together in their thinking" is contradicted by Table 8, just as it failed to find support in equivalent data for the 1960 Term. There are, indeed, no less than eight closer pairs than Douglas-Black; and both Douglas and Black are closer to Warren and to Brennan than they are to each other. However, it is true that the closest group of four justices consists of the Black-Warren-Brennan triad, plus Douglas.

The most notable of the remaining affinity relationships are the .51 for the White-Clark pair; and Stewart's .57 separation from Frankfurter and .75 from Whittaker, plus the Frankfurter-Harlan distance of .87. It is apparent, however, that there are no triads, or larger groupings, among these remaining six justices, which do not involve substantial separation between some of the included pairs. The most general statement that can be made is that three general points of view may be identified:

I. The *liberal* attitude, characteristic of the relatively closely grouped quadruple, of whom Warren was the most typical representative, at a minimal average distance of .42 from his colleagues Brennan, Black, and Douglas.

II. The *idiosyncratic* attitude, characteristic of the Clark-White pair, who are relatively close to each other, and relatively widely separated from all of the other justices, as an examination of the three-dimensional space depicted in Figure 3 makes evident.

III. The *conservative* attitude, characteristic of the remaining four justices, and best typified by Stewart, whose average distance from Whittaker, Frankfurter, and Harlan, was

.78—a measure which suggests that the conservatives were roughly twice as far apart from each other, in their attitudes in general, as were the liberals.

The greatest difference in attitude is that between Douglas and Harlan, who are maximally separated at a distance of 1.82. Harlan is also the justice who is most different from Black, Warren, Brennan, and White, while it is Douglas whose attitude is most dissimilar from Whittaker, Frankfurter, Clark, and Stewart, as well as from Harlan.

If we seek an "average" justice whose point of view best typifies that of the Court as a whole, there are two possibilities: Brennan, whose average distance from all of his colleagues is .96; and Stewart, whose average distance also is .96. However, the range of the distances separating Stewart from the rest of the Court is .71, considerably less than Brennan's range of 1.06. When we take both the mean and the range of the psychological distances into account, Stewart thus clearly emerges as the most typical member of the Court, a position that he also occupied in the 1960 Term. Such a finding is not inconsistent, of course, with the findings of scale analysis, and it accords with the configuration shown in the three-dimensional space of Figure 3. The most atypical justice during the 1961 Term was Harlan who, separated by an average distance of 1.39 from his colleagues, entertained the most generally extreme views of any of the justices.

Table 8 also permits us to make a direct inference concerning a question which, in the past, there has been a tendency to approach by a variety of indirect routes. To what extent do the views of Byron White replicate those of Charles Whittaker, the man to whose position on the Court he succeeded? Not very closely, according to these data. Their separation of 1.24 is greater than the mean, for all pairs, of 1.15; and White and Whittaker are no closer together than either of them is, on the average, to the rest of his colleagues. This finding is to some extent qualified and explained by the C and E scales, which show that White and Whittaker both were rather neutral toward civil liberty issues, but that White was considerably more liberal in his

attitude toward economic policy than was Whittaker, who concluded his services on the Court, in perfect accord with his position in other recent terms, as the anchor man on the E scale.

IV. PREDICTIONS FOR THE 1962 TERM

The Reapportionment Cases. It is anticipated that during the 1962 Term, the Court will announce its decision on the merits in regard to several cases challenging state legislative reapportionment. Some of these cases already have been docketed, and others may be docketed and decided during the course of the term. We recognize that there are many specific differences among the state constitutional provisions, the facts and formulae for legislative districting, and the consequences for the two-party system, presented by the cases coming to the Court from different states. Probably the Michigan case, *Beadle* v. *Scholle*, presents the most extreme libertarian claim for the extension of the equal protection clause of the Fourteenth Amendment to require representation by population of both houses of the state legislature, notwithstanding a recently-adopted state constitutional amendment and a pending referendum on a new state constitution, both of which are to the contrary.

Nevertheless, the assumption that one would have to make, on the basis of the theory discussed in this paper, is that the justices will vote in the decision of these reapportionment cases in response to their fundamental attitudes toward civil liberty, and more particularly, to that component of the C scale —the political equality subvariable—to which the reapportionment issue is most directly related. There have been too few cases, in recent terms, to make possible independent scaling of the political equality subvariable. But our assumption is that it lies, as a scale axis, midway between the C and E axes in Figure 3, since legislative reapportionment has such obviously important implications for public policy-making affecting economic as well as political rights and interests.

On the basis of that assumption, together

with the predictions that we already have made . . . concerning judicial rankings during the term, we shall predict that:

In its decision in *Beadle* v. *Scholle*, the Court will either deny *certiorari* to the decision of the Michigan Supreme Court in *Scholle* v. *Hare*,[28] or else affirm it on the merits by a division of 5–4, with Douglas, Black, Goldberg, Warren, and Brennan voting in the majority, and the remaining justices in dissent.

The Court will not reverse any of the pro-reapportionment decisions of lower courts in states other than Michigan,[29] nor will it affirm any of the anti-reapportionment decisions of lower courts presently docketed.[30]

Since none of the other cases presently docketed raise a more extreme claim of entitlement to political equality than does *Beadle* v. *Scholle*, and several of them raise claims that are less extreme, the voting divisions of the Court in those cases that are decided on the merits will range from 5–4 to 8–1; Douglas, Black, Goldberg, Warren, and Brennan will be in the majority, and Harlan will dissent, while the remaining three justices who join the majority will do so in the sequence: White, Clark, Stewart.

CONCLUSION

In conclusion, it should be understood that it will indeed be remarkable if all of the predictions stated above can be validated, in the decision-making behavior of the justices

---

[28]367 Mich. 176, 116 N.W. 2d 350 (1962).
[29]*Gray* v. *Sanders*, No. 112, 31 *U.S.L. Week* 3012 (U.S. July 3, 1962) (probable jurisdiction noted, 370 U.S. 921 (June 18, 1962)) [Ga.]; *Reynolds* v. *Sims*, No. 508, 31 *U.S.L. Week* 3147 (U.S. Oct. 30, 1962) (docketed Oct. 12, 1962) [Ala.]; *Price* v. *Christian*, No. 539, 31 *U.S.L. Week* 3157 (U.S. Nov. 6, 1962) (docketed Oct. 19, 1962) [Okla.]. The first two cases are appeals from federal district courts; the third is on certiorari to the Oklahoma Supreme Court.
[30]*W.M.C.A.* v. *Simon*, No. 460, 31 *U.S.L. Week* 3103 (U.S. Oct. 2, 1962) (docketed September 26, 1962) [N. Y.]; *Wesberry* v. *Vandiver*, No. 507, 31 *U.S.L. Week* 3147 (U.S. Oct. 30, 1962) (docketed Oct. 12, 1962) [Ga.]; *Vann* v. *Frink*, No. 540, 31 *U.S.L. Week* 3157 (U.S. Nov. 6, 1962) (docketed Oct. 19, 1962) [Ala.]; *Maryland Committee for Fair Representation* v. *Tawes*, No. 554, 31 *U.S.L. Week* 3146 (U.S. Oct. 30, 1962) (docketed Oct. 24, 1962) [Md.]. The first three of these cases are appeals from federal district courts; the fourth is an appeal from the Maryland Court of Appeals

---

as observed and measured and reported by some other analyst or analysts using the theory and methods of analysis that have been explained in this paper. It will be even more remarkable if most of these predictions *cannot* be validated, or if any of them prove to be extremely wide of the mark. The predictions relate to the kinds of continuities in judicial behavior which, although here confined to the empirical data for a single appellate court that hardly is a typical one, can nevertheless be expected to exist in other appellate courts as well. It should thus be possible to extend the scope of inquiries along the lines described above in order to increase our systematic knowledge about courts and judges in general. To be of maximal significance, such systematic knowledge about judicial behavior will be, of course, not *empirical* knowledge but *theoretical* knowledge.[31]

---

[31]This is the distinction which, more than any other, separates the skilled practitioner, the "legal expert" of whom we wrote earlier in this paper, from the behavioralist. The sophisticated lawman, in the tradition of legal realism, predicts on the basis of his specialized empirical knowledge; while the behavioralist, in the tradition of modern science, predicts on the basis of his theoretical knowledge.

[*Editors' note:* The Supreme Court disposed of the reapportionment cases cited above in the 1962 and 1963 terms. All the predictions were correct!]

---

36 THE THEORY OF THE LIBERAL MIND

Glendon Schubert

A point of criticism that is almost certain to be levied against this research is that it is based upon the *S–R* (stimulus-response) model of behaviorist psychology and learning theory; and that, as a consequence, I have greatly oversimplified the true attitudinal relationships of and among the justices. I think that the most appropriate response to such an accusation is to point out that the model of the atom may also be said to greatly

Reprinted by permission of the publisher from Glendon Schubert, *The Judicial Mind: The Attitudes and Ideologies of Supreme Court Justices 1946–1963* (Evanston: Northwestern University Press, 1965), pp. 286–288.

oversimplify the physical universe; and doubtless the concepts of gene and chromosome do violence to the intricate complexities of heredity, particularly in a context of environmental influences. The test of the value of a scientific model, concept, or theory is not *whether* it oversimplifies empirical reality; but rather, what effect it has upon our understanding of that reality. The lawyer's model of judicial decision-making, which is based upon traditional logic and depends upon the *stare decisis* norm for its *deus ex machina*, is also a vast oversimplification of empirical reality. If we must choose between *S–R* and *stare decisis* conceptualism, our criterion should be: Which helps us the better to acquire valid and reliable understanding about how and why judges make their decisions?

Even if we assume that a psychometric model is appropriate, there is still the question: Which, among competing concepts of factorial interpretation, ought to be preferred by lay analysts—such as myself—of judicial psychology? My own approach has been eclectic. . . . My methodology was constructed to help resolve the theoretical questions in which I was interested. . . .

. . . Neither attitudes nor ideologies have any essence; such dimensions are strictly hypothetical constructs which are invoked to help explain the manifest observable regularities and discontinuities in the voting behavior of United States Supreme Court justices. I do not for a moment delude myself in thinking that I have boxed the compass of Supreme Court decision-making, by offering an interpretation exclusively in socio-psychological terms, and at that, one confined to judicial attitudes toward policy values. Other studies of human behavior indicate a high probability that their attitudes toward and relationships with each other, with wives, with secretaries, with friends, and so on, have an influence upon their decisions; and although such influences necessarily are within the scope of what is measured by the phi matrices, they are *dehors* the attitudinal scales, and they certainly are *dehors* the strictly psychological interpretation that I have provided. . . . It seems likely that the health—both physical and mental—of the justices has an influence

upon their decisions; also their ethnic origins, religion, political affiliation, indeed, their whole life experience. But every one of these other sources of variance can be conceptualized as an indirect influence upon a respondent's attitudes toward policy values, and hence, an appropriate subject for future research into the question: What are the factors which condition attitudes and ideologies? In focusing as I have done upon attitudes and ideologies that are oriented toward issues of public policy, these other influences have been sublimated rather than lost; they are omitted from my analytical framework, but not from the empirical field of potentially observable events. . . .

My study of the judicial mind, subject to these caveats, shows that modern liberalism as a political ideology has as its primary content two scalable attitudinal dimensions. One of these, the political scale, measures attitudes toward personal rights; and the other, the economic scale, measures attitudes toward property rights. The combinations of attitudes of Supreme Court justices, that is, their ideologies—are such that the attitudinal relationship among the justices characteristically is not linear but rather is elliptical. This elliptical structure of judicial attitudes is of fundamental importance, because it makes possible the relatively high degree of consensus that is prerequisite to the Court's performance of its role in the larger political system. The fact that there are two major attitudinal dimensions means that differently constructed majorities can and do form on different issues; if there were only a single major dimension, it would be much more likely that the Court would be divided between a permanent majority and a permanent minority. Moreover, about a third of the issues resolved by the Court are *not* closely related to liberalism and conservatism; and the elliptical structure of ideologies makes it possible for the extremes of liberalism and conservatism to meet on common ground—as they do—when the issue is (for example) freedom of religious belief, or its opposite: rendering what is due unto Caesar, the collection of the public tithe through the income tax. . . .

Part 4
Output

The outputs of the federal judicial system are of two types; (1) the decisions in particular cases and (2) the policies which underlie them. These decisions and policies are the end products of the conversion process.

Of all the subjects treated in this book, the reader is probably most familiar with the decisions and policies which constitute output. The typical course on constitutional law focuses on this material as articulated in Supreme Court opinions. We, therefore, shall not review this material here even though we too shall focus on the Supreme Court. Instead we shall consider the two aspects of output in a manner different from conventional treatments.

First, we shall look at the problem of predicting decisional output. Here the concern, to a large extent, is with determining which side wins. In the second section we turn from the decision to a consideration of the policies which underlie specific decisions and how court-fashioned policies differ from those made by other institutions in the larger political system.

A. Predicting Decisional Output

All who study and work with the courts of the federal judicial system are concerned with explaining and even predicting unique decisions for specific legal and fact situations. This is true both for lawyers, who must advise clients, and for social scientists involved in studying judicial behavior. Obviously, the ability to explain or predict rests on the degree to which one's conception of how judges decide cases corresponds to reality. In Part 3, on Conversion, many of the approaches which have been used for undertaking this task were discussed. As will be remembered, however, they rest on diverse assumptions. Often, the characteristics of the system or data emphasized by one approach is disregarded in others. How, then, does one decide on the relative merits of different approaches? There are at least two different ways of approaching this question. The first is formal analysis. This involves looking at the assumptions of the model and the methodologies used and then seeing whether these are adequate for explaining judicial behavior. The second involves testing the approach or model for its predictive value. This means asking whether accurate predictions of decisions can be made.

The following selection by Sidney Ulmer reviews many of the approaches used for explaining Supreme Court decisions. He discusses the assumptions each rests on, the methodologies used, and the special problems associated with each. He then considers their predictive ability. This selection, therefore, provides an opportunity for bringing into perspective most of the approaches presented earlier.

37 MATHEMATICAL MODELS FOR PREDICTING JUDICIAL BEHAVIOR

S. Sidney Ulmer

In his volume on *Judicial Behavior,* Glendon Schubert refers to three philosophical models for predicting judicial decisions: the legal norm, the legal fact, and the legal discretion models.[1] In general, the legal norm model assumes that "facts are facts" and that judges are unlikely to disagree fundamentally as to the facts in a given situation. There may be disagreement about the legally relevant facts, but if so it is a function of improper choice of legal norm. Procedural norms serve the function of initially narrowing the facts, but those finally chosen as relevant will depend on the criteria which the court decides should prevail. This model, therefore, maximizes norm certainty and minimizes fact uncertainty. Such maximization constitutes the prediction problem.

The legal fact model suggests that facts are not as easily determined as the legal norm model implies. When judges disagree it is not over norms, but over the facts made relevant by the chosen decision rules. Thus, this model emphasizes that judges are likely to disagree about what has happened before a case reaches the court and to attribute disagreement concerning outcome to differential perception. Clearly, the legal fact model minimizes disagreement about norms and defines the prediction problem as maximization of fact recognition.

The suggestion that neither legal fact nor legal norm models are adequate is a feature of the legal discretion model. This approach assumes that the discretion left to the judge makes the prediction of decisions on the basis

of legal facts and norms unreliable. Consequently, emphasis is on minimizing such considerations as guides to action. This view is attributed to Hans Kelsen and his Pure Theory of Law, but Kelsen, while implying the operation of other variables, did not investigate their nature or their impact.

Schubert also refers to a modified legal discretion model which appears to take up where Kelsen leaves off—that is, it emphasizes the discretion of the judge, but assumes its exercise in some patterned fashion. If these individual patterns are sufficiently understood, then reliable prediction of individual votes is thought possible.

Whereas the legal norm and legal fact models are predictive schema, the legal discretion model asserts the impossibility of prediction or at least suggests that the problem is multidimensional and perhaps incapable of solution since the well springs of discretion are so exceedingly complex. Or to put it another way, this model emphasizes why we cannot predict rather than suggesting how we might go about a difficult task. Consequently, I think the legal discretion model one genus, the legal norm and fact models another.

The modified legal discretion model is of still a third variety for it, in effect, is many models or theories each emphasizing some particular factor or set of factors impinging upon decisional outcome. This is not merely a matter of approaching the subject from the perspectives of cultural anthropology, political sociology and social psychology or of approaching the prediction problem from different levels of analysis. This latter view, which Schubert asserts, reflects his adoption of attitude as the key ingredient or category in terms of which all other facets of explanation can be treated. Indeed, he says that: "One can understand and explain—at least, at a first level of initial comprehension— everything about judicial decision-making on the basis of attitudinal similarities and differences of the individuals in the decision-making group."[2]

Reprinted by permission of the author and the University of Virginia Press from "Mathematical Models for Predicting Judicial Behavior," paper delivered at the Conference on Mathematical Applications in Political Science, Virginia Polytechnic Institute, July 2, 1966, pp. 1–13, 15–28.

[1] Glendon Schubert, *Judicial Behavior: A Reader in Theory and Research* (1964), pp. 443 ff.

[2] Schubert, *op. cit.*, p. 445.

Of course, if by attitude we mean a consistent set of opinions regarding a given item or set of items, and we can assume that all individuals have such "opinion sets," then for any given decision, outcome consistent with at least one such "opinion set" seems likely. But John Sprague has suggested that "any found relationship may be characterized as an attitude under some construction of the facts."[3] He illustrates this point with the case of a judge who votes in some way out of loyalty to the executive who appointed him.

Professor Sprague's comment does not suggest any refutation of the statement attributed to Schubert unless the latter's remark is limited to the "issue in the case." For a judge may have an attitude toward the relationship of an office-holder to one who appointed him. But, presumably, Schubert's use of the concept is more restricted than such a general usage would allow. And, thus, non-attitudinally based decisions must be recognized as a possibility and if so recognized, attempts at explanation would be in order. Yet, Schubert has suggested in print that ". . . from the point of view of predicting judicial decision-making, the attitudinal approach takes the position that, given complete knowledge of the attitudes of a set of judges toward the issue or issues that they purport to resolve in a case, the analyst predicts the behavior of the judges on the basis of the imputed differentials in their attitudes."[4] This statement could be taken as Schubert's answer to the question: Attitude toward what? For it specifies the issue or issues to be resolved. This would rule out decisions

based upon the attitude of a judge to the president who appointed him. Whether this approach gives better prediction is, of course, an empirical question. But I think it clear that the modified legal discretion model is not a single attitudinal model with multiple levels. It is, in fact, a set of discretion models —some attitudinally based and some not.

Quantitative models for predicting judicial behavior can be classified in terms of what is to be predicted, the variables to be used, and the methods by which interrelationships are to be evaluated. Figure 1 gives a more detailed breakdown of this classificatory scheme. Obviously, the categories of this instrument could be given greater depth. We have extended them sufficiently to pick up the major quantitative models so far developed. Applying this scheme to the work of Kort, Tanenhaus, . . . Schubert, and Ulmer, we can identify five model types: ACB (Class 1); ACC (Class 2); ACD (Class 3); ABCD (Class 4); and ABBA (Class 5).

FIGURE 1

I. Dependent variables
  A. Decision of Court
    (1) on merits of case
    (2) other
  B. Decision of Individual Judge
    (1) on merits of case
    (2) other
II. Independent Variables
  A. Attributes
  B. Opinions—Attitudes
  C. Contextual—environmental stimuli
III. Analytical Models
  A. Psychometric
  B. Primitive—Quantitative (PQ)
  C. Boolean
  D. Regression
    (1) Normal
    (2) Discriminant

---

[3]John Sprague, Voting Patterns on the United States Supreme Court: Cases in Federalism, 1889–1959. Unpublished Ph.D. dissertation, Stanford University, 1964, p. 4. Although I think that Sprague puts his finger on the problem, I would approach it in a slightly different fashion. The relevant questions, as I see them are:
(a) Does a given judge have any consistent set of opinions toward an item or item set?
(b) If so, what is the identification of the items or item sets?
(c) If identified, which of the opinion sets are relevant for a given decision?
(d) If more than one opinion set is consistent with outcome, what is the relative degree to which each impinges on decision?
[4]Schubert, op. cit., p. 446.

II

Class 1 models are basically exploratory but early quantitative approaches to the prediction problem. Such models have been used by Kort, Nagel, and the present author. Each focused on the decisions of the Supreme Court on the merits in formal cases. Each identified contextual-environmental stimuli as the independent variables. Each used a relatively primitive form of quantitative analysis.

In 1962 this author attempted to explain the factors leading the Supreme Court to rule for or against Negro petitioners in jury exclusion cases.[5] Negro defendants are not entitled, under the Constitution, to have one or more Negroes on every jury by which they are tried. But in interpreting the fair trial implications of the 14th Amendment, the Supreme Court has consistently held that Negroes are entitled to a jury system from which they are not intentionally and systematically excluded solely on account of race and color. The reading of the relevant cases suggested that a determination of the matter depended upon the factual situation. The language used by several of the judges indicated that the exclusion of Negroes from state juries as a matter of chance was in no way illegal or unconstitutional. The problem seemed to be to discover how the Supreme Court separated chance exclusion from that which could be described as intentional and systematic in terms of race.

There were sufficient hints in the opinions of the judges for one to consider the possibility that the court was comparing two populations. The first was the total qualifying population from which juries or jury lists were drawn; the second was the grand or petit jury from which exclusion had been charged. But the relevant consideration for each of these populations was the ratio of whites to Negroes in each case. This ratio was expressed by an index of racial heterogeneity. The index figures for each population were then compared to see whether a difference of the observed magnitude would be expected by chance more than five times in 100. With this approach, we were able to explain outcome in all cases save one in the period 1935–1960.

A more ambitious attempt at predicting Supreme Court decisions mathematically was undertaken by Fred Kort in 1957.[6] Kort attempted to show that in certain areas of constitutional law it was possible to identify the factual elements influencing decision, derive numerical weights for these elements in a given set of cases, and to predict correctly decisions in later cases of the same type. The model he designed for this purpose ignored the reasoning of the judges and the changing composition of the Supreme Court even though 25 justices sat in the period analyzed. Nevertheless, using right to counsel cases for the period 1932–1947 for deriving factors and weights, Kort was able to predict, without error, all decisions in such cases in the period 1947–1956.

Professor Schubert has commented at some length on Kort's assumption that facts determine decision. According to Schubert, this is a kind of mechanical jurisprudence in which controlling facts replace controlling rules. Schubert defines facts as ". . . assertions about the observation of events that someone has perceived to have occurred in the real world." Having heard such assertions from lawyers and litigants, Supreme Court justices must then draw their inferences. It is Schubert's belief, however, that the ". . . judge's inference will be a function, inescapably, of his own attitude toward the value he selects as the criterion for perception of the fact."[7] This leads him to the conclusion that judges dominate and control facts, not vice-versa. Few would deny, of course, that attitudes and perceptions are key variables in interpreting reality. But Kort's focus is not on that question. Essentially, his inquiry has to do with the consistency of the relationships between fact and case outcome. Whether a set of decisions can be separated in terms of a set of variables chosen by an analyst is an empirical question. Kort clearly shows that such a separation is possible with his right to counsel data.

Franklin Fisher has discussed Kort's initial

---

[5]S. Sidney Ulmer, "Supreme Court Behavior in Racial Exclusion Cases: 1935–1960," *American Political Science Review*, Vol. 56 (1962), pp. 325–330.

[6]Fred Kort, "Predicting Supreme Court Decisions Mathematically: A Quantitative Analysis of the Right to Counsel Cases," *American Political Science Review*, Vol. 51 (1957), pp. 1–12.
[7]Schubert, *op. cit.*, p. 451.

predictive effort in more formal terms.[8] Having identified n factors to be responsible for decisional outcome, we can define a variable X_1 which takes the value 1 or 0 depending on the presence or absence of a given factor in a given case. Since such a variable must be defined for each factor, the number of variables $(X_1, X_2, X_3 \ldots X_n)$ equals the number of factors. The prediction problem, then, is to find a set of numbers (preferably positive) $A_1, A_2, A_3 \ldots A_n$ such that the expression:

$$A_1 X_1 + A_2 X_2 + A_3 X_3 \ldots A_n X_n$$

gives a higher value for cases decided for defendants than for cases decided to the contrary. This is basically a problem of finding a hyperplane which cuts a geometrical space such that all *pro* points fall on one side of the plane and all *con* points on the other.

Figure 2 shows a hyperplane cutting a two dimensional space. This diagram suggests that a weight of 6+ on either factor will give a *pro* decision regardless of the weight of the second factor. The converse, obviously, is not true. A weight of less than 6 on either factor will not necessarily give a *con* decision. Given such a weight on one factor, case outcome will be determined by the weight on the other factor with which it is to be combined. However, the diagram does suggest that a weight of less than 3 on both factors will produce a *con* result. In sum, then, the condition under which the hyperplane provides a perfect division is what Fisher calls condition 1: i.e., that should we observe a *pro* case with a certain number of the factors present, then we must never observe a *con* case with the same factors present. This, of course, assumes perfect consistency. Keeping in mind that the model assumes positive and monopolar weights, once the relative weight of a factor to other factors is determined, a given level on the numerical index assures a *pro* decision.

Kort's initial predictive effort provided relative factor weights which separated his

[8]Franklin M. Fisher, "The Mathematical Analysis of Supreme Court Decisions: The Use and Abuse of Quantitative Methods," *American Political Science Review*, Vol. 52 (1958), pp. 321–328.

FIGURE 2

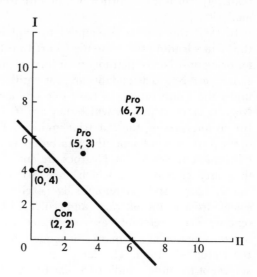

pro and *con* cases perfectly. However, this is one of many hyperplanes that might have performed such a function with equal success. This can be seen quite clearly in Figure 2. Although the hyperplane drawn there cuts each axis at the value of 6, the *pro* and *con* cases used in this example could be separated equally well if the intersecting values were 5 and 5, 5 and 6, 6 and 8, 6 and 7, etc. In short, the slopes of the lines and by definition the number of hyperplanes are infinite in number. This suggests that a particular weighting scheme may provide prediction but tell little about the true importance of the various factors. Fisher's analysis also implies that a successful predictive device does not assure us that the factors used were perceived by the judges nor whether high weight factors were more important than those of low weight. Consequently, the addition and subtraction of factors may have no effect on one's ability to predict case outcome. . . .

To his rather impressive analytical tour de force, Fisher has added some comments concerning the use of quantitative predictors in analyzing Supreme Court behavior. Essentially, his main point is that in those areas in which such predictors can be successful, they aren't needed. For, he says, if we can construct a perfectly predicting weighting scheme, the cases involved are covered by clear precedents. This comment suggests a gross misunderstanding of the judicial process. A perfectly predicting weighting scheme, at the least, identifies factors in terms of which prediction is to be made. The discovery of "clear precedent" is not always so easy. And legal analysis will not tell us whether our "clear precedent" is perceived and responded to by a given judge any more than quantitative analysis will provide that information for weighted factors in a predictive model. Moreover, Fisher fails to recognize the value of non-perfectly predicting weighting schemes. The question, always, is whether a given theory will explain a given set of facts. We are generally interested in the extent to which such is the case and an inadequate match is likely to lead to attempted improvement.

In spite of his generally pessimistic conclusion, however, Fisher's analysis is important for clarifying some of the problems associated with this kind of work. . . .

Each of the [two] class 1 models suffers in some respect if we accept the prediction problem as defined by Fisher. Ulmer's model (1) is not appropriate for the relative weighting of variables which in combination determine decisional outcome. . . . Kort's model (1) does not provide the "best" systematic method for placing the hyperplane in the geometric space. Later analytical schemes have remedied each of these shortcomings.

III

The only class 2 model considered in this paper is Kort's Boolean Model (2). . . .

The distinctive characteristic of the Boolean model is its concern only with logical relations; it does not assign numerical weights. As in Kort's Model (1), facts are used as independent variables. But no assumption as to the linearity (additive quality) of the facts is necessary. And the model avoids the postulate that the scoring system used for the variables is the "best" for placing cases on a numerical index. Otherwise, however, the Boolean Model makes a similar inquiry. Thus Kort recommends it in those cases in which one may be interested in predicting outcome in a case involving a combination of facts that have not appeared although using facts that have appeared in other combinations.

Since the facts used in the model are monopolar, a *pro* decision may be anticipated in any case having a set of facts which includes the smallest combination giving a *pro* decision. Or, to put it another way,

$$R\,(C_1) \geq R\,(C_2) \rightarrow D_{pro} \leftrightarrow R\,(C_2) \rightarrow D_{pro}.$$

This says that the rank of a case that is equal to or higher than the rank of a second case implies a decision for defendant if and only if the rank of the second case implies a *pro* decision. For example, consider five cases with four facts distributed as follows:

Cases	Facts	Rank	Decision
C_1	$f_1 f_2 f_3 f_4$	1	Pro
C_2	$f_1 f_2 f_3$	2	Pro
C_3	$f_1 f_2$	3	Pro
C_4	$f_1 \quad f_3$		Con
C_5	$f_2 \quad f_4$		Con

If a case characterized by a set of facts and a *pro* decision is compared to a case containing the same facts plus at least one more, the latter is said to have a higher rank than the former. Ranking our *pro* cases, we get the order C_1, C_2, C_3. Applying the above statement —we assert that if the rank of C_1 is equal to or higher than the rank of C_2, then a *pro* decision is expected if and only if the rank of C_2 gives a *pro* decision. Since C_1 is ranked first, C_2 second, and C_2 is *pro*, C_1 must be decided in the same direction to maintain consistency. The prediction equations can be written

$$D_{pro} \rightarrow f_1 \wedge f_2$$
$$D_{con} \leftrightarrow \, \sim (f_1 \vee f_2).$$

Obviously, the application of this method to large numbers of variables necessitates the use of computer facilities. But the complexity of large numbers does not appreciably affect the simplicity of the prediction equation, although it motivates the use of set and sub-set notation. Thus, an analysis of 100 variables would probably be prohibitive without machine help. The prediction equation, on the other hand, could be written simply as:

$$D_{pro} \leftrightarrow f_1 \wedge (f_3 \vee f_4) \vee (L3, Sa)$$
$$\vee (L8, Sb) \wedge (L12, Sc)$$

where: $Sa = f_5 - f_{15}$; $Sb = f_{16} - f_{75}$;
$$Sc = f_{76} - f_{100}.$$

We have remarked that the Boolean Model does not derive numerical weights for the operating factors. But in a different sense, a weighting is achieved. For a higher ranked case may be conceptualized as having a sum of weights that exceeds that of lower ranked cases. What we do not know is the contribution that each factor makes toward correct prediction. Figure 3 is a diagram representing the possible combinations of two facts in a geometrical space. Unity indicates the fact is present, zero indicates its absence. The four possibilities are:

$$f_1(1,0); f_2(0,1); f_1 f_2(1,1);$$
and $$\sim (f_1 f_2)\,(0,0).$$

FIGURE 3

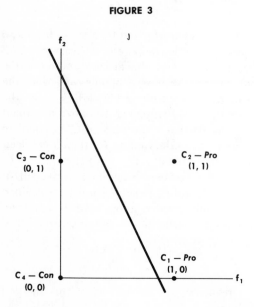

The rank of the pro cases would be C_1, C_2. Since C_1 is *pro*, C_2 must be decided the same way. Similarly, since C_3 is a *con* case, C_4 must be characterized in the same fashion. This tells us that the hyperplane must cut to the left of C_1 and to the right of C_3. But clearly,

the Boolean Model gives no guidance as to a more precise location or slope of the line. Thus it may be compared to Kort's model (1) which determined the slope systematically but used a formula developed by experimentation. While that attempt has received legitimate criticism, it recognized the problem and the need for a solution, in contrast to the Boolean Model which ignores these matters.

IV

Our class 3 and 4 models address themselves specifically to this problem by utilizing some form of regression analysis. Normal regression models have been used by Tanenhaus, *et al.* [and] Kort (3). . . . Tanenhaus and his students have investigated the process by which the Supreme Court accepts or rejects *certiorari* applications. They began by assuming that Rule 19 does not provide a satisfactory explanation for the Court's exercise of its *certiorari* jurisdiction; that the pressure on the justices' time is such that only cursory attention can be given to most *certiorari* applications; and that a substantial percentage of *certiorari* applications are so frivolous as to merit no attention at all. Given the validity of these postulates, their hypothesis—that a group of cues exist which warn a justice when a case needs serious study—is imminently reasonable.

Unlike the models discussed earlier, the cue regression model makes no attempt to predict outcome in cases decided on the merits. Nor do the authors try to predict the response of the Court to *certiorari* applications in particular cases. Instead of a dichotomy between cases to be decided for and against a litigant, the cue model is used to dichotomize the percentage of applications that will be granted as opposed to those that will be refused. The key considerations are said to be the presence or absence of the Federal government as a party, civil liberty questions, and dissension in the lower courts. Various combinations of these factors were used by the authors to predict that 7 to 80 per cent of the *certiorari* applications studied would be granted. This work is clearly outside the stream of thought developed by Kort for the reasons suggested above but also because the "legally relevant facts" are not identified as cues. Application of the Cue model showed that the presence of three cues gave a prediction of 80 per cent approval as compared to a rate of 70 per cent for party and civil liberties only, and 45 per cent for the presence of party alone. In Boolean terms, these three relationships would be quite logical in that cases containing party and civil liberties were approved at a higher rate than those containing party alone and cases containing all three had a still higher rate of approval predicted. The same logical relations hold when we examine the total pattern. But since only three of eight patterns led to a prediction rate higher than 50 per cent, most of the cases containing the other five configurations were decided against the petitioner. Since we are not told the number of cases associated with each of the eight patterns, we cannot calculate how many were mis-predicted in the sample available. However, it is quite clear that successful prediction rates varying from 7 to 80 per cent are somewhat below the rates attained by Kort and others who have applied normal regression models to judicial data. This, of course, is not to denigrate in any way the imaginative theoretical implications of this work. It is to suggest that contextual-environmental variables may be discovered which will account for Supreme Court decisions on *certiorari* applications more consistently than this cue regression model permits.

A third predictive model developed by Fred Kort is an improved version of his initial approach.[9] For his focus is still on the decisions of collegial courts in cases decided on their merit and his independent variables are still contextual—environmental stimuli, specifically, the legally relevant facts of the case. Moreover, the assumptions underlying the earlier conceptualization of the judicial decision-making process remain unchanged. But the third model features a normal regression analysis which provides solutions for most of the problems inherent in the earlier work.

Using cases from the United States Supreme Court and the Connecticut Supreme Court, Kort identified from 19 to 23 facts in cases involving right to counsel, involuntary confession, and workmen's compensation. These facts were then scored and put through a normal regression analysis to determine their approximate numerical weight. A unique characteristic of the process, however, was the method by which the facts were scored. Since a regression analysis of 19 to 23 variables is quite involved, some method of "weeding out" those that are marginally productive is desirable. One way of doing this is to correlate each variable with decision for the defendant. A small number of variables with high coefficients could then be chosen for analysis. Kort, however, adopted a standard data reduction device for this kind of problem, i.e., he put the initial scores through a factor analysis thereby reducing the number of variables to five in the workmen's compensation cases and nine in each of the other categories.

The next step in the analysis employed the factor loadings to restate the variables in terms of the factors using a method which reveals "how much of each factor" is present in each case. Using the factor estimates as independent variables, the multiple regression analysis provided weights which enabled prediction of case outcome. For the observed value of the dependent variable, Kort used the number of votes in favor of the petitioner or plaintiff. Since the estimated value of the case was obtained by analysis, the prediction was actually in terms of the number of votes cast for the petitioner in a given case. Thus, Kort was able to say that "If the correlation between the 'observed values' and the 'estimated values' can be accepted as significant, it can be concluded that the decision of a case, which is represented by the case weight [number of votes predicted for petitioner], is—at a specifiable degree of probability—a function of the combination of factors (the restated combinations of variables)."[10]

Since any observed value of five or more in

[9]Fred Kort, "Content Analysis of Judicial Opinions and Rules of Law," in Schubert (ed.), *Judicial Decision Making* (1963), pp. 133–197.

[10]*Ibid.*, p. 164. . . .

full decisions of the Supreme Court means victory for the plaintiff, *pro* or *con* outcome could be anticipated on the basis of the number of votes predicted for petitioner. On that criterion, Kort shows a success rate of 88.4 per cent in the involuntary confession cases; 82.9 per cent in the right to counsel cases; and 82.3 per cent in the workmen's compensation cases. . . .

V

In class 5 we have a single model, the psychometric, a framework in which the dependent variables are decisions of courts or judges in formal cases.[11] The psychometric is the only model which adopts opinions and attitudes as the independent variables from which decision is to be predicted. This model is an extension of the various applications of Guttman scales to Supreme Court cases which [Schubert] began. . . Initial scaling of these cases was motivated by the desire to investigate certain attitudinal hypotheses and more specifically the question of consensual cognition of the issues presented for decision. In a paper written in 1960, this author used the results of civil liberty scales compiled for 1956–1960 to predict the rank order of the justices on the civil liberty scale for the 1961 term. This prediction held up at the .001 level for the 1961 scale subsequently prepared. But, perhaps more striking, it was affirmed also by a 1961 civil liberty scale prepared independently by Schubert. Professor Schubert also predicted the rank order of the judges on three scales using 1962 cases and is the only person to date who has attempted to predict specific case outcome using the psychometric model.

Unlike those who have predicted the percentage of *certiorari* decisions to be approved or those who have concentrated on separating decided cases into *pro* and *con* groupings, Schubert forecast the following Supreme Court actions in the area of legislative reapportionment: (1) that in the case of *Beadle* v. *Scholle,* the Court would deny certiorari to the Michigan Supreme Court in *Scholle* v. *Hare* or affirm that decision with Douglas, Black, Goldberg, Warren, and Brennan in the majority; (2) that no *pro* reapportionment decisions of courts other than the Michigan Court would be reversed nor would any then docketed anti-reapportionment decisions be reversed; and (3) that viewing *Beadle* v. *Scholle* as the most "extreme claim of entitlement to political equality" of docketed cases, the voting divisions in other cases would run from 5-4 to 8-1 with Douglas, Black, Goldberg, Warren, and Brennan in the majority and White, Clark, and Stewart joining the majority in that sequence.

Certainly we must marvel at Schubert's courage in making predictions with such specificity. Of all the model builders we have discussed to this point, none have . . . predict[ed] the votes of individual judges. Yet, precedent can be found in legal circles. In 1962, Fred Rodell, a Yale Law School professor, predicted the vote of the Justices in *Baker* v. *Carr.*[12] Of the eight votes cast, Rodell forecast seven correctly. This result was accomplished, he tells us, by analyzing the personal predilection of each judge as a man. Rodell suggests that such factors as education, temperament, economic status, etc. shape judicial decision-making but the complexity of the ways in which such factors combine to produce choice is said to be beyond ". . . the predictive capacity of even the most intricately attuned and adjusted calculating machine. . . ." This amounts to a claim that he, Rodell, has done what an "intricately attuned and adjusted calculating machine" could not.

Be all that as it may—Rodell's qualitative approach and Schubert's quantitative effort identify many of the same variables. For Rodell and the judicial behavioralists emphasize the relationship of human variations to decisional variations. This emphasis contrasts with that of Kort . . . [who sees] less subjectivity in the judicial process. But the difference is one of degree only since none

---

[11]Glendon Schubert, "Prediction from a Psychometric Model," in Schubert (ed.), *Judicial Behavior: A Reader in Theory and Research* (1964), pp. 548–587.

[12]Fred Rodell, "For Every Justice, Judicial Deference Is a Sometime Thing," *Georgetown Law Journal,* Vol. 50 (1962), pp. 700–708.

would deny the effects of human variation on the outputs of the legal system. Schubert and Rodell also agree on the importance placed on judicial attitudes but disagree as to the possibility of systematic and quantitative analysis of these attitudes for predicting court decisions.

How successful is prediction based on attitudes? In regard to Schubert's forecasts for *Beadle* v. *Scholle, certiorari* was denied as predicted. As for the other two predictions, one case was decided in each category. In both instances, the prediction was affirmed. Obviously, there is a measure of success here. But we may inquire, as we did of Rodell, how the result was accomplished. Basically, the forecasts for the reapportionment cases were based upon several ʾassumptions: (1) that the Justices would vote in the decision of the reapportionment cases ". . . in response to their fundamental attitudes toward civil liberty, and more particularly, to that component of the C Scale—the political equality sub-variable—to which the reapportionment issue . . . [was] most directly related;" (2) that the most extreme claim of political equality in cases then docketed was present in the case of *Beadle* v. *Scholle;* (3) that the attitudes of the most liberal members of the Supreme Court were such that extreme claims of political equality were acceptable and (4) that the most liberal members of the Court were Douglas, Black, Goldberg, Warren and Brennan.

Compared to Rodell's qualitative approach, Schubert's model is obviously superior. Moreover, the application of the model for predicting specific decisions is imaginative. But the limitations of the psychometric approach for forecasting court decisions are more than any analyst could be expected to overcome. The model is not a rigorous, systematic, and replicative system for relating dependent and independent variables. That judges will vote in terms of attitudes may be tentatively accepted as a working postulate. But the degree of "extremism" attached to the claim in *Beadle* v. *Scholle* is subjectively determined. That being so, the view that subsequent extreme claims will be acceptable to certain individuals is difficult to interpret. The cutting point between the justices to whom a claim is acceptable and those to whom it is unacceptable is drawn here prior to decision. In scaling, the ranks of the justices are determined only after their votes have been cast. This is a crucial difference.[13] . . .

---

[13]Scales may permit us to show that given a set of civil liberty cases, the votes will differentiate the justices and that those relative differences will be stable over time. They may enable us to infer that given a similar set of cases, the relative differences will be maintained. But none of this will allow us to predict in a systematic fashion those cases in which a given judge will vote *pro* defendant and those cases in which he will decide to the contrary. In short, the psychometric model is not well suited to predicting specific court decisions and I see no reason to distort what has been a useful model in other areas for that purpose.

B. Policy as Output

Political science writing on the federal judicial system has heavily and properly emphasized the policy-making function of courts. This is especially true for writing about the Supreme Court. Concomitant with this emphasis, however, has been the recognition in most of the literature that judicial policy-making differs in form and even scope from policy-making by such other political institutions as Congress, the federal bureaucracy, and the Presidency. The unique characteristics and limitations of judge-made policies are considered in this section.

The following selection by Richard S. Wells and Joel B. Grossman explores the concept of judicial policy-making. They review some of the literature in this area and then present their own concept of judicial policy-making. In so doing, the authors discuss how judicially made policies differ from (and are similar to) those made by the other institutions within the larger American political system. This is a question which we shall also consider in the two concluding parts of this book.

38   THE CONCEPT
OF JUDICIAL POLICY-MAKING

Richard S. Wells
and Joel B. Grossman

During a recent interview, a Texas lawyer was asked to distinguish between the functions of the United States Supreme Court and lower federal courts. He replied: "The Supreme Court is a policy court; the others are law courts." Though his distinction between the policy roles of upper and lower courts is not persuasive, his characterization does point to the practicing lawyer's hard-eyed realism, which is suspended only on those ceremonial occasions when it is fitting and proper to invoke the spirit of John Marshall or lament the lost strands of enduring principle.

This same realism toward the policy function of courts has lately been shared by public law specialists in American political science. The "political" or "process" approach to the study of legal institutions has resulted in a generation of students who generally agree on the major elements of what might be termed "the judicial process." One of these is "policy" action by the Court, and there is clear consensus among advocates of the process approach that the concept of policy-making is central to any understanding of the Supreme Court. . . .

Acceptance of the policy function of courts has been so general that most process-oriented scholars have simply failed to examine policy as a concept; it is one of the inarticulate major premises of political jurisprudence. The current approach has emphasized the personal interactions and motivations of judicial action, but has not yet devoted particular attention to an examination of the critical conceptual elements of policy formation. This is an especially curious oversight when one considers the frequency with which the concept of judicial policy-

Reprinted from *Journal of Public Law*, XV, No. 2 (1966), pp. 286–295, 298–307 by permission of the publisher. Some footnotes have been omitted, others renumbered.

making is mentioned in the literature on the subject.

At least two reasons account for the fact that the policy function has been ignored or avoided in favor of strictly process aspects. First, the headlong flight of the process approach from traditional concern with doctrinal analysis took the understandable route of determining just what forces combined to shape whatever results the Court enunciated. This concern with the institutional and political genesis of doctrine drew attention from the results of the process under examination, or assumed a certain type of result in order to determine how it was achieved. . . .

Related to this first reason is the iconoclasm of the process approach. The process school attempted to shatter the myth of rule-oriented jurisprudence and attempted to portray the judiciary as a pattern of human behaviors, rather than a mechanical linkage of rules and precedents. . . .

A second reason underlying the avoidance of policy examination in public law has been the adoption of tools of research which were not suitable for such endeavors. Such tools as cumulative scaling, bloc analysis, and small group theory were primarily suited to the measurement and observation of interactions among individual Justices, rather than the general outputs of the Court. These otherwise fruitful techniques have generally stopped short of relating behavior to policy outputs. For example, none of the studies of the leadership qualities of Chief Justices Taft, Hughes, or Warren has demonstrated any connection between their alleged dominance and the achievement of their policy goals. Nor, in light of the techniques used, could they have been expected to do so! On the other hand, studies using cumulative scaling and related techniques have sought to establish a connection between judicial values and policy outcomes. But as we will argue below, such a connection is a poor substitute for a linkage between process and policy.

For several reasons, then, the process approach has not dealt with the concept of policy, other than to give it honorable mention. But this critique is not intended to denigrate the process approach. In fact, it is recognized that there could be no effective study of judicial policy activity and outcomes without a process foundation. But it should also be recognized that current research and exploration generally terminate at that point where the judicial process most importantly relates to the social and political structure. Our effort is to examine one concept of policy which affords this linkage between process and policy. Accordingly, Part I describes some of the ways in which the concept of policy has been used in current research, and offers a definition of policy designed to facilitate this linkage; Part II explores the occasions and conditions for judicial policy action; [and] Part III considers the forms and limitations of such action. . . . We make no pretense of claiming that what follows is a replacement for current research, or even a model of the judicial policy function. Rather, it is intended as an initial exploration, at a high level of generality, of the types of relationships that might be included in such a model. Whether the relationships we depict are at all useful in building that model is a question that can be answered only with the accumulation of empirical data.

I. CURRENT CONCEPTIONS OF JUDICIAL POLICY-MAKING

If current conceptions of judicial policy-making may be compared to market commodities, contemporary students live in a buyer's market: the selection is wide, the prices vary, and the qualities differ. Most frequently the concept is only stated and not defined. If it is defined, the reference and meaning are ambiguous. For example, a recent major study defined a "policy-oriented judge" as one "who is aware of the impact which judicial decisions can have on public policy, realizes the leeway for discretion which his office permits, and is willing to take advantage of this power . . . to further particular policy aims."[1] Sometimes the policy function of the Supreme Court seems to be equated with the overall behavior of the Court, as in Becker's notion that it includes "all legal decisions whose principles concern either a substantial segment of the existing population within the jurisdiction of the court . . . or the distribution, boundaries, modifications, etc., of the powers, rights, duties, and privileges of governmental or public institutions."[2] Dahl suggests that judicial policy-making is distinguished by the element of effective choice where there is at least some uncertainty of outcome.[3] While none of these definitions is irrelevant to an understanding of judicial policy-making, none establishes a sufficiently broad criterion by which policy functions may be meaningfully described.

Efforts at describing the properties of judicial policy-making can be assigned to two separate, but not mutually exclusive, categories: (1) efforts to compare judicial policy-making to nonjudicial policy-making, and (2) efforts to compare judicial policy-making to other judicial functions. This second category can be further and usefully subdivided into comparisons based on (a) values, goals, motivations, and conscious intent of the judges; (b) the intended scope or impact of the policy decision; (c) the number and identity of the participants; and (d) the legal or constitutional content of the decisions.

A. Judicial vs. Nonjudicial Policy-Making. Well known analogies between judicial and legislative policy functions have appeared in the studies of Rosenblum and Peltason,[4] but Jacob is the only writer who has compiled a fairly systematic catalog of comparisons.[5] Although his frame of reference is more in state and trial courts than in the Supreme Court, Jacob's observations are nonetheless a useful point of departure. He argues that judicial policies, as compared to nonjudicial policies, have a narrower scope;

[1]Murphy, *Elements of Judicial Strategy* 4 (1964).

[2]Becker, *Political Behavioralism and Modern Jurisprudence* 78 (1964).
[3]Dahl, "Decision-Making in a Democracy: The Supreme Court as National Policy-Maker," 6 *J. Pub. L.* 279 (1957).
[4]Rosenblum, *Law as a Political Instrument* 10–11 (1955); Peltason, *Federal Courts in the Political Process* 5, 22–24 (1955).
[5]Jacob, *Justice in America* 17–33 (1965).

are often directed at governmental agencies, rather than the public at large; have a more ambiguous impact than legislative policies; do not encompass areas such as foreign affairs, taxation rates, and appropriations; and are frequently retroactive. His is a strong and forceful argument for major conceptual differences between judicial and nonjudicial policy functions. By way of contrast, Peltason has emphasized the similarities between legislative and judicial policy actions; Schubert has noted that "adjudicative" policy-making is not only not peculiarly judicial, but not peculiarly governmental;[6] Shapiro has noted that the property of incrementalism is shared by all policy-makers;[7] and Sayre and Kaufman have suggested that policy functions are similar in judicial and nonjudicial governmental agencies.[8] The comparative merits of these definitions will be discussed below.

B. Judicial Policy-Making vs. Other Judicial Functions. Virtually all of the definitions in this category share the assumption, stated by Schubert, that "policies [made by judges] reflect those values that are preferred, for the time being, by such decision-makers." But they differ in details over the scope and extent of the impact of personal values on the policy process, as well as in attributing conscious or unconscious intent to judges in converting their values to policy outcomes. For example, Jacob has argued that policy-making involves a conscious intent by judges, implying at least the presence of some sort of rational, planning element in the policy-making process. This view is shared by Schubert, who argues that in such major fields as reapportionment or segregation it is not inaccurate to talk of policy development over a twenty or thirty year period.[9] On the

other hand, Shapiro's emphasis on the incremental and nonrational framework of judicial decisions would refute the long-range planning aspect and at least challenge the "conscious policy choice" criterion.

Some distinctions are based on the scope or impact of judicial decisions. Jacob has argued that there is a distinction between policy-making and norm-enforcement, the former being limited to the larger, "public" issues, and the latter comprising those more numerous, but essentially private, disputes which allegedly have little impact on the body politic. He also argues that policy-making is distinguished from norm-enforcement by its primary focus on relationships between government agencies, or between agencies and individuals, whereas norm-enforcement is seen as directed primarily at individuals. Jacob is the only writer to emphasize the possible importance of the question of scope of participants, rather than the nature of the issues. He suggests that these "larger" issues which comprise the policy-making segment of judicial activity can be further delineated by the increased participation of interest groups and others who have a stake in the court's decision, but who are not litigants.

Related to these distinctions are those which define judicial policy-making in terms of the law or precedent content of particular decisions. Many, including Dahl . . . and Pritchett,[10] have adopted the Holmes-Cardozo argument and distinguished between those decisions governed by precedent and those in which the judge has greater discretion. Dahl, for example, argues that the critical point is "the extent to which a court can and does make policy decisions by going outside established 'legal' criteria found in precedent,

---

[6]Schubert, *Judicial Policy-Making* 2 (1965).

[7]Shapiro, "Stability and Change in Judicial Decision-Making: Incrementalism or *Stare Decisis*?", 2 *L. Trans. Q.* 134, 136 (1965).

[8]Sayre & Kaufman, *Governing New York City* 553 (1960).

[9]Schubert, *op. cit., supra* note 6, at 145. Schubert is talking primarily in institutional terms, but it is also not inaccurate to talk of individual judges who have set long-range policy goals for themselves. These goals may be general, as Mr. Chief Justice Taft's attempt to mold an integrated and cohesive Court which would protect property rights, or quite specific, as Mr. Justice Black's

twenty-year campaign to "incorporate" the Bill of Rights into the fourteenth amendment.

[10]Pritchett, "Division of Opinions among Supreme Court Justices," 35 *Am. Pol. Sci. Rev.* 890 (1941), in *Judicial Behavior* 323 (Schubert ed. 1965). It is also interesting to note the use of a similar distinction by current Justices. For example, Mr. Justice Harlan, dissenting in *United States* v. *Guest,* 86 Sup. Ct. 1170, 1180 (1966), asserts that the "right involved [the right to travel free from private interference] being as nebulous as it is, . . . it is necessary to consider it in terms of policy as well as precedent." *Id.* at 1185.

statute, and constitution." Jacob's division between policy and norm-enforcement would seem to fall into this category, although his assertion that policy and norm-enforcement decisions *cannot* be differentiated on the amount of discretion exercised would seem to be at least in partial contradiction.

Other writers have found an overlapping, if not identity, between law and policy decisions. Murphy, for example, argues that "law is . . . one of the chief vehicles for carrying public policy into effect,"[11] while a famous article by Schubert, describing the Supreme Court's FELA decisions as "policy without law," implies that policy decisions without a "law" base are unusual, if not suspect.[12] On the other hand, Hurst takes the position that even if a court is merely applying precedent, it is making or enforcing a decision which has policy consequences.[13]

Distinctions are also made on the basis of output classifications. Schubert, for example, argues that there is "a major policy-making function inherent in the judiciary's role of interpreting the Constitution in relation to the guarantees of personal and property rights and to the federal division of powers." In an earlier book, he used the term "policy-making" to apply only to judicial review of some congressional and presidential actions, apparently excluding court decisions regulating commerce, or dealing with civil liberties or racial discrimination.[14]

Even from this sketchy description it is apparent that conceptions of judicial policy-making vary greatly. Many are incompatible with each other; others are cut from the same conceptual cloth, but vary in qualifying details. Within this assortment of distinctions one may discern various common difficulties.

First, it must be said that most of these definitions are "culture bound" in the sense that they reflect a widely held bias about the Supreme Court's proper role in the political system. This bias—clearly carried over from traditional scholarship—reflects a felt necessity to make distinctions which prevent claiming too much for the political conception of judicial action. As Dahl points out, "if the Court were assumed to be a political institution . . . it would be taken for granted that members of the Court would resolve questions of fact and value by introducing assumptions derived from their own predispositions. . . ." But since its public image as a strictly legal institution demands, at least for public consumption, a different kind of treatment, descriptions of the Court's policy role still attribute to it the illegitimacy best expressed in Holmes's statement that policy occurs when "a judge reads his conscious or unconscious sympathy with one side or the other *prematurely* into the law."[15] (Emphasis added.)

A second difficulty with most of these definitions is that they are primarily judge-centered, reflecting very strongly the personal values and motivational emphasis of current behavioral research. With this emphasis it is difficult, if not impossible, to consider the policy function in a perspective of the entire political system; the fact that policy-making is essentially a response to demands from the political system for certain types of judicial action is lost on a policy conception which sees the process centering on a conversion of personal values into policy outputs.

Third, those definitions which rest on output distinctions, such as those between policy and precedent or constitutional and other types of decisions, suffer from two basic flaws. They are essentially static definitions, and their criteria do not sufficiently distinguish judicial from other policies. For example, none faces the fact that while judges make constitutional policies, not all constitutional policies are made by judges. There are large areas of constitutional development which have received almost no Supreme Court guidance, yet continue to serve as effective

[11]Murphy, *Wiretapping on Trial* 7 (1965).
[12]Schubert, "Policy without Law: An Extension of the *Certiorari* Game," 14 *Stan. L. Rev.* 284 (1962).
[13]Hurst, *The Legal Process* 90 (1961).
[14]Schubert, *Constitutional Politics: The Political Behavior of Supreme Court Justices and the Constitutional Policies They Make,* chs. 5, 6 (1960).

[15]Holmes, "Law and the Court," in *Collected Legal Papers* 295 (1920).

guideposts of political and social behavior.[16]

Fourth, and finally, these definitions, with the exception of Jacob's catalog, are partial and segmented. They hinge on important but isolated aspects of the policy process, but fail to convey adequately the dynamics (and limits) of that process. There is no attempt to relate inputs to outputs, no linkage between the manner in which policy decisions are made and the results of those decisions. For example, there is both merit and heuristic value in the widely held distinction between precedent and policy. But is it a distinction which best illuminates the Court's policy function?

As an alternative to current policy descriptions, we suggest taking a somewhat broader view of the judicial policy function, a view that will facilitate better comparisons to non-judicial policy activity, as well as provide the basis for a better understanding of the judicial process. The guiding conception which supports our approach is that policy consists of a complex of action which is planned, taken, or tolerated by political institutions (or individuals) in the course of their coping with social, political, or economic problems. Policy is therefore conceptualized as (1) a problem-solving *endeavor* or *enterprise* in which conscious articulation and choice of alternatives is directed to the removal or change of conditions which combine to form an identifiable problem, or (2) a way of living with a problem with no effort at immediate or drastic solution —either due to lack of resources or low priority—but constant vigil to maintain the *status quo*. Since for us policy constitutes an "enterprise" in solving problems, it connotes not only the determination of a course of action by deciding among competing considerations of social advantage, but also the implementation of that action and the opportunity for occasional review and marginal adjustments, individual exceptions, and, sometimes, major changes.

In taking this broad view of policy and applying it to the judiciary, we are rejecting the

"policy-norm enforcement" and "precedent-policy" distinctions, as well as the notion that policy can be differentiated from other judicial actions by a differing array of participants. And, as already stated, we cannot accept the frequently stated identity between the value expressions of the judges and the policy outputs of courts. Of course, this approach has the vices of its virtues; some will argue that it excludes nothing, includes everything, and is therefore not useful. But all the necessary distinctions and delineations can be made within its framework, and, pending further empirical study, a broad approach seems preferable.

In following this conception of the judicial policy function, we are not unmindful of the difficulties in trying to bring both trial and appellate courts under the same conceptual umbrella. That there are functional differences between the two is undeniable, but we feel that the utility of a unified approach to judicial policy-making outweighs the problems. And, in fact, it may be a virtue of this approach that it eliminates the necessity for analytical distinctions, such as those listed by Jacob, which were conceived with the special functions of trial courts in mind. For example, it is true that a much larger portion of trial court calendars is taken up with cases of essentially local or individual interest. But regardless of scope or impact, cases handled by the judiciary are problem-solving endeavors, a property which is not lost when a judge finds controlling precedent to guide his disposition of the case.

A second cause of the asserted differences between appellate and trial court policy activity is the greater jurisdictional discretion of appellate courts. It is said that appellate courts avoid routine cases which present no novel questions and call for the exercise of little or no discretion. Aside from the lack of empirical evidence for such a proposition, it makes no sense to say that policy cannot be made through the application of settled law, for the mere decision to apply that law—or to depart from it—is a policy decision. Furthermore, if policy is seen as a process of which implementation and feed-back are important

[16]The development of free speech doctrines prior to 1918, or the regulation of the economy after 1937 are examples.

parts, and not just as the initial choice between competing values, and if the entire judicial system in any one jurisdiction is seen as a piece of complex but essentially unified policy machinery, then this distinction falls.

If we are to consider judicial policy-making as an enterprise in problem-solving, further delineations and distinctions can and must be made. This is particularly important if this conception is to serve as a stimulus for behavioral research into judicial policy formation. We must explore those occasions and situations in the political system which facilitate judicial policy pronouncements. Furthermore, we must investigate the forms of judicial policy actions and the relationship of these forms to policy outcomes. In short, we must explore the multiplicity of relationships which constitute the policy *process*. Within the confines of this analysis, no attempt at relating process relationships to policy outcomes can be made. But, by outlining some of the important relationships, a basis for studying policy outcomes will have been established. From these broad outlines perhaps at least an initial evaluation of this approach to judicial policy-making can be attempted.

II. THE OCCASIONS OF JUDICIAL POLICY

The view that policy-making on the Supreme Court is similar to that of other political institutions in its problem-solving functions does not preclude attention to the unique properties or optimum conditions which define the exercise of judicial power in the making of public policy. The same types of considerations which make plans for revamping federal policies toward Indian problems debatable, draw attention to comparable considerations in the area of judicial policy-making. . . .

An obvious set of conditions is that which emphasizes certain types of relationships within the structure of government itself, making judicial policy action the clear way to deal with given problems. For example, the interrelations among the federal courts make the Supreme Court the obvious formu-lator of policy through its control, subject to congressional veto, of the rules of civil and criminal procedure, and its continuing surveillance of the federal courts.[17] . . .

As it determines the procedures of the federal courts and has at least some say in the jurisdictional division of power among them, so, too, the Court is peculiarly suited for determining many types of informal relationships between other agencies and the Court. For example, its highly personal and symbiotic relationship with the Solicitor General's office effectively controls and limits the Government's litigational activity at the highest level. Likewise, under its original jurisdiction powers, it shares with Congress the power to determine the mutual rights and obligations of competing states to the use and control of natural resources.

Another set of conditions creating occasions for judicial policy formulation concerns what might be seen as a political request for action by the Supreme Court. Lower courts have statutory ways of making these requests, such as the writ of certification. But Congress has occasionally made such requests through the drafting of laws so ambivalent as to make necessary a judicial determination in the area of policy involved. The Sherman Act of 1890 was nothing less than a direct congressional request for judicial policy action, and *Muskrat* v. *United States*[18] was no less than a judicial refusal to accept detailed policy responsibility in the area of the distribution of Indian lands. Recently, the Court has accepted the "buck" as it was passed in the form of the Civil Rights Act of 1965, empowering the Attorney General to initiate suits in the federal courts to test the validity of poll tax laws.

---

[17]This control is accomplished both by case law, as exemplified by the decisions in *Erie R.R.* v. *Tompkins*, 304 U.S. 64 (1938), and *McNabb* v. *United States*, 318 U.S. 332 (1943), and by the creation and amendment of the rules themselves. It should be noted that this latter type of policy-making, which is clearly nonadjudicative in nature, has never won unanimous approval from the Justices. Mr. Justice Black's dissent from the 1966 rule amendments, on the ground that they represent an unconstitutional exercise of judicial power, makes this point. Mr. Justice Black's Statement, 86 Sup. Ct. 204 (yellow pages 1966).

[18]219 U.S. 346 (1911).

A readily perceived occasion for judicial policy arises whenever situations present the problem of determining the dividing line between governmental power and individual rights. In a sense, judicial innovation is reduced in the area of criminal law, at least in comparison to the private law areas of torts and contracts; but the Court obviously plays an expanding role in the broad determination of what sanctions society may apply in the deterrence of criminal behavior. The Supreme Court can, of course, limit congressional policies governing crimes and punishments through its powers of judicial review, but judicial policy-making in regard to federal criminal procedures lies primarily in statutory interpretation and creation of rules of evidence and procedures. With the criminal process in state courts, the Supreme Court is limited to imposing constitutional limitations, but recent practice has shown that procedural or evidentiary rules of the federal courts can easily become constitutional limitations on the states. Despite the recent furor over Supreme Court rulings on the admissibility of confessions and illegally seized evidence, policy formation in the criminal law area is perhaps most peculiarly suited to judicial techniques.

A related set of occasions for judicial policy action involves the determination of individual rights in the broader context of political and social relationships. This is particularly acute where individual members of minority groups challenge locally discriminatory policies, and where, because of constituency pressures, other policy-making bodies are unwilling to act. . . .

Judicial policy action is also possible, or necessary, in the solution of disputes which are essentially nonlegal in character or which have but a small legal content, but which, for strategic reasons, have been expanded or contracted in scope and form to permit judicial action. For example, in the area of civil rights, the jury trial is seen as an obstacle by one side and as a protective device by the other. The strategic virtues of protecting—or attacking—the jury trial were best articulated in the Barnett contempt case,[19] which presented the Supreme Court with a policy dilemma of the first order. Faced with the paradoxical problem of civil rights groups attacking an institution long felt to be a major protective device for individuals, the Court hedged and came up with a solution that satisfied nobody and only postponed determination of the important issues. But the point is that no national policy on the status of jury trials in contempt cases could be developed without judicial participation; and this participation, though limited to particular legal questions, was sought as a partial solution to a much wider range of civil rights problems.

Finally, an occasion for judicial policy action occurs when the existing norms governing a particular relationship are either ambiguous or become obsolescent with the passage of time or the development of new technology. Perhaps the most famous example was the movement away from the common-law fellow servant rule of negligence to a policy of full responsibility by employers or manufacturers for their employees or products. And, even today, further modifications lead toward a concept of implied warranty of manufactured goods to replace older judicial rules. A parallel example would be the increased concern over the legal and moral implications of artificial methods of birth control and insemination. . . .

Obviously, the occasions for judicial policy-making are varied and depend upon circumstances that are suited to the abilities and resources that political society requires and provides for judges. The gaps in judicial policy activity are instructive in understanding the nature and limitations of judicial policy-making. . . . These would include policies over space development and exploration, most aspects of foreign policy, foreign trade policies, census questions, medicare (although the over-all constitutionality of the program will undoubtedly have to undergo a constitutional baptism), the amount of the national debt, measures to curb inflation, the

---

[19] *United States* v. *Barnett*, 376 U.S. 681 (1964).

call up of military reserves and the assignment of troops to Viet Nam, and the seniority system in Congress.

These areas differ in many, but not all, respects from those in which judicial policy action is tolerated or encouraged. . . . Most of these policy decisions require extensive technical knowledge, a constant flow of information, and a capacity for constant supervision. Furthermore, there is but a minimal legal content on which a court could attach its policy preferences. Indeed, there are peripheral questions in these areas which could be subject to judicial policy action: due process limitations on census questions, constitutionality of medicare exemptions and allocations, devaluation of the currency as a default on the national debt, the legal rights of persons in standby or inactive military reserve categories, or the rights of Congress to protect activated reservists by establishing a moratorium on their debts and mortgages. But the very marginal relationship of these questions to the central policy issues emphasizes the Court's limitations of function. A more precise description of these limitations constitutes the next section. . . .

III. THE LIMITATIONS OF FORM, LEGITIMACY, AND RESOURCES

It has been suggested above that the occasions of judicial policy-making exist in response to certain types of societal conditions, designated either by explicit allocations of power in the political system, or by the system's need for certain types of policy decisions which are easily directed and particularly suited to the judicial process. But these opportunities for judicial policy action also carry with them limitations—some trivial, some severe—on the form, scope, and effectiveness of judicial policy action. Assessing the impact of these factors on judicial policy-making potential is the next step in laying the groundwork for a discussion of the linkage between policy and process.

In accord with our definition of policy-making as a problem-solving enterprise, let us focus on three overlapping segments of that enterprise: (1) problem detection and the determination of suitability for judicial policy action, (2) the determination of legitimacy, and (3) resources and effectiveness of judicial policy action. Within this frame of reference we will consider the major factors with which any theory of the judicial policy function would have to contend.

A. Judicial Problem Detection. The rules of judicial problem detection are highly particularized and formalized. To be considered available for solution, problems must have a specified legal or constitutional content (either raising a question of federal or constitutional law, or coming within the Court's diversity jurisdiction), and must be framed in a way which translates all policy questions into questions of law. Furthermore, the problem must involve a specific type of adversary relationship between the parties; one must allege a direct, personal injury and must claim relief which the Court has the power to grant. As a limited alternative in a small number of equity cases, the requirement that actual injury be alleged is suspended if a showing of prospective and irrevocable harm can be made; but the judicial remedy, or policy action, available is proportionately reduced from punitive to restorative action. Additionally, there is the requirement that the problem must have evaded proper solution through a specified number of prior stages, and that all other remedies be exhausted. And, finally, the request for a judicial policy solution should be couched in minimal terms sufficient to settle the particular dispute between the parties. To this requirement there is some leeway, such as the institution of class actions, or the involvement of amici curiae, whose arguments may underscore the interests of people or groups other than actual parties. Even where the Court takes the opportunity to speak more broadly than the facts of a particular case merit, it runs the risk of having its policies ignored or diluted as being mere obiter dicta.[20] These factors

[20]*Cf.* the famous rules of self-limitation set down by Mr. Justice Brandeis in a concurring opinion in *Ashwander* v. *Tennessee Valley Authority,* 297 U.S. 288 (1936).

define "availability" only; from the cases which satisfy all requirements, the Supreme Court has virtually complete discretion in choosing those cases which it will hear, and those issues for which it will make policy determinations.

It is clear from even this cursory description that problems which are solvable by Supreme Court action must conform to rigid and narrow specifications which still define only the outer limits of policy potential. The Court's considerable discretion in choosing the types of policy problems it will hear parallels that of other governmental agencies, and, paradoxically, even exceeds them in some ways. For the Court does not have many constituency pressures to *limit* its choices, and there is no instance on record where the Court has encountered serious difficulties because of inaction. The Court is perhaps better insulated from pressures demanding *some* policy action than any other body; it can pick and choose, waiting for the right time and the right case. The Court may be aware of a problem for a long time before acting upon it.

But if the Court has the advantage of waiting for problems to mature before deciding them, it has the converse problem of frequently not getting to a problem until a fairly late stage, by which time its policy alternatives may be seriously narrowed. This narrowing may result from the actions or conditions of the parties, as when cases become moot; but, most importantly, it comes from the fact that the questions which the Court permits itself to decide are often superficial or marginal to the root of the problem.

These factors also generally preclude innovation by the Court. Many aspects of problems, as well as many problems themselves, remain nonjusticiable and outside the scope of judicial policy determination. But there is a potential for occasional innovation which is not lost on policy-oriented judges. There is an exceptional case, such as *Jones* v. *Opelika*,[21] where a bloc of Justices will openly invite litigation giving them the opportunity to reverse a prior decision; but most judicial

policy innovation occurs in a more subtle manner. As the Court reverses old rules or suddenly begins accepting certain types of cases, it is effectively announcing that it is henceforth available for the resolution of these types of disputes. This was the situation in the wake of *Baker* v. *Carr*,[22] and perhaps most obviously in the sit-in cases.[23] In the first instance a generation-old ban on judicial action was reversed with a strong allusion to the substantive views of the Justices on the subject. In the sit-in cases, the apparent willingness of the Justices to decide in favor of the demonstrators (without subscribing to their claims of full constitutional protection) was a stimulus to continued and intensified protest activity, as well as a signal that favorable policy results could be expected through continued litigation. . . .

The converse of these propositions is also true. When the Court announces that it no longer considers certain types of questions suitable for judicial exposition, as it did with economic regulation cases in *West Coast Hotel* v. *Parrish*[24] and *Wickard* v. *Filburn*,[25] the market for judicial policy action in such areas becomes noticeably depressed, although the Court will occasionally take a case to reaffirm its reluctance or refusal to grant relief in cases in that category.

B. The Concern for Legitimacy. The determination of the legitimacy of judicial policy action is unusual because, to an unusual degree among policy-making bodies, the Court is the determiner of the legitimacy of its own actions—as well as being charged with the unique task of determining the legitimacy of the actions of others. Legitimacy is not just a legal term, but refers to form as well as substance, to conformity with technical procedures as well as fulfillment of popular expectancy. The Supreme Court is (or has

[21]316 U.S. 584 (1942).

[22]369 U.S. 186 (1962).

[23]*Garner* v. *Louisiana*, 368 U.S. 157 (1961), and *Hamm* v. *Rock Hill*, 379 U.S. 306 (1964), were among the many sit-in cases. The Supreme Court's apparent willingness in *Garner* to hear such cases and its obvious sympathy with the demonstrators clearly stimulated further litigation.

[24]300 U.S. 379 (1937).

[25]317 U.S. 111 (1942).

been) the most self-conscious policy-making body—so much so that many policy actions are taken only after a tedious and repetitive recital of precedents purporting to confer legitimacy on the action being taken.

What concerns us most about legitimacy in this paper is the relationship of the problems of acquiring legitimacy to policy actions. The Court's intensive concern with legitimacy severely affects and limits (a) the types of problems it will consider and (b) the potential solutions to those problems. The evidence for the first proposition is abundant; any familiarity with the Court's practices and its rigorous attention to the details of jurisdiction, justiciability, and standing brings recognition of this fact. Evidence for the second proposition is harder to find, but not impossible to obtain. A study of the differences between the alternative solutions suggested by the parties to a case and the policy response by the Court should demonstrate the Court's caution in stepping too close to the line of demarcation. Such caution is most often existent in those areas where the Court has not been previously active, or where it is carving out new jurisdictional territory for itself. In such situations, best exemplified by the sit-in cases, the gap between the relief sought and the remedy offered is likely to be greatest.[26]

C. Limitations on Policy Resources. The limitations on judicial policy capabilities which stem from inadequate resources include those of problem detection and legitimacy; but they also include (a) lack of adequate information on which to base broad policy

judgments, (b) lack of means to control the actions of all parties to a particular problem, (c) lack of effective devices for implementation, (d) lack of capacity for continuous surveillance of policy impacts and effectiveness, and (e) lack of capacity to absorb policy feedback and make corrective adjustments.

The problem of information limitation, which has been alluded to in the previous section, is, paradoxically, a self-imposed handicap. Operating within the bounds of the adversary system limits the Court to communicating only with the parties to the case (and occasional *amici*), and further limits it to communicating in form and language designed more to circumscribe than to illuminate the issues. There are exceptions to this proposition, as when the Court accepts a "Brandeis Brief" type of argument, appoints a special master to sift through the technicalities of a dispute over water or oil rights, or hires a professional economist to aid in the solution of a complicated antitrust case. But the central fact remains that judicial policy action flows not from a broad-ranging inquiry into the problems and prospective solutions, but from a narrow-gauged encounter.

The problem of inadequate information, compounded by the Court's inadequate facilities for controlling the behavior of all parties to the problem, makes a severe dent in the Court's policy potential. Of course, the Court is not unique in having problems of implementation; but it does have unique problems. First, appellate courts, at least, are limited to on-the-record, formal policy actions; they almost never meet or see the parties to the case, and have no opportunity to take advantage of the well-known aids of personal persuasion and informal sanctions. Lower court judges do have greater opportunity for contact and, with the development of the pretrial conference, for persuasion as well. But such opportunities cover only a fraction of the cases where such techniques could be utilized. This is not to say that there is no interchange between the Supreme Court and the litigants; the oral argument provides some opportunity, as does an occasional Court directive for

---

[26]The demonstrators sought constitutional protection, based on the fourteenth amendment, for their actions, while the Supreme Court steadfastly refused to offer more than reversals based on a bewildering variety of technicalities. The Court was extremely careful not to approve the expanded concept of state action urged by the demonstrators, though Justices Douglas and Goldberg argued for a Fourteenth Amendment solution. See *Bell* v. *Maryland,* 378 U.S. 226 (1964). Since these cases were argued during debate on what became the Civil Rights Act of 1964, there was considerable reluctance on the part of the Justice Department—and some of the Justices as well—to undercut the expected congressional action with a judicial solution.

reargument of certain specified questions. Second, the sanctions available to the Supreme Court for compelling conformity with its policy directives are dependent on the cooperation of a widespread and diverse group of lower court judges who do not stand in a completely hierarchical relationship to the Supreme Court, and who have significant latitude in following these directives. Third, the requirement that most decisions and opinions be couched in the form of a directive to the litigants results in a built-in ambivalence for others who may or may not be affected. Fourth, except where the Court retains jurisdiction of the case, it cannot on its own motion reopen the case to make marginal adjustments in its original policy decision. It cannot do this in any case; but, even if permissible, it would be difficult unless the Court could also effect some sort of continuous surveillance of the results and impacts of the policy decision. It is dependent on the original parties to the case, or subsequently interested or affected parties, to reopen an issue which has not been resolved satisfactorily. Thus, the Court has no opportunity, except in unusual circumstances, to receive and assess the feedback from its policy decisions; and even when it does get a feedback reaction, it is likely to be in a different case with different facts, different parties, and different considerations to be weighed; and the distance between the Court and the problem grows. Precisely how these factors will affect the policy output of the Court is an empirical question which cannot be answered here; but it can be noted that certain types of policies, because of their self-executing character, are least likely to be affected. On the other hand, policies which are formulated most broadly and which require the most implementation are likely to be frustrated the most.

Part 5
Feedback

Most traditional analyses of the judiciary consider the final rendering of decisions to specific cases as the end of the judicial process. But systems theory warns us that these case outputs are not the end. Outputs have an impact on the system's environment and spawn new inputs for future processing. This phenomenon is called feedback.

Our discussion of feedback shall be limited to the Supreme Court for two reasons: (1) Supreme Court decisions as the "final say" of the federal judicial system have the widest ramifications for the larger political system. They can be expected, therefore, to generate the greatest amount of feedback activity; (2) Materials of equivalent quality and richness are unavailable for lower court decisions.

Most Supreme Court decisions resolve not only individual disputes, they also act as declarations of judicial policy. After such a decision is announced it is analyzed in law reviews and newspapers. It is discussed by public officials and political candidates. Carrying out the policy announced both in the particular case decided and in similar cases may require activity by executive officials, lower court judges, legislators, and ultimately private citizens. This complex of comment and action, which influences the judiciary in its future handling of similar and related cases, constitutes the feedback we shall consider.

Six sources of feedback have been chosen for analysis in this part. They are the Lower Courts, the Press, Law Reviews, Congress, the President, and Public Officials.

Before turning to a consideration of specific feedback activities, a comment on the analytical implications resulting from our focusing on the Supreme Court should be made. In effect, we shall be looking at feedback to the Supreme Court as a subsystem rather than feedback to the entire federal judicial system. In most of the sections which follow, the results of this analytical shift are trivial. It is only when we consider feedback from the lower courts that it achieves importance. Under the term, "The Lower Courts," are included both the lower federal and the state judiciaries. Even though the lower federal courts lie within the federal judicial system and the state courts lie outside its boundaries, both lie outside the boundaries of the Supreme Court subsystem. Differences in recruitment, jurisdiction, and constitutional position give the state courts greater leeway in objecting to Supreme Court policies than is available to the lower federal courts. The effect, however, is probably not great enough to make state court feedback qualitatively different from lower federal court feedback. Furthermore, these two similar types of judicial feedback have usually been studied together. Thus they are grouped together in the following section.

A. The Lower Courts

The Supreme Court heads the formal judicial hierarchy. For other federal courts it is the hierarchical superior with the authority to determine both the content of the law and the procedures to be followed. Through its appellate role, the Court can correct the lower courts when they err in these matters. For the state courts the Supreme Court plays a similar supervisory role in matters touching on federal law. Even the determination of what are "matters touching on federal law" is one long since decided in the Supreme Court's favor.

From this formal analysis of American judicial structure instances of feedback from the lower courts might seem only marginal and of dubious legitimacy. A closer examination casts doubt on such a conclusion. It is considered legitimate for lower court judges to criticize the Court verbally as long as their decisions are not affected. Such feedback can be found in the dicta of judges applying Supreme Court policies to cases where they disapprove of the policy's content. Lower court criticism can also be observed in the "off-the-bench" remarks of judges. Probably the most dramatic recent example of such feedback occurred in the 1958 report by the Conference of State Chief Justices. This report (adopted by a vote of 36–8) criticized the Court for a lack of self-restraint in the field of federal-state relations. Significantly, however, this criticism was prefaced by the statement: "[O]ur obligation to seek to uphold respect for law . . . [does not] impose upon us an obligation of silence when we find ourselves unable to agree with pronouncements of the Supreme Court (*even though we are bound by them*). . . ."[1]

As a type of professional criticism such feedback from lower court judges does, of course, carry weight both with those within the legal community and those outside of it. It may lend support to those with direct power over the Court, such as congressmen or the President, in their attempts to subvert Court policies. It may encourage local officials and private citizens to non-obedience, thus slowing the impact of Court decisions. It may even encourage lower court judges themselves to non-obedience.

The hierarchical position of the Supreme Court does not guarantee automatic compliance by the lower judiciary. The Court faces problems of non-obedience by its subordinates analogous to those faced by the bureaucratic superior in dealing with his subordinates. Non-obedience as a form of feedback can alter the impact and even the content of Supreme Court policies if both widespread and prolonged. In the two readings that follow we shall look at both criticism and non-obedience as types of feedback emanating from the lower courts. The article by Walter Murphy presents a general overview of the extent of negative comment and avoidance of Supreme Court decisions coming from both state and federal judges. The Note from the *Harvard Law Review* gives in detail the extent to which state courts have avoided the effect of Supreme Court decrees in specific cases heard on appeal and remanded back with instructions.

---

[1]Conference of Chief Justices, *Report of the Committee on Federal-State Relationships as Affected by Judicial Decisions,* reprinted by the Virginia Commission on Constitutional Government. Italics added.

39 LOWER COURT CHECKS ON THE SUPREME COURT

Walter F. Murphy

The Supreme Court typically formulates general policy. Lower courts apply that policy, and working in its interstices, inferior judges may materially modify the High Court's determinations.[1] . . .

The line between evasion and defiance is always difficult to draw, and when in 1954 the Supreme Court declared Jim Crow legally dead, the attitude of many segregationist state judges shifted perceptibly. Yet the manner in which Southern judicial resistance has been expressed is significant. These judges have criticized the *School Segregation* decisions on and off the bench; they were among the leaders of the movement in the 1958 Conference of State Chief Justices to reprimand the Supreme Court.[2] They have given moral support and, one may guess, perhaps legal advice to Southern political leaders. But when pressed, no state supreme court has yet failed to concede that the School Segregation cases are the law of the land and binding on lower courts. Resistance of state supreme courts (and, though not universally, of state lower courts[3]) has taken three specific forms: (1) refusing to expand the school decision to other areas; (2) upholding the constitutionality of state efforts to evade compliance; and (3), in line with the state chief justices' censure, balking at Supreme Court decisions in related areas of race and of federal-state relations.

Two recent cases illustrate a combination of these resistance methods. The School Segregation decisions of 1954 seemed to spell final victory for a Negro named Virgil Hawkins who for over five years had been seeking admission to the University of Florida law school. A week after *Brown* v. *Board*, the Supreme Court sent the *Hawkins* case back to the Florida supreme court for reconsideration in light of the public school decisions. The Florida high court did reconsider and declared: "We deem it to be our inescapable duty to abide by this decision of the United States Supreme Court interpreting the federal constitution." A majority of the state justices, however, felt that "sound judicial discretion" required them to withhold issuance of a mandamus requiring immediate admission, in order to determine the effects of integration at the university.

Disappointed at this further delay, Hawkins took his case back to the Supreme Court, which entered a new order stating that the factors it had spelled out as allowing delay in desegregating grammar and high schools

Reprinted by permission of the author and publisher from Walter F. Murphy, "Lower Court Checks on Supreme Court Power," *American Political Science Review*, LIII (1959), pp. 1018–1031. Some footnotes have been omitted and others renumbered.

[1]Much lower court leeway is created by the fact that since Supreme Court opinions often represent a compromise among divergent approaches and views of individual Justices, there are sometimes multiple threads running through an official opinion which are inconsistent with the dominant pattern of thought. Even where a judge wishes to hew strictly to the High Court's line he may be left in doubt as to what was dogma and what was dicta. Alpheus T. Mason's *Harlan Fiske Stone: Pillar of the Law* (New York: The Viking Press, 1956) is studded with examples of opinion compromises. See especially the intra-Court memoranda and draft opinions in *Home Building and Loan Association* v. *Blaisdell*, 290 U.S. 398 (1934), and *Colgate* v. *Harvey*, 296 U.S. 404 (1935), found at pp. 360–365 and pp. 399–402 of Mason's book.

[2]Chief Judge Frederick W. Brune of Maryland, chairman of the Chief Justices' committee which prepared the critical report, has officially denied that any attack on the School Cases was intended. (*New York Times*, January 8, 1959, 30:1.) There can be no doubt, however, that the Supreme Court's racial decisions had a great deal to do with the attitude of the state judges. See the speech of Charles Alvin Jones, Chief Justice of Pennsylvania, reported in *Harvard L. Record*, October 23, 1958.

[3]The extreme example is that of the Birmingham, Alabama, judge who not only refused to follow the Supreme Court's racial decisions but also declared the Fourteenth Amendment unconstitutional. (*New York Times*, March 23, 1957, 14:4–5.) Perhaps the most vindictive remarks from the bench about the Supreme Court in its current crisis were made by the Alabama judge whose decision regarding voluntariness of a confession had been reversed in *Fikes* v. *Alabama*, 352 U.S. 191 (1957): "The opinion is the voice of the Supreme Court of the United States, but the hand is the hand of the NAACP. The opinion of the majority of the Court speaks the truth neither as to the facts nor as to the law. The opinion offends and is repugnant to judicial sensibilities." Quoted in 103 *Cong. Rec.* 4012 (85th Cong., 1st Sess., March 19, 1957).

did not apply at the professional school level. Once again the case went back to the Florida supreme court, and once again that tribunal, via three opinions for the majority and two for the dissenters, interpreted its way out of ordering Hawkins's immediate admission. The majority expressed a belief, based on the report of a special commissioner, that violence would be the result of even limited integration of the law school. The opinion added, "we cannot assume that the Supreme Court intended to deprive the highest court of an independent sovereign state of one of its traditional powers, that is, the right to exercise a sound judicial discretion as to the date of the issuance of its process in order to prevent a serious public mischief."

In *Williams* v. *Georgia*, the Georgia supreme court handled a different type of racial issue with considerably more bluntness. A Negro, convicted of murder in a state court, managed to obtain review by the United States Supreme Court. In arguing the case, the state attorney conceded that Negroes had been excluded from the jury panel and therefore that the defendant had been denied a fair trial. The state attorney contended, however, that since the defense had not challenged the method of jury selection within the time limits set by Georgia law, no substantial federal question was presented. The Supreme Court found that a real constitutional issue was involved, but declined to exercise its jurisdiction. The majority of the Justices stated that they could not imagine that the "courts of Georgia would allow this man to go to his death as the result of a conviction secured from a jury which the State admits was unconstitutionally impaneled." Instead of reversing the Georgia supreme court, the federal Supreme Court simply remanded the case for further consideration.

The Georgia supreme court disposed of the remand by a three paragraph opinion whose resistance can be gauged from the declaration in the opening paragraph: "we will not supinely surrender sovereign powers of this State." Speaking for all seven justices, the Georgia chief justice erroneously held that the United States Supreme Court had found

itself without jurisdiction, and on that finding reaffirmed the conviction. The Negro was electrocuted. . . .

[F]ederal court defiance [is] less likely than state, but district and circuit judges are not mere pawns in the judicial game. They sometimes lash out in caustic criticism, too. In 1958, for example, the Court of Appeals for the Ninth Circuit reversed the conviction of a pair of communist leaders on the basis of the Supreme Court's narrow interpretations of the Smith Act in *Yates* v. *United States*. Judge Chambers remarked tartly that the court would have upheld the validity of the convictions on the basis of past practice had not the Supreme Court changed the law. "One may as well recognize that the Yates decision leaves the Smith Act, as to any further prosecutions under it, a virtual shambles—unless the American Communist Party should witlessly set out to reconstitute itself again with a new 'organization'."

The reactions of a number of lower federal judges to the state chief justices' censure of the Supreme Court were no more subtle. The *U. S. News and World Report* polled all district and circuit judges, asking if they agreed or disagreed with the report of the state chief justices. Only 128 of 351 answered: 59 of them expressed approval, 50 disapproval, and 19 voiced no opinion.

Another channel of criticism, more discreet but also more directly pointed toward securing remedial congressional action, is the Judicial Conference,[4] either at the national or circuit level. The Judicial Conference of the United States several times in recent years has endorsed bills to reverse Supreme Court decisions allowing relatively liberal opportunities for state prisoners to seek *habeas*

---

[4]28 U. S. C. §331 provides that every year the Chief Justice of the United States shall call a meeting of the chief judges of each circuit, the chief judge of the Court of Claims, and a district judge from each circuit. This conference is directed to make a survey of the business of the courts of the United States and to submit to Congress a report including any suggestions for improvements. 28 U. S. C. §333 establishes similar rules for a judicial conference in each circuit. See Judge John J. Parker, "The Integration of the Federal Judiciary," *Harv. L. Rev.*, Vol. 56, p. 563 (1943).

corpus in federal courts. But it was the Judicial Conference for the District of Columbia Circuit which struck one of the harshest blows with this weapon.

At the close of its 1956 term the Supreme Court had, in *Mallory* v. *United States*, extended the application of its libertarian decision in the earlier *McNabb* case. *McNabb* had ruled that confessions secured as a result of questioning during a prolonged period of delay between arrest and arraignment could not be used as evidence in a federal court. While the delay in *McNabb* had been several days, in *Mallory* less than eight hours had elapsed between arrest and confession. Nevertheless, the Court held that even this shorter period fell within the prohibition against "unnecessary delay" in arraignment imposed by Rule 5(a) of the Federal Rules of Criminal Procedure. Frankfurter's unanimous opinion conceded that "circumstances may justify a brief delay," but the police must "arraign the arrested person as quickly as possible so that he may be advised of his rights and so that the issue of probable cause may be promptly determined." The Federal Rules were declared to allow "arresting officers little more leeway than the interval between arrest and the ordinary administrative steps required to bring a suspect before the nearest available magistrate."

This decision, resulting as it did in the freeing of a chronic criminal who had just been found guilty of a brutal rape, stirred up a hornet's nest in Congress as well as more tactfully expressed displeasure among lower court judges. At its next meeting, the Judicial Conference for the District of Columbia Circuit, the circuit in which *Mallory* had originated, endorsed pending legislation which would have rewritten Rule 5(a) so as to erase the *McNabb-Mallory* holdings.

District Judge Alexander Holtzoff, the trial judge in the *Mallory* case and a Department of Justice careerist years before, was even sharper than the Judicial Conference in his opposition to the Supreme Court decision. In reply to a letter from a Senate subcommittee, the judge, who had acted as secretary to the advisory committee which had assisted the Court in drafting the Federal Rules, supplied some of the pertinent legislative history of Rule 5(a). He reported that the advisory committee had considered adding a subsection to Rule 5 to the effect that confessions obtained during an "unnecessary delay" between arrest and arraignment should be inadmissible. The committee, however, had rejected this proposal because it felt that such exclusions would punish the public more than delinquent police officials. In similar oral testimony before another Senate subcommittee, Judge Holtzoff was deferential to the Supreme Court, but no less firm in his conviction that the Court had erred in *Mallory*. He reminded the Senators that *Mallory* was based not on constitutional but only on statutory interpretation. While such interpretation was within the power of the High Court, "it is equally within the power of the Congress to change this principle by legislation."

The later handling of the *Mallory* decision, without new legislation, provides a classic example of the power of inferior judges to reshape legal doctrine expounded by the Supreme Court. By means of explaining, limiting, and distinguishing, the district and circuit judges in the District of Columbia have been able to permit the use in evidence of a high percentage of confessions secured during delays in arraignment.[5]

Retired Associate Justice Stanley Reed, recalled to temporary duty on the Court of Appeals, and District Judge Holtzoff played prominent parts in this process. In *Porter* v. *United States*, Reed, who had dissented from

---

[5]Senate Subcommittee on Constitutional Rights, *Hearings on Confessions and Police Detention*, 85th Cong., 1st Sess. (March 7, 11, 1958). . . . contain a collection of 13 lower court decisions, many of them otherwise unreported, interpreting *Mallory*. For other opinions applying or avoiding that case, read: *United States* v. *White*, 153 F. Supp. 809 (1957); *United States* v. *Valente*, 155 F. Supp. 577 (1957); *United States* v. *Hodges*, 156 F. Supp. 313 (1957); *United States* v. *Armpriester*, 156 F. Supp. 134 (1957); *Mullican* v. *United States*, 252 F. 2d 398 (1958); *Smith* v. *United States*, 254 F. 2d 751 (1958); *Edwards* v. *United States*, 256 F. 2d 707 (1958); *Washington* v. *United States*, 258 F. 2d 696 (1958).

Confessions were ruled admissible in 16 of these 21 cases.

McNabb, shifted emphasis from the accused's right to be promptly arraigned to the accused's right not to be inflicted with the "serious stigma" of arraignment until the police had made "some pertinent and definitive inquiry." In this manner Reed was able to sustain admission of statements made during a 17-hour interval between arrest and arraignment.

Holtzoff continued his respectful resistance by closely limiting the value of *Mallory* as a binding precedent to the specific facts of the case. In overruling objections to a confession obtained during a short period of questioning (less than 45 minutes) before arraignment, Holtzoff stated: "An opinion of a court is not to be treated and read as an essay in determining the rule of law to be evolved therefrom. . . . The process is limited to collating not the statements in the various decisions and opinions, but the precise rulings." On this basis, he concluded:

While there are some statements in the opinion of the Court that are somewhat broader than the precise holding, the actual rule that can be deduced from the [Mallory] case in the light of the facts there involved, is that a period from 2:30 P.M. until 10:00 P.M.,—about seven and one-half hours, —is too long an interval and constitutes an unreasonable delay in bringing a prisoner before a committing magistrate.[6]

In this opinion Holtzoff brought out the underlying difference here between the lower courts and the Supreme Court. *Mallory* and its predecessors were concerned with the rights of the individual. If the Court was engaging in a balancing process, its thumb was on the side of the defendant's rights. Holtzoff and many of his colleagues in the District of Columbia circuit preferred to see the judicial thumb, if not off the scales, at least shifted to the side of the general public. Where the Supreme Court had been viewing the conflict as between a defendant's constitutional rights and police administration, the lower courts saw the clash as between an individual's rights to technical procedures and the public's right to basic protections. . . .

The Supreme Court had spoken in *Mallory*, and while its opinion obviously did not set precise or very narrow limitations on lower court discretion, it did impose broad restrictions on the number and kinds of decisional alternatives open to federal judges. On the other hand, many problems come before lower courts on which the Supreme Court has not yet passed judgment. In deciding such cases, these tribunals can do, once removed, what the Supreme Court itself occasionally does in an analogous situation. For the High Court's question "What would the Founding Fathers or Congress have willed had they foreseen the case at bar?" the lower courts can substitute "What would the Supreme Court have visualized the Framers or Congress as willing had the Supreme Court foreseen this case?" This kind of speculation comes close to giving oneself a blank check.

Further complications enter when judges sense shifts in Supreme Court policy. Two schools of thought tell lower courts how to handle such problems. One, represented by the late Jerome Frank, feels that "when a lower court perceives a pronounced new doctrinal trend in Supreme Court decisions, it is its duty, cautiously to be sure, to follow not to resist it." In a footnote to this statement, Frank added: "To use mouth-filling words, cautious extrapolation is in order."

Judge John J. Parker provided one of the most dramatic occasions of an inferior court's declining to follow an explicit Supreme Court precedent. In 1940, in the *Gobitis*[7] case, the High Court had with only one dissenting vote sustained the authority of Pennsylvania to compel children of Jehovah's Witnesses attending public schools to salute the flag, despite First Amendment and First Commandment scruples. Just two years later a case with almost identical facts arose in West Virginia, but, in the teeth of *Gobitis*, Judge Parker held the regulation invalid. This was not defiance. Parker noted that three of the *Gobitis* majority had confessed error[8] and that

---

[6]*United States* v. *Heideman and Brennan*, 21 F.R.D. 335, 338 (1958).

[7]*Minersville School District* v. *Gobitis*, 310 U.S. 586 (1940).
[8]*Jones* v. *Opelika*, 316 U.S. 584, 623–624 (1942).

two others had retired, leaving the flag salute supporters a minority of three. "Under such circumstances and believing, as we do, that the flag salute here required is violative of religious liberty when required of persons holding the religious views of plaintiffs, we feel that we would be recreant to our duty as judges, if through a blind following of a decision which the Supreme Court itself has thus impaired as an authority, we should deny protection to rights which we regard as among the most sacred of those protected by constitutional guarantees."[9]

But prediction is a risky enterprise, and while Parker's nose-counting turned out to be correct, other guesses, however informed, can be and have been wrong.[10] This is the reasoning behind the views of the more conservative school of thought which holds that inferior judges should follow doubtful precedents until the Supreme Court specifically voids them. As Chief Judge Calvert Magruder of the First Circuit has recently said: "We should always express a respectful deference to controlling decisions of the Supreme Court, and do our best to follow them. We should leave it to the Supreme Court to overrule its own cases." In keeping with this philosophy Judge Magruder called Parker's decision in the second flag case "an unseemly thing."

Magruder was taking an instrumental rather than an ideological position, however. He admitted that when a new situation arises a lower court has two choices: either to concentrate on previous Supreme Court opinions and milk available dicta for possible guidance, or to strike out afresh and give its own opinion of what the law should be. And Magruder confessed that he himself had used both methods. He conceded further that on one occasion where he was using the second method "it was necessary to deal somewhat roughly, though very respectfully," with an explicit Supreme Court decision which he thought "shaky."

Perhaps the most significant portion of Judge Magruder's address was his open acknowledgment that lower court jurists, although mindful of their obligation to the Supreme Court, were sometimes simply unwilling to follow the Justices in their interpretation of the law. As an example the judge cited a 1957 decision of his court limiting the definition of a seaman under the Jones Act. The Supreme Court had summarily reversed the Court of Appeals, but, Magruder frankly stated, were the issue to come up once more, "I am afraid that we shall again 'stick our necks out' and say, as a matter of law, that the man is not a seaman, thereby courting another probable reversal by the Supreme Court."

The power of prediction evidently confers considerable latitude on its user. He may be discerning what he believes the future does hold, what he hopes the future will hold, or what he judges the future should hold. Such guessing can influence the Supreme Court, or Congress, and it can also embarrass both by creating not just one but, by the time certiorari is granted and the case heard on review, a whole series of *faits accomplis*. On the other hand, refusal to accord official recognition to changing doctrine can also confer power. Disavowal of authority may be used to conceal or at least to give good form to

[9]*Barnette* v. *West Virginia*, 47 F. Supp. 251, 253 (1942). It is worth noting that it had been Parker's strict adherence to Supreme Court precedent in an anti-labor case some fifteen years earlier which had alienated organized labor and helped defeat Senate confirmation of his nomination to the Surpeme Court. The case was *United Mine Workers* v. *Red Jacket Consolidated Coal & Coke Co.*, 18 F. 2d 839 (1927). For details see Subcommittee of the Senate Committee on the Judiciary, *Hearings on the Confirmation of Hon. John J. Parker*, 71st Cong., 2d Sess. (April 5, 1930).

[10]In *Gardella* v. *Chandler*, 172 F. 2d 402 (1949), Judge Frank thought that the Supreme Court had turned into an "impotent zombi" its 1922 decision (*Federal Baseball Club* v. *National League*, 259 U.S. 200) that professional baseball was beyond the scope of congressional regulatory power, and consequently outside the reach of the Sherman Act. In 1953, however, the Supreme Court continued baseball's anti-trust immunity, though not affirming all that the earlier case had implied. *Toolson* v. *New York Yankees*, 346 U.S. 356. Even more to the point was the slap the Court administered in *Spector Motor Service* v. *McLaughlin*. 323 U.S. 101 (1944). A majority of the Court of Appeals for the Second Circuit (including Judge Frank) had detected a "new doctrinal trend" of the Supreme Court regarding state taxation of interstate commerce, and invalidated a Connecticut tax. In reversing this decision, the majority opinion, written by Justice Frankfurter, rebuked the lower court for its over-hasty anticipation.

serious disagreement with Supreme Court policy. In South Carolina, District Judge George Bell Timmerman, Sr., father of the governor, twice after 1954 insisted on applying the rule of *Plessy* v. *Ferguson* to bus segregation, asserting that the school cases had only involved education and not transportation. "One's education and personality," Timmerman said disdainfully, "is not developed on a city bus."[11]

The authority to make findings of fact gives trial judges extensive power which appellate tribunals can only partially control. And in the *School Segregation Cases*, the Supreme Court broadened the scope of this inherent authority by specifically directing the exercise of the widest sort of judicial discretion, guided only by the flexible formula "with all deliberate speed." . . .

Such a policy constitutes a manifestation of faith as well as an invitation for assumption of power. And occasionally a judge will seize the full implications of this invitation. Flying directly in the face of the desegregation ruling, and even after one reversal by the Court of Appeals, District Judge William H. Atwell declined to order Dallas, Texas, to set a date for integration because this would cause "civil wrongs." Lest his own feelings be mistaken, Atwell declared: "I believe that it will be seen that the [Supreme] Court based its decision on no law but rather on what the Court regarded as more authoritative, modern psychological knowledge. . . . It will be recalled that in 1952, Mr. Justice Frankfurter

said it was not competent to take judicial notice of 'claims of social scientists'."[12] . . .

The lower courts can and do check the Supreme Court, but the Supreme Court can act to counter lower court power. While it cannot fire and hire new personnel as the President can sometimes do, the Court can review and reverse inferior judges. This is important beyond any effect on a particular case. Judges, no more than other men, enjoy the prospect of public correction and reprimand. The Supreme Court can put added bite to this psychological whip by sarcasm and scathing criticism of its own. Alternatively, the Court may resort to more diplomatic means as it did in *Williams* v. *Georgia*. But the limitations on such efforts at peaceful coexistence were clearly spelled out when the Georgia supreme court not only refused to review Williams' conviction but also declined to recognize any federal jurisdiction.

In a more subtle fashion, the Supreme Court may nip evasions by means of gratuitous legal advice, a method which almost touches the tabu against advisory opinions. Thus after the final Florida decision in the *Hawkins* litigation, the United States Supreme Court denied *certiorari*; it added the notation, however, that this denial was not intended to prejudice the right of Hawkins to take his case to a federal district court. The NAACP got the hint and won a compromise victory in a relatively short time.[13] . . .

When confronted with systematic evasion the Supreme Court could, as a last resort,

---

[11]*Flemming* v. *South Carolina Gas & Electric Co.*, 128 F. Supp. 469, 470 (1955). After the Court of Appeals reversed Timmerman, 224 F. 2d 752 (1955), he tried to salvage something by ruling that if not currently law, at least *Plessy* had been law at the time the bus dispute had begun. 1 *Race Rel. L. Rep.* 679 (1956). This, too, was reversed, 239 F. 2d 277 (1956). See also Timmerman's bitter statements dissenting in *Bryan* v. *Austin*, 148 F. Supp. 563 (1957).

Not to be outdone by Timmerman's *bon mot* about buses and personality, Judge Walter Hoffman of the U. S. District Court for Eastern Virginia, in throwing out a suit against segregated rest rooms in a state courthouse, remarked: "The underlying reasons for the rejection of the 'separate but equal' doctrine would not appear to be applicable to toilet facilities. . . ." *Dawley* v. *Norfolk*, 159 F. Supp. 642, 648 (1958). In spite of this sardonic piece of humor, Hoffman has rigidly followed the letter and spirit of *Brown* v. *Board*.

[12]*Bell* v. *Rippy*, 146 F. Supp. 485, 486 (1956). The earlier decision is reported at 133 F. Supp. 811 (1955), and the reversal, *sub nom. Brown* v. *Rippy*, at 233 F. 2d 796 (1956). This second decision, of course, was also reversed, *sub nom. Borders* v. *Rippy*, 247 F. 2d 268 (1957), but this did not end the matter. Atwell immediately went to the opposite extreme and ordered Dallas schools integrated in the middle of the academic year. 2 *Race Rel. L. Rep.* 985 (1957). This decision was also reversed by the Court of Appeals, 250 F. 2d 690 (1957).

[13]Even this victory is significant for the thesis of this article. The federal district court first refused to allow Hawkins to introduce any evidence. The Court of Appeals reversed, *Hawkins* v. *Board*, 253 F. 2d 752 (1958). The final result of nine years of litigation was an injunction forbidding the University to deny entrance to its *graduate* schools because of race. The district court, however, refused to order Hawkins's admission, 162 F. Supp. 851 (1958).

invoke its inherent power to punish for contempt in order to coerce either state or federal judges. But this is as unlikely to be used as is the impeachment and removal power of Congress. More probably, the Court would . . . cast all technicalities aside and bring the full weight of its constitutional authority to bear on the substantive issues in the dispute. Or, if the case had originated in a federal court, it might act as it did in 1958 and make the final determination of the problems itself.[14] Faced with such counter-measures, lower courts would no doubt retreat in an effort both to save face and to salvage as much as possible, realizing that the battle could be continued in the administrative and legislative processes much more easily if a final showdown in the judicial process were avoided.

In such a fashion this aspect of judicial decision-making comes full circle. The Supreme Court must take into account the reaction of inferior judges, and lower courts must attempt to divine the counter-reaction of the Supreme Court. Meanwhile, both must keep a wary eye on public opinion and maneuverings within the other branches of government to ascertain how these will affect the policy concerned. Judges have not solved the dilemmas caused by this feedback process, nor have administrators. And if power can be checked only by power, it may be healthy for the continued existence of limited government if neither judicial nor administrative officers ever fully resolve these conflicts.

40 EVASION OF SUPREME COURT MANDATES BY STATE COURTS

The Harvard Law Review

After reviewing the decision of a state court, the Supreme Court of the United States fre-

Reprinted by permission of the publisher from Note, "Evasion of Supreme Court Mandates in Cases Remanded to State Courts Since 1941," *Harvard Law Review*, LXVII (1954), pp. 1251–1259. Copyright 1954 by The Harvard Law Review Association. Footnotes have been omitted.

[14] *Yates* v. *United States*, 356 U.S. 363 (1958).

quently reverses and remands the case for further proceedings. The customary mandate permits further action "not inconsistent with" the decision of the Court. From the October Term 1941 to the close of the October Term 1951, the Court disposed of 175 cases in this way. In forty-six of them there was further litigation, and in slightly less than half of these cases the party successful in the Supreme Court was unsuccessful in the state court following the remand. . . .

Instances of Doubtful State Court Action.—In *Radio Station WOW, Inc.* v. *Johnson*, the plaintiff, a member of a society which owned a radio station, sued in a Nebraska court to set aside as fraudulent a lease by the society to a corporation. The Nebraska court set the lease aside, called for an accounting, and ordered the lessee to take all other steps necessary to return the parties to their original situation. The Supreme Court, reviewing the decision on a writ of certiorari, concluded after some discussion that it had jurisdiction. It recognized the authority of the state court to determine the issue of fraud, but held that since the FCC had already transferred the license to the lessee, an immediate transfer of the station facilities to the lessor would result in an unwarranted disruption of broadcasting operations. The Court considered the resulting conflict between FCC power and that of the state court a federal question. It reversed and remanded, deciding that a proper accommodation would be achieved if the Nebraska decree were modified to allow the parties with due speed to initiate proceedings before the Commission. After the remand the state court asserted that the Supreme Court, having no jurisdiction to decide questions of state property law, had invaded the field of state court authority, and rendered an "advisory" opinion, which would be disregarded. The state court did not suggest that the Supreme Court had misunderstood the facts or the basis for the state decision. Rather, it reexamined the jurisdictional question which the Court considered at length. This disposition cannot be supported by the independent non-federal ground rule, because the question of Supreme Court jurisdiction is clearly a federal one.

The state court relied partly on the opinion of Chief Justice Marshall in *Davis* v. *Packard*, in which the Court affirmed a state court's refusal to alter a judgment which had been reversed by the Supreme Court. The New York court had affirmed a judgment against the defendant, who claimed federal constitutional immunity from state court proceedings because of his diplomatic status. In its first review of the litigation the Supreme Court held that the defendant was entitled to diplomatic immunity, and remanded the case to the New York court to "conform its judgment" to the Supreme Court's opinion. On remand the state court held that it had no jurisdiction under New York law to reverse the original judgment, because the claim of diplomatic immunity did not appear in the record of lower court proceedings; but it pointed out that state procedure did provide a way in which the lower court judgment could be changed. When the Supreme Court reviewed the case the second time, it noted that a remedy existed, agreed that the jurisdiction of the state court had not been extended by the mandate, and held that its action was proper. But the Supreme Court made it clear that it would not sanction a reexamination of the federal question of diplomatic immunity which it had once decided. In the *WOW* case the Nebraska court did not advert to any analogous jurisdictional obstacles and did reexamine a federal question. Therefore its decision does not find support in *Davis* v. *Packard* and is clearly inconsistent with the mandate of the Supreme Court.

Another Nebraska case, *Hawk* v. *Olson,* also presents a question of compliance. Hawk, who had been convicted of murder and sentenced to life imprisonment, petitioned a Nebraska court for a writ of habeas corpus, alleging that his rights under the Federal Constitution had been violated and he had been wrongly imprisoned. The denial of the writ was affirmed by the state supreme court, which held that the petition contained only conclusions of law and that, in any event, the proper remedy for one in Hawk's situation was a writ of error *coram nobis*. The Supreme

Court reversed and remanded the case, holding that petitioner's allegations were sufficient to entitle him to a hearing on the merits. On remand the state court asserted that it would adhere to its original position that the petitioner was seeking the wrong remedy under local law. It concluded that this provided an independent non-federal ground adequate to support its first decision. Ordinarily the question of the proper remedy to vindicate a constitutional right is one of state law, and if the state court bases its decision on this ground the Supreme Court will not review the case. Although the Court recognized that the state decision had been based, at least in part, on the remedy sought by Hawk, it did not discuss the possibility that this would constitute an independent non-federal ground for the decision; nor does it appear to have decided the question *sub silentio.* Thus the case differs from the *WOW* case, where the Supreme Court had explicitly decided the federal question which the state court reexamined in order to affirm its earlier judgment. Also, if *Davis* v. *Packard* retains any vitality, it appears to support the Nebraska court, which seemed to assert it was without jurisdiction so long as Hawk insisted on *habeas corpus.* Thus it probably should not be said that the state court acted improperly in the *Hawk* case.

A different problem of evasion occurred in *Ashcraft* v. *Tennessee.* Coerced confessions were admitted as evidence in a murder trial, and the state supreme court affirmed the resulting convictions. The United States Supreme Court held this violative of due process and reversed and remanded the case. At the second trial the court admitted evidence of statements made by the defendants during the thirty-six hour detention period held coercive by the Supreme Court. These convictions also were reversed by the Court after the Supreme Court of Tennessee had affirmed them. The Supreme Court of the United States made it clear that its original mandate had been interpreted far too narrowly. The slight changes in the evidence used to obtain the convictions were not sufficient to produce a different result. So narrow a reading of the mandate results either in the inefficiency inherent in reexamination by the Supreme Court, as in *Ashcraft,* or ultimate denial of federally protected constitutional rights.

In *Wieman* v. *Updegraff,* the Supreme Court reversed Oklahoma's highest court, which had affirmed an order enjoining the payment of salaries to state teachers who refused to take the legislatively prescribed loyalty oath. The Court based its reversal on the ground that the oath did not incorporate the element of scienter[1] and therefore violated the Due Process Clause. On remand to the Oklahoma court, the case was further remanded to a lower court for action pursuant to the mandate of the Supreme Court. The lower court took it upon itself to revise the loyalty oath by introducing the element of scienter. However, all but one of the teachers still refused to take the oath and the salaries were not paid. Immediate review by writ of mandamus was denied in the state supreme court. Though the lower court's action may raise due process problems different from the one decided by the Supreme Court, or be open to objection as poor judicial administration, it does not seem inconsistent with the mandate. It was rather an attempt to obey the mandate and at the same time implement the policy expressed by the state legislature.

In *Lavender* v. *Kurn,* an FELA action in a Missouri court, the jury returned a verdict for the plaintiff. The state supreme court reversed and entered judgment for the defendant, holding that some evidence was improperly admitted, and that there was not sufficient acceptable evidence to support the verdict, but the United States Supreme Court reversed the judgment of the Missouri court on the ground that there was sufficient evidence to support the verdict even without the objectionable evidence. It refrained from discussing the question whether that evidence should have been excluded. After remand, the state court reasserted its former view that the evidence had been erroneously admitted, reversed the trial court's judgment, and sent the case back for a new trial. At this point the

plaintiff sought Supreme Court review, arguing that the mandate had called for reinstatement of the jury's verdict. But the Court denied a motion for leave to file a petition for mandamus and denied *certiorari* because of the lack of a final judgment. The parties then reached a settlement as the new trial was about to begin. Three justices dissented from the denial of leave to file for a writ of mandamus, probably because they regarded it as arguable that there had been an evasion. Though the state court's action may have proceeded on the theory that, even if the unobjectionable matter would have supported a verdict for the plaintiff, the objectionable evidence so influenced the jury as to warrant a reversal, it seems to have acted improperly. The Supreme Court's treatment indicated that the Court thought the error, if there had been one, was harmless. Whether or not the state court agrees in this estimate, it seems improper for it to reexamine the question once the Supreme Court has decided it.

Kedroff v. *St. Nicholas Cathedral* again raised the problem of compliance. In an action for the possession of a Russian Orthodox cathedral, the New York Court of Appeals awarded judgment to the plaintiff, a representative of a church group which had seceded from the administrative control of the Patriarch of Moscow. The court based its decision on a local statute purporting to transfer control of Russian Orthodox Church properties to the plaintiff's group. On appeal, the Supreme Court held the statute violative of due process, and reversed and remanded. The New York court ordered a new trial, basing its decision on the state law of trusts, rather than the statute. At this point the defendant unsuccessfully attempted to secure a writ of mandamus from the Supreme Court to the New York court, by asserting that the mandate had been violated. The Supreme Court had said that, except when it was shown that the clergy had been selected invalidly, the internal administration of the churches was outside the competence of the civil courts. The New York court argued that this "passing comment" need not prevent it from applying the local law of trust administration.

[1][knowledge, or knowing action]

Thus the case presents the problem of the proper effect of Supreme Court dictum, following a remand. While a narrow interpretation of the mandate may be improper, giving effect to dictum would, in some situations, violate the policy against advisory opinions, because legal effect would be given to language not tested in litigation.

In order to determine whether the result could be supported by local property law, the state court directed the lower court to ascertain whether the religious trust property was presently well administered and whether the clergy had been properly selected. It seems probable that the Supreme Court's decision was not intended to remove the traditional right of state courts to adjudicate these questions. Therefore such a non-federal ground would not have been lacking in "fair support" if raised earlier in the litigation. But a dissent in the New York court argued that that court had violated the mandate by raising at this stage of the litigation, contrary to ordinary New York practice, questions which had no basis in the record. Though this may not itself be evasive, the New York court indicated that it was adopting this measure to ensure that the ultimate result of the litigation would conform to local policy as enunciated by the state legislature. Even if these factors combine to make the court's disposition an evasive one, it is possible that findings of fact at the new trial will bring the case outside the rule announced by the Supreme Court; and this might also occur, in any event, during a later suit. For example, if the defendant had been invalidly selected by his ecclesiastical superiors, presumably he would not be entitled to the premises. It is not clear whether the Supreme Court in subsequent proceedings would take into consideration the findings of such a trial. On the one hand, it might disregard them because of the evasion; on the other hand, it might consider the evaluation of newly discovered facts more important than prompt compliance with the mandate.

It seems clear that a state court acts inconsistently with the mandate of the Supreme Court when it rejects the Court's decision as to its own jurisdiction or any other federal question. And, though no precise standards can be enunciated, a very narrow interpretation of the mandate should also be considered improper. However, if the state court discovers an independent non-federal ground which has not been rejected by the Supreme Court, it may properly base the decision on it. There is authority that a state court may properly decide that a statute which the Supreme Court declared unconstitutional was misinterpreted by the Supreme Court and, as properly construed, is not objectionable. And even if the court reinterprets the statute, there appears to be no evasion. It may be an evasion to order a new trial for the purpose of sustaining the original judgment on a theory not found in the record. But if a change of fact occurs after the remand which would probably have resulted in another conclusion by the Supreme Court if it had taken place before review, there seems no reason why the state court should not interpret the mandate in the light of the new circumstances.

B. The Press

To most citizens the press is the sole source of information about judicial decisions, policies, and actors. Even the legal scholar probably first learns of court decisions from his daily newspaper. As Douglass Cater[1] notes, however, the press is not a neutral channel of information in reporting government policy-making. More or less consciously reporters and editorial writers seek to determine policy as well as report it. The judiciary is not immune from such treatment. The selection of what deci-

[1] *The Fourth Branch of Government* (Boston: Houghton Mifflin Co., 1959).

sions to report and the manner in which they are presented in news accounts, editorials, and political cartoons to a large degree structures the citizen's perception of the court and its policies.

Most newspaper coverage of the Court, however, is unsophisticated and biased towards the sensational. As a result, the press has little direct impact on Supreme Court decision-making. But the press does influence the manner in which other political decision-makers such as Congressmen and state legislators view the Court—both directly and through constituency reaction. Indirectly, therefore, press activity affects Court policies. It may generate criticism and action within institutions that can alter judicial policies.

The following selection by Chester A. Newland discusses the methods and backgrounds of the reporters who cover the Supreme Court.

41 PRESS COVERAGE OF THE U.S. SUPREME COURT

Chester A. Newland

[R]espect for the Supreme Court and law in general depends increasingly upon popular appreciation of the inherent merits of the Court's work. At the same time legal concepts and institutions are subjected to an ever diminishing time span of technical and social change which imposes heavy pressures upon the Court and upon the American people whose ultimate support the Court needs. Great obligations are placed upon the high court justices and media of mass communications by these circumstances.

This is a study of how these obligations were treated by the Court and leading representatives of the American press in the Court's October Term, 1961. . . . [R]eporting in the metropolitan press of two major cases is analyzed. That is followed by brief examination of wire service coverage of the 1961 Term generally. . . .

This problem of press coverage of the Supreme Court was publicly recognized by Mr. Justice Clark after the close of the 1961 Term when the Court found itself engulfed by a rising tide of public criticism over the Prayer

Reprinted with permission of the author and publisher from "Press Coverage of the United States Supreme Court," *Western Political Quarterly*, XVII (1964), pp. 15–16, 23–34. Some footnotes omitted and others renumbered.

case, decided June 25, 1962.[1] Justice Clark explained that popular misunderstanding was the cause of discontent, and he laid much of the blame on newsmen. Pressure on reporters to communicate the ruling rapidly with numerous other opinions announced the same day was described by Clark as the chief cause of inaccuracy. Clark's criticism of the press was answered immediately by representatives of the Associated Press and United Press International. The AP's reporter at the Court for the past eighteen years, Paul Yost, said: "We had it 100% accurate. We stuck right to the opinion and dealt specifically with what the opinion said." Washington Bureau Manager for UPI, Julius Frandsen, retorted that the reporting was "remarkably good," and suggested that Clark was evidently "confusing what news agencies have written with what certain members of Congress and the Clergy were saying." Charlotte Moulton, UPI reporter at the Court since 1949, suggested that the particular problem noted by Justice Clark might result from an "emotional accompaniment" which causes people to "read into the stories certain inaccuracies" when they touch on the sensitive matter of religion.

Although it illustrates the problem of public opinion of the Supreme Court's work especially well, reporting of the Prayer case and the reaction to it was only a small part

[1]*Engel* v. *Vitale*, 370 U.S. 421 (1962).

of the total communications responsibilities of the justices and the press during the October Term, 1961. In all, 1,062 cases on the regular docket and 1,510 on the miscellaneous docket were handled by the Court in the 1961 Term, and of those 125 went through the long route from filing to acceptance for review, oral argument, and final decision. The press covers each step in this process, eliminating on its own those cases which newsmen think merit no reports and identifying the significant aspects of others for reporting to local, regional, or national publics. At the same time, reactions to opinions (often solicited) are reported, individual judges and the Court as an institution are described and analyzed, conjectural articles are formulated, and editorials and political cartoons are published which may either promote public understanding or obscure the actual work of the Court.

. . .

REPORTING
OF REAPPORTIONMENT[2]
AND PRAYER CASES

An examination of press coverage of the two Supreme Court decisions of the 1961 Term which commanded greatest public interest discloses salient features of the task of communicating information of Court actions to the American people. These two decisions were those on Reapportionment and School Prayer. News coverage of the latter opinion has been subjected to brief study by journalists, largely as a consequence of Justice Clark's criticism. . . . The Reapportionment case represented a far more significant action by the Court, however. News coverage of these two opinions by 63 leading metropolitan daily newspapers was examined to provide basic information for this study.[3] These

[2]*Baker* v. *Carr,* 369 U.S. 186 (1962).
[3]The 63 newspapers selected are all of those principal dailies from the nation's 42 largest metropolitan areas which are kept by the Library of Congress. The newspapers are, in alphabetical order of their states: *Birmingham News; Arizona Republic; Los Angeles Times; San Diego Union; San Francisco Chronicle; San Francisco Examiner; Denver Post; Washington Post; Washington Star; Atlanta Constitution; Atlanta Journal; Chicago American; Chicago Sun Times; Chicago Tribune; Indianapolis News; Indianapolis Star; Courier Journal; Louisville Times; Times Picayune;*

newspapers were examined for the two one-week periods when these Court decisions received greatest attention: Reapportionment, March 26—April 2, 1962; and Prayer, June 25—July 2, 1962.

Before summarizing that survey of major metropolitan newspapers, it is essential to examine the Court opinions themselves. These opinions provide keys to understanding the communications problems involved and discloses that the Supreme Court justices were themselves the sources of some confusion in the reporting of these two vital cases.

In both the Reapportionment case and the Prayer case the Court suffered from sharp division of opinion. This has come to be expected in the difficult policy choices involved in the Supreme Court's work, with non-unanimous opinions in from two-thirds to three-fourths of written opinions in recent years. But in these cases the justices' opinions revealed more than judicial division over legal principles: the opinions in each case reflected confusion and sharp criticism better designed to promote public misunderstanding than enlightenment. The justices themselves recognized this grave shortcoming in their performances. In a concurring opinion in *Baker* v. *Carr,* Mr. Justice Clark complained: "One emerging from the rash of opinions with their accompanying clashing of views may well find himself suffering mental blindness. . . . One dissenting opinion, bursting with words that go through so much and conclude with so little contemns the majority action as 'a massive repudiation of the experience of

Baltimore News Post and *Sunday American; Baltimore Sun; Boston Globe; Boston Herald; Christian Science Monitor; Detroit Free Press; Detroit News; Minneapolis Star; Minneapolis Morning Tribune; Kansas City Star; Kansas City Times; St. Louis Globe Democrat; St. Louis Post-Dispatch; Omaha World-Herald; Buffalo Evening News; New York Herald Tribune; New York Times; Wall Street Journal; Rochester Democrat and Chronicle; Newark Evening News; Newark Star-Ledger; Cleveland Plain Dealer; Cleveland Press; Columbus Citizen Journal; Columbus Evening Dispatch; Toledo Blade; Daily Oklahoman; Oregonian; Oregon Daily Journal; Philadelphia Evening Bulletin; Philadelphia Inquirer; Pittsburg Post-Gazette; Pittsburg Press; Dallas News; Dallas Times-Herald; Fort Worth Star-Telegram; Houston Post; San Antonio Express; Memphis Commercial Appeal; Virginian Pilot; Seattle Post-Intelligencer; Seattle Daily Times; Milwaukee Journal; Milwaukee Sentinel.*

our whole past. . . .' " Mr. Justice Stewart likewise noted: "The separate writings of my dissenting and concurring Brothers stray so far from the subject of today's decision as to convey, I think, a distressingly inaccurate impression of what the Court decides." Both Clark and Stewart were concurring in Brennan's majority opinion when they commented, as quoted above. Douglas also found it necessary to write a separate concurring opinion. Finally, Frankfurter and Harlan each wrote dissents, with Harlan criticizing "variants of expression" in Frankfurter's opinion, which, he said, "becloud analysis."

Careful reading of the six opinions in the Reapportionment case reveals no ground for disagreement with the above remarks. There is no question here that while the justices sharply disagreed, they were individually concerned with the law of the case. But when opinions open with such sharp crossfire as above, news reporters and the public at large are likely to lose sight of the law in what appears (to the uninitiated at least) to be a battle of men and not of law. . . .

Division in the Prayer case resulted in even greater confusion. While separate opinions sometimes provide useful alternative expositions of legal concepts, the individual opinions in this case were such that apparently even the justices did not fully understand one another. Basis for the most extreme and unplausible public criticisms of the majority opinion are to be found in the dissent by Mr. Justice Stewart; and Justice Douglas' unrestrained remarks in a concurrence provide equally ample fuel for critics. It was Justice Douglas, not news reporters and Court critics, who first raised the point that numerous common ceremonial observances of a religious type might be barred by the logic of this decision. Before any critic outside the Court spoke of them, Douglas mentioned such practices as the Court's traditional invocation and congressional prayers as possible ceremonies to be ended. It appears that Douglas' opinion was partially a response to Justice Stewart's dissent. Stewart's opinion mentioned the major religious-type practices of American government which later became the

chief examples relied upon by critics: the Supreme Court ceremony; the third stanza of "The Star-Spangled Banner"; the Pledge of Allegiance to the Flag; and the motto, "In God We Trust." Taken together, these two opinions could do nothing less than produce serious misapprehensions and create general public confusion. Black's majority opinion failed to make it clear that the sensational consequences discussed by his brethren were not contemplated by his opinion. . . .

Wire service coverage of the Reapportionment and Prayer cases provided most of the reports used by the 63 newspapers studied. Of 25 evening papers examined, 23 published news reports of the Reapportionment decision on the Monday when it was announced. Principal stories in 14 of these papers were from AP, in 5 from UPI, in 2 by staff writers for the papers (*Evening Star* [Washington] and *Philadelphia Evening Bulletin*), and in one from the *Herald Tribune News Service*. Day-one stories on the Prayer case appeared in 17 of these evening papers. Principal stories in 10 were from AP, 4 from UPI, 2 "compiled from wire service," and one, in the *Washington Star*, by a staff reporter. Throughout the seven-day periods studied, AP reports were used at least twice as often as UPI stories. Day-two stories on both cases were too varied and numerous for quantification to be meaningful, but wire service reports were still most numerous in the Prayer case. Starting on day-two a sharp difference is discernible in the reporting of the two cases: reports by local staff writers were as common as wire service reports on the Reapportionment opinion, with detailed analyses or conjecture of possible local results; wire service reports of church and political leaders in Washington, New York, and other eastern cities were more numerous on the Prayer case, together with frequent reports of interviews of local critics.

Because of the central role of the wire service reports in publicizing these opinions, that coverage merits initial comment, although more detailed examination of the wire service reports is postponed to a later section. Here, the concern is only with "what the readers got" by way of wire service stories printed in the 63 newspapers studied. These are the stories as they appeared, after repeated editing.

Published day-one wire stories from AP and UPI on both cases were edited versions of the stories written largely in advance by [Paul] Yost and [Charlotte] Moulton. Background information on each case and conjecture about its importance filled the reports, with less attention to the Court's reasoning. The few day-one reports taken from wire services on the Prayer case were generally sketchy, but, though brief, some were largely accurate. For example, the page one lead story in the *Cleveland Press* on June 25, 1962, was a UPI report which stressed what Justice Clark later said was the heart of Justice Black's majority opinion: "[Justice Black] said that the court agrees with the contention of parents who opposed the practice that the establishment clause was violated because the prayer was composed by governmental officials as part of a governmental program to further religious beliefs." The story incorrectly reported also, however, that the basis of the decision was the religious freedom clause. Similarly, a page one story from AP on June 25 in the *Blade* (Toledo, Ohio), included three quotations from Justice Black, showing as clearly as possible from the Court's opinion that the issue was a governmentally composed prayer.

Starting with day-two stories and throughout the remainder of the week, however, reports drawn from wire services generally departed far from the Court's action and stressed reaction instead. The most striking feature of the reporting is that even Tuesday morning stories, the first printed by the particular newspapers involved, virtually ignored what the Supreme Court had said, and generally even what it had decided, and reported instead on national, state, and local reactions and conjecture. Day-two and later lead reports on Reapportionment were more frequently by local newspaper staff writers and newspaper bureau personnel than from wire services. On the Prayer case, wire reports of national level reaction were numerous and often on extreme views, completely obscuring

the Court's opinion in most newspapers. Besides reports of reaction, however, the Associated Press did send out the text of the Prayer opinions, and eleven newspapers published substantial portions of it. No text of opinions in the Reapportionment case was sent out by the wire services, but the *New York Times* printed substantial parts of the text, and the *Evening Star* (Washington) published Justice Stewart's opinion.

Emphasis on reaction instead of the Court's actual opinions was not simply the result of wire service reporting. On Reapportionment, the decision produced an immediate reaction in the form of legal actions and comments by state and local officials. This case had been closely watched, and local people, including journalists, were generally prepared for a fast response to the result. For example, the *Dallas Times-Herald* published a detailed day-one front page story on apportionment in Texas. Many metropolitan newspapers had been concerned with reapportionment already and were similarly prepared with extensive background data. In Atlanta, local officials filed a case on the same day as the Court's opinion, and other local court actions soon followed in other cities. While local actions were numerous, reaction in Washington was relatively mild, except from rural congressmen and Georgia's two senators who were elected under the threatened county unit system. News reports thus stressed state and local reactions, and they were generally written by local newspaper reporters or wire service bureau personnel.

Reaction in the Prayer case differed sharply from that above, and it was reported differently. Solicited opinions of political and religious spokesmen and of uninformed people in general dominated the news. Unlike the Reapportionment situation, few were prepared in advance for a planned response to this opinion. Metropolitan newspapers and political leaders who were elected state-wide lacked the personal involvement which was present in apportionment. Wire service reports provided quotations from national figures, but local journalists also solicited uninformed opinions from ministers and local citizens for publication in newspapers where no accurate report of the Court's action ever appeared. This was apparently not due to unavailability of accurate information; the Court's opinions were available from AP in the metropolitan areas, but only eleven newspapers published the opinions. The uninformed reactions were apparently thought by many local editors to possess greater news value.

Newspapers could hardly be expected to ignore much of the reaction. Often the sources were eminent men whose views commanded attention. For example, the president of the American Bar Association attacked the opinion on the Tuesday after it was delivered. He was reported as saying that the opinion would require elimination of the motto, "In God We Trust," from coins. It may be expected that journalists would report such a speech if made by the man so honored by other members of the Bar, and that many people would assume that the ABA president should understand a Supreme Court opinion before speaking if anyone should. A similar reaction came from the Chief Justice of Indiana's high court, who was reported as saying that the First Amendment is only a restriction on Congress. Although displaying unbelievable ignorance of constitutional law, if he said that, such a spokesman could hardly be ignored. Pennsylvania's Chief Justice John C. Bell, Jr., was interviewed by a journalist and reportedly said that the "First Amendment sometimes aids reds and criminals more than other citizens." In Boston, Harvard Law Professor Mark De Wolfe Howe was pictured on page one of the *Boston Globe*, June 27, 1962, and quoted as saying: "Justice Black's opinion is ridiculous. It has no social, political or historical validity." Roman Catholic cardinals unanimously attacked the opinion with strongly worded indictments. Many Methodist and Episcopal leaders, and a few Baptists, like Billy Graham, joined in the chorus of criticism.

The Court's defenders were few, and except for President Kennedy, they were scarcely noted when they spoke. Arthur Goldberg, then Secretary of Labor, urged support of the Court in a speech at Roanoke, Virginia, but his remarks were reported in only one of the 63 papers examined.[4] The Solicitor General defended the Court's opinion in Chicago, but his statement also made only one paper.[5] The one defense of the Court which received front page coverage in many papers was that by President Kennedy at his news conference on June 27. Several Jewish, Unitarian, and many Baptist leaders also spoke out in support of the Court on the local level, but few of their remarks were circulated nationwide.

While the critics talked and won headlines, the justices observed their traditional silence and were largely ignored. Finally, in August Justice Clark spoke out in defense of the Court at the American Bar Association convention, but his remarks won little publicity.

Content of news reports is only one aspect of newspaper communication of Court actions. News headlines, editorials, political cartoons, and featured analysts are also significant. Comparative emphasis in reporting of the Reapportionment and Prayer cases is disclosed by all these factors. Of the 63 newspapers examined, 29 gave noticeably greater space and prominence to the Prayer case and only seven to the Reapportionment case (by far the more important) than to the other opinion. Also, West Coast newspaper coverage on both cases was extremely sketchy and uninformative as compared to that of Eastern and Southern newspapers. Day-one stories were decidedly less prominent than day-two stories. In short, the sketchy but somewhat accurate day-one stories of Court action received much less space and headline prominence than day-two stories on reaction. Apparently day-one stories tend to be crowded in at the last minute, whereas follow-up stories are given deliberate prominence.

Headlines were generally misleading on both opinions, though the most serious distortions were on the Prayer case. On apportionment the headlines often stressed city voters winning and "conservatives" losing,

---

[4] *Virginian-Pilot*, June 30, 1962, p. 2.
[5] *Chicago Daily Tribune*, June 29, 1962, p. 9.

i.e., "High Court Decides for City Voters" (*Arizona Republic*); "Urban voters Win in Supreme Court" (*San Diego Union*); "Rural Conservatives to Lose Vote Power" (*Omaha World-Herald*); "Supreme Court Decision May End Rural Edge" (*Oregonian*); "Gerrymandering Hit, City Voters Get Hearing Right" (*Christian Science Monitor*). Even when headlines were wrong, as in the *Christian Science Monitor*'s reference to gerrymandering, the stories were sometimes exceptionally accurate, as in that newspaper. The headlines in the Prayer case were seriously misleading in most newspapers, i.e., "No Praying in Schools, Court Rules" (*Indianapolis News*); "Possible End to Christian, Jewish Holy Day Activity in Public Schools as Court Bans N.Y. Prayer" (*Baltimore Sun*); "Prayer Ruling Gives Jolt to School Religious Rites" (*Boston Globe*); "Supreme Court Outlaws Prayers in Public Schools" (*Detroit Free Press*); "No Prayers in Schools, Supreme Court Orders" (*Dallas Morning News*). Some headlines were accurate, as in the *Buffalo Evening News:* "Supreme Court Voids N.Y. State School Prayer;" such headlines were rare.

Editorial comments on these opinions were extensive. Of the 63 papers studied, 38 favored the apportionment opinion; 10 opposed it; and 12 published editorials which were neutral or confused. Of those supporting the opinion, the *Washington Post* and the *Atlanta Journal* each published four editorials in one week on the opinion; three editorials each were published in the *Atlanta Constitution, Minneapolis Star, Philadelphia Inquirer,* and the *Milwaukee Journal.* Nine of the 38 papers favoring the opinion published two supporting editorials in one week. Editorial support was generally based on a desire to provide greater urban voting power, and, more particularly, reapportionment in the urban areas represented by these newspapers. Despite the revolutionary change in law, opposing editorials were generally mild; they objected to federal infringement on state government affairs. The opposition newspapers were: the *Arizona Republic; Indianapolis News; Times Picayune; Boston Herald; Omaha World-Herald; Wall Street Journal; Dallas Times-Herald;* and

the *Fort Worth Star-Telegram.* Some of the newspapers which generally oppose such court intervention in political affairs traditionally under state control were torn between their usual "states rights" views and the opinion which favored their urban readers. The *Dallas Morning News,* for example, praised the result, condemned the Court's intervention, and then said: "The COURT, in this instance, is not taking away a state's right or a state's power; it merely admonishes the state to exercise it." One newspaper, the *Birmingham News,* published five editorials in one week which were neutral in expression but which tended to favor the result. The *Buffalo Evening News* published an editorial cartoon critical of the decision and an editorial which was neutral. Only 4 other of the 63 newspapers published editorial cartoons opposed to the decision; 16 published cartoons favoring the decision; 3 of these published editorials which were neutral.

Twenty-seven of the 63 newspapers[6] studied published editorials opposed to the Prayer decision; 16 favored it in editorials; and 11 were more or less neutral. The strongest opposition came from papers in the northern midwest. Contrary to common newspaper reports, more southern papers were neutral or favorable to the opinion than opposed it. Editorial cartoons were more numerous on the Prayer case than on Reapportionment. Twenty papers published critical cartoons; 12 published favorable cartoons. The *Philadelphia Evening Bulletin* favored the decision editorially, but it published two of its own cartoons which were critical. Two newspapers with neutral editorials published hostile cartoons.

One important aspect of individual newspaper coverage of these opinions is the relationship between informative reporting and editorial views. This is particularly true in the Prayer case, because public criticism of that decision has been attributed to misunderstanding arising from poor news coverage.

---

[6]Three of these newspapers were closed by strikes in June and not published: *Minneapolis Star, Minneapolis Morning Tribune,* and *Milwaukee Sentinel.*

Of the 11 newspapers which published substantial excerpts from the text of the justices' opinions, three opposed the decision editorially. One of these newspapers, the *Washington Star*, published four hostile editorials and two hostile cartoons in one week; yet it is difficult to see how this criticism could arise from ignorance due to poor news coverage. The *Star* published a partial text of opinions on day-two (Tuesday) as well as a sketchy but generally accurate day-one report. Thus the Court's opinion was also available to the many critics in Congress. This suggests that the justices' opinions and irresponsible but informed politicians may be as much at fault as the news coverage, if misunderstanding is a reason for public criticism of the Supreme Court. Both the *Kansas City Star* and the *Baltimore Sun* also opposed the decision while publishing the text of opinions and generally restrained and informative news stories. Even one Hearst newspaper, the *Seattle Post-Intelligencer*, ran informative though sketchy reports . . . along with its exceptionally hostile and misleading page one editorials written by William Randolph Hearst, Jr. for all Hearst papers.

Eight of the 11 newspapers which published partial texts of the Prayer opinions supported Black's views: *The Denver Post; Washington Post; Louisville Times; Christian Science Monitor; New York Times; Rochester Democrat and Chronicle; Norfolk Virginian-Pilot;* and the *Milwaukee Journal*. The newspapers which editorially supported the Court were also more restrained in wording of headlines and publication of excessively distorted criticisms than were the papers which opposed the decision.

News columnists featured in the 63 newspapers examined included several who analyzed these opinions, but there is no apparent relationship between the newspapers' views or news coverage on these cases and those of their syndicated columnists. David Lawrence commented on these opinions more frequently in these papers than any other writer. He was critical of the Reapportionment decision and mildly supported the Prayer decision, often on opposite sides of the issues from the newspapers involved. *New York Times* News Service articles by James Reston, Arthur Krock, and Anthony Lewis were used by a few papers; these same papers generally opposed the Prayer decision editorially.

The most informative and accurate news reports and analyses on these opinions were by Anthony Lewis of the *New York Times* and James Clayton of the *Washington Post. Christian Science Monitor* editorials and reports, some by-lined Richard L. Strout, and *Atlanta Journal* and *Constitution* reports were also perceptive.

WIRE SERVICE REPORTS

A comprehensive survey of newspaper reporting of the Reapportionment and Prayer cases reveals that journalists can and do sometimes provide fast and somewhat accurate reports of Supreme Court decisions. But such reports were generally obscured in one of those cases by unrestrained reporting of uninformed and extreme reactions and use of misleading headlines. News media were not altogether at fault. Much of the blame belongs to irresponsible political, religious, and Bar leaders, and some must also fall on the justices themselves for their own unrestrained and uncraftsmanlike opinions. Yet, the wire services play such a critical role as midwives between the Court and newspapers that their work deserves separate assessment.

Four major hazards are present in wire service coverage of the Supreme Court: (1) untrained personnel assigned to cover the Court; (2) speed; (3) multiple bureau editing under pressures of competition by journalists who lack backgrounds for understanding the Court's work; and (4) brevity. Examples of these from the reporting of the 1961 Term illustrate their seriousness.

Experienced reporters now represent AP and UPI on that beat. . . . but their original selection was based only on their high ability as journalists without provision for special preparation for their Court work. Because of multiple editing of wire service reports, it is impossible to know whether important technical errors enter into stories when first written at the Court or later at the Bureaus. Errors in reports of the 1961 Term which seem attributable to either the primary reporting or the editing included the following on the Prayer case. The first UPI Bulletin read: "The Supreme Court ruled today that daily recital of an official state prayer in public schools, even though non-compulsory, offends the religious freedom guarantees in the Constitution." In fact, the decision concerned the establishment clause, not religious freedom. Yet, the first UPI lead story at 12:29 P.M. opened with a similar, misleading sentence: ". . . unconstitutional because it violates the religious freedom guaranteed in the Bill of Rights. . . ." Informed readers could excuse such an error, perhaps, since the UPI story included a clear quotation from Justice Black stating the basis for his decision. But apparently newspaper editors are not well informed on this important constitutional provision since this obvious error was left in published stories and repeated several times during the week. Wire service reports also confuse other legal terms which are common in the everyday work of the Court. For example, on an important memorandum case announced April 2, 1962, *In Re Zipkin,* the Court said: "The Writ of Certiorari is dismissed as improvidently granted." Even on so simple a matter as this, the AP incorrectly reported as follows: "The Supreme Court dismissed today an appeal by Michail Zipkin. . . ." In another memorandum case of wide interest, announced June 18, 1962, *Young* v. *Motion Picture Association*, the AP referred repeatedly to the petition as an appeal and also as a complaint. Such errors are numerous in the wire service stories on Court actions of the 1961 Term.

Pressures for speed and brevity result in unbalanced and uninformative reporting. On June 25, 1962, the day of the Prayer case, decisions were handed down with opinions in a total of 16 cases and in 257 memorandum cases. Although several of these decisions were of unusual significance, most were obscured by reports of reaction to the Prayer case. Although a subject of proper disagreement, it would not be far wrong to describe the Brown Shoe case as equal in importance

to any matter decided that day. Yet the case went almost unreported outside the Washington, D.C., and New York newspapers. The UPI Bulletin at 12:37 P.M. June 25 reported it as follows: "The Supreme Court handed the government a major antitrust victory today by upholding an order divorcing two shoe companies." Only an unusually informed reader would know anything from reading that. The AP sent out a 240-word report on the decision by 12:40 P.M., but it was practically unused by newspapers. In its June 25 night lead on the Supreme Court, AP treated this major decision with one short paragraph. The same night lead devoted two paragraphs to two other decisions also. One concerned barring from the mails magazines appealing to homosexuals, a case which received wide publicity, generally under a UPI lead. The only other case widely reported was *Robinson* v. *California*, the California narcotics addict case. At the same time that most court actions were largely ignored, the Associated Press ran a steady sequence of reactions on the Prayer case on June 25.

Examination of sequences of wire service stories reveals two serious faults in their reporting which apparently grows out of competition: choosing sensational material over more significant cases for reports and blowing up of stories to sensational dimensions. These are faults in bureau editing, not simply results of speed in reporting. Two examples from reporting in February and June, 1962, clearly illustrate these problems.

On February 19, 1962, in a one sentence memorandum opinion, the Supreme Court affirmed a decision of a U.S. District Court that Louisiana could not close some of the schools in the state to avoid desegregation while leaving others open.[7] This was one of the most important decisions of the entire term and was reported as such in the UPI night lead on the Court that Monday under the by-line of Charlotte Moulton, the reporter at the Court. The Associated Press handled that case in the more customary way. At

[7] *St. Helena Parish School Board* v. *Hall* 368 U.S. 515 (1962).

11:39 A.M., AP moved an "urgent" story of 180 words, noting the decision: "The Supreme Court tagged unconstitutional today another of the numerous acts of the Louisiana Legislature designed to aid in the state's fight against racial integration of its schools. . . ." At 1:54 P.M. it again ran the story: "The Supreme Court declared Louisiana's local option law unconstitutional today and termed the state's statute a 'transparent artifice . . . designed to deny Negroes their declared constitutional right to attend desegregated public schools.' " The big trouble in that report is that the U. S. Supreme Court's opinion did not say that. All that the Court said was: "Per curiam: The motion to affirm is granted and the judgment is affirmed." Apparently the bureau editor erroneously attributed the more sensational language to the Supreme Court when in fact it was a quote gleaned in advance from the District Court opinion by Paul Yost and included in his story on the case. A third AP story at 2:50 P.M. corrected this error: "Louisiana's local option school law was declared unconstitutional today. Without comment, the Supreme Court unanimously affirmed a lower court decision. . . ." In its night lead on the Court, AP devoted only one absurdly inaccurate sentence to the decision: "For the seventh time since December 12, 1960, [the Court] upheld unanimously the decision holding unconstitutional an act of the Louisiana legislature aimed at helping the State's fight against racial school integration." Like the error in the 1:54 P.M. story, this mistake apparently grew from accurate wording in Yost's original advance report: "Today's action was the seventh since Dec. 12,1960 in which the Supreme Court ruled against Louisiana moves to block integration." These mistakes, which display serious lack of knowledge of the Court, are not the only deficiency in the AP's report. A greater fault was that while one inaccurate paragraph in the night lead was devoted to this most vital decision, twelve paragraphs were devoted to a lead story on a less important criminal case in which a district court was ordered to hear an Alcatraz prisoner's motion to vacate and set aside a forty-year sentence he was serving for a bank robbery.

C. The Law Reviews

Law reviews are a major source of professional comment and criticism of Supreme Court activity. They are edited by the best senior students of their respective law schools. Issues typically contain unsigned articles called "Notes" written by the individual editors. The signed articles, however, particularly in the reviews of such prestigious law schools as Chicago, Columbia, Harvard, and Yale, are frequently written by some of the most renowned law professors, judges, and legal administrators in the country. Often they deal directly with Supreme Court policies. Many, in fact, resemble the briefs one finds in appellate review. Such articles typically discuss the problems created by the present state of the law in a particular field and argue for changes or developments which should occur. Frequently such articles become the subject for further law review comment and criticism. The law reviews, therefore, present the members of the Court with a type of professional criticism to which judges are thought to be particularly sensitive.

In recent years it has not been uncommon to find law review articles cited in the footnotes of Supreme Court opinions as sources of authority. Not all members of the Court have indulged in this practice. It has been severely attacked by more conservative lawyers as "unprofessional." Despite this charge, review articles continue to be read and cited by the members of the Court. Their persuasiveness cannot be denied. Anthony Lewis, for example, in *Gideon's Trumpet*, argues that law review criticism of the right to counsel rule articulated in *Betts* v. *Brady* was in part responsible for its abandonment in *Gideon* v. *Wainwright*.[1]

The following selection by Chester A. Newland is a quantitative study of the reviews most commonly cited and the justices who use them as authority.

[1] *Gideon's Trumpet* (New York: Random House, 1964), pp. 105–117. *Betts* v. *Brady,* 316 U.S. 455 (1942); *Gideon* v. *Wainwright*, 372 U.S. 335 (1963). Note that the Betts rule essentially stated that in a case involving a capital crime a defendant must be provided counsel by the state if he cannot afford to hire his own. In a noncapital case, it was suggested in the Betts decision, the state must provide counsel for an impoverished defendant only if (1) the complexity of the law, (2) the intellectual capacity of the defendant, (3) the mood of the populace, or (4) some other unusual set of circumstances made an adequate defense by the defendant highly unlikely. In Gideon, the Court discarded the Betts rule and stated that the state is required to provide counsel for an impoverished defendant in both capital and noncapital cases.

42 LAW REVIEWS AND THE SUPREME COURT

Chester A. Newland

Even the most casual perusal of the court reports will show that legal periodicals have been cited by the Supreme Court of the United States and by judges of some other courts in the past several years in proportions that are sharply increased over those of three decades ago. . . . This article summarizes the actual proportions in which legal periodicals were cited by the Supreme Court during the period from the October Term, 1924, through the October Term, 1956, and it briefly describes the reliance on legal periodicals in a few cases selected for illustration. . . .

I. QUANTITATIVE SUMMARY

The extent of judicial reliance on legal periodicals . . . may be shown most readily in a quantitative summary. Although much vital information about the role of legal periodicals is obscured by such an abridged survey, four factors about the influence of legal periodicals can be observed from a quantitative analysis. These factors are:

(1) the frequency of citation, indicating the growth of reliance by the Court on legal periodicals; (2) the justices who have most often cited legal periodicals; (3) the law reviews which have been cited most frequently and the range of legal periodical and related sources cited;[1] and (4) the authors who have been cited most frequently. Following this quantitative summary, some qualitative factors will be noted in analyses of the influence of legal periodicals in a few cases.

Frequency of Citation of Legal Periodicals. As shown in Table 1, the citation by the Supreme Court of legal periodical writing increased slowly during the first fifteen years included in this examination. Then the frequency of citation increased sharply beginning with the October Term, 1939. During the five years from the October Term, 1939, through the October Term, 1943, legal periodicals were cited in opinions (opinions of the Court, concurring, and dissenting opinions) in 17 percent of the total number of written opinions. The percentage for the subsequent five terms was 28, and for the five terms from 1949 through 1953 the percentage was 26. Although these figures are not a sure measure of the influence of legal periodicals on the Supreme Court, they do show that the

Reprinted from "Legal Periodicals and the United States Supreme Court," *Midwest Journal of Political Science*, III, no. 1, 1959, by Chester A. Newland by permission of the Wayne State University Press. Some footnotes omitted, others renumbered.

[1] In the tables which follow, several journals such as the *American Political Science Review* and the *American Historical Review* are included with legal periodicals as related sources.

TABLE 1   Totals of Cases in Which Legal Periodicals and Related Sources Were Cited in Opinions of the United States Supreme Court, October Terms, 1924–1956, and Totals of Periodical Sources Cited

Term	Opinions	Periodicals	Term	Opinions	Periodicals	Term	Opinions	Periodicals
1924	1	1	1936	9	16	1947	31	93
1925	3	4	1937	7	32	1948	27	125
1926	3	5	1938	7	27	1949	23	76
1927	2	2	1939	27	66	1950	19	40
1928	2	8	1940	14	26	1951	25	57
1929	3	4	1941	30	73	1952	24	57
1930	1	2	*1942	1	1	*1953	1	1
1931	6	58	1942	25	106	1953	21	74
1932	11	30	1943	32	68	1954	20	37
1933	7	22	1944	30	72	1955	26	69
1934	9	21	1945	44	114	1956	27	63
1935	4	6	1946	42	112			

*Special Terms of the Court.

frequency of citation of periodicals has measurably increased during the past 20 years.

Supreme Court Justices and Legal Periodicals. Table 2 shows the totals of opinions in which justices on the Court cited legal periodicals during the period from 1924 through 1956 and the "per-term average" of total opinions in which each justice cited articles. In Table 3 the totals of articles cited by 13 justices who have most frequently cited legal periodicals are shown.

Some weaknesses in the type of summary attempted in these tables are apparent. Most obvious are the differences in length of tenure among the justices. This is taken into account in the "per-term averages" listed in Table 2. Closely related to the differences in tenure is the factor of the particular periods when the justices were on the Court. In addition, vital factors which appear only in a qualitative analysis of opinions are submerged in these frequency tabulations. Quite often, for example, articles which are cited in an opinion have little or no influence.

The tables reveal some interesting information at a glance, however. Rutledge's name, for example, is conspicuous for the relatively large number of articles cited, especially considering his short length of service. Equally conspicuous from Table 3 is the large number of articles cited by Brandeis, especially of articles not cited in briefs filed in the cases.

This reflects Brandeis' well-known practice of completing considerable original research in preparation of his opinions. These tables also show quite clearly that the citation of legal periodical writing has become general among the Supreme Court justices since 1939.

It is interesting to compare the justices who have frequently cited law reviews with those who have seldom cited them in an effort to determine whether any correlations exist between a grouping on this basis and other common classifications. The clearest difference in reliance on legal periodicals among the justices, so far as group classification is concerned, appears to be related to the differences in their dispositions toward the changes in the law which accompanied the adoption in this country of the social welfare philosophy associated with the New Deal. The seven justices who most frequently cited legal periodicals, for example, were all Roosevelt appointees: Frankfurter, Douglas, Black, Jackson, Rutledge, Reed, and Murphy. The "dissenters" during the [early] thirties—Justices Brandeis, Stone, and Cardozo—cited legal periodicals much more often than other members of the pre-Roosevelt Court, while the five justices who held out most firmly against the New Deal—McReynolds, Van Devanter, Butler, Sutherland, and Roberts—cited practically no law review writing. Later groupings of the justices according to divi-

TABLE 2   Totals of Opinions in Which Justices Cited Legal Periodicals (October Term, 1924–October Term, 1956)

Justice	Court Opinion	Dissent	Concurrence	Total	Per-Term Average*
Frankfurter	57	35	13	105	5.5
Douglas	51	18	4	73	3.8
Black	43	27	2	72	3.6
Reed	45	10	1	56	2.9
Jackson	37	11	6	54	4.1
Rutledge	30	16	6	52	7.4
Murphy	23	7	1	31	3.1
Brandeis	19	9	2	30	2.0
Stone	21	7	0	28	1.3
Burton	20	4	0	24	2.0
Clark	16	4	0	20	2.8
Vinson	16	1	1	18	2.6
Cardozo	14	1	0	15	2.1
Warren	9	2	0	11	2.8
Harlan	4	4	1	9	3.0
Hughes	7	0	0	7	0.7
Brennan	3	2	0	5	5.0
Minton	4	0	0	4	0.6
Byrnes	3	0	0	3	3.0
Butler	0	2	0	2	0.1
Holmes	2	0	0	2	0.3
Taft	1	0	0	1	0.1
Sutherland	1	0	0	1	—
Sanford	1	0	0	1	0.1
Roberts	1	0	0	1	—
McReynolds	1	0	0	1	—
Van Devanter	0	0	0	0	0.0
McKenna	0	0	0	0	0.0
Totals	429	160	37	626	

*The "per-term averages" were arrived at by dividing the total of opinions for each justice by his total terms (including partial terms) on the Court during the period covered. When below 0.1, the average is not shown unless it is 0.0.

sions of opinions, however, reveal no marked differences in their reliance on law reviews. For example, Black, Douglas, Rutledge, and Murphy as a group did not differ much in the extent to which they relied on legal periodicals from Frankfurter, Jackson, and Reed as a group.

There is little evidence of a unique relationship between the fact that some justices were ex-law professors and the extent to which they cited law reviews or the particular periodicals which they cited. At the time when "the repressive cruelty of prejudice" (to borrow from Cardozo) still generally forbade the citation of law review writing, Justice Stone sometimes relied on legal periodicals, but he cited them in only a few opinions. Frankfurter, Douglas, and Rutledge each frequently cited legal periodicals, and Frankfurter and Douglas each cited the journals published by the schools with which they were earlier associated more frequently than they cited other law reviews. But these facts do not necessarily indicate that the reliance on law reviews by these justices was associated with their earlier law school experiences. Justices Black, Jackson, and Reed also cited law reviews in numerous opinions, and, like

TABLE 3 Totals of Articles Cited by 13 Justices Who Have Most Frequently Cited Legal Periodicals

Justice*	Court Opinion Article		Dissent Article		Concurrence Article		Total Article		Grand Total
	Not in Brief	In Brief	Not in Brief	In Brief	Not in Brief	In Brief	Not in Brief	In Brief	
Frankfurter	109	17	68	9	16	3	193	29	222
Douglas	67	31	25	8	4	0	96	39	135
Black	99	27	64	8	4	2	167	37	204
Reed	97	31	22	5	1	0	120	36	156
Jackson	113	18	21	3	26	2	160	23	183
Rutledge	54	15	43	4	13	13	110	32	142
Murphy	39	4	11	2	0	0	50	6	56
Brandeis	53	5	66	0	3	0	122	5	127
Stone	36	14	23	0	2	0	61	14	75
Burton	20	13	8	0	1	0	29	13	42
Clark	22	10	8	0	0	1	30	11	41
Vinson	28	9	0	1	2	1	30	11	41
Cardozo	22	5	1	1	0	0	23	6	29

*Arranged in the order in which they appear in Table 2.

Frankfurter and nearly all of the other justices, they also cited the *Harvard Law Review* most often.

Legal Periodicals Cited by the Supreme Court. Although over 100 legal periodicals and related sources have been cited in Supreme Court opinions, a few reviews have been clearly most influential. When the practice of citing legal periodicals began, Justice Brandeis referred to the *Harvard Law Review* nearly as often as he cited all other law journals combined. And with the exceptions of two justices, the *Harvard Law Review* has remained the most frequently cited periodical among those who refer most often to law reviews. It has been cited twice as often as the *Yale Law Journal*, the second most-cited periodical. The following list shows the fifteen legal periodicals which were cited most often in Supreme Court opinions between the October Term, 1924, and the October Term, 1956, and the number of times each was referred to:

Harvard Law Review, 399
Yale Law Journal, 194
Columbia Law Review, 176
Michigan Law Review, 65
Northwestern University (Illinois) Law Review, 47

Cornell Law Quarterly, 32
Law and Contemporary Problems, 32
Virginia Law Review, 29
University of Pennsylvania Law Review, 23
Minnesota Law Review, 23
Texas Law Review, 17
California Law Review, 15
Georgetown Law Journal, 15
American Bar Association Journal, 14
George Washington Law Review, 14

Legal Writers Cited by the Supreme Court. The citation in court opinions of legal writers (by name) follows a pattern similar to that of references to law reviews. A few law writers have been frequently cited, but many others have been referred to only one or two times. The ten authors who have been cited most often by name and the total number of such references made to each (either to periodical articles or books) are as follows:

Felix Frankfurter, 28
Charles Warren, 27
Thomas Reed Powell, 21
Erwin N. Griswold, 16
James M. Landis, 16
Zechariah Chafee, 16
Edward S. Corwin, 11
Edmund M. Morgan, 11
Roscoe Pound, 10

Edwin Borchard, 9
Besides such widely recognized legal scholars as these, the justices have often cited little-known sources and unsigned writings.

II. ILLUSTRATIVE CASES

While the quantitative summary above shows the proportions in which law reviews have been cited, detailed qualitative analyses of opinions, sources cited, and briefs filed in cases are necessary to show the actual influence of legal periodicals. In this brief survey, four familiar cases chosen for illustration must substitute for such a detailed examination of these materials.

Erie Railroad v. *Tompkins*. Justice Brandeis' 1938 opinion in *Erie Railroad* v. *Tompkins*[2] is probably the most widely-known instance of judicial reliance on legal periodical writing. In overruling the 96-year-old precedent of *Swift* v. *Tyson*[3] even when counsel made no attempt to have Justice Story's venerable opinion changed, Brandeis relied heavily on a *Harvard Law Review* article by Charles Warren.[4] Twenty-one other articles were also cited in Brandeis' *Erie Railroad* opinion.

After reviewing several criticisms of Justice Story's interpretation of Section 34 of the Judiciary Act of 1789, Brandeis called attention to Charles Warren's research. Brandeis said ". . . it was the more recent research of a competent scholar, who examined the original document, which established that the construction given to it by the Court was erroneous; and that the purpose of the section was merely to make certain that, in all matters except those in which some federal law is controlling, the federal courts exercising jurisdiction in diversity of citizenship cases would apply as their rules of decision the law of the State, unwritten as well as written." The decisive influence of Warren's article in Brandeis' interpretation of the Judiciary Act of 1789 could hardly be made more plain than as stated here.

Warren's *Harvard Law Review* article contained a history of the progress of the Judiciary Act of 1789 through Congress, and of the variations of the final Act from the original draft bill. Warren's article was based upon materials discovered in the archives of the United States which had never before been examined. One part of his research concerned Section 34 of the Judiciary Act. On the basis of the evidence gathered, Warren said:

> It now appears from an examination of the Senate Files, however, that if Judge Story and the Court had had recourse to those Files in preparing the decision in *Swift* v. *Tyson*, it is highly probable that the decision would have been different, and that the word "laws" in Section 34 would have been construed to include the common law of a State as well as the statute law. This conclusion will probably be reached by anyone who examines the original slip of paper on which the amendment containing Section 34 was written, and which is, with little doubt, in Ellsworth's handwriting.[5]

Warren included the evidence to support this conclusion in his article—including a photostat copy of Section 34 of the Judiciary Act as originally drafted. Justice Brandeis did not discuss Warren's research or his conclusions in the *Erie Railroad* case. He simply cited the article as a reference, as noted above, in holding Justice Story's interpretation to be erroneous.

To understand fully the role of legal periodicals in the development of which *Erie Railroad* was a part, it is necessary to examine other cases which preceded and followed it. For example, Warren's article was first cited ten years earlier by Justice Holmes in his dissent in the *Taxicab* case.[6] Referring to Charles Warren in his dissent, Holmes said: "An examination of the original document by a most competent hand has shown that Mr. Justice Story probably was wrong if anyone is interested to inquire what the framers of the instrument meant." After the *Taxicab* case, criticism of *Swift* v. *Tyson* became wide-

---

[2]304 U.S. 64 (1938).
[3]16 Pet. 1 (1842).
[4]Charles Warren, "New Light on the History of the Federal Judiciary Act of 1789," *Harvard Law Review*, XXXVII (1923), 49–132.

[5]Warren, *ibid*, p. 85.
[6]*Black and White T. & T. Co.* v. *Brown and Yellow T. & T. Co.*, 276 U.S. 518 (1928).

spread. In *Erie Railroad*, Justice Brandeis cited several articles containing these criticisms. Then, following *Erie Railroad*, numerous articles on the change were published in legal periodicals, and some of these in turn were cited in opinions in subsequent cases. . . .

O'Malley v. Woodrough. *O'Malley* v. *Woodrough*[7] is another familiar case which illustrates the pressure which may be exerted through law school journals for changes in the law. Justice Frankfurter wrote the majority opinion in this case upholding the taxation of the compensation of judges of courts of the United States. Frankfurter supported his opinion primarily by citing English court practices and by noting "wide and steadily growing disfavor from legal scholarship and professional opinion" of *Evans* v. *Gore*[8] expressed in legal periodicals.

In *Evans* v. *Gore*, decided in 1920, the Court had held the taxation of salaries of federal judges to be unconstitutional. Criticism of this and subsequent such decisions became widespread in the law reviews, and it was this criticism which Frankfurter cited to support his view in *O'Malley* v. *Woodrough*. These articles had been used in a similar fashion in the *Brief* for the United States.

Frankfurter's first reference was to a *Yale Law Journal* comment, signed C. E. C. (Dean Charles E. Clark of the Yale Law School), in which the author described "serious" effects of *Evans* v. *Gore*.[9] The second criticism noted was in Edward S. Corwin's annual review of constitutional law in the *American Political Science Review*.[10] Corwin examined the larger implications of *Evans* v. *Gore*, concluding that it fell into the pattern of undesirable restrictions of the Sixteenth Amendment.

The third article cited, by David Fellman, was published in the *Iowa Law Review* shortly before *O'Malley* v. *Woodrough*.[11] Fellman examined in detail the problems of constitutional interpretation which had arisen out of judicial compensation clauses in state and federal constitutions. He also summarized the views of English judges in dealing with the problem. Commonwealth cases analyzed by Fellman were cited by Frankfurter to support the Court's opinion. In fact, Fellman's article contained most of the materials relied upon by Frankfurter, and Fellman's suggestion of a course of policy for American law paralleled the direction taken by the Court.

In addition to other law review articles by Charles L. B. Lowndes, Thomas Reed Powell, and W. S. Holdsworth, Frankfurter cited six law review case notes without mentioning the nature of the material referred to. Three of these were unsigned case notes, two were signed case notes, and one was a note on a South African Court decision on the taxation of judges' salaries. The five notes on American decisions were critical of the exclusion of judges' salaries from income taxation. . . .

Justice Frankfurter's use of legal periodicals in *O'Malley* v. *Woodrough* is typical in one respect. It illustrates his sensitiveness in some matters to the opinion of legal scholarship. Frankfurter often cites expressions of opinion of recognized legal scholars to support his opinions. However, he appears to have relied more heavily on the legal periodicals cited in this opinion than he customarily does, and he also referred to more articles than usual in this case.

Duncan v. Kahanamoku. The principal question in *Duncan* v. *Kahanamoku*[12] was whether the Hawaiian Organic Act gave military forces power to supplant all civilian laws and to substitute military for judicial trials during a period of martial law characterized by routine conditions of peace. In narrowing the matter before the Court, Justice Black cited several articles and books on martial law. He then turned to an examina-

[7]307 U.S. 277 (1939).
[8]253 U.S. 245 (1920).
[9]Charles Edward Clark, "Further Limitations upon Federal Income Taxation," *Yale Law Journal*, XXX (1920), 75–80.
[10]Edward S. Corwin, "Constitutional Law in 1919–1920," *American Political Science Review*, XIV (1920), 635, 641–644.

[11]David Fellman, "The Diminution of Judicial Salaries," *Iowa Law Review*, XXIV (1938), 89–126.
[12]327 U.S. 304 (1946).

tion of the legislative history of the Organic Act.

From his study of the legislative history of the Act, Black concluded that Congress had "expressed a strong desire to apply the Constitution without qualification." The chief source relied upon by Black in support of this opinion was a *Columbia Law Review* article by John P. Frank on the problems of martial law in Hawaii.[13] An analysis of Frank's article and of Black's opinion indicates that the article was probably the primary source of the Court's information. Justice Black quoted the identical materials summarized by Frank from the legislative history of the Organic Act. He relied upon the sources cited by Frank, and he followed the article's style of notation. Yet, Frank's article itself was cited in a manner which suggests that it was only supplementary to the Court's views.

John P. Frank's article is of added interest because of its central theme. The thesis of the article was that martial law in Hawaii was a disgraceful rule by the caprice of generals. The author suggested that military rule was being maintained not so much out of concern for security [but] as to facilitate firm control over the labor force. During the period when this article was written, Frank was an attorney in the Department of the Interior. Although he made clear that the views expressed did not purport to represent either the official or unofficial views of Interior, the article clearly supported the position of the Governor of the Islands and of the Interior Department. In this light, two other aspects of the article are of interest when compared to Justice Black's opinion. First, the Court not only relied upon the article for information, but it also followed the line of reasoning employed by Frank. Second, John P. Frank specifically commented on the *Duncan* case in his article. In fact, he analyzed the issues to be settled by the Court in the case and the questions which it raised.

Senior v. *Braden*. The final case selected to illustrate the manner in which legal periodicals have been cited in Supreme Court opinions is *Senior* v. *Braden*,[14] in which the articles cited were of small influence. *Senior* v. *Braden* was the only instance during the period covered in this study in which Justice McReynolds cited law reviews in an opinion. He referred to two articles published in the *Columbia Law Review* in 1917 on the rights of the *cestui que trust*. McReynolds' reference to these articles is interesting since one of the articles was written by Harlan Stone when he was at Columbia Law School, and McReynolds bluntly rejected its argument.

The first *Columbia Law Review* article, by Professor Austin Wakeman Scott of Harvard Law School, contained an analysis of the nature of the rights of the *cestui que trust* leading to the conclusion that the interest of a holder of a land trust certificate is an interest in real property.[15] Stone's article was written two months after Scott's, and it contained an analysis of the same subject leading to . . . [a] quite different conclusion. . . .[16]

The conflicting views of the law reflected in Scott's and Stone's articles met directly in *Senior* v. *Braden*. Through Justice McReynolds, the Court held in this case that the interest of a holder of a land trust certificate is an interest in real property and that it is therefore not subject to a state intangible property tax. In successfully arguing this position, attorneys for the appellant had cited Professor Scott's article. They also noted Stone's conflicting views but added Supreme Court decisions in opposition. McReynolds rejected Stone's view, which was advanced by the appellees, with the brief comment that "some writers do give it approval because of supposed consonance with general legal principles." The "some writers" referred to was Stone. McReynolds also cited a *Cincinnati Law*

---

[13]John P. Frank, "Ex Parte Milligan v. The Five Companies: Martial Law in Hawaii," *Columbia Law Review*, XLIV (1944), 639–668. . . .

[14]295 U.S. 422 (1935).

[15]Austin Wakeman Scott, "The Nature of the Rights of the *Cestui Que Trust*," *Columbia Law Review*, XVII (1917), 269–290.

[16]Harlan F. Stone, "The Nature of the Rights of the *Cestui Que Trust*," *Columbia Law Review*, XVII (1917), 467–501.

Review article in his *Senior* v. *Braden* opinion. He relied on it as a source of information on pertinent written opinions of the Attorney General of Ohio. Justice Stone dissented in an opinion in which he repeated some of the views expressed in his earlier *Columbia Law Review* article. However, he did not refer to the article in his opinion.

III. CONCLUSION

This acutely limited selection of cases sketched for illustration reveals that significant qualitative factors may be lost in the strictly quantitative summary of the citation of legal periodicals contained in the first part of this article. In most cases the law review articles which are cited are minor references in the justices' opinions. On the other hand, they are sometimes influential sources, as in *Erie Railroad* v. *Tompkins*. The justices differ in their manner of citing law reviews, and individual justices use these sources in a variety of ways in different opinions. Many of the references to frequently cited journals like the *Harvard Law Review* are inconsequential, whereas a single reference to a seldom-cited law review may be an influential source in an opinion. Only a detailed qualitative analysis of the role of law reviews in individual opinions will reveal these factors. However, this quantitative summary shows in broad outline the growth in influence of legal periodicals in the judicial process.

D. Congress

Congressional feedback in its policy orientations is similar to feedback from the press and the law reviews. It may be aimed at hindering or promoting past Supreme Court decisions or even forcing new Court policies. Like feedback from the press and law reviews, Congressional feedback may be merely verbal. There is hardly a Court decision of moment that is not both praised and criticized within Congress. It is likely that the members of the Court are not oblivious to such comment.

Congress has at its disposal means much stronger than words for influencing Court behavior, however. Through its powers as a coordinate branch of government Congress may directly and indirectly affect the impact, development, and even content of Court policies. Through its power over nominations the Senate has blocked appointments to the Supreme Court because of the presumed policy orientations of the nominees. Congress has changed the size, jurisdiction, and rules of procedure of the Court. Congress, both through its role in initiating Constitutional amendments and by passing legislation, has overruled Supreme Court policies and even explicit decisions. Every bill, in fact, that becomes law in which there is a Constitutional question generates litigation to which sooner or later the Court must respond.

In the relationship between Congress and the Court it is hard to say which institution has the upper hand. Certainly, those who state unequivocally that the Court has the "final say" are wrong. This is emphasized in the following selection from the *Harvard Law Review* which details Congressional overrulings of Supreme Court decisions through legislation between 1945 and 1957. This selection gives examples of overt Congressional responses to Court policies found unacceptable by the legislature. Much more difficult to document is the covert influence that Congress has on judicial decision-making. Men have not been nominated to federal judgeships because of anticipated Senate rejection. Cases have been denied *certiorari* or decided narrowly because negative Congressional response seemed likely. It is in this area of anticipated reactions that Congress' presence is probably of greatest importance. In reading the following selection this fact must be kept in mind.

43 CONGRESSIONAL REVERSAL OF SUPREME COURT DECISIONS

The Harvard Law Review

As significant as the decisions of the Supreme Court may sometimes be, its determinations have not always been final. The judicial mandates of one generation have been undone by those of the next. In some cases the Court's constitutional interpretations have been "reversed" by constitutional amendment. In many more instances Congress has intervened and, by passing new legislation, has reversed decisions of the Court interpreting statutes and otherwise administering the federal system. The interplay of legislative and judicial power since the end of the Second World War is of especial interest. By that time the New Deal had run its course, leaving behind a general acceptance of the relatively new and expanded role of the federal government. The post-1945 congressional response to judicial action may best be seen in those cases that were a focus of public or academic controversy.

A tabulation of the situations in which the Court and Congress have disagreed[1] shows that the Court was twice "reversed" by Congress after it had upheld individual rights against the imposition of federal power; no

Reprinted by permission of the publisher from Note, "Congressional Reversal of Supreme Court Decisions: 1945–1957," *Harvard Law Review,* LXXI (1958), pp. 1324–1336. Copyright 1958 by The Harvard Law Review Association. Some footnotes have been omitted, others renumbered.

[1]"Disagreement" for the purposes of this tabulation means that Congress passed a bill the intent and effect of which was to modify substantially the legal result of a specific Supreme Court decision. Whether the bill became law is regarded as irrelevant to the existence of the "disagreement."

decision restricting individual liberty was overturned. In at least five cases the Court was reversed after sustaining federal jurisdiction against claims that state power should prevail; in only one case did Congress modify a judicial decision refusing to extend federal power at the expense of state jurisdiction. In at least ten instances Congress reversed[2] decisions of the Court which favored government regulation of economic activity over self-regulation by the parties concerned; in only one case did Congress act to modify a Court decision denying federal authority to regulate an industry, and this case is of doubtful significance.

Though this sampling of cases is small, the consistent position taken by the Court implies that more than chance has been at work. Analysis of the individual cases will show, however, that any alleged political predisposition of the Court represents far too simple an account of the phenomenon. The results also cannot be explained on the apparently plausible hypothesis that the postwar Congresses have merely been undoing proper judicial interpretations of earlier statutes the federal legislature no longer favors. Although much of the congressional activity reported . . . did modify the effects of decisions construing New Deal social-welfare legislation, the decisions of the Court in these cases were not compelled by the statutes construed, for in most instances their meanings were uncertain and their legislative histories silent. The interaction between Congress and the Court was, in fact, the product of many causes, and cannot be explained by any single operative principle or simple political preference.

[2]If several cases on the same subject are treated by Congress as a unit, these cases are counted as a single reversal.

I. INSTITUTIONAL DIFFERENCES BETWEEN CONGRESS AND THE COURT

Out of the total of twenty-one instances of congressional reversal discovered, six cannot be viewed primarily as a conflict between the two branches of government. Rather, Congress was able to take into account policy factors that the Court could not properly have considered in ruling on property disputes or in applying a clear statutory directive. For example, in *United States* v. *South-Eastern Underwriters Ass'n*, the Court held, for the first time, that the insurance industry operated in interstate commerce and was therefore subject to the antitrust laws. Rather than enforce competition in the industry with these laws, Congress decided to prohibit certain specific restrictive practices and return to the industry its immunity from the antitrust laws to the extent that the industry was regulated by the states—a move which had the calculated effect of inducing forty-one states to enact some type of regulatory statute. In two other instances the Court's announced or anticipated applications of the antitrust laws were also contravened by Congress for essentially legislative reasons.[3]

The considerations of property law and national sovereignty that led the Court in *United States* v. *California* to rule that title to

submerged lands seaward of the low-tide mark was in the United States derived from doctrines which dated from the earliest days of the nation. The Court could not weigh the sectional interests involved in oil industry politics which prompted Congress three times to pass and President Truman twice to veto bills quit-claiming to the states the federal government's interest in the submerged lands. This pattern of legislative reconsideration in the light of policy factors that could not properly be presented to the Court was repeated on two more occasions, one involving an application of the Chandler Act,[4] and the other, the Natural Gas Act.[5]

II. DOMINANT PURPOSE AS A GUIDE TO STATUTORY CONSTRUCTION

The scope and standards of legislative programs are, of necessity, frequently described in general terms. Only with the guidance of an ascertained legislative purpose can the courts interpret a statute properly in the numerous and varied situations to which the statute may apply. However, seven of the instances in which the Court's construction of statutes was modified by Congress suggest that the Court placed too great an emphasis on a single dominant purpose and failed to limit this purpose when it clashed with other national

---

[3]In the first instance, Congress tried to reverse the decisions in *Clayton Mark & Co.* v. *FTC*, 336 U.S. 956 (1949), affirming by an equally divided Court, *Triangle Conduit & Cable Co.* v. *FTC*, 168 F. 2d 175 (7th Cir. 1948), and *FTC* v. *Cement Institute*, 333 U.S. 683 (1948), the combined effect of which was substantially to outlaw the basing-point price system. The attempted reversal, S. 1008, 81st Cong., 2d Sess. (1950), was vetoed by President Truman, S. Doc. 184, 81st Cong., 2d Sess. (1950). In the second instance, Congress anticipated what it thought would be the successful prosecution of an antitrust action by the state of Georgia against several railroads to enjoin their alleged conspiracy to set rates discriminatory toward its citizens, by amending the Interstate Commerce Act, 62 Stat. 472 (1948), 49 U.S.C. §5b (1952), over the veto of President Truman, S. Doc. 169, 80th Cong., 2d Sess. (1948). These amendments validated carriers' rate agreements if approved by the ICC. Georgia's suit was subsequently dismissed on stipulation of both parties. *Georgia* v. *Pennsylvania R.R.*, 340 U.S. 889 (1950) (memorandum opinion).

[4]C. 575, §1, 52 Stat. 840 (1938) (now 64 Stat. 24 (1950), 11 U.S.C. §96(a) (1952)). Drawing what seems a necessary conclusion from the statute, the Court held in *Corn Exchange Nat'l Bank & Trust Co.* v. *Klauder*, 318 U.S. 434 (1943), that a transfer of accounts receivable could be treated as a preference if the transfer had not been perfected against attack by a hypothetical bona fide purchaser. An amendment to the Bankruptcy Act, 64 Stat. 24 (1950), 11 U.S.C. §96(a) (1952), incorporated the recommendations of the American Bar Association and the National Bankruptcy Conference, see H.R. Rep. No. 1293, 81st Cong., 1st Sess. 5 (1949), that this decision be overruled because it constituted a serious handicap to commercial financing by use of nonnotification assignment of accounts receivable.

[5]52 Stat. 821 (1938), 15 U.S.C. §717(b) (1952). In *Phillips Petroleum Co.* v. *Wisconsin*, 347 U.S. 672 (1954), and *Interstate Natural Gas Co.* v. *FPC*, 331 U.S. 682 (1947), the Court held that the FPC had jurisdiction to regulate the price of gas sold to interstate pipelines by the producers and gatherers of natural gas. Congress twice tried to exempt these sales from FPC regulation.

policies or with reasonable and well-established private institutional arrangements. Particularly was this true in a series of cases arising under the Fair Labor Standards Act of 1938.

In *Bay Ridge Operating Co.* v. *Aaron*, a longshoremen's union and an employer group had been operating for many years under a collective-bargaining agreement under which all time outside of the daylight, week-day hours was paid at a time-and-a-half "overtime" rate. The purpose and substantial effect of this arrangement were to coerce the employers to shift all possible work into "regular" hours. Against the wishes of their own union, a group of employees brought suit under section 16(b) of the FLSA, seeking overtime payment under the statutory formula of "one and one-half times the regular rate" for working time in excess of forty hours per week. Since the particular employees involved had worked shifts that only partly coincided with the weekday, daylight hours, their pay had been computed under the collective-bargaining agreement's "regular rate" plus "overtime" for part of their first forty hours. They argued that the statutory "regular rate" should be construed to mean "average rate for the first forty hours," so that they would be entitled to include the contract "overtime" in the base rate to which the statutory overtime would be added, thus giving them "overtime on overtime." Their claim was upheld by a five-to-three decision of the Court which emphasized that the purposes of the FLSA were to compensate employees for the added strain of long hours and to spread employment by discouraging extra work for a few employees. The Court reasoned that in those relatively few instances in which a longshoreman worked an overlapping shift, these statutory objectives would be thwarted by the collective-bargaining agreement; the wage rate on such a shift would not increase after the initial forty-hour work week had elapsed, and so the penalizing effect of the statute would not be felt. As Mr. Justice Frankfurter's dissent pointed out, the decision of the Court ignored the "facts of industrial life" and upset an established arrangement which achieved, in an industry based on transient employment, the closest practical approximation of the results intended by the FLSA. Far from compelling the Court's result, the statute left "regular rate" undefined; the term should have been construed not merely by reference to the broad legislative purpose but also in the light of the bona fide and reasonable definition current among those subject to the act. Congress agreed with the dissent by retroactively redefining the disputed words to include the meaning contended for by both the union and employer.

Similarly, Congress, in the Portal-to-Portal Act of 1947, reversed three more decisions in which the Court had interpreted provisions of the FLSA. Section 7(a) of the act granted statutory overtime for work in excess of the normal forty-hour "work week." Although an established custom in the industry had excluded from the definition of "work week" the widely varying time spent by each individual worker in donning work clothes and walking from the shop entrance to the work site, the Court, in *Anderson* v. *Mt. Clemens Pottery Co.*, held that such time must be included in the "work week" because the purpose of the FLSA was to compensate each employee for "all time during which [he is] . . . required to be on the employer's premises. . . ." That this purpose might be qualified by a congressional desire not to require onerously complex bookkeeping or not to disrupt reasonable industrial custom was not seriously considered by the Court. Furthermore, just as in *Bay Ridge Operating Co.* v. *Aaron*, the crucial word was left undefined in the FLSA and so could have been interpreted in accord with industrial usage. The impact of this ruling was heightened by two other decisions which had previously been announced. In *D. A. Schulte, Inc.* v. *Gangi* and *Brooklyn Sav. Bank* v. *O'Neil*, the Supreme Court had subordinated the usual public policy in favor of peaceful settlement of disputes and held that claims for unpaid overtime plus the liquidated damages granted by the FLSA could not be compromised, since compromises would unduly limit the "purpose of the Act, which . . . was to secure for the lowest paid segment of the Nation's workers a subsistence wage. . . ." The combined effect of these three decisions was to expose employers to back-pay claims totaling well in excess of five billion dollars. They were all reversed retroactively by a single statute, which also contained an express rebuke to the Court for its interpretations of the FLSA.

Congress, in 1949, modified the effects of still a third series of cases in which the Court had dictated a broad application for provisions of the FLSA. As passed in 1938, the act covered employees in "any process or occupation necessary to the production" of goods for interstate commerce, but exempted agricultural workers and workers in "any retail or service establishment the greater part of whose selling or servicing is in intrastate commerce." To carry out the act's central purpose of improving substandard labor conditions, the Court in *Martino* v. *Michigan Window Cleaning Co.* broadly construed the initial grant of coverage to hold that the services of a local window-washing contractor whose customers manufactured goods shipped in interstate commerce were "necessary" to the production of those goods and therefore subject to the act. In *Roland Elec. Co.* v. *Walling,* decided earlier in the same term, the Court narrowly construed the "retail or service" exemption to include only the sale of goods or services "to an ultimate consumer for his personal use," thereby denying the exemption to a local contractor who supplied electricians' services to nearby commercial and industrial establishments. In *Farmers Reservoir & Irrigation Co.* v. *McComb,* the agricultural exemption was denied to a farmers' irrigation co-operative. The results in this last series of cases seem to flow again from too great a concentration on the act's dominant purpose without a sufficient balancing of the conflicting legislative objectives embodied expressly in the statutory exemptions and, perhaps, in the "necessary" requirement, although this requirement may be interpreted as having been intended to extend the coverage of the act to the limits of the commerce

power—an interpretation that would justify the decision in *Martino.* The Court's subordination of these secondary purposes led it to suggest that almost any resort to the exemptions by an employer was tantamount to an evasion and should be prohibited. Congress rejected these decisions in 1949 when it amended the FLSA by explicitly exempting farmer-owned irrigation cooperatives, by limiting the application of the act to employees whose work is "directly essential," rather than "necessary," to the production of goods for interstate commerce, and by spelling out the retailer exemption in considerable detail.

The many instances in which the Court has leaned too heavily on the central purpose in its construction of this single piece of legislation suggest that the Court may have been influenced by a sympathy for the social objectives of the FLSA. Moreover, the repetition of this same emphasis in cases arising under the Social Security Act, National Labor Relations Act, and Nationality Act of 1940, may also indicate a sympathy for statutes designed to benefit classes of people that might be regarded as politically weak. The Social Security Act established a social-insurance program for "employees," which program was funded by payroll taxes levied against the "employees" and their "employers." In an effort to fashion a definition of "employee" in accord with the purpose of the legislation, the Court, in a series of three cases . . . elaborated, as the measure of coverage, a test of "economic reality." The Court did not define the legislative purpose which gave rise to this test, but apparently thought the act was intended to provide economic security for the maximum number of workers economically unable to provide it for themselves. But a definition based exclusively on the overall objective of social security is incomplete; it fails to take into account the limitations imposed by the tax procedure set up to fund the benefit payments. And it is precisely in the borderline area where the Court was attempting to frame definitional standards that these procedural limitations become important; coverage has to stop when the employment relation is so transient or informal that the maintenance of the necessary records and the withholding of taxes by the employer is administratively impracticable. Since the Court's decisions took no account of this limitation, they were bound to have an expansive effect on the act's coverage. This was impressed upon Congress when the Treasury proposed to implement the Court's decisions with a new series of regulations imposing a withholding tax on many additional "employers." Congress reacted by reaffirming the common-law definition of "employee." This reaction was motivated by hostility, not to the expansion of coverage, but to the vague judicial criteria which afforded little predictability and gave too little weight to the employer's administrative difficulties. Two years later Congress put into effect its own plan expanding the coverage of the act.

The Court's attempt to define "employee" as the term appeared in section 2(3) of the National Labor Relations Act also met with reversal in subsequent congressional legislation. In *Packard Motor Car Co.* v. *NLRB*, the Court held, five to four, that the term embraced foremen, thus affording them the NLRB's protection in their efforts to bargain collectively. The dissenting justices rejected this interpretation after a searching examination of the act's legislative history and an exploration of the profound effect of the majority's decision. The majority, on the other hand, stressed the NLRA's dominant purpose to promote collective bargaining and expressly declined to consider the fact that this purpose, unless qualified, would extend the Board's jurisdiction up through the managerial ranks to senior executives. To the charge that its decision would effect a major change in accepted patterns of industrial relations, the majority replied that "it is for Congress, not for us, to create exceptions or qualifications at odds with [the act's] . . . plain terms." The Labor Management Relations Act created such an explicit exception for supervisory employees three months later.

The final instance in which the Court's overemphasis on a dominant purpose led to a reversal by Congress was *Bindczyck* v. *Finucane.* Seven days after a Maryland court had rendered a judgment of naturalization pursuant to the Nationality Act of 1940, that court exercised its normal power to set aside its own judgments at any time prior to the end of the term and annulled as fraudulently obtained the citizenship status it had just conferred. On *certiorari* to the Supreme Court, the petitioner's citizenship was reinstated on the ground that the procedure for revoking naturalization set out in section 338 of the Nationality Act, though its terms dealt only with the revocation of citizenship, impliedly prohibited a state court from annulling its own naturalization judgments. As originally enacted, the detailed procedural safeguards provided in section 338 were designed to prevent a naturalized citizen from having his status revoked in a hasty or fraudulent proceeding. This central purpose would, according to the majority, be compromised if state courts were permitted to follow their own rules for setting aside judgments. The dissent argued that the majority's departure from the usual policy of not interfering with the functioning of the state judiciary could not be justified by a remote inference from the general statutory objective, especially when this objective would suffer so slightly under the state procedures. Congress restored the power of the state courts a year later in section 340(j) of the Immigration and Nationality Act.

III. FACTORS MOST LIKELY TO PROVOKE CONGRESSIONAL RESPONSE

Although similarities can be observed in the public reaction to the Court's decisions in the remaining cases, the methods by which the Court arrived at its decisions form no general pattern. In *United States* v. *Cardiff,* the Court held that inspection provisions of the Federal Food, Drug, and Cosmetic Act were too vague to permit the conviction of a food processor who had refused to allow a federal inspector to enter his plant. The "vagueness" consisted of an apparent inconsistency between two provisions; read literally, they might have made criminal only the revocation of permission to inspect, leaving the choice of whether to grant permission in the first instance purely voluntary. This construction, of course, made nonsense of the act's purpose, and both the agency and the industry had assumed for fifteen years that Congress had intended inspection to be compulsory. Under these circumstances, the Court's conclusion that the statute did not give fair warning is difficult to justify. Congress reacted the following year by amending the statute to make explicit the compulsory character of inspection.

In three instances Congress acted to restore the law to its original state after the Court had reversed established judicial doctrines. Prior to *United States* v. *Wunderlich,* most government contracts included a "disputes" clause which provided for "final and conclusive" determination of disagreements by the head of the contracting agency. Since 1878, however, the courts had accorded finality only to agency decisions untainted by "fraud or such gross mistake as would necessarily imply bad faith" and had found such "fraud" when there was no substantial evidence to support the agency action. The Court in *Wunderlich* reversed this line of decisions by holding that an intent to deceive must be proved before the action of the agency head could be reversed. Congress, fearing the impact of *Wunderlich* on bidding prices for future government contracts, enacted a standard for judicial review of agency determinations even broader than that prevailing before *Wunderlich.*

Toucey v. *New York Life Ins. Co.* dealt with judicially created exceptions to section 265 of the Judicial Code of 1911, which prohibited federal courts from enjoining state-court proceedings except in certain bankruptcy matters. Although recognizing the existence of one well-established judicial exception to section 265, the Court refused in *Toucey* to approve the practice prevailing in many of the lower federal courts of staying the prosecution in a state court of a cause which already had been litigated in a federal tribunal. When the Judicial Code was recodified in 1948, the accompanying committee report indicated that section 2283 was intended to "overrule" the construction given by the Court in *Toucey* to

former section 265. In *Cline* v. *Kaplan,* the Court ruled that a party against whose property a trustee in bankruptcy had asserted a claim could withdraw from the summary jurisdiction of the bankruptcy court at any time before judgment. Prior to this decision, most courts had assumed that a defendant who argued on the merits impliedly consented to the court's jurisdiction. Congress amended the Bankruptcy Act to reinstate the previous majority practice in order that "sound procedure" be restored.

In two instances, the Court apparently misconceived the purpose of a statutory provision and forced Congress to enact new legislation redefining its previous intent. In *Schwegmann Bros.* v. *Calvert Distillers Corp.,* the Court held that the Sherman Act barred a liquor manufacturer from imposing his fair-trade prices on a dealer who was not a party to a resale-price-maintenance contract. Although the Miller-Tydings amendment to the Sherman Act had provided that "nothing herein . . . shall render illegal contracts or agreements prescribing minimum prices for resale," and the virtually unanimous understanding of these words was that they validated the nonsigner provisions of state fair-trade laws, the Court concluded that the exemption from the antitrust laws covered only the parties to the price-maintenance contracts. The McGuire Act, enacted a year later, specifically validated these nonsigner provisions. In *FPC* v. *East Ohio Gas Co.,* the Court affirmed the FPC's assertion of jurisdiction over a state-regulated distributor of natural gas whose intrastate pipeline connected with an interstate line at the state border. The provision of the Natural Gas Act which exempted from FPC jurisdiction "the local distribution of natural gas or . . . the facilities used for such distribution," was construed to include only low-pressure mains in the immediate vicinity of the consumer. A vigorous dissent pointed out that since the Natural Gas Act had been passed at the request of the gas-consuming states, Congress could hardly have intended that the FPC assert jurisdiction in an area already subject to regulation by these states. The act was amended in 1954 to exempt specifically companies whose rates were being regulated by a state.

The final instance of congressional reversal to be examined is *Wong Yang Sung* v. *McGrath*, in which the Court held that the Administrative Procedure Act's requirement of an independent hearing examiner was applicable to alien-expulsion hearings. Congress exempted such hearings from this requirement nine months later, ostensibly to save the cost of implementing it for the thousands of "wetbacks" along the Mexican border.

Unlike the social-welfare legislation discussed previously, this group of cases evidences no single method of statutory interpretation; whether the Court's decisions were justified or not, those decisions were arrived at in many different ways. However, with the exception of *Wong Yang Sung* v. *McGrath*, . . . all the cases have one common characteristic: to a significant extent the Court's interpretation was at odds with a pre-existing "common understanding." The subsequent legislative reversal was largely a return to the status quo, and comparatively free from the usual political stresses involved in legislating social change. Moreover, with the possible exception of *Toucey* v. *New York Life Ins. Co.*, the state of the law after the Court's action was so clearly contrary to the interests or understandings of all the politically articulate groups concerned that there was near unanimity in seeking legislative reversal. A reference to the social-welfare instances of congressional reversal shows that most of these instances also shared these characteristics. Both the union and the employer group opposed the Court's redefinition of "regular rate" in *Bay Ridge Operating Co.* v. *Aaron*. The cumulative effect of the decisions in *Brooklyn Sav. Bank* v. *O'Neil*, *D. A. Schulte, Inc.* v. *Gangi*, and *Anderson* v. *Mt. Clemens Pottery Co.* was to create such a staggering burden of potential liability for back-wage claims that no political group seriously contended that legislative relief was not a necessity. The scope of coverage of the FLSA and of the Social Security Act, as determined in the cases involving the definition of "employee" under these acts, although not entirely uncontroversial, were certainly not strongly contested national issues when Congress acted to reverse the Court. And, in both instances, the proponents of the modifying legislation maintained that a "common understanding" was being restored. The one obvious exception to this analysis within the social-welfare cases was the decision in *Packard Motor Car Co.* v. *NLRB*. Though the subject of bitter controversy, the result was reversed in the Labor Management Relations Act.

E. The President

Those holding Presidential office also have views of Supreme Court policies. Like Congress, the President has very strong powers for affecting the development and impact of judicial policies. Some of these powers are formal; others are informal.

Over the history of the Court, justices have been appointed on the average of one every twenty-three months. The President determines who will be nominated to fill these vacancies. As Robert Dahl has noted, "Presidents are not famous for appointing Justices hostile to their own views of public policy."[1] This was also, it will be recalled, noted in the readings on judicial selection in Part I.

A more subtle use of Presidential power is seen in how aggressively a president responds to Supreme Court policy pronouncements. The way he uses his prestige, his ability to initiate new legislation, his command over federal officials, even his

[1] Robert A. Dahl, *Pluralist Democracy in the United States* (Chicago: Rand McNally, 1967), p. 156.

appointments to the lower federal judiciary may forward or retard compliance. In certain areas of the law, the President has played an important role in determining how the law would develop. By picking the "right cases" to prosecute, the executive can influence whether a legal rule will be broadened or narrowed. Developments in the interpretation of the Antitrust Acts, for example, seem as much due to the aggressiveness of different administrations in prosecuting cases as they are due to Court decisions.

The two selections that follow give examples of how presidents have sought to use their powers to shape Supreme Court policies. The selection by President Franklin Roosevelt is from his radio address to the nation explaining the necessity for his "court-packing" plan. The second selection gives President Eisenhower's first public reaction to the Supreme Court's decision in *Brown* v. *Board of Education*.[2]

[2]347 U.S. 483 (1954).

44   THE PRESIDENT ATTACKS THE COURT

Franklin D. Roosevelt

. . . The American people have learned from the depression. For in the last three national elections an overwhelming majority of them voted a mandate that the Congress and the President begin the task of providing that protection [from the grave effects of economic depression]—not after long years of debate, but now.

The courts, however, have cast doubts on the ability of the elected Congress to protect us against catastrophe by meeting squarely our modern social and economic conditions.

We are at a crisis in our ability to proceed with that protection. It is a quiet crisis. There are no lines of depositors outside closed banks. But to the far-sighted it is far-reaching in its possibilities of injury to America.

I want to talk with you very simply about the need for present action in this crisis—the need to meet the unanswered challenge of one-third of a nation ill-nourished, ill-clad, ill-housed. . . .

When the Congress has sought to stabilize national agriculture, to improve the conditions of labor, to safeguard business against unfair competition, to protect our national

Reprinted from President Roosevelt's radio address to the nation, March 9, 1937, as contained in the appendix to Senate Report No. 711, 75th Cong., 1st Sess. (1937).

resources, and in many other ways to serve our clearly national needs, the majority of the Court has been assuming the power to pass on the wisdom of these acts of the Congress—and to approve or disapprove the public policy written into these laws. . . .

We have, therefore, reached the point as a nation where we must take action to save the Constitution from the Court and the Court from itself. We must find a way to take an appeal from the Supreme Court to the Constitution itself. We want a Supreme Court which will do justice under the Constitution—not over it. In our courts we want a government of laws and not of men.

I want—as all Americans want—an independent judiciary as proposed by the framers of the Constitution. That means a Supreme Court that will enforce the Constitution as written—that will refuse to amend the Constitution by the arbitrary exercise of judicial power—amendment by judicial say-so. It does not mean a judiciary so independent that it can deny the existence of facts universally recognized. . . .

What is my proposal? It is simply this: Whenever a judge or justice of any Federal court has reached the age of 70 and does not avail himself of the opportunity to retire on a pension, a new member shall be appointed by the President then in office, with the approval, as required by the Constitution, of the Senate of the United States.

That plan has two chief purposes: By bringing into the judicial system a steady and continuing stream of new and younger blood, I hope, first, to make the administration of all Federal justice speedier and therefore less costly; secondly, to bring to the decision of social and economic problems younger men who have had personal experience and contact with modern facts and circumstances under which average men have to live and work. This plan will save our National Constitution from hardening of the judicial arteries. . . .

45   THE PRESIDENT RESPONDS TO *BROWN* v. *BOARD OF EDUCATION*

Dwight D. Eisenhower

Harry C. Dent of the *Columbia (S.C.) State*—"Mr. President, do you have any advice to give the South as to just how to react to this recent Supreme Court decision banning segregation, Sir?"
President Eisenhower—"Not in the slightest. I thought that Governor [James F.] Byrnes

Reprinted from the unofficial transcript of the Presidential news conference of May 19, 1954, as reported in *The New York Times*, May 20, 1954, p. 18. Authorized Presidential statements are in quotation marks, all others are in indirect discourse.

[of S.C.] made a very fine statement when he said, 'Let's be calm and let's be reasonable and let's look at this thing in the face.'"

"The Supreme Court has spoken and I am sworn to uphold their—the constitutional processes in this country, and I am trying—I will obey."
Sarah McClenden of the *El Paso Times*—"Mr. President—"
Mr. Dent—"Mr. President, one more question. Do you think this decision has put Mr. Byrnes and Mr. Byrd [Senator from Virginia] and other Southern leaders who supported the Republican ticket in 1952 on the political hot spot, so to speak, since it was brought out under the Republican Administration?"
President Eisenhower—"The Supreme Court, as I understand it, is not under any administration."
Mr. Dent—"Thank you."
Miss McClenden—"Sir, along that same line, do you expect that this ruling will, however, alienate many of your Southern supporters politically?"
President Eisenhower—This was all he would say: He had stood, so far as he knew, for honest, decent government since he had been first mentioned as a political figure. He was still standing for it, and they [the President's Southern supporters] would have to make their own decisions as to what they [the Supreme Court] decided. . . .

F.   Public Officials

The Supreme Court tends to accept a case on appeal or *certiorari* if the litigants represent a large class of similarly situated people. Supreme Court decisions, therefore, can contain policies affecting large segments of the population. Even if the class affected is only a minority, this still might mean thousands or even millions of citizens in a country the size of the United States. With decisions that mark a change in the law as heretofore known, the members of the Court have no way of insuring that each individual affected will modify his behavior to reflect this change. In some cases the Court need not worry about this problem. It is insured by the actions of those benefiting from the new Court policy. This is most true with policy areas where the classes affected are well organized and/or endowed with the resources necessary to push the advantage offered them. Labor-management relations is an example of such a policy area.

In other policy areas realization of Court policy is not as easy. This is most true with decisions attacking traditional patterns of behavior supported by widespread agreement by those politically active in the community. A case which demonstrates this well is *Brown* v. *Board of Education.*[1] There are still vast numbers of Negroes who have not yet benefited from the policy announced in this case in 1954. This is so despite the fact that Congress, the President, and most of the lower judiciary, have attempted to carry out the Court's decree.

In such areas of the law, citizen compliance rests primarily on local public officials. Behavior by them which produces a lack of compliance is an important aspect of feedback. Noncompliance can have serious ramifications for the future development of the law. What these will be is not always predictable. With the law of race relations, for example, widespread noncompliance to the *Brown* decision may have stimulated the Court into delving into other patterns of discrimination.[2]

With other areas of the law, widespread noncompliance may lead to judicial retreat or forbearance. In the area of church-state relations, for example, *Zorach* v. *Clauson*[3] signaled at least a momentary retreat on the part of the Court regarding the role of the public schools in religious training.

The following two readings concern compliance by local officials in areas where Supreme Court policies were, or are, controversial. The first, by Frank J. Sorauf, deals with an area of the law (religious training and the public schools) where the line between the permissible and the forbidden was (at least until *Engel* v. *Vitale*[4]) unclear. Sorauf's article, published three years before the *Engel* decision, describes the feedback from *Zorach* v. *Clauson* which ultimately became an input relevant for *Engel* and subsequent decisions. The second selection is by Michael J. Murphy, former Police Commissioner of the City of New York. This article not only discusses compliance but it is also a feedback datum itself. Murphy, as a former public official, makes a plea for a shift in Supreme Court policies dealing with the administration of criminal law.

[1]347 U.S. 483 (1954).
[2]Justice Potter Stewart, for example, observed in an interview with one of the editors, that perhaps it was the Court's involvement with racial discrimination which led it subsequently to look at the political discrimination caused by the malapportionment of state legislatures.
[3]343 U.S. 306 (1952).
[4]370 U.S. 421 (1962).

46 *ZORACH* v. *CLAUSON:* THE IMPACT OF A SUPREME COURT DECISION

Frank J. Sorauf

It has become a commonplace that the Constitution is what the Supreme Court says it is. Scholars of American constitutional law have, therefore, focused their studies largely on the Court's opinions as indices of the Con-

stitution's current meaning. But however well established may be the Court's role as the expounder of the constitutional document, the impact of a decision will depend on many individuals and circumstances far beyond the confines of the Court. This paper will examine the effects of the decision in *Zorach* v. *Clauson*[1] on public policy in the seven years since its announcement. It will attempt to follow the repercussions of one Supreme Court decision through the entire political process within one area of political conflict—

Reprinted by permission of the publisher and author from Frank J. Sorauf, "Zorach v. Clauson: The Impact of a Supreme Court Decision," *American Political Science Review,* LIII (1959), pp. 777–791. Some footnotes omitted, other renumbered.

[1]343 U.S. 306 (1952).

in this case the conflict over church-state relationships.

The impact of the *Zorach* decision on state court decisions, on administrative rulings, on legislative action, and on the educational policies of local school districts may also be viewed as a case study in federalism. Within the federal system, what limits affect the power of the Court to dictate adherence to the Constitution throughout the states? How effectively does it function as an instrument of national supremacy? How responsive are state and local authorities to shifting constitutional interpretations?

I. THE DECISION

Despite considerable diversity in detail, "released time" programs of religious education have one principle in common: release from ordinary class-room attendance for students wishing to attend religious classes. Generally one hour a week is set aside for the purpose, and those students whose parents do not elect the religious classes for them are herded to study halls or given make-work exercises for the hour. The classes provided by the religious bodies of the community are referred to in religious education circles as "weekday church schools."

From a modest beginning shortly before World War I the released time movement expanded irregularly through the '20s and '30s, and then surged ahead dramatically in the wartime and post-war religious renaissance. In the late '40s, however, one Mrs. Vashti McCollum pressed a suit through the Illinois courts and to the Supreme Court of the United States, challenging the constitutionality of the released time program of the Champaign schools, as a breach in the wall of separation between church and state. The Supreme Court, in an 8–1 decision, agreed.[2] Justice Black, speaking for the Court, noted: "Here not only are the State's tax-supported public school buildings used for the dissemination of religious doctrines. The State also affords sectarian groups an invaluable aid in that it helps to provide pupils for their

religious classes through use of the State's compulsory public school machinery. This is not separation of Church and State."

Public reaction to the *McCollum* decision was distinctly hostile. A number of communities across the country defied the Court and continued to hold religious classes in school rooms. A brief examination of the periodical indexes for the next few years indicates the extent of the wrath and condemnation heaped on the Court in leading journals. More particularly, in the constitutional uncertainty about released time that the *McCollum* case created, school districts and religious bodies began to cast about for acceptable programs and to test in the courts the applicable limits of the *McCollum* rule. During this period of constitutional sparring another test case, *Zorach* v. *Clauson*, emerged from Brooklyn.

This case questioned the released time program of the New York City schools. Unlike the Champaign plan the New York program required that religious classes be held off the school premises, that all costs (even of application blanks) be borne by the organizations, and that there be no announcements or comments on the program during regular school sessions. The churches were, however, to make weekly attendance reports to the schools. Taxpayer-parents challenged the arrangement on the ground that the weight and influence of the public schools were placed squarely in support of released time, since the program depended on the schools' suspending classes and enforcing attendance. The New York courts swept aside these contentions to uphold it. In a 6–3 decision the U.S. Supreme Court sustained the state courts and the New York plan itself.

Writing for the majority, Justice Douglas first dismissed the argument that coercion had been used to get students into religious classes, and then turned to expound a theory of the separation of church and state quite at odds with the Court's earlier statement of an absolute separation in the *Everson*[3] and *McCollum* cases:

[2] *McCollum* v. *Board of Education*, 333 U. S. 203 (1948).

[3] *Everson* v. *Board of Education*, 330 U. S. 1 (1947).

The First Amendment, however, does not say that in every and all respects, there shall be a separation of Church and State. Rather, it studiously defines the manner, the specific ways, in which there shall be no concert or union or dependency one on the other. That is the common sense of the matter. Otherwise the state and religion would be aliens to each other—hostile, suspicious, and even unfriendly.

For further support Douglas listed current instances of church-state cooperation, noting that even the Supreme Court's sessions begin with a plea for Divine guidance. Following this enunciation of new doctrine, he uttered his frequently quoted dictum on religion in American life and institutions:

We are a religious people whose institutions presuppose a Supreme Being. . . . When the state encourages religious instruction or cooperates with religious authorities by adjusting the schedule of public events to sectarian needs, it follows the best of our traditions. For it then respects the religious nature of our people and accommodates the public service to their spiritual needs. To hold that it may not would be to find in the Constitution a requirement that the government show a callous indifference to religious groups. That would be preferring those who believe in no religion over those who do believe. . . . [W]e find no constitutional requirement which makes it necessary for government to be hostile to religion and to throw its weight against efforts to widen the effective scope of religious influence.

Government must, therefore, not coerce religious observance, but it may cooperate with religious bodies, accommodate itself to their convenience, and even encourage programs of religious instruction. "[I]t can close its doors or suspend its operations," Douglas wrote, "as to those who want to repair to their religious sanctuary for worship or instruction. No more than that is undertaken here." In conclusion Douglas reaffirmed the *McCollum* precedent and distinguished the facts there at issue from those before the Court.

Each of the three dissenters spoke individually. Justice Black, the Court's spokesman in the *Everson* and *McCollum* cases, could find no significant differences between the Brooklyn and Champaign programs—at least not enough to justify upholding the Brooklyn plan. He concluded by reaffirming his doctrine of an absolute separation, pressing its wisdom upon the Court. Justice Frankfurter argued the coercive elements of a system in which the non-religious student was compelled to remain in school and regretted that the appellants had been denied an opportunity to prove coercion in the lower courts. Justice Jackson's dissent—which can at best be called intemperate—deals as much with the Court itself as with religious education. After reiterating the argument that the program rested on state coercion, Jackson turned to remind his "evangelistic brethren" that "what should be rendered to God does not need to be decided and collected by Caesar." He agreed, too, that the distinction between the Champaign and Brooklyn programs was "trivial, almost to the point of cynicism," and concluded his philippic by supposing that the majority opinion would "be more interesting to students of psychology and of the judicial processes than to students of constitutional law."

So much for the case and decision itself. We turn now to the impact of the *Zorach* decision on released time programs and on church-state relations in general.

II. INITIAL REACTION AND RECEPTION

The friends of released time reacted immediately to the *Zorach* decision with extravagant praise. It was tritely hailed as the "*magna carta* for the weekday religious education movement," "a landmark in the history of America," and "a great piece of jurisprudence." Justice Douglas was saluted for averting the dangers of advancing secularism. Even the date of the decision was commemorated: "during the week of April 28 each year . . . some weekday classes hold special observances and contribute to a fund to help bring weekday church schools to communities which do not have them."

In their attempts to explain the general doctrine of church-state relations in the *Zorach* decision to their readers and members, the supporters of released time programs were generally agreed in their interpretations. Most noted with triumph that the decision "radically revised the Everson-McCollum doctrine on 'separation'" and that the Court had had to retreat from its unrealistic doctrine of complete separation. One well-known religious educator went so far as to observe that "the principle of friendly co-operation between the state and religious bodies was substituted for that of absolute separation" and that the whole issue of separation "may be said to be wide open."

Enthusiasm and wide-sweeping interpretation also marks these commentators' development of the narrow legal issues in the decision. The "shadow of illegality has been dispelled," the decision "removes the apparent stigma that weekday religious education has been under in the minds of many," the decision "established without a doubt the legality of releasing pupils from the public schools"— so went announcements of the good tidings. At least in the initial burst of optimism, the local religious leader or educator might easily have gathered that all released time programs had been sanctioned and that the *McCollum* precedent was no more. For instance, one commentator noted simply that the Court "reversed" itself in the *Zorach* case, and another thought it had "cut the heart out of the McCollum decision" and "greatly modified, if not virtually overruled" it. To be sure, Erwin L. Shaver, the generally recognized leader of the released time movement, cautioned that there was "no contradiction" between the two cases, explaining the "seeming reversal" on the basis of two differing sets of facts. His was, however, a lone counsel of caution.

The exuberance of released time advocates was matched by the disappointment of its opponents. Varied in approach, their comments reflected both a generalized dissatisfaction with the decision, and a desire to minimize its effect. The *Christian Century* in its initial editorial reaction went to great pains to point out that the New York program differed fundamentally from the one invalidated in Champaign. Unlike the favorable commentaries, it concluded that the *McCollum* prece-

dent had certainly not been overruled. It also thought, contrary to the supporters, that Justice Douglas's opinion "will not clarify the church-and-state issue, but will produce much future litigation." *Church and State*, publication of the Protestants and Other Americans United for the Separation of Church and State, ran only a brief news item devoted largely to excerpts from the dissenting opinions.

For his part, Professor R. Freeman Butts attempted to underplay the Court's dictum, quoted above, by distinguishing between "we as a people" and "we as a government" and by insisting that "we as a government" must be neutral on all religious issues. Another authority on school law, while deploring that the Court had "really muddied" the waters of constitutional doctrine in the *Zorach* case, nonetheless concluded that it was not a reversal of the earlier Champaign precedent. Finally, some among the opponents of released time avoided or ignored the force of the *Zorach* decision entirely. The chairman of the Anti-Defamation League, for instance, has observed that the *Zorach* decision reaffirms the doctrine of church-state separation laid down in the earlier *Everson* and *McCollum* cases.

This brief excursion into the reactions to the *Zorach* decision indicates that representatives of interest groups on the two sides of the issue have, by perceiving within the bounds of a distinct frame of reference, really divided the Court's precedent into two sharply contrasting images. Readers who overlap these self-selected audiences are confronted by two "precedents" rather than one. Whether *McCollum* was reversed or followed, whether the separation doctrine is clarified or confused, whether all or only some released time programs have judicial approval seems to depend on the commitments one brings to his appraisal of the decision.

III. THE IMPACT ON RELEASED TIME PROGRAMS

The impact of a Supreme Court decision should be most obvious in its direct and primary effect on the policies in question. In this instance the *Zorach* opinion, touted as a "magna charta" for the released time movement, rescued certain programs from the constitutional limbo to which they presumably had been consigned by the *McCollum* case. The empirical question, then, is whether it has in fact stimulated and accelerated the growth of these programs. This turns out to be not an easy question to answer.

Aggregate statistical totals of the number of children receiving released time religious training are impossible to come by. Several commentators seem to agree that after the *McCollum* decision in 1948 the released time programs fell off by some 20 per cent, accounting for a pupil loss of about 10 per cent. By 1953 the total attendance was variously estimated between 2,000,000 and 2,500,000—back just about to the pre-*McCollum* total. Three to five years later, leaders of the movement were setting enrolments at about 3,000,000 in programs in over 3,000 communities in 45 or 46 states. All of the losses after the *McCollum* decision were apparently recouped by 1953, and in the last five years enrolments have risen to an all-time high. Dr. Shaver sums up the growth in recent years as "a modest increase since 1952, although not a great one."

Enrolment statistics from scattered states and communities also confirm the general impression of a modest over-all growth since *Zorach*, with more substantial increases in some instances. The United Lutheran Church, for example, reports a 28 per cent growth in weekday church schools and a 13 per cent increase in pupils between the years 1951 and 1953. And if one accepts various data from the state of New York at face value, enrolments there have doubled, from 225,000 in 1952 to 450,000 in 1956.

Accounts of the impact of *Zorach* in specific communities supplement these statistical indications. The school board in Pittsfield, Massachusetts, was reported (in a journal that can hardly be called friendly) to have inaugurated a released time program immediately after the decision of the Brooklyn case. "Protestant and Jewish leaders represented in the local Council of Churches withdrew their formal opposition to the plan after the April 28 Supreme Court decision upholding the New York system of 'released time,' but voted not to participate themselves during the coming school year." Finally, in these community policy debates the impact of the decision is reflected in the determination of some religious groups to press their newly won advantage. The *New York Times* reported in late 1952 the efforts of the United Lutheran Church "at increasing church pressure on public schools to permit children to receive weekday religious education under the released-time system."

The ability of local authorities to begin released time programs may depend to some extent on the willingness of state legislatures to authorize or tolerate them. Yet no new legislation on the subject has been enacted by any state since the *Zorach* case decision. Bills to authorize released time programs in New Hampshire were beaten down in the 1953, 1955, and 1957 legislative sessions. Similar proposals have also been introduced in the Michigan and Arizona legislatures with similar results. Evidently, the Court's permissive opinion has failed to influence legislative policy-making in the states. However, enabling legislation is not usually necessary; only 13 states have laws expressly permitting absence for religious instruction. In most states the localities simply begin their programs under the regular educational authority with some vague assurances that they are not violating any state statutory or constitutional restrictions on religious education. Even in Virginia, where released time flourishes as in no other state, no explicit state authority for it exists.

In these circumstances the states' attorneys general, as the construers and appliers of state limitations, assume an important role in charting the legal progress of released time programs. Here the impact of *Zorach* is easier to assess. In only four instances, apparently, has a state attorney general found occasion to mention the *Zorach* precedent in dealing with released time or similar programs of religious education. The attorney general of Iowa upheld a released time plan in Dubuque that was virtually identical to the Brooklyn plan. An opinion in Indiana reaffirmed the constitutionality of a state statute that an earlier attorney general had held to be in grave doubt after *McCollum*. Here again there were no significant differences between the program authorized and the one the Court upheld in *Zorach*. Thirdly, the Vermont attorney general in 1954 cited *Zorach* v. *Clauson* in holding unconstitutional any religious classes in the schools during school hours. He hastened to add, however, that there would be no federal or state constitutional objection to classes held off school premises and made available to all sects. Finally, the Oregon attorney general referred to *Zorach* somewhat ambiguously in holding that local school boards are not free under the Oregon released time law to refuse requests for a released time program in a local community. Reports persist that attorneys general in several other states have informally decided such issues since 1952, but these are unconfirmed and too sketchy and fugitive to deal with here.

To round out the picture, mention ought also to be made of the uncertainties the decision has created. In relaxing the stringencies of the *McCollum* decision, it has still not resolved the status of such a program as Utah has adopted. Released time classes in that state extend to five hours a week, receive high school credit in some parts of the state, and are taught by special, state-accredited teachers. A learned observer therefore suggests:

> Elements showing some degree of control by the state of released time teachers, the degree of identification and coercion inherent in granting credit, some danger of unconstitutional administration, a possibility of attack on the ground of state preference for one religion, plus an unusual amount of time allowed for religious studies tend toward a stronger case for unconstitutionality than *Zorach*.

This compilation indicates that the impact of *Zorach* on local policy decisions has been a tonic to the movement, although it has hardly revolutionized the pattern of religious education.

IV. THE ISSUE OF COMPLIANCE

It is no secret that after the *McCollum* decision, and despite it, many communities continued to hold released time classes in public school buildings. The most conservative estimate places noncompliance at 15 per cent of the programs, and other estimates run up to 40 and 50 per cent in some states. Five years later in the *Zorach* case the Court reaffirmed the *McCollum* ruling but offered the localities a clearly constitutional alternative: religious education off school premises. Have local religious and educational groups met the Court halfway and given up released time in the school room?

The answer is "no—not entirely." In 1956, a knowledgeable authority on school law wrote that "school systems in virtually every state violate in some way the legal principles concerning religious instruction in the public schools." Some of the violations are unwitting, he wrote, but knowing violators include "some persons holding responsible church or school positions." Apart from such generalizations, precise estimates of noncompliance are not easy to make. Apparently, all or most of the programs run by the Virginia Council of Churches still use school rooms, many communities in Texas do also, and there are many reports of school room use in scattered places. Released time programs are conducted in school rooms in five Pennsylvania counties of which I am aware. Finally, *Religious Education* two years ago disclosed that a casual poll of released time programs indicated that 32 per cent were still holding classes in school buildings, although some were paying token rentals of from $5 to $100 a year.

Uncertainty about what constitutes noncompliance complicates this assessment. The transparent ruse of "renting" community educational facilities for five dollars a year is an obvious evasion of the *Zorach* rule. But what of holding religious instruction in schools during the lunch hour? Or after school hours? Or what of giving high school credit for Bible classes? Or of holding released time classes in publicly owned community centers? Or of giving class credit for

TABLE 1 Judgments of 50 Pennsylvania School Superintendents on the Unconstitutionality of Released Time Plans

Released Time Plan	Responses of "Unconstitutional"	% "Unconstitutional"
1. Classes in school rooms, taught by regular teacher	49	98
2. Classes in school rooms, taught by representatives of religions	47	94
3. Classes in school rooms, taught after regular school hours	41	82
4. Classes taught off school premises by representatives of religions	8	16
5. Classes taught off school premises when all classes dismissed	1	2

otherwise acceptable released time programs? Apparently, in this "twilight area," the very groups that are most adept in expanding aid to religion by analogous application of the precedent have been unwilling at the same time to apply the limitations of *Zorach*.

Dr. Shaver and the Division of Christian Education of the National Council of Churches, to be sure, have clearly and repeatedly urged compliance. The very vigor of their urgings may, in fact, be taken as some indication of the degree of noncompliance. In a 1956 speech Shaver urged the need for dispelling:

. . . the mood of illegality which still pervades the weekday church school movement in some quarters. Much of this is due to the same attitude of defiance or indifference to decisions of the Supreme Court that one finds in the segregation issue. Such an attitude toward the Zorach decision should be opposed just as strongly as the non-conforming attitude toward the segregation decision.

Other writings and speeches of his repeatedly urge local religious groups to refuse the help of school authorities in recruiting and registering students, to avoid the use of public school machinery and buildings for any aspect of the program, and to refrain from trying "to 'get by' with legal infractions because their communities may not object."

Conceivably, what appears to be noncompliance to an outside observer may be only the ignorance of some local officials. To get some limited information on this possibility, I sent questionnaires to the county superintendents of schools in Pennsylvania's 67 counties. One question confronted them with five possible forms of released time program and asked them to mark the alternatives they thought the Supreme Court would presently consider unconstitutional. The results, summarized in Table 1, indicate that nearly all the 50 county superintendents who responded to this question were well aware of the prevailing constitutional law on released time. If anything, they lean to a rigid interpretation of separation, as their overwhelming judgment on the uncertain third alternative indicates.[4] If this degree of constitutional sophistication prevails in the other states, noncompliance with the *Zorach* decision must be knowing evasion. In fact, in Pennsylvania the five county superintendents indicating classroom use for released time in their counties are even more aware of the constitutional niceties in this area than the average superintendent.

V. THE PRECEDENT EXPANDS

The impact of the *Zorach* rule does not stop with its direct consequences. Contrary to the gloomy expectations of Justice Frankfurter

[4]A total of 59 of 67 answered the questionnaire, although only 50 responded to this question. A total of 33 superintendents reported that they have released time programs in their counties, and 26 reported they do not. Of the 33 counties with released time, at least five still use school rooms, and two use community centers. The respondents making "correct" judgments on the issues of constitutionality are evenly divided between counties with released time programs and those without.

and others, there has been no further ardent rash of released time litigation following *Zorach*, nor has the decision fired up old debates on the issue. All sides in the general controversy over church-state relations have apparently decided that released time is now a settled issue, and have shifted their efforts to more advanced proposals. In this shifting of debate the *Zorach* decision has served both as legal precedent and political symbol and has had, consequently, a far-reaching influence quite beyond the particular facts on which it originally rested. The possibility of exactly this sort of application of the decision prompted the editors of the official organ of the National Council of Churches to warn:

. . . it is perhaps inevitable that some will uncritically assume that now "anything goes." This unwarranted implication will and ought to be stoutly resisted. This decision deals only with a specific case before the court. The decision says nothing explicitly about public aid to parochial schools, about required Bible reading and prayer in the public schools, or about the chaplaincy system of the Armed Services, military hospitals and government schools.

But their advice went unheeded.

At the very least, the *Zorach* precedent has been applied by analogy to validate or support varieties of religious education other than released time programs. When, for instance, the New York Board of Regents in March, 1955, recommended the injection of moral and spiritual values into the public school curricula of the state, it cited the *Zorach* dicta to buttress its assumptions about the relevance of religious education to the Republic. One scholar, proposing programs of teaching "about" religion in a "non-denominational" manner in the public schools, surmises that in light of the *Zorach* decision "there is good reason to believe that non-indoctrinational study of religion as a part of the culture will not fall under the ban." Speaking also of this kind of program, another scholar appraises the *Zorach* decision and declares that now "we have *carte blanche* to do what we think is morally, educationally, and philosophically sound in this field on the college level." For another commentator permissive cooperation is quickly transformed to compulsory alliance:

If, as the Court said, the state follows the best of our traditions when it encourages religious instruction or cooperates with religious authorities by adjusting the schedule of public events to sectarian needs (off public property), how much more faithful to American tradition is the state when it requires that its own schools teach America's [religious] heritage to its young citizens and future guardians of our Republic?

Similar expansions of the *Zorach* rule to cover other issues of religion in education have occurred in the courts. A Massachusetts court in reaffirming the legality of Bible reading in the public schools drew attention to *Zorach* as sanctioning a similar religious activity in the school. A year later the Kentucky Court of Appeals held that employment of members of religious orders, wearing religious garb and symbols, to teach in public schools did not violate the church-state separation. In so holding, it cited the *Zorach* case as an example of the Supreme Court's approval of analogous aid to religion. The Tennessee Supreme Court also recently ruled that reciting the Lord's Prayer, reading a verse of the Bible, or singing an "inspiring song" in the public schools did not breach the constitutional separation. In the course of its opinion the Court cited *Zorach*, but only to refer to its insistence that in cooperating with religion government be "neutral when it comes to competition between sects."[5]

The outward expansion of the *Zorach* precedent does not stop here. Courts and interest groups have taken its new doctrine of a "part-way" separation of church and state to expand the permissible area of government aid to and cooperation with organized religion. At the minimum some commentators edge cautiously away from the new doctrine to

[5]*Carden* v. *Bland*, 288 S.W. 2d 718 (1956), p. 722. I should also note that in one state case the *Zorach* decision was used to deny an expansion of church-state cooperation. The New Jersey Supreme Court held the distribution of Gideon Bibles in the public schools to be preferential aid for some religious sects. See *Tudor* v. *Board of Education*, 100 A. 2d 857 (1953). This is, however, the only instance of the restrictive use of the precedent in state or federal courts of which I am aware.

assert that "the legality of a friendly governmental attitude toward religious sects and institutions is now solidly affirmed." And at the other extreme, one scholar found in the *Zorach* decision proof that the separation of church and state can in reality amount to a denial of religious liberty: "If and where a community feels so strongly about religion in relation to the education of its children that it insists on some token of religious faith within the school, what we are dealing with is an elemental demand for religious liberty." The California Supreme Court, in ruling that aid to religions in the form of property tax exemptions was not unconstitutional, also took note of the [U.S. Supreme] Court's new and relaxed doctrine of separation.

Beyond these influences on other forms of religious education and on the issue of church-state relations, the precedent has spread slowly outward to touch more general questions of religious liberty. And no part of the decision has contributed so much to this inflation of the precedent as Justice Douglas' gratuitous assertion that "we are a religious people whose institutions presuppose a Supreme Being." One could, in fact, discuss the *Zorach* decision simply as a study in the misadventures of a dictum, for the courts have been as uncritical and unrestrained as laymen in embracing it.

The Pennsylvania Supreme Court, for instance, turned to it to support its contention that "immoral" has a sufficiently precise and definite meaning for statutory use. A Federal district court used the dictum to support a denial of a petition for naturalization to an atheist who refused to take the statutory oath of allegiance. In the *Zorach* case, wrote the judge, the Supreme Court "has not deemed it to be old fashioned to declare, 'We are a religious people whose institutions presuppose a Supreme Being.'" The same phrase has also helped a New York judge find meaning for "immorality" in a concurring opinion, and in another case supported the upholding of a pledge of allegiance to "one nation, under God." Similarly, a member of the New York Board of Regents notes that in the *Zorach* ruling the Court proclaimed that "belief and dependence upon Almighty God is still the basic law of this great nation." So the Court's dictum is turned from a statement of social fact to a constitutional imperative.

Finally, one ought to note that the *Zorach* precedent has in the hands of laymen expanded curiously in another direction. From its pages the friends of released time have fashioned two spurious constitutional doctrines. One of these comes from Erwin Shaver, who in several of his writings has read the Court's decision to demand rather than permit released time in the states. "It is now," he writes, "the 'unalienable right' of every parent of a public school child, if he so requests it, to have his child excused for 'religious observance and education.' In no state or local community can this right be denied." The other is voiced by a number of partisans who have convinced themselves that the decision "reaffirms the right of parents to determine the content and method of their children's education," and that "parental rights in education—a longstanding American tradition—received new vindication" in the decision. There has been no judicial support for these two constitutional excursions.

The impact of *Zorach* beyond the bounds of the facts it decided and the rules it enunciated illustrates how Supreme Court precedents, as soon as they leave judicial hands, enter another realm of policy-making and become symbols in political debate and deliberation. A certain expansion and exaggeration of doctrine in this process is normal and expected. But the expansion is encouraged and accelerated when the decision is as freighted with sweeping dicta and legal homilies as *Zorach*. It is no overstatement to say that in their rush to embrace Justice Douglas's comforting words the friends of the decision have smothered its legal distinctions.

VI. THE PRECEDENT VANISHES

On the other hand, there have been several instances where the *Zorach* decision has, surprisingly, been ignored when directly relevant; and ignored not only by interested groups and individuals but also in opinions of state courts and attorneys general. Since

1953 several such courts and officials have omitted mention of the *Zorach* rule in deciding the very questions of religious education and separation in which technicians of the law might be expected to consult the precedent. The fact that one finds the *Zorach* precedent serving in unlikely cases and failing to serve in other, more likely ones, lends credence to the old proposition that, contrary to the canons of jurisprudence, judges may deduce precedents from decisions.

The Virginia Supreme Court of Appeals, in holding state payments to sectarian training schools invalid, in 1955 cited the *Everson* and *McCollum* cases as the last words on the separation of church and state. And a dissent in a Kentucky case in 1956 cited the *Everson* case at length on the issue of separation without mentioning the Court's relaxation of the doctrine in *Zorach*. In response to a 1954 query about the denominational use of public school facilities, with or without rental fee, the Nevada attorney general held such practices to breach the separation of church and state. After confessing he could find no cases deciding these particular facts, he cited the general dicta of the *Everson* and *McCollum* cases without mentioning the Court's less rigorous standards in *Zorach*. Finally, the Illinois attorney general, approving the holding of sectarian classes on school premises by regular school teachers before or after school hours, did not mention *Zorach*. The *McCollum* precedent stands curiously alone in his opinion, even though for this purpose it is probably a less favorable precedent than *Zorach*.

VII. IN CONCLUSION

Initially, a precedent such as *Zorach* v. *Clauson* legalizes certain policies within the states, and interested parties and officials of the state apply the precedent to identical or similar programs. This much is the immediate and intended result of the Court's action, and it can be measured in terms of the growth of the program. More important, however, may well be the secondary impact of the decision on new and unsettled issues. The expansion of the *Zorach* precedent illustrates the tendency of an opinion to radiate consti-

tutional sanctions far beyond its original boundaries. Its history ought also to suggest that a Supreme Court precedent is in no sense an objective fact, that its interpretations and application depend as much on the goals and involvements of the groups concerned as on the words of the decision itself. To rephrase the old saw, the precedent in reality consists of what influential partisans and decision-makers say the Supreme Court says it is.

In effect, the *Zorach* precedent represents a continuation and extension, rather than a resolution, of conflict in the arena of church-state relations. By altering the balance among the contending interests, the decision has reframed the issue, shifted somewhat the focus of the conflict, triggered new interest group activity, and brought other policy-making organs into action. Released time programs are sanctioned and grow modestly with greatly diminished opposition, and their proponents take a cue from *Zorach* to press for new policies in the area of greater lenience the Court appeared to open up in the decision. So a decision such as this, especially one so thickly larded with popular dicta, creates a political and constitutional climate which encourages new goals and further innovations in aid to religion, thereby leading to the next test case. Beyond resolving old policy conflicts, then, the precedent has been used to advance and sanction new policy goals.

The evidence of non-compliance with the *Zorach* ruling indicates the limited effectiveness of the Court in maintaining constitutional uniformity within the federal system. Especially in religiously homogeneous communities where there are no dissident elements strong enough to protest or begin court action, the *McCollum* and *Zorach* rules are evaded and ignored. Although centralized judicial review of the litigation of such controversies has brought some uniformity of doctrine, the highly decentralized machinery of compliance thwarts real national uniformity of practice.

Finally, this analysis of the impact of *Zorach* v. *Clauson* illustrates once again that the doctrines of sociological jurisprudence cut two ways. Doubtless the Court felt forced by prevailing values to retreat in the *Zorach* case from its earlier absolutist position on the separation of church and state. But in so accommodating the mores of the time, it has created a symbol and an endorsement—the *Zorach* precedent—that is at the moment reshaping and molding the very values which the Court will have to attend to in later decisions.

47 PROBLEMS OF COMPLIANCE BY THE POLICE

Michael J. Murphy

When one looks at the problems which judicial review of law enforcement activities presents to police departments, it is evident that there are many areas in which there are presently diverse and often conflicting opinions by courts in different parts of the country. In general the problem of compliance contains a number of factors which must be met by law enforcement administrators.

In the first place we must determine what the rule is. Statutory provisions are usually relatively easy to interpret and enforce. The difficulty arises over case law. Therefore, [this] discussion . . . will be largely in the areas where the police are experiencing difficulty in implementing the decisions handed down by the Supreme Court.

The question of interpretation presents an extremely complex situation to law enforcement. Procedural problems, such as search and seizure . . . are largely based today on decisions which are sometimes vague and not readily susceptible of interpretation.

Thus the practical application of the rules laid down in the decisions becomes very vexing to the police administrator. Instructions must be formulated which are fully understandable and which are relatively

Reprinted by permission of *The Texas Law Review* and Fred B. Rothman & Co. from Michael J. Murphy, "The Problem of Compliance by Police Departments," *Texas Law Review*, XLIV (1966), pp. 939–946. Some footnotes omitted, others renumbered.

simple. An illustration of the problem of formulating such instructions for the front line of law enforcement arises when we consider that different lower courts in various areas of our country have differed in their interpretation of cases such as *Escobedo*.

Even when a fairly comprehensive and explicit interpretation of the practical implementation of a decision is arrived at, the problem of dissemination of this information down through a chain of command so that it is thoroughly understood is one requiring great skill in communications. Many of the larger police departments make substantial efforts in this direction and have the assistance of skilled legal advisors within their own framework. Many others have to depend upon prosecutors, who sometimes are not able to take on the task of interpreting and instructing police, and still others are left completely to their own devices with no real guidance available.

When the information is disseminated, there must be continuous supervision of the activities of the particular unit of law enforcement as to the field application of the instructions. This means, of course, that the superior officers must have a thorough knowledge of the problem and the many facets of experiences which can arise within these problems in the day-to-day work of the department. They must review time and time again the actions of subordinates, explain and reexplain, warn and admonish, and in general keep a tight rein on the methods of operation.

In the field of civil law the penalty for misinterpretation of statutes or cases is measured in dollars and cents. The loss of a case for a client is a loss which can be readily measured. However, in the field of law enforcement misinterpretation may result in loss of life, loss of job, or loss of the particular case. At the present time, the thousands of man-hours devoted to a complex case and the strenuous efforts to curtail a criminal career which threatens the peace and safety of a community can all go down the drain with one minor misinterpretation of a complex legal decision made by an officer acting in good faith.

Unlike the situation in civil law, where extensive research can be done in advance, where preparation is possible, and where time is not of the essence, the law enforcement officer on the street, meeting a complex situation which requires a decision in a split second, must rely entirely on his own knowledge, training, and instinct to enable him to evaluate and act immediately with the proper procedure.

These are the general observations which I have to make on the problem of compliance by law enforcement agencies, but at this juncture I wish to point out some of the specific areas which are troubling the police.

I. SEARCH AND SEIZURE

The resolution of the issue of whether or not the exclusionary rule would or should be imposed on the states as a constitutional mandate through the due process clause by *Mapp* v. *Ohio*[1] is now some four and one-half years behind us. I can think of no decision in recent times in the field of law enforcement which had such a dramatic and traumatic effect as this. It is quite clear that the effects of *Mapp* are still being felt and will continue to be felt in law enforcement procedures, attitudes, and techniques. As the then commissioner of the largest police force in this country I was immediately caught up in the entire problem of reevaluating our procedures, which had followed the *Defore* rule,[2] and modifying, amending, and creating new policies and new instructions for the implementation of *Mapp*. The problems were manifold. I dwell on the details of this impact in terms of the administration of a large police force so that you may understand that the decisions arrived at in the peace and tranquillity of chambers in Washington, or elsewhere, create tidal waves and earthquakes which require rebuilding of our institutions sometimes from their very foundations upward. Retraining sessions had to be held from the very top administrators down to each of the thousands of foot patrolmen and detec-

tives engaged in the daily basic enforcement function. Hundreds of thousands of man-hours had to be devoted to retraining 27,000 men. Every hour in the classroom was an hour lost from the basic function of the police department: the protection of life and property on the street.

On behalf of the New York City Police Department as well as law enforcement in general, I state unequivocally that every effort was directed and is still being directed at compliance with and implementation of *Mapp*. While there was, and perhaps should have been, some grumbling and bitter realization that the criminal element had again gained an advantage, although clearly not so intended by the Court, there was also and more importantly a good faith effort to conform to this new interpretation of the Constitution. The best example of the sincerity of law enforcement is the fact that in New York City, where search warrants had been rarely used prior to *Mapp*, from the period of the summer of 1961 to the present some 17,889 search warrants have been obtained. Figures at times do not have the dramatic illustrative effect they deserve, but for every one of these warrants one must conjure up an image of hours devoted to drafting of the applications, locating an available magistrate, traveling to his chambers, persuading him of the validity of the application, traveling back to the scene of the investigation and, at times, finding that because of the period taken to obtain the warrant the bird has flown. I will not bore you with the mechanical problems of finding available typists in the dead of night when all good civilian employees are resting from their daily labors and persuading them to take the curlers out of their hair, report to their offices, and provide the police agencies with the particular skills. Nor is it a proper subject for this paper to discuss the subsequent incredibly high number of lost man-hours spent in opposing motions to controvert or suppress.

The imposition of the exclusionary rule continues, however, to plague law enforcement in its practical implementation. In this vital field where factual situations vary so

---

[1] 367 U.S. 643 (1961).
[2] *People* v. *Defore*, 242 N.Y. 13, 150 N.E. 585 (1926).

much, which is usually the case when one deals with human beings, both as enforcers of the law and as suspects, aspects of the incident which appear to the police officer to be simply "technicalities" can have substantial and unfortunately too often adverse effects on the results of his course of conduct. The following are two illustrative examples of this point.

Police officers, with probable cause to arrest a suspect for robbery, went to a hotel where he was staying only to be informed that he was not in. They explained to the room clerk their purpose and concern, because the man was known to have a weapon, and they were admitted to his room. The suspect was not present, but the officers found his gun, a clip, and cartridges for it. The man was arrested at a later date. The Court ruled that the search for and seizure of the gun, cartridges, and clip was unreasonable, struck down the subsequent conviction of the defendant, and ordered a new trial. The state will never be able to use the weapon in evidence at a retrial, although the accused's possession of it obviously would have been a strong piece of circumstantial evidence tending to prove his guilt of the robbery. Had the accused been in his room, the search and seizure would have been reasonable because it would be considered incidental to his lawful arrest. The gun then could have been properly admitted in evidence and his conviction would have been upheld—and some police officer might have lost his life in apprehending the suspect.

In the second case the defendant and two companions, who had been sitting in a parked car in a downtown location since 10:00 p.m. one night, were arrested for vagrancy at 4:00 a.m. the following morning. After they had been booked, the police searched their car and found two loaded revolvers, caps, women's stockings (one with mouth and eye holes), rope, pillow slips, and an illegally manufactured license place equipped to be snapped over another plate. The conviction for conspiracy to rob a bank was set aside, the court holding that the search and seizure of the articles was improper because the

car had not been searched at the time of the arrest. Thus very convincing evidence against the defendant could never be used. As Judge Cardozo said, "The criminal is to go free because the constable has blundered." Or has he? It is true that if the police had searched the car at the location where the arrest was made rather than at the station house, the court might well have upheld the validity of the search. But this kind of technicality is very difficult to explain to a police officer who is confronted with a situation at 4:00 a.m. in the morning when for his own safety, never knowing whether or not there are additional confederates in the immediate area, he should remove the suspects and the car from the scene immediately to a location where a proper and thorough search can be made. A semi-deserted darkened street is not the best atmosphere for conducting a professional inquiry.

II. PROBABLE CAUSE

Flowing from the *Mapp* case is the issue of defining probable cause to constitute a lawful arrest and subsequent search and seizure. This continues to be a most vexing problem in law enforcement and is one that cannot be resolved by general principles and definitions. We have not been able to develop instructional material of sufficient specificity to enable the officer to make a proper determination in all cases. Indeed the courts have not been able to formulate rules which are adequate guidelines for the practical application on the firing line. Rather, confronted with a particular fact situation, the Supreme Court has often divided sharply on whether or not the circumstances before it in a cold record constitute probable cause.

In a number of cases where experienced police officers have decided on the circumstances that probable cause was present to justify a lawful arrest and subsequent search, the court has held differently. Assume that the following fact situation had been presented to you on your bar examination: Police officers in the early morning hours arrested an individual they had had under surveillance for several weeks and found in his possession a narcotic drug, to wit, heroin. On questioning, the suspect stated that he had bought the contraband some few hours before from a man who owned a laundry on a particular street. Going immediately to the laundry, the officer rang the bell, which was answered by a man conforming to the description given by the initial suspect. After some colloquy the officer identified himself, broke down the door when it was slammed in his face, and pursued the second suspect into his bedroom. No narcotics were found on the premises, and while the laundry owner denied that he ever sold narcotics, he stated that he knew a man named "Johnny" who was in the business. He described the house on Eleventh Avenue where Johnny lived and described a bedroom in those premises where "Johnny kept about a piece" of heroin (which is approximately one ounce); he also said that he and Johnny had used some of the drug in this bedroom the night before. The officers went immediately to that address, entered the house, and found Johnny in the bedroom. Johnny gave them about an ounce of heroin which he later stated he had purchased from Wong Sun. The officers then went to the apartment of Wong Sun and arrested him; no narcotics were discovered in his apartment. Assume further that objections were made to the admission in evidence of the statements of the laundry man suspect in his room, the narcotics found in the home of Johnny, and a pretrial statement made by Johnny and Wong Sun.

I have with malice aforethought set forth in some detail this factual description in order to illustrate the complexity of the circumstances which so often confront law enforcement officers, who also must cope with the underlying, ever-present consideration that time is of the essence in pursuing leads as they appear and develop.

What is the proper and legal resolution of the issues in this case? It is rather obvious that I have not created this hypothetical question from my own imagination, but have presented simply the facts of *Wong Sun* v. *United States*.[3] The view of a majority of the

[3]371 U.S. 471 (1963).

Supreme Court was that there was no probable cause to enter the laundry or arrest its occupant and that his statements in his room should be suppressed as the fruits of the prior illegal action. The Court did not resolve the further issue of whether or not the other pretrial statements should be excluded as having been tainted.

It is, however, of extreme importance to note that four Justices of the Court dissented in a rather vigorous opinion. Mr. Justice Clark, writing on behalf of those who disagreed with the majority, recognized the problems faced by law enforcement officers quite accurately and his concern with the majority view is rather evident in the following excerpt from his opinion:

The Court has made a Chinese puzzle out of this simple case involving four participants: Hom Way, Blackie Toy, Johnny Yee and "Sea Dog" Sun. In setting aside the convictions of Toy and Sun it has dashed to pieces the heretofore recognized standards of probable cause necessary to secure an arrest warrant or to make an arrest without one. Instead of dealing with probable cause as involving "probabilities," "the factual and practical considerations of everyday life on which reasonable and prudent men, not legal technicians, act," . . . the Court sets up rigid, mechanical standards, applying the 20–20 vision of hindsight in an area where the ambiguity and immediacy inherent in unexpected arrest are present. While probable cause must be based on more than mere suspicion, . . . it does not require proof sufficient to establish guilt. . . . The sole requirement heretofore has been that the knowledge in the hands of the officers at the time of arrest must support a "man of reasonable caution in the belief" that the subject had committed narcotic offenses. . . . That decision is faced initially not in the courtroom but at the scene of arrest where the totality of the circumstances facing the officer is weighed against his split-second decision to make the arrest. This is an everyday occurrence facing law enforcement officers, and the unrealistic, enlarged standards announced here place an unnecessarily heavy hand upon them. I therefore dissent.[4]

Again, in *Beck* v. *Ohio*[5] the Court was unable to resolve with unanimity what would

[4]*Id.* at 498–99 (dissenting opinion).
[5]379 U.S. 89 (1964).

appear to be a rather simple issue of probable cause. In this case the arresting officer had known of the defendant's record for gambling violations and had received information from an informant that the defendant was involved in the "numbers game." A search at a police station uncovered clearing house slips "beneath the sock of his leg."

It is rather basic but perhaps necessary in this discussion to point out that the highest court of the state of Ohio had found probable cause for the arrest and search. The majority of the Supreme Court, however, apparently applying the same general test for probable cause used by the Ohio court, reached the opposite result. The dissent in this case pointed out the problems created by rejecting the findings of fact and law of other courts, particularly highest state courts. In referring to this particular issue, Mr. Justice Clark stated:

The Court ignores these findings entirely. Where the highest court of a State after detailed and earnest consideration determines the facts and they are reasonably supportable, I would let them stand. And I would, of course, give the same respect to findings of probable cause by United States district courts when approved by United States courts of appeals. Otherwise, this Court will be continually disputing with state and federal courts over the minutiae of facts in every search and seizure case. Especially is this true if the Court disputes the findings *sua sponte* where, as here, no attack is leveled at them.[6]

The picture is muddled further to the eyes of dedicated, properly motivated police officers when they are confronted with a case such as *Ker* v. *California*.[7] It is unnecessary to describe the detailed and complicated facts for the purposes of this point. I need say only that many experienced law enforcement people, not only police but prosecutors as well,

would have expected the Supreme Court to reverse the conviction because of lack of probable cause. However, the Court here was content simply to state:

While this Court does not sit as in *nisi prius* to appraise contradictory factual questions, it will, where necessary to the determination of constitutional rights, make an independent examination of the facts, the findings, and the record so that it can determine for itself whether in the decision as to reasonableness the fundamental—*i.e.*, constitutional—criteria established by this Court have been respected. The States are not thereby precluded from developing workable rules governing arrests, searches and seizures to meet "the practical demands of effective criminal investigation and law enforcement" in the States, provided that those rules do not violate the constitutional proscription of unreasonable searches and seizures and the concomitant command that evidence so seized is inadmissible against one who has standing to complain. . . . Such a standard implies no derogation of uniformity in applying federal constitutional guarantees but is only a recognition that conditions and circumstances vary just as do investigative and enforcement techniques.[8]

What is probable cause? Can it be defined and explained in such a manner that it lends itself to concrete application of the multitude of problems which daily confront the hundreds of thousands of police officers in daily contact with the millions and millions of citizens in this country? Perhaps we can do no more for the police officer who asks for guidelines than to tell him generally what the rule is, give him a sampling of instances where the Supreme Court has or has not found probable cause, and then in effect advise him "use your own best judgment." But what we must add to this is a further comment to our police: you may be found to have erred, but where you act reasonably and in good faith we will not condemn or find fault or engage in recriminations.

[6]*Id*. at 99 (dissenting opinion).
[7]374 U.S. 23 (1963).

[8]*Id*. at 34.

Part 6
The Judiciary
and the Larger
American Political System

The federal judiciary thus far has been treated as a system complete within itself. Although it is an open system subject to inputs and feedback generated from the outside, its boundaries are fairly distinct. In our analysis there has been no question about the fact that the President, the Congress, federal and state bureaucrats and public officials lie outside these boundaries. It is obvious, however, that the federal judiciary is only one of several institutions in the nation making political policies. As but one policy-making institution among many, the federal judiciary can be viewed as a subsystem of the larger American political system. The role played by the federal judiciary—and the Supreme Court in particular—in this larger political system is considered by Robert Dahl in the final selection of this collection.[1]

[1]Several excellent studies of the Supreme Court are also concerned with this. See, for example, Loren P. Beth, *Politics, the Constitution and the Supreme Court* (New York: Harper & Row, 1962); Robert G. McCloskey, *The American Supreme Court* (Chicago: University of Chicago Press, 1960); and Arthur E. Sutherland, *Constitutionalism in America* (New York: Blaisdell Publishing Co., 1965).

48 THE SUPREME COURT'S ROLE IN NATIONAL POLICY-MAKING

Robert A. Dahl

. . . In the course of its one hundred and sixty-seven years, in eighty-five cases, the Court has struck down ninety-four different provisions of federal law as unconstitutional, and by interpretation it has significantly

Reprinted by permission of publisher from Robert A. Dahl, *Pluralist Democracy in the United States* (Chicago: Rand McNally & Co., 1967), pp. 155–164. This is an updated version of "Decision-Making in a Democracy: The Supreme Court as a National Policy-Maker," *Journal of Public Law*, VI, No. 2 (1957), pp. 279–295.

modified a good many more. It might be argued . . . that in all or in a very large number of these cases the Court was . . . defending the legitimate constitutional rights of some minority against a "tyrannical" majority. There are, however, some exceedingly serious difficulties with this interpretation of the Court's activities.

To begin with, it is difficult to determine when any particular Court decision has been at odds with the preferences of a national majority. Adequate evidence is not available, for scientific opinion polls are of relatively recent origin; and, strictly speaking, national elections cannot be interpreted as more than an indication of the first choice of about 40 to 60 per cent of the adult population for certain candidates for public office. The connection between preferences among candidates and preferences among alternative public policies is highly tenuous. On the basis of an election, it is almost never possible to adduce whether a majority does or does not support one of two or more *policy* alternatives about which candidates are divided. For the greater part of the Court's history, then, there is simply no way of establishing with any high degree of confidence whether a given alternative was or was not supported by a majority or a minority of adults or even of voters.

In the absence of relatively direct information, we are thrown back on indirect tests. The ninety-four provisions of federal law that have been declared unconstitutional were, of course, initially passed by majorities of those voting in the Senate and in the House. They also had the President's formal approval. One could, therefore, speak of a majority of those voting in the House and Senate, together with the President, as a "law-making majority." It is not easy to determine whether a law-making majority actually coincides with the preferences of a majority of American adults, or even with the preferences of a majority of that half of the adult population which, on the average, votes in congressional elections. Such evidence as we have from opinion polls suggests that Congress is not markedly out of line with public opinion, or at any rate with such public opinion as there is after one discards the answers of people who fall into the category, often large, labeled "no response" or "don't know." If we may, on these somewhat uncertain grounds, take a law-making majority as equivalent to a "national majority," then it is possible to test the hypothesis that the Supreme Court is shield and buckler for minorities against tyrannical national majorities.

Under any reasonable assumptions about the nature of the political process, it would appear to be somewhat naive to assume that the Supreme Court either would or could play the role of Galahad. Over the whole history of the Court, one new Justice has been appointed on the average of every twenty-three months. Thus a President can expect to appoint two new Justices during one term of office; and if this were not enough to tip the balance on a normally divided Court, he would be almost certain to succeed in two terms. For example, Hoover made three appointments; Roosevelt, nine; Truman, four; Eisenhower, five; Kennedy in his brief tenure, two. Presidents are not famous for appointing Justices hostile to their own views on public policy; nor could they expect to secure confirmation of a man whose stance on key questions was flagrantly at odds with that of the dominant majority in the Senate. Typically, Justices are men who, prior to appointment, have engaged in public life and have committed themselves publicly on the great questions of the day. As the late Mr. Justice Frankfurter pointed out, a surprisingly large proportion of the Justices, particularly of the great Justices who have left their stamp upon the decisions of the Court, have had little or no prior judicial experience. Nor have the Justices—certainly not the great Justices—been timid men with a passion for anonymity. Indeed, it is not too much to say that if Justices were appointed primarily for their 'judicial' qualities without regard to their basic attitudes on fundamental questions of public policy, the Court could not play the influential role in the American political system that it does in reality play.

It is reasonable to conclude, then, that the policy views dominant on the Court will never be out of line for very long with the policy views dominant among the law-making majorities of the United States. And it would be most unrealistic to suppose that the Court would, for more than a few years at most, stand against any major alternatives sought by a law-making majority. The judicial agonies of the New Deal will, of course, come quickly to mind; but President Franklin D. Roosevelt's difficulties with the Court were truly exceptional. Generalizing over the whole history of the Court, one can say that the chances are about two out of five that a President will make one appointment to the Court in less than a year, two out of three that he will make one within two years, and three out of four that he will make one within three years (Table 1). President Roosevelt had unusually bad luck: he had to wait four years for his first appointment; the odds against this long interval are about five to one. With average luck, his battle with the Court would never have occurred; even as it was, although his "court-packing" proposal did formally fail, by the end of his second term in 1940, Roosevelt had appointed five new Justices and he gained three more the following year: Thus by the end of 1941, Mr. Justice Roberts was the only remaining holdover from the pre-Roosevelt era.

two elections before the decision was handed down and may well have weakened or disappeared in the interval. In these cases, then, the Court was probably not directly challenging current law-making majorities.

Of the twenty-four laws held unconstitutional within two years, eleven were measures enacted in the early years of the New Deal. Indeed, New Deal measures comprise nearly a third of all the legislation that has ever been declared unconstitutional within four years of enactment.

It is illuminating to examine the cases where the Court has acted on legislation

TABLE 1   The Interval between Appointments to the Supreme Court, 1789–1965

Interval in Years	Number of Appointments	Percentage of Total	Cumulative Percentage
Less than 1 year	38	41	41
1	22	24	65
2	10	11	76
3	9	10	86
4	6	6.5	92.5
5	6	6.5	99
12	1	1	100
Total	92	100	100

Note: The table excludes six Justices appointed in 1789. It includes only Justices who were appointed and confirmed and served on the Court. All data through 1964 are from *Congress and the Nation*, 1452–1453.

It is to be expected, then, that the Court would be least successful in blocking a determined and persistent lawmaking majority on a major policy. Conversely, the Court is most likely to succeed against "weak" law-making majorities: transient majorities in Congress, fragile coalitions, coalitions weakly united upon a policy of subordinate importance or congressional coalitions no longer in existence, as might be the case when a law struck down by the Court had been passed several years earlier.

An examination of the cases in which the Court has held federal legislation unconstitutional confirms these expectations. Over the whole history of the Court, about half the decisions have been rendered more than four years after the legislation was passed (Table 2). Thus the congressional majorities that passed these laws went through at least

within four years of enactment—where the presumption is, that is to say, that the law-making majority is not a dead one. Of the twelve New Deal cases, two were, from a policy point of view, trivial; and two although perhaps not trivial, were of minor importance to the New Deal program.[1] A fifth involved the NRA, which was to expire within three weeks of the decision.[2] Insofar as the uncon-

[1]*Booth* v. *United States*, 291 U.S. 339 (1934), involved a reduction in the pay of retired judges. *Lynch* v. *United States*, 292 U.S. 571 (1934), repealed laws granting to veterans rights to yearly renewable term insurance; there were only twenty-nine policies outstanding in 1932. *Hopkins Federal Savings & Loan Assn* v. *Cleary*, 296 U.S. 315 (1935), granted permission to state building and loan associations to convert to federal ones on a vote of 51 per cent or more of votes cast at a legal meeting. *Ashton* v. *Cameron County Water Improvement District*, 298 U.S. 513 (1936), permitted municipalities to petition federal courts for bankruptcy proceedings.
[2]*Schechter Poultry Corp.* v. *United States*, 295 U.S. 495 (1935).

TABLE 2   Supreme Court Cases Holding Federal Legislation Unconstitutional: by Time between Legislation and Decision

	Supreme Court Cases Involving:					
Number of Years	New Deal Legislation		Other		All Federal Legislation	
	N.	%	N.	%	N.	%
2 or less	11	92	13	17.5	24	28
3–4	1	8	13	17.5	14	16
5–8	0	0	20	27	20	24
9–12	0	0	10	14	10	12
13–16	0	0	7	10	7	8
17–20	0	0	2	3	2	2
21 or more	0	0	8	11	8	10
Total	12	100%	73	100%	85	100%

stitutional provisions allowed "codes of fair competition" to be established by industrial groups, it is fair to say that President Roosevelt and his advisors were relieved by the Court's decision of a policy that they had come to find increasingly embarrassing. In view of the tenacity with which FDR held to his major program, there can hardly be any doubt that, had he wanted to pursue the policy objective involved in the NRA codes, as he did for example with the labor provisions, he would not have been stopped by the Court's special theory of the Constitution. As to the seven other cases,[3] it is entirely correct to say, I think, that whatever some of the eminent Justices might have thought during their fleeting moments of glory, they did not succeed in interposing a barrier to the achievement of the objectives of the legislation; and in a few years most of the constitutional dogma on which they rested their opposition to the New Deal had been unceremoniously swept under the rug.

The remainder of the thirty-eight cases where the Court has declared legislation unconstitutional within four years of enactment tend to fall into two rather distinct groups: those involving legislation that could

reasonably be regarded as important *from the point of view of the law-making majority* and those involving minor legislation. Although the one category merges into the other, so that some legislation must be classified rather arbitrarily, probably there will be little disagreement with classifying the specific legislative provisions involved in eleven cases as essentially minor from the point of view of the law-making majority (however important they may have been as constitutional interpretations).[4] The specific legislative provisions involved in the remaining fifteen cases are by no means of uniform importance, but with one or two possible exceptions it seems reasonable to classify them as major policy issues from the point of view of the law-making majority.[5] We would expect that cases involv-

[3]*United States* v. *Butler*, 297 U.S. 1 (1936); *Perry* v. *United States*, 294 U.S. 330 (1935); *Panama Refining Co.* v. *Ryan*, 293 U.S. 388 (1935); *Railroad Retirement Board* v. *Alton R. Co.*, 295 U.S. 330 (1935); *Louisville Joint Stock Land Bank* v. *Radford*, 295 U.S. 555 (1935); *Rickert Rice Mills* v. *Fontenot*, 297 U.S. 110 (1936); *Carter* v. *Carter Coal Co.*, 298 U.S. 238 (1936).

[4]*United States* v. *Dewitt*, 9 Wall. (U.S.) 41 (1870); *Gordon* v. *United States*, 2 Wall. (U.S.) 561 (1865); *Monongahela Navigation Co.* v. *United States*, 148 U.S. 312 (1893); *Wong Wing* v. *United States*, 163 U.S. 228 (1896); *Fairbank* v. *United States*, 181 U.S. 283 (1901); *Rassmussen* v. *United States*, 197 U.S. 516 (1905); *Muskrat* v. *United States*, 219 U.S. 346 (1911).

[5]*Ex parte Garland*, 4 Wall. (U.S.) 333 (1867); *United States* v. *Klein*, 13 Wall. (U.S.) 128 (1872); *Pollack* v. *Farmers' Loan & Trust Co.*, 157 U.S. 429 (1895), rehearing granted 158 U.S. 601 (1895); *Employers' Liability Cases*, 207 U.S. 463 (1908); *Keller* v. *United States*, 213 U.S. 138 (1909); *Hammer* v. *Dagenhart*, 247 U.S. 251 (1918); *Eisner* v. *Macomber*, 252 U.S. 189 (1920); *Knickerbocker Ice Co.* v. *Stewart*, 253 U.S. 149 (1920); *United States* v. *Cohen Grocery Co.*, 255 U.S. 81 (1921); *Weeds, Inc.* v. *United States*, 255 U.S. 109 (1921); *Bailey* v. *Drexel Furniture Co.*, 259 U.S. 20 (1922); *Hill* v. *Wallace*, 259 U.S. 44 (1922); *Washington* v. *Dawson & Co.*, 264 U.S. 219 (1924); *Trusler* v. *Crooks*, 269 U.S. 475 (1926).

TABLE 3 Number of Cases Involving Legislative Policy Other than Those Arising under New Deal Legislation Holding Legislation Unconstitutional within Four Years after Enactment

Interval in Years	Major Policy	Minor Policy	Total
2 or less	11	2	13
3 to 4	4	9	13
Total	15	11	26

ing major legislative policy would be propelled to the Court much more rapidly than cases involving minor policy, and, as the table above shows, this is in fact what happens (Table 3).

Thus a law-making majority with major policy objectives in mind usually has an opportunity to seek ways of overcoming the Court's veto. It is an interesting and highly significant fact that Congress and the President do generally succeed in overcoming a hostile Court on major policy issues (Table 4). It is particularly instructive to examine the

cases involving major policy. In two cases involving legislation enacted by radical Republican Congresses to punish supporters of the Confederacy during the Civil War, the Court faced a rapidly crumbling majority whose death knell as an effective national force was sounded after the election of 1876. Three cases are difficult to classify and I have labeled them "unclear." Of these, two were decisions made in 1921 involving a 1919 amendment to the Lever Act to control prices. The legislation was important, and the provision in question was clearly struck down,

TABLE 4 Type of Congressional Action Following Supreme Court Decisions Holding Legislation Unconstitutional within Four Years after Enactment (Other than New Deal Legislation)

Congressional Action	Major Policy	Minor Policy	Total
Reverses Court's Policy	10[a]	2[d]	12
Changes Own Policy	2[b]	0	2
None	0	8[e]	8
Unclear	3[c]	1[f]	4
Total	15	11	26

Note: For the cases in each category, see footnote 6.

[6]a. *Pollock* v. *Farmers' Loan & Trust Co.*, 157 U.S. 429 (1895); *Employers' Liability Cases*, 207 U.S. 463 (1908); *Keller* v. *United States*, 213 U.S. 138 (1909); *Hammer* v. *Dagenhart*, 247 U.S. 251 (1918); *Bailey* v. *Drexel Furniture Co.*, 259 U.S. 20 (1922); *Trusler* v. *Crooks*, 269 U.S. 475 (1926); *Hill* v. *Wallace*, 259 U.S. 44 (1922); *Knickerbocker Ice Co.* v. *Stewart*, 253 U.S. 149 (1920); *Washington* v. *Dawson & Co.*, 264 U.S. 219 (1924).
b. *Ex parte Garland*, 4 Wall. (U.S.) 333 (1867); *United States* v. *Klein*, 13 Wall. (U.S.) 128 (1872).
c. *United States* v. *Cohen Grocery Co.*, 255 U.S. 81 (1921); *Weeds, Inc.* v. *United States*, 255 U.S. 109 (1921); *Eisner* v. *Macomber*, 252 U.S. 189 (1920).
d. *Gordon* v. *United States*, 2 Wall. (U.S.) 561 (1865); *Evans* v. *Gore*, 253 U.S. 245 (1920).
e. *United States* v. *Dewitt*, 9 Wall. (U.S.) 41 (1870); *Monongahela Navigation Co.* v. *United States*, 148 U.S. 312 (1893); *Wong Wing* v. *United States*, 163 U.S. 228 (1896); *Fairbank* v. *United States*, 181 U.S. 283 (1901); *Rassmussen* v. *United States*, 197 U.S. 516 (1905); *Muskrat* v. *United States*, 219 U.S. 346 (1911); *Choate* v. *Trapp*, 224 U.S. 665 (1912); *United States* v. *Lovett*, 328 U.S. 303 (1946).
f. *Untermyer* v. *Anderson*, 276 U.S. 440 (1928).

but the Lever Act terminated three days after the decision and Congress did not return to the subject of price control until the Second World War, when it experienced no constitutional difficulties arising from these cases (which were primarily concerned with the lack of an ascertainable standard of guilt). The third case in this category successfully eliminated stock dividends from the scope of the Sixteenth Amendment, although a year later Congress enacted legislation taxing the actual income from such stocks.

The remaining ten cases were ultimately followed by a reversal of the actual policy results of the Court's action, although not necessarily of the specific constitutional interpretation. In four cases, the policy consequences of the Court's decision were overcome in less than a year. The other six required a long struggle. Workmen's compensation for longshoremen and harbor workers was invalidated by the Court in 1920; in 1922, Congress passed a new law which was, in its turn, knocked down by the Court in 1924; in 1927, Congress passed a third law, which was finally upheld in 1932. The notorious income tax cases of 1895 were first somewhat narrowed by the Court itself; the Sixteenth Amendment was recommended by President Taft in 1909 and was ratified in 1913, some eighteen years after the Court's decisions. The two child labor cases represent the most effective battle ever waged by the Court against legislative policy-makers. The original legislation outlawing child labor, based on the

before it began to meet so much resistance in the states remaining that the enterprise miscarried. In 1938, under a second reformist President, new legislation was passed twenty-two years after the first; this a Court with a New Deal majority finally accepted in 1941, and thereby brought to an end a battle that had lasted a full quarter-century.

The entire record of the duel between the Court and the law-making majority, in cases where the Court has held legislation unconstitutional within four years after enactment, is summarized in Table 5.

A consideration of the role of the Court as defender of minorities, then, suggests the following conclusions:

First, judicial review is surely inconsistent with democracy to the extent that the Court

TABLE 5   Type of Congressional Action after Supreme Court Decisions Holding Legislation Unconstitutional within Four Years after Enactment (Including New Deal Legislation)

Congressional Action	Major Policy	Minor Policy	Total
Reverses Court's Policy	17	2	19
None	0	12	12
Other	6*	1	7
Total	23	15	38

*In addition to the actions in Table 4 under "Changes Own Policy" and "Unclear," this figure includes the NRA legislation affected by the *Schechter Poultry* case.

commerce clause, was passed in 1916 as part of Wilson's New Freedom. Like Franklin Roosevelt later, Wilson was somewhat unlucky in his Supreme Court appointments; he made only three appointments during his eight years, and one of these was wasted, from a policy point of view, on Mr. Justice McReynolds. Had McReynolds voted "right," the subsequent struggle over the problem of child labor need not have occurred, for the decision in 1918 was by a Court divided five to four, McReynolds voting with the majority. Congress moved at once to circumvent the decision by means of the tax power, but in 1922, the Court blocked that approach. In 1924, Congress returned to the engagement with a constitutional amendment that was rapidly endorsed by a number of state legislatures

simply protects the policies of minorities from reversal or regulation by national majorities acting through regular law-making procedures.

Second, however, the frequency and nature of appointments to the Court inhibits it from playing this role, or otherwise protecting minorities against national law-making majorities. National law-making majorities—i.e., coalitions of the President and a majority of each house of Congress—generally have their way.

Third, although the court evidently cannot hold out indefinitely against a persistent law-making majority, in a very small number of important cases it has succeeded in delaying the application of a policy for as long as twenty-five years.

Table of United States
Supreme Court
Cases*

*Page and footnote citations are in *italics*.